ArtScroll Tanach Series®

A traditional commentary on the Books of the Bible

Rabbi Nosson Scherman / Rabbi Meir Zlotowitz
General Editors

A PROJECT OF THE

Mesorah Heritage Foundation

Tehillim

PSALMS / A NEW TRANSLATION WITH A
COMMENTARY ANTHOLOGIZED FROM TAL-
MUDIC, MIDRASHIC AND RABBINIC SOURCES.

Published by
Mesorah Publications, ltd

Volume IV

Commentary and Overview by
Rabbi Avrohom Chaim Feuer

Translation by
Rabbi Avrohom Chaim Feuer
in collaboration with
Rabbis Nosson Scherman *and* Meir Zlotowitz

FIVE VOLUME
PERSONAL SIZE EDITION
First Impression . . . June 1996
Second Impression . . . March 1998
Third Impression . . . April 2002
Fourth Impression . . . November 2003

Published and Distributed by
MESORAH PUBLICATIONS, Ltd.
4401 Second Avenue
Brooklyn, New York 11232

Distributed in Europe by
LEHMANNS
Unit E, Viking Industrial Park
Rolling Mill Road
Jarrow, Tyne & Wear NE32 3DP
England

Distributed in Australia & New Zealand by
GOLDS WORLD OF JUDAICA
3-13 William Street
Balaclava, Melbourne 3183
Victoria Australia

Distributed in Israel by
SIFRIATI / A. GITLER — BOOKS
6 Hayarkon Street
Bnei Brak 51127

Distributed in South Africa by
KOLLEL BOOKSHOP
Shop 8A Norwood Hypermarket
Norwood 2196, Johannesburg, South Africa

THE ARTSCROLL TANACH SERIES
TEHILLIM / PSALMS
PERSONAL SIZE EDITION VOL. IV
© Copyright 1977, 1985, 1996 by MESORAH PUBLICATIONS, Ltd.
4401 Second Avenue / Brooklyn, N.Y. 11232 / (718) 921-9000 / www.artscroll.com

---

ISBN
PERSONAL SIZE — FIVE VOLUME SET 0-89906-383-7

Typography by CompuScribe at ArtScroll Studios, Ltd.
4401 Second Avenue / Brooklyn, N.Y. 11232 / (718) 921-9000

Printed in the United States of America by Noble Book Press
Bound by Sefercraft Quality Bookbinders, Ltd., Brooklyn, NY

*T*his volume is dedicated to the glowing
memory of our beloved grandparents

Naftali Ringel

נפתלי זאב בן אברהם מרדכי ז״ל   ח׳ אייר ת״ש

Blima Golda Ringel

בלימה גולדה בת ישראל צבי ע״ה   כ׳ טבת תש״מ

*T*hey were filled with love for Torah,
the Jewish people, and the land of Israel.

*Our grandfather longed to be in Eretz Yisrael
and actually lived there for a time.
He was plucked from this life as a young man,
before we knew him — but our grandmother carried on.*

*With love and wisdom, warmth and piety,
she nurtured by deed and example.
She was the classic Jewish matriarch, and was blessed
with the years to see the nachas of her labors.*

תנצב״ה

Joyce and Eric Austein
Debra and Elliot Tannenbaum
Judy and Martin Braun
Aliza and Shlomie Liechtung
Mindy and David Greenberg

❧

and Families

86 מזמור פו

This is no ordinary composition, for David himself describes it as a תְּפִלָה, prayer. Indeed, these verses describe the essential purpose of prayer, which should be not so much to obtain the desired assistance from God as to reassure the supplicant that God is near in all moments of distress and danger. The awareness of God's intimate concern and close attention to a man's troubles is itself the response to his supplications (R' Hirsch).

David composed this prayer as a supplication to God to save him from his many enemies (Malbim). Specifically, it was the threat of King Saul which aroused David to express his feelings before God (Radak). But David did not seek mere safety from his foes. Rather he yearned for the opportunity to enhance the glory of God in the eyes of the entire word, for David recognized that the ultimate purpose of his existence was the glorification of God's Name.

From this psalm we derive some of the most striking passages of our liturgy which proclaim this theme. One of them is: אֵין כָּמוֹךָ בָאֱלֹהִים אֲדֹנָי וְאֵין כְּמַעֲשֶׂיךָ, There is none like You among the gods, my Lord, and there is nothing like Your works (v. 8). This verse is recited as the Torah scroll is taken from the Holy Ark to be read in public, for the Divine teachings contained in the Torah are the most splendid and impressive of all God's works.

א תְּפִלָּה לְדָוִד הַטֵּה־יהוה אָזְנְךָ עֲנֵנִי כִּי־עָנִי

ב וְאֶבְיוֹן אָנִי: שָׁמְרָה נַפְשִׁי כִּי־חָסִיד אָנִי
הוֹשַׁע עַבְדְּךָ אַתָּה אֱלֹהַי הַבּוֹטֵחַ אֵלֶיךָ:

1. תְּפִלָּה לְדָוִד — *A prayer of David.*

Malbim explains that תְּפִלָּה, *prayer*, is not simply a plea to God to fulfill bodily needs, but rather it is a fervent outpouring of the soul which yearns to soar heavenward and cleave to its Maker.

Ayalah Sheluchah notes that it is significant that this psalm of David has been placed in the middle of a series of works composed by Korach's sons (psalms 84, 85, 87, 88). [Indeed, this is the only work in the entire third *Book of Tehillim* that is ascribed specifically to David (*Toras Chesed*).] *Ayalah Sheluchah* explains that in the previous psalm, Korach's sons prescribe a formula for spiritual fulfillment: חֶסֶד וֶאֱמֶת נִפְגָּשׁוּ, *kindness and truth met* (85:11). In this psalm, David corroborates this formula, for he feels confident that God will come to his aid, כִּי חָסִיד אָנִי, *for a man who practices kindness am I.*

הַטֵּה ה׳ אָזְנְךָ עֲנֵנִי — *HASHEM, incline Your ear, answer me.*

[Elsewhere we find that the plea *incline Your ear* is addressed to God as אֱלֹהִים, *the Dispenser of Strict Justice* (31:3, 71:2; *Daniel* 9:18), rather than as ה׳, *the Dispenser of Mercy.* Even when this request is made of Hashem, in His manifestation of mercy (as in *II Kings* 19:16 and *Isaiah* 37:17), *incline Your ear* is followed by another request, וְשָׁמַע, *and hear.* It is for man to ask that God listen; God decides whether and when to respond. Here, however, when David was in danger and felt an urgent need for help, he added the plea עֲנֵנִי, *answer me,* immediately.]

כִּי עָנִי וְאֶבְיוֹן אָנִי — *For I am poor and needy.*

In these verses David enumerates five compelling reasons why God should answer his prayer. First, as a fugitive he is in a pitiful position, and it is God's way to save the helpless (*Malbim*).

[This declaration appears three other times — in 40:18, 70:6 and 109:22. However, David's claim of abject poverty is puzzling, since he belonged to one of Judah's wealthiest and most distinguished families.] *Radak* explains that although David did possess ample funds, this wealth was inaccessible to him while he was a fugitive. In seclusion, he subsisted on provisions secretly supplied by his family and tribesmen. On foreign soil, he was dependent upon the aid of foreign monarchs, such as Achish, king of the Philistines.

[Furthermore, although David might have had sufficient wealth to support himself, he was incapable of feeding his entire army of followers.]

According to *Metzudos*, David means that he has humbled himself in prayer before God, like a *poor and needy* man.

Eretz HaChaim notes that since David donated his wealth and the booty which he acquired to the Temple treasury in order to finance the building of the Temple, he was indeed impoverished. [See *Overview* to *Tehillim*, vol. I, part VI.]

2. שָׁמְרָה נַפְשִׁי — *Guard my soul.*

Zohar (*Pinchas*) observes that the proper grammatical usage should be שְׁמוֹר, addressing God in the male gender. David uses the female form שָׁמְרָה to stress the letter ה׳, one of the letters in the Four-Letter Name, which appears in it. This alludes to the fact that his soul deserves protection because it is Godly; in effect it is a fragment of the Divine Name of ה׳, *HASHEM.*

כִּי חָסִיד אָנִי — *For a devout man* [or: *a man who practices kindness*] *am I.*

A second reason to help me, is because You repay a man measure for

A prayer of David,
HASHEM, incline Your ear, answer me;
for I am poor and needy.
² Guard my soul, for a devout man am I;
save Your servant — O You, my God —
who trusts You.

---

measure; עִם חָסִיד תִּתְחַסָּד, *with a devout man You act devoutly* (18:26). Therefore, shall destruction be the reward of my devotion? *(Malbim).* [1]

I reached the pinnacle of devotion when my enemies cursed and insulted me, and I listened to them patiently. I could easily have taken revenge, but I remained silent *(Rashi).*

Indeed, notes *Meiri,* David worded his request carefully; he doesn't seek the preservation of his body, but the protection of his soul, for he is determined that it should remain the soul of a devout man. Therefore, he prays, "Do not allow my soul to be overwhelmed by hatred or revenge. Let me continue to treat my enemies with compassion, despite their malice towards me."

Radak cautions us not to look askance at David's apparent self-glorification, for David truly *was* exceptionally pious. His devotion to God was quite

extraordinary; although he occasionally erred, his heart remained upright, and he repented of his sins immediately. His enemies made every effort to harm him, yet David sought their welfare; they rejoiced at his failures, yet he was gladdened by their moments of success. David confronted his enemies with the claim that he was a devout person only so that they might learn from his example, not because he sought personal glory.

R' Hirsch provides a vivid and accurate portrait of the devout חָסִיד: He is a selfless man who neglects his own needs and devotes himself to the welfare of others. He does not seek his own privileges or advantages but pursues the guarantee of the rights of his fellow men.

הוֹשַׁע עַבְדְּךָ אַתָּה אֱלֹהַי הַבּוֹטֵחַ אֵלֶיךָ — *Save Your servant — O You, my God — who trusts You (Radak).*

David now offers a third reason why

---

1. The *Talmud (Berachos* 4a) records David's claim to outstandingly devout conduct in detail: "Am I not devout? All the monarchs of the east and west sleep through the first three hours of the day, but *at midnight I arise to give thanks to You* (119:62)."

Others maintain that David said, "Am I not devout? All other monarchs of the east and west display their regal splendor, but I soil my hands with post-natal blood and tissue, which I examine in order to determine whether a woman is ritually pure. Furthermore, before making any decision, I consult my rabbi and teacher, Mefiboshes, so that he may evaluate my rulings."

Pnei Yehoshua (Berachos 4a) explains that undoubtedly David's piety, devotion, and meticulous *mitzvah* observance were also manifested in many other ways. David merely singled out these examples, to illustrate his unique devotion in fulfilling his duties as King of Israel.

When Israel first demanded of the prophet Samuel that he appoint a king for them, they were motivated by a desire to imitate the gentile form of monarchy: *Appoint for us a king who will rule us like all the nations (I Samuel* 8:5). Thus Saul's ill-conceived reign was doomed from the start. David's monarchy was intended to rectify this distortion by presenting an authentically Jewish monarchy, which would emphasize the king as the nation's spiritual leader.

Therefore, David emphasized the contrast between his spiritual devotion, and the hedonistic abandon of the gentile kings. Because of this merit, he begged God to save him from Saul's fate.

ג-ד חָנֵּנִי אֲדֹנָי כִּי־אֵלֶיךָ אֶקְרָא כָּל־הַיּוֹם: שַׂמֵּחַ

ה נֶפֶשׁ עַבְדֶּךָ כִּי־אֵלֶיךָ אֲדֹנָי נַפְשִׁי אֶשָּׂא: כִּי־

אַתָּה אֲדֹנָי טוֹב וְסַלָּח וְרַב־חֶסֶד לְכָל־

ו קֹרְאֶיךָ: הַאֲזִינָה יהוה תְּפִלָּתִי וְהַקְשִׁיבָה

ז בְּקוֹל תַּחֲנוּנוֹתָי: בְּיוֹם צָרָתִי אֶקְרָאֶךָּ כִּי

ח תַעֲנֵנִי: אֵין־כָּמוֹךָ בָאֱלֹהִים ׀ אֲדֹנָי וְאֵין

God should save him: he has placed his trust solely in God. If God abandons such a loyal believer, His own honor will be tarnished (Malbim).

The *Zohar (Pinchas)* draws our attention to the odd usage הַבּוֹטֵחַ אֵלֶיךָ which literally means *who trusts 'to' You.* The customary form is בָךְ הַבּוֹטֵחַ, *who trusts 'in' You.* David implies: I have complete confidence in You, Hashem, because I come אֵלֶיךָ, *to You,* every night at midnight to offer prayers of penitence and hope.

3. חָנֵּנִי אֲדֹנָי כִּי אֵלֶיךָ אֶקְרָא כָּל הַיּוֹם — *Show me favor, O my Lord, for to You do I cry out all the day.*

A fourth reason to save David is that he is consistent; he cries out to God *always,* in every situation, and never turns to any other source of salvation. Furthermore, David does not claim to be deserving, but appeals to God for a *favor* (Malbim).

כָּל הַיּוֹם — *All the day.*

[The simple meaning of the phrase is that David prayed constantly.] *Rashi* explains that in a deeper sense, David alludes to Israel's tragic exile. The word כָּל, *all,* in connection with יוֹם, *day,* adds the connotation that every part of the twenty-four hour period is included. In the figurative sense, the phrase *all the day* represents every aspect of the exile, which is as bright as day for the Jews' wicked enemies, but as dark as night for the downtrodden nation of Israel (cf. *Berachos* 1:5).]

4. שַׂמֵּחַ נֶפֶשׁ עַבְדֶּךָ — *Gladden the soul of Your servant.*

Release me from my present agony, (Radak) because agony damages the soul and I must protect my soul, which is destined to ascend and rejoin its Creator. Since *unto You, my Lord, I lift up my soul,* I seek to return it to You in perfect condition (Maharit; Yaavetz Hadoresh).

כִּי אֵלֶיךָ אֲדֹנָי נַפְשִׁי אֶשָּׂא — *For unto You, my Lord, I lift up my soul* [i.e., in prayer, Targum].

Radak suggests three possible interpretations for *I lift up my soul:* (a) I implore You with all my soul; (b) I place all my hopes only in You, with all my soul; and (c) I offer You my soul as a complete sacrifice; I am totally dedicated to You.

According to *Nora Tehillos,* to lift one's soul means to activate all one's latent energies and abilities in order to come closer to God.

5. כִּי אַתָּה אֲדֹנָי טוֹב וְסַלָּח — *For You, my Lord, are good and forgiving.*

Radak comments that God is טוֹב, *good,* to all men, as stated in 145:9: טוֹב ה' לַכֹּל, *HASHEM is good to all.* According to *Targum* and *Ibn Ezra,* however, God is טוֹב, *good,* only to those who are themselves good and righteous.

God is סַלָּח, *forgiving,* to sinners (Ibn Ezra; Radak) who repent and return to the ways of the Torah (Targum).

If God would forgive only once or at occasional intervals, He would be described as a סוֹלֵחַ, i.e., one who forgives. Since, however, He forgives man constantly, without interruption, He is called סַלָּח, i.e., the very essence of forgiveness (R' Yoseif Titsak).

³ *Show me favor, O my Lord,*

     for to You do I cry out all the day.

⁴ *Gladden the soul of Your servant,*

     for unto You, my Lord, I lift up my soul.

⁵ *For You, my Lord, are good and forgiving,*

     and abundantly kind to all who call upon You.

⁶ *Give ear, HASHEM, to my prayer,*

     and heed the sound of my supplications.

⁷ *On the day of my distress I call upon You,*

     for You will answer me.

⁸ *There is none like You among the gods, my Lord,*

וְרַב חֶסֶד לְכָל קֹרְאֶיךָ — *And abundantly kind to all who call upon You.*

You are kind to all — even to the most corrupt and wicked — the moment they repent and call out to You (*Radak*).

Ordinarily, if one man wrongs another and then asks for forgiveness, the injured party may be willing to forgive him, but he will not easily forget the offense. Thus, the victim will tend to avoid the man who once wronged him. God's forgiveness is far greater. When an offender repents, not only will God completely erase his sin, but He will even shower the penitent with abundant kindness (*Ohel Yaakov*).

6. הַאֲזִינָה ה' תְּפִלָּתִי — *Give ear, HASHEM, to my prayer.*

Malbim explains that תְּפִלָּה, *prayer,* is an outpouring of the soul which yearns to be released from the narrow confines of the flesh, so that it may soar heavenward to its Divine source (see *comm.* to v. 1).

וְהַקְשִׁיבָה בְּקוֹל תַּחֲנוּנוֹתָי — *And heed the sound of my supplications.*

According to *Malbim*, תְּחִנָּה, *supplication,* unlike תְּפִלָּה, *prayer,* is a plea that God fulfills man's bodily needs. Once a man gains Divine attention through prayer for spiritual liberation, God becomes receptive to all his wishes — even requests for the

fulfillment of his mundane needs.

7. בְּיוֹם צָרָתִי אֶקְרָאֶךָ כִּי תַעֲנֵנִי — *On the day of my distress I call upon You, for You will answer me.*

I do not call upon You in vain; nor do I summon you in order to put You to the test. I call upon You only when I am in real distress and have no other recourse (*Ibn Ezra*).

8. אֵין כָּמוֹךָ בָאֱלֹהִים אֲדֹנָי — *There is none like You among the gods, my Lord.*

The gods refers to the celestial powers, such as the angels (*Targum*), or to the luminaries, i.e., the sun, moon, and stars. The idolators who worship these forces imagine that they have independent strength. Indeed, the Almighty did invest these forces and bodies with the ability to influence events, but they are merely the agents of the Lord, and they have no power to act on their own (*Radak*).

Meiri points out a special feature that characterizes the one all-powerful, true God. It is useless to pray to any other forces, for they cannot hear or respond; but when a man addresses himself to God, He *does* hear and respond to his prayer, as Moses emphasized in the Torah (*Deuteronomy 4:7*): *What nation is there so great, that has God so near to it as is HASHEM, our God, whenever we call upon Him?*

ט כְּמַעֲשֶׂיךָ: כָּל־גּוֹיִם | אֲשֶׁר עָשִׂיתָ יָבוֹאוּ |

י וְיִשְׁתַּחֲווּ לְפָנֶיךָ אֲדֹנָי וִיכַבְּדוּ לִשְׁמֶךָ: כִּי־

גָדוֹל אַתָּה וְעֹשֵׂה נִפְלָאוֹת אַתָּה אֱלֹהִים

יא לְבַדֶּךָ: הוֹרֵנִי יהוה | דַּרְכְּךָ אֲהַלֵּךְ בַּאֲמִתֶּךָ

יב יַחֵד לְבָבִי לְיִרְאָה שְׁמֶךָ: אוֹדְךָ | אֲדֹנָי אֱלֹהַי

יג בְּכָל־לְבָבִי וַאֲכַבְּדָה שִׁמְךָ לְעוֹלָם: כִּי־חַסְדְּךָ

וְאֵין כְּמַעֲשֶׂיךָ — *And there is nothing like Your works.*

None of the celestial forces can match Your works. Since You created them, You certainly can do everything which they can do and You can also undo anything they do. The celestial forces can only do Your bidding (*Radak*).

כָּל גּוֹיִם אֲשֶׁר עָשִׂיתָ יָבוֹאוּ וְיִשְׁתַּחֲווּ לְפָנֶיךָ אֲדֹנָי — 9. *All the nations that You made will come and bow down before You, my Lord.*

[Since our God is truly incomparable and no other force is anything like Him, why don't all the nations recognize this manifest truth? In fact, God has deliberately shaped events in a way which allows men to delude themselves by attributing power to helpless objects.]

Only in the Messianic era will God's omnipotence be evident to all and there will be no room for error (*Radak; Meiri*).

וִיכַבְּדוּ לִשְׁמֶךָ — *And [they] shall glorify Your Name.*

The nations that surround Israel will see that God will release His People from their stranglehold in a miraculous manner. Amazed and overwhelmed, they will spread the word of the marvels to all other nations, who will then hasten to pay homage to Hashem (*Ibn Ezra*).

כִּי גָדוֹל אַתָּה וְעֹשֵׂה נִפְלָאוֹת — 10. *For You are great and work wonders.*

God's most wondrous work is man. His body is so fragile, yet it functions as a living organism and as host to the heavenly soul (see *Bereishis Rabbah* 81:3; *Shulchan Aruch, Orach Chaim* 6).

אַתָּה אֱלֹהִים לְבַדֶּךָ — *You alone, O God.*

On the very first day of Creation, God performed His greatest wonder by creating matter from nothing — *ex nihilo.* No other force existed at that time, for even the angels were not created until later. (R' Yochanan says that the angels were fashioned on the second day; R' Chanina maintains that they were formed on the fifth day.)

A human monarch or ruler requires the assistance of many nobles, servants, or aides, yet the King of kings created the world all by Himself (*Rashi* based on *Bereishis Rabbah* 81:3).[1]

הוֹרֵנִי ה' דַּרְכְּךָ — 11. *Instruct me, HASHEM, in Your way.*

[See comm. to 27:11.] My faith has been based on a received tradition, and I adhere to this tradition with complete trust. Now I ask You to fortify my faith by providing me with insight into Your

---

1. Furthermore, God continues to perform countless wonders for man all by Himself, i.e., in secrecy. The recipient is oblivious to God's kindness.

For instance, when Jacob 'deceived' Isaac and 'stole' the blessings from Esau, Jacob was in great danger of getting caught, because Esau was about to come home from the hunt. But every time Esau trapped an animal, God sent an angel to release it, so that Esau would be delayed in the forest. At the very moment that Jacob left Isaac's tent, Esau entered. Jacob was unaware of these miracles, for *You ... work wonders, You alone, O God* (*Tanchuma HaKadum, Parashas Ki Sisa*).

and there is nothing like Your works.

⁹ *All the nations that You made*
will come and bow down before You, my Lord,
and shall glorify Your Name.

¹⁰ *For You are great and work wonders;*
You alone, O God.

¹¹ *Instruct me, HASHEM, in Your way,*
that I may walk in Your truth,
dedicate my heart to fear Your Name.

¹² *I will thank You, my Lord, my God,*
with all my heart,
and I will glorify Your Name forever.

¹³ *For Your kindness toward me is great,*

---

dominion over all aspects of nature. Thus instructed, I will follow *in your way* (*Radak*).

David begged God, "If ever You see me straying from the path of righteousness, force me back to the straight way!" This may be compared to a case of two oxen: the yoked one walked straight and plowed, but the unyoked one strayed and accomplished nothing. The farmer then put a yoke on the shiftless ox, and thenceforth it never failed him (*Midrash Shocher Tov*).

אֲהַלֵּךְ בַּאֲמִתֶּךָ — *That I may walk in Your truth.*

I know that I shall not arrive at the truth all at once. You will instruct me step by step, so that I will eventually walk straight (*Radak*).

The essence of God's truth can be comprehended only through the study of Torah (*Eretz HaChaim*). Through Torah, man perceives the way of God which is evident in simple nature. Afterwards, man learns to appreciate the hidden scheme of God's *truth,* which directs the course of nature (*Malbim*).

יַחֵד לְבָבִי לְיִרְאָה שְׁמֶךָ — *Dedicate my heart to fear Your Name.*

Now my heart wavers in indecison

and trembles in fear. Brace my heart to follow Your way without any deviation (*Radak*).

[When I finally understand how the myriad elements and events of the universe are united in one comprehensive Divine plan, my sense of conviction will be complete and unshakeable.]

12. אוֹדְךָ אֲדֹנָי אֱלֹהַי בְּכָל לְבָבִי — *I will thank You, my Lord, my God, with all my heart.*

When my faith in You becomes wholehearted (v. 11), I will be capable of thanking You *with all my heart,* for I will attribute my well-being and success to You alone (*Radak*).

I will praise You with both aspects of my personality — both the Good and the Evil Inclinations (*Midrash Shocher Tov*).

וַאֲכַבְּדָה שִׁמְךָ לְעוֹלָם — *And I will glorify Your Name forever.*

[I recognize that Your quintessential Name is not אֱלֹהִים, *God, Dispenser of Strict Justice,* but ה׳, *HASHEM, Dispenser of Mercy,* and that is the Name I glorify.]

13. כִּי חַסְדְּךָ גָּדוֹל עָלָי — *For Your kindness toward [lit. upon] me is great.*

There is a distressing human tend-

גָּדוֹל עָלָי וְהִצַּלְתָּ נַפְשִׁי מִשְּׁאוֹל תַּחְתִּיָּה:
אֱלֹהִים זֵדִים קָמוּ־עָלַי וַעֲדַת עָרִיצִים בִּקְשׁוּ
נַפְשִׁי וְלֹא שָׂמוּךָ לְנֶגְדָּם: וְאַתָּה אֲדֹנָי אֵל־
רַחוּם וְחַנּוּן אֶרֶךְ אַפַּיִם וְרַב־חֶסֶד וֶאֱמֶת:
פְּנֵה אֵלַי וְחָנֵּנִי תְּנָה־עֻזְּךָ לְעַבְדֶּךָ וְהוֹשִׁיעָה

יד

טו

טז

ency to beg for help in times of distress, but not to remember the savior after the passage of time. Often we discover that after God has lifted a man from the depths of despair, he fails to show appreciation. As he becomes increasingly successful, this man views God's past help as less and less significant. David, however, declares that the more God's *kindness* comes *towards* him, the greater God's goodness appears to be (*Tehillos Hashem*).

וְהִצַּלְתָּ נַפְשִׁי מִשְּׁאוֹל תַּחְתִּיָּה — *And You rescued my soul from the nethermost depth.*

David said, "Adulterers are condemned to the lowest level in hell. I was accused of committing adultery with Bath Sheba, but You absolved me of guilt and sent the prophet Nathan to inform me (*II Samuel* 12:13): *HASHEM has also forgiven your sin, you shall not die*" (*Rashi; Midrash Shocher Tov*).

This also alludes to שְׁאוֹל, Saul, who sought to send David down to שְׁאוֹל, the nethermost depth, i.e., the grave (*Radak*).

14. אֱלֹהִים זֵדִים קָמוּ עָלַי — *O God, transgressors have risen up against me.*

This refers to Doeg and Achitophel (*Rashi; Midrash Shocher Tov*). They are called זֵדִים because they pursued David בְּמֵזִיד, *willfully*, unlike those who chased David only under duress. Many men in Saul's army, for example, pursued David only because they feared Saul (*Radak*).

וַעֲדַת עָרִיצִים בִּקְשׁוּ נַפְשִׁי — *A company of ruthless men sought my soul.*

Not only do my enemies seek my physical destruction, they also seek to

ruin the moral perfection of *my soul* (*Ibn Yachya*).

[See comm. to 37:35 for the definition of עָרִיץ.]

וְלֹא שָׂמוּךָ לְנֶגְדָּם — *And they have not set You before them.*

Those who threaten me fail to remember that You commissioned the prophet Samuel to anoint me as king. If they would keep this fact in mind, they would not dare to defy Your decree (*Rashi; Midrash Shocher Tov*).

15. וְאַתָּה אֲדֹנָי אֵל רַחוּם וְחַנּוּן — *But You, my Lord, are God, Merciful and Compassionate.*

[David now explains that although vicious men pursue him he has no fear because he can depend on God's mercy.]

[This description of God is based on the Thirteen Attributes of Divine Mercy, which were revealed to Moses after the Jews sinned with the Golden Calf. These Attributes begin: אֵל ה' ה', *HASHEM, HASHEM, God*, רַחוּם וְחַנּוּן, *Merciful and Compassionate* (*Exodus* 34:6-7). Here the Name אֲדֹנָי, *my Lord*, is substituted for the two Names ה' ה'. Seven of the Thirteen Attributes are mentioned in this verse. The commentary to this verse is based on the ArtScroll volume, *Tashlich and the Thirteen Attributes*, pp. 16-20.]

The Name אֵל, *God*, denotes the most intense mercy. This powerful degree of mercy is reserved exclusively for the very righteous who sometimes err without intending to flout God's will, but then repent immediately. For such men, God is willing to disregard the laws of nature in order to perform miracles of salvation (*Milchemes Mitzvah*).

and You rescued my soul
from the nethermost depth.
¹⁴ *O God,*
transgressors have risen up against me,
A company of ruthless men sought my soul,
and they have not set You before them.
¹⁵ *But You, my Lord,*
are God, Merciful and Compassionate,
Slow to Anger,
Abundant in Kindness and Truth.
¹⁶ *Turn to me and show me favor,*
give Your might to Your servant,

The Name רַחוּם, *Merciful*, expresses the idea that even when a man must be punished, if he merely calls out to God for mercy, God will ease the intensity of his suffering (*Sforno*, Exodus 34:6).

חַנּוּן, *Compassionate*, finds its root in the word חֵן, *charm*, which is related to חִנָּם, *free of charge*. God is compassionate and aids even those unworthy of kindness. If they make a sincere request, God responds although they lack the merit with which to pay for His kindness (see *Berachos* 7a).

אֶרֶךְ אַפַּיִם — *Slow to Anger.*
Literally, אֶרֶךְ means *long*, signifying that God is not short-tempered. He takes a *long* time to grow angry in order to afford the sinner an opportunity to repent before it is too late (*Rashi*).

Tosafos (Eruvin 22a) explains that אַפַּיִם is the plural of אַף, *countenance, face.* God has two 'faces': to the wicked man, He displays a benign, smiling face, and He showers him with prosperity. Finally, if the wicked man dies unrepentant, he suffers eternal damnation.

To the righteous man, however, God displays an angry countenance. God punishes his slightest sins in This World, but waits אֶרֶךְ, *a long time*, before rewarding the righteous man for his good deeds. After having purged the righteous person of guilt in This World,

God smilingly gives him his eternal reward in the World to Come.

וְרַב חֶסֶד — *(And) Abundant in Kindness.*
For those who lack personal merits, God draws upon His abundant store of kindness (*Rashi*).

If the scales of justice are exactly balanced and a man's merits and sins are equal, God, in His abundant kindness, will tilt the scales toward the man's merits (*Rosh HaShanah* 17a).

וֶאֱמֶת — *And Truth.*
This signifies that God insures that His promises are fulfilled. He never reneges on His word and can be trusted to reward the deserving (*Rashi*).

16. פְּנֵה אֵלַי וְחָנֵּנִי — *Turn to me and show me favor.*
David pleaded, "Master of the Universe, turn away from all of Your other responsibilities and give me Your undivided attention, so that I will receive Your full mercy" (*Midrash Shocher Tov*).

תְּנָה עֻזְּךָ לְעַבְדֶּךָ — *Give Your might to Your servant.*
Intensify Your concern for me and provide me with heightened intellectual capacity and superior physical strength so that I may overcome my enemies (*Meiri*).

יז לְבֶן־אֲמָתֶךָ: עֲשֵׂה־עִמִּי אוֹת לְטוֹבָה וְיִרְאוּ
שֹׂנְאַי וְיֵבֹשׁוּ כִּי־אַתָּה יהוה עֲזַרְתַּנִי
וְנִחַמְתָּנִי:

וְהוֹשִׁיעָה לְבֶן אֲמָתֶךָ — *And save the son of Your handmaid.*

David's mother's name was Natzeves bas Adael (*Bava Basra* 91a).

David mentions his mother rather than his father here because before and after birth a child's entire being is more deeply intermeshed with his mother than with his father.

Judaism teaches that man has free will and is responsible for his actions and decisions. Nevertheless, a person's ancestry and upbringing *do* have an important effect on one's character and ideas; a mother's influence is particularly significant in this respect. David identifies himself both as עַבְדְּךָ, *Your servant,* and as בֶּן אֲמָתֶךָ, *the son of Your handmaid,* implying: I am Your servant of my own free will, yet my development was influenced by the fact that my mother was Your devoted *handmaid* (*Radak*). [See also 116:16: אֲנִי עַבְדְּךָ בֶּן אֲמָתֶךָ, *I am Your servant, son of Your handmaid.*]

Rashi explains that a slave who had

been born a free man to free parents retains some pride even after he is sold into servitude, whereas a slave born to a slave mother is completely humble. David declares that he achieved the ultimate level of humility before God because he is a *servant* who was born to a pious mother who was herself a humble *handmaiden* to God.

17. עֲשֵׂה עִמִּי אוֹת לְטוֹבָה וְיִרְאוּ שֹׂנְאַי וְיֵבֹשׁוּ — *Display for me a sign for good, so that my enemies may see it and be ashamed.*

David asked, "Please display publicly that You have forgiven my sin, so that my enemies will see it and be put to shame." However, God did not show this sign to David in his own lifetime, but waited until David's son, Solomon, dedicated the Temple. During the dedication, the gates of the Temple refused to open until Solomon invoked the merit of David's blessed memory (*Rashi,* based on *Shabbos* 30a; see *comm.* and footnote to 24:7).[1]

---

1. The word אוֹת means a *letter* of the alphabet as well as a *sign.*

   Chida (*Rosh David*) notes that throughout the *Book of Chronicles* David's name is spelled with an extra letter י — דָּוִיד [see *I Chronicles* 2:15, *et. al.*].

and save the son of Your handmaid.

¹⁷ Display for me a sign for good,
so that my enemies may see it and be ashamed,
For You, HASHEM, will have helped
and consoled me.

Chida observes that the initial letters of אוֹת לְטוֹבָה וְיִרְאוּ שׂנְאַי can be rearranged to form the name שָׁאוּל, *Saul*, David's most dangerous enemy. David asked God to demonstrate his personal innocence of Saul's charges.

כִּי אַתָּה ה' עֲזַרְתַּנִי וְנִחַמְתָּנִי — *For You, HASHEM, will have helped and consoled me.*

When Absalom and Achitophel threatened me, You *assisted me* through the efforts of Chushai HaArki (*II Samuel* 16:16-17:15). When I was grieved by the incident with Bath Sheba, You *consoled me* with the message transmitted by Nathan the prophet (*II Samuel* 12:13): *HASHEM has also forgiven Your sin; You shall not die* (*Midrash Shocher Tov*). [David concludes this psalm with a fervent prayer, "Since You have been kind to me in the past, I beseech You now for a final message of consolation and redemption."]

Ir Binyamin explains that David's arch-enemy was דּוֹאֵג, *Doeg*, whose name had the same numerical value as David's, i.e., fourteen. Doeg's wickedness so revolted David that he abhorred even this slight semblance of parity with his evil foe. Therefore, David asked Hashem to add a letter to his name, thereby changing its numerical value. God added a י, bringing the value to twenty-four.

The number twenty-four alludes to one of David's major accomplishments: the division of the *Kohanim* into twenty-four groups who served in the Temple for a week at a time on an alternating basis.

[For further discussion of the extra letter in David's name, see *Get Pashut* 129:21 and *Kiryas Chanah David* (p. 147) by R' Tzvi Ferber.]

Sefer Chassidim (346) observes that דָּוִיד is the numerical equivalent of אֹהֲבָיו, *those who love Him* (i.e., Hashem). Since David's enemies are God's enemies, they will be shamed by the fact that David is referred to as 'God's beloved.'

Korach denied the sovereignty and superior sanctity of Moses, Aaron, and the other leaders of Israel. He protested, "The entire congregation is holy, all of them, and HASHEM is among them. Why then do you elevate yourselves above the congregation of HASHEM?" (Numbers 16:3). He also refused to recognize that the Land of Israel is holier than any other land. At that point, Korach's sons refused to join his revolt; instead they composed a song to extol the unique virtues of the Land of Israel and the city of Jerusalem (Toras Chessed). In this way they gave credence to the concept that just as some locations are better suited to the service of God than others, so too are certain men, such as Moses, better suited for the spiritual leadership of the nation than others.

א לִבְנֵי־קֹרַח מִזְמוֹר שִׁיר יְסוּדָתוֹ בְּהַרְרֵי־
ב קֹדֶשׁ: אֹהֵב יהוה שַׁעֲרֵי צִיּוֹן מִכֹּל מִשְׁכְּנוֹת
ג יַעֲקֹב: נִכְבָּדוֹת מְדֻבָּר בָּךְ עִיר הָאֱלֹהִים
ד סֶלָה: אַזְכִּיר | רַהַב וּבָבֶל לְיֹדְעָי הִנֵּה פְלֶשֶׁת

1. שִׁיר מִזְמוֹר לִבְנֵי קֹרַח — *By the sons of Korach, a song with musical accompaniment.*

This psalm, which praises the gates of the holy Temple — HASHEM loves the gates of Zion (v. 2) — was inspired by an event in the life of Korach's family. The sons of Korach were particularly concerned with these gates. As noted in the *Prefatory Remarks* to psalm 79, *Midrash Shocher Tov* explains that Assaf was distressed when his father, Korach, was swallowed into the bowels of the earth (*Numbers* 16:31-33). Assaf lost all hope for his father's return, until he received a prophetic vision that the gates of the Temple would also be swallowed by the earth when the rest of the Sanctuary was destroyed. The vision concluded with the very same gates being raised from the earth to their former glory.

Then Assaf declared ecstatically, ''He who will descend to the bowels of the earth to retrieve the Temple's gates will also raise my father Korach'' (*Alshich*).

יְסוּדָתוֹ בְּהַרְרֵי קֹדֶשׁ — *Whose foundation is in the holy mountains.*

This composition was based on and dedicated to the mountains of Jerusalem and Zion (*Rashi*). Specifically, the Psalmist was inspired by Mount Zion, Mount Moriah (the Temple Mount), and the others mountains surrounding Jerusalem (such as the Mount of Olives). In 125:2, David, too, emphasizes the hilly terrain of this city, *Jerusalem, surrounded by mountains, and HASHEM surrounds His nation* (*Radak*).

[The impressive mountains represent special Divine providence and protection for Jerusalem.]

Indeed, these mountains form the foundation for the entire world, for tradition teaches that the first part of earth created at the genesis of the universe was the אֶבֶן שְׁתִיָּה, *foundation stone,* a rock in the Holy of Holies. From that rock, the earth expanded and spread outward to form the globe (see *Yoma* 55b; *Eretz HaChaim*).

According to *Midrash Shocher Tov*, Judaism is founded on two *holy mountains;* Mount Sinai and Mount Moriah. In the former, our tradition was transmitted, on the latter it was preserved.

Targum interprets הַרְרֵי קֹדֶשׁ as an allegory describing our ancient forefathers [for the pious and holy Patriarchs tower above ordinary men as mountains tower over the plains].

Indeed, יְסוּדָתוֹ may be read as a contraction of the words יְסוֹד דָתוֹ, *the foundation of His faith,* for the Patriarchs established the Jewish faith, which still stands as firm as a mountain (*Rav Yosef Titzak*).

2. אֹהֵב ה׳ שַׁעֲרֵי צִיּוֹן — *HASHEM loves the gates of Zion.*

The gates of every city took on particular importance because the local court and yeshivah were located there (*Radak*). But the most noteworthy gate in *Eretz Yisrael* was that of the Temple, for there the Great Sanhedrin convened as the supreme authority in Jewish life (*Sforno*).

The gates of the Temple had special significance because they were also the portals to heaven; through these gates the prayers of Jews throughout the world ascended heavenward, and through these gates heavenly blessings descended upon Israel (*Dorash Moshe*).

There were actually thirteen gates in the wall surrounding the Temple

87
1-4

By the sons of Korach,
    a song with musical accompaniment,
whose foundation is in the holy mountains.
    ² HASHEM loves the gates of Zion
        more than all the dwellings of Jacob.
    ³ Glorious things are spoken of you,
        O city of God, Selah.
    ⁴ I mention Rahav and Babylon to my acquaintances,

(*Middos* 2:6): a gate symbolizing each
of the twelve tribes and one general gate
for everyone. The prayers of each tribe
ascended through its specific gate
(*Migdal David*; see *Magen Avraham,
Orach Chaim* 68).

So precious were the gates that when
the enemy destroyed the entire Temple
God did not allow these gates to be
burned. Rather they were swallowed
into the ground, where they remain
intact to this day. In the future they will
be raised again and incorporated into
the Third and final Temple (*Zera
Yaakov*).

מִכֹּל מִשְׁכְּנוֹת יַעֲקֹב — *More than all the
dwellings of Jacob.*

Although God certainly loves these
private homes of the Jewish people — as
Scripture states (*Numbers* 24:5), *How
goodly are your tents, O Jacob, your
dwellings, Israel* — God prefers the *gates
of Zion* (*Radak*).

According to the Talmud (*Berachos*
8a), צִיּוֹן is to be interpreted as מְצֻיָּן,
outstanding, distinguished. God loves
the select academies where Torah is
studied constantly with utmost dedication by distinguished scholars even
more than He loves the synagogues and
ordinary study halls; for the elite
academies are spiritual centers comparable to the holy Temple which was
permanently established in Zion,
whereas the synagogues and study halls
are but מִשְׁכְּנוֹת יַעֲקֹב, *dwellings of Jacob,*
where God is sought at specific times
rather than continuously.

3. נִכְבָּדוֹת מְדֻבָּר בָּךְ — *Glorious things*

are spoken of you.

Indeed, in 48:3 the sons of Korach
describe the city of Jerusalem in the
most rapturous terms: *Fairest of sites,
joy of all the earth, Mount Zion.* This
description denotes the physical beauty
of the holy metropolis and the
perfection of its climate (*Radak*; see
comm. of *Radak* to 48:3).

According to *Midrash Shocher Tov,*
this phrase refers to the spiritual
excellence of the city. The most *glorious*
and distinguished scholars and teachers
were attracted to Jerusalem — especially
during the reign of King Hezekiah who
made the city an unsurpassed Torah
center.

עִיר הָאֱלֹהִים סֶלָה — *O city of God, Selah.*

Midrash Shocher Tov continues that
the most *glorious thing* about Jerusalem
was that מְדֻבָּר בָּךְ, *You are spoken of,*
i.e., only in the Temple in Jerusalem was
God's Name uttered explicitly, in all its
glory; elsewhere, substitute names had
to be used to describe Him. Thus, only
Jerusalem deserves the title *city of God.*
[See ArtScroll volume, *Bircas Kohanim,*
p. 32.]

4. אַזְכִּיר רַהַב וּבָבֶל לְיֹדְעָי — *I mention
Rahav and Babylon to my acquaintan-
ces.*

The translation follows *Sforno,
Akeidas Yitzchak,* and *R' S. R. Hirsch,*
who interpret this verse to mean: If I
praise the great empires of Rahav and
Babylon for the contributions their great
men made to civilization and culture,
then my acquaintances can challenge me
by mentioning the accomplishments of

ה וְצוֹר עִם־כּוּשׁ זֶה יֻלַּד־שָׁם: וּלֲצִיּוֹן | יֵאָמַר
אִישׁ וְאִישׁ יֻלַּד־בָּהּ וְהוּא יְכוֹנְנֶהָ עֶלְיוֹן:

ו יהוה יִסְפֹּר בִּכְתוֹב עַמִּים זֶה יֻלַּד־שָׁם סֶלָה:

ז וְשָׁרִים כְּחֹלְלִים כָּל־מַעְיָנַי בָּךְ:

Philistia, Tyre, and Kush, which have also fostered at least one noteworthy individual who has brought honor to his native land.

The literal meaning of רַהַב is *arrogant*. The word is related to רָחָב, *wide, extended,* and to רַב, *much, great,* because the arrogant have an overinflated self-image [see comm. to 40:5, וְלֹא פָנָה אֶל רְהָבִים].

The boastful empire of Egypt is called רַהַב by the prophet *Isaiah* (31:7): *Egypt shall offer assistance in vain and to no purpose, therefore I have called these people,* רַהַב, *boasters.* (See also *Isaiah* 51:9; *Psalms* 89:11; and *Job* 9:13 and 26:12.)

הִנֵּה פְלֶשֶׁת וְצוֹר עִם כּוּשׁ — *Behold there are Philistia and Tyre, with Kush.*

Megalleh Amukos explains that since God scattered נִיצוֹצוֹת, *sparks* [of Divine sanctity], throughout the world, even the pagan nations hold such sparks in their midst. Therefore, even such peoples as *Philistia, Tyre* and *Kush* — who are far removed from true faith — possess a few praiseworthy men of noble character. These rare individuals serve as the repository of the scattered Divine 'sparks.'

זֶה יֻלַּד שָׁם — [*Saying:*] "*This one was born there.*"

Since the emergence of a great man is a rare occurrence among the gentile nations, these individuals are singled out, and people remark, זֶה, *this one,* is special and different from everyone else (*Ibn Ezra; Meiri*).

The *Maggid of Dubno* points out that every country has certain special conditions which benefit its inhabitants. However, a country is usually beneficial only for natives who are accustomed to its climate and atmosphere. Therefore,

the nations praise their notables, saying, *this one was born here.* The land of Israel, however, has a beneficial effect on all those who enter its borders, even if they are not natives.

The special benefits of other countries are physical properties which aid only those men whose bodies were fashioned on the soil of that particular land. But the unique benefits of the Holy Land are universal spiritual gifts (*Kol Yaakov*).

5. וּלֲצִיּוֹן יֵאָמַר אִישׁ וְאִישׁ יֻלַּד בָּהּ — *But of Zion it can be said:* "*Man after man was born in her.*"

[Unlike the other lands,] Zion produces one man of stature after another, constantly (*Ibn Ezra; Radak*).

This phenomenon may be attributed to the fact that Zion is the source of all human life. The first man was created at the Temple Mount, from the earth where the altar was destined to stand (*Rambam, Hilchos Beis HaBechirah* 2:2). Therefore, the finest forms of human life emanate from that area (*Alshich*).

The Talmud (*Kesubos* 75a) explains that the double usage אִישׁ וְאִישׁ [lit. *a man and a man*] denotes that the inhabitants of the Holy Land are twice as great as those of other countries. The example of R' Yirmiah is cited. When he lived in Babylon, he was an inferior student who failed to comprehend his lessons, but when he went up to Israel, his talents developed so fast that he soon was far superior to his peers who remained in Babylon.

The Talmud (*ibid.*) offers another explanation of the double usage אִישׁ וְאִישׁ. Two types of people can be called children of Zion, both the person who was actually born there and the non-

behold there are Philistia and Tyre, with Kush,
Saying: "This one was born there."
⁵ *But of Zion it can be said:*
"Man after man was born in her,"
and He Himself will establish her as the most high.
⁶ *HASHEM will select — when He inscribes nations —*
This one was born there, Selah.
⁷ *And singers and flute players alike shall say,*
"All my essence is in You."

---

native who always yearned to live there.[1]

Targum says that the expression refers to Zion's two extraordinary kings, David and Solomon.

Rashi (comm. to Kesubos 75a) explains this verse as a prophecy of the future, for in the Messianic era, all the empires and nations will appreciate those people born in Zion. Whenever they identify a native of Zion trapped in exile, they will eagerly escort him home.

ווהוא יכוננה עליון — *And He Himself will establish her as the most high.*

God originally made Zion the foremost location on earth. The Psalmist now prays for the day when Zion will once again be recognized as supreme (Radak).

6. ה' יספר בכתוב עמים — *HASHEM will select* [lit. *count*] — *when He inscribes* [lit. *writes*] *nations.*

In the future, Hashem will determine the fate of the nations who deserve to be condemned, and He will *inscribe the nations* in the Book of Death. But at the same time, He will take note that

throughout the exile, many good Jews have been lost, some were forced to adopt other religions, while others assimilated. In the future, God will uncover and *select* [i.e., *count*] these lost Jews and declare, "*This one was born there* [i.e., in Zion], and he has no relationship to the gentiles" (Rashi).

Ibn Ezra and *Radak* interpret this as a reference to the dawn of history, when God recorded the number of noteworthy men who would appear in the world. He determined that only a handful would come from the gentile nations, whereas many would be born to Israel and to Zion.

Ibn Ezra concludes that the skies serve as the ledgers in which God keeps His records.

זה ילד שם סלה — *This one was born there, Selah.*

Targum translates סלה as forever and interprets these verses as a reference to the Davidic monarchy that flourished in Zion (see *Targum* to v. 5). Thus the verse would mean that the royal dynasty *born there* [i.e., anointed in Zion] will endure forever.

---

1. At the time of the British mandate over Palestine, the authorities were very strict about illegal immigration, and they enforced a very rigid quota limiting the number of Jews who could enter the land. However, if a Jew declared that he had been born in Palestine, then he was given permission for reentry and was not subjected to the quota.

A group of desperate Jews contacted Rav Yosef Chaim Sonnenfeld. They were foreign born, but the only way for them to enter *Eretz Yisrael* was by declaring themselves to be born there. Although the Rav was a scrupulously honest man, he permitted these people to make their declaration. "The Talmud teaches that both the man born in Zion and the man who yearns to live there equally deserve to be called children of Zion," he explained [Ha'ish al HaChomah, vol. II, p.154].

7. וְשָׁרִים כְּחֹלְלִים — *And singers and flute players alike.*

Zion is a perfect city which lacks no form of wisdom, culture or art. Zion is even the cradle of skilled singers and musicians (*Rashbam*). These are all destined to sing God's praises [when Zion is recognized as the Divine metropolis] (*Radak*).

Ibn Ezra notes that a large orchestra consisting of many musicians ordinarily accompanies one or several vocalists. In the future, however, so many people will be inspired to sing God's praises that the number of שָׁרִים, *singers*, will be כְּחֹלְלִים, *equal to the number of instrumentalists.*

Yalkut Eliezer translates חֹלְלִים as *flutes.* He points out that not everyone will be privileged to sing God's praises. The egotistical man who takes pride in his voice and seeks acclaim for his talent

will not sing before God. Only שָׁרִים, *singers*, who are humble and consider themselves כְּחֹלְלִים, *like flutes*, i.e., mere instruments in the hands of God, will be worthy to sing the Divine praise.

כָּל מַעְיָנַי בָּךְ — [*Shall say,*] *"All my essence is in You."*

The translation follows *Rashi*. *Radak* and *Metzudos* contend that the root of מַעְיָנַי lies in the word עִיּוּן, *study, research.* Thus the verse would mean: My entire life is dedicated to carefully scrutinizing and evaluating Your ways.

Ibn Ezra and *Radak* also suggest that this word is related to מַעְיָן, *wellspring*, implying: My heart constantly overflows with songs and music to You, O God. *Midrash Shocher Tov* adds that just as a fountain constantly discharges fresh water, so does Israel constantly transmit new songs of praise to Hashem.

Israel's exile and dispersion were Divinely ordained as instruments to spur Israel's spiritual development in the pursuit of excellence. In exile, the lonely, insecure Jew is compelled to turn to a Divine source of strength in order to find security and a purpose for his life. The exile is exceptionally close to God, for no secular national loyalties interfere with his devotion to God. Ideally, the holiness of Eretz Yisrael should have brought the people to heightened perceptions of God and to fulfillment of their spiritual potential. But instead of utilizing the land to enhance their development, they allowed themselves to become creatures of the earth. Therefore they were exiled so that they would realize that their 'home' is the Torah, not a parcel of real estate; and their success depends on mitzvos, not on a plow.

Despite the opportunity for spiritual development which galus (exile) offers, depression, disgrace, and doom threaten the suffering wanderer. In the following verses, Korach's sons vividly depict the agonies of galus and express Israel's yearning for Divine redemption.

א שִׁיר מִזְמוֹר לִבְנֵי קֹרַח לַמְנַצֵּחַ עַל־מָחֲלַת
ב לְעַנּוֹת מַשְׂכִּיל לְהֵימָן הָאֶזְרָחִי: יהוה אֱלֹהֵי
ג יְשׁוּעָתִי יוֹם־צָעַקְתִּי בַלַּיְלָה נֶגְדֶּךָ: תָּבוֹא
ד לְפָנֶיךָ תְּפִלָּתִי הַטֵּה אָזְנְךָ לְרִנָּתִי: כִּי־שָׂבְעָה

1. שִׁיר מִזְמוֹר לִבְנֵי קֹרַח — *A song with musical accompaniment by the sons of Korach.*

Alshich explains that this song refers to the suffering of the exile and to the yearning for redemption and reconstruction. This theme was especially significant to the sons of Korach because they knew that when the Temple is rebuilt both its gates and their father will ascend from the bowels of the earth. [See *Prefatory Remarks* to psalm 87.]

עַל מָחֲלַת לְעַנּוֹת — *Upon Machalas Le'annos.*

This term describes the pitiful state of Israel in exile. The Jews suffer from a מַחֲלָה, *sickness*, of heart because they yearn for the Holy Land. At the same time, they are לְעַנּוֹת, *afflicted*, by travails and persecutions in exile (*Rashi*).

Midrash Shocher Tov identifies מַחֲלַת with מְחִילָה, *forgiveness*. The Holy One, Blessed is He, said to David, "Sing my praises and I will forgive you, because לְעַנּוֹת, you have been afflicted."

Meiri identifies the מָחֲלַת as a special musical instrument that moves the listener to anguish and tears. Its music serves לְעַנּוֹת, *to afflict*, and upset the listener so much that he is prepared to repent with utter sincerity.

מַשְׂכִּיל — *A Maskil.*

Wherever a hymn is described as a *Maskil* it means that the composer prepared himself to be the recipient of a prophetic inspiration. An orator with a powerful voice was designated to announce the message. As the spirit of prophecy came to the composer, he transmitted the message to the orator, who then repeated it aloud to the assembled masses (*Rashi*).

לְהֵימָן הָאֶזְרָחִי — *By Heiman the Ezrahite.*

Scripture makes reference to two men who were called Heiman. In *I Chronicles* 6:18, we read: *From the sons of Kehas* [the Levite] *was Heiman the singer* [the chief singer (*Metzudos*)] *the son of Joel the son of Samuel* [the prophet].

Ibn Ezra cites *R' Yeshua*, who identifies the author of this psalm with Heiman the Levite. Furthermore, *R' Yeshua* suggests that אֶזְרָחִי is cognate with אֶזְרָח, *permanent resident* (see *Targum*). He explains that throughout *I Chronicles* we find that the majority of Temple singers were the sons and descendants of Heiman; therefore, Heiman is rightfully described as an אֶזְרָח, *permanent resident*, of the Temple.

A second man named Heiman is introduced in *I Chronicles* 2:6 in a listing of the descendants of the tribe of Judah. There he is recorded as the son of Zerach, the son of Judah [see *Genesis* 38:30]. *Rashi* and *Radak* identify the author of this psalm with that Heiman. According to their view, he is called the אֶזְרָחִי, *Ezrahite*, because of his father זֶרַח, *Zerach*.

Heiman the son of Zerach was a brilliant musician whose extraordinary intellect is apparent from the fact that Scripture (*I Kings* 5:11) says of Solomon, the wisest of all men, that he was even wiser than Heiman and his wise brothers. Heiman and his brothers were called בְּנֵי מָחוֹל, *people of song and music*, because they composed a number of songs that were incorporated into the *Book of Psalms*.[1]

2. ה' אֱלֹהֵי יְשׁוּעָתִי — *HASHEM, God of*

1. *Rashi* here takes pains to emphasize that Heiman was a gifted musician rather than a singer.

A song with musical accompaniment
by the sons of Korach,
for the conductor, upon Machalas Le'annos,
a Maskil by Heiman the Ezrachite.
² *HASHEM, God of my salvation,*
by day I cried out, by night I am before You.
³ *Let my prayer come before You,*
incline Your ear to my cry.

---

my salvation.

O God, You are responsible for every salvation I have experienced throughout my lifetime (*Sforno*).

Israel said to the Holy One, Blessed is He, "Our hopes and aspirations are concentrated on You alone!"

God responded, "In that case, I am compelled to save you!" (*Midrash Shocher Tov*).

יוֹם צָעַקְתִּי בַלַּיְלָה נֶגְדֶּךָ — *By day I cried out, by night [I] am before You.*

Although I cried out to You all day long, I continue to cry out at night (*Rashi*).

Rav Hirsch perceives in these four words a summary of the state of the Jews in exile: by day, the downtrodden Jew would struggle for his existence, while his enemies heaped derision upon him. But as the working day waned and night fell, the Israelite would return to his family, to his community, to the houses of study and prayer, and to communion with God. At night the Jew found knowledge and understanding, comfort and courage, strength and inspiration for his life's mission which God had assigned him.

3. תָּבוֹא לְפָנֶיךָ תְּפִלָּתִי — *Let my prayer come before You.*

The *Talmud* (*Eruvin* 65a) states that just as a drunken person cannot pray with proper concentration, so, too, Jews can be excused for failing to pray properly because of the emotional distress they suffer from the exile (see *Rashi* and *Maharsha*, ibid.). Israel therefore cries out, "Since I continue to pray to You as best I can — despite this exemption — please *let my prayer come before You*" (*Chomas Anach*).

הַטֵּה אָזְנְךָ לְרִנָּתִי — *Incline Your ear to my cry.*

Usually רִנָּה refers to a cry of joy, an exclamation of the soul. Israel pleads with God, "Despite the suffering of exile, I find joy in Your Presence and cry out in ecstasy. [Therefore, please *incline Your ear to my cry*]" (*Toras Chessed*).

Rav Hirsch defines רִנָּה as the soul's response, sometimes joyous and sometimes sorrowful, to any outside stimulus.

Rashi explains that the sons of Korach composed and arranged this song to be sung to the instrumental accompaniment of Heiman. *Rashi* is compelled to say this because he maintains that Heiman was *not* a Levite but a descendant of Judah, and, as Rambam (*Hilchos Klei HaMikdash* 3:3) rules, only Levites were permitted to sing in the Temple. *Rambam* states that Israelites of untainted lineage were permitted to provide musical accompaniment for the Levites, although they were forbidden to sing. Thus Heiman, the Judean, could not *sing* in the Temple, but he *could* serve as a musician.

The Talmud (*Bava Basra* 15a) offers the view that the Heiman mentioned in *I Kings* (who was only slightly less wise than Solomon) is none other than Moses, who was completely נֶאֱמָן, *faithful* (cognate with הֵימָן) to God (*Numbers* 12:7). According to the Talmud, another Heiman composed this psalm. *Rabbeinu Gershom* (*Bava Basra* 15a) identifies him as the grandson of Samuel, who was a Levite.

[See also commentary to 89:1 for further opinions regarding the term הָאֶזְרָחִי, *the Ezrachite*.]

ה בְּרָעוֹת נַפְשִׁי וְחַיַּי לִשְׁאוֹל הִגִּיעוּ: נֶחְשַׁבְתִּי

ו עִם־יוֹרְדֵי בוֹר הָיִיתִי כְּגֶבֶר אֵין־אֱיָל: בַּמֵּתִים

חָפְשִׁי כְּמוֹ חֲלָלִים | שֹׁכְבֵי קֶבֶר אֲשֶׁר לֹא

ז זְכַרְתָּם עוֹד וְהֵמָּה מִיָּדְךָ נִגְזָרוּ: שַׁתַּנִי בְּבוֹר

ח תַּחְתִּיּוֹת בְּמַחֲשַׁכִּים בִּמְצֹלוֹת: עָלַי סָמְכָה

ט חֲמָתֶךָ וְכָל־מִשְׁבָּרֶיךָ עִנִּיתָ סֶּלָה: הִרְחַקְתָּ

4. כִּי שָׂבְעָה בְרָעוֹת נַפְשִׁי — *For my soul is sated with troubles.*

I resemble a man whose hunger has been satisfied, for the agonies of exile have caused me to lose my appetite (*Nora Tehillos*).

וְחַיַּי לִשְׁאוֹל הִגִּיעוּ — *And my life has reached the Lower World.*

Because the miseries of exile have destroyed my appetite for life, I do nothing to sustain my physical well-being. Therefore, I find myself on the brink of utter ruination and death (*Nora Tehillos*).

5. נֶחְשַׁבְתִּי עִם יוֹרְדֵי בוֹר — *I was reckoned with those who descend to the pit.*

In exile, the downtrodden Jews became a symbol of failure and worthlessness. The gentiles jeer at us in our pitiful state and predict that such an oppressed, despised people will descend to the depths of hell (*Toras Chessed*).

הָיִיתִי כְּגֶבֶר אֵין אֱיָל — *I was like a man without strength.*

My hopelessness in exile has sapped ־e of strength. I must bear insult and ־njury, yet I utterly lack the energy to ־trike back at my persecutors (*Sforno*).

־ בַּמֵּתִים חָפְשִׁי — *[I am] among the dead ־vho are free.*

Since I have nothing from this world, I am like a dead man, who is completely divorced [i.e., free] from the earthly concerns and temptations that tend to

enslave the spirit (*Rashi*). [Since people tend to ignore the ideas of a pauper, he is considered 'dead', in the sense of being devoid of influence.]

The Talmud (*Nedarim* 64a) states that a poor man is considered dead. Nevertheless, it is his very poverty that *frees* the exiled Jew from his burden of sin, for poverty is a form of suffering which purges the soul (*Zera Yaakov*).

According to *Radak*, these words represent the exile's wish: "I would rather be reckoned among the dead, who are free from all burdens, than to continue to live as a slave of the wicked."[1]

כְּמוֹ חֲלָלִים שֹׁכְבֵי קֶבֶר אֲשֶׁר לֹא זְכַרְתָּם עוֹד — *Like the corpses lying in the grave, whom You remember no more.*

Targum renders חָלָל as a man who was murdered by the sword [see *Numbers* 19:16]. His corpse was abandoned in the field and no one cared enough to seek out his murderers in order to avenge his death (*Sforno*).

Just as such a corpse lies forgotten in an unmarked grave, so Israel seems to be forgotten in exile. It appears as if God intends never to rescue Israel from the deathlike state of *Galus* (*Radak*).

וְהֵמָּה מִיָּדְךָ נִגְזָרוּ — *But they were cut off by Your hand.*

Though a *corpse* may lay ignored and forgotten, the suffering of Israel in exile is completely different. For it was You who decided to punish Your people by

1. Death is tragic in that it robs man of the opportunity for repentance and self-improvement through the study of Torah and the fulfillment of its precepts. The *Midrash* (*Ruth Rabbah* 3:1) comments: In this world, a small person can become great and a great person can falter and become small. But in the World to Come, no one changes.

⁴ For my soul is sated with troubles,
        and my life has reached the Lower World.
⁵ I was reckoned with those who descend to the pit,
        I was like a man without strength —
⁶ Among the dead who are free,
        like the corpses lying in the grave,
whom You remember no more;
        but they were cut off by Your hand.
⁷ You placed me in the lowest of pits,
        into utter darkness,
        into shadowy depths.
⁸ Upon me Your wrath weighed down,
        and all Your crashing waves afflicted me,
        Selah.
⁹ You estranged my friends from me,

---

exiling them and permitting them to sink to the brink of death. Accordingly, Israel is not forgotten; its redemption will come (*Radak*).

Sforno identifies נגזרו as cognate with גְּזֵירָה, *decree*, which implies: It was You who decreed Israel's fate.

7. שַׁתַּנִי בְּבוֹר תַּחְתִּיּוֹת — *You placed me in the lowest of pits.*

Exile is worse than death, for death is called שְׁאוֹל תַּחְתִּית, *the lower world* (comparative), whereas exile is termed *the lowest of pits* (superlative), which indicates that it is like death many times over (*Radak*).

בְּמַחְשַׁכִּים בִּמְצֹלוֹת — *Into utter darkness, into shadowy depths.*

A prison contains many dungeons. The lowest dungeon, deep in the bowels of the earth, is the darkest and the dampest. The hopeless exile resembles this terrible black hole (*Nora Tehillos*).

8. עָלַי סָמְכָה חֲמָתֶךָ — *Upon me Your wrath weighed down.*

Whenever You visit Your wrath upon the world, it is primarily directed towards me, and I bear the brunt of Your anger (*Rashi, Sforno*).

וְכָל מִשְׁבָּרֶיךָ עִנִּיתָ סֶּלָה — *And all Your crashing waves afflicted [me], Selah.*

[The waves which crash upon the shore in rapid, relentless succession symbolize the constant troubles which batter the world from all sides without any respite. No matter where Israel turns, the nation finds neither rest nor refuge from suffering.]

9. הִרְחַקְתָּ מְיֻדָּעַי מִמֶּנִּי — *You estranged my friends from me.*

Some commentators maintain that this refers to the gentiles, whom God caused to become estranged from Israel. When Israel was a sovereign state, firmly established on its own soil, the gentiles appeared friendly. But when Israel was exiled, the gentiles became hostile.

Others say that this describes the breakdown of the cordial relations between one Jew and another, for each individual was so overwhelmed by his personal woes that he had no time to care about his neighbor's problems (*Radak*).

Sforno translates מְיֻדָּעַי as *the famous and distinguished* among us (יְדוּעִים), for Israel once produced world-renowned

מִיְדָעַי מִמֶּנִּי שַׁתַּנִי תוֹעֵבוֹת לָמוֹ כָּלֻא וְלֹא

י אֵצֵא: עֵינִי דָאֲבָה מִנִּי עֹנִי קְרָאתִיךָ יְהוָה

יא בְּכָל־יוֹם שִׁטַּחְתִּי אֵלֶיךָ כַפָּי: הֲלַמֵּתִים

תַּעֲשֶׂה־פֶּלֶא אִם־רְפָאִים יָקוּמוּ ׀ יוֹדוּךָ סֶּלָה:

יב הַיְסֻפַּר בַּקֶּבֶר חַסְדֶּךָ אֱמוּנָתְךָ בָּאֲבַדּוֹן:

יג הֲיִוָּדַע בַּחֹשֶׁךְ פִּלְאֶךָ וְצִדְקָתְךָ בְּאֶרֶץ נְשִׁיָּה:

יד וַאֲנִי ׀ אֵלֶיךָ יְהוָה שִׁוַּעְתִּי וּבַבֹּקֶר תְּפִלָּתִי

scholars, but the travails of exile destroyed the educational system that trained these intellectual giants.

שַׁתַּנִי תוֹעֵבוֹת לָמוֹ — *You made me abominable* [lit. *abominations*] *to them.*

Since each Jew became indifferent to his brothers, it appeared as if they regarded one another as abominable (*Radak*).

כָּלֻא וְלֹא אֵצֵא — *I was jailed and could not leave.*

This indifference grew to the extent that Jews would not even visit the sick. It appeared as if they were imprisoned in shackles which prevented them from looking in on a sick friend (*Ibn Ezra*).

10. עֵינִי דָאֲבָה מִנִּי עֹנִי — *My eye is grieved by affliction.*

Targum translates דָאֲבָה as *it sheds tears* [דָבָה being cognate with זָבָה, *flowing*].

Midrash Shocher Tov observes that poverty (עֹנִי) and tears cause a man's eyes to sink deep into their sockets. In this fashion the eye reflects *grief* and *affliction.*

קְרָאתִיךָ ה' בְּכָל יוֹם — *I called upon You, O HASHEM, every day.*

Throughout the exile You manifested Yourself with the Name אֱלֹהִים, *the Dispenser of Justice.* Nevertheless, I called upon You always as ה', *the Dispenser of Kindness,* for I never lost faith in Your mercy (*Dorash Moshe*).

שִׁטַּחְתִּי אֵלֶיךָ כַפָּי — *I stretched out my hands to You.*

When a person prays for mercy he should raise his hands high in a gesture of supplication and helplessness. Scripture relates that when Amalek attacked Israel, Moses raised his hands high in prayer, and that Israel was triumphant whenever he did (*Exodus* 17:11). The Talmud (*Rosh HaShanah* 25b) comments that whenever Moses lifted his hands, all of Israel's spirits soared in anticipation of Divine assistance (*Olelelos Yehudah*).[1]

11. הֲלַמֵּתִים תַּעֲשֶׂה פֶּלֶא — *Will You work wonders for the dead?*

Why, O God, do You refrain from working miracles for me? Do You

---

1. Praying with raised hands is found often in Scripture [e.g., *I Kings* 8:22], yet because this form of prayer has become prevalent among gentiles, it has fallen into disfavor among Jews. This rejection of a previously acceptable mode of worship has its basis in the Torah. During the time of the Patriarchs the erection of a מַצֵּבָה [*matzeivah*], *standing stone or pillar* [i.e., a single stone erected as an altar, usually used for libations rather than animal sacrifice], was considered a valid means of offering thanksgiving to the Creator. On three occasions Scripture records that Jacob set up *matzeivos* (*Genesis* 28:18; 31:45 and 35:14). Yet we are taught (*Deuteronomy* 16:22): *Do not set up a matzeivah for yourself, that which HASHEM, your God, despises.* Rashi explains that although in the time of the Patriarchs the *matzeivah* was acceptable, it became prohibited when such altars became the standard mode of Canaanite idol worship [see ArtScroll *Bereishis*, p. 1242]. Similarly, praying with upraised hands, although not forbidden, has fallen into disuse in the synagogue service (R' Akiva Eiger, *Orach Chaim* 89; see ArtScroll *Bircas Kohanim*, p. 31).

> You made me abominable to them,
>
> I was jailed and could not leave.
>
> 10 My eye is grieved by affliction,
>
>   I called upon You, O HASHEM, every day,
>
>   I stretched out my hands to You.
>
> 11 Will You work wonders for the dead?
>
>   Will the feeble arise and
>
>   offer You thanks? Selah.
>
> 12 Can Your kindness be recounted in the grave?
>
>   Or Your faithfulness in utter ruin?
>
> 13 Can Your wonders become known in the dark?
>
>   Or Your righteousness in the land of oblivion?
>
> 14 But I — to You, HASHEM, have I cried,

reserve Your wonders for the wicked who are considered as dead even while they live? (Rashi).

Are You waiting for us to die in the agony of exile before You decide to act on our behalf? Please do not delay, for Your miracles are wasted on the dead; as it is said (115:17), It is not the dead who will praise God (Radak).

אִם רְפָאִים יָקוּמוּ יוֹדוּךָ סֶּלָה — Will the feeble arise and offer You thanks?

The gentiles are רָפָה, feeble, in their resolve to serve You, for they refused the opportunity to accept the Torah and mitzvos. Will You perform miracles for people who ignore You? (Rashi).

According to Radak and Targum, the רְפָאִים are the dead whose bodies have decomposed in the grave. These weak corpses are unable to arise from their graves. [We believe in תְּחִיַּת הַמֵּתִים, the resurrection of the dead, but that is an extraordinary event of the future, whereas the Psalmist here speaks of man's everyday experience. See Radak, cited in Commentary to verse 6, who speaks of corpses that in natural terms will never live again, despite our faith that God will eventually 'remember' and resurrect the dead.]

12. הַיְסֻפַּר בַּקֶּבֶר חַסְדֶּךָ — Can Your kindness be recounted in the grave?

What will You gain by allowing us to perish in exile? Will we be able to praise You once we sink to the grave? (Rashi).

אֱמוּנָתְךָ בָּאֲבַדּוֹן — Or Your faithfulness in utter ruin?

The body decays in the grave and sinks into ruin (Radak).

The Talmud (Eruvin 19a) says that אֲבַדּוֹן is one of the seven names of Gehinnom. [Thus, the exile will estrange us from אֱמוּנָה, faith, in You; then, spiritually ruined, we will descend to hell.]

13. הֲיִוָּדַע בַּחֹשֶׁךְ פִּלְאֶךָ — Can Your wonders become known in the dark?

Again and again this query is posed, for the suffering man cries out repeatedly, searching desperately for an answer (Radak).

וְצִדְקָתְךָ בְּאֶרֶץ נְשִׁיָּה — Or Your righteousness in the land of oblivion?

The dead man is swiftly forgotten and sinks into oblivion (Radak).

14. וַאֲנִי אֵלֶיךָ ה' שִׁוַּעְתִּי — But I — to You, HASHEM, have I cried.

I cleave to You under all circumstances. Even when adversity causes me to sink like a dead man, I still propel my spirit heavenward as I plead for Your assistance (Tehillos Hashem).

The Zohar (Sh'mos) differentiates

טו תְקַדְמֶךָ: לָמָה יהוה תִּזְנַח נַפְשִׁי תַּסְתִּיר
טז פָּנֶיךָ מִמֶנִּי: עָנִי אֲנִי וְגֹוֵעַ מִנֹּעַר נָשָׂאתִי
יז אֵמֶיךָ אָפוּנָה: עָלַי עָבְרוּ חֲרוֹנֶיךָ בִּעוּתֶיךָ
יח צִמְּתֻתֻנִי: סַבּוּנִי כַמַּיִם כָּל־הַיּוֹם הִקִּיפוּ עָלַי
יט יָחַד: הִרְחַקְתָּ מִמֶנִּי אֹהֵב וָרֵעַ מְיֻדָּעַי
מַחְשָׁךְ:

between שַׁוְעָה, *cry*, and צְעָקָה, *scream*. A
cry is a form of prayer in which the
supplicant articulates precisely the type
of יְשׁוּעָה, *salvation* (cognate with שַׁוְעָה),
he needs. A *scream*, however, is merely
a wordless wail of עָקָא, the
onomatopoetic Aramaic word for *pain*.

The שַׁוְעָה, *cry*, is the initial stage of
the prayer process, which culminates
when repeated tears and shouts have
weakened the supplicant to the point
that his lips can no longer move. He is
then considered to be a man whose heart
is torn with remorse. Such deep
sincerity has the power to reverse even
the harshest Heavenly decree which
may have been issued against the
supplicant. [See *Malbim on Exodus*
2:23.]

וּבַבֹּקֶר תְּפִלָּתִי תְקַדְמֶךָ — *And in the
morning my prayer will greet You.*

Every morning, my prayers precede
my other activities (*Radak*). I ignore my
personal concerns, so that I may pursue
spiritual perfection (*Dorash Moshe*).

15. לָמָה ה' תִּזְנַח נַפְשִׁי — *Why,
HASHEM, should You abandon my
soul?*

Considering the extent of my
devotion to You, why do You persist in
ignoring my passionate prayers?
(*Radak; Sforno*).

תַּסְתִּיר פָּנֶיךָ מִמֶנִּי — *Why should You
conceal Your face from me?*

Why do You pay no attention to my
prayers? (*Radak*).

My face should be a reflection of the
glory of Your countenance, for I was
created in Your image (צֶלֶם אֱלֹהִים).
Why, then, do You conceal Your holy
face from me? (*Tehillos Hashem*).

16. עָנִי אֲנִי וְגֹוֵעַ מִנֹּעַר — *Afflicted am I,
and close to death since youth.*

The translation follows *Radak*, who
paraphrases: My life has been an
endless chain of tragedy from earliest
youth to old age. Nevertheless, I have
not forsaken You, my Lord, although I
have tottered on the brink of death.

Shaarei Chaim observes that mankind was stripped of immortality after
Adam's sin. Thus, the moment a child is
born, he starts his pre-destined journey
leading to the day of death. The
Psalmist describes this curse most
vividly with the words גֹוֵעַ מִנֹּעַר, I am ...
close to death since youth.

Rashi and *Menachem* identify מִנֹּעַר
as cognate with the verb לְנַעֵר, *to
vigorously shake* or *beat out*, thus
suggesting: I am on the verge of a
violent death which will forcefully
thrust my soul from my body.

נָשָׂאתִי אֵמֶיךָ אָפוּנָה — *I have borne Your*

and in the morning my prayer will greet You.

¹⁵ *Why, HASHEM, should You abandon my soul?*
   Why should You conceal Your face from me?
¹⁶ *Afflicted am I, and close to death since youth,*
   I have borne Your horrors
   and feel constant dread.
¹⁷ *Your rages have gone over me,*
   Your terrors have flayed me.
¹⁸ *They surround me like water all day long,*
   they encircle me in unison.
¹⁹ *You estranged from me friend and companion,*
   my dearest ones in obscurity

---

horrors and feel constant dread.

Rashi explains that אֵמוּנָה is related to אוֹפָן, *base* or *setting*: I have grown so accustomed to horror that I remain set in a constant state of shock.

Metzudos relates אֵמוּנָה to פָּנוּי, *empty, unoccupied*, thus suggesting: I am so pre-occupied with horrible experiences that my mind is empty of all other thoughts.

Radak and *Sforno* perceive the root of אֵמוּנָה as פֶּן, *perhaps*, which suggests: Bitter experience has conditioned me to live in a state of constant insecurity, by the fear that פֶּן, *perhaps*, I shall die.

17. עָלַי עָבְרוּ חֲרוֹנֶיךָ — *Your rages have gone over me.*

Every type of punishment which You inflicted upon the world has smitten me (*Sforno*).

בְּעוּתֶיךָ צִמְּתֻתוּנִי — *Your terrors have flayed me.*

The repetition of the letter ת indicates repeated flaying without respite (*Radak*).

18. סַבּוּנִי כַמַּיִם כָּל הַיּוֹם — *They surround me like water all day long.*

Just as the oceans surround the earth, these enemies surround me (*Radak*).

הִקִּיפוּ עָלַי יָחַד — *They encircle me in unison.*

My enemies were united in their hatred for me (*Targum*).

19. הִרְחַקְתָּ מִמֶּנִּי אֹהֵב וָרֵעַ — *You estranged from me friend and companion.*

[Compare with v. 9.] Israel's dearest friend is the eagerly awaited Messiah, and it appears as if God is delaying, rather than hastening, his arrival (*Chazah Zion*).

מְיֻדָּעַי מַחְשָׁךְ — *My dearest ones [are] in obscurity* [lit. *in darkness*].

My best friends are alienated from me; they seem to be hiding from me in a dark, obscure place (*Radak*).

[The Psalmist concludes this composition with this gloomy remark, which underscores the saddest aspect of exile — the intense feeling of loneliness and abandonment which plagues the downcast wanderer. The Jew has no friends, no one he can trust. The world turns its back on Israel and is content to let the Jewish people fade from the arena of history into eternal oblivion. This miserable experience serves as a lesson to Israel that our nation survives only by miracles and we have no one to trust in save our Father in Heaven.]

This composition unfolds the lengthy tale of bitter exile, not so much for the nation as a whole, but for its outstanding heroes.

The very first Hebrew, Abraham, was a fugitive from those who sought to obliterate God's Name. Powerful kings and hostile nations rose up to defy God and to torment Abraham, God's representative on earth.

Later, a king arose to lead the holy nation dedicated to God. David, the model king, was also persecuted by those who wished to obliterate God's Name.

This psalm records the pact that God struck with David. The Almighty promised that if David and his offspring would remain true to Him, He would be true to them. But if the seed of David would betray the covenant, exile and suffering would be their lot.

The third Book of Psalms concludes with the heartening message expressed in the final verse of this psalm: Blessed is HASHEM forever, Amen and Amen.

מַשְׂכִּיל לְאֵיתָן הָאֶזְרָחִי: חַסְדֵי יהוה עוֹלָם

אָשִׁירָה לְדֹר וָדֹר | אוֹדִיעַ אֱמוּנָתְךָ בְּפִי: כִּי

אָמַרְתִּי עוֹלָם חֶסֶד יִבָּנֶה שָׁמַיִם | תָּכִן

אֱמוּנָתְךָ בָהֶם: כָּרַתִּי בְרִית לִבְחִירִי

1. מַשְׂכִּיל לְאֵיתָן הָאֶזְרָחִי — *A Maskil by Eisan the Ezrachite.*

[For the explanation of *Maskil*, see 32:1.]

Rashi says that Eisan was one of five brothers who were famous musicians in the Temple, as stated in *I Chronicles* 2:6, *And the sons of Zerach: Zimri and Eisan and Heiman and Kalkol and Dara.* [Thus *Ezrachite* means 'of the family of Zerach' (see commentary to 88:1).] *Radak* adds that *Eisan the Ezrachite* was one of the wisest men who ever lived; his wisdom was surpassed only by that of Solomon (*I Kings* 5:11).

Targum, based on the *Talmud* (*Bava Basra* 14b), identifies Eisan as the Patriarch Abraham, for he was אֵיתָן [lit. *strong*] in his faith (*Aggadah Bereishis* 55). Since Abraham traveled from Chaldea in the מִזְרָח, *east*, in order to spread belief in God, he was called הָאֶזְרָחִי, *the Ezrachite* [lit. *the easterner*].

Radak explains that this psalm bemoans the length of the exile. The main feature of the exile is the nullification of the Jewish sovereignty vested in the monarchy of the House of David. Therefore, the Psalmist here speaks in terms of David and his seed.

Rav Shlomo Atiyah reconciles the various opinions regarding this psalm's authorship. In Abraham's time, he was despised by the Godless monarchs who feared his powerful lessons of faith in the One God. Abraham's nephew Lot was also a disseminator of the Patriarch's religious teachings. An alliance of four kings attacked Sodom and took Lot into captivity (*Genesis* 14:12). Abraham pursued the kings, defeated them and liberated Lot. At that time, he composed this hymn on the theme of captivity in the hands of the enemies of God.

Many centuries later, David was captive in a trap set by the treacherous people of the city of Ke'ilah. God delivered him from this trap and, in this psalm, David recorded the feelings of a liberated captive (see *I Samuel* 23:4-13).

When David composed this psalm, he based his words on the feelings expressed by the Patriarch Abraham in his earlier work. [Perhaps David commissioned the famous musician Eisan the Ezrachite to execute a composition based on Abraham's theme.]

2. חַסְדֵי ה' עוֹלָם אָשִׁירָה — *Of HASHEM's kindness I will sing forever.*

Abraham was the personification of kindness, as the prophet *Michah* 7:20 teaches: תִּתֵּן ... חֶסֶד לְאַבְרָהָם, *Bestow ... kindness to Abraham* (*Eretz HaChaim*).

In appreciation of God's kindness, Abraham dedicated himself to performing acts of kindness for others. For example, he invited all wayfarers to dine at his table and placed a sumptuous repast before them. Before he gave them permission to begin the meal, however, he asked that they pay homage to the master of the house.

When the guests began to lavish thanks upon Abraham, he stopped them saying, "I am not the master here. It is the one God who rules heaven and earth who is your kind host!"

According to the *Zohar* (*Parashas Vayechi*), the kindness of God was displayed to Abraham when the Almighty tested him with ten tests which made Abraham אֵיתָן, *strong*, steadfast in his faith.

לְדֹר וָדֹר אוֹדִיעַ אֱמוּנָתְךָ בְּפִי — *To every generation, with my mouth I will make your faithfulness known.*

Malbim explains that אֱמוּנָה, *faith-*

A Maskil by Eisan the Ezrachite.

² Of HASHEM's kindness I will sing forever;
to every generation, with my mouth
I will make your faithfulness known.
³ For I said, "The world is built on kindness;
the heavens — You establish Your faithfulness
in them."
⁴ I made a covenant with My chosen one,

---

fulness, refers to the constant and reliable course of natural events, while God's supernatural deeds are called חֶסֶד, kindness (see comm. to 36:6). Thus, the phrase לְדֹר וָדֹר, to every generation, which describes the normal passage of time and the natural progression of events from one era and generation to the next, is the proper description for God's faithfulness. However, חֶסֶד, kindness, is supernatural, and is not bound by the natural limits of time; it extends לְעוֹלָם, forever; or for eternity, i.e., beyond time.

3. כִּי אָמַרְתִּי עוֹלָם חֶסֶד יִבָּנֶה — For I said, "The world is built on kindness ..."

The translation follows Targum and Rashi. Midrash Shocher Tov said that at the time of Creation, the world was tottering like a chair which had only three legs until God propped up the world with a fourth 'leg' — kindness.[1]

[Indeed, God's sole purpose in creating the world was to benefit mankind. God gave men a chance to serve Him only so that He could then reward them with Divine kindness.]

An alternate translation renders the word עוֹלָם, not as the world but as

forever i.e., God will build with kindness forever the throne of David, so as to insure the continuity of his dynasty for all time (Rashi; Radak; Ibn Ezra; Sforno).

שָׁמַיִם תָּכִן אֱמוּנָתְךָ בָהֶם — "... The heavens — You establish Your faithfulness in them."

Just as the heavens endure forever, so will Your faithful promise to David last for eternity, as Scripture states (I Samuel 7:13), I will establish his royal throne forever (Rashi; Radak; Ibn Ezra).

Malbim explains this according to his commentary concerning the previous verse: when the world was first built, everything God did was חֶסֶד, kindness (i.e., extraordinary and supernatural), because at the moment of creation, the laws of nature were not yet in force. But after God created these universal laws of nature, then, You established Your faithfulness (i.e., the dependable, predictable natural order) even in heaven.

4. כָּרַתִּי בְרִית לִבְחִירִי — I made a covenant with My chosen one.

---

1. *Shimon the Tzaddik* used to say that the entire world is supported by three things: the study of Torah, the service of God, and the performance of kindness (*Avos* 1:2).

So important is kindness that when Abraham displayed the slightest lapse in חֶסֶד he was severely punished. In the introduction to *Zohar* it is related that Abraham invited all of the nobles and notables to the party he made on the day that his son Isaac was weaned. Satan sought to disrupt the celebration by disguising himself as a beggar standing at Abraham's door, waiting for some food. Abraham was completely pre-occupied with his guests and did not notice the pauper. Sarah too was busy with her well-wishers. Satan then went before the heavenly tribunal and condemned Abraham for this lack of kindness. Incensed, God decreed that Abraham would be put to the test with the sacrifice of Isaac, and that Sarah would die when she mistakenly heard that Isaac had been slaughtered.

ה נִשְׁבַּעְתִּי לְדָוִד עַבְדִּי: עַד־עוֹלָם אָכִין זַרְעֶךָ
ו וּבָנִיתִי לְדֹר־וָדוֹר כִּסְאֲךָ סֶלָה: וְיוֹדוּ שָׁמַיִם
ז פִּלְאֲךָ יְהוָה אַף־אֱמוּנָתְךָ בִּקְהַל קְדֹשִׁים: כִּי
מִי בַשַּׁחַק יַעֲרֹךְ לַיהוָה יִדְמֶה לַיהוָה בִּבְנֵי
ח אֵלִים: אֵל נַעֲרָץ בְּסוֹד־קְדֹשִׁים רַבָּה וְנוֹרָא
ט עַל־כָּל־סְבִיבָיו: יהוה | אֱלֹהֵי צְבָאוֹת מִי־

The 'faithfulness' of the previous verse is the Divine covenant described here. Nathan the Prophet informed David that God had made a covenant assuring him that (v. 5) his seed would retain their royal status forever (Rashi; Radak).

According to some commentators, this refers to God's covenant with Abraham, for he was also God's chosen one, as the prophet states (Nechemiah 9:7): You are the One who chose Abram and made his name Abraham (Tehillos Hashem).

נִשְׁבַּעְתִּי לְדָוִד עַבְדִּי — I have sworn to David, My servant.

I promised David that I would maintain the covenant I made with his forefather Abraham (Chazah Zion).

Radak observes that although God never formally swore to David, God's word is as reliable and binding as an oath.

5. עַד עוֹלָם אָכִין זַרְעֶךָ — "For eternity I will establish your seed …"

Nathan promised David (I Chronicles 17:10), HASHEM will build you a house. This refers to the eternal dynasty of the House of David (Radak).

וּבָנִיתִי לְדֹר וָדוֹר כִּסְאֲךָ סֶלָה — "… And I will build your throne for generations, Selah."

[Your children will not be mere figureheads but they will wield all the royal power symbolized by the throne.]

6. וְיוֹדוּ שָׁמַיִם פִּלְאֲךָ ה' — Then the heavens will gratefully praise Your wonders, HASHEM.

The establishment of the throne of

David is the occasion for great joy and thanksgiving; even the heavens will burst into praise (Midrash Shocher Tov).

How do the heavens offer praise and thanks to God? When the planets, stars and celestial bodies follow a precise course without deviation, this inspires all who behold them to sing God's praise (Radak; see comm. to 19:1).

אַף אֱמוּנָתְךָ בִּקְהַל קְדֹשִׁים — Also Your faithfulness in the assembly of holy ones.

The holy ones are the angels responsible for the motion of all heavenly bodies (Radak; Ibn Ezra).

Tehillos Hashem cites the Rabbis' statement that there is a certain holy angel which has a thousand mouths, each mouth containing a thousand tongues which give praise to God's faithfulness.

7. כִּי מִי בַשַּׁחַק יַעֲרֹךְ לַה' — For who in the sky can be compared to HASHEM…?

The heathens worship the planets and the stars in the sky. But how can any of these heavenly bodies be compared to HASHEM, since even the heathens themselves admit that God once created all of the celestial host! All admit that it is God who empowers the celestial bodies (Radak).

[See Rambam (Hilchos Avodas Kochavim 1:1, 2) for an explanation of man's early descent from belief in God to idolatry. See also footnote to ArtScroll Bereishis 5:1.]

יִדְמֶה לַה' בִּבְנֵי אֵלִים — Be likened to HASHEM among the angels?

> *I have sworn to David, My servant:*
>
> 5 *"For eternity I will establish your seed;*
>   *and I will build your throne*
>   *for generations, Selah."*
>
> 6 *Then the heavens will gratefully praise*
>   *Your wonders, HASHEM,*
> *also Your faithfulness*
>   *in the assembly of holy ones.*
>
> 7 *For who in the sky can be compared to HASHEM;*
>   *be likened to HASHEM among the angels?*
>
> 8 *God Who is dreaded in the hiddenmost*
>   *counsel of the holy ones,*
>   *and is awesome over all who surround Him.*
>
> 9 *HASHEM, God of Legions —*
>   *who is like You, O Strong One, God?*

The translation follows *Targum*. However, *Radak* comments that the אֵלִים are the angels and the בְּנֵי אֵלִים [lit. *the sons of angels*] are the planets and heavenly bodies which are controlled by the angels and are therefore considered their sons. [See comm. to 29:1.]

8. אֵל נַעֲרָץ בְּסוֹד קְדֹשִׁים רַבָּה — *God Who is dreaded in the hiddenmost counsel of the holy ones.*

[The root ערץ means *dread*, as in *Deuteronomy* 1:29, לֹא תַעַרְצוּן.]

Our translation follows *Rashi* and *Ibn Ezra*, who perceive רַבָּה [lit. *very much*] as a modifier of סוֹד, *counsel*. According to *Radak*, however, רַבָּה modifies נַעֲרָץ, to indicate that God is *very much* dreaded. *Metzudos* contends that רַבָּה describes קְדֹשִׁים, signifying *the very holy ones.*

Alshich explains that this refers to the Rabbinic tradition that when the ministering angels gather daily to proclaim God's sanctity with the words קָדוֹשׁ, קָדוֹשׁ, קָדוֹשׁ, *Holy! Holy! Holy!*, they are seized with an awesome dread. Trembling, they emit a fiery perspiration which turns into a flaming river, as

it were.

This proves that the righteous men are greater than the angels, for Abraham spoke to God and was not overwhelmed as were the angels. The angel stands before God only at intervals, whereas the truly righteous man constantly concentrates his attention on his Maker and is not startled by God's presence.

וְנוֹרָא עַל כָּל סְבִיבָיו — *And is awesome over all who surround Him.*

This idea was introduced in 50:3, וּסְבִיבָיו נִשְׂעֲרָה מְאֹד, *And His surroundings are exceedingly turbulent.*

The Talmud (*Yevamos* 121a) explains that God's gaze is fixed on the righteous, for they are closest to Him. Their slightest flaws are closely examined, and God exacts *awesome* judgment upon *all who surround Him.*

According to *Radak* and *Meiri*, this refers to the ministering angels who attend God in the heavenly tribunal, and surround Him.

9. ה' אֱלֹהֵי צְבָאוֹת מִי כָמוֹךָ חֲסִין יָהּ — *HASHEM, God of Legions — who is like You, O Strong One, God?*

Hashem, You are the Creator who

י כָּמוֹךָ חֲסִין | יָהּ וֶאֱמוּנָתְךָ סְבִיבוֹתֶיךָ: אַתָּה
מוֹשֵׁל בְּגֵאוּת הַיָּם בְּשׂוֹא גַלָּיו אַתָּה
יא תְשַׁבְּחֵם: אַתָּה דִכִּאתָ כֶחָלָל רָהַב בִּזְרוֹעַ
יב עֻזְּךָ פִּזַּרְתָ אוֹיְבֶיךָ: לְךָ שָׁמַיִם אַף־לְךָ אָרֶץ
יג תֵּבֵל וּמְלֹאָהּ אַתָּה יְסַדְתָּם: צָפוֹן וְיָמִין אַתָּה
יד בְרָאתָם תָּבוֹר וְחֶרְמוֹן בְּשִׁמְךָ יְרַנֵּנוּ: לְךָ

originally brought the Legions of creatures into being and You alone are the חֲסִין, *Strong One*, who continues their existence (*Radak*).

[God perpetuates the existence of His creations even if they defy Him.] The Talmud (*Gittin* 57a) relates that Titus the Roman blasphemed God, entered the Holy of Holies, and rolled out a Torah scroll upon which he lay with a prostitute. Afterwards he slashed the sacred פְּרוֹכֶת, *curtain*, with his sword. Rabbi Abba Chanin said: Despite all this, God withheld His wrath until the appropriate moment, because He is חֲסִין, *Strong One*, who patiently bears the evils of His creatures.

Since matrimony assures the perpetuation of mankind, the Order of the *Mishnah* and *Talmud* dealing with marriage is called חוֹסֶן, *strength* (*Shabbos* 31a). The *Midrash* (*Ruth Rabbah* 3:6) notes the intricacy of the Divine design for marriage and the propagation of progeny.

God, the Strong One, arranged events so that precisely as the funeral procession of Boaz's first wife was bearing her coffin from the city of Bethlehem, Ruth — who was destined to be Boaz's second wife [and the great-grandmother of David] — was entering that city (see *Maharzu* to *Ruth Rabbah* 3:6).

וֶאֱמוּנָתְךָ סְבִיבוֹתֶיךָ — *And Your faithfulness is Your surrounding.*

Hashem is surrounded by holy angels who attest to His *faithfulness* (*Radak*). [Indeed, when the Almighty makes a promise, He dispatches His ministering angels to fulfill the Divine pledge.]

10. אַתָּה מוֹשֵׁל בְּגֵאוּת הַיָּם — *You rule the towering* [lit. *pride*] *of the sea.*

In the preceding verses, the Psalmist described God's mastery over the heavenly forces; now he depicts God's rule over the earth below.

The גֵאוּת, *pride*, of the sea refers to the fact that the sea waters would tower over the land and flood the earth, if God did not *rule* the waters and confine them within their boundaries, as 33:7 states, כֹּנֵס כַּנֵּד מֵי הַיָּם, *He assembles like a mound the waters of the sea* (*Radak*).

God exercises similar control over all His creations (*Sforno*).

בְּשׂוֹא גַלָּיו אַתָּה תְשַׁבְּחֵם — *When it raises its waves, You calm them.*

Although the root שבח usually refers to *praise* or *improvement*, it can also mean *to becalm*, or *to still*, as in מְשַׁבֵּחַ שְׁאוֹן יַמִּים, *Who calms the roar of the seas* (65:8). When the waves hit the seashore and threaten to overwhelm the loose sand, *You calm the waves* and restrain them.

Your mastery over the water was most evident when You split the Sea of Reeds. Then waves of water piled up in walls which threatened to collapse at any moment; yet, as long as Israel was crossing the sea, You stilled the waves (*Radak*).

11. אַתָּה דִכִּאתָ כֶחָלָל רָהַב — *You crushed the arrogant like a corpse.*

רָהַב, *arrogant*, refers to the proud Egyptian empire [see comm. to 87:4 and 40:5]. *You crushed* [them] *like a corpse* when You allowed the water to cascade upon them (*Radak*).

בִּזְרוֹעַ עֻזְּךָ פִּזַּרְתָ אוֹיְבֶיךָ — *With Your*

And Your faithfulness is Your surrounding.

¹⁰ *You rule the towering of the sea,*
   when it raises its waves, You calm them.

¹¹ *You crushed the arrogant like a corpse,*
   with Your mighty arm You scattered Your foes.

¹² *Yours are the heavens, Yours, too, is the earth;*
   the world and its fullness — You founded them.

¹³ *The north and the south — You created them;*
   Tabor and Hermon sing joyously in Your Name.

¹⁴ *Yours is the arm with power;*

---

mighty arm You scattered Your foes.

Ordinarily, those who drown at sea are not washed ashore for a number of days. This was not true of the Egyptians; God caused their corpses to be washed ashore and scattered along the beaches immediately, so that the Israelites could see that their pursuers were dead and that God had assured their own salvation (Radak).

12. לְךָ שָׁמַיִם אַף לְךָ אָרֶץ — *Yours are the heavens, Yours, too, is the earth.*

Now the Psalmist notes God's mastery over *both* heaven and earth. All creatures instinctively recognize and praise the sovereignty of God (Radak).

תֵּבֵל וּמְלֹאָהּ אַתָּה יְסַדְתָּם — *The world and its fullness — You founded them.*

The inhabited portion of the earth is called תֵּבֵל [see comm. to 24:2]. God endowed this area with an abundant *fullness* of resources so that man could live in comfort (Radak).

13. צָפוֹן וְיָמִין אַתָּה בְרָאתָם — *[The] north and [the] south [lit. right] — You created them.*

The word יָמִין, *right*, describes the *south.* When Scripture speaks of directions, it starts with the east, (which is called קֶדֶם, *beginning*) for the day *begins* in the east with sunrise. When one faces the east, his יָמִין, *right hand*, is towards the *south* (Metzudos).

In this verse, the Psalmist

demonstrates that God is not only Master of heaven above and earth below, but also Ruler of all four directions of the world (Radak).

תָּבוֹר וְחֶרְמוֹן בְּשִׁמְךָ יְרַנֵּנוּ — *Tabor and Hermon sing joyously in Your Name.*

Tabor is one of the most famous mountains because of its height and width. *Hermon* is also called שְׂנִיר, *Senir.* *Rashi* to *Deut.* 3:9 comments that *Senir* was the Canaanite word for snow. The Canaanites gave this name to Hermon because, due to its height, it is capped with snow the year round [see *comm.* to 42:7].

Whoever views these impressive peaks is overwhelmed by the majesty of God's creation and bursts forth in song of praise. Since these mountains inspire song, it is considered as if the peaks themselves sing God's praise (Radak).

14. לְךָ זְרוֹעַ עִם גְּבוּרָה — *Yours is the arm with power.*

Your power supports the entire world as *Deuteronomy* 33:27 states וּמִתַּחַת זְרֹעֹת עוֹלָם, *And underneath are the everlasting arms* (Radak).

Your זְרוֹעַ, *arm*, serves as the defense of Israel, while Your גְּבוּרָה, *power*, is the offensive against those who defy You (Sforno).

Some men have physical strength but lack courage, but You have both זְרוֹעַ, *a mighty arm*, and גְּבוּרָה, *a powerful, brave heart* (Yaavetz Hadoresh).

טו זְרוֹעַ עִם־גְּבוּרָה תָּעֹז יָדֶךָ תָּרוּם יְמִינֶךָ: צֶדֶק

וּמִשְׁפָּט מְכוֹן כִּסְאֶךָ חֶסֶד וֶאֱמֶת יְקַדְּמוּ

טז פָנֶיךָ: אַשְׁרֵי הָעָם יוֹדְעֵי תְרוּעָה יהוה

יז בְּאוֹר־פָּנֶיךָ יְהַלֵּכוּן: בְּשִׁמְךָ יְגִילוּן כָּל־הַיּוֹם

יח וּבְצִדְקָתְךָ יָרוּמוּ: כִּי־תִפְאֶרֶת עֻזָּמוֹ אָתָּה

יט וּבִרְצוֹנְךָ °תָּרִים קַרְנֵנוּ: כִּי לַיהוה מָגִנֵּנוּ

°תָּרוּם ק' יט

תָּעֹז יָדְךָ תָּרוּם יְמִינֶךָ — *Your hand will be strengthened, Your right hand uplifted.*

Normally, when a physical organ is taxed over an extended period of time, it grows weaker and weaker, but *Your hand seems to gain strength the longer it is uplifted* (Yaavetz Hadoresh).

15. צֶדֶק וּמִשְׁפָּט מְכוֹן כִּסְאֶךָ — *Righteousness [or: charity] and justice are Your throne's foundation.*

Having established the fact that God is sovereign over the entire universe, the Psalmist goes on to emphasize that God's dominion is eternal; the Divine throne is a symbol of permanence. The universe will continue to exist (despite its flaws), because God is *righteous* and *just*. Just as a mortal monarch sits on His throne devising ways to better the lot of his subjects, so too God's *righteousness* and *justice* lead Him to grant us special loving care (Radak).[1]

חֶסֶד וֶאֱמֶת יְקַדְּמוּ פָנֶיךָ — *Kindness and truth precede Your countenance.*

These traits are always available to You, and You do not hesitate to employ them for the benefit of mankind (Radak).

16. אַשְׁרֵי הָעָם יוֹדְעֵי תְרוּעָה — *Praises to the people who know the teruah.*

[This translation of אַשְׁרֵי follows Targum and is explained in comm. to 1:1].

Previously the Psalmist described God's kindness to David; now he speaks of God's care for the entire nation. The *teruah* blast of the *shofar* is a symbol of triumph in battle. First the soldiers blow the terrifying, broken *teruah* note in order to intimidate the enemy; then they sound the *teruah* as a sound of victory (Radak).

The *teruah* note also has a spiritual element. On Rosh Hashanah, Israel appeases God with the *shofar* blast, which is the inspiration for the order of Rosh Hashanah prayers. When God hears the *teruah* and sees the Jews' repentance, He rises from His throne of Strict Justice and sits on His throne of Mercy, because He is filled with compassion (Rashi, based on Vayikra Rabbah 29:4).

Maharam Ibn Gabbai points out that the verse does not read שׁוֹמְעֵי תְרוּעָה, *who hear the teruah*, but יוֹדְעֵי תְרוּעָה, *who know the teruah*, which indicates that they are aware of the inner power of the *teruah* which can influence a sinner to repent.

Metzudos derives תְרוּעָה from רֵעַ, *friend*. Thus, the Psalmist praises the

---

1. The *Talmud* (Bava Basra 11a) teaches that all of the deeds of *righteousness* (i.e., charity) and *justice* which a man performs are stored in the base of God's celestial throne.

King Monbaz of the Hasmonean dynasty was extremely devout. When his realm suffered a year of terrible famine, he gave away his own fortune and the fortune he inherited from his royal ancestors in order to provide food for the poor. When his shocked friends and relatives questioned the wisdom of this action, Monbaz retorted, "My forebears stored their wealth in a place where other men could take it. However, I have stockpiled a treasury of merits which is far removed from human grasp, for Scripture states, *Charity* (צֶדֶק) *and justice are the foundation of Your throne.*"

> Your hand will be strengthened,
>> Your right hand uplifted.
> ¹⁵ Righteousness and justice
>> are Your throne's foundation,
> Kindness and truth
>> precede Your countenance.
> ¹⁶ Praises to the people who know the teruah;
>> HASHEM, in the light of Your countenance
>> they walk.
> ¹⁷ In Your Name they rejoice all day long,
>> and through Your righteousness they are exalted
> ¹⁸ For You are the splendor of their power
>> and through Your favor
>> our pride will be exalted.
> ¹⁹ For to HASHEM belongs our shield,

nation that knows how to achieve a closeness to God.

ה׳ בְּאוֹר פָּנֶיךָ יְהַלֵּכוּן — HASHEM, in the light of Your countenance they walk.

The man who is spiritually awakened by the *teruah* blast clearly perceives Divine truths which illuminate his path and prevent him from stumbling (*Radak*).

Imros Tehoros says that *those who know the teruah* are the worshipers who were moved by its impact on the previous Rosh Hashanah and keep its echo reverberating in their consciousness throughout the year. Thus, these men *walk in the light of [God's] countenance* at all times, in periods of sorrow and of happiness.

17. בְּשִׁמְךָ יְגִילוּן כָּל הַיּוֹם — In Your Name they rejoice all day long.

Despite the agony of exile, Israel rejoices in the fact that You lend Your name to them even when they are despised and downtrodden (*Yosef Tehillos*).

וּבְצִדְקָתְךָ יָרוּמוּ — And through Your righteousness they are exalted.

When they perform Your *mitzvos*, which are acts of *righteousness*, they are exalted and elevated over all other nations (*Zekan Aharon*).

18. כִּי תִפְאֶרֶת עֻזָּמוֹ אָתָּה — For You are the splendor of their power.

Jews do not glory in their own strength, but take pride in Your strength (*Ibn Ezra*).

וּבִרְצוֹנְךָ תָּרוּם קַרְנֵנוּ — And through Your favor our pride will be exalted.

When You favor Israel by lending them Your strength, they will gain mastery over all other nations and will thereby be exalted (*Radak*).

19. כִּי לַה׳ מָגִנֵּנוּ — For to HASHEM belongs our shield.

Although a Jewish king is the protection and shield of the nation, he is not independent; he belongs to God. Such submission to God was personified by King David and King Solomon (*Radak; Ibn Ezra*).

כ וְלִקְדוֹשׁ יִשְׂרָאֵל מַלְכֵּנוּ: אָז דִּבַּרְתָּ בְחָזוֹן
לַחֲסִידֶיךָ וַתֹּאמֶר שִׁוִּיתִי עֵזֶר עַל־גִּבּוֹר
כא הֲרִימוֹתִי בָחוּר מֵעָם: מָצָאתִי דָּוִד עַבְדִּי
כב בְּשֶׁמֶן קָדְשִׁי מְשַׁחְתִּיו: אֲשֶׁר יָדִי תִּכּוֹן עִמּוֹ
כג אַף־זְרוֹעִי תְאַמְּצֶנּוּ: לֹא־יַשִּׁא אוֹיֵב בּוֹ וּבֶן־

וְלִקְדוֹשׁ יִשְׂרָאֵל מַלְכֵּנוּ — *And to the Holy One of Israel belongs our king.*

The Messiah, the scion of David and Solomon and a symbol of sanctity, will also be completely devoted to Hashem.

20. אָז דִּבַּרְתָּ בְחָזוֹן לַחֲסִידֶיךָ — *Then You spoke in a vision to Your devout ones.*

There is a difference of opinion as to whether *Your devout ones* refers to Nathan the prophet and Gad the Seer (Rashi; Sforno); to the Temple musicians, such as Heiman and Eisan, who were called men of prophecy (Ibn Ezra); or to Samuel the prophet (Radak).

The *Midrash* (Vayikra Rabbah 1:4) suggests that three other men can be described as חֲסִידֶיךָ: Abraham, Moses and David. The Patriarch Abraham was devoted to God and God spoke to him in a vision, as recorded in Genesis 15. Moses, too, was extremely devout. He perceived God with a vision free of all distortion, the clearest perception possible for any human being. David, the devoted servant of God, also perceived his Maker in a vision as indicated by our verse.

וַתֹּאמֶר שִׁוִּיתִי עֵזֶר עַל גִּבּוֹר — *And [You] said, "I have set assistance upon the mighty one ..."*

You, O God, instructed Gad and Nathan to tell David that Your aid would always be at his disposal (Rashi).

You instructed Samuel to tell Israel that You entrusted the mighty David with the responsibility of coming to Israel's aid (Radak).

You told David that You would aid him in slaying the mighty Goliath (Sforno) and in overcoming the *mighty* King Saul (Arugas HaBosem).

In the course of his career David

fought eighteen battles; thirteen were for the sake of the entire nation, and five were for personal reasons. [Radak identifies each of these battles.] In all of David's campaigns, God came to his aid.

When Abraham pursued the four kings who captured Lot, he also emerged triumphant, with God's aid (Vayikra Rabbah 2:4).

[All the heroes described above fit *Targum's* definition of גִּבּוֹר: *a mighty Torah scholar.*]

הֲרִימוֹתִי בָחוּר מֵעָם — *I have exalted the one chosen from among the people.*

[The Midrash, cited in the commentary to the first stich of this verse, understands the verse as alluding to Abraham, Moses and David.]

Abraham was singled out from the masses of humanity to represent God, as Scripture states (Nechemiah 9:7), אַתָּה הוּא ה' הָאֱלֹהִים אֲשֶׁר בָּחַרְתָּ בְּאַבְרָם, *You are HASHEM, the God, Who chose Abram* (Vayikra Rabbah 1:4).

Moses was surrounded by many men worthy of leadership — Aaron and his sons, Betzalel, Chur, the princes of the twelve tribes, and the seventy elders of Sanhedrin — yet God chose Moses to lead the Jewish people (Tanchuma, Vayikra 3).

David was chosen from among his many brothers, the sons of Jesse (Radak).

21. מָצָאתִי דָּוִד עַבְדִּי — *I found David, My servant.*

There are three instances in which it is said that God *found* something. He found Abraham, as Scripture states, וּמָצָאתָ אֶת לְבָבוֹ נֶאֱמָן לְפָנֶיךָ, *And You found his heart faithful before You* (Nechemiah 9:8). He found David (as

and to the Holy One of Israel belongs our king.

²⁰ *Then You spoke in a vision to Your devout ones,*
and said, "I have set assistance
upon the mighty one,
I have exalted the one chosen
from among the people.
²¹ *I found David, My servant;*
with My holy oil I anointed him;
²² *With whom My hand shall be established,*
My arm, too, shall invigorate him.
²³ *The enemy shall not extort from him,*
nor the iniquitous person afflict him.

recorded here), and He found the Israelites to be loyal to Him after their long sojourn in the Wilderness (*Bereishis Rabbah* 29:3).

The *Midrash* explains this with a parable. While traveling, a king noticed that a precious jewel had fallen from his crown. He assembled his entire entourage and ordered them to collect all the dirt on the road they had traveled. Then they carefully sifted through the dirt until they found the jewel. Similarly, precious souls [i.e., Abraham, David and the Jews of the wilderness] were lost among the worthless masses who surrounded them, but God caused these precious individuals to emerge (*Bereishis Rabbah* 39:10).

Lot was the ancestor of David. Lot's older daughter was the mother of Moab and David's great-grandmother was Ruth the Moabite. Lot and his family were almost lost in the evil and decay of Sodom. At the last minute, however, God saved Lot, for the sake of his noble descendant, David. Thus, it can be said that David was found in Sodom, centuries before his actual birth (*Bereishis Rabbah* 41:4).

בְּשֶׁמֶן קָדְשִׁי מְשַׁחְתִּיו — *With My holy oil I anointed him.*

Although it was Samuel who actually anointed David, God also played an active role in the ceremony; even before Samuel tilted his horn to anoint David, the oil miraculously bubbled from its container onto David's head, as an indication of God's eagerness to anoint David (*Chomas Anoch*).

22. אֲשֶׁר יָדִי תִּכּוֹן עִמּוֹ — *With whom My hand shall be established.*

God's hand grows weary, so to speak, when He sustains the wicked, for they deplete the amount of Divinity in the world and detract from God's strength. But when God supplies the righteous with energy, He Himself, so to speak, grows stronger and more securely established, for the righteous increase and enhance God's sanctity on earth (*Alshich*).

אַף זְרוֹעִי תְאַמְּצֶנּוּ — *My arm, too, shall invigorate him.*

[A self-perpetuating cycle is established: as the righteous man adds to God's strength, God reinforces the righteous man all the more.]

23. לֹא יַשִּׁיא אוֹיֵב בּוֹ — *The enemy shall not extort from him.*

Extort is used in the sense of dominate; to act like one who forcefully demands payment (*Rashi; Radak; Ibn Ezra*).

וּבֶן עַוְלָה לֹא יְעַנֶּנּוּ — *Nor the iniquitous person afflict him.*

כד עוֹלָה לֹא יַעֲנֶנּוּ וְכַתּוֹתִי מִפָּנָיו צָרָיו:
כה וּמְשַׂנְאָיו אֶגּוֹף: וֶאֱמוּנָתִי וְחַסְדִּי עִמּוֹ וּבִשְׁמִי
כו תָּרוּם קַרְנוֹ: וְשַׂמְתִּי בַיָּם יָדוֹ וּבַנְּהָרוֹת
כז יְמִינוֹ: הוּא יִקְרָאֵנִי אָבִי אָתָּה אֵלִי וְצוּר
כח יְשׁוּעָתִי: אַף־אָנִי בְּכוֹר אֶתְּנֵהוּ עֶלְיוֹן
כט לְמַלְכֵי־אָרֶץ: לְעוֹלָם °אֶשְׁמוֹר־לוֹ חַסְדִּי
ל וּבְרִיתִי נֶאֱמֶנֶת לוֹ: וְשַׂמְתִּי לָעַד זַרְעוֹ וְכִסְאוֹ

°אֶשְׁמָר־ ק׳

The wicked man will not be able to inflict physical pain on David (Radak).

24. וְכַתּוֹתִי מִפָּנָיו צָרָיו — *And I will smash his tormentors from before him* [lit. *from before his face*].

The face of the king is a majestic reflection of God's image. When the king's tormentors see his face, they are overcome with awe, and beaten down by his grandeur. Consequently, the king has no need to exert physical force against them (Alshich).

וּמְשַׂנְאָיו אֶגּוֹף — *And strike those who hate him.*

Malbim explains that the מְשַׂנֵּא causes others to hate the person he hates; he tries to alienate everyone from his enemy. In return, God punishes the מְשַׂנֵּא with a מַגֵּפָה, *contagious plague*, (related to אֶגּוֹף) which requires that he be quarantined, isolated and alienated from everyone.

25. וֶאֱמוּנָתִי וְחַסְדִּי עִמּוֹ — *But My faithfulness and My kindness shall be with him.*

I displayed *My kindness* to David by choosing him as My king, and I proved *My faithfulness* by fulfilling My promise to perpetuate his reign throughout his own lifetime and the lives of his descendants (Radak).

Furthermore, I promised both Abraham and David that they would be a faithful source of *kindness* for the world, for God vowed to bless the entire world in their merit (Tehillos Hashem).

וּבִשְׁמִי תָּרוּם קַרְנוֹ — *And through My Name his pride shall be exalted.*

When David calls upon My Name and asks for My assistance I will always respond and exalt his honor and pride (Radak).

26. וְשַׂמְתִּי בַיָּם יָדוֹ — *I will set his hand upon the sea.*

Since *I rule the towering of the sea* (v. 10), I have the power to grant David dominion over the seafaring nations (Ibn Ezra).

Indeed, Hiram, the king of Phoenicia, sent gifts and tribute to David's son Solomon via the sea (I Kings 5:23); he dispatched barges of cypress and cedar wood from Lebanon to Israel (Radak).

וּבַנְּהָרוֹת יְמִינוֹ — *And upon the rivers his right hand.*

David and Solomon also dominated Aram, a nation on the other side of the Euphrates River. Aram sent immense wealth across the river, as tribute to these Jewish kings (Radak).

27. הוּא יִקְרָאֵנִי אָבִי אָתָּה — *He will cry to Me, 'You are my Father; ...'*

Recognizing that God alone invested him with power, the king will draw close to God, as a son clings to his father (Ibn Ezra; Radak).

אֵלִי וְצוּר יְשׁוּעָתִי — *'... My God and the Rock of my salvation!'*

Although a son usually makes many requests of his father, King David will ask only one thing of God: that He be his *salvation* from danger (Alshich).

²⁴ *And I will smash his tormentors from before him,*
   and strike those who hate him.
²⁵ *But My faithfulness and My kindness*
      shall be with him,
and through My Name
      his pride shall be exalted.
²⁶ *I will set his hand upon the sea,*
   and upon the rivers his right hand.
²⁷ *He will cry to Me, 'You are my Father;*
   my God and the Rock of my salvation!'
²⁸ *I will also make him first-born,*
   supreme over the earth's kings.
²⁹ *Forever I shall preserve My kindness for him,*
   and My covenant shall remain true to him.
³⁰ *And I shall establish his seed eternally,*

---

28. אַף אֲנִי בְּכוֹר אֶתְּנֵהוּ — *I will also make him first-born.*

David is considered first-born because he was the first monarch of the House of David, Israel's Divinely ordained dynasty. Since Saul's reign was aborted prematurely, he did not merit this title *(Ibn Ezra).*[1]

Ramban (Genesis 49:10) explains that if Saul had proven worthy, his posterity would have retained a limited degree of sovereignty, perhaps over his own tribe of Benjamin or even over the other descendants of Rachel, Ephraim and Menashe. But the primary rulers would have been the House of David.

עֶלְיוֹן לְמַלְכֵי אָרֶץ — *Supreme over the earth's kings.*

David was placed above all other kings simply because he acknowledged that God is the supreme Ruler of the world *(Ibn Ezra).*

29. לְעוֹלָם אֶשְׁמָר לוֹ חַסְדִּי — *Forever I shall preserve My kindness for him.*

I was kind to Abraham when I made him a source of blessing for the entire world *(Tehillos Hashem).*

I was kind to David when I made him king. This kindness will endure forever *(Radak).*

וּבְרִיתִי נֶאֱמֶנֶת לוֹ — *And My covenant shall remain true to him.*

[I entered into covenants with Abraham and David, and I shall keep them forever.]

30. וְשַׂמְתִּי לָעַד זַרְעוֹ — *And I shall establish his seed eternally.*

The dynasty of David will endure *(Radak).* [David's good deeds will also last forever for they are like seeds which result in future crops. Similarly, David's good deeds became the basis for the deeds of his descendants throughout history.]

---

1. David was the youngest of Jesse's sons, yet he is called *first-born* because, just as the first-born receives two portions of his father's estate, David received two portions of Divinely ordained royalty: sovereignty in this world and sovereignty in the World to Come *(Midrash Shocher Tov).*

לא אִם־כְּיָמֵי שָׁמַיִם: אִם־יַעַזְבוּ בָנָיו תּוֹרָתִי
לב וּבְמִשְׁפָּטַי לֹא יֵלֵכוּן: אִם־חֻקֹּתַי יְחַלֵּלוּ
לג וּמִצְוֹתַי לֹא יִשְׁמֹרוּ: וּפָקַדְתִּי בְשֵׁבֶט פִּשְׁעָם
לד וּבִנְגָעִים עֲוֹנָם: וְחַסְדִּי לֹא־אָפִיר מֵעִמּוֹ וְלֹא
לה אֲשַׁקֵּר בֶּאֱמוּנָתִי: לֹא־אֲחַלֵּל בְּרִיתִי וּמוֹצָא
לו שְׂפָתַי לֹא אֲשַׁנֶּה: אַחַת נִשְׁבַּעְתִּי בְקָדְשִׁי

— **וְכִסְאוֹ כִּימֵי שָׁמַיִם** — And his throne like the days of heaven.

Only on earth does man experience alternating intervals of darkness and light; in heaven, however, eternal Divine light creates unending daytime (Alshich).

31. אִם יַעַזְבוּ בָנָיו תּוֹרָתִי — If his sons forsake My Torah.

My covenant with the House of David is based on the study of Torah, which they dare not forsake (Ibn Yachya).

וּבְמִשְׁפָּטַי לֹא יֵלֵכוּן — And walk not in My judgments.

The term מִשְׁפָּטִים refers to commandments that are readily understood and appreciated by the human mind. Examples of such commandments are the requirement to honor parents and the injunction against murder (Ibn Yachya).

32. אִם חֻקֹּתַי יְחַלֵּלוּ — If they profane My statutes.

[The precepts known as חֻקִּים, decrees, have special sanctity, because these laws are not readily comprehensible by the human intellect. Man's intelligence cannot understand why the פָּרָה אֲדֻמָּה, red cow, should remove contamination or why it should be forbidden to wear a mixture of wool and linen. Only one who recognizes God's ineffable sanctity will faithfully fulfill His statutes. Therefore, the abandonment of the statutes is deemed a profanation of sanctity.]

וּמִצְוֹתַי לֹא יִשְׁמֹרוּ — And keep not My commandments.

[Although the word מִצְוֹת, commandments, is often used in the general sense of good deeds, it also has the more specific meaning (as in this verse), Torah precepts which are fulfilled by performing a specific act.] This refers to the positive commandments (Ibn Ezra) [the performance of which requires constant vigilance and effort].

33. וּפָקַדְתִּי בְשֵׁבֶט פִּשְׁעָם וּבִנְגָעִים עֲוֹנָם — Then I will punish with the rod their transgression, and with plagues their iniquity.

The prophet Nathan prophesied to David concerning the future of his son Solomon (II Samuel 7:14): I [God] will be his Father and he will be My son, if he commits iniquity I will rebuke him with the rod of man and with plagues which befall the sons of Adam. The Rabbis explain that the rod of man refers to the King of Aram, who smote Solomon; the plagues of the sons of Adam refers to Ashmedai, the king of the demons who plagued Solomon (Rashi).

The Talmud teaches that repentance and the holiness of Yom Kippur effect complete atonement for certain sins. However, more serious transgressions, such as those which incur the death penalty, can only be atoned for through physical pain and suffering, which cleanse the soul (Yoma 86a). In such cases, repentance and Yom Kippur remove only half of the sin; the rod and plagues remove the other half

> *and his throne like the days of heaven.*
> ³¹ *If his sons forsake My Torah*
> *and walk not in My judgments;*
> ³² *If they profane My statutes,*
> *and keep not My commandments;*
> ³³ *Then I will punish with the rod*
> *their transgression,*
> *and with plagues their iniquity.*
> ³⁴ *But My kindness I shall not remove from him,*
> *and I will not betray My faithfulness.*
> ³⁵ *I shall not profane My covenant,*
> *the utterance of My lips I shall not alter.*
> ³⁶ *One thing I swore by My holiness —*

(Yerushalmi Yoma 8:7).

34. וְחַסְדִּי לֹא אָפִיר מֵעִמּוֹ — *But My kindness I shall not remove* [lit. nullify] *from him.*

I shall not take the monarchy from David (Radak).

וְלֹא אֲשַׁקֵּר בֶּאֱמוּנָתִי — *And I will not betray My faithfulness.*

... and I will continue to be faithful to his children (Radak).[1]

35. לֹא אֲחַלֵּל בְּרִיתִי — *I shall not profane My covenant.*

Even if David or his descendants will nullify the covenant made at Mt. Sinai, I will not profane the covenant I made with him (Radak).

וּמוֹצָא שְׂפָתַי לֹא אֲשַׁנֶּה — *The utterance of My lips I shall not alter.*

The principle has been established that whenever God promises a punishment He can nullify the promise if circumstances change so that the punishment becomes unwarranted. If God promises a reward, however, He keeps His word even if changed circumstances indicate that the reward is no longer deserved (Dorash Moshe).

36. אַחַת נִשְׁבַּעְתִּי בְקָדְשִׁי — *One thing I swore by My holiness.*

I swore by My Holy Name (Targum). I swore by the holy heavens which endure forever (Ibn Ezra). Radak translates, I swore by My own sanctity.

1. Rambam (Hilchos Melachim 1:7) rules: The moment David was anointed, he acquired the crown of royalty for himself and for his male descendants forever ... but the monarchy was guaranteed only for those descendants who would be worthy of it, as it is stated (132:12), *If your sons will safeguard my covenant* ... However God also promised David that no matter how unworthy his descendants, the monarchy would never be entirely stripped away from his seed, as it is written, *If they profane My statutes* ... *Then I will punish with the rod their transgression* ... *But my kindness I shall not remove from him* ... *I would not be deceitful to David* ... *His seed will endure forever.*

The Brisker Rav (Chiddushei HaGriz LaLevi, II Samuel 21:17) proves that the promise was made to David a number of years prior to the birth of Solomon and that it applied only to the seed of Solomon but not to the descendants of David's other sons. If David had been killed before he had the opportunity to beget Solomon, then the entire promise would have been null and void. Therefore David's officers and army protected his life with extra care prior to Solomon's birth, so that this special covenant would not be endangered.

לז אִם־לְדָוִד אֲכַזֵּב: זַרְעוֹ לְעוֹלָם יִהְיֶה וְכִסְאוֹ
לח כַשֶּׁמֶשׁ נֶגְדִּי: כְּיָרֵחַ יִכּוֹן עוֹלָם וְעֵד בַּשַּׁחַק
לט נֶאֱמָן סֶלָה: וְאַתָּה זָנַחְתָּ וַתִּמְאָס הִתְעַבַּרְתָּ
מ עִם־מְשִׁיחֶךָ: נֵאַרְתָּה בְּרִית עַבְדֶּךָ חִלַּלְתָּ
מא לָאָרֶץ נִזְרוֹ: פָּרַצְתָּ כָל־גְּדֵרֹתָיו שַׂמְתָּ

אִם־לְדָוִד אֲכַזֵּב — *That I would not be deceitful to David.*

I will not allow his dynasty to be interrupted (*Rashi*).

37. **זַרְעוֹ לְעוֹלָם יִהְיֶה** — *His seed will endure forever.*

They shall retain the status of royalty for all time (*Radak*).

[From the time of David's anointment, no one other than a descendant of the House of David could become king of all Israel, nor could any other dynasty have more than temporary status.]

וְכִסְאוֹ כַשֶּׁמֶשׁ נֶגְדִּי — *And his throne shall be like the sun before Me.*

Just as the sun shines endlessly, David's line will be eternal (*Radak*).

Judges 5:31 states וְאֹהֲבָיו כְּצֵאת הַשֶּׁמֶשׁ בִּגְבֻרָתוֹ, *Those who love Him* [i.e., God] *are like the sun emerging in full force.*

The name David spelled out fully, דָּוִיד [rather than דָּוִד], has the numerical value of 24, which equals the value of אֹהֲבָיו, *those who love Him,* because David was the most forceful and energetic lover of Hashem; David's passion for God burned like the flaming sun (*Sefer Chassidim;* see footnote to 86:17).

38. **כְּיָרֵחַ יִכּוֹן עוֹלָם** — *Like the moon, it shall be established forever.*

Sometimes the moon shines brightly, sometimes its visibility is reduced, and sometimes it fades from sight altogether. The House of David undergoes similar changes. When David's descendants are obedient to God, they shine brilliantly [like the full moon], but when they defy God, their light is extinguished. Nevertheless, they will never be completely rejected from

the monarchy, just as the moon waxes, wanes and is temporarily lost from sight, but does not disappear forever (*Radak*).

The royalty of Israel resembled the cycle of the moon. Its first cycle endured for thirty generations, just as the month has thirty days. The light of Jewish monarchy began to rise in the days of the Patriarch Abraham, whom the Canaanites called a *godly prince* (*Genesis* 23:5). David (whose name has the numerical value of fourteen) lived fourteen generations after Abraham and resembled the nearly full moon. Solomon was the fifteenth generation; during his reign, the royal House of David reached its zenith, resembling the full moon. Then the House of David fell into a decline (like the waning moon); finally it underwent a total eclipse, with the exile of King Tzidkiyahu of Judea, who lived thirty generations after Abraham. Nebuchadnezzar blinded King Tzidkiyahu (*II Kings* 25:7), symbolizing the total disappearance of the moon's light.

Therefore, as we sanctify the new moon each month, we proclaim דָּוִד מֶלֶךְ יִשְׂרָאֵל חַי וְקַיָּם, *David, King of Israel lives on and endures!* (*Rabbeinu Bachya, Genesis* 38:30). [See *Overview* to Vol. I, part VIII.]

וְעֵד בַּשַּׁחַק נֶאֱמָן סֶלָה — *"... And the witness in the sky is faithful, Selah."*

Both the sun and the moon bear testimony to the eternal nature of the House of David. As long as these luminaries continue to shine in the sky, David's dynasty will endure. Thus it will last forever, for the prophet Jeremiah proclaims (*Jeremiah* 33:20), *So that I would not be deceitful to David.*

37-41　³⁷ *His seed will endure forever,*
and his throne shall be like the sun before Me.
³⁸ *Like the moon, it shall be established forever,*
and the witness in the sky is faithful, Selah.''
³⁹ *But You have abandoned and rejected;*
You have been angry with Your anointed;
⁴⁰ *You nullified the covenant of Your servant;*
You profaned to the ground his crown;
⁴¹ *You breached all his fences;*

---

says HASHEM: If you can break My covenant with the day and My covenant with the night that there should not be day and night in their season, then also My covenant may be broken with David, My servant, that he should not have a son to reign upon his throne (Rashi).

39. וְאַתָּה זָנַחְתָּ וַתִּמְאָס — *But You have abandoned and rejected.*

[Verses 20-38 contained the proclamation that God expressed in a vision to His devout ones (v. 20), promising that He would remain faithful to the House of David. Now the Psalmist records his response to that oath.]

Radak explains that in this verse the Psalmist appears to be launching into a lengthy condemnation of God, accusing the Almighty of betraying the covenant which He made to David. *Ibn Ezra* relates that in Spain there was a great scholar who found this section of the psalm so blasphemous that he refused to read it or hear it. *Ibn Ezra* himself maintains that this diatribe against God was *not* uttered by the Psalmist. According to *Ibn Ezra*, the Psalmist merely recorded the words of the malicious idolaters, who hurled curses and insults at Hashem.

Radak is of the opinion that these verses are indeed the Psalmist's words. The Psalmist is not questioning God's

faithfulness, for he remains confident that God will fulfill His oath to David. Rather, the Psalmist's query is — now that the Jews are plunged into the depths of a seemingly endless exile, it appears as if God's oath will never be fulfilled; why does God allow world events to develop in such a way that man might blasphemously conclude that God has betrayed His own solemn oath? Why does God not manifest His fidelity to David's descendants in order to preserve the sanctity of His Name?

הִתְעַבַּרְתָּ עִם מְשִׁיחֶךָ — *You have been angry with Your anointed.*

[It appears as if You will never bring about the advent of the long awaited Messiah, the scion who will continue the dynasty of David, *Your anointed*.]

40. נֵאַרְתָּה בְּרִית עַבְדֶּךָ — *You nullified the covenant of Your servant.*

This refers to the covenant which God made with Abraham (*Alshich*) [and with David].

חִלַּלְתָּ לָאָרֶץ נִזְרוֹ — *You profaned to the ground his crown.*

[Israel's monarchy, symbolized by the crown, has been degraded.]

41. פָּרַצְתָּ כָל גְּדֵרֹתָיו — *You breached all his fences.*

Fences refers to the walls and fortifications [which David] built in Jerusalem (*Rashi*).

מב מִבְצָרָיו מְחִתָּה: שַׁסֻּהוּ כָּל־עֹבְרֵי דֶרֶךְ הָיָה

מג חֶרְפָּה לִשְׁכֵנָיו: הֲרִימוֹתָ יְמִין צָרָיו הִשְׂמַחְתָּ

מד כָּל־אוֹיְבָיו: אַף־תָּשִׁיב צוּר חַרְבּוֹ וְלֹא

מה הֲקֵמֹתוֹ בַּמִּלְחָמָה: הִשְׁבַּתָּ מִטְּהָרוֹ וְכִסְאוֹ

מו לָאָרֶץ מִגַּרְתָּה: הִקְצַרְתָּ יְמֵי עֲלוּמָיו הֶעֱטִיתָ

מז עָלָיו בּוּשָׁה סֶלָה: עַד־מָה יהוה תִּסָּתֵר

מח לָנֶצַח תִּבְעַר כְּמוֹ־אֵשׁ חֲמָתֶךָ: זְכָר־אֲנִי מֶה־

מט חָלֶד עַל־מַה־שָּׁוְא בָּרָאתָ כָל־בְּנֵי־אָדָם: מִי

שִׂמְתָּ מִבְצָרָיו מְחִתָּה — *You turned his strongholds into debris.*

Strongholds refers to the ramparts around הַר הַבַּיִת, *the Temple Mount*, and מְצוּדַת צִיּוֹן, *the Tower of Zion* (Rashi).

42. שַׁסֻּהוּ כָל עֹבְרֵי דָרֶךְ — *All wayfarers plunder him.*

Since Jerusalem, the city of David, was left without walls and fortifications, it has been plundered by robbers and brigands (Radak; Ibn Ezra).

הָיָה חֶרְפָּה לִשְׁכֵנָיו — *He became a disgrace to his neighbors.*

This represents a dramatic reversal of the formerly exalted status of the House of David, which once ruled over all the neighboring states. Now David's descendants have become slaves to the neighboring kings (Radak).

43. הֲרִימוֹתָ יְמִין צָרָיו — *You exalted the right hand of his tormentors.*

You promised David *My arm, too, shall invigorate him* (v. 22), but now You appear to be strengthening David's enemies (Radak).

הִשְׂמַחְתָּ כָּל אוֹיְבָיו — *You gladdened his foes.*

David's glory had been universal, as Scripture states, *And David's renown spread out to all the lands, and HASHEM placed his fear upon all the nations* (I Kings 14:17). Now, however, David's enemies rejoice in his downfall (Radak).

44. אַף תָּשִׁיב צוּר חַרְבּוֹ — *You even turned back the edge of his sword.*

[The threatening sword is no longer pointed at David's enemies, but at David himself.]

וְלֹא הֲקֵמֹתוֹ בַּמִּלְחָמָה — *And You did not uphold him in battle.*

[No longer do You support David in battle against his foes.]

45. הִשְׁבַּתָּ מִטְּהָרוֹ — *You brought an end to his splendor* [lit. *his purity*].

The Aramaic word for afternoon is טִיהֲרָא, literally, *pure, brilliant light*. The dazzling zenith of David's rule is likened to the luminous sun at high noon (Rashi), as verses 37-38 state, *and his throne shall be like the sun before Me; like the [full] moon, it shall be established forever* (Alshich).

Ibn Ezra comments that טָהֳרוֹ, *his purity*, refers to the Temple built by David's family, for this was the purest and holiest place on earth.

46. הִקְצַרְתָּ יְמֵי עֲלוּמָיו — *You shortened the days of his youth.*

Youth alludes to the productive, potent period of one's life, while old age alludes to the period of decline and infirmity. The 'good days' of David's dynasty were few, whereas the 'bad days' of his agony and exile were many (Radak).

You turned his strongholds into debris.

⁴² All wayfarers plunder him;
he became a disgrace to his neighbors.

⁴³ You exalted the right hand of his tormentors;
You gladdened his foes;

⁴⁴ You even turned back the edge of his sword,
and You did not uphold him in battle;

⁴⁵ You brought an end to his splendor,
and toppled his throne to the ground;

⁴⁶ You shortened the days of his youth;
You shrouded him in shame, Selah.

⁴⁷ How long, HASHEM,
will You hide Yourself forever?
Will Your wrath burn like fire?

⁴⁸ I remember — how short is my lifetime!
For what worthlessness have You created
all the sons of man?

הֶעֱטִיתָ עָלָיו בּוּשָׁה סֶלָה — *You shrouded him in shame, Selah.*

The House of David was constantly put to shame by its enemies, who taunted, "Where is the fulfillment of God's promise to perpetuate your dynasty?" (*Radak*).

47. עַד מָה ה' תִּסָּתֵר לָנֶצַח — *How long, HASHEM, will You hide Yourself forever?*

It appears as if You are totally oblivious to the agonies of our exile (*Radak*).

תִּבְעַר כְּמוֹ אֵשׁ חֲמָתֶךָ — *Will Your wrath burn like fire?*

[Your *wrath* continues to burn, resembling a perpetual fire.]

48. זְכָר אֲנִי מֶה חָלֶד — *I remember — how short is [my] lifetime!*

[See comm. to 17:14, 39:6 and 49:12 for a detailed definition of חֶלֶד as *decaying earth* or as a *short lifetime*.

Rashi relates חֶלֶד to חֲלוּדָה, *rust*, for the word describes this transitory world, which can readily decay and rust away.]

I languish in an exile which appears to be interminable. Since I know that my lifetime is very *short*, I have given up hope of seeing the end of the exile (*Ibn Ezra*).

עַל מַה שָׁוְא בָּרָאתָ כָל בְּנֵי אָדָם — *For what worthlessness have You created all the sons of man?*

Life is truly an empty, worthless experience if it is lived without a lofty goal. [The Jews' goal is to prepare the way for the advent of David's descendant, the Messiah.] The existence of the Jewish people in exile has meaning only insofar as it contributes to the eventual reinstatement of the royal House of David. But if there is absolutely no hope of the Messiah's arrival, then life becomes devoid of all meaning, and man's creation was in vain (*Sforno*).

גֶּבֶר יִחְיֶה וְלֹא יִרְאֶה־מָּוֶת יְמַלֵּט נַפְשׁוֹ מִיַּד־

נ שְׁאוֹל סֶלָה: אַיֵּה | חֲסָדֶיךָ הָרִאשֹׁנִים | אֲדֹנָי

נא נִשְׁבַּעְתָּ לְדָוִד בֶּאֱמוּנָתֶךָ: זְכֹר אֲדֹנָי חֶרְפַּת

נב עֲבָדֶיךָ שְׂאֵתִי בְחֵיקִי כָּל־רַבִּים עַמִּים: אֲשֶׁר

חֵרְפוּ אוֹיְבֶיךָ | יהוה אֲשֶׁר חֵרְפוּ עִקְּבוֹת

נג מְשִׁיחֶךָ: בָּרוּךְ יהוה לְעוֹלָם אָמֵן | וְאָמֵן:

---

49. מִי גֶּבֶר יִחְיֶה וְלֹא יִרְאֶה מָּוֶת — *What man lives and will never see death?*

Since it is inevitable that I must die in the near future and the exile is far from ended, it appears that I will never witness the redemption. If so, all the misery which I suffered in exile appears to be for naught (*Ibn Ezra*).

יְמַלֵּט נַפְשׁוֹ מִיַּד שְׁאוֹל סֶלָה — *And will rescue his soul from the power* [lit. *hand*] *of the Lower World? Selah.*

[No man is invulnerable. Anyone who sins will fall into *the Lower World*, a euphemism for death and hell.]

50. אַיֵּה חֲסָדֶיךָ הָרִאשֹׁנִים אֲדֹנָי — *Where are Your early* [lit. *first*] *acts of kindness, my Lord?*

At first You generously swore to David that You would preserve his line, but now You seem to be abandoning that oath (*Radak*).

נִשְׁבַּעְתָּ לְדָוִד בֶּאֱמוּנָתֶךָ — *Those You pledged to David in Your faithfulness.*

You promised to bring the Messiah, and therefore we await his arrival (*Ibn Ezra*).

51. זְכֹר אֲדֹנָי חֶרְפַּת עֲבָדֶיךָ — *Remember, my Lord, Your servant's disgrace.*

This refers to the disgrace heaped upon Israel by the gentile nations, who taunt us by saying, "You shall never experience salvation" (*Ibn Ezra; Radak*).

שְׂאֵתִי בְחֵיקִי כָּל־רַבִּים עַמִּים — *Borne in my bosom — from the entire multitude of nations.*

The translation follows *Rashbam* and *Radak* who explain that the word חֶרְפַּת, *disgrace*, which appears earlier in the verse, applies here as well, i.e., the disgrace borne by Israel was inflicted by all the nations.

Although they insult me, I bear my disgrace in silence and keep my anguish to myself (*Lachmei Torah*).

89

49-53

⁴⁹ *What man lives and will never see death,*
and will rescue his soul
from the power of the Lower World? Selah.
⁵⁰ *Where are Your early acts of kindness, my Lord?*
Those You pledged to David
in Your faithfulness.
⁵¹ *Remember, my Lord, Your servant's disgrace —*
borne in my bosom —
from the entire multitude of nations.
⁵² *Those who disgrace are Your enemies, HASHEM,*
those who disgrace the footsteps
of Your Messiah.
⁵³ *Blessed is HASHEM forever, Amen and Amen.*

---

52. אֲשֶׁר חֵרְפוּ אוֹיְבֶיךָ ה׳ — *Those who disgrace are Your enemies, HASHEM.*

The prime target of their insults is the Messiah whom You will send to redeem Israel (*Radak*).

אֲשֶׁר חֵרְפוּ עִקְּבוֹת מְשִׁיחֶךָ — *Those who disgrace the footsteps of Your Messiah.*

At the conclusion of the exile, the Messiah will arrive. This period of time is called עִקְּבוֹת הַמָּשִׁיחַ, literally, *the footsteps of the Messiah,* because just as the עָקֵב, *heel,* is at the bottom of the body, the advent of Messiah will occur when the world has sunk to the nadir of its history (*Radak*).

Morality will deteriorate to the extent that man will have 'the face of a dog'; this means that people will have the audacity of a wild beast, which shows no regard for anyone and growls at every passerby. In the time of עִקְּבוֹת הַמָּשִׁיחַ, when *Messiah's footsteps are*

heard, חוּצְפָּא יַסְגֵּא, *brazen audacity will increase,* in unprecedented proportions. Students will defy their teachers, children will curse their parents, and all authority will be ridiculed (*Sanhedrin 97a; Sotah 49b*).

53. בָּרוּךְ ה׳ לְעוֹלָם אָמֵן וְאָמֵן — *Blessed is HASHEM forever, Amen and Amen.*

As the composition comes to its conclusion, the holy spirit, which enveloped the Psalmist, inspires him to see that the long desperate exile *would* come to an end and that Israel *would* emerge in glory (*Radak*).

Therefore, the Psalmist hastens to correct any misconception which may have been bred by the harsh words of this psalm, i.e., despite my complaints and protests over the bitter exile I still bless God forever and He is doubly blessed, *Amen and Amen* (*Metzudos*).

T he fourth book of Psalms commences with eleven consecutive works composed by Moses (Psalms 90-100). Rashi explains that these correspond to the eleven blessings which Moses bestowed upon eleven of the tribes as enumerated in Deuteronomy 33. The tribe of Simeon was excluded from Moses' blessings because the Simeonites had led the orgy that resulted in the death of thousands of Jews (see Numbers 25:1-15).

Midrash Shocher Tov demonstrates how the theme of each of the eleven psalms relates to a specific tribe. Psalm 90 speaks of repentance, as indicated in the third verse: You reduce man to pulp and You say, "Repent, O sons of man!" In his blessings, Moses blessed Reuben first, saying, "Let Reuben live and not die" (Deuteronomy 33:6), referring to Reuben's sin and to his subsequent repentance [see Genesis 35:22 and ArtScroll comm.]. With his sincere remorse and penitence, Reuben introduced the principle of complete repentance to the world (Bereishis Rabbah 84:19). Thus, this psalm relates to Reuben, the symbol of repentance.

According to the Talmud (Bava Basra 14b), when David composed the Book of Psalms he drew upon the works of ten scholars, including Moses. Rashi explains that Moses' contribution to Tehillim was these eleven psalms.

Radak explains that David found these eleven psalms in an old manuscript which had been traditionally ascribed to the authorship of Moses. David then adapted and incorporated them into his Book of Psalms. David dedicated this work to those crushed under the burden of exile. He speaks of man's frailty and of the brevity of his existence.

Ultimately, man can find solace only in the fact that God has been a dwelling place ... for us in all generations (verse 1) and that He welcomes penitents to dwell with Him.

א תְּפִלָּה לְמֹשֶׁה אִישׁ־הָאֱלֹהִים אֲדֹנָי מָעוֹן
ב אַתָּה הָיִיתָ לָּנוּ בְּדֹר וָדֹר: בְּטֶרֶם | הָרִים יֻלָּדוּ
וַתְּחוֹלֵל אֶרֶץ וְתֵבֵל וּמֵעוֹלָם עַד־עוֹלָם אַתָּה
ג אֵל: תָּשֵׁב אֱנוֹשׁ עַד־דַּכָּא וַתֹּאמֶר שׁוּבוּ בְנֵי־

1. תְּפִלָּה לְמֹשֶׁה אִישׁ הָאֱלֹהִים — *A prayer by Moses, the man of God.*

Radak cites Rav Saadiah Gaon's view that לְמֹשֶׁה means *to Moses* and refers to the group of Levites who were Moses' descendants and served as musicians in the *Beis HaMikdash.*

However, most commentaries agree that Moses himself composed this psalm (see *Prefatory Remarks*). The appellation *man of God* alludes to the two aspects to Moses' being: when he was on earth, Moses was an אִישׁ, *a man*, of flesh and blood but when he ascended Mount Sinai and survived without food for forty days, he resembled אֱלֹהִים, *God*, in that he was divorced from physical matter (*Devarim Rabbah* 11:4).[1]

Midrash Shocher Tov challenges the claim that Moses wrote this series of eleven psalms on the grounds that everything Moses wrote was incorporated into the Torah. If Moses had authored them, why were these works excluded from the Torah and designated as psalms?

Ibn Ezra explains that Moses was the only prophet who saw every Divine vision with complete clarity, free from any distortion (see *Yevamos* 49b). In addition, Moses communicated these visions with perfect purity and clarity. Consequently, every word he uttered was considered as emanating from God. These psalms, however, were not a direct vision from God, *Ibn Ezra* notes. Rather, they were Moses' own ideas,

conceived under the influence of Divine inspiration. Therefore, these psalms are not on the prophetic level of Torah [see footnote to verse 10].

אֲדֹנָי מָעוֹן הָיִיתָ לָּנוּ בְּדֹר וָדֹר — *My Lord, a dwelling place have You been for us in all generations.*

You have provided us with a place of refuge in every situation of danger and distress (*Rashi; Radak*).

The *Talmud* (*Megillah* 29a) states that since the שְׁכִינָה, *Holy Presence of God*, accompanied the Jews wherever they wandered in exile, God and Israel always dwelled together (*Tehillos Hashem*).

The Sages (*Megillah* 29a) taught that God specifically dwells in the synagogues and houses of study. Indeed, *Rabbi Elazar HaKappar* states that in the Messianic Era, these holy dwellings which were built all over the world by the exiled Jews are destined to be uprooted and relocated in the Holy Land.

2. בְּטֶרֶם הָרִים יֻלָּדוּ — *Before the mountains were born.*

The Psalmist addressed the Creator: When it was revealed before You that Your nation was destined to sin, You introduced the power of repentance to the world. Since repentance was so important, You created it even *before the mountains were born* (*Targum*).

וַתְּחוֹלֵל אֶרֶץ וְתֵבֵל — *And You [had not yet] convulsed the earth and the inhabited land.*

1. *Sifri* (*VeZos HaBerachah* 1) lists ten men who elevated themselves beyond the limits of their physical nature and sanctified their bodies to the extent that they merited the title אִישׁ הָאֱלֹהִים, *man of God:* Moses (here and *Deut.* 33:1), Elkanah (*I Sam.* 2:27, see *Rashi*), Samuel (*ibid.* 9:10), David (*II Chron.* 8:14), Shemayah (*I Kings* 12:22), Edo (*ibid.* 13:1, see *Rashi*), Elijah (*II Kings* 1:13), Elisha (*ibid.* 4:9), Michah (*I Kings* 20:28, see *Rashi*) and Amotz (*II Chron.* 25:7, see *Radak*).

A prayer by Moses, the man of God:
My Lord, a dwelling place
have You been for us in all generations.
² Before the mountains were born
and You had not yet convulsed the earth and the
inhabited land,
and from before the world to the end of the world
You are God.
³ You reduce man to pulp
and You say, "Repent, O sons of man."

The word בְּטֶרֶם, *before,* applies to this stich as well as the preceding one (*Rashi*).

The Psalmist describes the formation of the earth. He does not mention the creation of the heavens because the celestial beings are eternal, whereas the message of this psalm is that even the most solid of earthly formations is finite and destructible (*Radak*).

וּמֵעוֹלָם עַד עוֹלָם אַתָּה אֵל — *And from [before the] world to [the end of the] world You are God.*

You created the power of repentance even before the existence of sin, and this power will endure as long as the world continues under Your sole control (*Beis Elokim*).

3. תָּשֵׁב אֱנוֹשׁ עַד דַּכָּא — *You reduce man*

to pulp [lit. *You turn man back until he is crushed*].

The term אֱנוֹשׁ refers to *man* as a frail, limited creature. See *Malbim* to 8:5.

You bring afflictions upon man until *You* turn his strength and arrogance to frailty and humility. Then his pride is crushed (*Rashi*).

You remind the youth that someday he will enter a period of דַּכָּא, *decline* and old age, and that eventually he will have to answer for his actions (*Radak; Ibn Ezra*).

וַתֹּאמֶר שׁוּבוּ בְנֵי אָדָם — *And You say, "Repent* [lit. *return], O sons of man."*

You constantly remind men that they will *return* to the dust from where they came (*Radak; Ibn Ezra*), and that they should therefore *repent* without delay (*Rashi*).[1]

1. All day, every day, God's right hand is outstretched to encourage and welcome those who must repent. He announces, "Repent, O sons of man! ..." Ben Azai said: Come and see the power of repentance, for it can utterly transform a man. Shimon ben Lakish was a highway robber who stole from travelers with the aid of two cohorts. Finally, Shimon left his cohorts in the hills and returned to the God of his fathers with all his heart. He fasted and prayed constantly, he gave much charity to the poor, and he studied Torah with tremendous concentration. Henceforth he was known as Rabbi Shimon ben Lakish (Reish Lakish). The day he died, his two cohorts also died; but Rabbi Shimon was given a portion in the Garden of Eden, while his two cohorts were condemned to hell.

The cohorts protested, "Does God show favoritism? Shimon was a partner in our crimes, so why is he in the Garden of Eden while we are in hell?"

God replied, "He repented while you did not!"

"If so," cried the pair of robbers, "we too will now repent."

But God rejected their proposal, explaining, "Repentance is only accepted while a man is alive; afterwards it is too late!"

This may be likened to a man who wishes to make a sea voyage: he must prepare provisions before he embarks, for it will be impossible for him to acquire them once he is at sea (*Pirkei D' Rabbi Eliezer,* Chapter 43).

ד אָדָם: כִּי אֶלֶף שָׁנִים בְּעֵינֶיךָ כְּיוֹם אֶתְמוֹל כִּי
ה יַעֲבֹר וְאַשְׁמוּרָה בַלָּיְלָה: זְרַמְתָּם שֵׁנָה יִהְיוּ
ו בַּבֹּקֶר כֶּחָצִיר יַחֲלֹף: בַּבֹּקֶר יָצִיץ וְחָלָף
ז לָעֶרֶב יְמוֹלֵל וְיָבֵשׁ: כִּי־כָלִינוּ בְאַפֶּךָ
ח וּבַחֲמָתְךָ נִבְהָלְנוּ: שַׁתָּ עֲוֹנֹתֵינוּ לְנֶגְדֶּךָ

[You demonstrate that the sinner is merely אֱנוֹשׁ, a term that denotes man's fragility and limitations. After man repents, however, he soars to the level of בְּנֵי אָדָם, sons of man (lit. *Adam*), and achieves the perfection which Adam enjoyed before he sinned.]

4. כִּי אֶלֶף שָׁנִים בְּעֵינֶיךָ כְּיוֹם אֶתְמוֹל כִּי יַעֲבֹר — *For a thousand years in Your eyes are but a bygone yesterday* [lit. *like yesterday when it will pass*].

As explained in the preceding verse, man should not allow his pride to lead him to sin for he is destined to be *crushed* by old age [i.e., he will become infirm and restricted]. Even if a person is blessed with extraordinary longevity [which might induce an unwarranted sense of pride], he should not lose sight of his ultimate end. For no man can live more than one thousand years. Moreover, even if a person were to live one thousand years, this should not make him proud before God, because to the Eternal One a millennium is akin to a mere day (*Radak*).

וְאַשְׁמוּרָה בַלָּיְלָה — *And like a watch in the night.*

According to *Radak*, this further minimizes the relative importance of man's maximum lifespan of one thousand years. Not only is a millennium less significant than a single Divine day, but it is even comparable to a mere *watch in the night* [which consists of only three or four hours, as discussed in *Berachos* 3a].

Rashi, however, maintains that one day of God consists of less than one thousand years, for God warned Adam not to eat of the tree of knowledge,

saying, "For on the day you eat of it, you will surely die" (*Genesis* 2:17), which implies that Adam's entire lifespan was considered a single day in God's eyes. When Adam's life ended after 930 years (*Genesis* 5:5), it was the end of God's day. Thus, one thousand years in God's eyes are like *one yesterday plus a short watch in the night* composed of seventy years.

5. זְרַמְתָּם — *You flood them away.*

Not only are the days of man few (verse 4), but they also pass by quickly. You made them flow away like a זֶרֶם, *rushing stream* (*Radak*).

Man accomplishes nothing in his brief sojourn. The term זְרַמְתָּם is a contraction of three words: זָרוּ מֵתוּ תַּמּוּ, *They were alienated, they died, they vanished.* This implies that all of man's material pursuits are futile (*Midrash Shocher Tov*).

שֵׁנָה יִהְיוּ — *They become sleep-like.*

The transitory nature of human existence may be likened to a dream which forms in a man's mind while he sleeps, but then vanishes abruptly without leaving a trace (*Radak*).

What is the length of the average lifespan? In verse 10, the Psalmist notes that *the days of our years* [i.e., the average lifespan] ... *are seventy years.* The duration of the Babylonian exile was also seventy years. The Psalmist describes this interval in the following terms: *When HASHEM will return the captivity of Zion, we will be like dreamers* (126:1). Thus we see that the seventy years of man's life are considered to be no more than a fleeting dream (*Rashi*).

⁴ For a thousand years in Your eyes
are but a bygone yesterday,
and like a watch in the night.

⁵ You flood them away, they become sleep-like,
by morning they are like grass that withers.

⁶ In the morning it blossoms and then it withers,
by evening it is cut down and brittle.

⁷ For we are consumed by Your fury;
and we are terrified by Your wrath.

⁸ You have set our iniquities before Yourself,

בַּבֹּקֶר כֶּחָצִיר יַחֲלֹף — By morning they are
like grass that withers [lit. will change].

חָצִיר is a species of grass which
readily dries out and withers in a span
of only a few hours. If it blossoms at
night, it withers by morning. If, as in
the next verse, it blossoms in the
morning, it withers by evening (see
Malbim to 37:2).

The חָצִיר remains moist and fresh all
night, until the sun rises in the morning
and dries it out. Similarly, man is
initially fresh and full of vitality but in a
short time, he withers and wrinkles
(Radak).

Targum paraphrases this verse: If
man does not heed the call to repent,
then You will cause a זֶרֶם, flow [i.e., a
powerful force], of death to engulf him,
and the sinner will become as one asleep
forever. And when the new era of the
World to Come dawns upon mankind,
the sinner will be cut off like withered
grass.

6. בַּבֹּקֶר יָצִיץ וְחָלָף — In the morning it
blossoms and then it withers [lit.
changes].

The translation of חָלָף follows Rashi
and Ibn Ezra, who liken man's lifespan
to the passage of time between the
morning and the night. According to
this analogy, the bloom of youth does
not even survive the dawn of life.

Targum, Radak and Meiri, however,
render חָלָף as to flourish, literally to
change, from strength to strength.

Thus, throughout early life man seems
to blossom, but when he reaches middle
age he starts to fade. Here middle age
corresponds to high noon, when the sun
beats down and dries out the blossom.

לָעֶרֶב יְמוֹלֵל וְיָבֵשׁ — By evening it is cut
down and brittle [lit. dried out].

The daytime sun dries out the grain
until it becomes brittle and crumbles to
the touch (Meiri). [Similarly, man
deteriorates rapidly in old age, until he
reaches the point of total collapse.]

7. כִּי כָלִינוּ בְאַפֶּךָ — For we are consumed
by Your fury.

Now the Psalmist turns his attention
to the special perils of the exile (Radak),
for if mortal men are vulnerable in times
of tranquility, they are certainly in even
greater danger when they are exposed to
the Divine fury unleashed in exile (Eitz
Yosef).

וּבַחֲמָתְךָ נִבְהָלְנוּ — And we are terrified by
Your wrath.

The word אַף of the first stich
describes an externally displayed anger.
[Rashi (to Exodus 5:8) explains that the
word אַף, fury, also means nose. Among
the most prominent physical manifesta-
tions of anger are flaring nostrils and
heavy nasal breathing.] In contrast,
חֵמָה, wrath, is a hostile, violent feeling
which is kept inside (Malbim).

8. שַׁתָּ עֲוֹנֹתֵינוּ לְנֶגְדֶּךָ — You have set our
iniquities before Yourself.

Although man forgets quickly, God

ט עֲלֻמֵנוּ לִמְאוֹר פָּנֶיךָ: כִּי כָל־יָמֵינוּ פָּנוּ
י בְעֶבְרָתֶךָ כִּלִּינוּ שָׁנֵינוּ כְמוֹ־הֶגֶה: יְמֵי־
שְׁנוֹתֵינוּ בָהֶם שִׁבְעִים שָׁנָה וְאִם בִּגְבוּרֹת |
שְׁמוֹנִים שָׁנָה וְרָהְבָּם עָמָל וָאָוֶן כִּי־גָז חִישׁ

remembers everything forever (Rav
Yoseif Titzak).

Since our past sins remain before You
eternally, You never stop punishing us
for them (Radak).

עֲלֻמֵנוּ לִמְאוֹר פָּנֶיךָ — Our immaturity [lit.
youth] before the light of Your
countenance.

The translation of עֲלֻמֵנוּ follows the
opinion of Targum and Rashi that it is
cognate with עֶלֶם, youth. The Psalmist
refers to sins committed in the
immaturity of youth.

Ibn Ezra and Radak relate this word
to נֶעְלַם, vanished, or concealed,
suggesting that even the sins which
have vanished from our memory are still
remembered clearly by God.

9. כִּי כָל־יָמֵינוּ פָּנוּ בְעֶבְרָתֶךָ — For all our
days passed by because of Your anger.

We never experienced a good day.
Our time was wasted because You
punished us in Your anger (Radak).

Dorash Moshe quotes the Zohar,
which explains that if a man spends his
time properly, each and every day of his
life adds a new dimension of spiritual
growth to his personality. This growth
is reflected on his countenance which
then constantly increases in radiance.
Moreover, if man wastes his time by
sinning, the day is lost. It passes out of
the sinner's grasp and storms up to the
Heavenly Tribunal in anger. The wasted
day testifies before God, whose anger is
then aroused against the sinner. Only if
the sinner repents will his wasted day
[which passed away] be returned to him.

כִּלִּינוּ שָׁנֵינוּ כְמוֹ הֶגֶה — We consumed our
years like a fleeting word.

The spoken word has no permanence; once it leaves the mouth, it
vanishes into thin air (Ibn Ezra).

Similarly, our years vanished without
a trace; our efforts left no enduring
impression. Since history will not
remember our contributions, we are
condemned to oblivion. Our accomplishments are so insignificant that they
may be likened to a child's scribbles on a
chalkboard, which are swiftly erased
(Meiri).

10. יְמֵי שְׁנוֹתֵינוּ בָהֶם שִׁבְעִים שָׁנָה — The
days of our years — among them are
seventy years.

I.e., the years we spend surrounded
by the iniquities and immaturity
mentioned in verse 8 (Rashi).

The Talmud (Moed Katan 28a) says
that the average lifespan is sixty years;
thus the man who reaches seventy has
achieved שֵׂיבָה, ripe old age.

Vilna Gaon notes an allusion to this
in our verse: he explains that the
numerical value of יְמֵי, days, is 60 and
refers to שְׁנוֹתֵינוּ, our years, denoting the
average lifespan. According to this
interpretation, בָהֶם, among them, refers
to those few extraordinary individuals
'among' the masses who live seventy
years.

The Talmud (Yevamos 64b) derives
from this verse that in earlier generations man had lived longer than seventy
years, for when David said, the days of
'our' years ... are seventy years, he
implied that those in previous generations had enjoyed longer lifespans.

Tosafos (Yevamos 64b) questions this
statement on the grounds that
authorship of this psalm is attributed to
Moses, who lived 120 years. Tosafos
answers that although the bulk of this
psalm was composed by Moses, this
verse must be ascribed to David, who
lived only to the age of seventy (see

> *our immaturity before the light*
> *of Your countenance.*
>
> ⁹ *For all our days passed by because of Your anger,*
> *we consumed our years like a fleeting word.*
> ¹⁰ *The days of our years —*
> *among them are seventy years,*
> *and if with strength — eighty years;*
> *their proudest success is but toil and pain,*

---

commentary to the next stich of this verse).

וְאִם בִּגְבוּרֹת שְׁמוֹנִים שָׁנָה — *And if with strength — eighty years.*

According to most commentaries, Moses composed this psalm. Yet, as Scripture states, *Moses was one hundred and twenty years old when he died, his eye was not dim nor was his natural vitality diminished* (Deuteronomy 34:7). If Moses lived so long how could he say that men live only seventy or eighty years?

Radak explains that since Moses realized that he was an exception to the rule, he spoke of the lifespan granted the majority of men.

Ibn Ezra suggests that until he reached eighty, Moses, like other men, grew weaker and weaker with age. He

composed this psalm as he approached the age of eighty. At that time, his vitality was ebbing and he felt that only an infusion of גְּבוּרֹת, *strength*, would enable him to continue living.

[When he reached the age of eighty, Moses received an extraordinary infusion of youthful energy and vitality, because at that time he was chosen to lead the Jewish people out of Egypt, to receive the Torah, and to lead the Jews to the Promised Land. This Divine mission so invigorated him that his health and strength remained undiminished until the moment of his death.][1]

וְרָהְבָּם עָמָל וָאָוֶן — *Their proudest success is but toil and pain.*

Anything man accomplishes during his brief sojourn on earth is meaningless —

---

1. [The commentary to verse 1 raised an important question: all of the words of Moses were said on the highest plane of prophetic clarity. Thus, they were fit to be included in the text of the Torah proper, which is the most sacred of Jewish books. Why then was this composition not included in the Torah but relegated to the Book of Psalms, which is less sacred?

According to *Ibn Ezra's* theory [cited in the above commentary] that this psalm was written before Moses was eighty years old, we can propose an answer to this question. God endowed Moses with clear prophetic vision because he needed it to lead the Jews out of Egypt and to receive the Law at Sinai. This psalm was an earlier work, written before Moses received this vision.

Harav Yaakov Kaminetsky, שליט״א, endorses this explanation and corroborates it with the *Midrash* (*Shemos Rabbah* 5:22) which says that the oppressed Jews would derive comfort during their Egyptian bondage from the study of certain מְגִלּוֹת, *scrolls*, which uplifted their spirits from Sabbath to Sabbath. Since the *Midrash* does not identify these scrolls, many opinions are offered by the commentaries. *Harav Kaminetsky* suggests that these scrolls contained the eleven psalms which Moses composed. These psalms exhorted the Jews to repent and to trust that God would eventually punish their wicked taskmasters.

Moses composed these psalms in his youth, when he first witnessed the bondage of Israel, before he attained his full prophetic stature. [See gloss of *Rav Matisyahu Strashun* to *Bava Basra* 14a.]]

יא וַנָּעֻפָה: מִי־יוֹדֵעַ עֹז אַפֶּךָ וּכְיִרְאָתְךָ עֶבְרָתֶךָ:

יב לִמְנוֹת יָמֵינוּ כֵּן הוֹדַע וְנָבִא לְבַב חָכְמָה:

יג שׁוּבָה יהוה עַד־מָתָי וְהִנָּחֵם עַל־עֲבָדֶיךָ:

יד שַׂבְּעֵנוּ בַבֹּקֶר חַסְדֶּךָ וּנְרַנְּנָה וְנִשְׂמְחָה בְּכָל־

טו יָמֵינוּ: שַׂמְּחֵנוּ כִּימוֹת עִנִּיתָנוּ שְׁנוֹת רָאִינוּ

---

less, *for it soon passes away* (Rashi). Life involves constant עָמָל, toil, to solve problems and אָוֶן, painful exertion, to provide sustenance and protection (Sforno).

כִּי גָז חִישׁ וַנָּעֻפָה — *For it is cut off swiftly and we fly away.*

The translation of גָז as *cut off* follows *Ibn Ezra* and *Metzudos*. However, *Rashi, Radak* and *Sforno* render גָז as *to pass away.* In any case, the sense of the phrase is that man's success is fleeting. It leaves him when his life flies away as he dies and is buried.

11. מִי־יוֹדֵעַ עֹז אַפֶּךָ — *Who knows the power of Your fury?*

Since human life is so brief, who has the opportunity to learn the full extent of Your fury? (Rashi). Who has the power to restrain Your fury? (Targum). Who knows how to guard himself from Your wrath once it is unleashed? (Radak; Ibn Yachya).

Meiri identifies the *fury* referred to here as the fury which stirred God to cast the Jews into exile. Who can predict how long God's fury will persist and how long the exile will endure?

וּכְיִרְאָתְךָ עֶבְרָתֶךָ — *As You are feared so is Your anger.*

The fear which You arouse in men is intense. Just as You inspire a powerful fear in man, so do You display a most potent anger that You use to punish the wicked (Rashi).

Radak translates: To the extent that a man fears You, Your anger is aroused against him, for Hashem scrupulously disciplines those who are close to Him, and He is angered by their slightest sin. [See commentary to 50:3 and 89:8.]

12. לִמְנוֹת יָמֵינוּ כֵּן הוֹדַע — *According to the count of our days so make known.*

In former times, when man's lifespan was long, God had ample opportunity to reveal Himself to man (Rashi), but now man's sojourn on earth is brief and he is preoccupied with countless cares and problems which disturb his thoughts. Thus, to compensate for the brevity of man's present lifespan, intensify Your revelation to him, so that he may more readily comprehend the truth (Sforno).

Indeed, the brevity of יָמֵינוּ, *our days,* is alluded to in the very next word, כֵּן, which has a numerical value of seventy, for as verse 10 states, *the days of our years ... are seventy years* (Chazah Zion; also see gloss to *Rashi's* printed comm.).

Radak suggests that this request also alludes to the length of the exile. No one knows its actual duration, for even the prophecy of David concerning our future redemption is shrouded in inscrutable calculations.

Midrash Shocher Tov emphasizes that once a person recognizes how brief life is, he will hasten to repent. Rabbi Eliezer would admonish his disciples, ''Repent one day before you die!''

The disciples asked, ''Does a person know the day of his death?''

Rabbi Eliezer replied, ''Precisely! Man never knows when his end is near. Therefore, repent every day, lest you die on the morrow!''

וְנָבִא לְבַב חָכְמָה — *Then we shall acquire* [lit. *bring*] *a heart of wisdom.*

The word נָבִא is a verb from the root בּוֹא, *to bring.* When we realize how brief life is, we will try harder to acquire

for it is cut off swiftly and we fly away.

¹¹ Who knows the power of Your fury?
    As You are feared so is Your anger.
¹² According to the count of our days
        so make known,
            then we shall acquire a heart of wisdom.
¹³ Return, HASHEM, how long?
    And relent concerning Your servants.
¹⁴ Satisfy us in the morning with Your kindness,
        then we shall sing out and rejoice all our days.
¹⁵ Gladden us according to the days You afflicted us,

---

wisdom which will guide our hearts. David asked (39:5), *Let me know, O HASHEM, my end, and the measure of my days, what is it? (Radak; Meiri).*

Radak also suggests an interpretation in which the word נָבִא functions as a noun — *the prophet.* Thus the verse would mean: When the days of this world are finally counted out, we will witness the advent of the prophet Elijah, who will herald the advent of Messiah. The enlightened teachings of the prophet will *bring a heart of wisdom* to mankind, as Scripture states: *The earth shall be filled with the knowledge of HASHEM as water covers the sea (Isaiah 11:9).*

The *Talmud (Bava Basra 12a)* states that a wise man is greater than a prophet, because here even the נָבִא, *prophet,* is praised for his לֵב חָכְמָה, *heart of wisdom,* which indicates that *wisdom* is the supreme achievement. In addition, the *Talmud* teaches, the genuine scholar is endowed with a Holy Spirit which reveals to him many secrets of Torah (see *Ramban* and *Ritva, Bava Basra 12a).*

13. שׁוּבָה ה׳ עַד מָתָי — *Return, HASHEM, how long?*

Turn back Your anger (Rashi) and *return* to us. How long will You abandon us? *(Radak).*

How long will *the power of Your fury* (v. 11) keep us in exile? *(Sforno).*

וְהִנָּחֵם עַל עֲבָדֶיךָ — *And relent concerning Your servants.*

Do not persist in persecuting them, for they have suffered enough for their sins *(Rashi).*

14. שַׂבְּעֵנוּ בַבֹּקֶר חַסְדֶּךָ וּנְרַנְּנָה וְנִשְׂמְחָה בְּכָל יָמֵינוּ — *Satisfy us in the morning with Your kindness, then we shall sing out and rejoice all our days.*

Here youth is considered the morning of life. Thus: If You *satisfy us with kindness* in our early years, this will fortify us against the vicissitudes and sufferings of later life, and we will be able to *rejoice all our days* (Ibn Ezra; Meiri).

Interpreting this verse on a national level, *Alshich* points out that the author, Moses, led the nation at the dawn of its development. Moses begged God to perform miracles at the time of the Exodus from Egypt in order to strengthen the faith of the Jews throughout the difficult days of their history.

Radak perceives this verse as a reference to the dawn of the Messianic era, which will shine as brilliantly as the morning sun. At that time, we will be sated by God's kindness and we will never again experience any misery. Then *we shall sing out and rejoice all our days.*

15. שַׂמְּחֵנוּ כִּימוֹת עִנִּיתָנוּ — *Gladden us according to the days You afflicted us.*

טז רָעָה: יֵרָאֶה אֶל־עֲבָדֶיךָ פָּעֳלֶךָ וַהֲדָרְךָ עַל־
יז בְּנֵיהֶם: וִיהִי | נֹעַם אֲדֹנָי אֱלֹהֵינוּ עָלֵינוּ
וּמַעֲשֵׂה יָדֵינוּ כּוֹנְנָה עָלֵינוּ וּמַעֲשֵׂה יָדֵינוּ
כּוֹנְנֵהוּ:

In the preceding verse, the Psalmist implored Divine mercy during man's youth, in order to instill a positive attitude which will sustain him for the remainder of his life. Here the Psalmist continues: If, unfortunately, a man's youth turns out to be tragic and miserable, then at least make his old age glad, to compensate for his early sorrows (Maharam Almosnino).

Rashi comments: *Make us glad* in the Messianic era of the future for a duration of time which will equal the length of time that we suffered in exile in this world.

A great many opinions are offered by the *Talmud* (*Sanhedrin* 99a) to determine the duration of the Messianic era. Some say that it will last forty years corresponding to the number of years the Jews suffered in the wilderness,

— ... or 400 years corresponding to the years of the Egyptian bondage,

— ... or 365 years corresponding to the days of the solar year, for the burning sun is a symbol of fiery Divine retribution,

— ... or 7000 years [כִּימוֹת, *like the days* (of the week), and each day of God is 1000 years (see verse 4)].

שְׁנוֹת רָאִינוּ רָעָה — *The years when we saw evil.*

Let every one of *the days* wherein *You afflicted us* be reckoned as a complete year of evil, and repay us a year of gladness for each day of affliction (*Alshich*).

16. יֵרָאֶה אֶל עֲבָדֶיךָ פָּעֳלֶךָ — *May Your works be visible to Your servants.*

We look forward to the day when You will openly display Your love for Your servants (*Ibn Ezra*) with salvation and victory (*Radak*).

Specifically, we await the most monumental accomplishment of Jewish history: the final reconstruction of the third *Beis HaMikdash*. Actually, since the destruction of the second Temple, God has been slowly reconstructing the edifice in heaven. When it is completed, God will display His *works* by bringing the celestial Temple down to earth (*Dorash Moshe*).

וַהֲדָרְךָ עַל בְּנֵיהֶם — *And Your majesty upon their children.*

After God returns His presence to earth, we ask that He continue to dwell here for future generations so that our *children* and descendants will enjoy His glory. Indeed, we hope that His glory will be apparent soon, so that the fathers will still be alive to see it with their children (*Radak; Meiri; Sforno*).

90   *the years when we saw evil.*

16-17   ¹⁶ May Your works be visible to Your servants,
            and Your majesty upon their children.
            ¹⁷ May the pleasantness of my Lord, our God,
            be upon us —
            may He establish our handiwork for us;
            our handiwork, may He establish.

Dorash Moshe continues: After the Temple is reconstructed, God will gather in the scattered exiles, and Israel will return to the Holy Land. This will truly add glory to our nation, for as Scripture states, בְּרָב עָם הַדְרַת מֶלֶךְ, *In the multitude of people is the King's glory* (Proverbs 14:28).

17. וִיהִי נֹעַם אֲדֹנָי אֱלֹהֵינוּ עָלֵינוּ — *May the pleasantness of my Lord, our God, be upon us.*

May God delight us with the bliss of the Garden of Eden (*Targum*) so that man will accomplish great things without annoyance, frustration and wasted efforts (*Radak*).

This bliss can be achieved through a clear understanding of Torah, which is sweet intellectual enlightenment (*Sforno; Rashbam*).

Scripture (*Exodus* 39:43) relates that when Moses saw that the Jewish people completed the construction of the Tabernacle, he blessed them, saying, "May it find favor before God that He cause His Holy Spirit to descend upon Your handiwork." The children of Israel responded by affirming Moses' blessing, saying, *May the pleasantness of my Lord, our God, be upon us* (*Sifri, Pinchos* 28:8).

[Similarly, we look forward to witnessing God's Spirit in the third *Beis Hamikdash*.]

וּמַעֲשֵׂה יָדֵינוּ כּוֹנְנָה עָלֵינוּ — *May He establish our handiwork for us.*

Malbim observes that a builder who lays a physical foundation and builds an edifice upon it remains personally unchanged. However, the man who does the will of God and builds a *mitzvah* structure, adds breadth and depth to his own personality. Thus his efforts to fulfill the Torah's precepts are literally upon him.

וּמַעֲשֵׂה יָדֵינוּ כּוֹנְנֵהוּ — *Our handiwork, may He establish.*

We pray that everything we undertake will be a source of pride and glory for ourselves and for all mankind. Therefore, we ask that He establish our handiwork *upon us*, so that our deeds reflect glory on us, and that He establish the work of our hands for the benefit of all men (*Meiri; Ibn Yachya*).

The blessing of the Temple and the Tabernacle is not confined to Israel. Rather, it is the factor which lends solidarity and prosperity to the entire world. We pray that God return to this world and establish His blessed presence for all time (*Dorash Moshe*).

מזמור צא 91

This is the second psalm composed by Moses. He dedicated this composition to the tribe of Levi. This tribe in particular can be described as dwelling in the shadow of the Almighty, for the Levites spent their days in the insulated and sacred environment of the Temple courtyard (Radak).

According to the Midrash, Moses composed this work on the day he completed construction of the מִשְׁכָּן, Tabernacle, and these verses describe Moses himself, who entered the Divine clouds and was enveloped in the shadow of the Almighty.

At that moment, a great question arose: how could a Tabernacle with walls and curtains contain the Presence of the Almighty? The Master of the universe Himself explained, "The entire world cannot contain My glory, yet when I wish, I can concentrate My entire essence into one small spot. Indeed, I am Most High, yet I sit in a [limited, constricted] refuge — in the shadow of the Tabernacle constructed by Bezalel."

Throughout this composition, the Psalmist describes the devout man of faith who lives with God in his heart and who never leaves God's shadow. Such a man is the true hero of Jewish life to whom God pledges (v. 16), I will satisfy him with long life and show him My salvation.

א-ב יֹשֵׁב בְּסֵתֶר עֶלְיוֹן בְּצֵל שַׁדַּי יִתְלוֹנָן: אֹמַר
ג לַיהוה מַחְסִי וּמְצוּדָתִי אֱלֹהַי אֶבְטַח־בּוֹ: כִּי
הוּא יַצִּילְךָ מִפַּח יָקוּשׁ מִדֶּבֶר הַוּוֹת:

1. יֹשֵׁב בְּסֵתֶר עֶלְיוֹן — *Whoever sits in the refuge* [lit. *hidden* or *secret place*] *of the Most High.*

The person who scorns conventional forms of protection and seeks only the refuge provided by the Most High will find his faith rewarded. He will be enveloped by God's providence so that he can continue to seek holiness and wisdom without fear of those who would seek to do him harm: *He will* [truly] *sit in the refuge of the Most High* (Rashi).

[As explained in the *Prefatory Remarks*, this psalm was composed on the day Moses completed the construction of the Tabernacle. The final verse of the preceding psalm (90:17) was also composed then, when the work was done. Moses blessed Israel, and they responded by echoing his earlier wish: *May the pleasantness of my Lord, our God, be upon us — may He establish our handiwork for us; our handiwork, may He establish.* The Tabernacle is not considered to be truly *established* until *the Most High* dwells there and makes it His own, intimate *refuge.*]

Alshich interprets that the place where the *Most High* dwells is actually the heart of man; this is God's most sacred sanctuary.

Tehillos Hashem notes that the customary superscription giving the author's name is omitted from this psalm and that Moses' authorship is left unstated. This is due to his unsurpassed humility; he submerged his entire being in God and gave himself no credit. Since Moses secreted himself in *the shadow of the Almighty* this psalm does not mention his name.

בְּצֵל שַׁדַּי יִתְלוֹנָן — *He shall dwell in the shadow of the Almighty.*

The architect and builder of the Tabernacle was בְּצַלְאֵל, *Bezalel,* whose name is composed of the words בְּצֵל אֵל, *in the shadow of God.* Bezalel anticipated aspects of the Divine blueprint even before Moses gave him the necessary information. So amazed was Moses that he asked Bezalel, "Perhaps you reside *in the shadow of God?"* (*Berachos* 55a; see *Tanchuma, Vayakhel 3).*

Midrash Tanchuma (*Nasso 23)* states that Moses composed this psalm when he ascended Mount Sinai. Moses dwelt *in the secret refuge of the Most High* for three periods of forty days — a total of one hundred and twenty days. The numerical value of צֵל, *shadow,* is also one hundred and twenty.

[The fact that God is here referred to as שַׁדַּי is significant, for this Divine Name alludes to the fact that the Almighty, although infinite, confined Himself in a finite world. The *Talmud* (*Chagigah* 12a) explains that, at creation, the world continued to grow until God halted its expansion with the command, דַּי, *Enough!* This mortal world must be finite and limited!"[1]

---

1. When the Jewish people forsook God and worshiped idols in Egypt, they implied a belief that His Presence was not supreme everywhere on earth, but that various pagan deities were supreme in their own respective locations. Therefore, God bade Israel to build a Tabernacle that would symbolize the world in microcosm. The Presence of the Almighty filled the Tabernacle unmistakably and He declared, "Just as My presence permeates every inch of the Tabernacle, the miniature world, so too, it pervades every area and atom of the entire world even though it is hidden from human perception" [see ArtScroll, *Aseres HaDibros,* p. 44].

Kli Yakar (comm. to *Exodus* 35:30) cites the successful collection of money and materials for the construction of the Tabernacle. Moses was forced to issue a proclamation telling the

Whoever sits in the refuge of the Most High—
    he shall dwell in the shadow of the Almighty.
² I will say of HASHEM:
    He is my refuge and my fortress,
    my God — I will trust in Him.
³ That He will deliver you from the ensnaring trap,
    from devastating pestilence.

Had the creation been unlimited, the world would be perfect, filled with God's spiritual light. However, since this potential perfection was arrested, there are dark areas in the world where God's light is obscured (in the shadow) and His presence not readily evident. Only the devout man, the true believer, detects the presence of God even in the secrecy of the shadows. Only people like Moses and Bezalel can dwell with God even in the shadows formed by the Name that represents His hiddenness and still recognize that He is עֶלְיוֹן, Most High, everywhere.]

2. אֹמַר לַה' מַחְסִי וּמְצוּדָתִי — I will say of HASHEM: He is my refuge and my fortress.

The devout man who sits in the refuge of the Most High declares publicly that God is his refuge from all physical dangers, and his fortress, protecting him from all human enemies (Radak; Sforno).

Bamidbar Rabbah (12:3) states that Moses composed this verse as he ascended Mount Sinai. Whenever a person embarks upon a mission to increase good and sanctity in the world, the forces of evil struggle to interfere. Accordingly, demonic forces and hostile

angels of violence attempted to block Moses' path as he rose higher and closer to God. But Moses uttered God's Name [I will say of HASHEM: He is my refuge and my fortress] and all of these evil forces fled.

אֱלֹהַי אֶבְטַח בּוֹ — My God — I will trust in Him.

Not only do I find refuge in the Almighty when He appears as ה', the Dispenser of Divine Kindness, but I even trust Him when He manifests Himself as אֱלֹהִים, the Dispenser of Divine Justice (Olelos Yehudah).

3. כִּי הוּא יַצִּילְךָ מִפַּח יָקוּשׁ — That He will deliver you from the ensnaring trap. [See 141:9, שָׁמְרֵנִי מִידֵי פַח יָקְשׁוּ לִי וּמֹקְשׁוֹת פֹּעֲלֵי אָוֶן, Safeguard me from the trap which they set to ensnare me, and the snares of the doers of iniquity.]

מִדֶּבֶר הַוּוֹת — [And] from devastating pestilence (Radak).

[Elsewhere, הַוּוֹת has been translated treachery. (See comm. to 5:10, 38:13, 55:12.) Here it refers to a pestilence that causes such destruction that the world order is betrayed.] Ibn Ezra views הַוּוֹת as cognate with הֹוֶה, present, signifying a sudden pestilence which comes at this moment, without warning.

people to stop bringing contributions, for the material they had was enough [דַי] for all the work to be done, and left over (Exodus 36:6). The construction of the miniature world reflected that of the universe. Just as the universe expanded until God cried, "Enough," so the miniature world, in the form of contributions to build it, expanded until Moses cried, "Enough!" God limited the expansion of the real world so that He could confine His infinite Presence within finite boundaries to be close to man. The same was true of the miniature world of the Tabernacle [see Sfas Emes to Exodus 36:6 שֶׁנֶּת תרלז].

ד בְּאֶבְרָתוֹ | יָסֶךְ לָךְ וְתַחַת־כְּנָפָיו תֶּחְסֶה צִנָּה

ה וְסֹחֵרָה אֲמִתּוֹ: לֹא־תִירָא מִפַּחַד לָיְלָה מֵחֵץ

ו יָעוּף יוֹמָם: מִדֶּבֶר בָּאֹפֶל יַהֲלֹךְ מִקֶּטֶב יָשׁוּד

ז צָהֳרָיִם: יִפֹּל מִצִּדְּךָ | אֶלֶף וּרְבָבָה מִימִינֶךָ

4. בְּאֶבְרָתוֹ יָסֶךְ לָךְ — *With His pinion He will cover you.*

A bird uses its pinion (wing) to shelter its young (*Rashi*) or to fly it to safety (*Ibn Ezra*).

Bamidbar Rabbah (12:3) explains that the *pinion* resembles an arm: thus, God covers Israel with the merit of the Torah which had been given to Israel by His right arm (*Deuteronomy* 33:2).

Divrei Shlomo calculates that the numerical value of בְּאֶבְרָתוֹ equals 611, which is also the numerical value of the word תּוֹרָה, *Torah*. The stronger a bird's wings are, the higher it is propelled. Similarly, the more powerful a person's grasp of Torah wisdom, the higher his spirit ascends.

וְתַחַת כְּנָפָיו תֶּחְסֶה — *And beneath His wings you will be protected.*

Rashi (see comm. to 68:14) describes כָּנָף as *plume,* a bird's outer feathers, which are primarily ornamental, in contrast to the feathers it uses for flying. Every *mitzvah* a person performs is like a beautiful feather added to his plumage — a feather that will adorn him eternally (*Divrei Shlomo*).

צִנָּה וְסֹחֵרָה אֲמִתּוֹ — *Shield and armor will His truth be.*

Rashi describes the צִנָּה as a *shield* which protects its wearer incompletely whereas סֹחֵרָה, *armor,* [related to סְחַר, *circle*] totally surrounds its wearer [affording greater protection]. [See

comm. to 35:2 for a detailed discussion of these terms.]

Midrash Shocher Tov explains this homiletically: Torah, which is God's *truth,* is a *shield* and a זַיִן, *weapon,* for those who study it.[1]

[But casual Torah study is not sufficient. The word סֹחֵרָה alludes to the idea that the diligent student must treat Torah as סְחֹרָה, *precious merchandise,* which is guarded and examined carefully, in order to discover אֲמִתּוֹ, *His (God's) truth.*]

5. לֹא תִירָא מִפַּחַד לָיְלָה — *You shall not fear the terror of night.*

If you put your faith in God, fear will be banished from your heart (*Rashi*). The person who walks alone in the dark is usually terrified of the unknown forces he imagines to be lurking in the shadows [but he who walks with God never walks alone] (*Rashi*).

מֵחֵץ יָעוּף יוֹמָם — *[Nor] the arrow that flies by day.*

Man is most vulnerable to the sudden tragedies and misfortunes that fly at him without warning like swift *arrows* (*Radak*).

Targum identifies חֵץ as the *arrow* unleashed by the Angel of Death; since he fears no one, he cuts a man down even in broad daylight.

6. מִדֶּבֶר בָּאֹפֶל יַהֲלֹךְ — *Nor the pestilence that walks in gloom.*

---

1. *Abudraham* points out that all the letters of the alphabet are represented in this psalm with the exception of ז, *zayin,* which literally means *weapon,* because whoever recites this psalm with concentration and sincerity has no need for conventional military weapons.

Furthermore, *Abudraham* notes that the numerical value of ז is seven. This alludes to the fact that ordinarily this psalm is recited on Saturday night at the conclusion of *Maariv,* the Evening Prayer. Seven times a year [the Saturday nights preceding and during the festivals of Pesach (twice), Shavuos, Sukkos (twice), Rosh Hashanah and Yom Kippur], however, this psalm is deleted from the service due to festivals and special events which occur in the following week. [See footnote to verse 7.]

⁴ *With His pinion He will cover you,*
and beneath His wings you will be protected;
shield and armor will His truth be.
⁵ *You shall not fear the terror of night,*
nor the arrow that flies by day;
⁶ *Nor the pestilence that walks in gloom,*
nor the destroyer who lays waste at noon.
⁷ *A thousand will fall at your side*
and a myriad at your right hand,

Severe extremes of weather make a person susceptible to *pestilence* and disease. *Gloom* signifies darkness and severe cold, while צָהֳרַיִם, *noon*, mentioned at the end of this verse, symbolizes blazing heat (*Ibn Ezra*).

מִקֶּטֶב יָשׁוּד צָהֳרָיִם — *Nor the destroyer who lays waste at noon.*

In *Deuteronomy* 32:24 God threatens Israel that if they are errant He will smite them with קֶטֶב מְרִירִי, *bitter destruction.* This is interpreted to be destruction by demonic forces.

Ibn Ezra and *Radak* quote *Midrash Shocher Tov*, which relates יָשׁוּד to the word שֵׁד, *demon*, that causes man harm. [Ordinarily, demons operate only in the dark and flee from daylight (*Berachos* 3b), but the terrible destroyer, קֶטֶב, *lays waste* even in broad daylight, *at noon*.] *Radak* cites the חַכְמֵי הַמֶּחְקָר, *wise men of science*, who deny the reality of demons because there is no scientific proof for their existence.[1]

7. יִפֹּל מִצִּדְּךָ אֶלֶף וּרְבָבָה מִימִינֶךָ — *A thousand will fall at* [lit. *from*] *your side*

---

1. *Rambam* also questions the existence of demons. (See *Yoreh Deah* 179 and the *Vilna Gaon's* gloss there.)

It is strange that *Radak* should cite the opinion of the scientists who find no scientific proof for demons, for many Torah beliefs and concepts, such as the existence of angels and the occurrence of miracles, cannot be proven scientifically.

Harav Yaakov Kaminetsky, שליט״א, explains that in a discussion of an entirely spiritual phenomenon we certainly do not take the opinions of the scientists into consideration. However, even according to Rabbinical tradition, שֵׁדִים, *demons*, are not entirely spiritual. The *Talmud* (*Chagigah* 16a) explains that demons are distinguished by six features. In three respects they resemble angels: (a) they have wings; (b) they fly all over the world; and (c) they have prior knowledge of future events. In three respects, however, they are like men: (a) they eat and drink; (b) they procreate; and (c) they die, like mortals.

Because demons have physical properties similar to man's, *Radak* finds it noteworthy that these properties have not yet been discovered by scientific research.

Harav Kaminetsky notes that most rabbinic authorities agree that demons no longer bother men. Only in earlier days, when men were much holier, did God challenge them with the scourge of demons. Then, the loftier the man, the more the demons challenged him. The *Talmud* says in numerous places that demons attacked Torah scholars in particular. [See *Berachos* 6a.]

Demons serve to demonstrate to man that despite his coarse body, he can still strive to elevate himself to the level of an angel. Therefore, the more angelic a man becomes, the more the demons disturb him. Nowadays, men are too removed from angelic perfection to be affected by semi-angelic demons.

[The *Zohar* (*Vayikra* 277) explains that a demon is in a constant state of flux: he changes from demon to angel and from angel to demon in accordance with the actions of man, i.e., when people sanctify this earth by their righteous acts the forces of evil are transformed into forces of good. This occurred when the Tabernacle was dedicated as an abode for God's Presence on earth.]

ח אֵלֶיךָ לֹא יִגָּשׁ: רַק בְּעֵינֶיךָ תַבִּיט וְשִׁלֻּמַת
ט רְשָׁעִים תִּרְאֶה: כִּי־אַתָּה יְהוָה מַחְסִי עֶלְיוֹן
י שַׂמְתָּ מְעוֹנֶךָ: לֹא־תְאֻנֶּה אֵלֶיךָ רָעָה וְנֶגַע

and a myriad at [lit. *from*] *your right hand.*

The term מִצִּדְךָ, *at your side,* refers to the left hand; for since it is designated for just one *mitzvah — tefillin,* phylacteries — its power is relatively limited. The right hand, however, is the preferred one for the performance of all other *mitzvos;* therefore, its strength is enhanced and it can fell ten thousand (*Midrash Shocher Tov*).

According to *Rashi,* this means that thousands and myriads of demons will fall before the man who is shielded by God's truth.

Radak perceives this as a description of the enemies of Israel who fall before them in battle: Despite the fact that *the pestilence ... and the destroyer ... lay waste* (v. 6) *to a thousand ... at your left side and a myriad at your right hand,* nevertheless, *to you it* (i.e., the pestilence) *shall not approach.*[1]

אֵלֶיךָ לֹא יִגָּשׁ — *But to you it shall not approach.*

Midrash Shocher Tov explains that

the man of faith is shielded from the forces of evil by a vanguard of angels at his left hand and at his right. Ordinarily, a master who controls thousands of servants is expected to sustain them, but this *tzaddik* is not held responsible for his guardian angels; they are sustained by God alone. Therefore, they shall not approach you to demand payment.

Thus, the myriads of angels that are created by the *mitzvos* a man performs [see *Rambam, Hilchos Mezuzah* 6:13] will protect him from the myriads of attacking demons [see *comm.* and footnote, 34:8].

8. רַק בְּעֵינֶיךָ תַבִּיט — *You will merely peer with your eyes.*

You will peer and behold the destruction of the wicked who spurned God and refused to *sit in the refuge of the Most High* (*Radak*), but they will be helpless to harm you (*Metzudos*).

Alshich cites Talmudic instances that the Rabbis could punish someone by training their holy eyes on him, and the

1. The Talmud (*Shavuos* 15b) explains that it was possible to expand the city limits of the Holy City of Jerusalem and the territory of the Temple courtyards by following a carefully detailed ritual: The Song of Thanksgiving was recited to the accompaniment of musical instruments in every corner of the city and upon every large rock.

Then they would recite this psalm. Some call it שִׁיר שֶׁל פְּגָעִים, the *Song of the Demons,* because in this verse we read that thousands and tens of thousands of demons will fall. Others call it שִׁיר שֶׁל נְגָעִים, the *Song of the Plagues,* as we read, *nor will any plague come near your tent* (v. 10). This psalm was recited in order to cleanse the hitherto unsanctified area of all impure and evil forces. When plagues and demons are expelled, sanctity can be introduced (*Maharsha*).

The Talmud relates that Rabbi Yehoshua ben Levi recited this psalm before he went to sleep to insure his safety from the dangers of the night. Consequently, the Halachah stipulates that this psalm be said every night before retiring (*Orach Chaim* 239:1).

Furthermore, this psalm is recited after *Maariv,* the Evening service, at the conclusion of the Sabbath. *Tefillah L'Moshe* explains that when the sanctity of the Sabbath envelops the world, all evil forces are expelled; but when the Sabbath ends and sanctity departs, the demonic forces return. Therefore, the psalm is recited at once, to protect the world from harm. [However, when a festival occurs in the following week, the forces of evil are arrested by the holiness of the holidays and there is no need to recite this psalm following the Sabbath. See footnote to verse 4.]

but to you it shall not approach.

⁸ *You will merely peer with your eyes*
and you will see the retribution of the wicked.

⁹ *Because you have said, "HASHEM is my refuge,"*
you have made the Most High
your dwelling place.

¹⁰ *No evil will befall you,*
nor will any plague come near your tent.

---

sinner would disintegrate into a heap of bones. Thus, *you will merely peer with your eyes at the wicked for that will suffice to decimate them.* [See commentary of *Ohr Hachaim* to Exodus 11:4 for explanation of this concept.]

וְשִׁלֻּמַת רְשָׁעִים תִּרְאֶה — *And you will see the retribution of the wicked.*

Only a person who is delivered from danger because of his own merit is accorded the privilege of witnessing the downfall of his enemies. If he was saved only because of the merits of others [like Lot, who was saved from Sodom because of Abraham], the man is forbidden to witness the suffering that he, too, deserved to share (*Olelos Yehudah*). [See comm. to 118:7.]

9. כִּי אַתָּה ה׳ מַחְסִי — *Because you [have said], "HASHEM is my refuge."*

These are the Psalmist's words to the man of faith. The statement is recorded here in abbreviated form, as if it read: *Because you*, the man of faith, *have said, "HASHEM is my refuge"* you thereby made the Most High the dwelling place (i.e., the repository) of your faith (*Rashi; Ibn Ezra; Radak*).

עֶלְיוֹן שַׂמְתָּ מְעוֹנֶךָ — *You have made the Most High your dwelling place.*

[Although the body of the man of faith is on earth, his true abode is in heaven because that is where his heart, soul, and mind are concentrated. Thus, no harm can befall him, because the essence of his being is high above the grasp of earthlings.]

10. לֹא תְאֻנֶּה אֵלֶיךָ רָעָה — *No evil will befall you.*

Before the construction of the Tabernacle, the forces of evil were unchecked and they harmed all men. But the completion of the Tabernacle heralded a new era of purity and goodness, which swept away the influence of evil (*Midrash Shocher Tov*).

At that time, the מַזִּיקִים, *demons*, vanished [temporarily, see footnote to v. 6] from the earth and ceased to hurt human beings (*Bamidbar Rabbah* 12:3).

The *Talmud* (*Sanhedrin* 103a) interprets this as a blessing that the Evil Inclination should have no power over the devout man and that he should not be frightened by terrifying dreams or fantasies.

וְנֶגַע לֹא יִקְרַב בְּאָהֳלֶךָ — *Nor will any plague come near your tent.*

The *Talmud* (*Sanhedrin* 103a) perceives this as a blessing for domestic bliss [for tent signifies *household*]. May you raise worthy children and students, who will not shame you by acting improperly in public.

Tzror HaMor notes that this psalm contains one hundred and thirty words corresponding to the one hundred thirty years Adam separated from Eve after Cain killed his brother Abel. Since Adam did not procreate or produce anything good during that period of abstinence, he was responsible for the introduction into the world of plagues and demonic forces. This happened

יא לֹא־יְקָרֶב בְּאָהֳלֶךָ: כִּי מַלְאָכָיו יְצַוֶּה־לָּךְ
יב לִשְׁמָרְךָ בְּכָל־דְּרָכֶיךָ: עַל־כַּפַּיִם יִשָּׂאוּנְךָ פֶּן־
יג תִּגֹּף בָּאֶבֶן רַגְלֶךָ: עַל־שַׁחַל וָפֶתֶן תִּדְרֹךְ
יד תִּרְמֹס כְּפִיר וְתַנִּין: כִּי בִי חָשַׁק וַאֲפַלְּטֵהוּ
טו אֲשַׂגְּבֵהוּ כִּי־יָדַע שְׁמִי: יִקְרָאֵנִי | וְאֶעֱנֵהוּ

because he lacked the protection provided by the conjugal relationship: *tent* connotes *wife*. Therefore, the Psalmist blesses the man of faith with a *tent* so that no *plague will come near him*.

11. כִּי מַלְאָכָיו יְצַוֶּה־לָּךְ — *He will charge His angels for you.*

A man performs one *mitzvah* and God sends one angel to protect him, as 34:8 states: *The angel (singular) of HASHEM encamps around His reverent ones, and he releases them.* A man performs two *mitzvos* and God sends him two angels, as this verse states: *He will charge His angels* (plural) *for you.* If a person performs many *mitzvos* God gives him half of His own escort, as explained in the commentary to verse 7: *A thousand will fall at your side and a myriad at your right hand* [v. 7, see comm. ibid.]; a *myriad* is one-half of God's escort, as 68:18 states: *The chariot of God is twice ten thousand* (*Shemos Rabbah* 32:6).[1]

לִשְׁמָרְךָ בְּכָל־דְּרָכֶיךָ — *To protect you in all your ways.*

The *Talmud* (*Chagigah* 16a) teaches that these angels are not merely guardians, but witnesses as well. They observe every action and they are

destined to testify for or against the man under their protection when he comes before the Heavenly Tribunal after death.

12. עַל־כַּפַּיִם יִשָּׂאוּנְךָ — *They will carry you on their palms.*

The angels created by the *mitzvos* that you perform with your *palms* (i.e., giving charity and doing acts of kindness) will raise you above all dangers that lurk in your path (*Zera Raakov*).

פֶּן־תִּגֹּף בָּאֶבֶן רַגְלֶךָ — *Lest you strike your foot against a stone.*

Stone refers to the obstacles strewn in a man's way. The man of faith treads a clear path, free from all such obstacles, as if the forces of nature unite in their resolve to smooth his way as *Job* 5:23 states: כִּי עִם אַבְנֵי הַשָּׂדֶה בְרִיתֶךָ, *For you shall be in league with the stones of the field* (*Ibn Ezra; Radak*).

The *Talmud* (*Succah* 55a) lists seven allegorical names for the Evil Inclination. Among them is אֶבֶן, *stone*, because the Evil Inclination is the major obstacle in man's way. This *stone* will not disturb the man of faith (*Na'eh L'hodos*).

13. עַל־שַׁחַל וָפֶתֶן תִּדְרֹךְ — *You will tread upon the lion and the viper.*

1. *Tanna d'Bei Eliyahu Rabbah* (chapter 28) teaches that God's angels are reserved for those who are merely beginners in Torah and who have studied nothing more than the basic Scripture. However, advanced students of the Oral Law who have mastered the *Mishnah* and *Talmud* are escorted and protected by God Himself, for He loves these scholars as a father loves his own son.

This may be likened to the case of a king who traveled in the desert with his son. If the king noticed that the blazing sun was harming his son, he would not send a servant to the rescue. He himself would spread a protective canopy over his beloved child. Thus the Psalmist says of God, *HASHEM is your keeper, HASHEM is your shadow at your right hand … HASHEM will guard your going out and your coming in from this day and forever more* (121:5, 8).

¹¹ *He will charge His angels for you,*
to protect you in all your ways.
¹² *They will carry you on their palms,*
lest you strike your foot against a stone.
¹³ *You will tread upon the lion and the viper,*
you will trample the young lion and the serpent.
¹⁴ *For he has yearned for Me and I will deliver him;*
I will elevate him because he knows My Name.
¹⁵ *He will call upon Me and I will answer him,*

Kol Bo identifies שַׁחַל as a large, mature *lion*. The פֶּתֶן is an old, vicious *snake*.

The Talmud (*Berachos* 33a) relates that a poisonous snake was harming the populace, so Rabbi Chanina ben Dosa placed his heel on the opening of its pit. The snake bit his heel and died instantly. Rabbi Chanina hoisted it on his shoulder and brought it to the *Beis HaMidrash* (House of Study) where he addressed the students, "My sons, observe! It is not the snake which kills, it is sin which kills." [Thus, he who is free of sin may tread on a snake without fear.]

Then people said, "Woe unto the man who is attacked by a snake and woe unto the snake that attacks Rabbi Chanina ben Dosa!" [See *Shaarei Orah, V'zos Habrachah.*]

תִּרְמֹס כְּפִיר וְתַנִּין — *You will trample the young lion and the serpent.*

These two dangerous creatures hate each other. When they see each other they are aroused to murderous fury. Furthermore, if someone tramples upon either of them it is infuriated and poised to kill.

Despite the double danger of trampling on both of them at the same time, God will be at your side and you will pass through these perils unscathed (*Akeidas Yitzchak*).

14. כִּי בִי חָשַׁק וַאֲפַלְּטֵהוּ — *For he has yearned for Me and I will deliver him.*

Earlier the Psalmist promised that Hashem *will charge His angels for you* (v. 11). This verse records how God actually fulfilled His promise, telling His angels why He shows special favor to the man of faith (*Ibn Ezra; Sforno*).

The man of faith has displayed חֵשֶׁק, *yearning,* for God, which is greater than אַהֲבָה, *love,* for a lover's heart can love a number of people or things whereas one who *yearns* has only one desire, which excludes all else (*Rambam, Guide to the Perplexed,* Part III). Also, love fluctuates; it flourishes and fades intermittently whereas yearning remains consistently intense (*Rav Refael of Nurtzi*).

אֲשַׂגְּבֵהוּ כִּי יָדַע שְׁמִי — *I will elevate him because he knows My Name.*

9:11 states, *And those knowing Your Name will trust in You, for You forsake not those who seek You, HASHEM.* This describes those who know God's true, ineffable Name, and are permitted to use it to perform miracles and wonders. These people receive no benefit, gifts, or favors from other human beings for they put their faith in God alone.[1]

1. The Talmud (*Kiddushin* 71a) teaches that the Holy Name of the Almighty (with its proper pronunciation and *kavanah*) is composed of seventy two letters, and was revealed only to humble, pious men. *Tosefos Rid* cites *Yerushalmi* which describes them as men who never derived any benefit or gift from others. See Responsa of *Chasam Sofer* (*Orach Chaim* no. 198). [See ArtScroll *Hoshanos,* p. 84, and *Bircas Kohanim* pp. 45.]

עַמּוֹ־אָנֹכִי בְצָרָה אֲחַלְצֵהוּ וַאֲכַבְּדֵהוּ: אֹרֶךְ
יָמִים אַשְׂבִּיעֵהוּ וְאַרְאֵהוּ בִּישׁוּעָתִי:

God Himself will elevate and rescue such a man, because he *knows* — i.e., recognizes — God's Name as the only source of his salvation (*Dorash Moshe; Tehillos Hashem*).

15. יִקְרָאֵנִי וְאֶעֱנֵהוּ — *He will call upon Me and I will answer him.*

Yerushalmi (*Berachos* 9:1) explains that if a man in distress seeks the help of a human being, he will not storm into his potential protector's home abruptly. Rather he will go to the protector's gates and request an audience from the gatekeeper. There is no guarantee that the audience will be granted. However, no such procedure need be followed by those who seek protection from God. The Holy One, Blessed is He, declares, "If misfortune should befall you, do not cry out to the ministering angel Gabriel or to the ministering angel Michael! Cry out to Me, and I will answer you immediately!"

עַמּוֹ אָנֹכִי בְצָרָה — *I am with him in distress.*

This may be likened to a mother who was angry at her pregnant daughter. The mother went upstairs, leaving her daughter below. When the daughter went into labor and began to scream in pain, the mother, too, began to cry out. The neighbors were amazed by the mother's anguish and asked, "Are you giving birth with her?"

The mother replied, "Although my daughter angered me, I cannot bear to hear her scream, because her pain is my pain!"

So, too, when God was angered by Israel. He abandoned them and ascended to heaven. When He destroyed the Temple, however, He heard Israel's anguished cries. Then He cried with them, telling His ministering angels, "My children are suffering and I am suffering with them" (*Midrash Shocher Tov*).

I am with him in distress,
I will release him and I will honor him.
¹⁶ *I will satisfy him with long life*
and show him My salvation.

אֲחַלְּצֵהוּ וַאֲכַבְּדֵהוּ — *I will release him and I will honor him.*

In 50:15, the Psalmist said, וּקְרָאֵנִי בְּיוֹם צָרָה אֲחַלֶּצְךָ וּתְכַבְּדֵנִי, *Beseech Me in a day of distress, I will release you and you will honor Me.* This implies that if God releases someone, he must honor God for having done so. However, Moses, the author of this psalm, says that God will not only release a man of faith, He will even honor him. Furthermore, He will endow him and Israel with the power to conquer many great nations (*Radak*).

16. אֹרֶךְ יָמִים אַשְׂבִּיעֵהוּ — *I will satisfy him with long life* [lit. *length of days*].

I will fill out the days of the man of faith. His life will not be cut short in this world (*Ibn Ezra; Radak*).

[Moreover, some men live long lives that are full of frustration and disappointment, but this man will live a satisfying, meaningful life.]

וְאַרְאֵהוּ בִּישׁוּעָתִי — *And show him My salvation.*

He will witness the salvation I will bring about at the advent of the Messiah, at the time of the revival of the dead, and at the salvation of the World to Come (*Radak*).

Indeed, it is not God who needs salvation, but Israel; yet God calls Israel's victory *My Salvation* to emphasize that Israel's salvation is His as well (*Midrash Shocher Tov*). It is God's desire to display His Presence in this world, but if there were no Israel, no community of faith, [no Tabernacle and no Temple,] then there would be no place for God to reveal His glory and no one to appreciate Him. Therefore, God, Himself, is the beneficiary of Israel's salvation (*Tehillos Hashem*).

It is both unreasonable and unwise to pass judgment on a work of art before it has been completed; even a masterpiece may look like a grotesque mass of strokes and colors, prior to its completion. Human history is God's masterpiece. Physical creation was completed at the end of the sixth day, but the spiritual development of mankind will continue until this world ends, at the close of the sixth millennium. Thus it is both unfair and impossible to judge God's equity before the denouement of human history, despite the fact that history appears to be a long series of tragic injustices.

On the seventh day of the first week of creation, on the Sabbath, Adam surveyed God's completed work and he was stirred to sing of the marvelous perfection which his eyes beheld.

Similarly, when the panorama of human history is completed, the seventh millennium will be ushered in as the יוֹם שֶׁכּוּלוֹ שַׁבָּת, the day of everlasting Sabbath. At that time all Adam's descendants will look back and admire God's completed masterpiece.

This psalm speaks of man's bewilderment as he observes the inequity which is apparent in this world. It also tells of the joy he will experience when the inequities are resolved.

Therefore, the Talmud (Rosh Hashanah 31a) prescribes this as the שִׁיר שֶׁל יוֹם, the Song of the Day for the Sabbath, both in the song of the Levites in the Holy Temple and in the universal Sabbath liturgy.

א-ב מִזְמוֹר שִׁיר לְיוֹם הַשַּׁבָּת: טוֹב לְהֹדוֹת
ג לַיהוָה וּלְזַמֵּר לְשִׁמְךָ עֶלְיוֹן: לְהַגִּיד בַּבֹּקֶר
ד חַסְדֶּךָ וֶאֱמוּנָתְךָ בַּלֵּילוֹת: עֲלֵי-עָשׂוֹר וַעֲלֵי-

1. הַשַּׁבָּת שִׁיר לְיוֹם מִזְמוֹר — *A song with musical accompaniment for the Sabbath day.*

The *Pesikta* notes that the initial letters of these four words form לְמשֶׁה, *by Moses,* for this is the third of the eleven psalms which he composed.

Indeed, the Sabbath rest was a special gift which Moses bestowed upon the children of Israel. The *Midrash (Shemos Rabbah* 1:28) relates that Moses was distraught when he saw his beloved brethren suffering under Egyptian bondage without any respite. He approached Pharaoh and argued, ''A slave who works constantly cannot long survive. Therefore, you will certainly lose your Israelite slaves unless you allow them a free day each week.'' Pharaoh agreed, and Moses established Saturday as the day of rest. This event is commemorated in the Sabbath morning service in the passage משֶׁה יִשְׂמַח בְּמַתְּנַת חֶלְקוֹ, *Let Moses rejoice in the gift* [i.e., the Sabbath] *which is his portion (Iyun Tefillah; Chazah Zion).*

The enslaved Jews were particularly depressed by the fact that the wicked Egyptians flourished while the righteous Jews suffered. Moses composed this psalm to console his brethren.[1]

Many other sources attribute this psalm to Adam. *Pirkei D' Rabbi Eliezer* 19 reconciles both opinions; he maintains that after Adam composed the psalm, it was forgotten for many generations, until Moses rediscovered it.

Pirkei D' Rabbi Eliezer 20 explains that after Adam sinned, late in the afternoon of the sixth day, he was expelled from the Garden of Eden and he fell vulnerable to many forces of evil. Finally the holy Sabbath arrived and its sanctity protected Adam from these evil powers. Indeed the Sabbath saved Adam from death, because when God wanted to kill Adam for his sin, the Sabbath argued, ''Master of the universe, no man was killed on the first six days of creation. Why should killing begin on my day? Is this my sanctity? Is this my blessing?'' When Adam realized why he had been spared, he gave praise to the Sabbath day.

This psalm is also dedicated to the future world, which is described as יוֹם שֶׁכֻּלוֹ שַׁבָּת, *the day which is completely Sabbath,* for ordinary weekdays will not exist in that totally sacred world. At that time, all demonic forces will be destroyed and the evil inclination will be subdued (*Sifra, Bechukosai* 26:8). According to this source, the word שַׁבָּת is cognate with לְהַשְׁבִּית, *to finish,* or *to destroy,* referring to the destruction of all evil powers.

According to *Bereishis Rabbah* 22:28, after Cain killed Abel, he encountered his father Adam, who asked, ''How did the Heavenly Tribunal judge you?''

Cain replied, ''I repented and my punishment was lightened.''

Adam then exclaimed in dismay, ''I didn't realize that the power of repentance is so great!'' Immediately he composed this psalm for הַשַּׁבָּת יוֹם [word the שָׁב can be related to שָׁב, *to return* or *repent,* and the letters of הַשַּׁבָּת can be re-arranged to form the word תְּשׁוּבָה, *repentance.* Sabbath is the day for introspection and improvement].

1. See comm. and footnote to 90:10 which explain that Moses composed psalms 90-100, while the Israelites were still suffering in the bondage of Egypt. Moses recorded the psalms on scrolls and distributed them to his oppressed brethren. He encouraged them to take advantage of their Sabbath rest by studying these inspirational statements of faith in God's justice so that they might be able to face the rigors of the forthcoming week.

A song with musical accompaniment
for the Sabbath day:

² It is good to thank HASHEM,
and to sing praise to Your Name, O Exalted One.
³ To relate Your kindness at dawn,
and Your faith in the nights.

2. טוב להדות לה' — *It is good to thank HASHEM.*

Moses dedicated this psalm [the third in the series of eleven], to the tribe of יהודה, Judah. Judah had been named by his mother, Leah, for she said (Genesis 29:35), הַפַּעַם אוֹדֶה אֶת ה', *This time let me gratefully thank HASHEM* (see *Midrash Shocher Tov* and *Radak* to 91:1).

It is particularly *good to thank HASHEM* on the Sabbath. Throughout the week man is preoccupied with mundane pursuits which prevent him from concentrating on God's wonders. But on the day of rest, man's soul is liberated from its weekday shackles. Cleansed and purified, it can meditate upon the wonders of God's providence and His system of reward and punishment (*Radak; Meiri; Rashbam*).

The word להדות may also be translated *to confess.* When Adam repented his sin, he composed this psalm to teach all future generations that *it is good to confess to HASHEM* in order to achieve atonement and to be saved from *Gehinnom* (*Midrash Shocher Tov; Pirkei D' Rabbi Eliezer* 19).

וּלְזַמֵּר לְשִׁמְךָ עֶלְיוֹן — *And to sing praise to Your Name, O Exalted One.*

The human soul has its source on high. All week, the soul is enmeshed in the mundane, but on the Sabbath it returns to sing to God, the Most High (*Radak*).

[On the seventh day, when God completed His Creation, it was evident that He is the Sovereign of every aspect of the universe and that He is, indeed, the Exalted One.]

3. לְהַגִּיד בַּבֹּקֶר חַסְדֶּךָ — *To relate Your kindness at dawn.*

Adam sinned late in the afternoon of the sixth day. Suddenly he noticed the sun sinking beneath the horizon. He cried out bitterly, "Woe unto me! Because I sinned, God is plunging the world into eternal gloom!" The following morning (on the Sabbath), as Adam saw the light rising over the horizon, he was filled with tremendous joy, and gratefully offered sacrifices to God. Legions of ministering angels descended and sang songs of praise to the Sabbath, emphasizing man's obligation *to relate Your kindness in the morning,* i.e., for the sun which arose at dawn and illuminated the terrifying darkness of night. Adam survived only because he was sustained by God's faithfulness which brought him from darkness to light (*Avos D' Rabbi Nassan* 1).

וֶאֱמוּנָתְךָ בַּלֵּילוֹת — *And Your faith in the nights.*

This verse also refers metaphorically to the stark contrast between the gloom of exile and the bright dawn of redemption. [Moses encouraged the oppressed Jews not to be overwhelmed by their bondage, but to keep faith in the day-break of liberation.] Subsequent generations of Jewish exiles are encouraged to maintain their אֱמוּנָה, *faith,* in God, Who will surely usher in the light of redemption in the glorious Messianic age (*Rashi; Avos D' Rabbi Nassan* 1).

בֹּקֶר, *dawn,* is singular, while לֵּילוֹת, *nights,* is plural. When we recognize God's Hand, seemingly disparate events are perceived to be part of a consistent

ה נֵבֶל עֲלֵי הִגָּיוֹן בְּכִנּוֹר: כִּי שִׂמַּחְתַּנִי יהוה
ו בְּפָעֳלֶךָ בְּמַעֲשֵׂי יָדֶיךָ אֲרַנֵּן: מַה־גָּדְלוּ
ז מַעֲשֶׂיךָ יהוה מְאֹד עָמְקוּ מַחְשְׁבֹתֶיךָ: אִישׁ־

pattern. But when we are conscious only of exile and suffering, each successive travail seems to be a random event, unrelated to what comes before or after (ArtScroll Siddur, Kabbalas Shabbos).

4. עֲלֵי עָשׂוֹר וַעֲלֵי נָבֶל — *Upon the assor and upon the neivel.*

[See commentary to 33:2 for a detailed discussion of these instruments.] The עָשׂוֹר was a ten-stringed instrument which produced ten different tones. According to the *Talmud* (Arachin 13b), the כִּנּוֹר, *harp,* of the Temple had seven strings, but in Messianic times the harp will have eight strings, and in the World to Come, it will have ten. In 33:2, we find that the *assor* and the *neivel* are a single instrument, whose exquisite music makes inferior instruments seem נָבֶל, *withered and disgraced.*

Alshich explains that when Adam sinned God punished him with ten curses. All of these will be turned into blessings by the inspiring music of the final redemption.

[The name אָדָם, *Adam,* is composed of the initial letters of the names אָדָם, מָשִׁיחַ דָּוִד, *Adam, David, Messiah.* See Overview, *Tehillim* Vol. I.] Adam's sin brought the darkness of exile into the world. Some of the gloom was dispelled when the light of the Sabbath arrived and the angels sang to God to the accompaniment of these instruments.

David, whose lifespan of seventy years had been a gift from Adam, arose at midnight to sing psalms to God, accompanied by these same instruments. For David sought to dispel, through his psalms, some of the darkness and misery with we, his descendants, would suffer at the hands of their gentile oppressors in the bleak night of our exile.

The dark age of Jewish exile will end with the advent of the Messiah. However, the ultimate salvation will be experienced in the World to Come, which is the יוֹם שֶׁכֻּלּוֹ שַׁבָּת, *the day which is completely Sabbath.* At that time, the ten-stringed instrument will be played.

Midrash Shocher Tov explains that the number ten is always associated with God's presence, which graces all holy functions where a quorum of ten Jews gather.

Pesikta Rabbasi (21:3) understands this verse homiletically: the Jewish people are עֲלֵי עָשׂוֹר, literally *upon them ten,* for it is [incumbent] *upon them* to fulfill the *Ten* Commandments, and עֲלֵי נָבֶל it is [incumbent] *upon them* to accept martyrdom if necessary, for the sanctification of God's Name [thus becoming a נְבֵלָה, *corpse,* to fulfill God's will].

עֲלֵי הִגָּיוֹן בְּכִנּוֹר — *With singing accompanied by a harp.*

Literally, הִגָּיוֹן pertains to verbal expression [see 35:28]. Here it describes the lyrics of the songs of praise which will be sung to God, to the accompaniment of musical instruments (Radak; Midrash Shocher Tov).

The word הִגָּיוֹן also describes meditation and deep thought [see 1:2]. When a person immerses his mind in Torah study, this concentration produces rapturous melodies in praise of God. These melodies are even more beautiful than those of the harp (Tehillos Hashem).

This also alludes to the statement of the *Talmud* (Berachos 36): A harp was suspended over David's bed. At midnight, the north wind would blow through its strings and the harp would play by itself, awakening David to

⁴ *Upon the* assor *and upon the* neivel,
    with singing accompanied by a harp.
⁵ *For You have gladdened me, HASHEM,*
    with Your deeds,
    at the works of Your hands I will sing glad song.
⁶ *How great are Your deeds, HASHEM;*
    exceedingly profound are Your thoughts.

---

study Torah and to sing God's praises.

5. כִּי שִׂמַּחְתַּנִי ה' בְּפָעֳלֶךָ — *For You have gladdened me, HASHEM, with your deeds.*

Only on the Sabbath, the seventh day, were all of God's creative accomplishments evident. On that day, when the body rested, the mind could meditate upon the wonders of nature which God created. The symmetry and harmony of nature is a splendid spectacle which gladdens the heart (Radak; Ibn Ezra).

בְּמַעֲשֵׂי יָדֶיךָ אֲרַנֵּן — *At the works of Your hands I will sing glad song.*

The Zohar (Bereishis 45) explains that this refers to Adam, who was formed by God's own *hands.* God displayed before Adam's eyes the scholars, leaders and kings of each successive generation. When Adam saw that David was predestined to die immediately after his birth, Adam gave seventy years of his own life to David as a present. Therefore, David says here that he will *sing glad song* because of God's *handiwork,* referring to Adam, the one who was fashioned by God's hands and who gave David the gift of life.

This verse was also recited when the construction of the מִשְׁכָּן, *Tabernacle,* was completed, for this was Hashem's splendid accomplishment. Similarly, the construction of the בֵּית הַמִּקְדָּשׁ, *Holy Temple,* is called God's handiwork, over which Israel rejoices (Midrash Tanchuma, Pikudei).

6. מַה גָּדְלוּ מַעֲשֶׂיךָ ה' — *How great are*

Your deeds, HASHEM.

The Rabbis taught that although there are myriad species of animals, birds, and fish, no two species sound, look, or taste exactly alike (Sanhedrin 37a). This endless diversity proclaims the greatness of the King of kings, the Holy One, Blessed is He. When a man mints coins from a mold, they are all identical, but although the King of kings minted all men in the mold of Adam, no two men look exactly alike. Therefore Scripture attests, *How great are Your deeds, HASHEM* (Tanna D' Bei Eliyahu Rabbah 2).

מְאֹד עָמְקוּ מַחְשְׁבֹתֶיךָ — *Exceedingly profound are Your thoughts.*

When I contemplate [on the Sabbath day] the magnitude of creation, I realize *How great are Your deeds.* They are truly beyond my comprehension. Moreover, *exceedingly profound are Your thoughts.* I cannot fathom the reason for many phenomena. One perplexing question is why the Almighty created the world when He did, rather then earlier or later. The only answer for such a query is that God's will is utterly beyond our grasp (Radak).

God is constantly supervising and controlling every detail of creation, yet He has designed the universe so that all of His actions are hidden *deep* beneath a cloak of nature. Since God's hand is invisible, events appear to happen by themselves. This is all part of God's deep design for this world: it is a test to determine whether man will strive to detect God beneath His concealment

בַּעַר לֹא יֵדָע וּכְסִיל לֹא־יָבִין אֶת־זֹאת:
ח בִּפְרֹחַ רְשָׁעִים | כְּמוֹ עֵשֶׂב וַיָּצִיצוּ כָּל־פֹּעֲלֵי
ט אָוֶן לְהִשָּׁמְדָם עֲדֵי־עַד: וְאַתָּה מָרוֹם לְעֹלָם
י יְהֹוָה: כִּי הִנֵּה אֹיְבֶיךָ | יהוה כִּי־הִנֵּה אֹיְבֶיךָ

and to live his life in accordance with the Divine plan (Malbim).

7. אִישׁ בַּעַר לֹא יֵדָע — *A boor cannot know.*

[The בַּעַר is one who is completely devoid of knowledge and resembles the בְּעִיר, *beast*, as in 73:22: *I am senseless* (בַּעַר) *and know nothing, like a beast was I with You.* See commentary there and 49:11.]

The בַּעַר is oblivious to all the wonders of Hashem (Rashi).

Although such a person may appear to be an אִישׁ, *a man*, of dignity and stature in business and community affairs, he is nevertheless totally ignorant of God's designs (Norah Tehillos; Rabbeinu Bachya).

However, even the most ignorant man can be taught something. If the בַּעַר comes to the Rabbis and Sages, they will teach him Torah and demonstrate God's wonders, as the Psalmist (94:8) exhorts: בִּינוּ בֹּעֲרִים בָּעָם, *educate the senseless of the nation* (P'dRE 19; Midrash Shocher Tov; Zohar, Parshas Acharei).

וּכְסִיל לֹא יָבִין אֶת זֹאת — *Nor can a fool understand this.*

There is a marked difference between the כְּסִיל, *fool,* and the בַּעַר, *boor.* The כְּסִיל is not unintelligent; he may, in fact, have a brilliant mind. However, he is not interested in delving deeply into any subject. All his study is superficial (Rashbam; Ibn Yachya), because his intelligence is utilized to serve his insatiable lusts and desires. He despises

moral and ethical wisdom, for he fears that such knowledge will deprive him of his pleasures. [See Malbim on Proverbs 1:22 and ArtScroll commentary to 49:11.]

Whenever his studies or observations of nature lead the כְּסִיל to a truth which will force him to recognize God's binding authority, and to thus restrict his actions and deny himself pleasure, he seeks to *distort* this truth. The כְּסִיל cleverly seeks out one detail which he claims makes no sense; he uses this bogus problem as a pretext to discredit the preponderance of evidence before him. The Psalmist brilliantly exposes this ruse, saying, *nor can a fool understand* זֹאת, *this,* i.e., *this* one point which he claims is untenable. On the basis of this single question, the כְּסִיל casts aspersion on everything.

King Solomon disclosed this subterfuge in Proverbs 14:8, אִוֶּלֶת כְּסִילִים מִרְמָה, *the folly of the fools is* [in reality] *deceit* (Shiurei Daas of Telshe, Vol. I, footnote to p. 87).

8. בִּפְרֹחַ רְשָׁעִים כְּמוֹ עֵשֶׂב — *When the wicked bloom like grass.*

Another phenomenon that *a boor cannot know, nor can a fool understand* is the apparent success of the wicked in this world (Radak). Fools do not realize that the wicked prosper so that God can compensate them for their few merits before He destroys them (Rashi).[1]

[God requites the good and bad done by every individual. These rewards and

---

1. The Midrash (Esther Rabbah 6:2) strikingly explains the apparent success of the wicked: Behold! The enemies of God are raised up to meet their downfall! This may be likened to the vile galley slave who viciously cursed the king's beloved son. The king reasoned, "If I kill him, people will not take notice of it and they will learn nothing from it — for of what consequence is the life of a lowly galley slave?" Therefore, the king first promoted the slave to the rank of captain, then he elevated him to the post of governor-general. Only then, after giving him

⁷ *A boor cannot know,*
    nor can a fool understand this.
⁸ *When the wicked bloom like grass*
    and all the iniquitous blossom —
    it is to destroy them till eternity.
⁹ *But You remain exalted forever, HASHEM.*
¹⁰ *For behold! — Your enemies, HASHEM,*
    for behold! — Your enemies shall perish,

punishments may be meted out in this world or in the World to Come. However, God often rewards the wicked for their good deeds in this world deferring their punishments for the eternal World of Truth.]

וַיָּצִיצוּ כָּל פֹּעֲלֵי אָוֶן — *And all the iniquitous blossom.*

The wicked rise to success swiftly, like grass which sprouts overnight. Their existence is fleeting, however, and they are soon overtaken by death. The progress of the righteous man is slower and much less dramatic. The Psalmist notes, that *he shall flourish like a date palm* (verse 13), for the palm requires a long period of time for its growth, but its roots are solid and permanent (*Maharam Markado*).

Maharal infers that the duration of the period required for the maturation of any creature is in direct proportion to its distinction and value. Since the wicked have almost no value, they prosper quickly and fade quickly, passing into oblivion after the short span of a lifetime in this world. But the value of the righteous man is immeasurable. Throughout his lifetime, he is engaged in developing his unique qualities and his latent abilities. In fact, the righteous man does not even

complete his development in this world; his spiritual growth continues in the World to Come. [This fascinating corollary explains why insects are almost fully mature at birth and why many animals and birds can care for themselves within a few days or weeks of birth, whereas a human being is not self-sufficient until his teens. Since the human intellect far surpasses that of the beast, it requires a much longer maturation period.]

לְהִשָּׁמְדָם עֲדֵי עַד — *It is to destroy them till eternity.*

Destroyed forever means that they lose their portion in the World to Come (*Ibn Yachya*).

[Every success which the wicked enjoy brings them a step closer to their doom.]

9. וְאַתָּה מָרוֹם לְעֹלָם ה׳ — *But You remain exalted forever, HASHEM.*

Although the wicked appear successful in this world, this does not mean that God is not watching and controlling His creation. In the future, God will demonstrate how He recorded and judged every human action. At that time God will recompense every man in accordance with his deeds and reveal His presence to all men (*Radak*).

prominence and renown, did the king execute the rogue for his crime.

Similarly the Holy One, Blessed is He, elevates the wicked for their own detriment. An example is Haman. The Holy One, Blessed is He, said: ''Haman's original treachery occurred when he advised Ahasuerus to halt the construction of the Second Temple. But if I had punished Haman then, no one would have noticed that I meted out justice, for Haman was only a minor official. Therefore, I caused Haman to prosper and succeed so that he could hang [and teach the world a lesson in Divine retribution].''

יא יֹאבֵדוּ יִתְפָּרְדוּ כָּל־פֹּעֲלֵי אָוֶן: וַתָּרֶם כִּרְאֵים

יב קַרְנִי בַּלֹּתִי בְּשֶׁמֶן רַעֲנָן: וַתַּבֵּט עֵינִי בְּשׁוּרָי

יג בַּקָּמִים עָלַי מְרֵעִים תִּשְׁמַעְנָה אָזְנָי: צַדִּיק

יד כַּתָּמָר יִפְרָח כְּאֶרֶז בַּלְּבָנוֹן יִשְׂגֶּה: שְׁתוּלִים

10. בִּי הִנֵּה אֹיְבֶיךָ ה' כִּי הִנֵּה אֹיְבֶיךָ יֹאבֵדוּ — *For behold! — Your enemies, HASHEM, for behold! — Your enemies shall perish.*

The day will come when the wicked will receive their just punishment, because they are Your enemies (*Radak*).

A number of reasons are offered for the repetition of this prediction:

— The repetition strengthens the credibility of the prediction (*Radak*).

— We have heard what Hashem did to His enemies in the past, and we have even seen the punishment He metes out to evildoers (*Ibn Ezra*).

— This Divine destruction will be visited not only upon those enemies who have *spoken* against God, but also against those who have silently plotted against Him (*Ibn Yachya*).

— Both the enemies who destroyed the First Temple and those who devastated the Second Temple will perish (*Chazah Zion*).

יִתְפָּרְדוּ כָּל פֹּעֲלֵי אָוֶן — *Dispersed shall be all doers of iniquity.*

These are the villains who not only think and speak of evil, but who actually execute it (*Ibn Yachya*).

They will have no part in the World to Come, and thus they will be eternally *separated* from the company of the righteous (*Targum*).

11. וַתָּרֶם כִּרְאֵים קַרְנִי — *As exalted as a re'eim's shall be my pride.*

[See commentary to 22:22. The word רְאֵים has been translated variously as *ox, bison, buffalo, unicorn,* and *reindeer.* It is clear that the רְאֵים derives its name from the majestic horns which are its most distinctive feature. Ibn Ezra (22:22, where the word is spelled רֵמִים, *reimim,* without an א) derives from this

verse that these horns are רָם, *high, exalted,* taller than those of all other creatures, because the height of the *re'eim's* horn is used here as a measure of great exaltation.]

The Psalmist now speaks in first person, testifying for every devout believer who has lived to see the downfall of his enemies. He thanks God for giving him a *horn,* i.e., a symbol of pride and strength, as in *Deuteronomy* 33:17: *The horns of the re'eim are his horns, with them he will gore the nations* (*Radak*).

This verse refers to the Israelites' triumphant Exodus from Egypt, which proved that the oppression of the righteous at the hands of the wicked does eventually end and that the righteous ultimately receive their just reward. Thus all encouraging promises which Moses had made to Israel throughout the terrible bondage (and especially on the Sabbath day of rest) came to pass. This triumph is recorded twice in the Torah, in *Numbers* 23:22 and 24:8: אֵל מוֹצִיאָם מִמִּצְרַיִם כְּתוֹעֲפֹת רְאֵם לוֹ, *God has brought them out of Egypt, He has exhibited the strength of the re'eim.*

Just as the *re'eim* lifts its lowered horn with a single sudden jerk, so does Israel's salvation arise suddenly, without hesitation or delay (*Baal HaTanya*).

בַּלֹּתִי בְּשֶׁמֶן רַעֲנָן — *I will be saturated with ever-fresh oil.*

Whenever oil has been blended into another substance, it is said to be בָּלוּל בְּשֶׁמֶן, *saturated with oil* (*Leviticus* 2:5, *et al; Rashi*). Here it is used figuratively to describe the euphoria of the righteous man who is completely

dispersed shall be all doers of iniquity.

¹¹ As exalted as a re'eim's shall be my pride,
  I will be saturated with ever-fresh oil.
¹² My eyes have seen my vigilant foes;
  when those who would harm me
    rise up against me my ears have heard.
¹³ A righteous man will flourish like a date palm,
  like a cedar in the Lebanon he will grow tall.

---

satisfied, body and soul, with his triumph (*Radak; Metzudas David*).[1]

12. וַתַּבֵּט עֵינִי בְּשׁוּרָי — *My eyes have seen my vigilant foes.*

Ibn Ezra renders: I have witnessed their downfall.

See commentary to 5:9. The word שׁוּרָי is derived from שׁוּר, *watching closely,* as in אֲשׁוּרֶנּוּ וְלֹא קָרוֹב, *I watch him closely, but he is not near (Numbers 24:17; Radak).*

בְּקָמִים עָלַי מְרֵעִים תִּשְׁמַעְנָה אָזְנָי — *When those who would harm me rise up against me my ears have heard.*

I have been informed of their downfall (*Radak*). *Rashi* comments: My ears heard a heavenly voice proclaim that no matter how they try, *those who rise against me* will never annihilate me. The *Sefer Halkkarim* explains this homiletically: The wise man pays attention to all the criticism leveled against him, even if it comes from his avowed enemies, because he knows that there must be a measure of truth in their accusations. Thus the Psalmist wisely gazes upon himself through the eyes of his *vigilant foes,* and when evildoers raise criticism against him, his ears listen closely. Then he rectifies his faults and errors, so that eventually his enemies can find nothing to criticize;

they then become his friends.

13. צַדִּיק כַּתָּמָר יִפְרָח — *A righteous man will flourish like a date palm.*

[The Psalmist contrasts the wicked, who are like withered grass (verse 8), and the righteous, who resemble thriving trees.]

The Rabbis enumerate the many distinctive properties which make the palm tree a symbol of virtue and righteousness:

— The palm grows very straight, without bending, just as the righteous man remains upright and honest.

— The wood of the palm is free of knots, just as the righteous man is free of flaws.

— The palm's shady leaves and fronds are far off the ground, at the very top of the tree. Similarly, the reward promised the righteous is not immediate, but reserved for the distant future of the World to Come.

— Every part of the palm is useful: its fruits are eaten, its leaves and fronds are used in thatching, and its wood is used for construction. Similarly, each righteous Jew fulfills a special purpose (*Bereishis Rabbah* 41:1).

כְּאֶרֶז בַּלְּבָנוֹן יִשְׂגֶּה — *Like a cedar in the Lebanon he will grow tall.*

The *cedar* also symbolizes virtue and

---

1. *Yalkut Shimoni* (Samuel 124) understands this verse in reference to the anointment of David. Samuel had initially attempted to pour the horn of holy oil on the heads of each of David's seven brothers, but instead of flowing downward the oil recoiled back up to the horn [as a sign that none of these was the Divinely ordained monarch]. When Samuel tried to anoint David, however, the oil spurted miraculously from the horn and *saturated* David's head. David was anointed with *fresh oil,* which had not been previously used, since his brothers were unworthy of it (see footnote to 45:8).

צב

טו בְּבֵית יְהוָה בְּחַצְרוֹת אֱלֹהֵינוּ יַפְרִיחוּ: עוֹד
טו־טז
טז יְנוּבוּן בְּשֵׂיבָה דְּשֵׁנִים וְרַעֲנַנִּים יִהְיוּ: לְהַגִּיד
°עוֹלָתָה ק׳   כִּי־יָשָׁר יְהוָה צוּרִי וְלֹא־°עֹלָתָה בּוֹ:

righteousness. Furthermore, the unique properties of the cedar compensate for any deficiencies in the palm tree:

The wood of the palm is unsuitable for furniture and utensils, whereas the wood of the cedar is excellent for these purposes (Midrash Shocher Tov). [Similarly, the righteous man is admirably suited to be a vessel dedicated to the service of God.]

When the palm tree is cut down, its trunk dries in the ground. When the cedar is felled, however, its roots and stump remain alive, and a new cedar shoot will sprout in its place (Taanis 25a). [Similarly, righteousness is indestructible; if a righteous man is harmed, he will only grow stronger. If he is cut down, another righteous man will rise to take his place.

[However, the cedar lacks several of the palm tree's good qualities. Unlike the palm, the cedar does not grow straight and erect; it does not produce fruit; it has knots; its shade is near the ground, and not every part of the cedar can be used. Thus the righteous possess virtues which resemble the best features of both the palm and the cedar.]

14. 'שְׁתוּלִים בְּבֵית ה — Planted in the House of HASHEM.

In one significant respect, however, the righteous man differs from the palm tree and from the cedar, for these trees are rooted in the earth and grow upward, whereas the righteous man is rooted in the heavens and grows downward. The base of the human 'tree' is the soul, which is hewn from God's

celestial glory. The limbs of the body resemble the branches of a tree.

This world is compared to a פְּרוֹזְדוֹר, corridor, or a חָצֵר, courtyard, which serves as an entrance to an edifice, the spiritual World to Come. Therefore, the verse continues, in the courtyards of our God they will flourish; i.e., the righteous, who are rooted in Hashem's celestial House, will flourish on earth, which is the entrance to His House (Nefutzos Yehudah; Norah Tehillos).

Midrash Shocher Tov observes that this refers to the very young children who are carefully planted in God's house, the house of study and prayer, so that they will grow in Torah scholarship.

בְּחַצְרוֹת אֱלֹהֵינוּ יַפְרִיחוּ — In the court-yards of our God they will flourish.

This verse also describes the priests and Levites who flourish in the service which they render to God in the Temple courtyards. It is as if they give forth פְּרָחִים, flowers, for their service makes manifest the beauty of God's ways (Targum; Ibn Ezra).

Similarly, in the future, the righteous and the true scholars will dwell in the environs of the Holy Temple, where their comprehension of the Divine design will blossom (Radak).[1]

15. עוֹד יְנוּבוּן בְּשֵׂיבָה — They will still be fruitful in old age.

The Mishnah (Kannim 3:6) teaches that as an עַם הָאָרֶץ, an ignorant man, gets older, his mind becomes more confused. As a Torah sage gets older,

---

1. Rabbi Levi said that when King Solomon brought the holy Ark into the Beis HaMikdash, all the trees and cedars there became full of sap and gave forth succulent fruit, as Scripture states, Planted in the House of HASHEM in the courtyards of our God they will flourish. These fruits grew constantly and provided a very abundant source of income for the priests, until King Menashe (the wicked) sinned by bringing a pagan idol into the Holy of Holies, into God's presence. This caused all the trees to wither and die (Yerushalmi Yoma 4:4).

¹⁴ *Planted in the House of HASHEM,*
in the courtyards of our God they will flourish.
¹⁵ *They will still be fruitful in old age,*
full of sap and freshness they will be.
¹⁶ *To declare that HASHEM is just,*
My Rock in Whom there is no wrong.

---

however, his mind becomes clearer and more settled. *Job* 12:12 states: *With elders there is wisdom, and length of days brings understanding.*

Rambam explains there that the pursuit of physical comfort and gratification interferes with the development of the mind. As the ignorant man grows older, the demands of his body become more intense. Consequently, he increasingly neglects his mind more and becomes confused. But as the wise man ages, his body grows weaker and he ignores its desires all the more. As a result, his mind and soul improve, yielding abundant fruit (see *Sforno; Gevul Binyamin*).[1]

דְּשֵׁנִים וְרַעֲנַנִּים יִהְיוּ — *Full of sap and freshness they will be.*

Radak comments that this verse describes the Messianic age, when the Jews will achieve longevity. The time of life which is now considered old age will then be regarded as youth. The prophet *Isaiah* (65:20) predicts that at that time, if someone dies at the age of one hundred, people will say, that he died young. In the Messianic era, as people grow older they will simultaneously grow stronger and healthier.

16. לְהַגִּיד כִּי יָשָׁר ה׳ — *To declare that HASHEM is just.*

God controls and directs all events of human history for but one purpose: that in the future His Providence and guidance will become manifest and that men will then *declare that HASHEM is just.*

In this world, men hesitate to make a total commitment to God because they are confused by the suffering of the righteous and by the seeming success of the wicked. But, in the time of Messiah, all apparent iniquity and evil will be purged. The world will then achieve a purity like that of carefully refined metal. When the righteous cease to suffer and the wicked no longer succeed, it will be evident that God is upright. Then, God's ways will not only *be* just, they will be *perceived* as just — and we will join in declaring them to be so (*Radak*).

צוּרִי וְלֹא עַוְלָתָה בּוֹ — *My Rock in Whom there is no wrong.*

The word עַוְלָתָה, *wrong*, is written deficiently, without the letter ו. Thus the written form is עַלָתָה. The two forms of the word are equivalent, and the deficient spelling can also be found in *Job* 5:16: וְעַלָתָה קָפְצָה פִּיהָ, *And wrongdoing shut its mouth* (see also 58:3).

In this world it often appears as if

---

1. Rabbi Nehorai said: I would set aside every craft and profession in the world, and I would teach my son only Torah, because a profession is secure only as long as a person has the energy to pursue it. If he should fall sick or grow old, he would die of starvation. But Torah not only honors a man and protects him from harm in his youth, but it also provides him with a future and with security in old age. In describing the young Torah scholar, Scripture states: *Those who place confidence in HASHEM shall renew their strength, they shall mount up opinions as eagles, they shall run and not be weary, they shall walk and not tire* (*Isaiah* 40:31). And of the aged Torah scholar it says: *They will still be fruitful in old age, full of sap and freshness they will be* (*Kiddushin* 82a; *Yerushalmi Kiddushin*).

   Ibn Ezra (comm. to 90:10) says that until Moses reached eighty, he was like all other men

God's judgments and designs are *wrong* and unfair, but in the future it will be clear that He never betrayed the righteous; He was always their *Rock* and controlled all their affairs equitably (*Radak*).

Sefer Chassidim offers a concluding statement on this psalm: Moses died on the Sabbath, and David died on the Sabbath. Moses wrote the five books of the Torah, and David wrote the five books of the *Psalms* to strengthen the Jew's faith in Torah. Both Moses and David excelled in their recognition that God's judgment is completely righteous and fair. Thus both could declare with full confidence that *there is no wrong in Him.*

who grow weaker with age. At that time Moses' vitality was ebbing and he felt that only an extraordinary infusion of strength would enable him to continue living. [Indeed, at the age of eighty Moses accepted the call of God to lead the Jews out of Egypt and suddenly he discovered that in the merit of his mission his youthful vigor was renewed. This extraordinary vigor remained with him until the day he died as we read: *And Moses was one hundred and twenty years when he died, his vision was not dimmed nor was his vitality diminished.*]

Rav Eliyahu Lopian was almost eighty years old when he was invited to serve as *Menahel Ruchani* (spiritual director) in the Yeshiva of Zichron Yaakov [which later moved to Kfar Chassidim] in Israel. Rav Lopian consulted the *Chazon Ish* as to whether he could accept such a responsible position at his advanced age. The *Chazon Ish* encouraged him to accept the post, explaining that precisely such a mission of spreading the word of God would keep him young. As the Psalmist says: *They will still be fruitful in old age, full of sap and freshness they will be.* When? When they devote their lives *to declare that HASHEM is just* (*Lev Eliyahu*, Heb. ed., Vol. I, p. 16). [According to a family tradition, Rav Lopian was eleven years old when he attended the funeral of Rav Yisrael Salanter in 1883. Accordingly, he was in his ninety-eighth year when he passed away twenty years after accepting the position of *Menahel Ruchani.*]

מזמור צג 93

R ashi explains that this psalm is dedicated to the Messianic era, when all men will again recognize God's majesty.

This psalm is a direct continuation of Psalm 92, which concluded with the prediction that in the Messianic era men will declare that HASHEM is just, My Rock in Whom there is no wrong (92:16). At that time men will recognize that HASHEM [alone] reigns over all of creation and that He alone, גֵאוּת לָבֵשׁ, will have donned grandeur.

Unlike the arrogant gentile monarchs such as Pharoah of Egypt, Nebuchadnezzar of Babylon, and Sennacherib of Assyria — who considered themselves to be gods and who brazenly defied the Almighty — Messiah will be a monarch noted for his humility (Radak).

This psalm is the Song of the Day for the sixth day of the week (Rosh Hashanah 31a) because on that day God completed His work and donned [the] grandeur of His creation (Avos D' Rabbi Nassan 1:8).

Indeed, comments Rav Yaakov Emden, this psalm describes God as robing Himself in grandeur like one dressing in His Sabbath finery. Thus this work was designated as the Song of Friday when the footsteps of Sabbath begin to be heard.

On the sixth day Adam was created. God blew a breath of life into his nostrils and invested him with a Divine soul. When Adam stood and scrutinized God's amazing creation, he realized how awesome and wonderful it was. As he sang God's praises, Adam truly looked Divine, because he was a reflection of God's image. The creatures of the earth were filled with awe, for they imagined that Adam was their creator. When they gathered to bow to him in submission, however, Adam was incredulous. "Why do you bow to to me?" he asked: "Let us go together to pay homage to HASHEM, Who truly reigns. Let us robe the Creator in majesty." Then Adam led all the creatures in this song, HASHEM ... reigned, He ... donned majesty (Pirkei D' Rabbi Eliezer 11).

א יהוה מָלָךְ גֵּאוּת לָבֵשׁ לָבֵשׁ יהוה עֹז הִתְאַזָּר
ב אַף־תִּכּוֹן תֵּבֵל בַּל־תִּמּוֹט: נָכוֹן כִּסְאֲךָ מֵאָז
ג מֵעוֹלָם אָתָּה: נָשְׂאוּ נְהָרוֹת | יהוה נָשְׂאוּ
ד נְהָרוֹת קוֹלָם יִשְׂאוּ נְהָרוֹת דָּכְיָם: מִקֹּלוֹת |

1. הי מָלָךְ גֵּאוּת לָבֵשׁ — *HASHEM will have reigned, He will have donned grandeur.*

[The translation generally follows the view that this psalm reflects the pronouncements that will be made in the Messianic era. Accordingly, the past tense syntax of the psalm will be uttered in retrospect.]

Originally there was no physical matter; there was only the Spiritual essence of the Divine. God chose to cloak the spirit in a material robe. At each progressive stage of Creation, God donned an additional 'robe' of matter, which concealed His inner spirit. Simultaneously, however, new creatures were being fashioned and subjected to Hashem's reign. Thus each additional material 'robe' added another outward manifestation of God's *majesty* (Baal HaTanya).

Literally, גֵּאוּת means גַּאֲוָה, *arrogance.* This detestable characteristic would hardly seem to befit God, for, as Solomon says (Proverbs 16:5), תּוֹעֲבַת הי כָּל גְּבַהּ לֵב, *Every arrogant heart is an abomination to HASHEM.* Yet although pride is despicable when displayed by men, whose every talent and skill is a gift of God, Hashem Himself certainly deserves to be robed in גֵּאוּת, *pride,* for He is the source of all human accomplishments (Sefer HaIkkarim).

In man, arrogance is a contemptible trait, because man's power is limited at best. But to God גֵּאוּת, *grandeur,* is becoming because all forces owe their existence to Him while He is dependent on nothing (Midrash Shocher Tov).

Ramban elaborates on this theme in his ethical will, *Iggeres HaRamban,* explaining that the arrogant man is a rebel who defies the sovereignty of God.

Such a person steals the royal vestments which belong to God alone, for, as our verse states, *HASHEM will have reigned, He will have donned grandeur.*

לָבֵשׁ הי עֹז הִתְאַזָּר — *HASHEM will have donned might and girded Himself.*

[The לְבוּשׁ, *robe,* is the outward manifestation of God's glory. He displays (the) fact that He ... *donned might and girded Himself* with (the) strength to control all of nature and to subdue His foes. Indeed, God's *strength* is that He controls the course of world history. When Israel is in exile, this strength is concealed; when Israel is redeemed, however, God girds Himself and reveals His *Strength* (see Sforno).]

אַף־תִּכּוֹן תֵּבֵל בַּל תִּמּוֹט — *Even firmed the world that it should not falter.*

Even when *HASHEM will have girded Himself* with strength and violently cast the wicked out of the land, He will not let the earth falter into utter chaos and destruction (Sforno).

[At present, the fate of the inhabited land is uncertain. Beset by countless threats and dangers, it totters on the brink of disaster. But when the King Messiah reigns, stability will return to the land and it will bring joy in its wake (see Rashi).]

2. נָכוֹן כִּסְאֲךָ מֵאָז — *Your throne was established from of old* [lit. *from then*].

When the world is set firm (verse 1) in the Messianic era, then all will realize that *Your throne* [i.e., Your permanent control of the universe] *was established from of old* [i.e., from the first moment of Creation] (Radak) and that Your kingdom is not a new phenomenon.[1]

Furthermore, since Creation, Your

Hʌshem will have reigned,
He will have donned grandeur;
HASHEM will have donned might and girded Himself;
even firmed the world that it should not falter.
² Your throne was established from of old,
eternal are You,
³ Like rivers they raised, O HASHEM,
like rivers they raised their voice;
like rivers they shall raise their destructiveness.

dominion has not changed at all; from times *of old*, Your sovereignty has endured (*Norah Tehillos*).

מֵעוֹלָם אָתָּה — *Eternal are You.*

Indeed, Your existence predates the dawn of time at Creation; for You, O God, are eternal (*Radak*).

[Thus, all we see of God is the physical 'garment' He donned when time began at the dawn of Creation. No matter how much of God's greatness we think we understand, our limited intellect grasps but the minutest fraction of His infinite and eternal greatness, which transcends time and space.]

3. נָשְׂאוּ נְהָרוֹת ה' — *Like rivers they raised, O HASHEM.*

Rivers is a metaphor for the enemy hordes who seek to sweep Israel away. They raise their voices and threaten Israel with extinction (*Rashi*).

Specifically, this refers to the gentile nations who will gather outside the gates of Jerusalem for the final war of Gog and Magog. Their tumult will resemble the mighty roar of the river torrent, as the prophet (*Isaiah* 8:7) declares: *Now, therefore, behold my Lord raises up against them the waters of the river, powerful and abundant the*

king of Assyria and his splendor, and he shall overflow all his channels and overwhelm all his banks (*Radak*).

נָשְׂאוּ נְהָרוֹת קוֹלָם — *Like rivers they raised their voice.*

As *Sforno* explains the repetition of נָשְׂאוּ נְהָרוֹת, the first refers to the *uprising* of the gentiles against the First Temple, while the second refers to their uprising against the Second Temple. In 74:4, the Psalmist describes the second destruction: *Your tormentors roared amidst Your meeting place.*

יִשְׂאוּ נְהָרוֹת דָּכְיָם — *Like rivers they shall raise their destructiveness.*

The word דָּכְיָם derives from דָּכָא, *broken, shattered.* The enemy nations will *raise up* their forces to crash against Israel in an effort to shatter our nation (*Radak*).

Others interpret this as a prediction of the downfall of our enemies, for the first section of this verse is in past tense, whereas this section is in the future. In the past, נָשְׂאוּ נְהָרוֹת, *the rivers have risen* successfully against Israel. In the future, יִשְׂאוּ נְהָרוֹת, *the rivers will rise up* once again, but this time their arrogance will result in דָּכְיָם, their *crashing*, i.e., their failure and doom (*Tehillos Hashem; Shaloh*).

1. *Midrash Shocher Tov* teaches that Hashem's throne of glory is among the six things that existed in His thought even before the Creation of the world. The Throne of Glory, the King Messiah, the Torah, Israel, the Holy Temple, and repentance were the six things which antedated the Creation.

מַיִם רַבִּים אַדִּירִים מִשְׁבְּרֵי־יָם אַדִּיר בַּמָּרוֹם
ה יְהוָה: עֵדֹתֶיךָ | נֶאֶמְנוּ מְאֹד לְבֵיתְךָ נַאֲוָה־
קֹדֶשׁ יְהוָה לְאֹרֶךְ יָמִים:

4. מִקֹּלוֹת מַיִם רַבִּים אַדִּירִים מִשְׁבְּרֵי יָם —
*More than the roars of many waters,
mightier than the waves of the sea.*

You, O God, are *above the sounds of
great waters,* i.e., the threatening cries of
the hostile nations who wish to drown
us. You are stronger than the *powerful
breakers of the sea,* i.e., the mighty
forces of evil among the nations who
wish to crush us, *You are mighty on
high, HASHEM* (Rashi; Ibn Ezra).

Hirsch notes that the separating
accent over the word רַבִּים proves that
אַדִּירִים cannot be interpreted as an
adjective describing מַיִם, *water,* but
rather is the predicate of מִשְׁבְּרֵי יָם.

Tefillah L'Moshe notes that the
phrase שְׁבֶר הַיָּם is a figurative description of the calamities which have
befallen the Jewish people. *Lamenta-*
tions 2:13 states כִּי גָדוֹל כַּיָּם שִׁבְרֵךְ, *Your
ruin is as vast as the sea,* and *Alshich*
likens Israel's uninterrupted succession
of troubles to the incessant waves of the
ocean.

The *Midrash* says that the Lord Who
is destined to repair the שֶׁבֶר, *breakage,*
ruination, of the sea will also repair the
ruination of Israel, yet in what sense is
the sea ruined? The *Midrash* explains
that on the second day of Creation, God
separated the waters on earth from
those of the firmament in the heavens
(*Genesis* 1:7). At that time the lower
waters cried bitterly, because they were

being torn away from the celestial
presence of God. It was this division
which constituted their ruination.
However, the Lord is destined to repair
the ruination of the sea when His
presence descends to pervade the earth
with sanctity. Similarly, the Lord will
cure the breakage of Israel when he
recalls them from exile. At that time, it
will no longer be necessary to say *You
are mighty on high,* for His power will
pervade the lower earth as well.

אַדִּיר בַּמָּרוֹם ה׳ — *You are mighty on
high, HASHEM.*

Midrash Shocher Tov relates that the
Roman Emperor Hadrian sought to
fathom the depth of the ocean by
lowering measured ropes deeper and
deeper into the sea. Finally, after three
years, a heavenly voice announced,
'Hadrian's life will end [before his rope
does]!'

Another time, Hadrian tried to learn
how the waters praise the Holy One,
Blessed is He. He put men into glass
chests and lowered the chests into the
ocean. When the divers came up, they
reported: 'We have heard the waters of
the ocean sing the praise of the Holy
One, Blessed is He, saying, "*You are
mighty on high, HASHEM.*" '

According to *Tefillah L'Moshe,* this is
a lament rather than a song, for it means
that Hashem is *on high,* whereas the

⁴ More than the roars of many waters,
mightier than the waves of the sea —
You are mighty on high, HASHEM.
⁵ Your testimonies are exceedingly trustworthy,
about Your House, the Sacred Dwelling —
O HASHEM, may it be for lengthy days.

waters are below, far removed from His presence. Similarly, Israel suffers in exile, distant from God's presence.

5. עֵדֹתֶיךָ נֶאֶמְנוּ מְאֹד — Your testimonies are exceedingly trustworthy.

Your trustworthy prophets have attested to the truth of Your promise to rebuild Your House (i.e., the Holy Temple) and to fill it with the proper sanctity (Rashi; Radak).

The impact of these prophetic testimonies is far greater than the roars of many waters (Malbim).

לְבֵיתְךָ נָאֲוָה קֹדֶשׁ — About Your House, the Sacred Dwelling.

True, the fascinating and wondrous sounds of nature attest to the power of the Creator. Yet, if one only hears God in the sounds of the great waters, he fails to sense the immediacy of the Divine Presence. When the Temple is rebuilt, however, God's sacred presence will be manifested so miraculously that it will become evident that God's holiness pervades every inch of this earth. This sanctity that befits God, for it displays His Omnipresence (Malbim).

According to this interpretation, the word נָאֲוָה is, synonymous with נָאֶה, befitting, pleasing. Radak, however, translates נָאֲוָה as cognate with תַּאֲוָה, desire. He renders: In the future, all men will desire that Your house be filled with sanctity for all time.

ה׳ לְאֹרֶךְ יָמִים — O HASHEM, may it be for lengthy days.

This psalm closes with a plea that when the exceedingly trustworthy prophecies about the Third Temple are finally fulfilled, may it stand for lengthy days, i.e., for all time (Radak).

In his commentary to 91:1, Radak cites the view of Midrash Shocher Tov that Moses dedicated this psalm to the tribe of Benjamin, which dwelled in the shelter of Hashem, the King of the world. The Holy Temple, Beis HaMikdash, was built on the territory of Benjamin, in fulfillment of Moses' farewell blessing to this tribe: Beloved of HASHEM! he shall dwell in security near Him, He shall cover him all the time, and he shall dwell between His shoulders (Deuteronomy 33:12).

[Benjamin is admirably suited to project the גֵּאוּת, grandeur, of God as depicted in this psalm, for Benjamin never compromised his posture of Jewish pride in the face of our enemies. When the Patriarch Jacob encountered Esau, he and his eleven sons prostrated themselves before this wicked man in order to appease him (Genesis 33:6,7). Benjamin, who was yet unborn, was never subjected to such humiliation. Therefore, the Holy Temple, the גָּאוֹן, majestic pride of Israel (see Rashi to Leviticus 26:19) was built in Benjamin's territory.]

This is the fifth of the eleven psalms composed by Moses. He dedicated it to the tribe of Gad from which Elijah the prophet is descended [according to some sources. See Bereishis Rabbah 71:12 and Midrash Shocher Tov Psalm 90]. The tribe of Gad was renowned for its military prowess and its ability to punish the attacking enemy as we read in Jacob's blessing: Gad will recruit a regiment and it will retreat in its tracks (Genesis 49:19). And, of Gad, [Moses] said: He dwells like a lion, and tears off the arm [of the enemy] with the crown of the head (Deuteronomy 33:20). Similarly, Elijah will herald the advent of the Messianic era, when God will appear as אֵל נְקָמוֹת, the God of vengeance, who will punish the proud and cruel nations (see Radak 91:1).

The Talmud (Rosh Hashanah 31a) designates this psalm as the שִׁיר שֶׁל יוֹם, the Song of the Day for the fourth day of the week, on which God created the sun and the moon. In the future, the God of vengeance will punish the idolators who worshiped these celestial bodies. Moses composed this psalm as a prayer to bring that day of Messianic redemption and retribution closer (Radak).

א-ב אֵל־נְקָמוֹת יְהוָה אֵל נְקָמוֹת הוֹפִיעַ: הִנָּשֵׂא

ג שֹׁפֵט הָאָרֶץ הָשֵׁב גְּמוּל עַל־גֵּאִים: עַד־מָתַי

ד רְשָׁעִים| יְהוָה עַד־מָתַי רְשָׁעִים יַעֲלֹזוּ: יַבִּיעוּ

1. אֵל נְקָמוֹת ה' — *O God of vengeance, HASHEM.*

Despite the fact that God is ה', HASHEM, the Dispenser of Kindness, when the time comes to punish the wicked His kindness turns to נְקָמוֹת, *vengeance* (Alshich).

The Talmud (Berachos 58a) states that when a Jew sees the ruins of a pagan temple where idols were once worshiped he should exclaim, *O God of vengeance, HASHEM!*

אֵל נְקָמוֹת הוֹפִיעַ — *O God of vengeance, appear!*

In the course of history, God will have made a total of four appearances. He appeared to the Jews in Egypt as we read (80:2), *You Who leads Joseph [and his brethren in Egypt] like a flock, He Who is enthroned upon the Cherubim, appear!*

God appeared before the Jews when He presented them with the Torah at Sinai, as we read (Deuteronomy 33:2),

HASHEM came from Sinai ... He appeared from Mount Paran.

The worldwide war of Gog and Magog will herald the Messianic era, and God will appear in order to punish His foes as we read here, *O God of vengeance, appear!*

Finally when the Messianic era reaches its full glory God will appear as we read (50:2) מִצִּיוֹן מִכְלַל יֹפִי אֱלֹהִים הוֹפִיעַ, *Out of Zion, consummation of beauty, God appeared* (Sifri, VeZos HaBerachah 33:2).[1]

2. הִנָּשֵׂא שֹׁפֵט הָאָרֶץ — *Arise, O Judge of the earth.*

In order to punish the wicked, God will *arise* to the loftiest heights, as Obadiah 1:4 foretells: *"Though you soar aloft like the eagle and though you set your nest among the stars, from there I will bring you down,"* says HASHEM (Sforno).

הָשֵׁב גְּמוּל עַל גֵּאִים — *Render recompense*

---

1. A great chassidic master explained this verse with a parable:

Once there was a king who led a parade which displayed his power and glory. The crowds all cheered, except for one ragged little urchin who, in his ignorance, took the king to be a clown with a shiny hat. Looking for some fun, the urchin threw a rock which knocked off the king's dazzling crown. The royal guards wanted to kill the boy on the spot, but the king commanded them to take the boy to his palace, explaining, "If I execute him now, what will he have learned and what will I have gained?"

The king treated the boy like a prince and showed him every aspect of royal grandeur. He had him educated by the most brilliant scholars in the land.

After a while the pauper turned prince came to the king, distressed. "Royal sire!" the boy exclaimed, "Now I understand who you really are and I understand your exalted majesty! Indeed, I deserve to die a thousand deaths for the terrible insult I did you!"

"Enough", said the king, "the mental anguish you now experience is sufficient vengeance for your crime."

Similarly, if a man sins against God, what will the King of kings gain if He kills the offender on the spot? The offender sins because he is ignorant of God's majesty and sovereignty. The only way that אֵל נְקָמוֹת, *the God of vengeance,* will gain is if, הוֹפִיעַ, *He appears,* before the ignorant sinner and punishes him by revealing His sovereignty. The most potent vengeance is when the sinner realizes that he has committed the unthinkable crime of defying the King of kings.

This is the meaning of the Talmudic statement (Berachos 33a): Vengeance is a great thing because it appears between two Names of God, אֵל נְקָמוֹת ה', *God of vengeance, HASHEM,* i.e., the greatest vengeance is when God reveals to man the full extent of His Divine glory which is embodied in these two sacred Names.

O *God of vengeance, HASHEM,*
O God of vengeance, appear!
² *Arise, O Judge of the earth,*
render recompense to the haughty.
³ *How long shall the wicked — O HASHEM —*
how long shall the wicked exult?
⁴ *They speak freely, they utter malicious falsehood,*

---

to the haughty.

Of the future era the prophet (Isaiah 33:10) predicts: *Now I shall be exalted, now I shall arise!* At that time God will rise to *render recompense to* [destroy] *the haughty.*

[In the preceding psalm we read (v. 1), גֵּאוּת לָבֵשׁ מֶלֶךְ 'ה, *HASHEM will have reigned, He will have donned grandeur.* No man has the right to be proud, because all his talents and skills are Divinely given. The arrogant man is crediting himself with honor which rightfully belongs to Hashem alone. It is, so to speak, as if the proud are stealing God's robe. This sin of arrogance is so great, that God Himself is destined to *render recompense to the haughty.*]

3. עַד מָתַי רְשָׁעִים ה' — *How long shall the wicked — O HASHEM?*

We are already weary from the long exile and the success of the wicked; how much more can we endure? (Radak).

How much longer will You respond to the wicked with the Name 'ה, *the Dispenser of Kindness?* Is it not time to put an end to this kindness and to begin acting toward them as אֱלֹהִים, *the Dispenser of Strict Justice?* (Alshich; Tehillos Hashem).

Minchas Shai notes that a separating line (פָּסִיק) appears between the word רְשָׁעִים, *wicked,* and *HASHEM,* in order to keep wickedness at a distance from *HASHEM.*

עַד מָתַי רְשָׁעִים יַעֲלֹזוּ — *How long shall the wicked exult?*

If the wicked would sin and be shamed by their deeds, there would be hope that they would reconsider their evil ways and repent. But *the wicked exult* and enjoy their crimes tremendously; therefore, there is no reason to wait at length for their contrition, for they will never have any regrets (*Dorash Moshe*).

4. יַבִּיעוּ — *They speak freely.*

[The root נבע means *to flow freely, to gush.* The word is used in reference to the flow of water and the flow of words which pour out effortlessly, as in תַּבַּעְנָה שְׂפָתַי תְּהִלָּה, *My lips overflow with praise* (119:171). The wicked express their malicious lies without constraint and with complete ease of mind.]

יְדַבְּרוּ עָתָק — *They utter malicious falsehood.*

The translation follows *Rashi* to 31:19. *Donash, Radak,* and *Metzudos* there render *strong words.*

Zera Yaakov homiletically identifies עָתָק with עָתִיק, *ancient.* The Midrash relates that at first King Ahasuerus refused to harm the Jews for fear lest the God of Israel! He is old and feeble and has no strength left to retaliate.'' Thus, one of the most potent arguments of the evildoers is based on the *malicious falsehood* that God is עָתָק, *ancient,* and impotent.

ה יְדַבְּרוּ עָתָק יִתְאַמְּרוּ כָּל־פֹּעֲלֵי אָוֶן: עַמְּךָ

ו יהוה יְדַכְּאוּ וְנַחֲלָתְךָ יְעַנּוּ: אַלְמָנָה וְגֵר

ז יַהֲרֹגוּ וִיתוֹמִים יְרַצֵּחוּ: וַיֹּאמְרוּ לֹא יִרְאֶה־

ח יָּהּ וְלֹא־יָבִין אֱלֹהֵי יַעֲקֹב: בִּינוּ בֹּעֲרִים בָּעָם

ט וּכְסִילִים מָתַי תַּשְׂכִּילוּ: הֲנֹטַע אֹזֶן הֲלֹא

יִתְאַמְּרוּ כָּל פֹּעֲלֵי אָוֶן — *They glorify themselves, all workers of iniquity.*

Ibn Ezra identifies יִתְאַמְּרוּ, *they glorify themselves*, with אָמִיר, *the tallest stalk of wheat* (Isaiah 17:6). As such it is used as an idiom describing glorification and distinction, as in the words (Deuteronomy 26:17), אֶת ה' הֶאֱמַרְתָּ הַיּוֹם, *HASHEM You have magnified today* (Radak; Rashi).

[The wicked are not ashamed of their sins; on the contrary, they try to *glorify* their reputations by boasting that they are *workers of iniquity.*]

5. עַמְּךָ ה' יְדַכְּאוּ — *Your nation, HASHEM, they crush.*

Israel is called (Deuteronomy 9:26) עַמְּךָ וְנַחֲלָתְךָ, *Your nation and Your heritage.* The wicked oppress Israel as much as they can, trying to *crush* and *afflict* it. Those who are weak and defenseless, like the *widow, stranger,* and *orphans* (v. 6), they *murder* (Radak).

וְנַחֲלָתְךָ יְעַנּוּ — *And they afflict Your heritage.*

Israel is called God's, נַחֲלָה, *heritage,* because they are the heirs of a spiritual estate bequeathed to them from their patriarchal forefathers and they live in the Holy Land, which is the heritage of God (Divrei Shlomo).

Malbim explains that עִנּוּי is *affliction* of the spirit and therefore the word is used in connection with נַחֲלָה, which refers to the spiritual heritage of Israel.

However, עַמְּךָ, *Your nation,* refers to the physical mass of Israel, and so it is used in conjunction with the word יְדַכְּאוּ, *they crush,* i.e., they physically hurt the Jews.

6. אַלְמָנָה וְגֵר יַהֲרֹגוּ — *The widow and the stranger they slay.*

Ordinarily the term גֵר refers to a gentile *convert* to Judaism. *Radak* explains that in this case it refers to a Jew who moves to a new place. Lacking relatives and close friends, this *stranger* is vulnerable to all types of dangers and threats.

The citizens of the town are both godless and lawless, and so the unprotected stranger is *slain* without compunction.

Dorash Moshe notes that Israel in exile is likened to a grass widow whose husband abandoned her indefinitely and departed on a long journey. Nevertheless, the husband did promise to return someday. However, as long as the husband is gone the widow can be molested and slain.

וִיתוֹמִים יְרַצֵּחוּ — *And the orphans they murder.*

Tehillos Hashem explains the difference between הָרַג, *slaying,* and רָצַח, *murder.* The *widow* and *stranger,* who are mature adults, have the strength to resist their attackers. They must be ambushed and *slain* in a concealed place where they can be taken by surprise and the crime can go undetected. However, the weak and immature *orphan* is helpless. He can be *murdered* openly with no difficulty.

7. וַיֹּאמְרוּ לֹא יִרְאֶה יָּהּ — *And they say, ''YAH will not see ...''*

The Talmud (Eruvin 18b) explains that when the Temple was destroyed and God's power cut short, His Name was abbreviated from the four-letter Name, יה־ו־ה *HASHEM* to the two-

they glorify themselves, all workers of iniquity.

⁵ *Your nation, HASHEM, they crush,*
   and they afflict Your heritage.

⁶ *The widow and the stranger they slay,*
   and the orphans they murder.

⁷ *And they say, "YAH will not see,*
   nor will the God of Jacob understand."

⁸ *Understand! You boors among the nation,*
   and you fools, when will you gain wisdom?

⁹ *He Who implants the ear, shall He not hear?*

---

letter יָהּ, *YAH*. This is because God partially concealed His Presence at the time of anger and devastation. This concealment gives non-believers the opportunity to claim that *YAH* will not see and is detached from This World (*Zera Yaakov*).

וְלֹא יָבִין אֱלֹהֵי יַעֲקֹב — *"... Nor will the God of Jacob understand."*

[The Jewish people refer to Hashem as אֱלֹהֵי יִשְׂרָאֵל, *the God of Israel*, because the name Israel is symbolic of greatness and authority (see *Genesis* 32:29). But the gentiles refuse to recognize that our God is unique and omniscient. They associate Him with the Name יַעֲקֹב, *Jacob*, which is derived from עָקֵב, *heel* (*Genesis* 25:26), the lowest part of the body. The name Jacob also alludes to crookedness and treachery as in *Genesis* 27:38. Thus the gentiles defame the *God of Jacob* and delude themselves with the notion that He neither sees nor understands the crimes of man (see *Radak*).]

The wicked commit sins in the secrecy of their inner chambers, and they boast, "Who sees me? Who knows

about me?" But the Holy One, Blessed is He, searches out the most remote places with His candlelight and uncovers them (*Eliyahu Rabbah* 18).[1]

8. בִּינוּ בֹּעֲרִים בָּעָם — *Understand! You boors among the nation.*

When will you finally understand that God does see and know every detail of human affairs? (*Radak*). [See comm. to 92:7.]

וּכְסִילִים מָתַי תַּשְׂכִּילוּ — *And you fools, when will you gain wisdom?*

These כְּסִילִים, *fools*, are intelligent people, but, they despise genuine wisdom because knowledge of the truth makes demands on a person and forces him to discipline himself. Therefore the Psalmist asks them when *they will gain wisdom*, which is so readily in their grasp if they should only desire it (*Alshich*). [See comm. to 92:7.]

9. הֲנֹטַע אֹזֶן הֲלֹא יִשְׁמָע — *He Who implants the ear, shall He not hear?*

This verse holds the answer to the wicked who say (v. 7), "*YAH will not see, nor will the God of Jacob understand.*" The Psalmist proves the

---

1. The disciples of Rabban Yochanan ben Zakkai inquired of their master, "Why did the Torah punish the גַּנָּב, *burglar*, more than the גַּזְלָן, *robber*?" [The burglar must pay back בְּכֶפֶל, *double*, what he stole, whereas the robber pays back only the exact amount he took.]

The rabbi answered, "The robber openly accosts his victims. He fears no one, neither man nor God. But the burglar doesn't dare to rob openly; he sneaks into homes when no one is looking. Thus, he shows that he has more fear of man than of God. In effect, the burglar claims that God is blind to human crime, '*YAH will not see, nor will the God of Jacob understand*'" (*Bava Kamma* 79b; *Midrash Tanchuma Noach* 4).

‏י יִשְׁמָע אִם־יֹצֵר עַיִן הֲלֹא יַבִּיט: הֲיֹסֵר גּוֹיִם
‏יא הֲלֹא יוֹכִיחַ הַמְלַמֵּד אָדָם דָּעַת: יהוה יֹדֵעַ
‏יב מַחְשְׁבוֹת אָדָם כִּי־הֵמָּה הָבֶל: אַשְׁרֵי הַגֶּבֶר
‏אֲשֶׁר־תְּיַסְּרֶנּוּ יָּהּ וּמִתּוֹרָתְךָ תְלַמְּדֶנּוּ:

absurdity of such a claim: God is the artisan who fashioned the organs of sound and sight for man. Is it conceivable that God Himself should lack the ability which He implanted in His own creations? (Radak).

Therefore listen you wicked oppressors! Do you think that God, Who implanted the power of hearing in all men, is not capable of hearing, and that He is deaf to the anguished cries of all those innocents whom you torment? (Rashi).[1]

אִם יֹצֵר עַיִן הֲלֹא יַבִּיט — He Who fashions the eye, shall He not see?

The term יֹצֵר, fashions, is used in relation to the eye because light waves from the seen object focus on the retina, where an image is fashioned and transmitted to the brain (Rashbam).

10. הֲיֹסֵר גּוֹיִם הֲלֹא יוֹכִיחַ — He Who chastises peoples, shall He not rebuke?

[The Psalmist continues to deride the absurdity of those who deny God's intimate supervision of this world.] History has proven that God rebukes

the sinners. Did He not drown the sinners in the waters of the great Flood? Did He not overturn the entire city of Sodom when He could no longer tolerate their evils? How do the wicked delude themselves into believing that they will be spared from God's rebuke? (Radak).

According to Targum, גּוֹיִם, peoples, refer to the greatest of peoples — Israel. God gave the Torah to Israel in order to instruct and chastise them. Is it possible to believe that God will not rebuke them if they disregard the Torah's teachings?

הַמְלַמֵּד אָדָם דָּעַת — He Who teaches man knowledge.

God is the Creator who fashioned the human brain. Is it conceivable that He should not know everything which transpires inside of it? (Radak).

11. ה' יֹדֵעַ מַחְשְׁבוֹת אָדָם כִּי הֵמָּה הָבֶל — HASHEM knows the thoughts of man, that they are futile.

Indeed, God is keenly aware of every machination of the human intellect. Moreover, He knows that men imagine

---

1. The commentaries draw our attention to the seemingly odd word used to describe the creation of the ear, נֹטַע, implants. Rashbam says that this alludes to the complexity of the ear. Sound produces air waves which enter the ear and 'hammer' against the eardrum, causing it to vibrate. Behind the eardrum is the malleus, a small hammer-shaped bone. It vibrates and beats against the next bone, the incus, which is anvil-shaped. The sound is conducted deeper into the ear and finally to the brain by a complex series of bones, membranes, fibers and fluids, which are set into motion by 'hammering' vibrations.

In Hebrew the word describing the erection of a tent is נֹטַע, because the first step is to hammer a tent peg into the ground until it is נָטוּעַ, lit. implanted. The term for firm hammering, נֹטַע is borrowed here to describe the ear, which functions because of a complex system of hammering vibrations. [Interestingly, the Talmud (Kesubos 5a) likens the forefinger (which may be thrust into the ear) to a יָתֵד, tent peg.]

[The inner ear also makes it possible for man to maintain his sense of balance. Through an intricate system of shifting fluids and sensitive hair fibers, the inner ear sends messages to the brain, informing it of changes in the position of the head or body. The body automatically compensates for these changes and makes necessary adjustments to maintain balance. The sense of balance which is centralized in the אֹזֶן, ear, assures that a person's feet are securely נָטוּעַ, implanted, on the ground and that he can maintain stability.]

> *He Who fashions the eye, shall He not see?*
> ¹⁰ *He Who chastises peoples, shall He not rebuke?*
> *He Who teaches man knowledge.*
> ¹¹ *HASHEM knows the thoughts of man,*
> *that they are futile.*
> ¹² *Praises to the man whom YAH disciplines,*
> *and whom You teach from Your Torah.*

that He does not know what is in their minds. That idea is the most senseless and *futile* of thoughts because God is aware of everything (*Radak*).

Furthermore, this is precisely God's greatness. Not only is He familiar with the significant and important thoughts of man; He also knows and records their foolish and futile thoughts (*Meiri*).

Chomas Anach comments that the word אָדָם in our verse can allude to *Adam*, the first man, and הֶבֶל to his son *Abel*. That man's schemes are futile can be seen from the first human family. The *Midrash* (*Bereishis Rabbah* 22:7) teaches that Abel lived only fifty days before he was murdered by Cain. The numerical value of הֵמָּה equals fifty, the days of Abel's abbreviated lifespan, and proves that man's illusions of immortality are הֶבֶל, *futile*.

12. אַשְׁרֵי הַגֶּבֶר אֲשֶׁר תְּיַסְּרֶנּוּ יָּהּ — *Praises to the man whom YAH disciplines.*

The most forceful argument of the wicked who deny God's presence is this: If righteousness truly has value in God's eyes, why do the righteous suffer? The Psalmist answers: Hashem afflicts those whom He loves, and their suffering is for their benefit, as it says (*Deuteronomy* 8:5, 16), *You shall realize in your heart that as a man disciplines his son, so does HASHEM, your God, discipline you … so that He might afflict you and so that He might test you in order to benefit you in the end* (*Radak; Meiri*).

Similarly, Solomon said (*Proverbs* 3:12), *For HASHEM rebukes him whom He loves even as a father does to the son*

in whom he delights (*Midrash Shocher Tov*).

Midrash Tanchuma (*Ki Seitzei* 2) emphasizes that a person should show appreciation to God when he sees affliction coming upon him because suffering brings a person closer to God. [Suffering makes a person realize that the flesh is weak and that the pleasures of this world are fleeting. The only permanent and worthwhile love is the love of God. Suffering which brings a person closer to God is called יִסּוּרִין שֶׁל אַהֲבָה, *affliction of love*.]

Midrash Shocher Tov observes that suffering is more worthwhile than animal sacrifice. When a man sacrifices an animal to God he gives away only his money, but when a man suffers he gives away his own flesh and blood and comfort for the sake of the Almighty.

וּמִתּוֹרָתְךָ תְלַמְּדֶנּוּ — *And whom You teach from Your Torah.*

Suffering is considered an affliction of love only when it does not force a person to interrupt his Torah studies (*Rashi*).

Indeed, sometimes suffering can enhance a person's understanding and appreciation of Torah. The *Talmud* (*Berachos* 5a) teaches that Hashem bestowed three precious gifts upon Israel but they can be acquired only through suffering. These gifts are Torah, the Land of Israel and the World to Come (see *Midrash Shocher Tov*).

R' Bisna said: There is no person in the world who doesn't suffer. There is a man whose eye hurts and whose sleep is disturbed. There is a man whose tooth

יג לְהַשְׁקִיט לוֹ מִימֵי רָע עַד יִכָּרֶה לָרָשָׁע

יד שָׁחַת: כִּי | לֹא־יִטֹּשׁ יהוה עַמּוֹ וְנַחֲלָתוֹ לֹא

טו יַעֲזֹב: כִּי־עַד־צֶדֶק יָשׁוּב מִשְׁפָּט וְאַחֲרָיו כָּל־

טז יִשְׁרֵי־לֵב: מִי־יָקוּם לִי עִם־מְרֵעִים מִי־יִתְיַצֵּב

aches and whose sleep is disturbed. And there is a person who is so immersed in Torah that he cannot sleep. Those in pain are awake all night and he who studies is awake all night, but how fortunate is he who is awake because what disturbs him is his thirst for Torah knowledge (*Tanchuma HaKadum, Mikeitz* 16).

All of the above commentaries are based on a reading of the words as תְּלַמְּדֶנּוּ, *You* [God] *will teach* [Torah to] *him* [i.e., the student], even when he suffers.

An alternate reading is תְּלַמְּדֵנוּ, *You* [God] *teach us* [Israel] from *Your* Torah. The verse teaches the concept that suffering is beneficial and liberates a man from his lust for pleasures of the flesh (*Berachos* 5a).[1]

13. לְהַשְׁקִיט לוֹ מִימֵי רָע — *To give him rest from the days of evil.*

The suffering a person experiences when God disciplines him (v. 12) saves him *from days of evil* and punishment in Gehinnom (*Rashi*).

Alternatively, *Radak* interprets: *The days of evil* experienced by the wicked *give a rest* to the righteous people whom they persecute.

עַד יִכָּרֶה לָרָשָׁע שָׁחַת — *Until a pit is dug for the wicked.*

The righteous suffer in this world only עַד, *until,* the time of final

retribution, when *a pit is dug for the wicked* (*Rashi*).

Radak translates עַד as בְּעוֹד, *while,* i.e., God gives rest to the righteous *while* He simultaneously digs a pit for the wicked.

Rashbam perceives this entire verse as a sharp contrast to the preceding one: God vigorously disciplines those who learn Torah. They suffer in this world so that they may delight in the future world of rewards. However, God treats the wicked in the opposite fashion. He gives them complete *rest from the days of evil* in this world so that He may dig a deep pit in Gehinnom for them in the future!

14. כִּי לֹא יִטֹּשׁ ה' עַמּוֹ — *For HASHEM will not cast off His nation.*

Sforno and *Tefillah LeMoshe* identify עַמּוֹ, *His nation,* as the elite of the Jewish nation — the Torah scholars [who suffer deprivation in this world. They should not be discouraged by their lot because Hashem certainly will not cast them off. Their future reward is assured.

According to *Radak* and *Meiri,* the Psalmist offers reassurance to Israel in exile lest they feel that God *has cast off His nation.*

Elsewhere, the prophet makes a similar declaration (*I Samuel* 12:22): כִּי לֹא יִטֹּשׁ ה' אֶת עַמּוֹ בַּעֲבוּר שְׁמוֹ הַגָּדוֹל, *For HASHEM will not cast off His nation, for the sake of His Great Name.*

---

1. Rav Chama noticed a blind man deeply immersed in studying Torah [by heart]. He greeted him warmly, saying, "Peace unto you, free man!"

The blind man responded, "Are you implying that I was once a slave?"

"What I mean," explained the Rabbi, "is that you will be a free man in the World to Come" [i.e., free to enjoy all of its delights].

Rav Yudan said: The Torah teaches (*Exodus* 21:26, 27) that if a master knocks out the eye or the tooth of his Canaanite slave, the slave goes free. Now if suffering in one bodily organ can bring a man freedom, certainly suffering and pain which rack the entire body can release a man from the shackles of the flesh (*Bereishis Rabbah* 92:1; *Berachos* 5a).

13 To give him rest from the days of evil,
until a pit is dug for the wicked.
14 For HASHEM will not cast off His nation,
nor will He forsake His heritage.
15 For justice shall revert to righteousness,
and following it will be all of upright heart.
16 Who will rise up for me against evildoers?
Who will stand up for me

וְנַחֲלָתוֹ לֹא יַעֲזֹב — *Nor will He forsake His heritage.*

God will not abandon Israel in exile because the time will come to summon His people back to their homeland [which is God's *heritage*] (*Radak*).

Malbim diferentiates between עָזַב, to *forsake*, and נָטַשׁ, *cast off.* Casting off means a violent act of rejection. God will not do this to עַמּוֹ, *His nation*, i.e., the physical mass of people which He has chosen. *Forsaking* is a much milder act of discontinuing a once close relationship. God will not even *forsake* Israel casually because they are נַחֲלָתוֹ, His chosen spiritual *heritage*, the bearers of His teachings and tradition.

The *Midrash* (*Ruth Rabbah* 2:11) comments: Sometimes Hashem acts for the sake of His nation and His heritage, and sometimes He acts for the sake of His Great Name. When Israel is meritorious, Hashem acts for His nation and His heritage, but when it is undeserving, Hashem acts for His great Name. The Rabbis say: In the land of Israel, Hashem acts for the sake of His nation and His heritage [i.e. the Holy Land is the heritage He designated for His nation], but on foreign soil Hashem acts for the sake of His great Name.

15. כִּי עַד צֶדֶק יָשׁוּב מִשְׁפָּט — *For justice shall revert to righteousness.*

For the man who is basically good but who has erred slightly, God's justice decrees discipline and affliction, until the errant sinner repents of his errors

[even the most minor ones]. Then he will revert to [total] *righteousness*. Thus, the purpose of the justice was to lead the sinner to righteousness (*Rashi*).

Sforno perceives this as a reference to the conclusion of the exile, when the gentiles shall be taken to task with strict *justice* and God's mercy and favor shall *revert to the righteous* nation of Israel.

וְאַחֲרָיו כָּל יִשְׁרֵי לֵב — *And following it will be all of upright heart.*

I.e., after the upright of heart go through the final process of purification [through suffering], they will all assemble to receive their long-awaited reward (*Rashi*).

This contrasts dramatically with the lot of the wicked who are always rewarded *before* it, i.e., immediately in this world and before the World to Come for any slight merit they have obtained. However, all *of upright heart* are recompensed *following it*, i.e., after this world, in the World to Come (*Midrash Shocher Tov; Radak*).

16. מִי יָקוּם לִי עִם מְרֵעִים — *Who will rise up for me against evildoers?*

The Psalmist marshals further evidence of God's intervention in human affairs. The hearts of the gentile oppressors are filled with evil schemes against Israel and would *rise up* to aid us. It appears as if nothing can prevent the execution of their ugly plots, had HASHEM not been a help to me (v. 17) (*Radak*).

יז לִי עִם־פֹּעֲלֵי אָוֶן: לוּלֵי יהוה עֶזְרָתָה לִּי

יח כִּמְעַט | שָׁכְנָה דוּמָה נַפְשִׁי: אִם־אָמַרְתִּי

יט מָטָה רַגְלִי חַסְדְּךָ יהוה יִסְעָדֵנִי: בְּרֹב

שַׂרְעַפַּי בְּקִרְבִּי תַּנְחוּמֶיךָ יְשַׁעַשְׁעוּ נַפְשִׁי:

כ הַיְחָבְרְךָ כִּסֵּא הַוּוֹת יֹצֵר עָמָל עֲלֵי־חֹק:

כא–כב יָגוֹדּוּ עַל־נֶפֶשׁ צַדִּיק וְדָם נָקִי יַרְשִׁיעוּ: וַיְהִי

כג יהוה לִי לְמִשְׂגָּב וֵאלֹהַי לְצוּר מַחְסִי: וַיָּשֶׁב

עֲלֵיהֶם | אֶת־אוֹנָם וּבְרָעָתָם יַצְמִיתֵם

יַצְמִיתֵם יהוה אֱלֹהֵינוּ:

מִי יִתְיַצֵּב לִי עִם פֹּעֲלֵי אָוֶן — *Who will stand up for me against the workers of iniquity?*

Whose merit will protect me [i.e., Israel] against my iniquitous enemies? (*Rashi*).

Homiletically, the *Talmud* (*Sotah* 13a) attributes these words to God Himself. He lamented the death of Moses, His trusted servant, and asked who could take Moses' place as a foe of evil.

[No one ever combated the forces of evil as vigorously as Moses. He was, so to speak, God's partner in the work of fighting the wicked. He brought ten plagues upon Pharaoh; executed those who worshiped the Golden Calf; brought about the downfall of Korach, Dassan and Aviram, Balaam, and Kings Og and Sichon.]

17. לוּלֵי ... עֶזְרָתָה לִּי — *Had HASHEM not been a help to me.*

Without His help I could not have stood up against the *evildoers and workers of iniquity* (*Radak*).

Midrash Shocher Tov comments that whenever the word לוּלֵי is used it means that salvation was assured in the merit of Abraham and the other patriarchs; in the merit of Torah; in the merit of Jewish faith; and in the merit of God's Name.

כִּמְעַט שָׁכְנָה דוּמָה נַפְשִׁי — *My soul would*

soon have dwelt in silence.

[Another name for *Gehinnom* is דוּמָה (cognate with דְּמָמָה, *silence*) because in hell all souls are silenced whereas in heaven they are not, for they eternally sing God's praises. Had Hashem not helped me to withstand the influence of the evil men I would have succumbed to their ideas and been condemned to *Gehinnom*.]

Radak offers an alternate translation: My soul would have שָׁכְנָה, *been laid to rest*, and דוּמָה, *cut off*.

18. אִם אָמַרְתִּי מָטָה רַגְלִי — *If I said, "My foot is slipping."*

If the perils of exile threaten to make Israel falter, Hashem's kindness supports them, because God fortifies their hearts with courage which reinforces and strengthens their weakened feet (*Radak*).

חַסְדְּךָ ה' יִסְעָדֵנִי — *Your kindness, HASHEM, supported me.*

The way of God differs from the way of flesh and blood The way of flesh and blood is that men are eager to uphold others who are rich and successful, but if they notice that someone is falling they will help to push him down. However, the way of God is quite different. When God notices a man who grows arrogant because of riches and success, He pushes him down, but when God sees the lowly, downtrodden and

against the workers of iniquity?

¹⁷ Had HASHEM not been a help to me
my soul would soon have dwelt in silence.

¹⁸ If I said, "My foot is slipping,"
Your kindness, HASHEM, supported me.

¹⁹ When my forebodings were abundant within me,
Your comforts cheered my soul.

²⁰ Can the throne of destruction
be associated with You?
Those who fashion evil into a statute?

²¹ They organize themselves
against the soul of the righteous,
and the blood of the innocent they condemn.

²² Then HASHEM became a stronghold for me,
and my God, the Rock of my refuge.

²³ He turned upon them their own violence,
and with their own evil He will cut them off,
HASHEM, our God, will cut them off.

poor, He kindly upholds them (*Yalkut Shimoni*).

19. בְּרֹב שַׂרְעַפַּי בְּקִרְבִּי — *When my forebodings were abundant within me.*

The apparently endless exile has increased my pessimism and sorrow (*Radak*), and I live in constant fear of renewed prejudice and persecution (*Sforno*).

Elsewhere (139:23) we read, בְּחָנֵנִי וְדַע שַׂרְעַפָּי, *Try me and know my forebodings. Radak* (ibid.) points out that שַׂרְעַף is cognate with שָׂעִיף or סְעִיף, the *branches* of the tree which grow in separate sections. Thus, שַׂרְעַף denotes thoughts that are fragmented and have lost their unity and clarity due to distress, which shatters mental stability (see *Hirsch*).

תַּנְחוּמֶיךָ יְשַׁעַשְׁעוּ נַפְשִׁי — *Your comforts cheered my soul.*

Even when I seemed to be lost in exile, I did not panic because I was cheered by the comforting promise

which You made in the Torah (*Deuteronomy* 4:31), *For a God of mercy is HASHEM, your God; He will not let you loose nor will He destroy you* (*Sforno*).

The initial letters of שַׂרְעַפַּי בְּקִרְבִּי, *my forebodings ... within me*, תַּנְחוּמֶיךָ, *Your comforts*, form the word שַׁבָּת, Sabbath. Daily preoccupation with endless mundane affairs shatters a man's mental tranquility. Only on the Sabbath does one regain equanimity. Indeed, *Pirkei D'Rabbi Eliezer* 20 relates that because Adam observed the very first Sabbath day, he was protected from all evil and unsettling thoughts (see *Yoseif Tehillos*).

20. הַיְחָבְרְךָ כִּסֵּא הַוּוֹת — *Can the throne of destruction be associated with You?*

After having praised God Whose comforts cheered my soul through every vicissitude — an allusion to Israel's confidence in the fulfillment of the prophecies — the Psalmist contrasts

God's justice with the evil of such adversaries as Nebuchadnezzar. Can the throne of rulers who epitomize destruction be associated in any way with that of God? (Radak).

יֹצֵר עָמָל עֲלֵי חֹק — Those who fashion evil into a statute?

Evil becomes their very code of behavior (Rashi; Radak).

The evil of these villainous monarchs is not performed as an isolated act; rather, it is set down in their law books permanently as a legal statute (Meiri).

21. יָגוֹדּוּ עַל נֶפֶשׁ צַדִּיק — They organize themselves against the soul of the righteous.

The gentiles gather as גְּדוּדִים, regiments, to take the lives of the people of Israel (Rashi).

Alternatively, Radak suggests that the root גוד may be translated to cut up (see Daniel 4:20). In a judicial context, cutting is an idiom meaning to issue a clear-cut legal decision. The gentiles render such decisions when they enact spiteful laws to persecute the Jews.

וְדָם נָקִי יַרְשִׁיעוּ — And the blood of the innocent they condemn.

They trump up false charges against the innocent man to make it appear as if his condemnation is legal and justified (Rashi).

22. וַיְהִי ה׳ לִי לְמִשְׂגָּב — Then HASHEM

became a stronghold for me.

After the gentiles accused me falsely and condemned me based on those lies, Hashem came to my rescue and saved me from their schemes (Radak; Sforno).

וֵאלֹהַי לְצוּר מַחְסִי — And my God, the Rock of my refuge.

Since I put my full faith in God, He was my refuge (Tehillos Hashem).

23. וַיָּשֶׁב עֲלֵיהֶם אֶת אוֹנָם — He turned upon them their own violence.

Although this verse is written in past tense, it is a wish for the future (Radak). [The wish is so strong that the Psalmist regards it as an already accomplished fact.]

[The word אוֹן is cognate with אוֹנָאָה, torment.] Hashem will bring upon the gentiles the same kind of violence and injury which they themselves perpetrated against Israel (Ibn Yachya).

וּבְרָעָתָם יַצְמִיתֵם — And with their own evil He will cut them off.

Hashem will punish the gentiles even for the evil intentions which they harbored against Israel (Ibn Yachya).

יַצְמִיתֵם ה׳ אֱלֹהֵינוּ — HASHEM, our God, will cut them off.

This wish is repeated for greater emphasis (Radak). [Thus ends the psalm which opened with a plea for God to appear as the God of vengeance against Israel's enemies.][1]

---

1. As explained in the Prefatory Remarks, this psalm is the Song of the Day for the fourth day of the week. The custom is to continue to recite the first two verses of the following psalm (95) in addition to this one [this addition is printed in the text of the prayer book]. The reason for this addition is that we do not wish to conclude the inspiring Song of the Day on a negative note of the psalm's last verse: HASHEM, our God, will cut them off.

Harav Yaakov Kaminetsky שליט״א, points out that the two additional verses from psalm 95 are the introductory stanzas of קַבָּלַת שַׁבָּת, the welcoming of the Sabbath, which begins with לְכוּ נְרַנְּנָה, Come! Let us sing to HASHEM. These special verses are recited on Wednesday, the fourth day of the week, and three days before the Sabbath, as an allusion to the halachah (Orach Chaim 248:1) which requires one to begin to prepare for the Sabbath three days before the Sabbath arrives.

95 מזמור צה

This is the sixth of the eleven psalms which Moses composed. He dedicated it to the tribe of Issachar, a family of scholars who were constantly immersed in רְנָּה שֶׁל תּוֹרָה, the joyous song of Torah. (See Radak on 91:1.)

This psalm is composed of two parts. The first seven verses are the Psalmist's call to his people: Come with alacrity to sing to God, to praise Him, to thank Him, to acknowledge Him as the sole Creator and Guiding Force — of the universe in general and Israel in particular. True, in our present state of exile and subjugation we may seem to be forsaken, but this situation is only temporary — it can change, הַיּוֹם אִם בְּקֹלוֹ תִשְׁמָעוּ, today! if we but heed His call (v. 7).

The second section is in the form of a direct exhortation from God to Israel, in which He recalls the disastrous results of our ancestors' sins in the Wilderness and urges us not to emulate that course.

Only the joyous song of Torah study can lift Israel out of the present wilderness of exile. Surely Israel will be redeemed when every Jew turns to his brother and declares: "Let us strive for spiritual excellence and ecstasy and sing joyously to HASHEM!"

On the eve of the Sabbath, the holiest of days, when Israel is granted a glimmer of the future world of spiritual bliss, it is customary to welcome the Sabbath with the קַבָּלַת שַׁבָּת, the welcoming service that begins with this psalm and its call: Come! Let us sing to HASHEM [see footnote to verse 1].

א לְכוּ נְרַנְּנָה לַיהוָה נָרִיעָה לְצוּר יִשְׁעֵנוּ:
ב-ג נְקַדְּמָה פָנָיו בְּתוֹדָה בִּזְמִרוֹת נָרִיעַ לוֹ: כִּי
אֵל גָּדוֹל יהוה וּמֶלֶךְ גָּדוֹל עַל־כָּל־אֱלֹהִים:
ד אֲשֶׁר בְּיָדוֹ מֶחְקְרֵי־אָרֶץ וְתוֹעֲפוֹת הָרִים לוֹ:

1. לְכוּ — *Come* [lit. *go*].

The term לְכוּ, *come*, represents an enthusiastic appeal, urging someone to surrender his doubts or leave a course of action to which he has become attached. Forget your preoccupation with material concerns and heretical beliefs, the Psalmist urges, and join me in singing God's praises! *(Meiri).* [1]

Radak explains that this psalm refers to the future era of the Messiah when Israel will achieve a deeper awareness of God's power and omnipresence. Then every Jew will arouse his neighbor with the words of this psalm, urging him to praise the Almighty for the wonders He wrought during the epoch of Messianic triumph and redemption.

נָרִיעָה לְצוּר יִשְׁעֵנוּ — *Let us blow the shofar to the Rock of our salvation.*

I.e., let us all recognize God as the source of our strength and salvation. Let us demonstrate our faith and obedience in a dramatic and public fashion, just as the *shofar* is sounded publicly to announce the coronation of a new king *(Malbim).*

לה׳ ... לְצוּר יִשְׁעֵנוּ — *To HASHEM ... to the Rock of our salvation.*

The two different references to God represent calls to two different classes of people. Addressing the non-Jewish nations, the Psalmist describes God as *HASHEM*, the Four-Letter Name formed from the letters of הָיָה הֹוֶה וְיִהְיֶה, *Who was, Who is, and Who will be.* This Name suggests to all nations that He

brought everything into existence and is the Source of all life — past, present, and future. Israel, however, has a more personal awareness of God. To us, He is צוּר יִשְׁעֵנוּ, *the Rock of our salvation*, because He is the Protector of Israel throughout our history. No matter how imminent Israel's destruction has often seemed, God always prevented the 'inevitable' from happening *(Avnei Eliyahu).*

2. נְקַדְּמָה פָנָיו בְּתוֹדָה — *Let us greet Him* [lit. *precede His Presence*] *with thanksgiving.*

Before we sing joyously to HASHEM *(v. 1)* let us first go out to greet God and thank Him for His many acts of kindness on our behalf *(Be'er Avraham).*

בִּזְמִרוֹת נָרִיעַ לוֹ — *With praiseful songs let us pray* [lit. *cry*] *to Him.*

After we offer thanksgiving for the kindness that God dispensed in the past, we will pray for His continued kindness in the future *(Midrash Chachomim).*

3. כִּי אֵל גָּדוֹל ה׳ — *For a great God is HASHEM.*

While Israel languishes in exile, heretics dare to deny that Hashem is God. But in the Messianic era, God's presence and supervision will be clearly evident; then all will admit His greatness *(Radak).*

וּמֶלֶךְ גָּדוֹל עַל כָּל אֱלֹהִים — *And a great King above all heavenly powers.*

The אֱלֹהִים of this verse refers, of

1. Every week, on the eve of the Sabbath, the Jew abandons his pursuit of and preoccupation with the material world and envelops himself in the spirit of the Sabbath. The Sages of Talmudic times would don their finest clothing and get up with the approach of the Sabbath, saying, ''Let us go out to greet the Sabbath queen'' *(Shabbos* 119a).

This custom was broadened by the holy kabbalist masters of sixteenth century Safed who would literally walk out to the fields to greet the incoming Sabbath. The custom of reciting the six *mizmorim* (psalms 95-99 and 29), which is now known universally as *Kabbalas Shabbos* —

95
1-4

Come! — Let us sing to HASHEM,
let us blow the shofar
to the Rock of our salvation.
² Let us greet Him with thanksgiving,
with praiseful songs let us pray to Him.
³ For a great God is HASHEM,
and a great King above all heavenly powers.
⁴ For in His power
are the hidden mysteries of earth,
and the mountain summits are His.

course, to the angels and other forces through whom God exercises His mastery of the universe. He assigns one force to provide rainfall, another to heal the sick, a third to regulate the tides, and so on. But no matter how strong and independent these powers seem to be, He is their acknowledged King. Human beings, too, are called to inculcate themselves with this recognition (Radak).

R' Hirsch adds that this call is of particular relevance to Jews, who may easily consider themselves subservient in various lands and political councils.

Sforno explains that in the future, God will strip these angels of their powers. Then He Himself will supervise human affairs, without intermediaries, as Isaiah 24:21 prophesies: וְהָיָה בַּיּוֹם הַהוּא יִפְקֹד ה' עַל צְבָא הַמָּרוֹם בַּמָּרוֹם, And it shall come to pass on that day that HASHEM will command the high legions on high.

וּמֶלֶךְ גָּדוֹל — And a great King ...
The allusion to God as King is unique to Israel, for we find a distinction between the terms מֶלֶךְ, King, and מֹשֵׁל, Ruler. A king is one who reigns with the

consent of the governed, while a ruler exercises power without regard to the wishes of his subjects. To the nations, God is a מֹשֵׁל, Ruler; they would prefer the freedom to indulge their own passions, but they will ultimately be forced to accept God's sovereignty. To Israel, however, God is primarily a מֶלֶךְ, King, Whose rule is based on the consent and support of His subjects. Israel, therefore, blows the shofar, the traditional fanfare to the king, to express its voluntary, willing acceptance of God as King, not only as Ruler (Avnei Eliyahu).

4. אֲשֶׁר בְּיָדוֹ מֶחְקְרֵי אָרֶץ — For in His power are the hidden mysteries of earth.

Radak interprets מֶחְקְרֵי אָרֶץ as the depths of the earth. Accordingly, the intent of the verse is that God is Master of every part of the universe, from the lowest to the highest.

Literally, the world מֶחְקַר means examination, or investigation. Here it indicates that there are many natural phenomena which defy logic and human investigation, yet God understands every aspect of nature (Meiri).

Similarly, God examines the depths

the Friday night service of Welcoming the Sabbath — was instituted by Rav Moshe Cordovero (1522-1570), one of the greatest of Safed's company of mystics (Rav Yaakov Emden). From Safed, the new liturgy spread gradually until it was adopted in virtually all Jewish communities.

The common theme of these six psalms is that God is King of the universe; indeed, this echoes the theme of the Sabbath, which reminds us that God created heaven and earth in six days and rested on the seventh. Someone who recognizes God as Master of the material world

ה אֲשֶׁר־לוֹ הַיָּם וְהוּא עָשָׂהוּ וְיַבֶּשֶׁת יָדָיו יָצָרוּ:
ו בֹּאוּ נִשְׁתַּחֲוֶה וְנִכְרָעָה נִבְרְכָה לִפְנֵי־יהוה
ז עֹשֵׂנוּ: כִּי הוּא אֱלֹהֵינוּ וַאֲנַחְנוּ | עַם מַרְעִיתוֹ

of every human heart and knows man's deepest thoughts (Meir Tehillos).

וְתוֹעֲפוֹת הָרִים לוֹ — And the mountain summits are His.

The root of תּוֹעֲפוֹת is עוֹף, bird. This refers to the mountain peaks which are so high and remote that they are only accessible to the birds.

These mountain heights, which are so inaccessible to man without great effort and equipment, represent power. Thus, the sense of the verse is that all knowledge and all power are in His hands (Ibn Ezra).

According to Sforno, the mountain summits is a figurative phrase referring to the high and mighty monarchs [whose hidden mysteries and plots are unknown to common men, but are revealed to the Omniscient God].

5. אֲשֶׁר לוֹ הַיָּם וְהוּא עָשָׂהוּ ... — For His is the sea and He perfected [lit. made] it ...

Not only did God create the vast waters, but He also gathered them into distinct bodies of water called seas. Then His hands fashioned the countless kinds of animals and vegetables on the dry land.

All this proves that God is master of the heights (v. 3), the depths (v. 4), and everything in between. It is in His power to lift men and nations high or to demote them. Thus, although He banished Israel to the depths of exile, He is destined to raise the Jews to the heights of glory. At the time of redemption, they will praise Him (Radak).

Dorash Moshe perceives in this verse an allusion to the two stages of the expansion of the sea waters. At first, the sea was His: at creation, the waters covered only one-third of the earth, and two-thirds was dry land. When the generation of Enosh sinned and introduced idolatry into the world, God punished the world with a flood which permanently drowned another third of the land mass in sea water (Shemos Rabbah 23:5). At that time, He perfected it [i.e., He enlarged the dimensions of the sea and brought it to its optimum size].

עָשָׂהוּ ... יָצָרוּ — He perfected it ... [He] fashioned it.

Be'er Avraham explains that יְצִירָה, fashioning, denotes the shaping of the general outline and dimensions of an object whereas עֲשִׂיָּה, literally making, refers to completing an object, down to the last detail.

God purposely fashioned the dry land and the creatures that inhabit it in a way that left them imperfect. He entrusted the earth to the seventy nations and charged them with the task of bringing every creature in their domain to its ultimate perfection.

This does not apply to the sea, however. The sea is His [i.e., God's] alone, for He did not apportion it to any one of the seventy nations. Since He made it and perfected it, its creatures need not be refined by human hands. That is why fish do not require the ritual slaughter which is mandatory for kosher meat.

during the six working days is prepared to welcome His intense spiritual presence on the holy Sabbath.

The kabbalists note that these six psalms contain a total of sixty-five verses, the numerical value of the Name אֲדֹנָי, my Lord, for the psalms are intended to convey the teaching that the Lordship of God is constant (Avodas Yisrael). The numerical value of the first letters of the psalms is 430, equal to that of נֶפֶשׁ, soul, for the psalms are meant to imbue us with the spiritual exaltation and serenity which are indicative of the נְשָׁמָה יְתֵרָה, additional soul, which is granted to the Jew on the Sabbath (Rav Munk; see ArtScroll Siddur, Kabbalas Shabbos).

⁵ For His is the sea and He perfected it,
        and the dry land — His hands fashioned it.
⁶ Come! — Let us prostrate ourselves and bow,
     let us kneel before HASHEM, our Maker.
⁷ For He is our God
        and we are the flock He pastures

6. בֹּאוּ נִשְׁתַּחֲוֶה וְנִכְרָעָה נִבְרְכָה — *Come!
— Let us prostrate ourselves and bow,
let us kneel.*

Prostration involves falling to the
ground and stretching out full length;
bowing is the bending of the head and
upper body as we do in *Shemoneh Esrei
[Amidah]*; and *kneeling* is falling to the
knees (*Radak*).

R' Hirsch notes that the order of the
verse seems to be incongruous, since
bowing and kneeling come before
prostration. He explains that prostration
in our verse is to be understood
figuratively as total submission to God's
will. This attitude comes first, to be
followed by the physical acts of bowing
and kneeling.

Ibn Ezra and *Radak* say that this
refers to the future when God will be
recognized as *a great King* (v. 3) and
everyone will come to demonstrate
submission to Him.[1]

נִבְרְכָה לִפְנֵי ה' עֹשֵׂנוּ — *Let us kneel before
HASHEM, our Maker.*

Radak explains that בְּרַךְ means *to
kneel* on the בִּרְכַּיִם, *knees.*

Midrash Tanchuma (*Ki Savo* 1) notes
that the three terms for bowing

expressed in this verse correspond to the
three daily prayers. Moses saw through
prophetic vision that the Temple would
be destroyed and that sacrifices and
offerings would be discontinued;
therefore he composed prayers to take
their place.

Sfas Emes comments that *let us
prostrate* refers to the morning service
(שַׁחֲרִית), in which man begins the day
by dedicating his entire being to God's
service. *Let us bow* refers to the
afternoon service (מִנְחָה), when man
pauses in the midst of his daily activities
to pay homage to God. [Bowing alludes
to mid-day because a person bows from
the waist, the middle of the body.] *Let
us kneel* refers to the evening service
(עַרְבִית). When one sinks to his knees, it
appears as if he is returning to the earth
from which the first man once emerged.
Similarly, at night a man returns his
soul to his Maker and returns to his
source when he sinks into sleep.

7. כִּי הוּא אֱלֹהֵינוּ — *For He is our God.*

He is the Judge who decides to punish
the enemies who harmed us (*Radak*).
[Therefore we pay Him homage by

---

1. The *Midrash* (*Bereishis Rabbah* 56:2) points out that it was by virtue of the act of
הִשְׁתַּחֲוָאָה, prostration, that our people merited many great achievements, for example:
Abraham and Isaac returned safely from Mount Moriah because they prostrated themselves
there (*Genesis* 22:5); the Jews were redeemed from Egyptian bondage because they prostrated
themselves before God (*Exodus* 4:31); the Torah was given to Israel at Mount Sinai after they
prostrated themselves (*Exodus* 24:1); Hannah conceived Samuel because she prostrated
herself at the Tabernacle in Shiloh (*I Samuel* 1:3).

In the future, the scattered exiles will be gathered in because they will prostrate themselves,
as *Isaiah* (27:13) states: *And they will prostrate themselves before HASHEM at the holy
mountain in Jerusalem*. The Holy Temple will be rebuilt in this merit, as 99:9 states: *Exalt
HASHEM, our God, and prostrate before His holy mountain*. The dead are also destined to be
resurrected in this merit, as this verse states: *Come! Let us prostrate ourselves and bow ...
before HASHEM, our Maker.*

ח וְצֹאן יָדוֹ הַיּוֹם אִם־בְּקֹלוֹ תִשְׁמָעוּ: אַל־
תַּקְשׁוּ לְבַבְכֶם כִּמְרִיבָה כְּיוֹם מַסָּה בַּמִּדְבָּר:
ט אֲשֶׁר נִסּוּנִי אֲבוֹתֵיכֶם בְּחָנוּנִי גַּם־רָאוּ פָעֳלִי:
י אַרְבָּעִים שָׁנָה | אָקוּט בְּדוֹר וָאֹמַר עַם תֹּעֵי

---

prostrating and bowing before Him (v. 6).

וַאֲנַחְנוּ עַם מַרְעִיתוֹ וְצֹאן יָדוֹ — *And we are the flock He pastures and the sheep in His charge* [lit. *in His hand*].

The Psalmist reminds Israel that at the nation's inception, the Jews were a helpless flock of sheep led by the Divine Shepherd. He guided them with the staff of faith through the harsh wilderness into the Promised Land (Radak).

[Similar language appears elsewhere: וַאֲנַחְנוּ עַמְּךָ וְצֹאן מַרְעִיתֶךָ, *And we are Your nation and the sheep of Your pasture* (79:13), and וְאַתֵּן צֹאנִי צֹאן מַרְעִיתִי, *But you are My flock, the flock of my pasture* (Ezekiel 34:31). This teaches that although God granted Israel the freedom to enjoy the entire *pasture* of the Holy Land, God also controls Israel very closely and keeps His flock in His charge.]

הַיּוֹם אִם בְּקֹלוֹ תִשְׁמָע — *Today! if we but heed His call* [lit. *voice*].

The laudatory description of Israel as צֹאן יָדוֹ, *sheep in His* [personal, affectionate] *charge*, can be fulfilled immediately — הַיּוֹם, *today! if we but heed His call* (Vilna Gaon; Malbim).[1]

Vilna Gaon adds that this phrase also refers back to עֹשֵׂנוּ, *our Maker* (v. 6). The root עשה can refer to the perfect completion of an act [see commentary to verse 5]. By heeding God's call, Israel

will make it possible for God, our *Maker*, to have perfected His creation, thanks to man's deeds.

Radak explains: If we would only listen to His commands, God would repeat the miracles of the exodus from Egypt for us *even today*. All God asks is that we do not repeat the defiance of the Jews who tested Him immediately after He released them from bondage (*Radak*).

If all of Israel would repent even for one day, the son of David [the Messiah] would immediately arrive, as this verse attests: Even *today, if we but heed His call*. If all of Israel would observe a single Sabbath properly, the son of David would arrive. Scripture refers to the Sabbath as הַיּוֹם, *today* [lit. *the day*], i.e., the day *par excellence*] (*Exodus* 16:25), and the Psalmist assures Israel: Even *today* [the Messiah will come], *if we but heed His call* (*Yerushalmi Taanis* 1:1).

8. אַל תַּקְשׁוּ לְבַבְכֶם כִּמְרִיבָה — *Do not harden your heart as at Merivah.*

The Psalmist now alludes to various instances in which the Jews had defied God in the wilderness. In general, God considered that generation to be very difficult and stubborn as *Exodus* 32:9 states: *And HASHEM said to Moses, "I have seen this nation and behold it is a stiff-necked nation"* (*Sforno*).

Immediately after they left Egypt, the

---

1. In these words, *Rabbi Nachman of Bratzlav* detects an important principle for the proper service of God. Often a wave of inspiration stirs a man to dedicate himself completely to God's service. Yet this enthusiasm quickly subsides when he looks ahead and realizes how staggering a task it is to serve God properly and to constantly fulfill all the Divine requirements and demands.

The only way to avoid this disabling discouragement is to concentrate on serving God one day at a time and to ignore the obstacles of the morrow. Thus *today, if we but heed His call*, teaches man to serve God as if today were the only day in his life.

and the sheep in His charge —
today! if we but heed His call.
⁸ *Do not harden your hearts as at Merivah,*
as on the day of Massah in the Wilderness,
⁹ *When your ancestors tried Me;*
they tested Me, though they had seen My deed.
¹⁰ *For forty years I quarreled with a generation;*
then I said, "An errant-hearted people are they,

Jews refused to put their full faith in God. When they had no water, they did not hesitate to quarrel with God and to challenge Him. *Exodus* 17:7 states: וַיִּקְרָא שֵׁם הַמָּקוֹם מַסָּה וּמְרִיבָה עַל רִיב בְּנֵי יִשְׂרָאֵל וְעַל נַסֹּתָם אֶת ה׳ לֵאמֹר הֲיֵשׁ ה׳ בְּקִרְבֵּנוּ אִם אָיִן, *And they called the name of the place Massah and Merivah because of the quarrel* (מְרִיבָה) *of the Children of Israel and their testing* (מַסָּה) *of HASHEM, saying, "Is HASHEM among us or not?"* (Radak).

[See commentary to 78:18-20 for a detailed discussion of Israel's testing of God at Massah and Merivah.]

Ibn Ezra, however, interprets the phrase as a reference to מֵי מְרִיבָה, *the Waters of Strife,* where Moses was punished for striking the rock instead of speaking to it *(Numbers* 20:13). Accordingly, the word מַסָּה is not a place name; it is rendered *[day of] testing.*

בְּיוֹם מַסָּה בַּמִּדְבָּר — *As on the day of Massah in the wilderness.*

[Israel's conduct was all the more contemptible because it took place *in the wilderness,* where the Jews were privileged to witness God's miraculous providence many times each day. They were surrounded by wondrous clouds which protected them from heat and harm. They were led by amazing pillars of fire and clouds; and they were sustained by manna, the food of angels. How did they dare to test (מַסָּה) God and to doubt His presence and omnipotence?]

9. אֲשֶׁר נִסּוּנִי אֲבוֹתֵיכֶם — *When your ancestors tried Me.*

First they doubted God's ability to perform wonders in the wilderness. They repeatedly tested God, to see if He could sustain them *(Be'er Avraham).*

בְּחָנוּנִי גַם רָאוּ פָּעֳלִי — *They tested Me, though they had seen My deed.*

Even after God demonstrated His supernatural power and provided them with miraculous nutrition in the form of manna, they were not satisfied. Then *they tested* God's works and complained about what *they had seen,* lamenting *(Numbers* 21:5): *There is no bread nor is there any water and our soul loathes this miserable bread* [i.e., the manna] *(Be'er Avraham).*

10. אַרְבָּעִים שָׁנָה אָקוּט בְּדוֹר — *For forty years I quarreled with a generation.*

Ibn Ezra points out that throughout the bulk of the forty year sojourn, God did *not* communicate with Moses. Moses lost his prophetic vision [because a prophet is only granted Divine perception in the merit of the people whom he represents. If they quarrel with God and reject this instruction (as communicated by the prophet), the channels of prophecy become blocked, for God concludes that it is fruitless for His prophet to convey additional Divine directives to a rebellious people]

וָאֹמַר עַם תֹּעֵי לֵבָב הֵם — *Then I said, "An errant-hearted people are they …"*

Because the Israelites who left Egypt were not wholesome at heart, they

יא לֵבָב הֵם וְהֵם לֹא־יָדְעוּ דְרָכָי: אֲשֶׁר־
נִשְׁבַּעְתִּי בְאַפִּי אִם־יְבֹאוּן אֶל־מְנוּחָתִי:

refused to recognize God's power and interest in their welfare. It was not He Who was remiss — but their perception of Him. Therefore God decreed forty years of wandering during which all the adults of the generation would die (Radak).

Sforno attributes the distorted thinking of those Jews to their exposure to pagan thought and heretic ideologies, throughout the centuries of their exile in Egypt.

וְהֵם לֹא יָדְעוּ דְרָכָי — "... And they know not My ways."

The Talmud (Avodah Zarah 5b) cites the example of the generation of the wilderness to prove that no one fully comprehends the ways of his [intellectual] mentor until he has been under his tutelage for forty years, because at the end of the forty year sojourn, Moses told the people (Deuteronomy 29:2), And HASHEM did not give you a heart to understand, nor eyes to see, nor ears to hear, until this day (Alshich).

[God ought to have lead the Jews to the Holy Land by the swiftest and safest route, but they imagined that God was leading them towards danger and doom.] Therefore, they were oblivious to God's miracles and dreaded the thought of entering the Holy Land, which was strange and unknown (Radak).

11. אֲשֶׁר נִשְׁבַּעְתִּי בְאַפִּי — Therefore, I have sworn in My wrath.

The Children of Israel aroused My wrath because they corrupted themselves with false beliefs that they adopted from the idolators. Thus they ignored the miracles which I constantly performed for their sake and they knew not My ways (Sforno).

אִם יְבֹאוּן אֶל מְנוּחָתִי — That they shall not enter My land of contentment.

[Indeed the Jews did not deserve to enter the Promised Land, for God designed it as an abode of tranquility and prosperity, but the Jews despised it and maligned it as a place of danger and death (see Radak).]

The Talmud (Sanhedrin 110a) teaches that מְנוּחָתִי [lit. my rest] refers

and they know not My ways."

¹¹ *Therefore, I have sworn in My wrath,*
that they shall not enter
My land of contentment.

to the eternal rest and reward in the World to Come.

Rabbi Akiva maintains that the generation of the wilderness lost their share in the World to Come, for *Numbers* 14:29 states: *In this wilderness they shall perish and there they shall die.* Rabbi Akiva interprets this to mean: *They shall perish* from life in This World and *they shall die* and be cut off from the World to Come. Furthermore, he notes, God states: *I have sworn in My wrath that they shall not enter My land of contentment.*

Rabbi Eliezer, however, holds that the generation of the wilderness does have a portion in the World to Come. Since God swore in His *wrath*, as it were, He had the right to regret His words and to retract His oath when His anger abated.[1]

Rabbi Eliezer supports his opinion with the verse (50:5), *Gather Me My devout ones, sealers of My covenant through sacrifice.* He contends that the *devout ones* alludes to the Jews who left Egypt and followed God into the wilderness without pausing to make any preparations. Because they sealed a covenant with God through self-sacrifice, God will gather them into His presence in the World to Come.

[Similarly, God promised to gather from the exile all the *devout ones* of Israel who will be redeemed by the Messiah. In the future all of the devout will sing to Hashem and greet Him with intense thanksgiving.]

---

1. [Elsewhere (*Avos D'Rabbi Nathan* 36), Rabbi Yehoshua maintains that this oath was never intended for the entire nation. Rather, it was merely a condemnation of the מְרַגְּלִים, *spies*, and the other villains of that generation.

This means that the oath was conditional. As long as the Jews remained defiant towards God His wrath was kindled. After that rebellious generation received its recompense it surely repented, and God's wrath subsided. Thus His oath was cancelled because it was meant to last only as long as His wrath was aroused.]

This is the seventh psalm which Moses composed. *Midrash Shocher Tov* quotes *Rabbi Yehoshua ben Levi,* who said: I know to whom Moses dedicated the first six psalms because I heard it from my teachers. However, beyond that I received no tradition.

Ibn Yachya attempts to identify the tribes to whom the remaining five psalms (in this series of eleven) were dedicated. He explains that this psalm was dedicated to Zevulun, who rejoiced when he went out to earn a livelihood so that he could support his brother Issachar, who studied Torah (see *Deuteronomy* 33:18). Therefore, Zevulun would constantly sing to HASHEM a new song, thanking Him for the Divine blessing which resulted in his wealth.

Later, David adapted this psalm to his own circumstances. *Radak* comments that David recited it (together with psalm 105) when he brought up the Holy Ark from the house of Oved Edom (see II Samuel, chapter 6). Thus, this composition contains a deeper symbolism. The Ark had been held captive in Philistine exile and David sang joyously upon the occasion of its redemption. Similarly, when Israel is finally released from exile, the Jews will join the Messiah and exult: Sing to HASHEM a new song, sing to HASHEM, everyone on earth.

This psalm appears (with minor variations) in I Chronicles 16:23-33, where it is attributed to Assaf and his brothers. David appointed them to lead the thanksgiving to God on the day when David placed the Holy Ark in a tent before the presence of Hashem (see *Meiri*).

א שִׁירוּ לַיהוה שִׁיר חָדָשׁ שִׁירוּ לַיהוה כָּל־
ב הָאָרֶץ: שִׁירוּ לַיהוה בָּרְכוּ שְׁמוֹ בַּשְּׂרוּ
ג מִיּוֹם־לְיוֹם יְשׁוּעָתוֹ: סַפְּרוּ בַגּוֹיִם כְּבוֹדוֹ
ד בְּכָל־הָעַמִּים נִפְלְאוֹתָיו: כִּי גָדוֹל יהוה
ה וּמְהֻלָּל מְאֹד נוֹרָא הוּא עַל־כָּל־אֱלֹהִים: כִּי |
כָּל־אֱלֹהֵי הָעַמִּים אֱלִילִים וַיהוה שָׁמַיִם

1. שִׁירוּ לַה' שִׁיר חָדָשׁ — *Sing to HASHEM a new song.*

In the time of the Messiah, every man will arouse his neighbor to praise God with these words (*Radak*). [Thus, these same words serve as the introduction to many psalms which speak of the future. See 33:3, 40:4, 98:1, 149:1, and Isaiah 42:10.]

The *Midrash* (*Shemos Rabbah* 23:11) points out that throughout Scripture the word for song is שִׁירָה (which is the feminine form), but the *new song* of the future is in the masculine form, שִׁיר. The *Midrash* explains that in this world of adversity and struggle, every brief period of triumph and song is succeeded by a new tragedy. Since this pattern resembles the female cycle of pregnancy and childbirth, *song* takes the feminine form.

However, the song of the future is in the masculine form שִׁיר, because it describes the Messianic *song* of ultimate triumph after which no further misfortunes will be born [see *Rashi* to *Arachin* 13b and *comm.* to 33:3].

Radak paraphrases the aforementioned *Midrash*: all previous victories which Israel experienced were fragile and weak, like a female. Only the final victory will be sturdy, strong and enduring like a male.

שִׁירוּ לַה' כָּל־הָאָרֶץ — *Sing to HASHEM, everyone on earth.*

At that time the words of the prophet (Isaiah 66:22) will be fulfilled, *the new heavens and the new earth which I will make shall remain before Me.* At that time, all of mankind throughout *all the earth,* will sing *a new song to HASHEM* (*Sforno*).

In what respect will this song be new? *Alshich* explains that when good triumphed over evil in the past, evil was not utterly vanquished. For example, the impure spirit still pervaded the atmosphere of Egypt even after the Egyptians were annihilated at the sea. The same was true after Israel's other victories over their enemies. In the future, however, the atmosphere will be completely purged of every detrimental influence.

2. שִׁירוּ לַה' בָּרְכוּ שְׁמוֹ — *Sing to HASHEM, bless His Name.*

Bless God for the kindness He will display when gathering the exiles (*Sforno*).

בַּשְּׂרוּ מִיּוֹם לְיוֹם יְשׁוּעָתוֹ — *Announce His salvation daily.*

Do not be content with mere knowledge of God's salvation; unless the thrill of the event is recalled, it soon comes to be taken for granted. Instead, proclaim it publicly and remind one another of God's goodness, thereby renewing the joy that was felt when the miracle occurred (*Radak*).

Do not acknowledge God only for supernatural, openly miraculous interventions. Recognize that even seemingly innocuous *daily* events are Heavenly gifts (*R' Hirsch*).

3. סַפְּרוּ בַגּוֹיִם כְּבוֹדוֹ — *Relate His glory among the peoples.*

God will be glorious because He will honor and glorify Israel in the presence of all the nations [whereas previously

Sing to HASHEM a new song,
   sing to HASHEM, everyone on earth.
² Sing to HASHEM, bless His Name;
   announce His salvation daily.
³ Relate His glory among the peoples,
   among all the nations His wonders:
⁴ That HASHEM is great and exceedingly praised,
   awesome is He above all heavenly powers.
⁵ For all the gods of the nations are nothings,

Israel was downtrodden and despised in exile) (Radak).

בְּכָל הָעַמִּים נִפְלְאוֹתָיו — Among all the nations His wonders.

Norah Tehillos explains that גּוֹיִם, peoples, are bound only by ethnic similarity or geographic proximity. Their bonds are purely physical and they lack a common recognition of a deity. They are impressed by physical power and glory which they relate among themselves.

The nations, however, are united by a firm faith in one God. Since they possess deep spiritual awareness, they recognize God's supernatural wonders and they promulgate their beliefs to all other men of the spirit (see Malbim on 2:1).

4. כִּי גָדוֹל ה' וּמְהֻלָּל מְאֹד — That HASHEM is great and exceedingly praised.

Hashem is undeniably the Master of the Universe. His great power brings Him praise because He uses it to perform kindness and mercy to all (Sforno).

נוֹרָא הוּא עַל כָּל אֱלֹהִים — Awesome is He above all heavenly powers.

The אֱלֹהִים are the angels and the celestial forces which are closest to Hashem and which have the clearest comprehension of His awesomeness (Radak). He is awesome to them because He can change [or destroy] them at will (Sforno).

5. כִּי כָּל אֱלֹהֵי הָעַמִּים אֱלִילִים — For all the gods of the nations are nothings [or: idols].

Ibn Ezra traces the root of אֱלִיל to אַל, not, nothing, alluding to the fact that no man-made or man-designated deity has value. They are all nothings, completely worthless.[1]

[One must pause slightly between the words אֱלִילִים, nothings, and וַה׳, but HASHEM. The prefix ו, here translated but, has many meanings. The most

---

1. Sifra (Kedoshim 19) lists ten names which Scripture uses for idols. Each of these names alludes to a different aspect of the idols' worthlessness. They are called:
1) אֱלִילִים — because they are חֲלוּלִים, hollow and empty;
2) פֶּסֶל — because they are נִפְסָלִים, carved by men;
3) מַסֵּכָה — because they are נִיסוֹכִים, molten and poured into forms;
4) מַצֵּבָה — because they are נִצָּב, upright [and immobile];
5) עֲצַבִּים — because they are put together from עֲצָבִים, small pieces;
6) תְּרָפִים — because they are רָפִּים, weak, decadent and disintegrating;
7) גִּילוּלִים — because they are מְגוֹעָלִים, abominable;
8) שִׁקּוּצִים — because they are מְשׁוּקָצִים, disgusting;
9) חַמָּנִים — because their owners put them out to bake in the חַמָּה, sun; and
10) אֲשֵׁרִים — because they are described by their worshipers as מְתְאַשְּׁרִים, fortunate [but in reality lack intrinsic value].

י עָשָׂה: הוֹד־וְהָדָר לְפָנָיו עֹז וְתִפְאֶרֶת
ז בְּמִקְדָּשׁוֹ: הָבוּ לַיהוה מִשְׁפְּחוֹת עַמִּים הָבוּ
ח לַיהוה כָּבוֹד וָעֹז: הָבוּ לַיהוה כְּבוֹד שְׁמוֹ
ט שְׂאוּ־מִנְחָה וּבֹאוּ לְחַצְרוֹתָיו: הִשְׁתַּחֲווּ
לַיהוה בְּהַדְרַת־קֹדֶשׁ חִילוּ מִפָּנָיו כָּל־
י הָאָרֶץ: אִמְרוּ בַגּוֹיִם | יהוה מָלָךְ אַף־תִּכּוֹן

common one is *and*. Thus, if the two Hebrew words were read together it would seem חי״ו as if Hashem were being equated with the lifeless gods.]

וְהֹ׳ שָׁמַיִם עָשָׂה — *But HASHEM made heaven.*

He made them all by Himself. During the first six days of creation, *HASHEM made heaven* [on the second day of Creation] before He created the angels [later on the second day. See *Rashi* to *Genesis* 1:5] and the heavenly luminaries [on the fourth day of Creation], so that no one could say that God needed the angels to help Him create the wondrous heavens (*Tehillos Hashem*).

Radak points out that initially the idolators worshiped the sun, the moon and the stars. These celestial bodies are utterly insignificant when compared to God, because *HASHEM* [Himself] *made the heavens,* including these heavenly bodies, and the Creator certainly surpasses His creations.

6. הוֹד וְהָדָר לְפָנָיו — *Glory and majesty are before Him.*

In the future, God's praises will be so widespread that even the majestic and glorious stars will offer praise to the Creator. They will declare that their majesty is a reflection of Divine glory (*Radak*).

Malbim defines הוֹד as the intrinsic *glory* which is the true essence of God, whereas הָדָר is the external *majesty* which is visible to the observer.

Kedushas Levi points out that הָדָר literally means *to return* (in Aramaic-

Hebrew). God generously bestows vitality and הוֹד, *glory,* upon all of His creations. In gratitude, all of God's creations praise Him and reflect glory back to God. The glory which they *return* to God is called הָדָר; it is this which comes לְפָנָיו, *before Him.*

עֹז וְתִפְאֶרֶת — *Might and splendor in His Sanctuary.*

His Sanctuary refers to God's celestial Temple in the vault of the heavens, where the planets and constellations are in perpetual orbit (*Sforno; Meiri*). This *Sanctuary* proclaims God's *might* and *splendor* as 19:2 says: *The heavens declare the glory of God, and the expanse of the sky tells of His handiwork* (*Radak*).

Malbim defines עֹז as inner *might* which fortifies its possessor, whereas תִפְאֶרֶת refers to external *splendor* which impresses all who behold it.

7. הָבוּ לַה׳ מִשְׁפְּחוֹת עַמִּים — *Attribute to HASHEM, O families of nations.*

[The word הָבוּ is variously defined as *attribute, ascribe, give, prepare, bring, etc.* See commentary to 29:1.]

Having declared their idols worthless, the Psalmist tells the nations where they should direct their praises (*Rashi*).

Midrash Shocher Tov interprets this verse in a different vein. It is a reference to the future redemption, when all the gentile nations will bring gifts to the Messiah. Then the Messiah will tell them: "All I want of you is to bring me the Children of Israel, who are scattered among you." Thus: *Attribute to HASHEM, O you nations — the families* of Israel in your midst.

but HASHEM made heaven!

⁶ *Glory and majesty are before Him,*
might and splendor in His Sanctuary.

⁷ *Attribute to HASHEM, O families of nations,*
attribute to HASHEM honor and might.

⁸ *Attribute to HASHEM honor worthy of His Name,*
take an offering and come to His courtyards.

⁹ *Prostrate before HASHEM*
in His intensely holy place,
tremble before Him, everyone on earth.

¹⁰ *Declare among the peoples, "HASHEM reigns!"*
Indeed, the world is fixed
so that it cannot falter,

הָבוּ לַה׳ כָּבוֹד וָעֹז — *Attribute to HASHEM honor and might.*

All nationalities alike seek honor and might. The Psalmist urges them to realize how vain are their pretensions. Instead, let them ascribe all glory to God (R' Hirsch).

8. הָבוּ לַה׳ כְּבוֹד שְׁמוֹ — *Attribute to HASHEM honor worthy of His Name.*

This paraphrases *Deuteronomy* 32:3, where Moses said, כִּי שֵׁם ה׳ אֶקְרָא הָבוּ גֹדֶל לֵאלֹהֵינוּ, *When I call upon the Name of HASHEM, attribute greatness to our God* (Midrash Shocher Tov).

שְׂאוּ מִנְחָה וּבֹאוּ לְחַצְרוֹתָיו — *Take an offering and come to His courtyards.*

This refers to the courtyards of the Temple (Radak).

Chazah Zion maintains that this refers to the offering of human energy and resources which will be dedicated to Hashem when men become inspired to attribute all they have to God.

9. הִשְׁתַּחֲווּ לַה׳ בְּהַדְרַת קֹדֶשׁ — *Prostrate before HASHEM in His intensely holy place.*

Let the source of sanctity, the holy Temple, be more splendid than all other structures (Radak) [that men will serve God with intense awe and respect].

Indeed, the *Talmud* (Berachos 30a) says that the word הַדְרַת should be read as חֶרְדַת, awe. From this we learn that before one stands to pray, he should be imbued with a sense of awe and reverence.

חִילוּ מִפָּנָיו כָּל הָאָרֶץ — *Tremble before Him, everyone on earth.*

The nations who failed to fear God throughout the millennia of history will recognize His greatness in the Messianic era and will *tremble before Him* (Radak).

10. אִמְרוּ בַגּוֹיִם ה׳ מָלָךְ — *Declare among the peoples, "HASHEM reigns!"*

The families of the nations who *take an offering* (v. 8) will observe the *splendor* of the Temple. They will then return to their respective lands and announce to those who stayed behind, "We have seen with our own eyes that *HASHEM reigns!"* (Ibn Ezra; Radak)

אַף תִּכּוֹן תֵּבֵל בַּל תִּמּוֹט — *Indeed, the world is fixed so that it cannot falter.*

Before the Messianic era, the earth will be in a state of chaos and decay, as the prophet says (Isaiah 24:18-20): *The foundations of the earth shake, the earth is completely broken down, the earth crumbles away, the earth con-*

תֵּבֵל בַּל־תִּמּוֹט יָדִין עַמִּים בְּמֵישָׁרִים:
יא יִשְׂמְחוּ הַשָּׁמַיִם וְתָגֵל הָאָרֶץ יִרְעַם הַיָּם
יב וּמְלֹאוֹ: יַעֲלֹז שָׂדַי וְכָל־אֲשֶׁר־בּוֹ אָז יְרַנְּנוּ
יג כָּל־עֲצֵי־יָעַר: לִפְנֵי יהוה | כִּי בָא כִּי בָא
לִשְׁפֹּט הָאָרֶץ יִשְׁפֹּט־תֵּבֵל בְּצֶדֶק וְעַמִּים
בֶּאֱמוּנָתוֹ:

tinually falters, the earth reels to and fro like a drunkard (Ibn Ezra). [God will send the Messiah to bring stability to the world.]

Rashi (comm. to *I Chronicles* 16:30) observes that a mortal king exploits his power, for when he sees that his subjects fear him he seeks to increase their fear that he may destroy them and their homes. But when God, the King of Kings, sees that His creations fear and serve Him as they should, He lets them be. Indeed, God then brings additional stability to the earth, so that men will feel a sense of security. Thus, when *tremble before Him, everyone on earth* (v. 9), then He in turn will see to it that *the world is fixed so that it cannot falter.*

יָדִין עַמִּים בְּמֵישָׁרִים — *He will judge the nations with equity.*

[See 9:9, and 98:9.]

God will bring lasting peace to the world in the Messianic era, as *Michah* (4:3) foretells: *And He shall judge between many nations and reprove mighty peoples, even the distant; and they shall beat their swords into plowshares and their spears into pruning hooks, nation shall not lift a sword against nation, nor shall they learn war any more* (Radak).

God will also render judgment concerning each country's final recompense: the deserving nations will be duly rewarded, and the guilty ones will receive fair punishment (*Maharam Markado*).

11. יִשְׂמְחוּ הַשָּׁמַיִם וְתָגֵל הָאָרֶץ — *The heavens will rejoice and the earth will be*

glad.

Radak interprets this as a figurative allusion to the happiness which will sweep the universe at the advent of the Messianic era of eternal peace. As *Rashbam* observes: When there is peace people are filled with optimism.

Ibn Ezra explains that even the components of nature will signify their joy by carrying out the functions assigned to them by God. The heavens will give abundant rain and dew; the earth will give generous crops.

R' Hirsch vividly describes how mankind's eventual deliverance from sin will foster a comprehensive rejuvenation of nature, for an intimate and irrevocable bond ties nature's development to man's moral conduct. Moreover, if man fulfills his destiny, then all of nature, which exists only to serve man and his mission, will achieve its destiny and *raison d'etre*. Fields and pastures rejoice when their abundant gifts are utilized by man to please God. The heavenly bodies are glad when man uses their light to illuminate his sphere of righteous activity.

The Gaon of Vilna explains that שִׂמְחָה, *joy*, denotes the intense emotion of happiness which one experiences when encountering something completely new. Thus, *the heavens* may be described as rejoicing because they symbolize the realm of the spirit which is constantly refreshed and renewed. In contrast, גִּילָה, *gladness*, refers to the happiness evoked by that which is established and familiar. This term is appropriate for *the earth*, for the

He will judge the nations with equity.

¹¹ *The heavens will rejoice and the earth will be glad,*
the sea will roar with its fullness;

¹² *The field will exult and everything in it,*
then all the trees of the forest
will sing joyously —

¹³ *Before HASHEM, for He arrives,*
for He arrives to judge the earth.
He will judge the world with righteousness,
and nations with His faithful truth.

---

physical, material world has not changed since the six days of creation (*Eitz Yoseif*).

יִרְעַם הַיָּם וּמְלֹאוֹ — *The sea will roar with its fullness.*

Its fullness refers to the fish which fill the sea; they, too, will sing God's praises (*Radak*).

12. יַעֲלֹז שָׂדַי וְכָל אֲשֶׁר בּוֹ — *The field* [lit. *my field*] *will exult and everything in it.*

The animals of the field and the beasts of the wilderness will all exult together (*Radak*).

Alshich comments that when Adam sinned, God cursed the earth which Adam would thereafter have to cultivate for his sustenance. As *Genesis* (3:17) states: *Cursed is the ground because of you, in sorrow you shall eat of it all the days of your life.* In the future, however, this curse will be nullified and the fields will exult when they return to their original blessed state.

אָז יְרַנְּנוּ כָּל עֲצֵי יָעַר — *Then all the trees of the forest will sing joyously.*

R' Hirsch comments that the forest is the abode of the animal kingdom and the living trees serve the needs of these creatures. However, when people fell the trees and use them to build houses, the trees attain a higher destiny and they exult over this opportunity to achieve a more noble level of service.

When the earth was cursed, many flourishing fruit trees became barren; thenceforth entire species of trees brought forth only brambles and thorns. The *Talmud* (*Kesubos* 112b) teaches, however, that all of these barren trees will eventually produce luscious fruit and that those who behold this wonder *will sing joyously* (*Alshich; Lachmei Todah*).

Rashi explains that *the trees of the forest* symbolize the monarchs of the gentile nations. [With their strength and erect bearing, they resemble towering trees. They, too, are destined to recognize the sovereignty of Messiah, and they shall rejoice when he arrives.]

13. לִפְנֵי ה׳ כִּי בָא כִּי בָא לִשְׁפֹּט הָאָרֶץ — *Before HASHEM, for He arrives, for He arrives to judge the earth.*

The words כִּי בָא, *for He arrives,* are repeated because God's arrival will serve a dual purpose. First, He will redeem Israel. Second, He will punish the nations who tormented the Jewish people (*Ibn Yachya*).

Malbim offers another interpretation of the "two arrivals": First, He will manifest Himself in the functioning of nature when people recognize that the so-called Law of Nature is truly the concealed Hand of God. Second, God will be perceived as the One Who judges the deed of mankind.

יִשְׁפֹּט תֵּבֵל בְּצֶדֶק — *He will judge the world with righteousness.*

Hashem will show understanding and compassion when He judges them (Sforno).

וְעַמִּים בֶּאֱמוּנָתוֹ — *And nations with His faithful truth.*

In the future, all the predictions of the prophets will be fulfilled. Their prophecies concerning the redemption of Israel and the doom of the nations will prove to be *faithful* and accurate (*Arugos Habosem*).

[At that time, all men will unite to form a community of faith dedicated to proclaiming their belief in the One and Only God Who created heaven and earth and Who controls nature and history.]

I bn Yachya *observes that Moses dedicated this psalm, his eighth, to the tribe of Joseph (Ephraim and Menashe), from whom Joshua is descended. Joshua would conquer the land of Canaan in God's Name, and this victory is described in verse 1:* When HASHEM will reign, the land [of Canaan] will exult!

Fire will advance before him [Joshua] (verse 3) and the mountains [i.e., the mighty monarchs of Canaan] *will melt like wax (verse 5).*

This psalm also alludes to the future, as Midrash Avakir explains with a parable: A king had two servants. One burst out in song and laughter, while the other cried bitter tears. The king attempted to console his weeping servant, saying, "In my eyes you are both equal. Why do you cry?"

The servant replied, "My colleague lives with you and eats at your table. He certainly has good reason to sing. You have kept me at a distance and put my sustenance in the hands of others. Therefore, I cry!"

Similarly, God created both the heavens and the earth together. The heavens sing joyously, as 19:2 states: The heavens declare the glory of God. *The earth cries, however, and protests to the Holy One, Blessed is He, "The heavens are near You, and they enjoy the splendid radiance of Your presence. Futhermore, the Angel of Death has no power over the heavenly bodies and luminaries. But I am far from Your presence and subject to the authority of the Angel of Death. Therefore, I cry."*

Then HASHEM consoled the earth: "Fear not! In the future, your lot will improve, and you will have ample reason to rejoice, as the Psalmist says, When HASHEM will reign [i.e., when His Presence will fill the land], the earth will exult."

א יהוה מָלָךְ תָּגֵל הָאָרֶץ יִשְׂמְחוּ אִיִּים רַבִּים:
ב עָנָן וַעֲרָפֶל סְבִיבָיו צֶדֶק וּמִשְׁפָּט מְכוֹן
כִּסְאוֹ: אֵשׁ לְפָנָיו תֵּלֵךְ וּתְלַהֵט סָבִיב צָרָיו:
ד הֵאִירוּ בְרָקָיו תֵּבֵל רָאֲתָה וַתָּחֵל הָאָרֶץ:
ה הָרִים כַּדּוֹנַג נָמַסּוּ מִלִּפְנֵי יהוה מִלִּפְנֵי אֲדוֹן

1. יהוה מָלָךְ תָּגֵל הָאָרֶץ — *When HASHEM wi'l reign, the earth* [lit. *land*] *will exult.*

The previous psalm concludes, *He arrives to judge the earth. He will judge the world with righteousness, and nations with His faithful truth.* At that time, all will recognize that *HASHEM reigns* and that justice has returned to earth; then everyone *will be glad* (Yaavetz HaDoresh).

At first, only תֵּבֵל, a term referring to the developed areas of the *world*, will be judged, but eventually God's influence will spread throughout the אָרֶץ, *earth*, causing even the uncultured and uncivilized barbarians to be glad (Ibn Yachya).

Indeed, as King Solomon said (Proverbs 30:21-22), *For three things the earth is in upheaval ... for a slave who becomes a king.* This refers to the reign of a man who is unfit for royal authority; his rule is a tragic disaster. The opposite will be true *when HASHEM will reign.* Then — *the earth will exult* to be ruled by the perfect Monarch.

יִשְׂמְחוּ אִיִּים רַבִּים — *Numerous islands will be glad.*

Even the most remote islands will hear of God's glory (Radak). Small *islands* will have special reason to rejoice because they were defenseless against the larger nations, which made them into colonies and exploited their wealth. The Messiah will proclaim their independence, which will bring them joy (Rashbam).

2. עָנָן וַעֲרָפֶל סְבִיבָיו — *Cloud and dense darkness will surround Him.*

Since God rewards the wicked in This

World to recompense them for their few merits, it appears as if they are His favorites who *surround Him.* In the World to Come of the future, however, God will bring *cloud and darkness* (i.e. destruction) upon them (Radak).

Sforno and *Ibn Yachya* maintain that these words describe the way in which God's constant supervision of this world is obscured by the seemingly independent operation of the laws of nature (see *Malbim*).

צֶדֶק וּמִשְׁפָּט מְכוֹן כִּסְאוֹ — *Righteousness and justice are His throne's foundation.*

When people see that the wicked are rewarded, they question God's equity. But when they witness the ultimate destruction of the wicked, they will all attest that *righteousness and justice are His throne's foundation* (Radak).

3. אֵשׁ לְפָנָיו תֵּלֵךְ — *Fire will advance before Him.*

This alludes to the outbreak of the war of Gog and Magog (which precedes the advent of Messiah), as described in *Ezekiel* 38:22: *And I will punish him with pestilence and with blood. Torrential rain, hailstones, and sulfurous fire I will rain upon him* (Rashi).

God's avenging fire will go forth at the behest and under the direction of the Messiah, as *Isaiah* 11:4 states: *He shall smite the earth with the rod of his mouth and with the breath of his lips shall he slay the wicked.*

Similarly, *Midrash Shocher Tov* (psalm 2) explains that they will inform the Messiah, "This state has risen in revolt against you!"

The Messiah will respond, "Let the locust come to destroy that land!"

When HASHEM will reign, the earth will exult;
   numerous islands will be glad.
² Cloud and dense darkness will surround Him
   righteousness and justice
   are His throne's foundation.
³ Fire will advance before Him,
   and consume His enemies all around.
⁴ His lightning bolts will light up the world,
   the earthlings will see and tremble.
⁵ Mountains will melt like wax before HASHEM,
   before the Lord of all the earth.

Then the Messiah will receive a report, "This province is in rebellion!"

Whereupon the Messiah will command, "Let the Angel of Death come and slay them!" (Yaavetz HaDoresh)

וַתְּלַהֵט סָבִיב צָרָיו — *And consume His enemies all around.*

The flames of doom will completely surround the enemy, leaving him no avenue of escape (Radak).

4. הֵאִירוּ בְרָקָיו תֵּבֵל — *His lightning bolts will light up the world.*

Baalei Bris Avraham comments that this can be explained with the observation of the *Rambam* in his introduction to the *Guide to the Perplexed*. Rambam compares the dilemma of a man who is grappling with the uncertainty and mystery of life to the situation of a traveler who has lost his way on a dark and stormy night. At intervals, a bolt of lightning illuminates the darkness; for a brief moment, the lost traveler catches a glimpse of the path he must take. Similarly, man is lost in a sea of falsehood and desperately seeks the path of truth. Only on rare occasions does God illuminate a man's intellect with a flash of perception and truth, and it is this insight which guides man through the darkness which swiftly envelops him once again.

In the future, God will grant man perpetual insight and understanding, as the Psalmist here promises: *His lightning bolts* [constantly] *light up the* [inhabited] *world*, banishing doubts and misconceptions forever.

רָאֲתָה וַתָּחֵל הָאָרֶץ — *The earthlings will see and tremble.*

In the future, a great earthquake will convulse the Land of Israel (Rashi); all the nations of the earth will see it and tremble before this manifestation of God's might (Radak).

5. הָרִים כַּדּוֹנַג נָמַסּוּ מִלִּפְנֵי ה׳ — *Mountains will melt like wax before HASHEM.*

God will humble the arrogant nations who consider themselves to be as formidable as mountains (Ibn Ezra).

[Yet in 98:8, the Psalmist says that in the future יַחַד הָרִים יְרַנֵּנוּ, *mountains will exult together*. This can be explained as follows: the mountains, i.e., the nations that remain arrogant, will melt. However, those mountains which humbly unite with other mountains will exult.]

מִלִּפְנֵי אֲדוֹן כָּל הָאָרֶץ — *Before the Lord of all the earth.*

The arrogance of the mighty nations will melt when they realize that it is Hashem who is the אֲדוֹן, *Lord*, of the earth (Ibn Ezra).

ו כָל־הָאָרֶץ: הִגִּידוּ הַשָּׁמַיִם צִדְקוֹ וְרָאוּ כָל־

ז הָעַמִּים כְּבוֹדוֹ: יֵבשׁוּ | כָּל־עֹבְדֵי פֶסֶל
הַמִּתְהַלְלִים בָּאֱלִילִים הִשְׁתַּחֲווּ־לוֹ כָּל־

ח אֱלֹהִים: שָׁמְעָה וַתִּשְׂמַח | צִיּוֹן וַתָּגֵלְנָה בְּנוֹת

ט יְהוּדָה לְמַעַן מִשְׁפָּטֶיךָ יְהוָה: כִּי־אַתָּה יְהוָה
עֶלְיוֹן עַל־כָּל־הָאָרֶץ מְאֹד נַעֲלֵיתָ עַל־כָּל־

י אֱלֹהִים: אֹהֲבֵי יְהוָה שִׂנְאוּ רָע שֹׁמֵר נַפְשׁוֹת

יא חֲסִידָיו מִיַּד רְשָׁעִים יַצִּילֵם: אוֹר זָרֻעַ לַצַּדִּיק

6. הִגִּידוּ הַשָּׁמַיִם צִדְקוֹ — *The heavens will declare His righteousness.*

When the atmospheric conditions produced by the heavens cause harm to the wicked nations, they will, in effect, make a declaration of God's righteousness. Thus the prophet (*Ezekiel* 38:22) predicts that *torrential rains, great hailstones, fire and brimstone* will pour down upon them from heaven (*Radak*).

וְרָאוּ כָל־הָעַמִּים כְּבוֹדוֹ — *And all the nations will see His glory.*

When those who defied God are punished, *His glory* will be evident (*Radak*).

7. יֵבֹשׁוּ כָּל־עֹבְדֵי פֶסֶל הַמִּתְהַלְלִים בָּאֱלִילִים — *Humiliated will be all those who worship idols, who pride themselves in worthless gods.*

Alshich defines אֱלִילִים [from אֵל, *god*] as the spiritual forces in which the pagans believe, including the sun, moon, stars, angels, and spirits. Each of these celestial forces is represented by a man-made פֶסֶל, *graven image.* The pagans attributed their success to these deities. But when God smites the pagans and demonstrates that their deities are powerless to defend them, the pagans will be ashamed of the trust they placed in worthless graven images (*Radak*).

Moreover, the *Yerushalmi* (*Avodah Zarah* 4:7) says that in the future every idol will come before its worshipers and contemptuously spit in their faces. The

worshipers will be shamed and the idols (having completed their mission) will vanish from the earth.

The celestial bodies which the gentiles worship will also be shamed, as the prophet foretells in *Isaiah* 24:23: *The moon will be disgraced and the sun ashamed when HASHEM of Legions will reign on Mount Zion and in Jerusalem* (*Sforno*).

הִשְׁתַּחֲווּ־לוֹ כָּל אֱלֹהִים — *To Him all the powers* [or, *gods*] *will bow.*

The *Yerushalmi* (*Avodah Zarah* 4:7) continues: In the future, all the idols will kneel before God; then they will vanish. Those who worshiped these false gods will recognize the truth, and they too will prostrate themselves before the true God (*Radak*).

8. שָׁמְעָה וַתִּשְׂמַח צִיּוֹן — *Zion will hear and be glad.*

When the thunder and lightning roar and the fiery hailstones crash, all the nations will be terrified. But the inhabitants of Zion will rejoice, because God is judging their tormentors (*Radak*).

וַתָּגֵלְנָה בְּנוֹת יְהוּדָה — *And the daughters of Judah will exult.*

The Messiah, the Scion of David, is a descendant of the tribe of Judah. Therefore, *the daughters of Judah,* the Messiah's relatives, will have special reason to rejoice, upon his arrival (*Chazah Zion*).

⁶ *The heavens will declare His righteousness,*
    and all the nations will see His glory.

⁷ *Humiliated will be all those who worship idols,*
    who pride themselves in worthless gods;
    to Him all the powers will bow.

⁸ *Zion will hear and be glad,*
    and the daughters of Judah will exult;
    because of Your judgments, HASHEM.

⁹ *For You, HASHEM, are supreme above all the earth,*
    exceedingly exalted above all powers.

¹⁰ *O lovers of HASHEM — despise evil!*
    He guards the lives of His devout ones,
    from the might of the wicked he rescues them.

¹¹ *Light is sown for the righteous,*

לְמַעַן מִשְׁפָּטֶיךָ ה׳ — *Because of Your judgments, HASHEM.*

The Messiah will judge all the nations in the Valley of Jehoshaphat [in the vicinity of Judea], and all of Israel will rejoice when they see justice meted out to their tormentors (*Radak*).

9. כִּי אַתָּה ה׳ עֶלְיוֹן עַל כָּל הָאָרֶץ — *For You, HASHEM, are supreme above all the earth.*

When the graven images are shattered and the deities humbled (v. 7), everyone will realize that *You, HASHEM are alone supreme above all* the forces of *the earth* (*Radak*).

מְאֹד נַעֲלֵיתָ עַל כָּל אֱלֹהִים — *Exceedingly exalted above all powers.*

When men recognize God's sovereignty, He draws new strength, so to speak, and He becomes more *exalted* than ever (*Kiflayim L'Tushiah*).

10. אֹהֲבֵי ה׳ שִׂנְאוּ רָע — *O lovers of HASHEM — despise evil!*

[The man who cultivates a flourishing garden cannot let any weeds remain. Similarly, the man who seeks to implant the love of God in his heart must uproot every trace of evil from his personality.]

Some fear the wicked because they appear to be exceptionally prosperous and successful. Men of evil give the impression that God protects them. But God will demonstrate that *He is supreme … exceedingly exalted above all powers* (v. 9) when He topples the gods of the evildoers and demonstrates that they are helpless. At that time the *lovers of HASHEM* will *despise evil*, without any fear of reprisal or retribution (*Ibn Ezra*).

שֹׁמֵר נַפְשׁוֹת חֲסִידָיו — *He guards the lives of His devout ones.*

Even when Israel is in exile there is no reason to fear men of evil, because God always *safeguards the souls of His devout ones* (*Sforno*).

מִיַּד רְשָׁעִים יַצִּילֵם — *From the might of the wicked he rescues them.*

God does not interfere with the free will of *the wicked*, but he delivers *His devout ones* from the conspiracies which evildoers direct against them (*Alshich; Shaarei Hayosher*).

11. אוֹר זָרֻעַ לַצַּדִּיק — *Light is sown for the righteous.*

Rashi emphasizes that this should be

יב וְלְיִשְׁרֵי־לֵב שִׂמְחָה: שִׂמְחוּ צַדִּיקִים בַּיהוָה
וְהוֹדוּ לְזֵכֶר קָדְשׁוֹ:

understood literally: *light is sown*, and it is ready to sprout forth *for the righteous*. Even if but a little light is sown, they will later reap light in abundance (*Ibn Ezra*) in the days of the Messiah and in the World to Come (*Sforno*).

The *Midrash* (*Bamidbar Rabbah* 17:5) explains that every material object in Creation holds within itself the potential for spiritual purpose and growth. The righteous recognize that seeds of Spiritual Light are sown and concealed throughout the world, so that man may cultivate a rich harvest of *mitzvos*. Opportunities to fulfill the precepts of the Torah are everywhere, even in the most mundane acts.

Elsewhere, the *Midrash* (*Shemos Rabbah* 35:1) says that this verse refers to the original light which illuminated the world at the time of Creation. With this light, a man could see from one end of the world to the other. But God realized that wicked men might

someday use this light for corrupt purposes. Therefore, God hid this light in the Garden of Eden, where it is reserved as a reward for the righteous.

וְלְיִשְׁרֵי לֵב שִׂמְחָה — *And for the upright of heart, gladness.*

The *Talmud* (*Taanis* 15a) states that not everyone is destined to be blessed with *light*, and not everyone is destined to be blessed with *gladness*. Only the righteous will have light, and only the upright will merit gladness. Rashi explains that the upright are on a higher spiritual plane than the righteous [see *Rashi's* commentary on *Avos* 6:1 and *Maharsha* on *Taanis* 15a].

Sfas Emes (in his essays on Yom Kippur) explains that the upright person has perfected his personality to such an extent that he resembles Adam before his sin, as King Solomon teaches (*Ecclesiastes* 7:29): *God has made man upright [literally straight] but they sought many intrigues.* Man will rejoice *and for the upright of heart, gladness.*

¹² *Be glad, O righteous, in HASHEM,*
  and give grateful praise
  at the mention of His Holy Name.

when he regains his original purity and uprightness.

[Whereas the righteous man has perfected his relationship with God, the upright has also achieved perfection in his relationships with his fellow man. (See *Deuteronomy* 12:24 and *Rashi's* commentary there. See also *Netziv's* introduction to *Chumash Haamek Davar*.)

Therefore the צַדִּיק is mentioned here in the singular, because a *righteous man* can live alone and serve God. The יְשָׁרִים, *upright*, are referred to in the plural, however, because their lives are also dedicated to serving God by helping others.

The main concern of the righteous is with spiritual matters; therefore their reward is primarily reserved for the future World of the Spirit. Thus, *light is sown for the righteous* in the future. But the upright are dedicated to improving the lot of their fellow man in this world; therefore they are rewarded with

rejoicing in this world (see *Rambam* on *Mishnah Peah* 1:1 and on *Mishnah Avos* 2:1).]

12. שִׂמְחוּ צַדִּיקִים בַּה' — *Be glad, O righteous, in HASHEM.*

In the future, the influence of the Messiah will elevate everyone to higher spiritual levels. The *righteous* will then begin to rejoice and the *upright* will reach new heights of ecstasy, as we read in the liturgy for the High Holidays: וּבְכֵן צַדִּיקִים יִרְאוּ וְיִשְׂמָחוּ וִישָׁרִים יַעֲלֹזוּ, *And thus the righteous will see and rejoice and the upright will exult* (see *Siddur HaGrah* with commentary of *Siach Yitzchak*).

וְהוֹדוּ לְזֵכֶר קָדְשׁוֹ — *And give grateful praise at the mention of His Holy Name.*

Man will 'remember' God when Israel is released from exile. Then the entire world will recognize that it is God Who has superintended this momentous redemption (*Tehillos Hashem*).

I bn Yachya *explains that Moses dedicated this psalm to the tribe of Naftali, whom he blessed in* Deuteronomy 33:23: *Naftali satisfied with favor and full of HASHEM's blessing. The contentment of Naftali describes the universal abundance and peace which will envelop the earth in the Messianic era. The Children of Israel will then merit special tranquility and peace of mind, which will prompt them to sing to HASHEM. The* Midrash (Shemos Rabbah 23:5) *states that it is because of Abraham's unshakeable faith in God that his descendants will be privileged to sing this song, for nothing could disturb Abraham's serene trust in HASHEM, and his descendants inherited this sublime faith. King Solomon taught that faith is the prime ingredient of song, as the* Song of Songs (4:8) *states:* תָּשׁוּרִי מֵרֹאשׁ אֲמָנָה, *You shall sing from the heights of faith.*

א מִזְמוֹר שִׁירוּ לַיהוָה | שִׁיר חָדָשׁ כִּי־נִפְלָאוֹת
ב עָשָׂה הוֹשִׁיעָה־לּוֹ יְמִינוֹ וּזְרוֹעַ קָדְשׁוֹ: הוֹדִיעַ
ג יהוה יְשׁוּעָתוֹ לְעֵינֵי הַגּוֹיִם גִּלָּה צִדְקָתוֹ: זָכַר
חַסְדּוֹ | וֶאֱמוּנָתוֹ לְבֵית יִשְׂרָאֵל רָאוּ כָל־

1. מִזְמוֹר שִׁירוּ לַה׳ שִׁיר חָדָשׁ כִּי נִפְלָאוֹת
עָשָׂה — *A psalm, sing to HASHEM a new
song for He has done wonders.*

Midrash Tanchuma (Beshalach 10)
lists ten great songs of faith which
highlight Jewish history. This psalm is
destined to be the tenth and final song.[1]
[See comm. to 96:1 which explains that
the word שִׁירוּ, *song* in the masculine
gender, refers to the future.]

Other sources indicate that this song
was first sung at an earlier date.
Scripture relates that when the Holy
Ark was captured by the Philistines,
God plagued the Philistines until they
decided to return the Ark which had
brought them so much trouble. They
placed it on a new wagon drawn by two
oxen, and sent the oxen in the direction
of the territory of the Israelites.
Scripture states (*I Samuel* 6:12): וַיִּשַּׁרְנָה
הַפָּרוֹת בַּדֶּרֶךְ, *the oxen went straight
(יָשָׁר) on the path.* This also means that
the oxen sang שִׁירָה, *song,* as they went.
They turned their faces towards the
Holy Ark, and words of praise for
Hashem miraculously burst forth from
their lips (*Bereishis Rabbah* 54:4).

The *Talmud (Avodah Zarah* 24a)
cites numerous opinions as to the
identity of that song: according to one
opinion, it was psalm 93; others

maintain that it was psalm 99. *Rav
Shimon ben Lakish* contends that the
oxen sang psalm 98. This psalm is
known as מִזְמוֹרָא יְתָמָא, *the orphaned
psalm,* because it begins simply with the
word מִזְמוֹר, but is neither attributed to
any author, nor dedicated to any
specific event (see *Tosafos, Avodah
Zarah* 24a and commentary of *Mahari
Ibn Chaviv).*

[The fact that this psalm is not linked
to one author or event attests to its
universal quality. It is truly the psalm of
the future, when everyone, everywhere,
will walk יָשָׁר, *straight,* in God's ways
and will sing a שִׁיר, *song.* Every
creature, even the dumbest animal, will
turn towards God and recognize the
Torah as the focal point of all creation.
See Overview to Vol. I, part VII for a
discussion of songs sung by non-human
creatures.]

הוֹשִׁיעָה לּוֹ יְמִינוֹ וּזְרוֹעַ קָדְשׁוֹ — *His own
right hand and His holy arm have
helped Him.*

At the time of the redemption from
Egypt, God used only one hand, so to
speak, as *Exodus* 15:6 indicates: *Your
right hand, HASHEM, is glorious in
power; Your right hand, HASHEM,
shatters the foe.* In the future, however,

---

1. *Midrash Tanchuma* enumerates the first nine songs:
   (1) The song the Jews sang on the first night of Passover when they were redeemed from Egypt;
   (2) The Song of the Sea, when the waters split to permit Israel to cross and then returned to their beds to drown the Egyptians (*Exodus* 15:1-21);
   (3) the song dedicated to Miriam's well (*Numbers* 21:17-20);
   (4) Moses' final song before his death (*Deuteronomy,* 32);
   (5) Joshua's song of victory (*Joshua* 10:12);
   (6) Deborah's song of victory (*Judges* 5);
   (7) David's song of salvation from his enemies (*II Samuel,* 22 and *Psalms* 18);
   (8) David's song for the inauguration of the Temple (*Psalms,* 30);
   (9) King Solomon's Song of Songs;
   (10) this psalm.

A psalm, sing to HASHEM a new song
    for He has done wonders;
  His own right hand and His holy arm
    have helped Him.
  ² HASHEM has made known His salvation,
    in the sight of the peoples
    He revealed His righteousness.
  ³ He recalled His kindness
    and faithful pledge to the House of Israel;

He will redeem His people with both hands (*Ibn Yachya*).

[*Malbim* (*comm.* to 44:4) explains that the זְרוֹעַ refers to the *upper arm*, which moves the forearm and hand. The upper arm is the source of the hand's strength.

Scripture alludes to this relationship between the upper arm and the hand when describing God's actions on behalf of Israel. When the Children of Israel are righteous enough to stimulate Divine action, they are described as the זְרוֹעַ, *upper arm*, and God's performance is called יַד ה׳, *the hand of HASHEM*, which derives its strength from Israel's merits.

When Israel fails to merit Divine intervention, God's deeds are termed זְרוֹעַ ה׳, *the upper arm of HASHEM*, which derives its strength from God's own mercy.

In the redemption of the future, God will act with both the יַד, *hand*, and the זְרוֹעַ, *arm*, of salvation, for all the power will emanate from God's mercy, regardless of Israel's merits.]

2. הוֹדִיעַ ה׳ יְשׁוּעָתוֹ — *HASHEM has made known His salvation.*

At the time of redemption, Hashem will finally make known the precise date of the advent of the Messiah. From the earliest times, this date has been shrouded in secrecy, as *Deuteronomy* 32:34 states: *Is it not secreted with Me,*

sealed up in My treasuries? And the prophet *Daniel* (12:9) confirms: *These matters are obscured and sealed up* (*Sforno*).

This verse has a parallel passage in *Isaiah* 56:1 which reads: כִּי קְרוֹבָה יְשׁוּעָתִי לָבוֹא וְצִדְקָתִי לְהִגָּלוֹת, *For my salvation is near to come and my righteousness will be revealed.* This prophecy will be fulfilled by the Messiah (*Malbim*).

לְעֵינֵי הַגּוֹיִם גִּלָּה צִדְקָתוֹ — *In the sight of the peoples He revealed His righteousness.*

During the tragic exile of Israel, the persecuted Jews have sometimes been tempted to question God's equity and righteousness. But in the future it will be manifest that Israel deserved to be punished for its sins and that the redemption represents an act of pure Divine kindness (*Sforno*).

3. זָכַר חַסְדּוֹ וֶאֱמוּנָתוֹ לְבֵית יִשְׂרָאֵל — *He recalled His kindness and faithful pledge to the House of Israel.*

God is committed to Israel because of the merit of their forefathers, as stated in *Michah* 7:20: תִּתֵּן אֱמֶת לְיַעֲקֹב חֶסֶד לְאַבְרָהָם, *Give truth to Jacob, kindness to Abraham* (*Bereishis Rabbah* 73:2).[1]

Harav Vidal HaTzorfati explains that God acted with *kindness* towards Abraham when He promised him the Holy Land. Once the promise was made,

---

1. *Chomas Anoch* [quoting *Tashbatz* and *AriZal*] points out that the letters of the name יִשְׂרָאֵל, *Israel*, allude to the initials of the names of the three Patriarchs and four Matriarchs of

ד אַפְסֵי־אָרֶץ אֵת יְשׁוּעַת אֱלֹהֵינוּ: הָרִיעוּ

ה לַיהוה כָּל־הָאָרֶץ פִּצְחוּ וְרַנְּנוּ וְזַמֵּרוּ: זַמְּרוּ

ו לַיהוה בְּכִנּוֹר בְּכִנּוֹר וְקוֹל זִמְרָה: בַּחֲצֹצְרוֹת

ז וְקוֹל שׁוֹפָר הָרִיעוּ לִפְנֵי | הַמֶּלֶךְ יהוה: יִרְעַם

ח הַיָּם וּמְלֹאוֹ תֵּבֵל וְיֹשְׁבֵי בָהּ: נְהָרוֹת יִמְחֲאוּ־

ט כָף יַחַד הָרִים יְרַנֵּנוּ: לִפְנֵי־יהוה כִּי בָא

לִשְׁפֹּט הָאָרֶץ יִשְׁפֹּט־תֵּבֵל בְּצֶדֶק וְעַמִּים

בְּמֵישָׁרִים:

---

however, its fulfillment was not only a *kindness*, but also a matter of keeping *faith* with Jacob and his sons [who constitute *the House of Israel*].

Because of this commitment of Divine kindness and *faith*, God will deliver Israel from the present exile and announce the advent of the Messiah (*Radak*).

רָאוּ כָל אַפְסֵי אָרֶץ אֵת יְשׁוּעַת אֱלֹהֵינוּ — *All ends of the earth have seen the salvation of our God.*

All the nations witnessed the wonders which God wrought, yet they refused to accept His sovereignty. Only the *House of Israel* acclaimed God's salvation, and for this reason God always *remembered* to treat them with kindness and faith (*Kedushas Levi*).

4. הָרִיעוּ לַה' כָּל הָאָרֶץ — *Call out to HASHEM, all the earth.*

Even the gentile nations should *call out* for joy in recognition of Israel's salvation, because it is the salvation of the entire world as well. When Israel is allowed to live in peace, the hostilities which divide the nations will also cease,

ushering in an era of universal harmony (*Radak*).

AriZal points out that the initial letters of these four words form the acronym הֲלָכָה [*halachah*], *Torah law*. When *all the earth* becomes filled with the study and practice of *halachah*, the Messiah will be victorious [see footnote to 100:1] (*Noeh L'hodos*).

פִּצְחוּ וְרַנְּנוּ וְזַמֵּרוּ — *Open your mouths* [lit. *burst out*] *and sing joyous songs and play music.*

Radak and *Ibn Yachya* perceive the word פִּצְחוּ as cognate with פִּתְחוּ, *open up.* [For whereas the suffering of exile stifled Israel's ability to sing out to Hashem, the redemption will reopen the wellsprings of song.]

[Celebrate God's triumph in every way possible, like a joyous nation which goes forth to greet its victorious King (see *Sforno*).]

5. זַמְּרוּ לַה' בְּכִנּוֹר — *Strum* [lit. *play music*] *to HASHEM on a harp.*

Alshich points out that this music is used as a means of paying homage to Hashem. Therefore the player starts on

---

the Jewish nation:

י stands for יִצְחָק, *Isaac* [and יַעֲקֹב, *Jacob*];
ש stands for שָׂרָה, *Sarah*;
ר stands for רִבְקָה, *Rebecca*, and רָחֵל, *Rachel*;
א stands for אַבְרָהָם, *Abraham*; and
ל stands for לֵאָה, *Leah.*

The name יִשְׂרָאֵל itself, which is formed from these initials, is the spiritual title of the Patriarch Jacob [and his descendants].

all ends of the earth have seen
the salvation of our God.

⁴ *Call out to HASHEM, all the earth,*
open your mouths and sing joyous songs
and play music.

⁵ *Strum to HASHEM on a harp, with a harp*
and the sound of musical instruments.

⁶ *With trumpets and shofar sound,*
call out before the King, HASHEM.

⁷ *The sea and its fullness will roar,*
the world and those who dwell therein.

⁸ *Rivers will clap hands,*
mountains will exult together —

⁹ *Before HASHEM, for He will have arrived*
to judge the earth,
He will judge the world with righteousness
and nations with fairness.

---

the harp whose soft, fluid notes inspire a mood of rapture which enables the audience to melt before the presence of God.

בְּכִנּוֹר וְקוֹל זִמְרָה — *With a harp and [the] sound of musical instruments.*

Later, after creating a quiet atmosphere of intimacy and submission to God, the musicians add a vast array of instruments, building to a thunderous crescendo of chanted song. At that point the listeners soar to the thrilling heights of ecstasy (Alshich).

6. בַּחֲצֹצְרוֹת וְקוֹל שׁוֹפָר הָרִיעוּ לִפְנֵי הַמֶּלֶךְ ה' — *With trumpets and shofar sound, call out before the King, HASHEM.*

Come before God in His palace, the Holy Temple, and praise Him to the accompaniment of these powerful instruments (Radak).

Shaarei Chaim observes that the חֲצֹצְרוֹת, trumpets, are associated with joyous victory (as in Numbers 10:10), whereas the groaning or crying sound of

the שׁוֹפָר, shofar, connotes fear (Rosh Hashanah 26a), for as Amos 3:6 asks, Is it possible that the shofar could be blown in the city and the nation not tremble?

This verse teaches that man should harness all of his emotions, both fear and joy, in the service of God, because God is both הַמֶּלֶךְ, the King, who inspires dread, and ה', HASHEM, the Dispenser of Kindness, Who creates joy.

7. יִרְעַם הַיָּם וּמְלֹאוֹ תֵּבֵל וְיֹשְׁבֵי בָהּ — *The sea and its fullness will roar, the world [i.e., inhabited land] and those who dwell therein.*

[See comm. to 96:11.]

All will rejoice at the universal peace ushered in by the Messiah (Ibn Ezra).

Kiflayim L'Tushia observes that in this verse the Psalmist associates the sea with the inhabited land because as 24:1-2 states, HASHEM's is the earth and its fullness, the inhabited land and those who dwell in it. For He founded it upon seas [see commentary there].

8. נְהָרוֹת יִמְחֲאוּ כָף — *Rivers will clap hands.*

The sailors who navigate ships down the rivers will clap for joy (*Ibn Ezra*).

Hand clapping is associated with welcoming a king, as in *II Kings* 11:12: *They clapped their hands and proclaimed, "Long live the King!"* At the time of the final redemption the entire world will recognize and welcome Hashem as its King (*Radak*).

יַחַד הָרִים יְרַנֵּנוּ — *Mountains will exult together.*

Here the Psalmist associates the mountains with the rivers, as in 104:10: *He sends forth the watersprings in the rivers, between the mountains they flow* (*Kiflayim L'Tushia*).

[Homiletically, this verse may be interpreted: *Rivers will clap hands, together with mountains they will exult.* The mighty rivers are created from the confluence of small rivulets, formed by rain and melted snow, which flow down from the mountains. The water flow causes erosion of the rock formations and reshapes the mountains. Thus, the mountains shape the rivers and the rivers in turn shape the mountains. Because of this symbiosis, when the rivers praise God they are joined by the mountains.]

9. לִפְנֵי ה׳ כִּי בָא לִשְׁפֹּט הָאָרֶץ — *Before HASHEM, for He will have arrived to judge the earth.*

All will rejoice when God comes to bring justice to the earth (*Ibn Ezra*).

This verse parallels 96:13, except that there כִּי בָא is mentioned twice. There, the Psalmist alludes to the order and justice that God brought to the world during the eras of the First and Second Temples. Those reigns of justice were short-lived, however. Here, the Psalmist speaks to the era of the Third Temple, when God's reign of justice will be eternal (*Chazah Zion*).

יִשְׁפֹּט תֵּבֵל בְּצֶדֶק וְעַמִּים בְּמֵישָׁרִים — *He will judge the world with righteousness and nations with fairness.*

96:13 reads, *He will judge the world with righteousness, and nations, with His faithful truth,* whereas this verse states that God will judge *nations with fairness.*

Shaarei Chaim explains that these two terms refer to the two stages of human acceptance of Divine judgment. At first, man does not comprehend the equity of God's actions, yet he trusts in God's *faithful truth,* confident that God will not be treacherous.

However, as time progresses, events prove the equity and perfection of God's decisions and deeds. The climax of history will come when mankind recognizes that all of God's judgments were rendered *with fairness.* Then man will no longer need to rely on blind faith to accept Divine decrees, for their justice will be manifest to all.

מזמור צט 99

This psalm speaks of the future Day of Judgment, when God will call all of the depraved nations to task (Sforno). The cataclysmic war of Gog and Magog will take place during this period of judgment and retribution (Rashi; Radak). At that time, HASHEM will establish His universal reign, unchallenged by any nation on earth.

Ibn Yachya explains that Moses dedicated this psalm to the tribe of Dan. Moses blessed Dan, saying: Dan is a young [and powerful] lion, who leaps up from Bashan (Deuteronomy 33:22), for when HASHEM will reign, nations will tremble, and Dan will have the opportunity to conquer them in God's Name.

א יהוה מָלָךְ יִרְגְּזוּ עַמִּים יֹשֵׁב כְּרוּבִים תָּנוּט

ב הָאָרֶץ: יהוה בְּצִיּוֹן גָּדוֹל וְרָם הוּא עַל־כָּל־

ג הָעַמִּים: יוֹדוּ שִׁמְךָ גָּדוֹל וְנוֹרָא קָדוֹשׁ הוּא:

ד וְעֹז מֶלֶךְ מִשְׁפָּט אָהֵב אַתָּה כּוֹנַנְתָּ מֵישָׁרִים

ה מִשְׁפָּט וּצְדָקָה בְּיַעֲקֹב | אַתָּה עָשִׂיתָ: רוֹמְמוּ

יהוה אֱלֹהֵינוּ וְהִשְׁתַּחֲווּ לַהֲדֹם רַגְלָיו קָדוֹשׁ

ו הוּא: מֹשֶׁה וְאַהֲרֹן | בְּכֹהֲנָיו וּשְׁמוּאֵל בְּקֹרְאֵי

1. יהוה יִרְגְּזוּ עַמִּים מָלָךְ ה׳ — *When HASHEM will reign, nations will tremble.*

In the series of psalms beginning with psalm 96, the reign of God is mentioned three times: *HASHEM reigns! Indeed, the world is fixed so that it cannot falter* (96:10); *when HASHEM will reign, the earth will exult* (97:1); and here. Actually, Hashem's reign will begin at the war of Gog and Magog, when *the nations will tremble* before God's might. Then Hashem will fix the earth on the foundations of justice, and *the earth will exult* (Radak).

This epoch will also be the era of the Day of Judgment when the wicked will receive their recompense (Sforno).

יֹשֵׁב כְּרוּבִים תָּנוּט הָאָרֶץ — *[Before] Him Who is enthroned on Cherubim, the earth will quake.*

The earth is no longer settled and stable, as *Midrash Shocher Tov* comments: as long as Israel is in exile, God's sovereignty is incomplete, and the nations are powerful. When Israel is redeemed, however, God's dominion will be firmly established, nations will waver on the brink of doom.

When God sits on His Throne of Justice it is considered as if He is seated upon the Cherubim, as *Ezekiel* (10:1) states: *I looked and see! By the expanse which is above the heads of the Cherubim something like a sapphire stone, like the appearance of the form of a throne, appeared over them* (Sforno).

2. בְּצִיּוֹן גָּדוֹל ה׳ — *[Before] HASHEM Who is great in Zion.*

[See *comm.* to 47:3. Something גָּדוֹל, *great*, resembles a מִגְדָּל, *tower*, which rises to the sky but is based on earth. Thus does the Jewish people (Zion) view God. He is great and lofty, yet He is also involved in this mundane world.]

וְרָם הוּא עַל כָּל הָעַמִּים — *And Who is exalted above all nations.*

[The word רָם, *exalted*, refers to an elevated object such as a soaring bird which is completely divorced from the earth. Thus do gentile nations conceive of God: He is deemed aloof and remote. In the future, however, the nations will recognize that God is indeed involved in earthly affairs. Therefore, He is described as בְּצִיּוֹן גָּדוֹל ה׳, *a great King over all the earth* (47:3).]

3. יוֹדוּ שִׁמְךָ גָּדוֹל וְנוֹרָא קָדוֹשׁ הוּא — *They will gratefully praise Your Name, great and awesome, it is holy!*

Moses revealed *Your* [true] *Name* to Israel [see *Exodus* 6:2] and described You as *Great and Awesome*. The nations are also destined to recognize Your Name (Ibn Ezra) but they will conceive of You differently. Israel perceives Hashem's involvement in and control of all mundane affairs, whereas the gentiles think of God as קָדוֹשׁ, *holy* [lit. *separated*], and aloof from the details of human life (Alshich).

4. וְעֹז מֶלֶךְ מִשְׁפָּט אָהֵב אַתָּה כּוֹנַנְתָּ מֵישָׁרִים — *Mighty is the King Who loves justice, You founded fairness.*

A man who wields great power often regards himself as being above the law

When HASHEM will reign, nations will tremble;
        before Him Who is enthroned on Cherubim,
        the earth will quake.
² Before HASHEM Who is great in Zion,
        and Who is exalted above all nations.
³ They will gratefully praise Your Name,
        great and awesome, it is holy!
⁴ Mighty is the King Who loves justice,
        You founded fairness.
The justice and righteousness of Jacob,
        You have made.
⁵ Exalt HASHEM, our God,
        and prostrate before His footstool; He is holy!
⁶ Moses and Aaron were among His priests,

and tends to abuse his power by injuring others. However, the Holy One, Blessed is He, *loves justice;* therefore, He uses His might to enforce the strict letter of the law (*Midrash Shocher Tov*).

[The Jewish legal system, which God codified in the Torah, insures the dignity and worth of each individual. The law views all Jews as equals in order to demonstrate that all are the handiwork of One Creator, the sons of One Father in heaven. Thus the Psalmist emphasizes that the *Mighty King* in Whose image all are created *loves justice* and has therefore founded the sense of fairness in His creations.]

מִשְׁפָּט וּצְדָקָה בְּיַעֲקֹב אַתָּה עָשִׂיתָ — *The justice and righteousness of Jacob, You have made.*

According to one view this verse means that God will display His Divine *justice* when He redeems *Jacob* [i.e., the Jews] from exile. However, others maintain that the verse refers to God's *justice and righteousness* that was most evident when He gave the Torah to *Jacob* [i.e., the Jews] at Mount Sinai (*Radak*).

5. רוֹמְמוּ ה' אֱלֹהֵינוּ — *Exalt HASHEM, our God.*

This exhortation is addressed to the exiles: Publicize Your wondrous redemption throughout the entire world and encourage everyone to join you in praising God (*Sforno*).

וְהִשְׁתַּחֲווּ לַהֲדֹם רַגְלָיו קָדוֹשׁ הוּא — *And prostrate before His footstool; He is holy!*

[See parallel phrase in 132:7.]

Not only is God holy in heaven above, but also on earth below (*Alshich*).

Alternatively, God's footstool alludes to the Temple [see *Isaiah* 66:1] and He made it holy with His Presence (*Sforno*).

6. מֹשֶׁה וְאַהֲרֹן — *Moses and Aaron [were] among His priests.*

Radak and *Sforno* interpret בְּכֹהֲנָיו, *[were] among His priests,* to mean Moses and Aaron were the chosen and foremost *among God's priests.*

[Prior to Aaron's installation as High Priest, it was Moses who served in that capacity.] Before the מִשְׁכָּן, *Tabernacle,* was used for the regular daily service in the wilderness, it was dedicated and prepared over a seven day period

ז שָׁמוֹ קֹרְאִים אֶל־יהוה וְהוּא יַעֲנֵם: בְּעַמּוּד
עָנָן יְדַבֵּר אֲלֵיהֶם שָׁמְרוּ עֵדֹתָיו וְחֹק נָתַן־
ח לָמוֹ: יהוה אֱלֹהֵינוּ אַתָּה עֲנִיתָם אֵל נֹשֵׂא

(Radak). During that time, Moses served as its priest, performing all the rituals and services. He did not wear the traditional costume of the High Priest which consisted of eight garments, however; he only wore a pure white toga (Taanis 11b).

Throughout this period, Moses was initiating Aaron into the High Priesthood. He anointed Aaron and dressed him in his special garments (Midrash Hagadol, Bamidbar 7:1).

Others are of the opinion that Moses served as a High Priest [with Aaron] throughout the forty year sojourn in the wilderness (Shemos Rabbah 37:1).

Thus, the Psalmist here explains why one should *prostrate before His footstool* [i.e., the Temple] *for it is holy* (v. 5). The holiness of the Temple or Tabernacle is determined by the caliber of the people who serve there [i.e., if those who serve in the sacred environs reach a higher level of holiness, God's Presence will dwell there with greater intensity] and devout men like *Moses and Aaron* served God in the Tabernacle (Sforno).

וּשְׁמוּאֵל בְּקֹרְאֵי שְׁמוֹ — *And Samuel among those who invoke His Name.*

The Psalmist singles out Samuel because in certain respects his stature matched that of Moses and Aaron. These brothers were the greatest priests [and prophets] of their age, just as Samuel was the greatest prophet of his day. Samuel may have been the greatest

prophet of all time after Moses, as *Jeremiah* 15:1 states: *If Moses and Samuel should stand before Me* [i.e., in that order]. According to one Talmudic opinion (*Berachos* 31b), Samuel's stature was equal to that of Moses and Aaron [in certain respects].[1]

The *Talmud* (*Taanis* 5b) observes that all of Moses' accomplishments were enduring; none were destroyed in his lifetime. Similarly, Samuel's greatest achievement, the anointment of King Saul, was not destroyed in his lifetime, for although Saul deserved to lose his crown, he did not die until after Samuel's death.

Furthermore, Moses' strength derived from the fact that he was completely selfless in his service to the Jewish people. Moses never derived any personal profit or advantage from his position of leadership [see *Numbers* 16:15]. Similarly, Samuel's authority was above reproach because he took nothing from the people in return for his service [see *I Samuel* 12:3] (*Midrash Yelamdeinu*).

Finally, Samuel was a Levite, a descendant of the same family as Moses and Aaron (Radak).

[Samuel was also responsible for sanctifying the Tabernacle at Shiloh where he served as Levite. He was trained there by the High Priest, Eli.]

Samuel was the most prominent and successful of קֹרְאֵי שְׁמוֹ, *those who invoke His Name*; this refers to those

1. *Shaloh HaKadosh* (*Parashas Korach*) explains that undoubtedly no one ever equaled Moses, for Scripture clearly states: *And there arose no prophet ever equal in Israel equal to Moses* (*Deuteronomy* 34:10). However, Moses emphasized service devoted to obeying and pleasing God (בֵּין אָדָם לַמָּקוֹם) whereas Aaron stressed being friendly and helpful to his fellow man (בֵּין אָדָם לַחֲבֵרוֹ). Samuel dedicated himself to follow the examples of both Moses and Aaron by placing equal emphasis on service to God and kindness towards man. This is what the *Talmud* means when it says that Samuel was equal to both Moses and Aaron. [See *I Samuel* 2:26: *And the youth Samuel grew continuously and he was good both with HASHEM and also with men.*]

> *and Samuel among those who invoke His Name,*
> *they called upon HASHEM*
> *and He answered them.*
> *⁷ In a pillar of cloud He spoke to them;*
> *they obeyed His testimonies*
> *and whatever decree He gave them.*
> *⁸ HASHEM, our God, You answered them.*

who pray to Hashem and ask for Divine assistance (Sforno).[1]

קָרְאִים אֶל ה' וְהוּא יַעֲנֵם — *They called upon HASHEM and He answered them.*

God Himself intervened and answered the prayers of these three great men, rather than delegating an intermediary to fulfill their requests (Alshich).

7. בְּעַמּוּד עָנָן יְדַבֵּר אֲלֵיהֶם — *In a pillar of cloud He spoke to them.*

Ibn Ezra maintains that this refers only to Moses and Aaron, to whom God spoke in the wilderness through a pillar of cloud. Radak (based on Midrash Shocher Tov and Pesikta Rabbosi 14) explains that God also spoke to Samuel through a pillar of cloud.

Scripture relates (I Samuel 9:10-12) that Saul was searching for Samuel, who was known as the רֹאֶה, seer. A group of young girls pointed out Samuel's house to Saul. It was obvious that this was the prophet's home because a pillar of cloud hovered over Samuel's door (i.e., his home was so consecrated that it resembled the Tabernacle, where God's Spirit dwelled in a cloud].

Rav Saadiah Gaon points out that the clouds provide a sign to the prophet that all that he sees and hears is truly a prophetic message. When God speaks to the prophet, the entire expanse of the sky is perfectly clear, save for a single pillar of cloud which stands before the prophet's eyes [symbolizing God's presence].

שָׁמְרוּ עֵדֹתָיו וְחֹק נָתַן לָמוֹ — *They obeyed His testimonies and whatever decree He gave them.*

God revealed the entirety of His testimonies and statutes to Israel through Moses and Aaron who faithfully transmitted the Divine teachings without the slightest deviation (Ibn Ezra; Rav Saadiah Gaon).

8. ה' אֱלֹהֵינוּ אַתָּה עֲנִיתָם — *HASHEM, our God, You answered them.*

[Whenever Moses and Aaron prostrated themselves before You and begged You to forgive the children of Israel, You did not refuse their request (See Ibn Ezra).]

---

1. Vilna Gaon and Chida offer an alternative translation of קֹרְאֵי שְׁמוֹ, *those who were called* [i.e., named] *by his name* [i.e., Samuel's own name].

Aggadas Rhmuel Rabbosi (chapter 2) relates that over the period of one year, a heavenly voice went forth, proclaiming, "An extremely righteous soul is about to enter the world, and the child who bears this soul will be called, שְׁמוּאֵל, Samuel [from the two words אֵל שְׁמוֹ, *his name is God*]."

All mothers who bore males at that time gave their sons the name Samuel. However, the behavior of these infants soon proved that they were unworthy of this extraordinary name.

Finally, the prophet Samuel was born to a woman named Hannah. All who observed Samuel's conduct agreed that he was truly worthy of his lofty name.

The other boys who were קֹרְאֵי שְׁמוֹ, *called by his* [Samuel's] *name*, became Samuel's disciples. The Holy Spirit descended upon them, and they were known as בְּנֵי הַנְּבִיאִים, *the sons of the prophets*, i.e., the apprentice prophets.

ט הָיִיתָ לָהֶם וְנֹקֵם עַל־עֲלִילוֹתָם: רוֹמְמוּ יהוה
אֱלֹהֵינוּ וְהִשְׁתַּחֲווּ לְהַר קָדְשׁוֹ כִּי־קָדוֹשׁ
יהוה אֱלֹהֵינוּ:

אֵל נֹשֵׂא הָיִיתָ לָהֶם — *A forgiving God were You to them.*

Israel sinned with the Golden Calf and they sinned again by believing the evil report of the spies. In both instances, Moses invoked Divine compassion and God responded affirmatively, as *Numbers* 14:20 states: וַיֹּאמֶר ה׳ סָלַחְתִּי כִּדְבָרֶךָ, *And HASHEM said, "I have forgiven* [them] *as you* [Moses] *requested"* (Alshich).

וְנֹקֵם עַל עֲלִילוֹתָם — *But an Avenger for their iniquities.*

Chazah Zion explains: Despite the fact that You forgave the sins of Israel for the sake of their great leaders, You, O God, were very strict and unforgiving towards the leaders themselves. Moses and Aaron were punished because of the incident at *Merivah*, where Moses smote the rock instead of commanding it to give water. (See *Numbers* 20:11.)

The two elder sons of Aaron were killed for the transgression which they committed in God's sanctuary (*Leviticus* 10:1-2). The prophet Samuel was punished for having made a single statement which God deemed presumptuous. Samuel had described himself with the words, אָנֹכִי הָרֹאֶה, *I am the Seer* (*I Samuel* 9:19). Therefore God later demonstrated to Samuel that his vision was unclear [see Overview to Tehillim Vol. I, part II]. All of these incidents bear testimony to the statement made in verse 4: *Mighty is the King Who loves justice, You founded fairness. The justice and righteousness of Jacob, You have made.*

Chazah Zion concludes that during the Messianic era, God will also exercise this type of Strict Justice towards the wicked nations who persecuted the exiled Jews. God will take revenge for the suffering which they caused to the

> A forgiving God were You to them —
> but an Avenger for their iniquities.
> ⁹ Exalt HASHEM, our God,
> and prostrate before His holy mountain;
> for holy is HASHEM, our God.

Jews while the Jews themselves will be redeemed with glory and triumph as they were when God liberated them from Egypt.

רוֹמְמוּ ה׳ אֱלֹהֵינוּ וְהִשְׁתַּחֲווּ לְהַר קָדְשׁוֹ .9 — *Exalt HASHEM, our God, and prostrate before His holy mountain.*

[This stich is a duplicate of the first stich of verse 5, except that there it says *and bow to His footstool.* For, in that verse, the Psalmist only demonstrated that God's spirit dwells in the Temple. In the succeeding verses, the Psalmist proves that the Tabernacle and the Temple are actually the sources whence holiness emanates throughout the world. The vehicles for the dissemination of this sanctity are holy men such as Moses, Aaron and Samuel, who were deeply influenced by the sacred environment of the Tabernacle. Conse-

quently, the Psalmist now describes the Tabernacle/Temple as *His Holy mountain,* i.e., the source from which His holiness emanates.]

כִּי קָדוֹשׁ ה׳ אֱלֹהֵינוּ — *For holy is HASHEM, our God.*

The place where God's holy presence dwells is awesome and holy, as *Leviticus* 19:30 teaches: וּמִקְדָּשִׁי תִּירָאוּ, *And you shall fear My Temple* [lit. *My holy place*]. When a person is awestuck by God's holy dwelling place, he will eventually learn reverence for God Himself *(Radak).*

Reverence is inspired by the realization that *HASHEM, our God, is holy* and that although the righteous men who serve Him are holy, God treats them with strict justice. When this is recognized, God's holiness will be promulgated throughout the entire world *(Rashi).*

This psalm was sung in the Temple during the service of a קָרְבָּן תּוֹדָה, Thanksgiving offering, *an offering that one would bring in thanksgiving after having survived great danger.* Abudraham rules that one should recite this thanksgiving psalm every day, while standing, as part of the Pesukei D'Zimrah section of the prayer service (see Shulchan Aruch, Orach Chaim 51). Not a day of life goes by without danger, although man is usually oblivious of the threatening forces surrounding him. Unknown to man, God protects him from such dangers and performs countless miracles of salvation. For this constant deliverance, this psalm is recited in daily thanksgiving. However, just as the Todah offering itself was not brought on Sabbaths and festivals in the Temple, the psalm commemorating it is not recited on those days.

R' Hirsch explains that this song of thanksgiving deals with the gratitude that will be due to God in the Messianic age, when the world has reached perfection. Thus psalm 100 serves as a finale to the previous psalms concerning the approach of the Messianic era.

This is the last in the series of eleven psalms composed by Moses. Ibn Yachya says that Moses dedicated this psalm to the tribe of Asher, whom he blessed with special bounty (Deuteronomy 33:24): *May Asher be blessed with children, let him be favored by his brothers and let him dip his foot in oil.* Since the tribe of Asher was blessed so abundantly, it is certainly fitting that it should attest that HASHEM is good, His kindness endures forever (verse 5).

ק
א־ה

א מִזְמוֹר לְתוֹדָה הָרִיעוּ לַיהוָה כָּל־הָאָרֶץ:

ב עִבְדוּ אֶת־יְהוָה בְּשִׂמְחָה בֹּאוּ לְפָנָיו בִּרְנָנָה:

°וְלוֹ קְ ג דְּעוּ כִּי־יְהוָה הוּא אֱלֹהִים הוּא עָשָׂנוּ °וְלֹא

ד אֲנַחְנוּ עַמּוֹ וְצֹאן מַרְעִיתוֹ: בֹּאוּ שְׁעָרָיו |
בְּתוֹדָה חֲצֵרֹתָיו בִּתְהִלָּה הוֹדוּ לוֹ בָּרְכוּ

ה שְׁמוֹ: כִּי־טוֹב יְהוָה לְעוֹלָם חַסְדּוֹ וְעַד־דֹּר
וָדֹר אֱמוּנָתוֹ:

1. מִזְמוֹר לְתוֹדָה — *A song of thanksgiving.*

[The word תּוֹדָה can be translated in three ways: *thanksgiving, admission,* and *confession.*]

This psalm is recited while the תּוֹדָה sacrifice is offered (*Rashi*).

In the future, Israel will offer thanksgiving to God for all His kindness (*Radak*). The Midrash teaches that in the Messianic era, no sacrifices except the thanksgiving will be brought (*Vayikra Rabbah* 9:7). This refers to individual offerings that, by and large, are brought in atonement for sin. In those utopian times, people will no longer be tempted to sin (*Tiferes Zion*).

At that time, the nations of the world will give תּוֹדָה of God's omnipotence. They will all recognize His sovereignty, as Isaiah 45:23 foretells: *For unto Me* [God] *every knee shall bow, every tongue shall swear* (*Midrash Shocher Tov*).

The word תּוֹדָה is also cognate with וִדּוּי, *confession,* because in the future the wicked will confess their sins and God will forgive them. How different are the ways of God from the ways of man! If a human interrogator extracts a confession of guilt from an accused man, the man is condemned and punished. If the accused remains adamantly silent, however, his case is dismissed. Conversely, the man who confesses his guilt before God is pardoned, but he who stubbornly refuses to admit to his misdeed is severely punished (*Midrash Shocher Tov*).

הָרִיעוּ לַה' כָּל הָאָרֶץ — *Call out to HASHEM, all the earth.*

[See commentary to 98:4, where this phrase is also found.] *Call out to HASHEM* with prayers and blessings. *Megalleh Amukos* (239) notes that the Psalmist placed this stich in the one hundredth psalm as an allusion to the *halachah* [law] (*Menachos* 43a) that one is obligated to *call out to Hashem* by reciting one hundred benedictions every day.[1]

2. עִבְדוּ אֶת ה' בְּשִׂמְחָה — *Serve HASHEM with gladness.*

This statement appears to contradict 2:11: עִבְדוּ אֶת ה' בְּיִרְאָה, *Serve HASHEM in awe.* *Midrash Tanchuma* (*Noach*) explains that that verse refers to the gentiles, who serve God as slaves serve their master, in constant fear of punishment. This verse, however, refers

---

1. *Arizal* points that the initial letters of these four words form הֲלָכָה, *halachah.* The *Talmud* (*Berachos* 8a) states that since the Temple was destroyed, God had no interest in the world beyond the four cubits [i.e., the domain] of the study of *halachah.* Because of this, *halachah* has a special relationship to תּוֹדָה, *thanksgiving,* for, as noted above, in the future, God will have no interest in any form of Temple sacrifice brought by individuals except for the thanksgiving sacrifice. Thus, *halachah* and the thanksgiving offering are similar in that they both command God's full attention and interest (*Maharam Paprish*). [See comm. to 98:4.]

A song of thanksgiving.
Call out to HASHEM, all the earth.
² Serve HASHEM with gladness,
come before Him with joyous song.
³ Know that HASHEM, He is God,
it is He Who made us and we are His,
His nation and the sheep of His pasture.
⁴ Enter His gates with thanksgiving,
His courts with praise,
give thanks to Him, bless His Name.
⁵ For HASHEM is good, His kindness endures forever,
and from generation to generation
is His faithfulness.

---

to Israel, God's chosen and beloved people, who serve God as sons serve their father, with joyful confidence of His love and forbearance.

Sefer Chassidim reconciles the two verses thus: If a person is excessively happy, he should sober himself and remember the day of death. But if a person is somber and sad, he should gladden his heart with words of Torah, for as 19:9 teaches, *the orders of HASHEM are upright, gladdening the heart.*

בֹּאוּ לְפָנָיו בִּרְנָנָה — *Come before Him with joyous song.*

Don't hide your feelings, but display your joy as you come into God's presence (*Ibn Ezra*).

Specifically, this describes the joyous frame of mind a person must assume when he comes before God in prayer (*Midrash Shocher Tov*).

3. דְּעוּ כִּי ה׳ הוּא אֱלֹהִים — *Know that HASHEM, He is God.*

Israel should *serve HASHEM with gladness* (v. 2) because *HASHEM is* [the trustworthy] *God* on whom Israel can rely for their just recompense. The wicked, however, have no cause for joy, because they have earned no reward in the future (*Rashi*).

הוּא עָשָׂנוּ וְלוֹ אֲנַחְנוּ — *It is He Who made us and we are His.*

In this verse we find an example of קְרִי and כְּתִיב, *kri* and *ksiv*, i.e., the *kri*, or oral pronunciation, differs from the *ksiv*, or written spelling. The written form reads: *It is He Who made us,* וְלֹא אֲנַחְנוּ, *and not us*, i.e., we did not create our own soul. However, the word וְלֹא is pronounced as if it were spelled וְלוֹ, *and unto Him*, i.e., we are His. Thus, although the spelling differs in the *kri* and the *ksiv*, the basic interpretation is the same (*Minchas Shai*). [This teaches that it was Hashem Who created mankind *and not us*, and that since we are totally dependent on Him, *we are His*, in the fullest sense.]

Our complete dependence on God stems from our recognition of His role as Creator and stands in sharp contrast to the view of the heretics who arrogantly claim as did Pharaoh (*Ezekiel* 29:3), וַאֲנִי עֲשִׂיתִנִי, *and I have made myself* (*Ibn Ezra*).

עַמּוֹ וְצֹאן מַרְעִיתוֹ — *His nation and the sheep of His pasture.*

[See commentary to 79:13 and 95:7.]

After God created us He did not abandon us; He did not put us under the control of an angel [as He did the other nations]. Rather, we are *His nation,* under His personal surveillance. Furthermore, even without our asking, God nourishes and sustains us, just as a shepherd tends *the sheep of His pasture* (*Alshich*).

4. בָּאוּ שְׁעָרָיו בְּתוֹדָה חֲצֵרֹתָיו בִּתְהִלָּה — *Enter His gates with thanksgiving, His courts with praise.*

Although here the Psalmist uses בְּתוֹדָה, *with thanksgiving* [in the singular], in 56:13 we read אֲשַׁלֵּם תּוֹדֹת לָךְ, *I shall render thanksgiving offerings* [in the plural] *to You*. *Midrash Shocher Tov* [quoted by *Radak*] explains that that verse refers to two offerings, both of which are mentioned in this verse. In the Messianic era, all forms of atonement sacrifice will become obsolete [since men will be righteous, no sacrifices will be required to atone for their sins]. The תּוֹדָה, *thanksgiving offering*, however, will be retained so that men can show appreciation to God for providing an ideal world. Similarly, prayers of petition will be discontinued; since God will fulfill all men's needs, they will no longer have to petition Him, but prayers of תְּהִלָּה, *praise*, will still be recited in recognition of God's renewed kindness. [See footnote to 56:13.]

Alshich points out that the level of appreciation will rise progressively.

When the Jews reach the outer *gates* of the Temple they will offer *thanksgiving* but when they enter into the inner *courts* they will ascend to the highest crescendo of *praise*. *Chazah Zion* notes that the initial letters of בָּאוּ שְׁעָרָיו בְּתוֹדָה חֲצֵרֹתָיו form the word בְּשֶׁבַח, *with praise*.

5. כִּי טוֹב ה׳ לְעוֹלָם חַסְדּוֹ — *For HASHEM is good, His kindness endures forever.*

These are the words of *thanksgiving* and *praise* (v. 4) with which the Jews are destined to address God (*Ibn Ezra*).

HASHEM is good, but if a person fails to recognize His goodness, he should realize that God's *kindness* is often לְעַלֵם, i.e., which can be vowelized לְעַלֵּם, *concealed* from human vision (*Chazah Zion*).

וְעַד דֹּר וָדֹר אֱמוּנָתוֹ — *And from generation to generation* [lit. *until generation and generation*] *is His faithfulness.*

God faithfully keeps His promises. If one fails to see that fulfillment, however, he should not be dismayed. Rather he should realize that God's actions are not confined to one era, but continue throughout history. Thus, God may save His kindness from one *generation to* [another] *generation* (*Chazah Zion*).

The Sages of the Talmud (Pesachim 117a) teach us that in most
instances David elevated himself to the level of Divine exultation
upon the wings of his own song. In such cases the psalm is
superscribed מִזְמוֹר לְדָוִד, A song [first, and then inspiration came] to
David.

In a few instances, however, David achieved a pitch of rapture and
ecstasy without prior preparation through song. He secluded himself
and immersed his entire being in intense meditation. Oblivious to his
surroundings, David contemplated the wonders of God as
demonstrated in history and in nature. The result of this forceful
encounter of faith was a psalm of praise introduced as לְדָוִד מִזְמוֹר, To
David — a song, for inspiration first came to David through
meditation, and the result was a song.

This psalm describes how David secluded himself (verse 2): I will
walk wholeheartedly within my home; and how he yearned for the
truth of Divine revelation: I will discern the way of wholesomeness O
when will You come to me? (Alshich)

Throughout the psalm David reiterates his hatred for evil and his
sincere love of strict justice. Thus, for him Divine kindness and
justice are one and the same. David loves God unswervingly no
matter how the Almighty treats him; therefore, he can sing at all
times, to You HASHEM will I sing praise (verse 1).

א לְדָוִד מִזְמוֹר חֶסֶד־וּמִשְׁפָּט אָשִׁירָה לְךָ יהוה
ב אֲזַמֵּרָה: אַשְׂכִּילָה ׀ בְּדֶרֶךְ תָּמִים מָתַי תָּבוֹא
ג אֵלָי אֶתְהַלֵּךְ בְּתָם־לְבָבִי בְּקֶרֶב בֵּיתִי: לֹא־
אָשִׁית ׀ לְנֶגֶד עֵינַי דְּבַר־בְּלִיָּעַל עֲשֹׂה־סֵטִים
ד שָׂנֵאתִי לֹא יִדְבַּק בִּי: לֵבָב עִקֵּשׁ יָסוּר מִמֶּנִּי
ה רָע לֹא אֵדָע: מְלוֹשְׁנִי בַסֵּתֶר ׀ רֵעֵהוּ אוֹתוֹ

°מְלָשְׁנִי ק׳ ה

1. לְדָוִד מִזְמוֹר חֶסֶד וּמִשְׁפָּט אָשִׁירָה — *Of David — a song. Of kindness and justice will I sing.*

I.e., I will sing to You, O God, under all circumstances, no matter how You treat me. If You act with kindness, I will bless You with the benediction בָּרוּךְ הַטּוֹב וְהַמֵּטִיב, *Blessed [are You] who is good and does good.* If You treat me with strict justice, I will offer the benediction בָּרוּךְ דַּיַּן הָאֱמֶת, *Blessed [are You] the truthful Judge* (Rashi; based on Berachos 54a).

לְךָ ה׳ אֲזַמֵּרָה — *To You HASHEM will I sing praise.*

I will do everything to create public recognition of Your greatness (Sforno).

2. אַשְׂכִּילָה בְּדֶרֶךְ תָּמִים מָתַי תָּבוֹא אֵלָי — *I will discern the way of wholesomeness — O when will You come to me?*

I shall dedicate myself to discern the way of wholesome service of God, and I long to be able to attain this goal of perfection (Rashi; Ibn Ezra).

[The word תָּמִים, *wholesome*, or *unblemished*, describes God, as in הָאֵל תָּמִים דַּרְכּוֹ, *The God whose way is perfect* (18:31). Man should strive to emulate God's unblemished perfection, as David said in 18:33, וַיִּתֵּן תָּמִים דַּרְכִּי, *And Who kept my way perfect.*]

The way to wholesomeness starts with the improvement of one's deeds. They should be performed with innocence and faith, and they should be motivated solely by the desire to please God. The man of perfect innocence is consistent and does not deviate from his [righteous] manner and way (Malbim).

In time, a person's external actions influence his internal thoughts and attitudes, and the Holy Spirit of the perfect God settles in his heart. Then his mind is illuminated by Divine light (R' Bachya).

Eventually, this man shuns the company of men, with their incessant quarrels and strife. He secludes himself with God, Who now reveals Himself to him frequently, because his path and God's perfect way have merged into one. Ultimately this Man can arouse the Divine Spirit as easily as the accomplished musician can draw music from his harpstrings (Ibn Ezra).

אֶתְהַלֵּךְ בְּתָם לְבָבִי בְּקֶרֶב בֵּיתִי — *[Then] I will walk wholeheartedly within my home.*

In the privacy of my home as much as in the public gaze, I will sincerely seek to walk in the ways ordained by God (Radak).

Scripture teaches that when the prophet Elisha desired to draw the Divine Spirit upon himself, he secluded himself בַּבַּיִת אַחַת הֵנָּה וְאַחַת הֵנָּה וַיֵּלֶךְ, *and he walked in the house to and fro* (II Kings 4:35), because total concentration of heart and soul can bring about an intense encounter with God (Radak).

The paragon of wholehearted innocence was our first forefather, Abraham, to whom God said, הִתְהַלֵּךְ לְפָנַי וֶהְיֵה תָמִים, *Walk before me and be perfect* (Genesis 17:1). Abraham and the other Patriarchs became a *permanent resting for God's Holy Spirit*, and God never departed from them (R' Bachya; Chazah Zion).[1]

101
1-5

Of David — a song.

Of kindness and justice will I sing,
    to You HASHEM will I sing praise.
² I will discern the way of wholesomeness —
    O when will You come to me?
Then I will walk wholeheartedly
    within my home.
³ I will not place before my eyes any wicked thing,
    wayward actions I despised;
    it shall not cling to me.
⁴ A perverted heart shall be removed from me;
    I shall not know evil.
⁵ He who slanders his neighbor in secret
    — him will I cut down;

3. לֹא אָשִׁית לְנֶגֶד עֵינַי דְּבַר בְּלִיָּעַל — *I will not place before my eyes any wicked thing.*

According to *Radak*, my eyes means my mind's eye, i.e., my thoughts and intentions.

I train my thoughts on God above, and my intentions are pure. I seek nothing from my actions except to please God and to intensify His Holy Presence (*Malbim*).

עֹשֵׂה סֵטִים שָׂנֵאתִי — *Wayward actions I despised.*

Unfortunately, many people do not follow the straight and perfect path of faith. They סֹטֶה, *deviate*, and perfect their actions with selfish motives (*Rashi; Malbim*).

לֹא יִדְבַּק בִּי — *It shall not cling to me.*

David vows: "Not only will I not *act* perversely, but I will never allow a perverse thought to cling to my mind" (*Radak; Malbim*).

4. לֵבָב עִקֵּשׁ יָסוּר מִמֶּנִּי — *A perverted heart shall be removed from me.*

I have never befriended a perverse man. I cannot tolerate his company (*Radak*). This is because such a man is devious and manipulates other people to his own advantage (*Sforno*).

רָע לֹא אֵדָע — *I shall not know evil.*

Not only do I shun the company of the wicked, but I am simply ignorant of evil: my heart has no inclination toward evil, and I cannot even conceive an evil scheme. This resembles Adam before the sin. He was totally oblivious of evil and could not even imagine it (*Malbim*).

5. מְלָשְׁנִי בַסֵּתֶר רֵעֵהוּ אוֹתוֹ אַצְמִית — *He who slanders his neighbor in secret — him will I cut down;*

David declared: "I conduct my royal affairs with complete security and confidence in God, but godless monarchs are filled with anxiety and fear. To protect themselves they play

1. See *Rambam's Guide for the Perplexed*, Part III, chapter 51: The Patriarchs achieved the supreme degree of perfection ... their minds were so identified with the knowledge of God that He made a lasting covenant with each of them ... they had their minds filled exclusively with the Name of God, that is, with His knowledge and love ... even when they were at work, their hearts remained focused on the Name of God ... and they enjoyed the continual presence of God.

[The Patriarchs are described as יְשָׁרִים, upright (see *Avodah Zarah* 25a). In the commentary

אֲצָמִית גְּבַהּ־עֵינַיִם וּרְחַב לֵבָב אֹתוֹ לֹא

אוּכָל: עֵינַי | בְּנֶאֶמְנֵי־אֶרֶץ לָשֶׁבֶת עִמָּדִי הֹלֵךְ

בְּדֶרֶךְ תָּמִים הוּא יְשָׁרְתֵנִי: לֹא־יֵשֵׁב | בְּקֶרֶב

בֵּיתִי עֹשֵׂה רְמִיָּה דֹּבֵר שְׁקָרִים לֹא־יִכּוֹן

לְנֶגֶד עֵינָי: לַבְּקָרִים אַצְמִית כָּל־רִשְׁעֵי־אֶרֶץ

לְהַכְרִית מֵעִיר־יְהֹוָה כָּל־פֹּעֲלֵי אָוֶן:

one favorite against another. They encourage espionage and intrigue in their courts. Such kings welcome the slanderous tales which one courtier spreads about another and they eagerly seize upon the gossip and hearsay their spies bring them.

"I despise this!" says David. "I accept only the testimony of two reliable witnesses who appear publicly before the courts. Anyone who confides slanderous tales to me arouses my wrath and is swiftly punished" (Radak; see Pesachim 113a).

גְּבַהּ עֵינַיִם וּרְחַב לֵבָב אֹתוֹ לֹא אוּכָל — One with haughty [lit. high] eyes and an expansive [lit. wide] heart — him I cannot bear.

As Solomon said (Proverbs 21:4), רוּם עֵינַיִם וּרְחַב לֵב רִשְׁעִים חַטָּאת, A haughty look and an expansive heart are the sinful growth of the wicked. This describes the man whose lusts are boundless. He sets his sights on every type of pleasure and nothing is beyond his reach [for his eyes are high]. Furthermore, his heart is wide, i.e., his lust has no limits. There is room in his heart for every type of desire. This voluptuous man is so despicable that

God Himself cannot tolerate him (Radak).

From this verse, the Sages learned that when God sees an arrogant man He says: "He and I cannot exist together in the same world" (Sotah 5a).

6. עֵינַי בְּנֶאֶמְנֵי אֶרֶץ לָשֶׁבֶת עִמָּדִי — My eyes are upon the faithful of the land, that they may dwell with me.

I detest the wicked and expel them from my home and from my company. But I yearn for the companionship of the righteous so that I may observe and follow their fine example (Rashi).

What are the qualities of the faithful of the land? They keep the secrets entrusted to them and they return lost objects and articles which had been left with them for safekeeping (Derech Eretz Rabbah, chapter 2).

הֹלֵךְ בְּדֶרֶךְ תָּמִים הוּא יְשָׁרְתֵנִי — He who walks the way of wholesomeness — he shall serve me.

I will employ no ignorant man to serve me [for he may err and cause me to do something improper (see Berachos 52b)] (Sforno).

7. לֹא יֵשֵׁב בְּקֶרֶב בֵּיתִי עֹשֵׂה רְמִיָּה — In my house shall not dwell a worker of deceit.

to 97:11 it is explained that the upright excel not only in their relationship with God, but are also exemplary in their concern for their fellow men. Nevertheless, the Psalmist teaches us here that the ideal יָשָׁר maintains a state of rigid mental discipline in which his thoughts remain aloof from mundane concerns. Even when he is involved with other people and deeply enmeshed in their concerns, he concentrates primarily on divine thoughts and views himself as standing in the Presence of God.]

101
6-8

one with haughty eyes and an expansive heart —
    him I cannot bear.
⁶ My eyes are upon the faithful of the land,
    that they may dwell with me,
he who walks the way of wholesomeness —
    he shall serve me.
⁷ In my house shall not dwell a worker of deceit,
    one who tells lies;
    he shall not remain steadfast before my eyes.
⁸ Every morning I will cut down
    all the wicked of the land,
    to excise from the City of HASHEM all evildoers.

I will not appoint a deceitful man to any position in my royal household (*Radak*).

The deceitful will also be denied admission to the *Beis HaMikdash* (*Targum*).

דְּבֵר שְׁקָרִים לֹא יִכּוֹן לְנֶגֶד עֵינָי ... — *one who tells lies; he shall not remain steadfast* [lit. *be established*] *before my eyes.*

All men are destined to stand in God's presence in the World to Come, except for four groups of immoral men who will not enjoy this privilege. One of these groups consists of those who tell lies (*Sotah* 42a).

8. לַבְּקָרִים אַצְמִית כָּל רִשְׁעֵי אָרֶץ — *Every morning* [lit. *at the mornings*] *I will cut down all the wicked of the land.*

According to *Rashi* and *Radak*, this refers to this world, where King David waged war against evil. David says: "Little by little, day by day, *I will cut down all the wicked men of Israel*, who

deserve the death penalty."

Targum maintains that this refers to the World to Come, which is likened to a new *morning* which will dawn for all mankind.

לְהַכְרִית מֵעִיר ה' כָּל פֹּעֲלֵי אָוֶן — *To excise from the City of HASHEM all evildoers.*

David vows: "I will not tolerate a wicked man in any part of my realm, but especially not in the Holy City of Jerusalem" (*Radak*). The evildoers have a choice: they can either repent or be expelled from the holy environs (*Sforno*).

[This psalm, in effect, represents the royal charter upon which David established his sovereign state. The monarchy of David was one of justice and truth; it tolerated no abuse of power or privilege. Lawlessness and tyranny were banished from this realm for they were a gross contradiction to David's lofty standards, as he proclaimed (v. 6), *My eyes are upon the faithful of the land, that they may dwell with me.*]

David composed this psalm to express the feelings of the poor man enveloped in misery. In a deeper sense these verses describe the tragic state of Israel in exile, impoverished and downtrodden. The nation is poor both financially and spiritually (Radak; Ibn Ezra; Maharam Armaah).

Another aspect of Israel's poverty in exile is the poor response which their prayers receive from heaven. In better days God responded generously and in abundance, but now the blessings are meager and few (the Maggid of Koznitz). Similarly we lament (Lamentations 3:8): Though I would cry out and plead, He shut out my prayer. Rav Eliezer said: From the day the Temple was destroyed, the gates of prayer have been locked tight (Berachos 32b; Alshich).

However, this psalm ends with a prophecy of hope and redemption. Prosperity will return to Israel when they return to their permanent homeland to serve God eternally. Your servants' children shall be settled, and their children will be steadfast before You (v. 29).

א תְּפִלָּה לְעָנִי כִי־יַעֲטֹף וְלִפְנֵי יהוה יִשְׁפֹּךְ
ב שִׂיחוֹ: יהוה שִׁמְעָה תְפִלָּתִי וְשַׁוְעָתִי אֵלֶיךָ
ג תָבוֹא: אַל־תַּסְתֵּר פָּנֶיךָ | מִמֶּנִּי בְּיוֹם צַר לִי
ד הַטֵּה־אֵלַי אָזְנֶךָ בְּיוֹם אֶקְרָא מַהֵר עֲנֵנִי: כִּי־
כָלוּ בְעָשָׁן יָמָי וְעַצְמוֹתַי כְּמוֹ־קֵד נִחָרוּ:
ה הוּכָּה כָעֵשֶׂב וַיִּבַשׁ לִבִּי כִּי־שָׁכַחְתִּי מֵאֲכֹל

1. תְּפִלָּה לְעָנִי כִי יַעֲטֹף — *A prayer of the afflicted man when he swoons.*

The term עָטֹף is used to describe the person who has been weakened by suffering as in *Lamentations* 2:19: הָעֲטוּפִים בְּרָעָב, *those who swoon from hunger* (Ibn Ezra).

Literally עָטֹף means to *fold over* or *envelop*. The word provides a vivid description of the starving man who is bent over in pain (*Radak*).

Also עָטֹף means to be *cloaked* in a cape or a prayer shawl. The afflicted man is ashamed of his misery; he struggles to hide his shameful condition. Only when shrouded in the privacy of his prayer shawl does he *pour forth his supplication before HASHEM* (*Tehillos Hashem*).

Shevet Mussar explains that poverty is the most shameful and devastating affliction which plagues man because it is a contradiction and negation of the very purpose of man's creation.

The soul of every man has its origin in heaven, where it basks in Divine light and glory. But the soul did not earn this glory, and this unearned glory causes the soul shame. The soul is placed in a body and challenged by all the hardships of the mundane world so that it may succeed in earning its glory. If, in this world, a man is afflicted with poverty and is forced to beg for money he did not earn, then his descent to earth appears to be in vain for he continues to exist in shame.

The term עָנִי, *afflicted* or *poor*, describes both Israel in exile and David, the author of this psalm. *Midrash Shocher Tov* points to an apparent

contradiction: sometimes David refers to himself as a wealthy king and at other times he describes himself as a miserable pauper.

The *Midrash* explains that when David foresaw the illustrious and righteous kings who were destined to descend from him (such as Assa, Yehoshafat, Hezekiah, and Josiah), he considered himself to be a wealthy king; when David envisioned the wicked rulers who were to emanate from his family (such as Achaz, Menashe and Ammon), he deemed himself destitute.

וְלִפְנֵי ה' יִשְׁפֹּךְ שִׂיחוֹ — *And pours forth his supplication before HASHEM.*

The term שִׂיחַ describes a special form of prayer. *Malbim* (to *Genesis* 24:63, following *Abarbanel*) notes that שִׂיחַ literally means *speech*. It is used in the sense of words that flow in one's mind as he meditates, and also the flow of words as he prays.

HaKsav V'haKabbalah, however, comments that the term derives from שׁוּחַ, or as it is often spelled, סָח, which refers to *movement*. The word designates an act of removal as in מֵשִׁיחַ דַּעַת, *to remove one's attention,* from the task at hand. Thus, שִׂיחַ is prayer which relieves man from preoccupation with something else. The word is certainly most appropriate for the poor man whose prayer takes his mind off his financial problems. [See *ArtScroll Genesis* 24:63.]

2. ה' שִׁמְעָה תְפִלָּתִי — *HASHEM, hear my prayer.*

Please overlook the fact that my prayer is not properly organized or

A prayer of the afflicted man when he swoons,
and pours forth his supplication before HASHEM:

² HASHEM, hear my prayer,
and let my cry reach You!

³ Hide not Your face from me,
on the day of my distress incline Your ear to me;
on the day that I call answer me speedily.

⁴ For my days are consumed in smoke,
and my bones are shriveled as a hearth.

⁵ Smitten like grass and withered is my heart,
for I have forgotten to eat my food.

---

expressed. I am so overwhelmed by my affliction that I have no opportunity to prepare my prayers properly (Ibn Yachya).

וְשַׁוְעָתִי אֵלֶיךָ תָבוֹא — And let my cry reach You.

This request is especially necessary for those in exile who feel that no matter how much they pray, their prayer receives no response, because since the day the Temple was destroyed the heavenly gates of prayer have been locked tight (Berachos 32b; Alshich).

3. אַל תַּסְתֵּר פָּנֶיךָ מִמֶּנִּי בְּיוֹם צַר לִי הַטֵּה אֵלַי אָזְנֶךָ — Hide not Your face from me, on the day of my distress incline Your ear to me.

There are some days when the distress of poverty and exile is so crushing that those who suffer are on the verge of defying God and denying His providence and supervision. The miserable man asks that on those days God should reveal His presence to him and shed a ray of hope upon his broken heart.

The poor man does not necessarily ask God to release him from his poverty. He is willing to suffer and endure if only he would know that God listens to his cries and cares about his situation. This Divine concern is in itself an answer to his hardship (Alshich).

4. כִּי כָלוּ בְעָשָׁן יָמָי — For my days are consumed in smoke.

My poverty prevents me from accomplishing anything worthwhile. I waste my days in an endless search for sustenance. It is as if my days are consumed and lost, vanished like a disappearing puff of smoke (Radak; Maharam Arma'ah).

וְעַצְמוֹתַי כְּמוֹקֵד נִחָרוּ — And my bones are shriveled as a hearth.

[My sorrow is intensified by a constant feeling of burning frustration. This destroys my bones, i.e., the very essence of my being.]

5. הוּכָּה כָעֵשֶׂב וַיִּבַשׁ לִבִּי — Smitten like grass and withered is my heart.

The heart is the source of human vitality and strength. Frustration and poverty have sapped my heart of its strength, and this vital organ has withered like grass which dries up in the face of the blazing sun, as if the sun struck it down (Radak).

The severity of my condition has also stunted my intellectual development (Alshich).

כִּי שָׁכַחְתִּי מֵאֲכֹל לַחְמִי — For I have forgotten to eat my food [lit. bread].

[I have become so accustomed to accepting alms and charity, the bread of shame, that I have forgotten the delightful taste of hard earned bread, i.e., the fruit of my own labor.]

ו לַחְמִי: מִקּוֹל אַנְחָתִי דָּבְקָה עַצְמִי לִבְשָׂרִי:

ז דָּמִיתִי לִקְאַת מִדְבָּר הָיִיתִי כְּכוֹס חֳרָבוֹת:

ח-ט שָׁקַדְתִּי וָאֶהְיֶה כְּצִפּוֹר בּוֹדֵד עַל־גָּג: כָּל־

הַיּוֹם חֵרְפוּנִי אוֹיְבָי מְהוֹלָלַי בִּי נִשְׁבָּעוּ: כִּי־

אֵפֶר כַּלֶּחֶם אָכָלְתִּי וְשִׁקֻּוַי בִּבְכִי מָסָכְתִּי:

יא מִפְּנֵי־זַעַמְךָ וְקִצְפֶּךָ כִּי נְשָׂאתַנִי וַתַּשְׁלִיכֵנִי:

יב-יג יָמַי כְּצֵל נָטוּי וַאֲנִי כָּעֵשֶׂב אִיבָשׁ: וְאַתָּה

I am so preoccupied with my sorrow that I have completely lost my appetite (Radak).

6. מִקּוֹל אַנְחָתִי דָּבְקָה עַצְמִי לִבְשָׂרִי — *From the sound of my sigh my bone clung to my flesh.*

Radak notes that sighing and groaning take their toll on the human body and weaken it to the point where healthy muscles and fat are consumed and the shriveled skin clings to the bones. The people of Israel suffered in a similar fashion at the time of the Temple's destruction as we read (*Lamentations* 4:8), *Their skin has shriveled on their bones, it became dry as wood.*

7. דָּמִיתִי לִקְאַת מִדְבָּר — *I am like a ke'as of the wilderness.*

Radak identifies the *ke'as* as the bird known as קיק [*kik*], mentioned in the *Mishnah* (*Shabbos* 2:1) [however, *Rav ibid.*) translates קיק as *cotton*]. This undomesticated bird lives in the wilderness and it issues a sighing sound. The cries of Israel in exile resemble this mournful sighing.

הָיִיתִי כְּכוֹס חֳרָבוֹת — *I have become like the cos of the wasteland.*

This bird is mentioned in *Leviticus* 11:17 among the unclean fowl (*Ibn Ezra*) [and many identify it as the owl].

In exile, the devastated nation of Israel resembles this bird *in the wasteland* (*Radak*). Just as the *cos* stays away from habitated areas, exiled Israel was ostracized by the gentiles and kept

away from their places of habitation (*Maharam Arma'ah*).

8. שָׁקַדְתִּי וָאֶהְיֶה — *I persevere.*

The long exile resembles a dark night when a vigilant watchman must stand guard. Similarly the only reason that I, Israel, survived the *galus* is because *I persevered* and took pains to preserve my faith and my identity (*Radak*).

כְּצִפּוֹר בּוֹדֵד עַל גָּג — *Like a lonely bird upon a rooftop.*

Birds normally fly in flocks but in exile I resemble an estranged and rejected bird which always flies alone. When this bird alights upon the roof of a comfortable home, it yearns to enter the home but dares not lest it be captured and killed. Similarly, Israel in exile yearns to find a permanent home but dares not get too close to the gentiles lest they react adversely and punish Israel (*Radak*).

9. כָּל הַיּוֹם חֵרְפוּנִי אוֹיְבָי — *All day long my enemies revile me.*

[They search for any excuse to insult me.]

מְהוֹלָלַי בִּי נִשְׁבָּעוּ — *Those who ridicule me swear by me.*

My enemies make fun of me (*Rashi*), and when they wish to swear in vain they swear by my life, i.e., by the life of a Jew. Furthermore, all of the nations take up an oath to ally themselves against me, Israel (*Rav Vidal HaTzorfati*).

10. כִּי אֵפֶר כַּלֶּחֶם אָכָלְתִּי — *For I have*

⁶ From the sound of my sigh
　　my bone clung to my flesh.
⁷ I am like a ke'as of the wilderness,
　　I have become like the cos of the wasteland.
⁸ I persevere but I remain,
　　like a lonely bird upon a rooftop.
⁹ All day long my enemies revile me;
　　those who ridicule me swear by me.
¹⁰ For I have eaten ashes like bread,
　　and mixed my drink with tears.
¹¹ Because of Your anger and Your wrath —
　　for You have raised me high
　　and hurled me down.
¹² My days are like a lengthening shadow,
　　and I am withered like grass.

---

eaten ashes like bread.

We read (Lamentations 3:16), *He ground my teeth on gravel, He made me cower in ashes.* Rashi (there) explains that because the exiles had to knead their dough in pits dug into the ground, their bread was mixed with grit.

Radak observes that misery dulls the sense of taste to the point where everything tastes like ashes. Moreover, the bitter man turns pessimistic and paints everything black. To him, even the whitest bread appears to be black as ashes and coals (*Rav Vidal HaTzorfati*).

וְשִׁקֻּוַי בִּבְכִי מָסָכְתִּי — *And mixed my drink with tears* [lit. *with weeping*].

I relentlessly shed tears in such abundance that everything I drank was diluted with my tears. The word שִׁקֻּוַי is cognate with מַשְׁקֶה, *drink* (*Radak*).

11. מִפְּנֵי זַעַמְךָ וְקִצְפֶּךָ — *Because of Your anger and Your wrath.*

If not for *Your anger and wrath, I would not have been thrust into the* terrible experience of exile (*Radak*), for these words imply an anger that expresses itself in a curse and punishment (*Malbim*).

כִּי נְשָׂאתַנִי וַתַּשְׁלִיכֵנִי — *For You have raised me high and hurled me down.*

In order to throw something down with great force, one must first lift it up high. No nation ever fell as Israel did, because God first raised His people to the greatest heights of sanctity before casting them down, as we read (*Lamentations* 2:1), הִשְׁלִיךְ מִשָּׁמַיִם אֶרֶץ תִּפְאֶרֶת יִשְׂרָאֵל, *He cast down from heaven to earth the glory of Israel* (*Radak; Maharash Uzida*).

12. יָמַי כְּצֵל נָטוּי — *My days are like a lengthening shadow.*

As daylight fades away and dusk approaches, the shadows become longer and longer until everything is engulfed in darkness (*Rashi*). Similarly, Israel is enveloped in the dark tragedy of exile (*Radak*).

At first Israel imagined the continuation of the exile would bring some improvement in their status. Only later did they realize that the longer the exile, the closer they came to complete darkness and despair (*Alshich*).

וַאֲנִי כָּעֵשֶׂב אִיבָשׁ — *And I am withered like grass.*

יד יהוה לְעוֹלָם תֵּשֵׁב וְזִכְרְךָ לְדֹר וָדֹר: אַתָּה
תָקוּם תְּרַחֵם צִיּוֹן כִּי־עֵת לְחֶנְנָהּ כִּי־בָא
טו מוֹעֵד: כִּי־רָצוּ עֲבָדֶיךָ אֶת־אֲבָנֶיהָ וְאֶת־
טז עֲפָרָהּ יְחֹנֵנוּ: וְיִירְאוּ גוֹיִם אֶת־שֵׁם יהוה
יז וְכָל־מַלְכֵי הָאָרֶץ אֶת־כְּבוֹדֶךָ: כִּי־בָנָה יהוה

Even before I am engulfed in darkness I suffer. My vitality is sapped like the grass which withers in the sun (Radak; see comm., v. 5).[1]

13. וְאַתָּה ה' לְעוֹלָם תֵּשֵׁב — *But You, HASHEM, will be enthroned* [lit. *will sit*] *forever.*

Every captive of the long exile laments the fact that his days are so short and the chances of his living to see the redemption are very slim. Nevertheless, the exiles console themselves with the understanding that some day God will bring the redemption for their descendants because God endures forever (Radak).

Furthermore, God's special consideration for Israel will never change for He is *enthroned forever* in His position of love for the Jews (Ibn Ezra).

וְזִכְרְךָ לְדֹר וָדֹר — *And Your memory endures for all generations.*

The Jewish people will never forget God. In every generation they remem-ber to pray to God to bring about the redemption (Radak).

14. אַתָּה תָקוּם תְּרַחֵם צִיּוֹן — *You will arise and show Zion mercy.*

Although You will be [seated and] enthroned forever (v. 13), You will arise to do battle with the enemy for the sake of Zion (Ibn Ezra).

Despite Zion's status as a desolate ruin for many years, we are confident that You have not abandoned this holy site and *You will show Zion mercy* (Radak).[2]

כִּי עֵת לְחֶנְנָהּ כִּי בָא מוֹעֵד — *For it will be the time to favor her, for the appointed time will have come.*

There is a definite, predestined time when the redemption must come about. We do not know the precise time, but it is certain that when that time does come You will surely bring about the redemption (Radak).

15. כִּי רָצוּ עֲבָדֶיךָ אֶת אֲבָנֶיהָ — *For Your servants had cherished her stones.*

1. *Rabbeinu Yonah (The Gates of Repentance)* bemoans the blindness of the people who are completely oblivious to their ultimate fate. After a person reaches the second half of his life he begins to deteriorate. God fashioned the human body in this way so that man could have ample warning of his end. This warning is meant to provide a person with an opportunity to repent and mend his ways. Thus, in the second half of life, as man sinks towards the darkness of death, his eyesight begins to fade [*like a lengthened shadow*] and his hair dries and falls out [*like withered grass*]. God sends warnings, but man is foolish and pays them no heed. Man rushes towards his final hour unpenitent and unprepared.

2. The Talmud (*Menachos* 87a) states that even after the destruction of Zion, God guarded this sacred site by posting guardian angels around it, as the prophet (*Isaiah* 62:6) says: *Upon Your walls, O Jerusalem, I posted sentries all day and all night; they will never be silent; all those who remember HASHEM be not still!*

What do these angels say as they stand guard? Rava bar R' Shila says: They recite the verse, *You will arise and show Zion mercy.*

R' Nachman says: They recite the verse, *The builder of Jerusalem is HASHEM* (147:2).

What did the angels say before the destruction? Rava bar R' Shila says: They recited the verse, *For HASHEM has chosen Zion, it He desired for His dwelling place* (132:13) [and in the future, when the Temple is rebuilt, they will recite that verse once again (Rashi)].

13 But You, HASHEM, will be enthroned forever,
    and Your memory endures for all generations.
14 You will arise and show Zion mercy,
    for it will be the time to favor her,
    for the appointed time will have come.
15 For Your servants had cherished her stones,
    and been gracious to her dust.
16 Then the nations will fear the Name of HASHEM,
    and all the kings of the earth, Your glory.
17 For HASHEM will have built Zion,

The exiles pine for the opportunity to return to the Land of Israel and to kiss her very stones (Radak). Even if they are successful and prosperous in exile and live in splendid palaces, they prefer to return to the ruins and rubble of Jerusalem, where the very stones are sacred (Ibn Yachya).

Rashi cites the Midrash which relates that when the Babylonian king Nebuchadnezzar exiled Yehoyachin, the king of Judah [along with ten thousand outstanding Torah scholars], the exiles carried the stones and dust of Jerusalem with them so that they could use these materials to build a synagogue in Babylon. [The Talmud (Megillah 29a) describes this synagogue, which was located in the city of Nehardea, as the synagogue which was שָׁף וְיָתִיב, relocated and rebuilt. The holy spirit of God resided in that synagogue (see Rashi ibid.).][1]

וְאֶת עֲפָרָה יְחֹנֵנוּ — And been gracious to her dust.

The Talmud (Kesubos 112a) describes the amazing love which the Rabbis showed the Land of Israel: Rabbi Abba would kiss the rocks of Acre to show his affection. Rabbi Chanina would smooth any obstacles on the roadways of Israel. [He repaired anything which was not in order so that no one would have an excuse to complain about the highways of his beloved land (Rashi).]

Rabbi Ami and Rabbi Assi took great pains to assure their comfort in Eretz Yisrael so that they would never be tempted to complain about its climate and living conditions.

In the summer, they made sure not to be too hot. When the sun started to beat down on the place where they were learning they quickly ran to the comfortable shade. In the winter they got up from the cold shadows to sit and learn in the warm sun.

Rav Chiya bar Gamda would roll around in the dust of Eretz Yisrael to fulfill the dictate of this verse, For Your servants had cherished her stones, and been gracious to her dust.

16. וְיִרְאוּ גּוֹיִם אֶת שֵׁם ה׳ — Then the nations will fear the Name of HASHEM.

When they see the wonders of the future redemption (Rashi).

וְכָל מַלְכֵי הָאָרֶץ אֶת כְּבוֹדֶךָ — And all the kings of the earth, Your glory.

[When your glory will be revealed in full, all kings will stand in awe of it.]

17. כִּי בָנָה ה׳ צִיּוֹן — For HASHEM will have built Zion.

---

1. [When Sir Moses Montefiore made his first trip to Eretz Yisrael, he brought back a stone which he used as a pillow for his head in order to fulfill the words of this verse, For Your servants had cherished her stones.]

יח צִיּוֹן נִרְאָה בִכְבוֹדוֹ: פָּנָה אֶל-תְּפִלַּת הָעַרְעָר
יט וְלֹא-בָזָה אֶת-תְּפִלָּתָם: תִּכָּתֶב זֹאת לְדוֹר
כ אַחֲרוֹן וְעַם נִבְרָא יְהַלֶּל-יָהּ: כִּי-הִשְׁקִיף
מִמְּרוֹם קָדְשׁוֹ יהוה מִשָּׁמַיִם | אֶל-אֶרֶץ
כא הִבִּיט: לִשְׁמֹעַ אֶנְקַת אָסִיר לְפַתֵּחַ בְּנֵי
כב תְמוּתָה: לְסַפֵּר בְּצִיּוֹן שֵׁם יהוה וּתְהִלָּתוֹ

[The high point of the redemption drama will come about when Jerusalem is rebuilt.]

נִרְאָה בִכְבוֹדוֹ — *He will have appeared in His glory.*

[Only then will God's full glory be evident.]

18. פָּנָה אֶל תְּפִלַּת הָעַרְעָר — *He turned to the prayer of the devastated one.*

Rashi translates עַרְעָר as the *devastated one* based on 137:7, which relates that when the Edomites [Romans] destroyed the Temple and razed it to its very foundations, their battle cry was עָרוּ עָרוּ, *destroy, destroy* [see *Ibn Ezra*]. Alternatively, *Rashi* defines עַרְעָר as the *shout of protest.*

Radak and *Ibn Ezra* identify the עַרְעָר as a solitary tree which grows in the abandoned wilderness. [Thus עַרְעָר is cognate with עֲרִירִי, *childless* or *barren.* This lonely tree bears no fruit and no seeds so no other tree of its kind will grow in its vicinity.]

Midrash Shocher Tov says that the *prayer of the lonely* describes the supplications of the isolated exiles, who have no king and no prophet, no High Priest and no holy breastplate (אורים ותומים). The only sacred power left to the exile is the prayer which he offers to God.

וְלֹא בָזָה אֶת תְּפִלָּתָם — *And has not despised their prayer.*

Zohar (Vayechi) notes that this verse begins in the singular form, i.e., *the* [one] *prayer of the devastated 'one,'* and concludes in the plural, i.e., 'their' *prayer.* *Zohar* explains that when a man

prays by himself God rivets His scrutiny on the supplicant and his failings come to light. Indeed, God does not ignore or reject the prayer of the wretched individual; He does turn to it [פָּנָה] but after consideration and analysis of merit God may very well decide not to accept it.

However, whenever a group of Jews gathers to pray, God always views them favorably. He never despises their prayer.

Chazah Zion explains that whenever God observes a group of Jews, He identifies them with their glorious ancestry and in the merit of their forefathers they always curry Divine favor. Indeed, the initial letters of the phrase וְלֹא בָזָה אֶת תְּפִלָּתָם form the word אָבוֹת, *Patriarchs.*

19. תִּכָּתֶב זֹאת לְדוֹר אַחֲרוֹן — *Let this be recorded* [lit. *written*] *for the last generation.*

[Not only are the prayers of the exiles not despised (v. 18) and rejected, but they will be invested with historic significance to the point where every word is recorded for posterity. These passionate pleas will serve as an inspiration to all successive generations of Jews (see *Targum*).]

In addition, the triumphs and salvations which God brings to the Jews in exile will be recorded forever (*Rashi; Radak*).

וְעַם נִבְרָא יְהַלֶּל יָהּ — *So the newborn* [lit. *created*] *nation will praise God.*

In exile, the Jewish nation is considered as dead both politically and

102

He will have appeared in His glory.

18-22
¹⁸ He turned to the prayer of the devastated one
and has not despised their prayer.

¹⁹ Let this be recorded for the last generation,
so the newborn nation will praise God.

²⁰ For He gazed from His exalted Sanctuary;
from heaven to earth, HASHEM peered.

²¹ To hear the groaning of the prisoner,
to liberate those doomed to die.

²² To declare in Zion the Name of HASHEM,
and His praise in Jerusalem.

---

spiritually. In the *last generation* of Jewish history the downtrodden nation will experience political liberation and revival coupled with spiritual awakening and rebirth. A wave of repentance will sweep over Israel, and the penitents will be reborn. They will rededicate their lives to spreading the praises of God throughout the world (*Midrash Shocher Tov*).

20. כִּי הִשְׁקִיף מִמְּרוֹם קָדְשׁוֹ — *For He gazed from His exalted Sanctuary.*

The word הִשְׁקִיף, *gazed*, is used whenever God scrutinizes someone in order to ferret out his faults (see *Shemos Rabbah* 41:1). God *gazed* upon the wicked nations so that they may be condemned for their crime of destroying the Temple (*Ibn Yachya*).

ה' מִשָּׁמַיִם אֶל אֶרֶץ הִבִּיט — *From heaven to earth, HASHEM peered.*

At the same time, God looked down to earth benignly to sympathize with the plight of the Jewish people (*Rashi; Ibn Yachya*).

(See footnote to *Haamek Davar, Deuteronomy* 26:16.)

21. לִשְׁמֹעַ אֶנְקַת אָסִיר — *To hear the groaning of the prisoner.*

From heaven to earth HASHEM *peered* (v. 20) in order *to hear* and truly understand *the groaning of the prisoner,* i.e., the Jews who languish in captivity (*Ibn Yachya*).

לְפַתֵּחַ בְּנֵי תְמוּתָה — *To liberate* [lit. *to unshackle*] *those doomed to die.*

[As long as the Jews are in exile, they are at the mercy of their captors, who can murder them at any time.]

22. לְסַפֵּר בְּצִיּוֹן שֵׁם ה' — *To declare in Zion the Name of HASHEM.*

[God will liberate the condemned Jews of verse 21 so that they will have a new opportunity to live and publicize His greatness in Zion.]

Zohar (*Acharei Mos*) says that this refers to the study of Torah, which is both סְתִים וְגַלְיָא, *revealed and concealed.*

Apparently the Torah is nothing more than a series of laws and historic narratives which God *revealed* (גַלְיָא) to man. However, there is also a *concealed* (סְתִים) dimension. The letter formations which now appear as simple words in the Torah may be rearranged to form God's ineffable and holy Name. The secret of this rearrangement of the letters of the Torah will be revealed in the future, when Israel will *declare in Zion the Name of HASHEM* [see Introduction of *Ramban* on Torah].

וּתְהִלָּתוֹ בִּירוּשָׁלָיִם — *And His praise in Jerusalem.*

No one can fully praise God in this world while His Name and His accomplishments are concealed. Full praise must await the future revelation which will take place in the Holy Temple in Jerusalem (*Zohar, Acharei Mos*).

[1233] *Tehillim*

כג בִּירוּשָׁלָ͏ִם: בְּהִקָּבֵץ עַמִּים יַחְדָּו וּמַמְלָכוֹת

כד לַעֲבֹד אֶת־יְהוָה: עִנָּה בַדֶּרֶךְ °כֹּחוֹ קִצַּר יָמָי:

כה אֹמַר אֵלִי אַל־תַּעֲלֵנִי בַּחֲצִי יָמָי בְּדוֹר דּוֹרִים

כו שְׁנוֹתֶיךָ: לְפָנִים הָאָרֶץ יָסַדְתָּ וּמַעֲשֵׂה יָדֶיךָ

כז שָׁמָיִם: הֵמָּה | יֹאבֵדוּ וְאַתָּה תַעֲמֹד וְכֻלָּם

כַּבֶּגֶד יִבְלוּ כַּלְּבוּשׁ תַּחֲלִיפֵם וְיַחֲלֹפוּ:

כח-כט וְאַתָּה־הוּא וּשְׁנוֹתֶיךָ לֹא יִתָּמּוּ: בְּנֵי־עֲבָדֶיךָ

יִשְׁכּוֹנוּ וְזַרְעָם לְפָנֶיךָ יִכּוֹן:

---

23. בְּהִקָּבֵץ עַמִּים יַחְדָּו — *When nations gather together.*

[In the future the prophecy of *Isaiah* (56:7) concerning the nations will be fulfilled: *I will bring them to My holy mountain and gladden them in My House of Prayer ... for My House shall be called a House of Prayer for all nations.*]

וּמַמְלָכוֹת לַעֲבֹד אֶת ה' — *And kingdoms, to serve HASHEM.*

[Kings will no longer demand that their subjects serve them; rather they will insist that all of their people serve God.]

24. עִנָּה בַדֶּרֶךְ כֹּחִי — *He afflicted my strength on the way.*

Earlier (v. 12) the Psalmist recorded the complaints of Israel in exile and concluded with the lament, *My days are like a lengthening shadow, and I am withered like grass.* Then he began an inspired reverie in which he vividly described the glory of the future redemption (vs. 13-23). Now the Psalmist returns to Israel's woeful complaint. "I am so far removed from the Holy Land; the distance is so great! Even if the arrival of Messiah should be announced at this very moment I fear that my strength will give out before I reach Jerusalem because the journey is an arduous one" (Ibn Ezra).

קִצַּר יָמָי — *He shortened my days.*

Throughout the period of exile, incessant travel sapped my energy. Persecution and economic deprivation forced me to be constantly on the move in search of a safe haven of peace and prosperity. This endless exertion *shortened my days* (Radak) [as the *Talmud* (*Gittin* 70a) says: Three things sap a person's strength: fear, travel and sin].

25. אֹמַר אֵלִי אַל־תַּעֲלֵנִי בַּחֲצִי יָמָי — *I say, "O my God, do not remove me* [lit. *raise me*] *in the midst* [lit. *in the half*] *of my days."*

Throughout the duration of the exile, the people of Israel say; "O God, do not permit the enemy to annihilate us in the middle of our historic experience," for the history of Israel is inextricably bound up with God Himself, and of God it says, "You remain the same and Your years are endless" (Rashi).

בְּדוֹר דּוֹרִים שְׁנוֹתֶיךָ — *Your years endure through all generations* [lit. *for generation of generations*].

God promised that Israel would always serve Him. Since He exists forever, how can He bring Israel's history to an end? (Rashi).

[At the dawn of history, God displayed before Adam דּוֹר דּוֹר וְדֹרְשָׁיו, דּוֹר דּוֹר וַחֲכָמָיו, *each generation and its preachers, each generation and its scholars* (*Avos d'R' Nassan* chapter 31). If Israel were to be cut off in the middle of its history, these generations would

---

תהלים [1234]

²³ *When nations gather together,*
and kingdoms, to serve HASHEM.
²⁴ *He afflicted my strength on the way;*
He shortened my days.
²⁵ *I say, "O my God, do not remove me*
in the midst of my days —
Your years endure through all generations."
²⁶ *Previously, You laid the earth's foundation,*
and the heavens are Your handiwork.
²⁷ *They will perish but You will endure;*
all of them will wear out like a garment;
You will exchange them like a cloak
and they will pass on.
²⁸ *But You remain the same,*
and Your years are endless,
²⁹ *Your servants' children shall be settled,*
and their children will be steadfast before You.

never come into being.][1]

26. לְפָנִים הָאָרֶץ יָסַדְתָּ — *Previously, You laid the earth's foundation.*

After stating that God is eternal and that His existence has no end [*Your years endure through all generations*], the Psalmist declares that the eternal God also had no beginning because His existence was לְפָנִים, previous to, הָאָרֶץ, the earth [i.e., He is not limited to the confines of time and space] (Radak).

וּמַעֲשֵׂה יָדֶיךָ שָׁמָיִם — *And the heavens are Your handiwork.*

The Talmud (Chagigah 12a) and the Midrash (Vayikra Rabbah 36:1) record a debate as to the order of Creation. Beis Shammai say that God created the heavens before the earth, as it is written, *In the beginning of God's creating the heavens and the earth* (Genesis 1:1). The prophet (Isaiah 66:1) describes the heaven as God's throne and the earth as His footstool. Naturally, a king makes

himself a throne before he makes a footstool.

Beis Hillel cite our verse as proof that God created the earth first, as we read, *Previously, You laid the earth's foundation;* afterwards, *the heavens are Your handiwork.* This can be compared to the king who built himself a palace. First he built the bottom floor and only afterwards the roof.

Pirkei d'Rabbi Eliezer (ch. 11) provides a sequel to this debate: The schools of Shammai and Hillel were filled with righteous zeal by this discussion. God's presence descended upon all those who participated and both sides were inspired to accept the following solution: God created heaven and earth simultaneously. He stretched out His right hand and expanded the heavens. He extended His left hand and established the earth.

27. הֵמָּה יֹאבֵדוּ וְאַתָּה תַעֲמֹד — *They will perish but You will endure.*

1. *Chida* attaches deeper significance to this plea. David received seventy years of life from Adam [see Overview to Vol. I, part I]. According to the *Zohar* the three Patriarchs, Abraham,

Since heaven and earth are themselves creatures, not creators, they are subject to the ravages of time and are in a constant state of flux and change (*Malbim*).

וְכֻלָּם כַּבֶּגֶד יִבְלוּ — *All of them will wear out like a garment.*

Ramban (*Genesis* 1:2) describes a very thin substance — entirely devoid of form but having potential — which was the primary matter created from absolute nothingness by God. This substance is known as חוֹמֶר הַהִיּוּלִי, from the Greek *hyly* [matter]. It was from this *hyly* that He then formed and brought everything else into existence, clothing the forms and putting them into finished condition. All shapes and forms which we see and feel are merely *garments* cloaking the original *hyly*.

It was God's plan that these garments remain in existence for only a limited period of time, after which they wear out and vanish (*Malbim*).

Thus the prophet says (*Isaiah* 51:6), *The heavens shall vanish like smoke and the earth will wear out like a garment, and those who dwell in it shall die in like manner* (*Ibn Ezra*).

כַּלְּבוּשׁ תַּחֲלִיפֵם וְיַחֲלֹפוּ — *You will exchange them like a cloak and they will pass on.*

God can alter the appearance of the earth as easily as a man takes off one jacket and replaces it with another, and no creature can protest against Him or interfere with His designs (*Radak*).

28. וְאַתָּה הוּא — *But You remain the same* [lit. *You are He*].

External shapes and forms change but You *remain the same* — always (*Malbim*).

וּשְׁנוֹתֶיךָ לֹא יִתָּמּוּ — *And Your years are*

endless [lit. *shall never end*].

[For You are beyond the limitations of time.]

29. בְּנֵי עֲבָדֶיךָ יִשְׁכּוֹנוּ — *Your servants' children shall be settled.*

At the time of redemption, the descendants of Your original servants will return to the Holy Land and they will be settled there forever, never to be uprooted and sent into exile (*Radak*).

When everything in the world will wear out and perish, only the righteous children of the devoted forefathers will survive and flourish, for just as God is eternal all those who cleave to Him are eternal (*Malbim*).

וְזַרְעָם לְפָנֶיךָ יִכּוֹן — *And their children will be steadfast before You.*

They will bask in the glorious illumination of the Divine light forever (*Malbim*).

[This psalm is titled תְּפִלָּה לְעָנִי, *A prayer of the afflicted man* (v. 1), because exile causes spiritual and financial impoverishment for Israel.

Shevet Mussar (comm. to v. 1) explains that, in a deeper sense, man's mission on earth is to triumph over poverty of the spirit. Before it was placed in a human body, the soul stood before the Divine Presence in heaven and enjoyed spiritual bliss that it had never earned. The soul, so to speak, was like a beggar seeking undeserved charity. Then the 'impoverished soul' descended to be tempted and tested in the physical world, so that it could become deserving of spiritual reward.

Accordingly, the Psalmist concludes this chapter with the promise that by the end of the period of exile, Israel will have earned the privilege of standing *steadfast before God* to enjoy the spiritual reward for having withstood the challenges of life on earth.]

Isaac and Jacob, contributed an additional seventy years to David's life for a total of one hundred forty years.

When David was seventy and on the verge of death he begged of God, *Do not remove me in the half of* (חֲצִי) *my days.*

God responded, בְּדוֹר דּוֹרִים שְׁנוֹתֶיךָ, *Your years are made of double generations*, i.e., one year or generation of your life is equivalent to two ordinary years [because David slept very little and never wasted time, so he extracted from each day twice as much as any other man]. Thus, you, David, have lived a hundred forty years of life in a span of seventy years!

מזמור קג 103

In this psalm David thanks God for the greatest gift He bestowed
upon man — the soul. Without a soul man is merely a two-legged
creature competing against all other animals in the bitter struggle for
survival. With a soul, he becomes a reflection of the sacred heavens, a
semblance of the Divine.

The tragic irony of life is that people are often oblivious to their
own souls, unaware of the essence of their being and the true purpose
of their existence. All too often, this Divine fragment is smothered by
the flesh, this ray of eternal light is engulfed in darkness.

The fundamental lesson of Judaism is to foster an awareness of the
Divine Soul and to teach man how to enhance and enrich this most
precious possession so that it will be worthy of standing in God's
presence to praise Him.

Thus the Psalmist recites the refrain, repeated five times in this
psalm and the next, בָּרְכִי נַפְשִׁי אֶת ה׳, Bless HASHEM, O my soul!

א לְדָוִד ׀ בָּרְכִי נַפְשִׁי אֶת־יהוה וְכָל־קְרָבַי אֶת־
ב שֵׁם קָדְשׁוֹ: בָּרְכִי נַפְשִׁי אֶת־יהוה וְאַל־
ג תִּשְׁכְּחִי כָּל־גְּמוּלָיו: הַסֹּלֵחַ לְכָל־עֲוֹנֵכִי
ד הָרֹפֵא לְכָל־תַּחֲלֻאָיְכִי: הַגּוֹאֵל מִשַּׁחַת

1. לְדָוִד בָּרְכִי נַפְשִׁי אֶת ה' — *Of David,
bless HASHEM, O my soul.*

Throughout the *Book of Psalms*,
David praises God for the many gifts
which He lavished upon mankind. In
this psalm, as noted in the *Prefatory
Remarks*, he gives thanks for the
greatest gift of all — the human soul.
David repeats the refrain, *Bless
HASHEM, O my soul*, five times [verses
1, 2, 22 and 104:1, 35].

R' Yochanan explains that these five
repetitions correspond to the Five Books
of the Torah, which are a blessing for
the soul (*Vayikra Rabbah* 4:7).

R' Shimon bar Yochai (*Berachos* 10a)
explains that David detected five stages
in the soul's development and praised
God for His intricate plan. [Each of
these stages corresponds with one of the
Five Books of Moses.]

He first sang of the miraculous
process in which the embryo's soul is
introduced to this world and fused to its
flesh. No sculptor could emulate God's
ability to fashion a baby inside its
mother in such a way that it is
eventually capable of existing independently. Thus, to praise God for the
miracles of reproduction, David sang:
*Bless HASHEM, O my soul, and all that
is within me* [bless] *His Holy Name.*
[This stage corresponds with the *Book
of Genesis* which describes the birth of
the world and civilization.]

The second stage of the soul's
odyssey begins at birth, when it is
released from the womb and discovers
the endless expanse of the universe.
Then the soul recognizes that just as the
lofty heavenly bodies obey the bidding
of Hashem, so must the humble human

soul fulfill the Divine design and praise
God for the opportunities to serve Him
(see verses 20-22). [This stage reflects
the *Book of Exodus*, whose theme is
redemption and release from bondage.]

The third stage of the soul's
maturation begins when the infant is
nursed at its mother's breast. Then an
entirely new world begins to unfold —
the cycle of nourishment (see verse 2).
[The third stage corresponds with the
Book of Leviticus, which details the
dietary laws regulating nourishment. It
also describes the sacrificial service in
the Temple which God calls לַחְמִי, *My
bread*, i.e., spiritual sustenance for the
world.]

The soul reaches the fourth stage
when it begins to recognize the lifelong
struggle between good and evil. This
occurs at religious maturity, the time of
bar or *bas mitzvah* [age thirteen for
boys, twelve for girls], when a pure and
holy spirit enters the soul and
strengthens it to resist temptation (*Pnei
Yehoshua*). This fourth stage is
completed when the soul comprehends
that the downfall of evil and evildoers is
inevitable (see 104:35). [The soul's
fourth stage corresponds with the *Book
of Numbers*, which describes how the
Jews were counted when they came of
age and joined the army to fight the
enemy.]

The fifth and final stage of the soul's
journey occurs at death, when the soul
is finally released from the flesh (see
104:1). [The fifth and final stage of the
soul corresponds with the *Book of
Deuteronomy* which depicts the final
days and the death of Moses.][1]

1. *Pnei Yehoshua* (comm. to *Berachos* 10a) observes that the *Zohar* and other Kabbalistic
works identify the five phases of the soul's development as נֶפֶשׁ, רוּחַ, נְשָׁמָה, חַיָּה, יְחִידָה.
  In the womb, the Divine spark is called נֶפֶשׁ, *spirit* [cognate with נָשׁ, *resting*, because before

Of David, bless HASHEM, O my soul,
 and all that is within me — His Holy Name.
² Bless HASHEM, O my soul,
 and forget not all His kindnesses.
³ Who forgives all your sins,
 Who heals all your diseases.

וְכָל קְרָבַי אֶת שֵׁם קָדְשׁוֹ — *And all that is within me — His Holy Name.*

The recital of God's praise is not confined to the soul. The flesh, too, recounts God's wonders (Ibn Ezra). [Even the קְרָבַיִם, *innards*, the excretory organs, which constitute the coarsest part of the body, join the soul in singing God's praises.]

2. בָּרְכִי נַפְשִׁי אֶת ה' — *Bless HASHEM, O my soul.*

The Psalmist repeats the exhortation of the first phrase to emphasize that the soul should bless God again and again, without interruption (Ibn Ezra).

First bless God for His great sanctity, then bless Him for His goodness (Radak).

וְאַל תִּשְׁכְּחִי כָּל גְּמוּלָיו — *And forget not all His kindnesses.*

Bless God for His constant, ongoing goodness, and *forget not His* past kindnesses (Sforno).

The Talmud (Berachos 10a) perceives גְּמוּלָיו as cognate with גָּמוּל, *a nursing infant*. When David comprehended God's complex and generous system of sustaining all living creatures, including the helpless infant, he was stirred to bless his Creator.

3. הַסֹּלֵחַ לְכָל עֲוֹנֵכִי — *Who forgives all your sins.*

Not only does God promote the development and welfare of the soul, but He also protects it from pitfalls. Since man is capable of sin, God provided the soul with a method to repent and to gain forgiveness, in order that the soul might improve and flourish without impediment (Hirsch).

הָרֹפֵא לְכָל תַּחֲלוּאָיְכִי — *Who heals all your diseases.*

Some say that this refers to *diseases* of the body. From this we learn that

birth the soul has not yet been activated].

At birth, it is called רוּחַ, literally *wind* or *direction* [because the soul is now free to soar in any direction].

When the infant starts to nurse, the soul is called נְשָׁמָה [cognate with נְשִׁימָה, *the breath of survival*, because nourishment is essential for human survival].

Until the age of religious majority, *bar* or *bas mitzvah*, the soul is still relatively dormant. When a man or woman becomes obligated to perform *mitzvos*, God introduces a powerful יֵצֶר טוֹב, *good inclination*, into the soul, which activates it to serve God with dedication. Then the soul is called חַיָּה, *the live one*, because it receives new vigor and vitality.

When the soul finally comprehends that God is the only true power in the universe, the soul is referred to as יְחִידָה, *the one and only*. Most ordinary people never achieve this level of perception, for it is reserved for the righteous, who struggle all their lives to comprehend God. When they die and their souls are released from the distractions of the flesh, they can finally conceive of God as One and Only and their souls enter the sphere of יְחִידָה.

[The Midrash (Vayikra Rabbah 4:8) details the many ways in which the soul, which is a fragment of God, resembles Himself. For example, the soul permeates every fiber of the body, just as God's presence permeates the world; the soul sees everything, yet it remains unseen, just as God sees everything but remains invisible; the soul is fused to the flesh, yet it preserves its purity, just as God is totally involved in the affairs of the mundane world, but maintains His purity. The Midrash concludes: Let the pure soul come forth to offer praise to the pure God!]

ה חַיָּיְכִי הַמְעַטְּרֵכִי חֶסֶד וְרַחֲמִים: הַמַּשְׂבִּיעַ

ו בַּטּוֹב עֶדְיֵךְ תִּתְחַדֵּשׁ כַּנֶּשֶׁר נְעוּרָיְכִי: עֹשֵׂה

צְדָקוֹת יְהוָה וּמִשְׁפָּטִים לְכָל־עֲשׁוּקִים:

ז יוֹדִיעַ דְּרָכָיו לְמֹשֶׁה לִבְנֵי יִשְׂרָאֵל עֲלִילוֹתָיו:

God heals the body's diseases only after He has forgiven the iniquities of the soul (*Nedarim* 41a).

Others are of the opinion that *diseases* refers to the ailments of the soul, which has been corrupted by sin. God *heals* these *diseases* by providing atonement and forgiveness (*Megillah* 17b).

Similarly, David cried out (41:5), *"Heal my soul for I have sinned against You"* (*Radak*).

4. הַגּוֹאֵל מִשַּׁחַת חַיָּיְכִי — *Who redeems your life from the pit.*

Many times the sick man was on the brink of death, yet God, in His mercy, saved him from this *pit* (*Ibn Ezra*).

The vehicle for this miraculous redemption is the power of repentance, which can save the condemned man even at the last moment (*Radak*).

הַמְעַטְּרֵכִי חֶסֶד וְרַחֲמִים — *Who crowns you with kindness and mercy.*

The sinner repented because the *diseases* of his body made him aware of the sickness of his soul. Thus, a disease which originally appeared to be a degrading curse was later recognized to be a magnificent crown of blessing and a proof of God's *kindness* and *mercy* (*Radak*).

5. הַמַּשְׂבִּיעַ בַּטּוֹב עֶדְיֵךְ — *Who satisfies your mouth with goodness.*

The translation of עֶדְיֵךְ as *your mouth* follows *Radak, Ibn Ezra,* and *Metzudos*; it is based on 32:9, עֶדְיוֹ לִבְלוֹם, *to restrain his mouth.* The Psalmist here refers to the sick person who is disgusted by the mere sight of food, as in *Job* 33:19-20: *And he was chastened with pain·upon his bed ... so that his very being abhors bread and his soul* [despises] *tempting food.* When

God cures the invalid, his appetite will return and God will satisfy him with all kinds of good things (*Radak*).

Ibn Ezra alternatively renders עֶדְיֵךְ as *your adornments,* as in וַיִּתְנַצְּלוּ בְנֵי יִשְׂרָאֵל אֶת עֶדְיָם מֵהַר חוֹרֵב, *And the children of Israel stripped themselves of their ornaments from Mount Horeb* (*Exodus* 33:6).

Man's most exquisite ornament is his soul, and sickness serves to polish and refine the soul, so that it will be fit to be satisfied *with goodness,* i.e., spiritual enrichment [see commentary to verse 7].

Finally, *Targum* translates עֶדְיֵךְ as *your old age,* when man is crowned with the ornament of שֵׂיבָה, *a hoary head,* which is a sign of maturity. Suffering and struggle in the younger years bring glory to a man's old age when he has repented and learned from his mistakes. As the righteous man grows older, he improves and his mental capacity becomes more acute, as the *Talmud* (*Shabbos* 152a) states: As Torah scholars get older, their wisdom increases (*Rav Avraham Azulai*).

תִּתְחַדֵּשׁ כַּנֶּשֶׁר נְעוּרָיְכִי — *So that your youth is renewed like the eagle's.*

After the sick man repents and is healed by God, he becomes healthier than ever before, as *Job* 33:25-26 states: *His flesh shall be smoother than a child's, he shall return to the days of his youth. He shall pray to God and He will show him favor* (*Radak*).

Indeed, the *Talmud* (*Yoma* 86a) teaches that if a man repents out of love of God, his sins are transformed into merits and he becomes an entirely different person, passing from villainy to righteous vigor (*Rav Avraham Azulai*).

Birds molt and renew their feathers

103
4-7

⁴ Who redeems your life from the pit,
    Who crowns you with kindness and mercy.
⁵ Who satisfies your mouth with goodness,
    so that your youth is renewed like the eagle's.
⁶ HASHEM does righteous deeds,
    and judgments for all the oppressed.
⁷ He made known His ways to Moses,
    His accomplishments to the Children of Israel.

annually. Owing to this trait, the eagle [king of birds] is a prime example of renewed youth (Rashi).

Rav Saadiah Gaon and Radak perceive this as an allusion to the legendary eagle which flies higher than all other birds, close to the solar fire which generates tremendous heat. In an effort to cool off, the eagle plunges into the sea and pulls out its hot feathers. Later it emerges from the sea with a new set of feathers and appears to be reborn. This rite of renewal occurs once every ten years, throughout the eagle's lifespan of one hundred years. When the eagle reaches one hundred years of age, it soars to the sun and plunges into the sea for the last time.

[The eagle also symbolizes the future renewal of the world. Yalkut Shimoni (Isaiah 447) teaches that this world is destined to be covered with water from which a new, perfect world will emerge. While the process of renewal takes place beneath the surface, Hashem will fashion eagles' wings for the righteous. Then they will fly over the water — i.e., they will soar to new spiritual heights.]

6. עָשָׂה צְדָקוֹת ה׳ — *HASHEM does righteous deeds.*

The Psalmist determined that the sickness and suffering which afflict man are just (verse 3), for they cause penitence, after which the disease is healed. Now the Psalmist emphasizes that the 'illness-cure cycle' is only one phase of Hashem's performance of *righteous acts,* because Hashem controls all aspects of society and nature

according to strict rules of righteousness (Radak; Ibn Ezra).

וּמִשְׁפָּטִים לְכָל עֲשׁוּקִים — *And judgments for all the oppressed.*

In order to rescue *all the oppressed,* God issues *judgments* and punishments against those who oppress them (Radak; Ibn Ezra).

7. יוֹדִיעַ דְּרָכָיו לְמֹשֶׁה — *He made known His ways to Moses.*

The *judgments* and punishments which God inflicts are not haphazard. They follow a strict plan and pattern which God *made known to Moses* (Ibn Yachya). God revealed this pattern to Moses after Moses pleaded (Exodus 33:13): *Now, if I have found favor in Your eyes,* הוֹדִעֵנִי נָא אֶת דְּרָכֶךָ, *please make Your way known to me,* so that *I may know You* (Radak; Ibn Ezra; Sforno).

[When God responded favorably to this request, saying אֲנִי אַעֲבִיר כָּל טוּבִי עַל פָּנֶיךָ, *I will display all of my goodness before You* (Exodus 33:19), God fulfilled His role as He *Who satisfies Your 'ornament' with goodness* (verse 5). God passed before Moses and revealed to him the Thirteen Attributes of Divine Mercy and bid Moses to acquire these character traits which represent perfection, and 'ornament' the soul. The soul which is perfected in this manner is completely attuned to the ways of God and understands the rationale and the righteousness of all God's ways.]

לִבְנֵי יִשְׂרָאֵל עֲלִילוֹתָיו — *His accomplish-*

ח רַחוּם וְחַנּוּן יהוה אֶרֶךְ אַפַּיִם וְרַב־חָסֶד:
ט־י לֹא־לָנֶצַח יָרִיב וְלֹא לְעוֹלָם יִטּוֹר: לֹא
כַחֲטָאֵינוּ עָשָׂה לָנוּ וְלֹא כַעֲוֹנֹתֵינוּ גָּמַל

ments to the Children of Israel.

[When the Children of Israel accepted God's Torah at Sinai, they repented of their previous sins and idolatry. This penitence cured all their physical ailments, as the Rabbis taught: At Sinai, all the ailments of Israel were healed. (See *Shir HaShirim* 4:15 and comm. of *Rabbeinu Nissim* to *Nedarim* 7b.) Forty days later, Israel betrayed this pledge of penitence by offering their allegiance to the golden calf. The Almighty wished to annihilate the treacherous nation in a single moment of terrible retribution. All those who had been cured at Sinai returned to their previous state of sickness and infirmity (*Bamidbar Rabbah* 7:4). Only the impassioned protests of Moses turned God's anger to mercy. The climax of this pardon came when God displayed His Thirteen Attributes of Mercy to Moses.

The *Talmud* (*Rosh HaShanah* 17b) states that Rav Yochanan said: The Holy One, Blessed is He, wrapped Himself in a prayer shawl like a cantor and showed Moses the order of prayer, saying, "Whenever Israel sins, let them perform this order of service and I will forgive them."

Rav Yehudah said: A covenant has been struck between God and Israel that the Thirteen Attributes never go unanswered.]

Alshich emphasizes that the mere recitation of these Attributes is not sufficient. Rather, as Rav Yochanan stresses, "Let them *perform* this order of service," meaning that the Jews are required to imitate God's acts of kindness and mercy. [See Introduction to ArtScroll Tashlich.] Thus, God made עֲלִילוֹתָיו, *His accomplishments*, known to the children of Israel, in order that they might emulate Him and accomplish the same things.

8. רַחוּם וְחַנּוּן ה׳ — *Merciful and Compassionate is HASHEM.*

The Psalmist here enumerates a few of the Thirteen Attributes of Mercy. *Ibn Ezra* explains that it is by exercising these attributes that God heals the sick man. *Radak* says that it is these attributes which assure Israel's survival in exile.

The term רַחוּם, *Merciful*, refers to the fact that God ensures that our captors tolerate us and do not completely destroy us, despite the hostility they bear us.

The term חַנּוּן, *Compassionate*, refers to God's concern for our sustenance in exile; He manifests this compassion by wondrously providing for all our needs.

Others say that the attribute *Merciful* refers to God's mercy in averting moments of crisis or temptation which would overpower one's normal degree of self-control. Thus, this attribute refers to the mercy which God shows *before* a person is engulfed in a situation beyond his control (gloss to *Tosafos, Rosh Hashanah* 17b).

The attribute *Compassionate* is cognate with חֵן, *charm*, which is related to חִנָּם, *free of charge*. Since God is compassionate, He aids even those unworthy of His kindness. Unlike the attribute of mercy, which is exercised *before* a crisis, the attribute of compassion is exercised *during* a crisis. The *compassionate* God does not ignore the cries and pleas of a person who seeks to avoid sin but whose will-power is unequal to the task. God rescues him, although he is unworthy of such aid (*ibid.*; see introduction to *ArtScroll Tashlich*).

אֶרֶךְ אַפַּיִם — *Slow to Anger.*

Literally, אֶרֶךְ means *long*, indicating that God is not short-tempered. He

⁸ *Merciful and Compassionate is HASHEM,*
Slow to Anger and Abundantly Kind.
⁹ *He will not quarrel for eternity,*
nor will He forever bear a grudge.
¹⁰ *He has not treated us according to our sins*
nor repaid us according to our iniquities.

takes a long time to grow angry, in order to afford the sinner an opportunity to repent before it is too late (Rashi).

[The word אַפַּיִם is the plural of אַף, nose. When a person is enraged, his nose turns red and he breathes heavily. God controls this formidable and apparent fury.]

וְרַב חֶסֶד — And Abundantly Kind.

This attribute is directed toward those who lack personal merits. God compensates for their deficiency with His abundant store of kindness (Rashi).

If the scales of justice are precisely balanced, i.e., a man's merits and demerits are equal — God, in His abundant kindness, will tilt the scales towards merit (Rosh Hashanah 17a).

9. לֹא לָנֶצַח יָרִיב — He will not quarrel for eternity.

God exiled Israel because He quarreled with them, but this conflict shall not endure forever (Radak).

וְלֹא לְעוֹלָם יִטּוֹר — Nor will He forever bear a grudge.

The exiles suffer not only for their own sins, but also for the sins of their fathers and ancestors which caused God to exile the Jewish nation. However, we are confident that the merciful God will not bear a grudge against our forebears (and us) forever (Sforno).

Malbim differentiates between לָנֶצַח, for eternity, which represents the timelessness of the spiritual world and לְעוֹלָם, forever [which can also be translated for the world], which describes an unending situation in the physical world.

Malbim also differentiates between יָרִיב, quarrel, which refers to an open act of hostility, and יִטּוֹר, bear a grudge,

which refers to animosity which is harbored secretly.

Thus, He will not quarrel for, נֶצַח, eternity, means that God will fight with us and punish us in this עוֹלָם, physical world, so that we will be at peace with Him in נֶצַח, the eternal world of the spirit.

Nor will He bear a grudge, לְעוֹלָם, forever, means that in this physical world, God does not conceal His anger against us. He reveals it and openly quarrels with us, so that when we arrive at the eternal world of נֶצַח, the quarrel will cease.

10. לֹא כַחֲטָאֵינוּ עָשָׂה לָנוּ — He has not treated us according to our sins.

Ibn Ezra (verse 8) explains that this description corresponds to the Divine attribute נֹשֵׂא עָוֹן וָפֶשַׁע וְחַטָּאָה, Forgiver of iniquity, transgression and sin (Exodus 34:7).

Radak observes that this dimension of God's mercy is especially evident during Israel's exile: He has not treated us according to our sins, because, if He had, we would have been destroyed long ago.

According to Malbim, עָשָׂה, He has treated, connotes an action which is performed perfunctorily, without feeling. Similarly, a חֵטְא, sin [i.e., an error], is performed accidentally, without feeling. Thus the punishment for a sin should be dealt out measure for measure, without Divine animosity or revenge. In His extreme mercy, however, God has not punished our sins at all, even in such a mild fashion.

וְלֹא כַעֲוֹנֹתֵינוּ גָּמַל עָלֵינוּ — Nor repaid us according to our iniquities.

Malbim defines גָּמוּל as recompense

יא עָלֵינוּ: כִּי כִגְבֹהַּ שָׁמַיִם עַל־הָאָרֶץ גָּבַר חַסְדּוֹ

יב עַל־יְרֵאָיו: כִּרְחֹק מִזְרָח מִמַּעֲרָב הִרְחִיק

יג מִמֶּנּוּ אֶת־פְּשָׁעֵינוּ: כְּרַחֵם אָב עַל־בָּנִים

יד רִחַם יהוה עַל־יְרֵאָיו: כִּי־הוּא יָדַע יִצְרֵנוּ

for wrongdoing which is accompanied by feelings of revenge and bitterness.

For since עָוֹן, *iniquity*, is performed with feelings of lust and desire, it · deserves to be repaid with a harsh punishment which is motivated by feelings of hostility and revenge. Nevertheless, the Psalmist notes, the merciful God has *not repaid us* in the harsh fashion *according to our iniquities.*

11. כִּי כִגְבֹהַּ שָׁמַיִם עַל־הָאָרֶץ — *For, as high as heaven is above the earth.*

This indicates the extent of God's kindness. *Rabbeinu Bachya* questions this analogy, however, because it seems to place a limitation on God's infinite kindness, for, as *Lamentations* 3:22 states, חַסְדֵי ה׳ כִּי לֹא תָמְנוּ כִּי לֹא כָלוּ רַחֲמָיו, *HASHEM's kindness surely has not ended, nor are His mercies exhausted.*

R' Bachya and *Radak* explain that the Psalmist speaks here in human terms, for, to the average man, nothing seems greater than the height of the heavens.

Ibn Yachya interprets this metaphorically: *heaven* (the spiritual world) *is high above* (i.e., totally divorced from) *the earth* (the physical world). Similarly, as a result of His intense kindness, God will completely remove *our transgressions from us* (verse 12).

גָּבַר חַסְדּוֹ עַל יְרֵאָיו — *Has His kindness intensified towards those who fear Him.*

Zekan Aharon explains that the higher one goes into the heavens, the closer he comes to the source of God's kindness. Those *who fear God* are the ones who come closest to Him. Therefore, *His kindness has intensified* towards them.

12. כִּרְחֹק מִזְרָח מִמַּעֲרָב — *As far as east from west.*

The commentators ask why the Psalmist speaks of the distance between east and west rather than that between north and south.

Rav Yitzchak Arama observes that *east*, the direction from which the sun rises, symbolizes daytime, which is synonymous with purity from sin, whereas the west, where the sun sets, symbolizes the night, which is synonymous with evil. Thus the Psalmist implies that Israel will be purged and removed from sin just as day is removed from night.

Radak explains that the Psalmist speaks of the distance between east and west because this is more readily comprehended by human experience, for most travel around the globe is restricted to the inhabited temperate zone, which encircles the globe in an east-west direction.

The climate to the north and south of this belt is plagued by such extremes of temperature that few travelers ever experience the great distance between north to south.

[Man's familiarity with the sun's daily journey across the sky also facilitates his comprehension of the distance between east and west.]

הִרְחִיק מִמֶּנּוּ אֶת פְּשָׁעֵינוּ — *Has He distanced our transgressions from us.*

This, of course, only takes place after a person repents sincerely and turns his heart to God *(Ibn Ezra)*. [The closer one comes to God, the further removed he is from sin.]

13. כְּרַחֵם אָב עַל בָּנִים — *As merciful as a father to his children.*

No form of mercy is as intense as a

¹¹ *For, as high as heaven is above the earth,*
has His kindness intensified
towards those who fear Him.
¹² *As far as east from west,*
has He distanced our transgressions from us.
¹³ *As merciful as a father to his children,*
so has HASHEM shown mercy to
those who fear Him.
¹⁴ *For He knew our nature,*

father's mercy towards his child (Radak).[1]

Alshich, for example, relates the case of the captured highwayman who withstood the torture which had been calculated to wring a confession from his lips. When his captors threatened to torture the highwayman's son, however, the brigand immediately confessed.

Ibn Shuib observes that even when a father strikes his child, it is only in order that the child benefit from rebuke. This is the same reason why God punishes Israel, as *Deuteronomy* 8:5 states: *For as a father chastises his son so does HASHEM, your God, chastise you.*

רִחַם ה׳ עַל יְרֵאָיו — *So has HASHEM shown mercy to those who fear Him.*

[Maharil Diskin (Parashas Vayish-

lach) explains that God's blessing can sometimes become a curse. God knows that if certain people are granted prosperity, they will become arrogant and defy Him, or they will use their wealth to destroy their rivals and opponents. God knows that if He is merciful to such people He will eventually be compelled to withdraw His mercy and unleash His wrath. Therefore, God is *merciful* (only) *to those who fear Him* and who will continue to be worthy of His goodness.]

14. כִּי הוּא יָדַע יִצְרֵנוּ — *For He knew our nature.*

God is prepared to be merciful towards us and to remove our transgression from us (verse 12) because long ago, after He brought the great flood, He proclaimed (Genesis 8:21), "I

1. The *Midrash* (quoted in *Tehillas Hashem* and *Toras Chesed*) relates that when Joab, David's commander-in-chief, heard this statement he was incredulous. He went to David and challenged him, "How can you say that a father's mercy surpasses that of a mother? Certainly the love of a mother is unequaled because she suffers so much for her children! She goes through the pains of pregnancy, labor, and birth, and then she struggles so much to raise the children! Certainly, David, you must be wrong!"

Joab decided to go out into the world to test David's assertion. He traveled throughout Israel and found a poor family of twelve children, whom the father supported with great difficulty. Joab offered to make the father wealthy if only he would sell him one of his children. The father was outraged by this suggestion and chased Joab away. Joab then approached the mother. She finally agreed to the bargain and sold one of her children for one hundred golden dinarim.

When the weary father returned home that night and discovered his child's absence he was deeply grieved. He could not eat or drink because of his despair. He took the one hundred dinarim and pursued Joab. Then the father issued an ultimatum to Joab, "Either you take back the one hundred dinarim and return my son, or we fight until either you or I are slain!"

Joab returned the child and admitted that David had been correct in his estimate of a father's mercy, for a father expends all his energy and even endangers his life in order to support his child. Because the father's investment is so great, his love is very intense.

טו זָכוּר כִּי־עָפָר אֲנָחְנוּ: אֱנוֹשׁ כֶּחָצִיר יָמָיו
טז כְּצִיץ הַשָּׂדֶה כֵּן יָצִיץ: כִּי רוּחַ עָבְרָה־בּוֹ
יז וְאֵינֶנּוּ וְלֹא־יַכִּירֶנּוּ עוֹד מְקוֹמוֹ: וְחֶסֶד יהוה |
מֵעוֹלָם וְעַד־עוֹלָם עַל־יְרֵאָיו וְצִדְקָתוֹ לִבְנֵי
יח בָנִים: לְשֹׁמְרֵי בְרִיתוֹ וּלְזֹכְרֵי פִקֻּדָיו

will not continue to curse again the ground because of man, since the imagery of man's heart is evil from his youth." Therefore, King Solomon taught (Ecclesiastes 7:20): No man on earth is so wholly righteous that he [always] does good and never sins (Radak).

Radak (commentary to Genesis 8:4) observes that the word יֵצֶר literally means formation, because the יֵצֶר הָרַע, evil inclination, is formed together with man. The Rabbis taught that man acquires his evil inclination first; only later does he acquire his good inclination. For man is born without wisdom and with an inclination toward evil; only later does he become enlightened and begin to develop virtues. [See Piskei HaTosafos to tractate Nedarim, no. 62.]

זָכוּר כִּי עָפָר אֲנָחְנוּ — He remembers that we are dust.

As God told Adam (Genesis 3:19), כִּי עָפָר אַתָּה וְאֶל עָפָר תָּשׁוּב, "For dust are you, and to dust shall you return."

Man is composed of two aspects: the body and the soul. If he focuses primarily on the celestial realm of the spirit, then the soul is supreme and man resembles an angel. But if man focuses primarily on the coarse physical realm, then he will become akin to the animals and beasts (Radak).

God recognizes that our physicality drags us toward the animal aspect of our natures, and therefore He is lenient and merciful with us (Ibn Yachya).

15. אֱנוֹשׁ כֶּחָצִיר יָמָיו — Frail man — his days are like grass.

Frail man is not even as good as dust, for dust endures but man is like grass,

which dries quickly and disappears (Radak).

כְּצִיץ הַשָּׂדֶה כֵּן יָצִיץ — Like a sprout of the field, so he sprouts.

The lifespan of man is so brief that if he errs, he hardly has time to rectify his mistakes. Before man realizes it, youth slips away and is succeeded by old age and death. God recognizes the brevity of man's earthly sojourn and is inclined to have mercy on him (Radak).

16. כִּי רוּחַ עָבְרָה בּוֹ וְאֵינֶנּוּ — If a wind passes over it, it is gone.

The grass which sprouts is so fragile that a puff of wind dries it out and breaks it (Ibn Ezra).

Similarly, man is so weak that sickness or death can easily overcome him (Rashi).

וְלֹא יַכִּירֶנּוּ עוֹד מְקוֹמוֹ — And its site knows it no more.

[So insignificant is man that after he is gone he leaves no trace of his accomplishments, just as a blade of grass is totally forgotten after it withers.]

17. וְחֶסֶד ה' מֵעוֹלָם וְעַד עוֹלָם עַל יְרֵאָיו — But the kindness of HASHEM is forever and ever upon those who fear Him.

Ibn Ezra (verse 8) explains that this corresponds to one of the Thirteen Divine Attributes, נֹצֵר חֶסֶד לָאֲלָפִים, Preserver of Kindness for thousands of generations (Exodus 34:7). This means that the descendants of the righteous man will benefit from the merits of their ancestor for thousands (i.e., two thousand) of generations, on the condition that the descendants follow their ancestor's righteous example.

In Deuteronomy 7:9, however,

He remembers that we are dust.
¹⁵ *Frail man — his days are like grass,*
like a sprout of the field, so he sprouts.
¹⁶ *If a wind passes over it, it is gone,*
and its site knows it no more.
¹⁷ *But the kindness of HASHEM is forever and ever*
upon those who fear Him,
and His righteousness upon children's children.
¹⁸ *To those who keep His covenant,*
and to those who remember His commands
to fulfill them.

Scripture says that the merits of a righteous ancestor only extend for *one* thousand generations. The *Talmud* (Sotah 31a) explains that the merit of those who serve God out of intense love lasts two thousand generations, but the merit of יְרֵאָיו, *those who [merely] fear Him,* only endures for one thousand generations.

Radak cites an alternative opinion that this verse refers to the existence of the soul, rather than to the body. According to this view, it is the soul of those who fear God which will endure *forever,* even beyond thousands of generations.

The *Talmud* (Sukkah 49b) explains that the word חֶסֶד may also be translated as *charm* or *grace.* When a person finds unusual favor in the eyes of his fellow men this is a sign that he is one of the יְרֵאָיו, *those who fear God.*

וְצִדְקָתוֹ לִבְנֵי בָנִים — *And His righteousness* [or, *charity*] *upon children's children.*

Many opinions interpret צִדְקָתוֹ as a reference to the righteousness of man [rather than of God], i.e., to the charity which man performs. Thus, this verse contrasts the virtues of צְדָקָה, *charity,* with those of חֶסֶד, *acts of kindness.*

The *Talmud* (ibid.) lists three ways in which kindness surpasses charity. Firstly, charity is performed only with

money, whereas kindness is performed both with money and with personal acts of consideration. Secondly, charity is extended only to the poor, whereas acts of kindness benefit rich and poor alike. Thirdly, charity can be given only to the living, whereas kindness can be extended both to the living and to the dead [by attending to a person's burial, for example].

Therefore, the merit of a man's חֶסֶד, *kindness,* endures *forever and ever,* whereas the merit of his צְדָקָה, *charity,* extends only to *his children's children,* i.e., for three generations (Midrash Shocher Tov).

18. לְשׁמְרֵי בְרִיתוֹ — *To those who keep His covenant.*

When a person learns Torah with total concentration and remains oblivious to everything in the world he deserves the title שׁוֹמֵר הַבְּרִית, *Guardian of the Covenant.* The entire Jewish nation reached this lofty level of Divine service during the sojourn in the wilderness, when they were miraculously sustained by the manna and studied Torah without interruption (Midrash Shocher Tov).

וּלְזֹכְרֵי פִקֻּדָיו לַעֲשׂוֹתָם — *And to those who remember His commands to fulfill them.*

Midrash Shocher Tov continues:

יט לַעֲשׂוֹתָם: יהוה בַּשָּׁמַיִם הֵכִין כִּסְאוֹ
כ וּמַלְכוּתוֹ בַּכֹּל מָשָׁלָה: בָּרְכוּ יהוה מַלְאָכָיו
גִּבֹּרֵי כֹחַ עֹשֵׂי דְבָרוֹ לִשְׁמֹעַ בְּקוֹל דְּבָרוֹ:
כא בָּרְכוּ יהוה כָּל־צְבָאָיו מְשָׁרְתָיו עֹשֵׂי רְצוֹנוֹ:
כב בָּרְכוּ יהוה | כָּל־מַעֲשָׂיו בְּכָל־מְקֹמוֹת
מֶמְשַׁלְתּוֹ בָּרְכִי נַפְשִׁי אֶת־יהוה:

Once the Torah student leaves the sheltered environment of the House of Study to seek a livelihood, his immersion in study decreases and he becomes one of those *who [merely] remember[s] God's commands,* which he once studied so intently. [Nevertheless, he still deserves God's mercy and charity for he fulfills the commands.]

19. בַּשָּׁמַיִם הֵכִין כִּסְאוֹ — *HASHEM has established His throne in the heavens.*

According to *Ibn Ezra,* the Psalmist is here substantiating his claim that *HASHEM's kindness endures forever and ever* (verse 17) by stating that *His throne is established in the heavens* and will endure eternally. Consequently, God can continue to grant kindness forever.

וּמַלְכוּתוֹ בַּכֹּל מָשָׁלָה — *And His kingdom reigns over all.*

Midrash Shocher Tov observes that there are four 'rulers' in the world who are proud because they are exalted over others, but the Holy One, Blessed be He, is exalted even over these four. The bull is proud in his rule over the animal kingdom; the lion, in his rule over wild beasts; the eagle, in his rule over creatures which fly. Man, to whom God granted dominion over *all* creatures, is even prouder than the bull, lion, and eagle. God set the faces of these four 'rulers' into His Throne of Glory (see *Ezekiel* 1:10) and proclaimed: "Indeed all of you kings are exalted, but My kingdom reigns over all!"

20. בָּרְכוּ ה' מַלְאָכָיו — *Bless HASHEM, O His angels.*

The preceding verse emphasizes that God *rules over all.* Now the psalmist explains that the agents who carry out the commands of the Divine ruler are His blessed *angels* (*Ibn Ezra*).

Sforno identifies these *angels* as the prophets and Torah scholars, who represent God on earth.

גִּבֹּרֵי כֹחַ עֹשֵׂי דְבָרוֹ — *The strong warriors who do His bidding.*

[God endows the celestial *angels* with the strength necessary to fulfill *His bidding* and to control the events of the world.]

The righteous and devout men are also compared to *strong warriors,* as *Avos* 4:1 teaches: Who is truly strong? One who subdues his evil inclination (*Shevet Mussar*).

The *Midrash* (*Vayikra Rabbah*) explains that this verse especially refers to those who faithfully uphold the agricultural restrictions of שְׁמִיטָה, *the Sabbatical year.* Since God commanded that the land lie fallow for one full year, these men willingly allow their property to go to waste, despite the fact that they must pay taxes on the property which they cannot use. Because the devout man accepts all this with serene faith, he merits the title *strong warrior.*

[The *Midrash* (ibid.) emphasizes that upholding the sanctity of the seventh year is a feat that demonstrates remarkable stamina and endurance. Ordinarily a person is willing to sacrifice a generous sum for charity once a week or once a month, but in the seventh year, his sacrifice must be constant. For one whole year, every

19 *HASHEM has established His throne in the heavens,*
        and His kingdom reigns over all.
20 *Bless HASHEM, O His angels,*
        the strong warriors who do His bidding,
        to obey the voice of His word.
21 *Bless HASHEM, O His legions,*
        His servants who do His will.
22 *Bless HASHEM, all His works,*
        in all the places of His dominion.
        Bless HASHEM, O my soul.

---

minute of the day, he must stand by and watch his field go to waste. Such constant devotion resembles the service of angels who serve God without pause. From this we learn that man should serve God steadily, not merely in sporadic bursts of inspiration that quickly fade away and die out.]

לִשְׁמֹעַ בְּקוֹל דְּבָרוֹ — *To obey the voice of His word.*

The *angels* who are the *strong warriors* of God seek absolutely no reward for their service. They find ample satisfaction in the fact that they were given the opportunity *to obey the voice of His word* (Ibn Ezra).

This is proven by the fact that immediately after the angels do God's bidding they do not rest. Rather, they seek new opportunities *to obey the voice of His word* (Radak; Alshich).[1]

21. בָּרְכוּ ה' כָּל צְבָאָיו — *Bless HASHEM, O His legions.*

This refers to the *legions* of stars who are God's intermediaries for controlling the world (Ibn Ezra).

מְשָׁרְתָיו עֹשֵׂי רְצוֹנוֹ — *His servants who do His will.*

[These celestial bodies have no desire other than to serve Hashem.]

22. בָּרְכוּ ה' כָּל מַעֲשָׂיו בְּכָל מְקֹמוֹת מֶמְשַׁלְתּוֹ — *Bless HASHEM, all His works, in all the places of His dominion.*

Rivash (Responsa 157) quotes *Rav Yehuda HaLevi*, who explains that David is describing three worlds in descending order. The highest is that of the *angels* (verse 20). In the middle is the world of the stars and *legions* (verse 21), and at the bottom is this terrestrial world inhabited by מַעֲשָׂיו, *His works.*

Radak observes that the earth contains a vast variety of creations and *works* placed in many different regions — underground, in the water, in the air, etc. Therefore, in reference to Hashem's *works* the soul blesses Him *in all the places of His dominion.*

בָּרְכִי נַפְשִׁי אֶת ה' — *Bless HASHEM, O my soul.*

In this psalm the words *Bless HASHEM, O my soul* appear three

---

1. The *Talmud* (*Shabbos* 88a) notes that the verse begins with a description of angels who *do* (עֹשֵׂי) and concludes with a description of angels who *obey* (לִשְׁמֹעַ). This alludes to the Jew's enthusiastic reaction when God offered them the Torah at Sinai. The entire nation eagerly responded, נַעֲשֶׂה וְנִשְׁמָע, *We shall do and we shall obey* (Exodus 24:7).

At that moment, six hundred thousand ministering angels descended and set two crowns on the head of each Jew: one crown was for saying *we shall do* and one was for saying *we shall obey.*

times. *Alshich* explains that man is composed of elements gathered from the three worlds described in the first stich of this verse. His נְשָׁמָה, *soul,* is from the world of the angels. His נֶפֶשׁ, *living spirit,* is associated with the legions of stars which exercise a measure of control of human life. His גוּף, *body,* is from the lowly earth. Therefore, man is exhorted to bless Hashem for the three forms of goodness which were bestowed upon him *(Alshich).*

104 מזמור קד

 T his psalm is a continuation of the preceding one and echoes its refrain, *Bless HASHEM, O my soul!* Here, *David recounts the wonders of the six days of Creation and describes the splendor of the primeval light, the heaven and earth, the grass, the fish of the sea, the beasts of the field, and, finally, the crowning glory of Creation — man himself* (Ibn Ezra)

The *Midrash (Shemos Rabbah 15:22) says: In the Torah, Moses related many events without elaboration. They remained obscure until David came and explained them, as he did here by expanding upon the theme of Creation and illuminating its mysteries.*

Radak observes that every artist is motivated to produce works of art because he seeks personal acclaim and glory. However when God fashioned the world, His sole concern was man's welfare. Mere flesh and blood cannot grasp the profound motives of God, much less appreciate them. Only the soul can comprehend the altruism and selfless love of its Creator. Thus, the Psalmist calls upon his own spirit, Bless HASHEM, O my soul! For none but the soul could compose this blessing.

This psalm is the שִׁיר שֶׁל יוֹם, *Song of the Day, for Rosh Chodesh, the first day of the new month. Tur (Orach Chaim 423) explains that the Psalmist alludes to the new month in verse 19, He made the moon for festivals [see footnote there]. Zohar (Midrash HaNe'elam, Parshas Vayeira) says that the souls of the righteous people in Paradise recite this psalm every Rosh Chodesh (see Taamei HaMinhagim).*

א בָּרְכִי נַפְשִׁי אֶת־יהוה יהוה אֱלֹהַי גָּדַלְתָּ

ב מְאֹד הוֹד וְהָדָר לָבָשְׁתָּ: עֹטֶה־אוֹר כַּשַּׂלְמָה

ג נוֹטֶה שָׁמַיִם כַּיְרִיעָה: הַמְקָרֶה בַמַּיִם

עֲלִיּוֹתָיו הַשָּׂם־עָבִים רְכוּבוֹ הַמְהַלֵּךְ עַל־

ד כַּנְפֵי־רוּחַ: עֹשֶׂה מַלְאָכָיו רוּחוֹת מְשָׁרְתָיו

1. בָּרְכִי נַפְשִׁי אֶת ה׳ — *Bless HASHEM, O my soul.*

[See comm. to 103:1.]

אֱלֹהַי גָּדַלְתָּ מְאֹד ה׳ — *HASHEM, my God, You are very great.*

The Psalmist makes no attempt to define the extent of God's greatness; he says only that God is *very great.* Man can merely attempt to begin a recital of God's blessings, which are truly innumerable (*Ibn Ezra*).

Indeed, God was *great* even before the dawn of Creation, but there was no one to recognize and acknowledge His greatness. When He fashioned intelligent creatures who appreciated Him, however, God became *very great.*

Mortal kings have their portraits engraved on larger-than-life canvases. But the Almighty God etched His image and likeness into every molecule of the universe; the heavens, the earth, and the seas form a vast tapestry reflecting God's glory. Nevertheless, the Creator remains even larger than His creation (*Tanchuma, Parshas Vayechi*).

הוֹד וְהָדָר לָבָשְׁתָּ — *You have donned majesty and splendor.*

Malbim defines הוֹד as inner, personal *majesty,* and הָדָר as visible *splendor.*

Before Creation, the essence of God was completely spiritual. Then God, so to speak, clothed His spirit in layer after layer of matter. The process by which the spirit was cloaked and contained in matter is known as סוֹד הַצִּמְצוּם, *the mystery of* [progressive] *confinement,* meaning that God confined His infinite greatness to bring it within the capacity of man's limited perception (*Meor VaShemesh*). [Thus, God clothed His

inner spiritual *majesty* with layer upon layer of *splendor* in the form of His awesome Creation.]

[The corruption of mankind has tarnished the *splendor* of the Divine clothing. Therefore, we eagerly await the advent of the Messiah, who will restore the *majesty* and *splendor* of the world, as 21:6 states: הוֹד וְהָדָר תְּשַׁוֶּה עָלָיו, *majesty and splendor You conferred upon him.*]

2. עֹטֶה אוֹר כַּשַּׂלְמָה — *Cloaked in light as with a garment.*

Light was the very first creation on the first day. As such, it was the first cloak in which God concealed His spiritual essence (*Ibn Ezra*).

Ibn Yachya and *Vidal HaTzorfati* observe that when God created the primal light He also created the מַלְאָכִים, *ministering angels,* who are a pure spiritual force radiating light. The angels surround God as a cloak envelops the one who wears it. [See, however, commentary to *verse* 4.]

נוֹטֶה שָׁמַיִם כַּיְרִיעָה — *Stretching out the heavens like a curtain.*

God created the heavens on the second day, when He said (*Genesis* 1:6), *"Let there be a firmament in the midst of the waters;"* then *God called the firmament, "Heaven"* (*ibid. v.* 8; *Radak*).

Ibn Ezra (*Genesis* 1:6) explains that רָקִיעַ, *firmament,* means something that is stretched out and it refers specifically to the אֲוִיר, *atmosphere.* He esoterically explains that when the primal light intensified upon the earth and the [moisture-laden] wind evaporated [i.e.,

Bless HASHEM, O my soul,

HASHEM, my God, You are very great,

You have donned majesty and splendor;

² Cloaked in light as with a garment,

stretching out the heavens like a curtain;

³ Who roofs His upper chambers with water,

Who makes clouds His chariot,

Who walks on winged wind,

⁴ Who makes the winds His messengers,

---

spread out], the primal flame [of light] became the firmament.

3. הַמְקָרֶה בַמַּיִם עֲלִיּוֹתָיו — *Who roofs His upper chambers with water.*

Radak suggests that this refers to the upper firmament, as in *Genesis 1:7: And God made the firmament, and He separated between the waters which were beneath the firmament and between the waters which were above the firmament.*

Me'am Loez (Genesis 1:7) states that although the water above the firmament is of a spiritual nature, we are nevertheless obliged to believe that it is, indeed, water, as King David said: *Praise Him, heavens of heavens, and you waters that are above the heavens* (148:4).

However, *Radak* and *Ibn Yachya* interpret הַמְקָרֶה as *one who lays beams* [cognate of קוֹרָה, *beam*]. Thus, this verse refers to the clouds which are stretched out across the sky like *beams* and *rafters* [to shield the earth from the blazing sun].

Tanchuma (Parshas Vayechi) observes that when a mortal king builds his palace, he first constructs the floor and solid walls. Later, he covers it with a roof of stone, wood, and earth. But the Almighty God made the entire world His palace and began by constructing an apparently flimsy roof of clouds composed of mere water vapor.

הַשָּׂם עָבִים רְכוּבוֹ — *Who makes clouds His chariot.*

The constantly shifting *clouds* resemble a *chariot* pulled to and fro by a steed which is at its master's beck and call (*Radak*).

Indeed, God does appear to ride on clouds, as *Isaiah 19:1* states: *Behold, HASHEM rides upon a swift cloud and comes to Egypt.* Similarly, God said at Sinai (*Exodus 19:9*), *Behold, I am coming to you in a thick cloud* (*Exodus 19:9*).

However, God differs from mortal riders who are supported by their mounts, in that God supports His steed and infuses it with strength (*Midrash Shocher Tov*).

הַמְהַלֵּךְ עַל כַּנְפֵי רוּחַ — *Who walks on winged wind* [lit. *wings of wind*].

The clouds soar across the sky, driven by the wind, and they resemble swift winged birds (*Ibn Ezra*).

4. עֹשֶׂה מַלְאָכָיו רוּחוֹת — *Who makes the winds His messengers.*

Even the invisible, ever-shifting winds and breezes have immense significance. They are emissaries of God, performing His bidding as He controls the world. Thus, each breeze is ordained to serve a specific purpose (*Radak*).

Similarly, 148:8 speaks of רוּחַ סְעָרָה עֹשָׂה דְבָרוֹ, *a stormy wind which fulfills His word* (*Ibn Ezra*)

Midrash Shocher Tov translates מַלְאָכָיו as *His angels* and states that the angels were created on the Second day

ה אֵשׁ לֹהֵט: יָסַד־אֶרֶץ עַל־מְכוֹנֶיהָ בַּל־תִּמּוֹט
ו עוֹלָם וָעֶד: תְּהוֹם כַּלְּבוּשׁ כִּסִּיתוֹ עַל־הָרִים
ז יַעַמְדוּ־מָיִם: מִן־גַּעֲרָתְךָ יְנוּסוּן מִן־קוֹל
ח רַעַמְךָ יֵחָפֵזוּן: יַעֲלוּ הָרִים יֵרְדוּ בְקָעוֹת אֶל־
ט מְקוֹם זֶה | יָסַדְתָּ לָהֶם: גְּבוּל־שַׂמְתָּ בַּל־
י יַעֲבֹרוּן בַּל־יְשׁוּבוּן לְכַסּוֹת הָאָרֶץ: הַמְשַׁלֵּחַ

of Creation. [But see commentary to verse 2.]

מְשָׁרְתָיו אֵשׁ לֹהֵט — *The flaming fire His ministers.*

According to *Radak*, this refers to the blazing fires and flashes of lightning which streak through the sky.

Zohar (*Shemos* and *Terumah*) says that this refers to the fiery angels who stay near God in His inner chambers in order to minister to Him. However, the wind-like angels are God's *messengers*, and He sends them abroad to do His will.[1]

5. יָסַד אֶרֶץ עַל־מְכוֹנֶיהָ — *Who established the earth upon its foundations.*[2]

[The earth is actually the foundation of the entire universe, because God created everything only for the sake of man. Originally, God laid the foundation stone of the earth. It was called the אֶבֶן שְׁתִיָּה, because מִמֶּנּוּ הוּשְׁתַת הָעוֹלָם, *from it the earth sprang forth* (*Yoma* 54b). The earth continued to expand until God said, "It is enough." (See commentary and footnote to 91:1.)]

בַּל תִּמּוֹט עוֹלָם וָעֶד — *That it falter not forever and ever.*

[God allowed the expansion process to continue until the earth reached the proper size to support the quality and extent of life that He desired for it. After the expansion was arrested, the earth would never grow again.]

6. תְּהוֹם כַּלְּבוּשׁ כִּסִּיתוֹ — *The watery deep, as with a garment You covered it.*

The commentators are not in accord regarding the antecedent of *it* in this stich. *Ibn Ezra* understands it as a reference to the *watery deep* and translates: *You covered the watery deep with a garment*, i.e., the surface waters of the sea cover the very deep (תְּהוֹם) waters beneath them.

Radak views *it* as an allusion to *the earth* mentioned in verse 5. According to his explanation the word תְּהוֹם, *watery deep*, includes all waters from the surface down to the very depths. He explains that originally the waters *covered* the entire surface of the earth and enveloped it *as with a garment*. Only later, on the third day, did God gather the waters into one area, so that the dry land appeared (see *Genesis* 1:9).

עַל־הָרִים יַעַמְדוּ מָיִם — *Upon the mountains water would stand.*

1. *Rambam* (*Hilchos Yesodei HaTorah* 2:7) describes ten groups of celestial angels in ascending order. The highest angels are called חַיּוֹת הַקֹּדֶשׁ [*Chayos*], *the holy beasts*, which are next to God's celestial throne.

Of these angels the prophet *Ezekiel* 1:13 says: *As for the appearance of the Chayos, their appearance was like fiery coals, burning like the appearance of torches ... there was a brilliance to the fire, and from the fire went forth lightning.*

2. The three foundations upon which the world stands are תּוֹרָה, *Torah study*, עֲבוֹדָה, *Temple service*, and גְּמִילוּת חֲסָדִים, *acts of kindness* (*Avos* 1:2). An allusion to this may be found in the numerical equivalent of our verse, 1309, which is the same as the combined numerical equivalent of תּוֹרָה (611), עֲבוֹדָה (87), and גְּמִילוּת חֲסָדִים (611) (*Rabbi Avie Gold*).

the flaming fire His ministers,

⁵ *Who established the earth upon its foundations,*
that it falter not forever and ever.

⁶ *The watery deep, as with a garment You covered it,*
upon the mountains water would stand.

⁷ *From Your rebuke they fled,*
from the sound of Your thunder
they rushed away.

⁸ *They ascended mountains,*
they descended to valleys,
to the special place You founded for them.

⁹ *You set a boundary they cannot overstep,*
they cannot return to cover the earth.

¹⁰ *He sends the springs into the streams,*

Even now, there are huge mountains on the ocean floor covered by the deep waters (Rashi; Ibn Ezra).

7. מִן גַּעֲרָתְךָ יְנוּסוּן — *From Your rebuke they fled.*

When God cried out יִקָּווּ הַמַּיִם, *Let the waters gather* (Genesis 1:9), they all fled from where they were spread out and condensed into seas and oceans (Rashi).

מִן קוֹל רַעַמְךָ יֵחָפֵזוּן — *From the sound of Your thunder they rushed away.*

Rav Vidal HaTzorfati comments that this alludes to the splitting of the Sea of Reeds. During the six days of Creation, God informed the waters of the sea that they would split when Israel attempted to cross them. Therefore, centuries later, *they hastened away*, in obedience to the command which God thundered at them.

8. יַעֲלוּ הָרִים יֵרְדוּ בְקָעוֹת אֶל מְקוֹם זֶה יָסַדְתָּ לָהֶם — *They ascended* [lit. *will ascend*] *mountains, they descended to* [lit. *will descend*] *valleys, to the special* [lit. *to this*] *place You founded for them.*

[*Pirkei d'Rabbi Eliezer* and the *Zohar* teach that the earth was originally a plain, entirely submerged under water. Scarcely had God's words, *Let the*

waters gather (Genesis 1:9), been uttered, when mountains and hills appeared all over and the waters collected in the deep-lying valleys. But the waters threatened to overflow the earth until God forced them back into the sea, and encircled the sea with sand.]

9. גְּבוּל שַׂמְתָּ בַּל יַעֲבֹרוּן — *You set a boundary they cannot overstep.*

[Similarly, *Jeremiah* 5:22 states, "Do you not fear me?" says HASHEM, "Will you not tremble at My presence? For it is I who have placed the sand as a boundary for the sea, by an eternal decree that it shall not pass over it; and though its waves toss themselves, yet they cannot prevail, though they roar they cannot pass over it."]

בַּל יְשֻׁבוּן לְכַסּוֹת הָאָרֶץ — *They cannot return to cover the earth.*

[Whenever the sea is tempted to overflow its bounds, it beholds the sand and recoils, because it remembers God's rebuke, from which it fled during the six days of Creation.]

10. הַמְשַׁלֵּחַ מַעְיָנִים בַּנְּחָלִים — *He sends the springs into the streams.*

Radak vividly describes how God engineered the world's water supply as a

יא מַעְיָנִים בַּנְּחָלִים בֵּין הָרִים יְהַלֵּכוּן: יַשְׁקוּ
כָּל־חַיְתוֹ שָׂדָי יִשְׁבְּרוּ פְרָאִים צְמָאָם:
יב עֲלֵיהֶם עוֹף־הַשָּׁמַיִם יִשְׁכּוֹן מִבֵּין עֳפָאיִם
יג יִתְּנוּ־קוֹל: מַשְׁקֶה הָרִים מֵעֲלִיּוֹתָיו מִפְּרִי
יד מַעֲשֶׂיךָ תִּשְׂבַּע הָאָרֶץ: מַצְמִיחַ חָצִיר |
לַבְּהֵמָה וְעֵשֶׂב לַעֲבֹדַת הָאָדָם לְהוֹצִיא לֶחֶם

marvel of technical ingenuity which efficiently serves all human needs.

First, God designated the enclosed areas of the seas and oceans. Since these mammoth bodies of water are relatively still, they could have become huge, stagnant swamps because of all the plant and animal life which decays inside them. Therefore, God made the seas salty, to prevent such putrefaction.

On the land masses which were not covered by the sea, God provided rivers and springs of fresh, cold water. These streams have many uses, including human and animal consumption, irrigation of crops, cooling of the air, and the provision of moisture for parched organisms and for the atmosphere. In addition, the swift flow of the current serves as a source of energy. The spring waters do not remain in one place, but flow in streams. This clever design frees them from the threat of stagnation and decay.

בֵּין הָרִים יְהַלֵּכוּן — They flow between the mountains.

God made the rivers and streams flow in deep channels and river-beds so that they would be contained within protective banks. If they were to flow on flat plains without containment, they would cause property damage and injury (Radak).

11. יַשְׁקוּ כָּל חַיְתוֹ שָׂדָי — They water every beast of the field.

God has not neglected any place on earth. He has even provided a water supply for the parched desert, where underground streams form oases at which beasts can slake their thirst (Radak).

יִשְׁבְּרוּ פְרָאִים צְמָאָם — They quench the wild creatures' thirst.

The פְרָאִים are the wild creatures which inhabit the forsaken wilderness (see Jeremiah 2:24). God is concerned about them, for He cares for all creatures (Radak).

12. עֲלֵיהֶם עוֹף הַשָּׁמַיִם יִשְׁכּוֹן — Near them dwell the heavens' birds.

The birds congregate around the watering holes, to which they are especially attracted since they were originally created from the water, as Genesis 1:20 states: God said, ''Let the waters teem with creeping living creatures, and fowl that fly about over the earth across the expanse of the heavens'' (Radak).[1]

מִבֵּין עֳפָאיִם יִתְּנוּ קוֹל — From among the branches they give [forth] songs [lit. sound].

The Aramaic word for branches is עֲפָיָה as in Daniel 4:9 (Rashi). קוֹל, sound, alludes to קָל זְמָר, the sound of

1. Ramban (Genesis 1:20) connects the creation of bird life to the sea, because the creations of the fifth day emanated from the waters. He contends that had bird life been created from earth, it would have been mentioned on the sixth day. However, the view was debated by some Sages in the Talmud, Chullin 27b, who cited Genesis 2:19, as evidence that bird life sprang from רֶקַק, alluvial mud, which, as Ramban explains, is at the bottom of the ocean. Thus, even though mud is technically land, the creation of the birds is mentioned on the fifth day.

One Sage attempts to prove the relationship between birds and the sea from the fact that birds have scales on their feet resembling those of a fish (Chullin 27b).

they flow between the mountains;

¹¹ They water every beast of the field,
they quench the wild creatures' thirst.

¹² Near them dwell the heavens' birds,
from among the branches they give forth song.

¹³ He waters the mountains
from His upper chambers,
from the fruit of Your works the earth is sated.

¹⁴ He causes vegetation to sprout for the cattle,
and plants for the service of man,
to bring forth bread from the earth,

---

song (Targum). In their natural habitat, the birds chirp and sing with abandon and delight (Radak).

13. מַשְׁקֶה הָרִים מֵעֲלִיּוֹתָיו — *He waters the mountains from His upper chambers.*

The Psalmist continues his discussion of the creations of the third day. After God gathered all the waters in special areas, He caused the grass to grow on dry land. This grass flourished when watered by the rains. The Psalmist singles out the mountains because they are particularly dependent on the rains sent by God; the plains and valleys, however, can be cultivated and irrigated by man, thus decreasing their direct dependence on rain from God (Radak).

מִפְּרִי מַעֲשֶׂיךָ תִּשְׂבַּע הָאָרֶץ — *From the fruit of Your works the earth is sated.*

God's *works* alludes to the clouds whose *fruit* is the life-giving rain (Radak).

14. מַצְמִיחַ חָצִיר לַבְּהֵמָה — *He causes vegetation to sprout for the cattle.*

Since animals lack the intelligence and the physical ability to engage in agriculture, God causes *vegetation* to sprout for the cattle to eat (Rav Yoseif Titzak).

וְעֵשֶׂב לַעֲבֹדַת הָאָדָם — *And plants* [lit. *grass*] *for the service of man.*

Man, however, must perform עֲבוֹדָה, *service* and *labor*, in order to earn his daily bread. Prior to his sin, Adam could

eat the wild grass. Afterwards, however, Adam was cursed (Genesis 3:19): *By the sweat of your brow shall you eat bread* (Rav Yitzchak Aboab).

According to *Midrash Shocher Tov*, grass refers to flax, which man must process into thread and cloth for garments.

לְהוֹצִיא לֶחֶם מִן הָאָרֶץ — *To bring forth bread from the earth.*

Ibn Ezra (Genesis 3:19) observes that today, after Adam's sin, man is worse off than the animals, for their food requires no preparation. But before man can partake of food, he must first sow, thresh, knead, and bake his bread [see Pesachim 118a].

Before Adam's sin, whole loaves of fresh bread grew on trees and Adam had only to pick them. The Talmud (Shabbos 30b) records Rabban Gamliel's teaching that in the time of Messiah, the land of Israel will return to this level of perfection. Then the trees will produce loaves of baked bread every day, in fulfillment of the verse; *May a loaf of bread be in the land* (72:16).

For this reason, *halachah*, Torah and Rabbinic law, states that the blessing on bread should be הַמּוֹצִיא לֶחֶם מִן הָאָרֶץ, *Blessed are You ... Who brings forth bread from the earth*, to commemorate the perfection which prevailed before Adam's sin and which will be reinstated in the future.

טו מִן־הָאָ֑רֶץ: וְיַ֤יִן ׀ יְשַׂמַּ֬ח לְבַב־אֱנ֗וֹשׁ לְהַצְה֣יל
טז פָּנִ֥ים מִשָּׁ֑מֶן וְ֝לֶ֗חֶם לְבַב־אֱנ֥וֹשׁ יִסְעָֽד: יִשְׂבְּע֡וּ
יז עֲצֵ֣י יְ֭הֹוָה אַֽרְזֵ֥י לְ֝בָנ֗וֹן אֲשֶׁ֣ר נָטָֽע: אֲשֶׁר־שָׁ֭ם
יח צִפֳּרִ֣ים יְקַנֵּ֑נוּ חֲ֝סִידָ֗ה בְּרוֹשִׁ֥ים בֵּיתָֽהּ: הָרִ֤ים

Shulchan Aruch (Orach Chaim 167:4) rules that when one recites the blessing over bread he should hold the loaf in both hands, grasping it with all ten fingers. The number ten corresponds to the ten *mitzvos* which are involved in making bread. (These include the separation of *terumah*, *maaser*, *challah*, etc.) Furthermore, there are ten words in the blessing, *Who brings forth*, and ten words in this verse which speaks of bringing forth *bread from the earth*.

[Man can easily delude himself into thinking that he deserves the credit for producing bread because his toil was responsible for the many stages needed to process it into a loaf of bread. Moreover, he put all his talent and strength into the effort, symbolized by ten fingers. To counter this false impression *halachah* requires man to proclaim that God alone is responsible for growth and productivity. He is the Creator Who brought the world into being with ten utterances (*Avos* 5:1); and He continues to control everything in it. Therefore, at every one of the ten stages in the production of bread man demonstrates his gratitude to God by performing one of ten *mitzvos*. Finally, he grasps the bread with the ten fingers that were involved in its manufacture, and recites a blessing as if to proclaim: "We must praise God for this bread, for man is merely a tool in the hands of the Almighty, Who creates and produces everything."]

15. וְיַיִן יְשַׂמַּח לְבַב אֱנוֹשׁ — *And wine that gladdens man's heart.*

God creates the grapes from which wine is pressed. When drunk in sensible proportions, wine gladdens the heart and drives away melancholy. It heightens the intellect and even prepares the mind for prophecy (*Radak*).

But when used improperly and excessively, wine can cause יְלָלָה, whining and crying (*Sanhedrin* 70b).[1]

If the letter שׂ in יְשַׂמַּח is read as a שׁ, the entire word becomes יְשַׁמַּח, related to שְׁמָמָה, *destruction*, alluding to the potential danger of wine drunk in excess. With a שׂ, however, the word is יְשַׂמַּח, *makes glad*, referring to the positive qualities of wine drunk in moderation (*Yoma* 76b).

Indeed, the Sages of the *Talmud* (*Pesachim* 109a) derive a rule from this verse: אֵין שִׂמְחָה אֶלָּא בְּיַיִן, *there can be no true rejoicing without wine*. Therefore, this beverage should be present at all festival celebrations.

לְהַצְהִיל פָּנִים מִשָּׁמֶן — *To make the face glow from oil.*

When man drinks oil, his face shines. Also, when oil is burned in a lamp, it casts rays of light on the face (*Radak*).

The *Talmud* (*Horayos* 13b) teaches that one of the five things which cause a person to forget his learning is the practice of eating whole olives. Five things help a person remember that which he forgot, including the practice

1. Noah took a grapevine into the ark and replanted it after the flood. He produced wine from grapes and became drunk and caused himself humiliation (*Genesis* 9:12-20). In expounding on Noah's drunkenness *Midrash Tanchuma* (*Noach* 13) likens a drunkard to a lamb, a lion, a pig and a monkey:

Before man begins to drink he is as gentle as a lamb. After becoming mildly intoxicated, he feels as strong and fearless as a lion. When he drinks even more he vomits and wallows in his own filth like a pig. Finally the drinker loses all control; he shouts obscenities and dances wildly like a monkey.

¹⁵ *And wine that gladdens man's heart,*
to make the face glow from oil,
and bread that sustains the heart of man;
¹⁶ *The trees of HASHEM are sated,*
the cedars of Lebanon which He has planted;
¹⁷ *There where the birds nest,*
the stork — its home is among cypresses;

of drinking oil and wine and the smelling of fine spices. Rav Yochanan said: Just as whole olives can cause a man to forget all that he studied for seventy years, olive oil can cause a man to remember seventy years of study. Rava said: Wine and spices open the mind and make a man clever.

[This may be understood allegorically. The 'whole olive' alludes to the flesh and the outer husk of the fruit, whereas the 'olive oil' is its inner essence.

In the pursuit of knowledge a person should always strive to penetrate to the inner core of a subject in order to comprehend its essence. Never should the student 'swallow it whole,' i.e., study matters superficially, because that breeds misconception, and ignorance. Such confused knowledge is best forgotten, while clear knowledge of essentials should be remembered for a lifetime.]

וְלֶחֶם לְבַב אֱנוֹשׁ יִסְעָד — *And bread that sustains the heart of man.*

Bread is the staff of life; the only form of nutrition which can consistently sustain man. This lesson is mentioned in each of the three sections of Scripture: תּוֹרָה, *Pentateuch*, נְבִיאִים, *Prophets*, and כְּתוּבִים, *Writings*. The Pentateuch *Genesis* 18:5 records that when the three travelers appeared at Abraham's door, he told them, *"I will fetch a morsel of bread that you may sustain yourselves."* The Prophets (*Judges* 19:5) teaches: *Sustain your heart with a morsel of bread.* And in the Writings it is written: *Bread that sustains the heart of man* (*Bereishis Rabbah* 48:11).

[The term used here for *heart* is לְבָב, with a double ב, rather than לֵב. In Rabbinic homiletics לְבָב denotes the heart as the seat of two inclinations — good and evil (see *Mishnah Berachos* 9:1).]

16. יִשְׂבְּעוּ עֲצֵי ה' — *The trees of HASHEM are sated.*

God waters them generously with abundant rain (*Radak*).

Midrash Shocher Tov says that this refers to the trees which God originally planted in the Garden of Eden. Since God Himself was involved in this planting, they are called *the trees of HASHEM*.

Radak says that these trees grew so large that they can only be adequately described in Divine terms.

אַרְזֵי לְבָנוֹן אֲשֶׁר נָטָע — *The cedars of Lebanon which He has planted.*

Men plant fruit trees for human consumption but huge trees such as *the cedars*, which bear no fruit, are planted only by God. He fashioned plants in such a way that they need no human care. He supplies their forest soil with all the required nutrients and minerals and showers abundant rains upon them (*Radak*).

Midrash Shocher Tov states that the fruitless cedar was created solely to enhance the glory of Hashem because its splendid wooden beams were used in the construction of the Holy Temple, the *Beis HaMikdash*.

17. אֲשֶׁר שָׁם צִפֳּרִים יְקַנֵּנוּ — *There where the birds nest.*

The Psalmist continues to depict the genius of the Divine design. The value

הַגְּבֹהִים לַיְּעֵלִים סְלָעִים מַחְסֶה לַשְׁפַנִּים:

יט עָשָׂה יָרֵחַ לְמוֹעֲדִים שֶׁמֶשׁ יָדַע מְבוֹאוֹ:

כ תָּשֶׁת־חֹשֶׁךְ וִיהִי לָיְלָה בּוֹ־תִרְמֹשׂ כָּל־חַיְתוֹ־

of the great trees is quite evident after they are cut down: The large beams are ideal for construction and the smaller branches and chips serve as fuel for fires. Here, however, the Psalmist observes that while the cedar lives, it serves a vital function by providing a nesting place for the high-flying birds.

This demonstrates a fundamental concept underlying the Divine design of nature. The world is composed of four main categories of creations. In ascending order they are: דּוֹמֵם, *inorganic minerals*, צוֹמֵחַ, *vegetation*, חַי, *living* creatures of all kinds, and מְדַבֵּר *speakers*, i.e., human beings endowed with the gift of intelligent speech. Since the lower categories exist to serve the higher ones, the smallest creature of the higher order is more important than the most massive creature of the order beneath it. Thus the Psalmist suggests that God created the loftiest cedar trees only to provide nests for small birds (*Radak*).

חֲסִידָה בְּרוֹשִׁים בֵּיתָהּ — *The stork — its home is among cypresses.*

[Although the exact translation of חֲסִידָה, *chassidah*, is uncertain, most renderings use *stork*.][1]

The Psalmist singles out the *chassidah* because this large, high-flying bird nests only in tall trees like the cedar or cypress (*Radak*).

Midrash Shocher Tov understands this as an allusion to the Levites, who

are called חֲסִידִים [*chassidim*], *devout* and *kind* men (*Deuteronomy* 33:8). Their *home* was the Holy Temple, which was built of cedar and cypress [see *Song of Songs* 1:17].

18. הֶהָרִים הַגְּבֹהִים לַיְּעֵלִים — *High mountains for the wild goats.*

At first glance, the remote and barren mountains appear to serve no purpose; but in fact they were created to provide a habitat for the *wild* mountain *goats* (*Rashi; Radak*). [This runs counter to the secular theory of evolution, which teaches that organisms adapt to the specific nature of their particular environments. The Torah teaches, however, that the environment was created to suit the needs of the specific animals which were destined to live there. Evolution supposes that the high forms of life developed and emerged from lower forms which preceded them, but the Torah teaches that the lower forms of life or nature were created to serve the higher forms which were ordained to follow them. Thus, tall trees were created to serve the needs of high-flying birds. High mountains were formed to provide shelter for wild goats.]

The *Midrash* (*Bereishis Rabbah* 12:8) illustrates how God manipulates the environment to suit the needs of the creatures who inhabit it. Since the wild goat is a weak, defenseless creature, it

---

1. The *Talmud* (*Chullin* 63a) teaches that the חֲסִידָה, *chassidah*, received its name because it performs acts of חֶסֶד [*chesed*], *kindness* for its friends. *Rashi* (*Chullin* 63a) explains that this bird shares its food supply with others.

In *Leviticus* 11:19, the Torah lists it among the unclean fowl. *Ramban* observes that the unclean birds possess a cruel, predatory nature, which is transferred to those who consume them. For this reason, the Torah forbade these species. *Ramban* notes that the *chassidah*, which is noteworthy for its kindness, appears to contravene this theory that unclean animals are cruel.

Some commentaries explain, however, that since the *chassidah's* kindness does not extend beyond its own species, the Torah considers it cruel and unfit to eat, for kindness done only to one's own limited circle is more selfish than kind.

¹⁸ *High mountains for the wild goats,*
     rocks as refuge for the gophers.
¹⁹ *He made the moon for festivals,*
     the sun knows its destination.
²⁰ *You make darkness and it is night,*
     in which every forest beast stirs;

lives in the remote mountains in order to be protected from predators.

סְלָעִים מַחְסֶה לַשְׁפַנִּים — *Rocks as refuge for the gophers.*

Even the huge boulders and rocks which litter the wilderness and the plains have a purpose. God created huge rocks to protect the tiny gophers from the predatory birds which seek to swoop down on them (*Bereishis Rabbah* 12:8).

19. עָשָׂה יָרֵחַ לְמוֹעֲדִים — *He made the moon for festivals.*

The Psalmist now describes the creations of the fourth day. Then, *God made the two luminaries, the greater luminary* [the sun] *to dominate the day and the lesser luminary* [the moon] *to dominate the night (Genesis 1:16).*

Although the moon is the smaller of the two luminaries, it is mentioned first here because the night precedes the day. The moon is described as the controller of the seasons because the Jewish calendar of festivals is based on the lunar cycle as it relates to the solar cycle. At the moment of creation, *God said, "Let there be luminaries in the firmament of the heaven to separate between the day and the night; and they shall serve as signs, and for festivals, and for days and years" (Genesis 1:14).*[1]

שֶׁמֶשׁ יָדַע מְבוֹאוֹ — *The sun knows its destination.*

The daily orbit and the annual cycle of the sun is more regular than that of the moon, which seems to change and move in an erratic manner. The *Talmud* (*Rosh Hashanah 25a*) states: The sun knows where it is going; the moon does not (*Radak*).

[The precision of the sun's cycle demonstrates the skill and genius of the Creator, Who fashioned its flawless orbit.]

20. תָּשֶׁת חֹשֶׁךְ וִיהִי לָיְלָה — *You make darkness and it is night.*

After praising the creation of the luminaries which provide light, the Psalmist extols the darkness as well. God forbade certain ferocious beasts from going out to hunt in broad daylight, lest they harm man. God instilled an instinctive fear of man in these animals, as *Genesis 9:2* states: *The fear of you* [men] *and the dread of you shall be upon every beast of the earth.* Included in this *dread* is a fear of daylight.

Another benefit of the dark is that since darkness limits visibility, man and his domesticated animals are forced to rest at night.

Finally, the pattern of light and

---

1. The *Tur* (*Orach Chaim* 423) states that this psalm is recited as the Song of the Day for Rosh Chodesh, the Festival of the New Moon, because the Psalmist alludes to the New Moon in this verse: *He made the moon for the festivals.*[1]

Rav Yitzchak Aboab explains that these words are not merely a casual allusion to the new month. Rather, they set the tone of this entire composition, whose main theme is God's complete mastery over every aspect of creation. Throughout the monthly lunar cycle, the size of the moon visibly waxes and wanes, to demonstrate dramatically that God has total mastery over His creations. No other natural phenomenon conveys this message as vividly and forcefully as the moon's cycle. Thus, the theme of the New Moon complements the theme of this entire hymn of praise to the Master of Creation.

כא יָעַר: הַכְּפִירִים שֹׁאֲגִים לַטָּרֶף וּלְבַקֵּשׁ מֵאֵל

כב אָכְלָם: תִּזְרַח הַשֶּׁמֶשׁ יֵאָסֵפוּן וְאֶל־מְעוֹנֹתָם

כג יִרְבָּצוּן: יֵצֵא אָדָם לְפָעֳלוֹ וְלַעֲבֹדָתוֹ עֲדֵי־

כד עָרֶב: מָה־רַבּוּ מַעֲשֶׂיךָ | יהוה כֻּלָּם בְּחָכְמָה

כה עָשִׂיתָ מָלְאָה הָאָרֶץ קִנְיָנֶךָ: זֶה | הַיָּם גָּדוֹל

darkness is essential for the process of growth [i.e., photosynthesis] (Radak).

וּבוֹ תִרְמֹשׂ כָּל חַיְתוֹ יָעַר — *In which every forest beast stirs.*

The *Talmud* (*Bava Metzia* 83b) interprets this verse allegorically: This [material] world resembles the gloom and darkness of night, for the wicked men roam freely, like the beasts of the forest [which prey on weak, innocent victims].

21. הַכְּפִירִים שֹׁאֲגִים לַטָּרֶף — *The young lions roar after the[ir] prey.*

A כְּפִיר is a *young lion;* the mature animal is termed an אַרְיֵה. However, the כְּפִיר is older than the גּוּר, *the lion's whelp* (Radak).

When the *young lion roars at its prey,* the quarry becomes momentarily immobilized with fear, enabling the young lion to attack its victim (*Maharam Armaah*).

וּלְבַקֵּשׁ מֵאֵל אָכְלָם — *And to seek their food from God.*

God is the ultimate source of all food, for He initiated the cycle of natural causes which eventually brings nourishment to the lion. Therefore, when the lion seeks its prey, it is as if it seeks food from the hand of God (*Radak*).

Midrash Shocher Tov interprets figuratively: the כְּפִירִים are the כּוֹפְרִים, *heretics,* who deny the existence of God. According to this approach, *roar after prey* means that they prey upon and plunder their helpless victims, particularly the Jewish people. *And to seek their food from God* describes the Jewish people who depend on God for their sustenance. [See commentary to 34:11.]

22. תִּזְרַח הַשֶּׁמֶשׁ יֵאָסֵפוּן — *The sun rises and they are gathered in.*

When the darkness of night ends and the daylight emerges, the wild beasts come back to their caves to hide from the men who are now going forth to work (*Rashi; Radak*).

The *Talmud* (*Bava Metzia* 83b) perceives this as a continuation of the allegory begun in verse 20: in the future, the sun (i.e., success and reward) will rise and shine upon the righteous, while the wicked are gathered into the fires of hell.

וְאֶל מְעוֹנֹתָם יִרְבָּצוּן — *And in their dens they crouch* [lit. *recline*].

The *Talmud* (*ibid.*) continues that each righteous man will receive a unique reward [i.e., his own *den*] in accordance with his merit and virtue.

23. יֵצֵא אָדָם לְפָעֳלוֹ — *Man goes forth to his work.*

When *man goes forth to his work* by day, the beasts' hunting period ends. God, in His infinite wisdom, coordinates this timetable with precision (*Radak*).

The *Talmud* (*Bava Metzia* 83b) derives from this verse an important rule of labor relations and compensation: when the worker goes out to his place of employment in the morning it is on his employer's time; but the return of the worker to his home in the evening is on the employee's time. Furthermore, the worker is responsible to be at his place of work when the sun rises, and the employer must ensure that the worker is able to return to his home when the sun sets (see *Rashi* and *Tosafos, Bava Metzia* 83b, and *Midrash Shocher Tov*).

²¹ *The young lions roar after their prey,*
and to seek their food from God.
²² *The sun rises and they are gathered in,*
and in their dens they crouch.
²³ *Man goes forth to his work,*
and to his labor until evening.
²⁴ *How abundant are Your works, HASHEM,*
with wisdom You made them all,
the earth is full of Your possessions.
²⁵ *Behold this sea — great and of broad measure,*

וְלַעֲבֹדָתוֹ עֲדֵי עָרֶב — *And to his labor until evening.*

Midrash Shocher Tov interprets this allegorically: when the World to Come arrives, man, (i.e., the Jewish people who serve God) *will go forth* to receive the reward of his *work.* However, only the man who did not give up, but persevered in the service of God, will be rewarded, for man must *labor until evening* (i.e., until the moment of death).

24. מָה רַבּוּ מַעֲשֶׂיךָ ה׳ — *How abundant are Your works, HASHEM.*

Radak comments that מָה רַבּוּ, *how abundant,* has both a quantitative meaning (*how numerous*) and a qualitative meaning (*how great*).

Rabbi Akiva exclaimed: There are great creatures on land, and there are great creatures in the sea. If the denizens of the sea were to come up to the land, they would immediately perish, and if the creatures of the land were to enter the sea, they would immediately perish! *How abundant are Your works, HASHEM!* (*Chullin* 127a) [I.e., God, in His infinite genius and wisdom, has fashioned a complex world composed of creatures whose natures are completely different. The element and environment which is essential to one organism is fatal to another.]

כֻּלָּם בְּחָכְמָה עָשִׂיתָ — *With wisdom You made them all.*

No creature evolved by chance; every one was designed by God in His wisdom and demonstrates His omnipotence (*Sforno*).

מָלְאָה הָאָרֶץ קִנְיָנֶךָ — *The earth is full of Your possessions.*

God did not allow a single inch of space in the entire world to go to waste. Every spot is full of wondrous creations which testify to Hashem's absolute mastery over and complete possession of the world (*Radak*).

The *Kotzker Rebbe* observed that קִנְיָנֶךָ can also be translated homiletically as *ways to acquire You.* The world abounds with clear evidence of God's mastery; thus there are infinite opportunities for man to acquire a solid faith in the Almighty Creator.

25. זֶה הַיָּם גָּדוֹל וּרְחַב יָדָיִם — *Behold this sea* [lit. *this is the sea*] — *great and of broad measure* [lit. *hands*].

Radak explains that the Psalmist here describes the creations of the fifth day, the fish and the denizens of the sea. [Although the birds, too, were created on the fifth day, they were discussed earlier (*verse 17*), in relationship to the trees in which they nest, and which were created on the third day.]

The Psalmist had just marveled over the vastness of creation on land, exclaiming, *the earth is full of Your possessions (verse 24).* Now he declares that the *sea* is even larger and more

וּרְחַב יָדָיִם שָׁם־רֶמֶשׂ וְאֵין מִסְפָּר חַיּוֹת
כו קְטַנּוֹת עִם־גְּדֹלוֹת: שָׁם אֳנִיּוֹת יְהַלֵּכוּן
כז לִוְיָתָן זֶה־יָצַרְתָּ לְשַׂחֶק־בּוֹ: כֻּלָּם אֵלֶיךָ
כח יְשַׂבֵּרוּן לָתֵת אָכְלָם בְּעִתּוֹ: תִּתֵּן לָהֶם
כט יִלְקֹטוּן תִּפְתַּח יָדְךָ יִשְׂבְּעוּן טוֹב: תַּסְתִּיר
פָּנֶיךָ יִבָּהֵלוּן תֹּסֵף רוּחָם יִגְוָעוּן וְאֶל־
ל עֲפָרָם יְשׁוּבוּן: תְּשַׁלַּח רוּחֲךָ יִבָּרֵאוּן

amazing than the land, because it covers the major portion of the globe (Ibn Yachya).

שָׁם רֶמֶשׂ וְאֵין מִסְפָּר — *There are creeping things without number.*

The fish are far more prolific than any land creatures. They spawn millions of eggs and they reproduce constantly throughout the year (Radak)

חַיּוֹת קְטַנּוֹת עִם גְּדֹלוֹת — *Small creatures and great ones.*

[The inhabitants of the sea include both microscopic organisms and huge whales.]

26. שָׁם אֳנִיּוֹת יְהַלֵּכוּן — *There ships travel.*

God, in His great wisdom, endowed man with the skill to construct boats. Ships grant man access to the wealth of the sea [i.e., the fish] and also facilitate the development of lucrative overseas trading ventures (Radak).

לִוְיָתָן זֶה יָצַרְתָּ לְשַׂחֶק בּוֹ — *This Leviathan You fashioned to sport in it.*

Genesis 1:21 states: *and HASHEM created the great* הַתַּנִּינִם, *sea-giants.* The Talmud (*Bava Basra* 74b) identifies the sea-giants as the *Leviathan* and its mate. God slew the female and preserved her for the righteous in the Hereafter, for had these giants been permitted to multiply, their enormous bulk would not have allowed the world to continue its normal existence.[1]

Because the Leviathan is the largest sea creature, it rules the sea and eats any fish it pleases (Radak).

27. כֻּלָּם אֵלֶיךָ יְשַׂבֵּרוּן — *They all look to You with hope.*

[145:15 states: *The eyes of all look to You with hope, and You give them their food in its proper time.*] The creatures of both land and sea turn to You for sustenance. Although they lack intellect and do not realize that You, O God, are the Great Provider, we know that it is to You that their pleas and yearnings are directed (Ibn Yachya; Radak).

1. *Ritva* (comm. to *Bava Basra* 74b) cites the opinion that the Sages' account of two Leviathans, one of which God killed, is an allegory. It alludes to the highest Divine Wisdom which *Proverbs* 1:8 describes as לִוְיַת חֵן לְרֹאשֶׁךָ, *a graceful garland to adorn your head.* The allure of such wisdom can be as seductive as the charms of an attractive female. If the full Divine Wisdom were to remain accessible to man in this world, man might well become obsessed with its pursuit and abandon all physical activity, which is essential for the development of this earth. Therefore God removed the alluring female aspect of the Leviathan wisdom from this world so that men would continue to have a normal physical existence. This wisdom is stored up as a reward and delight for the righteous in the World to Come.

The *Talmud* (*Avodah Zarah* 3b) teaches that for three hours of each day, God amuses Himself, so to speak, with the Leviathan. This is based on an alternate interpretation of our text which renders לְשַׂחֶק בּוֹ, *You* [God] *sport with it* [Leviathan]. [According to *Ritva's* comment (above) this 'amusement' may be interpreted as God's delight upon contemplating the secret wisdom which He treasures for the righteous in the World to Come.] See *ArtScroll, Akdamus* pg. 128-129 for discussion of the sport with Leviathan.

> there are creeping things without number,
>   small creatures and great ones;
>
> ²⁶ There ships travel,
>   this Leviathan You fashioned to sport in it.
> ²⁷ They all look to You with hope,
>   to provide their food in its proper time.
> ²⁸ You give to them, they gather it in;
>   You open Your hand, they are sated with good.
> ²⁹ When You hide Your face they are dismayed,
>   when You retrieve their spirit they perish
>   and to their dust they return.

לָתֵת אָכְלָם בְּעִתּוֹ — *To provide their food in its [proper] time.*

Every species of life has a different feeding schedule, and You carefully provide each one with its food at the proper time (Ibn Yachya; Radak).

28. תִּתֵּן לָהֶם יִלְקֹטוּן — *You give to them, they gather it in.*

In times of famine and drought, You provide morsels of food for them to gather (Radak).

תִּפְתַּח יָדְךָ יִשְׂבְּעוּן טוֹב — *You open Your hand, they are sated with good.*

In times of plenty, You provide generously (Radak) [as 145:16 states, פּוֹתֵחַ אֶת יָדֶךָ וּמַשְׂבִּיעַ לְכָל חַי רָצוֹן, *You open Your hand and satisfy the desire of every living thing*].

Furthermore, *You open Your hand* repeatedly every day *to provide their food in its proper time* (verse 27; Ibn Yachya).

29. תַּסְתִּיר פָּנֶיךָ יִבָּהֵלוּן — *When You hide Your face they are dismayed.*

When You do not *open Your hand* and You deprive them of their daily bread, they become terrified and depressed, because they imagine that You have forgotten them (Ibn Ezra), and they have no one else to turn to for their sustenance (Radak).

Midrash Shocher Tov says: Were it not for the shadow of the Holy One,

Blessed is He, which protects a man, the demons would destroy him, as we read (Numbers 14:9): *Their shadow is removed from over them, but HASHEM['s shadow] is with us, fear them not.*

תֹּסֵף רוּחָם יִגְוָעוּן — *When You retrieve their spirit they perish.*

According to this translation, תֹּסֵף is cognate with אָסַף, *gather in*, and סָף, *come to an end* (Rashi; Ibn Ezra; Radak).

Zohar (Parshas Vayechi) relates תֹּסֵף, to תּוֹסִיף, *add* or *increase*. When a person is on the verge of death, his soul receives an additional wave of spiritual energy such as he never experienced throughout his lifetime. At that climactic moment, his spiritual perception is enhanced dramatically and he can perceive and comprehend mysteries of which he was previously unaware. God said, ''You cannot see My face, for no man shall see Me and live'' (Exodus 33:20). This means that although no man can see God in his lifetime, man *can* 'glimpse' God immediately prior to death.

וְאֶל עֲפָרָם יְשׁוּבוּן — *And to their dust they return.*

[As God told Adam: *For dust are you and to dust shall you return* (Genesis 3:19). And Solomon said: *All originate from dust and all return to dust* (Ecclesiastes 3:20).]

לא וַתְּחַדֵּשׁ פְּנֵי אֲדָמָה: יְהִי כְבוֹד יהוה
לב לְעוֹלָם יִשְׂמַח יהוה בְּמַעֲשָׂיו: הַמַּבִּיט
לָאָרֶץ וַתִּרְעָד יִגַּע בֶּהָרִים וְיֶעֱשָׁנוּ:
לג אָשִׁירָה לַיהוה בְּחַיָּי אֲזַמְּרָה לֵאלֹהַי
לד בְּעוֹדִי: יֶעֱרַב עָלָיו שִׂיחִי אָנֹכִי אֶשְׂמַח
לה בַּיהוה: יִתַּמּוּ חַטָּאִים | מִן־הָאָרֶץ וּרְשָׁעִים |
עוֹד אֵינָם בָּרְכִי נַפְשִׁי אֶת־יהוה הַלְלוּיָהּ:

30. תְּשַׁלַּח רוּחֲךָ יִבָּרֵאוּן — *When You send forth Your breath, they will be created.*

At the moment of man's death, God snatches the breath of life from him, but He will return it at the time of תְּחִיַּת הַמֵּתִים, *the resurrection of the dead.* When the dead bodies are recreated, their souls will be restored (*Radak*).

R' Azariah says: All souls are in the hands of God, as it says, *In His hand is the soul of every living thing, and the breath of all mankind* (*Job* 12:10). God has in His hand the key to the graves and the key to the repository of souls. In the future, God will open both the graves and the repository of souls; then He will return each soul to its respective body (*Pirkei D'Rabbi Eliezer* 34).

וַתְּחַדֵּשׁ פְּנֵי אֲדָמָה — *And You renew the surface of the earth.*

Radak refutes the mistaken view that God will not resurrect the old bodies, but will create new bodies in which to deposit these souls. The Sages teach that the *original* bodies will be renewed and brought back to life. [These bodies will appear exactly as they did before death, with all of their wounds and bruises, but God will immediately cure them (*Sanhedrin* 91a).] Therefore, the Psalmist says, *You renew the surface of the earth,* i.e., You bring the old, decayed bodies from the grave to the surface of the earth, and there You renew them.

31. יְהִי כְבוֹד ה' לְעוֹלָם — *May the glory of HASHEM endure forever.*

The Psalmist has completed his overview of the six days of creation, and he is overwhelmed by the scope of God's accomplishment. In profound awe, he exclaims, *"May the glory of HASHEM endure forever!"* (*Radak*)

יִשְׂמַח ה' בְּמַעֲשָׂיו — *Let HASHEM rejoice with His works.*

The Psalmist prays that *HASHEM* rejoice with all the *works* He created, because if He is displeased He may return the world to chaos and void. Indeed, initially, God was completely satisfied with creation, as *Genesis* 1:31 states: *And God saw all that He had made, and behold it was very good.* However, there have been many times in the course of history when God was profoundly saddened by His own creations. In the Messianic era and in the World to Come, God's joy in His works will be complete and constant (*Radak*).

[*Perek Shirah*, 'The Chapter of Song,' states that the theme song of the שְׁרָצִים, *creeping reptiles,* is this verse, to teach that God rejoices with all His works — even with the lowly, repulsive reptile.]

32. הַמַּבִּיט לָאָרֶץ וַתִּרְעָד — *He peers toward the earth and it trembles.*

God is the foundation of the earth, and He holds it firmly in His grasp. However, if He should merely look askance at the earth, it would tremble and shake (*Ibn Ezra*).

Yerushalmi (*Berachos* 9:2) points out that elsewhere God's gaze seems to be beneficial, rather than damaging, for the

³⁰ When You send forth Your breath,
         they will be created,
         and You renew the surface of the earth.
³¹ May the glory of HASHEM endure forever,
         let HASHEM rejoice with His works.
³² He peers toward the earth and it trembles,
         He touches the mountains and they smoke.
³³ I will sing to HASHEM while I live,
         I will sing praises to my God while I endure.
³⁴ May my words be sweet to Him —
         I will rejoice in HASHEM.
³⁵ Sinners will cease from the earth,
         and the wicked will be no more —
         Bless HASHEM, O my soul.
         Praise God!

Holy Land is described as: *A land where ... the eyes of HASHEM are always upon it* (Deuteronomy 11:12). This apparent discrepancy can be resolved as follows: when the Jews follow the ways of God and give tithes properly, they are fortified and blessed by God's benign gaze; when Israel defies God, however, and does not tithe its produce, they tremble when He looks at their land.[1]

יִגַּע בֶּהָרִים וְיֶעֱשָׁנוּ — *He touches the mountains and they smoke.*

This refers to the downfall of the wicked, as *Deuteronomy* 32:22 states: *For a fire is kindled in My wrath ... and it sets ablaze the foundations of the mountains* (Radak).

These words also have a positive connotation: when God gave the Torah at Sinai, *Exodus* 19:18 relates: *And*

Mount Sinai smoked all over because HASHEM descended upon it in fire and the smoke of it ascended like the smoke of a furnace (Rashi).

33. אָשִׁירָה לַה׳ בְּחַיָּי — *I will sing to HASHEM while I live.*

The Psalmist now concludes his composition, declaring that in recognition of all the wonders recounted in this psalm, he should sing to Hashem forever, all the days of his life (Ibn Ezra).

A person must seize the opportunity to praise God while he lives, because afterwards it is too late.

אֲזַמְּרָה לֵאלֹהַי בְּעוֹדִי — *I will sing praises to my God while I endure.*

["Making music in praise of God is the main purpose of my existence," said

---

1. Elijah asked Rav Nehorai: "Why do earthquakes come?"
   Rav Nehorai answered: "Because the Children of Israel fail to set aside tithes, as ordained."
   Elijah rejoined, "Although things appear to be as you say, earthquakes actually occur when the Holy One, Blessed be He, looks upon the theatres and the circuses of the nations of the earth where the non-Jews sit unperturbed, although God's Holy Temple is in ruins. At that time He wishes to lay the world to waste, as *Jeremiah* 25:30 states: *HASHEM does roar from on high and lets loose His voice from His holy dwelling, again and again He roars because of His habitation.* However, He does not destroy the entire world, instead, *He peers toward the earth and it trembles* (Midrash Shocher Tov).

David. Indeed, David's soul was originally destined to live no more than three hours but Adam bestowed seventy years of his life upon David so that David could compose songs of praise and penitence to God. See *Overview* to Vol. I, part I.]

34. יֶעֱרַב עָלָיו שִׂיחִי — *May my words be sweet to Him.*

The translation follows *Targum*, *Rashi*, and *Radak*. May God accept my prayers and supplications; and my most fervent wish is to rejoice in Him (*Sforno*).

אָנֹכִי אֶשְׂמַח בַּה' — *I will rejoice in HASHEM.*

In *verse* 31, the Psalmist prayed: *Let HASHEM rejoice with His works.* Now he adds, that we too should rejoice in Hashem. This implies that He will be our God, and we will be His faithful people (*Radak*).

35. יִתַּמּוּ חַטָּאִים מִן הָאָרֶץ וּרְשָׁעִים עוֹד אֵינָם — *Sinners will cease from the earth, and the wicked will be no more.*

Rabbi Judah and Rabbi Nechemiah differed in their explanation of these words. Rabbi Judah said that יִתַּמּוּ is related to תָּם, *upright.* Thus, may the sinners become תְּמִימִים, *upright*, and may *the wicked* [wicked] *no more.* Rabbi Nechemiah, however, said that יִתַּמּוּ is related to תּוֹם, *cease.* Thus, may the sinners actually perish from the earth and may the wicked actually be destroyed (*Midrash Shocher Tov*).

The *Talmud* (*Berachos* 10a) relates that a band of thugs in Rabbi Meir's neighborhood vexed him sorely, and Rabbi Meir wanted to pray for their death. But Rabbi Meir's wife, Beruriah, said to him, "How can you justify such a prayer? Do you think that Scripture says חוֹטְאִים, *sinners, will cease?* The verse actually says חַטָּאִים, which can also mean *sins will cease.* As soon as the sinners repent, sins and crimes will cease to be perpetrated and *the wicked will be no more,* for then everyone will be righteous." Accepting her argument, R' Meir prayed that the thugs would repent, and his request was answered.

בָּרְכִי נַפְשִׁי אֶת ה' הַלְלוּיָהּ — *Bless HASHEM, O my soul. Praise God!*

The word הַלְלוּיָהּ is a composite of הַלְלוּ יָהּ, *praise YAH* [for the implications of this particular Holy Name of God, see commentary to 94:7]. Whether it is to be written as one word (הַלְלוּיָהּ), two words (הַלְלוּ יָהּ) or with a hyphen (הַלְלוּ-יָהּ) is the subject of disagreement among the Talmudic Sages. No *halachic* consensus has ever been reached and different spellings are found in the printed editions of *Tehillim.* (See Commentary to 111:1 for further discussion of this point.)

Rabbi Samuel bar Abba observed that although this is the one hundred and fourth psalm, it is the first to include the word הַלְלוּיָהּ [*Hallelujah*], *Praise God.* This occurs after Scripture states: *The sinners will cease from the earth and the wicked will be no more.* Only then does the Psalmist declare, *Hallelujah,* because as Solomon said (*Proverbs* 11:10): *When the wicked perish, there is joyous song* (*Midrash Shocher Tov; Radak*).

105 מזמור קה

This psalm was composed on the day King David brought the Holy Ark from its temporary quarters in the home of Oved Edom to the holy city of Jerusalem, where it was installed with great ceremony and honor. The full details of the event are described in I Chronicles, chapter 16. Verses 8-22 of that chapter closely parallel the first fifteen verses of this psalm, while verses 23-33 of that chapter are an almost exact repetition of psalm 96.

Verse 7 there reads: On that day David determined the foremost activity to be the offering of thanks to HASHEM, under the direction of Assaf and his brothers. Rashi explains that Assaf would recite one verse of praise at a time, which would then be repeated by his fellow Levites.

In this composition, the Psalmist emphasizes that the Jews who escorted the Holy Ark are the seed of Abraham, His servant. Abraham's greatest accomplishment was that he traveled from place to place teaching and publicizing the Name of the One God. The Holy Ark of the Law also represents God's Name. Thus when David carried the Ark from place to place to the accompaniment of thanksgiving to the Almighty, he resembled his illustrious forebear, Abraham (Ibn Ezra).

Radak and Malbim (in the name of Seder Olam Rabbah) explain that the Levites sang psalm 105 each morning and psalm 96 each evening while the Holy Ark was housed in a temporary tent in Jerusalem. When Solomon built the Temple and the Ark was placed in its permanent abode, a perpetual order of songs was established. These were the Songs of the Day which were related to the respective days of the week and to each special festival.

א הוֹדוּ לַיהוה קִרְאוּ בִשְׁמוֹ הוֹדִיעוּ בָעַמִּים

ב עֲלִילוֹתָיו: שִׁירוּ־לוֹ זַמְּרוּ־לוֹ שִׂיחוּ בְּכָל־

ג נִפְלְאוֹתָיו: הִתְהַלְלוּ בְּשֵׁם קָדְשׁוֹ יִשְׂמַח לֵב

ד מְבַקְשֵׁי יהוה: דִּרְשׁוּ יהוה וְעֻזּוֹ בַּקְּשׁוּ פָנָיו

ה תָמִיד: זִכְרוּ נִפְלְאוֹתָיו אֲשֶׁר־עָשָׂה מֹפְתָיו

ו וּמִשְׁפְּטֵי־פִיו: זֶרַע אַבְרָהָם עַבְדּוֹ בְּנֵי יַעֲקֹב

1. הוֹדוּ לַה' קִרְאוּ בִשְׁמוֹ — *Give thanks to HASHEM, declare His Name* [lit. *call in His Name*].

With these words, David exhorted all those who joined his procession to honor and to accompany the Holy Ark (*Radak*).

Specifically, these words are directed at the Torah scholars, who have a special obligation to promulgate God's glory to the world and to tell both Jew and gentile that God is great and very kind.

God's nature and omnipotence are not mere abstractions, but a tangible reality. This recognition constitutes a dynamic force which fortifies those who possess it and protects them from evil (*Sforno*).

[For other interpretations of *calling in the Name of God* see ArtScroll Bereishis 12:8.]

הוֹדִיעוּ בָעַמִּים עֲלִילוֹתָיו — *Make His acts known among the nations.*

[As God's fame spreads throughout the nations, His power and dominion spread as well. Later in this psalm, the Psalmist explains that the purpose of the plagues which afflicted Egypt was to make God's acts known to the world.]

2. שִׁירוּ לוֹ זַמְּרוּ לוֹ — *Sing to Him, make music to Him.*

Sing with your mouths, *make music* with your instruments (*Ibn Ezra; Radak*).

Sing [before the Ark] in the morning, *make music* [before the Ark] in the evening (*Chazah Zion*).

שִׂיחוּ בְּכָל נִפְלְאוֹתָיו — *Speak of all His wonders.*

Believers — converse with one another! Relate all that you have experienced of God's wonders, and specifically of the wonders which you have seen in connection with the Holy Ark (*Radak*).

3. הִתְהַלְלוּ בְּשֵׁם קָדְשׁוֹ — *Glory in His Holy Name.*

Feel honored that you enjoy the protection and supervision of a patron as great as our God (*Rashi*).

Indeed, you have the unique opportunity to add sanctity to *His Holy Name* by giving glory to His Holy Ark (*Radak*).

Chazah Zion points out that God's Holy Name, אֲדֹנָי, *my Lord*, has a numerical value of sixty-five, which equals the value of הַלֵּל, *glory* or *praise*. [From this we can infer that our praise should always be directed to God and that He is the sole source of our glory.]

יִשְׂמַח לֵב מְבַקְשֵׁי ה' — *Be glad of heart, you who seek HASHEM.*

In the pursuit of material gain, happiness depends upon the attainment of one's aim; thus the seeker is dissatisfied because he lacks the object of his desire. Such is not so in the search for God, however, for in this case the seeking and the finding occur simultaneously. A person who dedicates himself to seeking God demonstrates that he has found God to be the ultimate good fortune; therefore he rejoices while he seeks (*Rav Yoseif Albo*).

4. דִּרְשׁוּ ה' וְעֻזּוֹ — *Search out HASHEM and His might.*

HASHEM's might is the Torah which was contained in the Holy Ark, as 78:61

105
1-6

Give thanks to HASHEM, declare His Name,
      make His acts known among the nations.

² Sing to Him, make music to Him,
      speak of all His wonders.

³ Glory in His Holy Name,
      be glad of heart, you who seek HASHEM.

⁴ Search out HASHEM and His might,
      seek His Presence always.

⁵ Remember His wonders that He wrought,
      His marvels and the judgments of His mouth.

⁶ O seed of Abraham, His servant,

---

states: וַיִּתֵּן לַשְּׁבִי עֻזּוֹ, *He placed His might into captivity* [i.e., the Philistines captured the Ark]. Thus, the Psalmist exhorts his listeners to direct their prayers to the resting place of the Tablets of the Covenant (*Radak*).

Sforno explains עוֹז as *God's mighty concern for and surveillance of his creations*. The more we search for Hashem, the *mightier* God's concern for us becomes.

בַּקְּשׁוּ פָנָיו תָּמִיד — *Seek His Presence always.*

[The search for God never ends, because the very process of searching is an end in itself (see commentary to verse 3).]

Chazah Zion explains that the act of seeking Hashem is equivalent to offering the קָרְבָּן תָּמִיד, *daily offering,* which was sacrificed in God's presence, in the Temple.

Midrash Shocher Tov teaches: If you seek an opportunity to welcome the countenance of God in this world and to stand in His Presence, then learn God's Torah in Eretz Israel!

5. זִכְרוּ נִפְלְאֹתָיו אֲשֶׁר עָשָׂה — *Remember His wonders that He wrought.*

The Psalmist exhorts Israel to thank God for all the wonders He wrought in the land of Egypt, in the wilderness, and in the land of Canaan since the time of its conquest. This remembrance was

spurred by the wonders which occurred when the Holy Ark was brought back from the Philistine captivity, because when a new wonder occurs, the beneficiary is obligated to recall all the miraculous events which preceded it (*Radak*).

מֹפְתָיו וּמִשְׁפְּטֵי פִיו — *His marvels and the judgments of His mouth.*

Before each plague struck Egypt, God pronounced judgment on the Egyptians and sealed their doom with the words of His mouth (*Radak*).

Each plague was clearly predicted before it struck. This precision demonstrated beyond a doubt that God was in control of the entire event (*Alshich*).

6. זֶרַע אַבְרָהָם עַבְדּוֹ — *O seed of Abraham, His servant.*

God was eager to demonstrate His might to the world for the sake of the Jews because they are the *seed of Abraham, His* [most faithful] *servant,* the first man in the world to fully accept all of God's commands (*Ibn Ezra*).

The corresponding verse in I *Chronicles* 16:13 reads זֶרַע יִשְׂרָאֵל עַבְדּוֹ, *The seed of Israel, His servant. Radak* explains that only the twelve sons of Israel/Jacob are considered the true *seed,* or spiritual heirs, of Abraham, for Abraham also fathered [unworthy] Ishmael and Isaac fathered [evil] Esau.

ז בְּחִירָיו: הוּא יהוה אֱלֹהֵינוּ בְּכָל־הָאָרֶץ
ח מִשְׁפָּטָיו: זָכַר לְעוֹלָם בְּרִיתוֹ דָּבָר צִוָּה
ט לְאֶלֶף דּוֹר: אֲשֶׁר כָּרַת אֶת־אַבְרָהָם
י וּשְׁבוּעָתוֹ לְיִשְׂחָק: וַיַּעֲמִידֶהָ לְיַעֲקֹב לְחֹק
יא לְיִשְׂרָאֵל בְּרִית עוֹלָם: לֵאמֹר לְךָ אֶתֵּן אֶת־
יב אֶרֶץ־כְּנָעַן חֶבֶל נַחֲלַתְכֶם: בִּהְיוֹתָם מְתֵי

But all of Jacob's sons were righteous bearers of the holy tradition of their great-grandfather Abraham; thus only they deserved to be called his *seed*.

בְּנֵי יַעֲקֹב בְּחִירָיו — *O children of Jacob, His chosen ones.*

As explained previously, none of Jacob's children was rejected or cast out of the fold; all were select, *chosen* men of the highest caliber (*Radak*).

Indeed, Abraham's life was spared in order that he could become the progenitor of Jacob and Jacob's children, God's *chosen ones*. Isaiah 29:22 alludes to this: *Thus says HASHEM to the House of Jacob — it was he* [i.e., Jacob] *who ransomed Abraham.*

Yalkut Shimoni relates that when Nimrod cast young Abraham into the furnace, God foresaw that Jacob was destined to be Abraham's descendant. Therefore, Abraham was miraculously rescued (*Chazah Zion*).

7. הוּא ה׳ אֱלֹהֵינוּ בְּכָל הָאָרֶץ מִשְׁפָּטָיו — *He is HASHEM, our God, over all the earth are His judgments.*

Although God's supervision and concern extend over all the earth, He maintains a very special interest in us, His Chosen people, for *He is our God* and we are His people (*Radak*).

8. זָכַר לְעוֹלָם בְּרִיתוֹ — *He remembered His covenant forever.*

God promised the Jews that the land of Israel would belong to them *forever.* Even when they are in exile, they are assured that their absence will not be permanent and that their return is forthcoming (*Radak*). Indeed, God guaranteed that they would own the

Holy Land even if they were not [completely] righteous or deserving (*Sforno*).

דָּבָר צִוָּה לְאֶלֶף דּוֹר — *The Word he commanded for a thousand generations.*

Deuteronomy 7:9 teaches that *HASHEM ... is the faithful God who safeguards the covenant and the kindness, to those who love Him and observe His commands, for one thousand generations* (*Rashi*).

Sforno comments that when Abraham entered into בְּרִית בֵּין הַבְּתָרִים, *the Covenant Between the Parts* (*Genesis* 15:7-21), God promised to always remember בְּרִית מִילָה, *the Covenant of Circumcision* (*Genesis* 17).

R' Hirsch perceives this as a reference to the acceptance of the Divine *word* at Sinai. That *word* will apply even to those Jews who live a thousand generations after the holy generation which originally accepted the Torah.

Midrash Shocher Tov cites an alternative reading of אֶלֶף as אַלּוּף, *leader*; thus God commanded His word to the leader of each generation. *Radak* maintains that this refers specifically to Abraham, the leader with whom God established the first covenant. [The leader of each generation is God's liaison with the masses. The leader understands the people as no one else does. *Rabbi Israel Salanter* observed that after death, every person will be judged by a Heavenly Tribunal composed of the souls of leaders of his own generation, because only they can appreciate the unique difficulties and challenges which confronted their contemporaries.]

> O children of Jacob, His chosen ones,
> ⁷ He is HASHEM, our God,
>   over all the earth are His judgments.
> ⁸ He remembered His covenant forever —
>   the Word He commanded
>   for a thousand generations —
> ⁹ that He made with Abraham
>   and His vow to Isaac.
> ¹⁰ Then He established it for Jacob as a statute,
>   for Israel as an everlasting covenant.
> ¹¹ Saying, "To you I shall give the Land of Canaan,
>   the lot of your inheritance."

---

9. אֲשֶׁר כָּרַת אֶת אַבְרָהָם — That He made with Abraham.

[All of the good things which God does for Israel throughout the generations are a result of His original covenant with Abraham.]

וּשְׁבוּעָתוֹ לְיִשְׂחָק — And His vow to Isaac.

Thus said the Lord to Isaac (Genesis 26:3), "Sojourn in this land and I will be with you and bless you; for to you and your offspring will I give all these lands and establish the oath that I swore to Abraham your father" (Radak).

Chazah Zion points out that although Isaac's name is usually spelled יִצְחָק with a צ, here it is spelled יִשְׂחָק with a שׂ. He explains that at the Covenant Between the Parts God informed Abraham of the Egyptian bondage, which was to last four hundred years beginning from the day of Isaac's birth (Genesis 15:13) Later, God mercifully reduced that figure to two hundred and ten years. The numerical value of the letter שׂ in יִשְׂחָק is 300, the numerical value of the צ in יִצְחָק is 90. The difference between these two figures is 210. Thus the very name יִצְחָק/יִשְׂחָק which in either spelling means he shall laugh, alludes to Isaac's joy that the years of bondage were reduced to two hundred and ten years.

10. וַיַּעֲמִידֶהָ לְיַעֲקֹב לְחֹק — Then He established it for Jacob as a statute.

God voluntarily made a covenant with Abraham and uttered a vow to Isaac (verse 9); but when Jacob established a special relationship with God, God's commitment to the holy nation became an iron-clad statute which had to be fulfilled, because the covenant had then become an established fact (Rashi; Malbim).

לְיִשְׂרָאֵל בְּרִית עוֹלָם — [And] for Israel as an everlasting [or: world] covenant.

Eventually, Jacob was elevated to a higher spiritual plane and was given the title Israel, which has the connotation, for you [i.e., Jacob] have striven with the Divine and with humans and have overcome (Genesis 32:29). At that time God enforced the ultimate covenant with Israel by stating that the entire עוֹלָם, world, and its history would be controlled by the conduct of Israel and his descendants (Malbim).

11. לֵאמֹר לְךָ אֶתֵּן אֶת אֶרֶץ כְּנָעַן חֶבֶל נַחֲלַתְכֶם — Saying, "To you I shall give the Land of Canaan, the lot of your inheritance."

The verse begins in the singular form לְךָ, to you, and ends in the plural נַחֲלַתְכֶם, your inheritance. Radak explains that God first addressed each

יג מִסְפָּר כִּמְעַט וְגָרִים בָּהּ: וַיִּתְהַלְּכוּ מִגּוֹי אֶל־
יד גּוֹי מִמַּמְלָכָה אֶל־עַם אַחֵר: לֹא־הִנִּיחַ אָדָם
טו לְעָשְׁקָם וַיּוֹכַח עֲלֵיהֶם מְלָכִים: אַל־תִּגְּעוּ
טז בִמְשִׁיחָי וְלִנְבִיאַי אַל־תָּרֵעוּ: וַיִּקְרָא רָעָב
יז עַל־הָאָרֶץ כָּל־מַטֵּה־לֶחֶם שָׁבָר: שָׁלַח
יח לִפְנֵיהֶם אִישׁ לְעֶבֶד נִמְכַּר יוֹסֵף: עִנּוּ בַכֶּבֶל

of the three Patriarchs individually, saying: "To you I shall give the Land of Canaan." Later, God addressed the entire congregation of Israel and referred to the holy land as *the lot of your inheritance* (in the plural).

12. בִּהְיוֹתָם מְתֵי מִסְפָּר — *When they were but few in number.*

When our forefathers first began to publicize God's name, *they*, their sons, [and their followers] *were but few in number*. [Nevertheless, they courageously proclaimed their unpopular beliefs.] Indeed, the sons of Jacob did not hesitate to attack the entire city of Shechem to punish them for their sins, even though the sons of Jacob were greatly outnumbered (Ibn Ezra; Radak).

כִּמְעַט וְגָרִים בָּהּ — *Hardly dwelling there.*

The translation follows *Radak*, who explains that the forefathers had complete and unswerving faith in God's promise to give them the land, despite the fact that they spent so little time on the holy soil. Abraham's sojourn in the land was twice interrupted by famine which forced him to go to Egypt and Philistia. Famine later sent Isaac to Philistia and finally sent Jacob and all his sons to Egypt for 210 years.

13. וַיִּתְהַלְּכוּ מִגּוֹי אֶל גּוֹי — *And they wandered from people to people.*

None of the Patriarchs were permanently settled in one place; they were constantly on the move (Rashi).

מִמַּמְלָכָה אֶל עַם אַחֵר — *From one kingdom to another nation.*

[The moving was particularly difficult because they not only changed

geographical locations, but also were confronted with the need to adjust to עַם אַחֵר, which literally means *different nation*. These cultures subscribed to strange ideologies which challenged the lesson of monotheism which the Patriarchs taught.]

14. לֹא הִנִּיחַ אָדָם לְעָשְׁקָם — *He allowed no man to rob them.*

[Since the Patriarchs represented justice and right, God protected them from wrong.]

וַיּוֹכַח עֲלֵיהֶם מְלָכִים — *And He rebuked kings for their sake.*

When Pharaoh took Sarah from Abraham, *HASHEM plagued Pharaoh and his house with great plagues* (Genesis 12:17). When Avimelech, king of the Philistines, took Sarah, Hashem completely restrained every orifice of each member of Avimelech's household (Rashi, Genesis 20:18).

15. אַל תִּגְּעוּ בִמְשִׁיחָי — *"Dare not touch My anointed ones ..."*

When Hashem reproved the kings who threatened His beloved Patriarchs, He warned them, "Dare not touch those whom I have anointed. They are appointed to represent me in this world. You mortal kings regard yourselves as monarchs, but the Patriarchs are the true rulers of the earth and must be accorded the honor due to anointed kings."

In this fashion, God came to Avimelech and Laban in dreams and warned them not to harm His favorites [see *Genesis* 20:3 and 31:24]. He smote Pharaoh and Avimelech when they

¹² *When they were but few in number,*
hardly dwelling there.
¹³ *And they wandered from people to people,*
from one kingdom to another nation.
¹⁴ *He allowed no man to rob them,*
and He rebuked kings for their sake:
¹⁵ *"Dare not touch My anointed ones;*
and to My prophets do no harm."
¹⁶ *He declared a famine upon the land,*
every staff of bread He broke.
¹⁷ *He sent a man before them,*
Joseph was sold as a slave.

overstepped their authority and attempted to take Sarah away from Abraham (Radak; Rashi).

וְלִנְבִיאַי אַל תָּרֵעוּ — *"... and to My prophets do no harm."*

All of the Patriarchs were *prophets* and deserved to be treated with reverence and awe. In particular, God admonished Avimelech when he took Sarah from Abraham, saying (Genesis 20:7), *"Now return the man's wife, for he is a prophet, and he will pray for you and you will live"* (Radak).[1]

16. וַיִּקְרָא רָעָב עַל הָאָרֶץ — *He declared a famine upon the land.*

The Divine plan of history ordained that the children of Israel sojourn in the land of Egypt. Therefore, God *declared a famine* throughout the lands of the world, including the land of Canaan where Jacob sojourned, so that Jacob would be forced to relocate himself in Egypt, where food was available (Rashi; Radak).

This famine struck even the land of Egypt, which was the most fertile and

productive of all lands, so that Joseph could rise to greatness through his brilliant plan of stockpiling Egypt's food during the years of abundance (Sforno).

כָּל מַטֵּה לֶחֶם שָׁבָר — *Every staff of bread He broke.*

God determined that Joseph would rule Egypt because everyone would depend on the grain which he had stored. A miracle occurred and anyone else who had hoarded food found that his supplies rotted [see *Rashi* on Genesis 41:55]. Thus, God *broke every* [other] *staff of bread* so that everyone would recognize that Joseph alone controlled the staff of life (Alshich).

17. שָׁלַח לִפְנֵיהֶם אִישׁ — *He sent a man before them.*

Joseph was sent to Egypt nineteen years before the famine began (Alshich).

לְעֶבֶד נִמְכַּר יוֹסֵף — *Joseph was sold as a slave.*

Many years later, in retrospect, Joseph reviewed all of the events which led to his ascent to greatness. His

1. The *Talmud* (Shabbos 119b) teaches that *dare not touch My anointed ones* refers to תִּינוֹקוֹת שֶׁל בֵּית רַבָּן, *the schoolchildren under their teacher's supervision.* [Since oil does not mix with water, it symbolizes unadulterated purity. Therefore, pure Jewish youth are akin to monarchs anointed with oil.]

And to My prophets do no harm refers to the Torah scholars [whose rigorous intellectual

°רַגְלָיו בַּרְזֶל בָּאָה נַפְשׁוֹ: עַד־עֵת בֹּא־דְבָרוֹ יט

אִמְרַת יהוה צְרָפָתְהוּ: שָׁלַח מֶלֶךְ וַיַּתִּירֵהוּ כ

מֹשֵׁל עַמִּים וַיְפַתְּחֵהוּ: שָׂמוֹ אָדוֹן לְבֵיתוֹ כא

וּמֹשֵׁל בְּכָל־קִנְיָנוֹ: לֶאְסֹר שָׂרָיו בְּנַפְשׁוֹ כב

brothers were tormented with guilt over the injustice which they had shown to him, but Joseph comforted them, saying (Genesis 45:5), ''Now, be not distressed, nor reproach yourselves for having sold me here for it was to be a provider that God sent me ahead of you'' (Rashi).

18. עֻנּוּ בַכֶּבֶל רַגְלוֹ — *They afflicted his foot with fetters.*

This occurred when Joseph was imprisoned for allegedly molesting the wife of his master Potiphar [*Genesis 39:20*] (Radak).

בַּרְזֶל בָּאָה נַפְשׁוֹ — *His soul was placed in irons.*

According to the plain meaning the *soul*, too, suffers when the body is put in chains (Radak).

The Midrash (Bereishis Rabbah 87:11) relates: For twelve months, the wife of Potiphar made advances to Joseph but he always ignored her. Whenever she came to talk to him he bent his head low and averted his gaze from her. In desperation, she ordered that an iron collar with razor-sharp edges be placed around Joseph's neck. This collar made it impossible for Joseph to bend his head, but he still closed his eyes and refused to gaze upon the seductive temptress. She pleaded with Joseph, ''Come, be with me! No

one will know, and we can conceal the affair.''

Joseph steadfastly refused, saying, ''How foolish is your offer! I would not even touch one of your unwed women, for they are forbidden to my people; how much more are you prohibited to me, since you are a married woman!''

19. עַד עֵת בֹּא דְבָרוֹ — *Until the time that His word came to pass.*

Joseph was tortured and enslaved *until the time* God ordained for *His word* to come to pass. *His word* refers to God's pronouncement to the Patriarchs that their descendants would come to Egypt. When that point of time arrived, Joseph was elevated to greatness and he invited Jacob to join him (Rashi).

אִמְרַת ה׳ צְרָפָתְהוּ — *The word of HASHEM made him pure.*

God decreed that Joseph be enslaved, tested, and imprisoned in order that these trials and obstacles might purify Joseph's soul and perfect his character (Rashi; Sforno).

Thus cleansed and purged, every word Joseph uttered was recognized as the pure truth and the word of God. Pharaoh eagerly accepted everything Joseph advised, and he exclaimed to his court (Genesis 41:38), ''Could we find another like him, a man in whom is the spirit of God?'' (Ibn Ezra).

training brings them close to God and to a comprehension of His holy spirit of prophecy].

Rav Levi said, ''The world continues to exist only by virtue of the words and breath of the innocent schoolchildren.''

Rav Pappa queried, ''And what of the breath of the mature, eminent scholars?''

Rav Levi replied, ''How can you compare our breath, which is tainted with sin, to their breath, which is pure and innocent?'' Rav Levi continued in the name of Rabbi Yehudah the Prince, ''It is forbidden to interrupt the [Torah] study of schoolchildren for any reason even for the building of the Holy Temple!''

Rav Levi said to Rabbi Yehudah the Prince, ''We have received a tradition from our forefathers: Any city which fails to establish a school where schoolchildren learn from their teacher should be destroyed; some say all the inhabitants should be excommunicated.''

¹⁸ *They afflicted his foot with fetters,*
his soul was placed in irons.
¹⁹ *Until the time that His word came to pass,*
the word of HASHEM made him pure.
²⁰ *The king sent word and released him,*
a ruler of nations — and he freed him.
²¹ *He appointed him master of his palace,*
and ruler of all his wealth.
²² *To imprison his princes at his whim,*

20. שָׁלַח מֶלֶךְ וַיַּתִּירֵהוּ — *The king sent word and released him.*

When the time came for Joseph to be freed, Pharaoh sent his servants to loosen Joseph's bonds (*Rashi*). Furthermore, *the king,* who was the supreme magistrate of the land and the highest authority of justice, ruled that Joseph had been imprisoned under false charges. He exonerated Joseph from all blame and *loosed him* from the onus of guilt which had besmirched his good name (*Sforno*).

Zohar (*Parshas Mikeitz*) cites 146:8, מַתִּיר אֲסוּרִים, ה', *Hashem releases prisoners,* as proof that neither Pharaoh nor any other king deserves credit for releasing captives. Therefore, *Zohar* interprets our verse, *The king sent word and released him,* in reference to Hashem, the King of kings, who sent word to Pharaoh, His representative on earth, to free Joseph.

מֹשֵׁל עַמִּים וַיְפַתְּחֵהוּ — *A ruler of nations — and he freed him.*

Joseph had been accused, condemned, and convicted by a very powerful noble, Potiphar, who was the chamberlain of Pharaoh, the captain of the guard (*Genesis* 39:1). Nevertheless, Pharaoh could overrule Potiphar's verdict, because he was the [supreme] *ruler of nations* and Potiphar's superior (*Sforno*).

21. שָׂמוֹ אָדוֹן לְבֵיתוֹ — *He appointed him master of his palace* [lit. *house*].

[Pharaoh said to Joseph, "You shall

be in charge of my palace and by your command shall my people be sustained" (*Genesis* 41:40).]

This refers to the internal operation of Pharaoh's household (*Ibn Yachya*).

וּמֹשֵׁל בְּכָל קִנְיָנוֹ — *And ruler of all his wealth.*

[Then Pharaoh said to Joseph, "Behold, I have placed you in charge of all the land of Egypt" (*Genesis* 41:41).]

Thus, Joseph's mandate was extended and he was empowered to conduct all matters of state, including economic programs, taxes, diplomacy, and war (*Ibn Yachya*).

22. לֶאְסֹר שָׂרָיו בְּנַפְשׁוֹ — *To imprison his princes at his whim.*

Pharaoh granted Joseph's every desire and sought to give him every pleasure (*Rashi*). Therefore, Joseph was free to act against his adversaries. First, he punished the wicked Potiphar, who had had him imprisoned unjustly (*Ibn Ezra; Radak*).

Midrash Shocher Tov relates that when Pharaoh elevated Joseph to the position of viceroy, all of the princes of the realm protested, "Shall a slave become a king?" After Joseph attained power, he imprisoned all of these antagonists. Joseph waited until his brothers arrived in Egypt and publicized the fact that Joseph came from the royal family of Israel. Then Joseph had these defiant princes severely punished for challenging his authority and undermining his rule.

כג וּזְקֵנָיו יְחַכֵּם: וַיָּבֹא יִשְׂרָאֵל מִצְרָיִם וְיַעֲקֹב גָּר

כד בְּאֶרֶץ חָם: וַיֶּפֶר אֶת־עַמּוֹ מְאֹד וַיַּעֲצִמֵהוּ

כה מִצָּרָיו: הָפַךְ לִבָּם לִשְׂנֹא עַמּוֹ לְהִתְנַכֵּל

כו בַּעֲבָדָיו: שָׁלַח מֹשֶׁה עַבְדּוֹ אַהֲרֹן אֲשֶׁר

כז בָּחַר־בּוֹ: שָׂמוּ־בָם דִּבְרֵי אֹתוֹתָיו וּמֹפְתִים

כח בְּאֶרֶץ חָם: שָׁלַח חֹשֶׁךְ וַיַּחְשִׁךְ וְלֹא־מָרוּ

וּזְקֵנָיו יְחַכֵּם — And make his elders wise.

Pharaoh's admiration for Joseph knew no bounds; he exclaimed (Genesis 41:39) "There can be no one so discerning and wise as you." Pharaoh declared that everyone — including Egypt's elders and savants — must consider himself Joseph's inferior and disciple (Radak; Ibn Ezra).

23. וַיָּבֹא יִשְׂרָאֵל מִצְרָיִם — Thus Israel came to Egypt.

God told Abraham that his descendants would be strangers in a foreign land (Genesis 15:13); therefore, Israel had to come to Egypt (Radak).

וְיַעֲקֹב גָּר בְּאֶרֶץ חָם — And Jacob sojourned in the land of Ham.

Radak observes that Mitzrayim, progenitor of the Egyptian nation, was the son of Ham (see Genesis 10:6).

24. וַיֶּפֶר אֶת עַמּוֹ מְאֹד — And He made His nation exceedingly fruitful.

Exodus 1:7 states: And the children of Israel were fruitful, and increased abundantly, and multiplied (Radak).

וַיַּעֲצִמֵהוּ מִצָּרָיו — And made them mightier than their oppressors.

Scripture concludes (ibid.): And they grew exceedingly mighty and the land was filled with them. The Jews became more powerful than the Egyptians themselves (Radak).

25. הָפַךְ לִבָּם לִשְׂנֹא עַמּוֹ — He turned their heart to hate His nation.

[Exodus 1:12 states: And they were disgusted by the children of Israel, because they saw that the Jews were spreading throughout the land and

infiltrating every stratum of society (see Sforno; Exodus 1:7).]

לְהִתְנַכֵּל בַּעֲבָדָיו — To plot against His servants.

[Pharaoh plotted against the Jews and said to his people, "Come, let us deal cleverly with them lest they multiply" (Exodus 1:10).]

26. שָׁלַח מֹשֶׁה עַבְדּוֹ — He sent Moses, His servant.

It was God's desire that the world attribute His wonders to Him and not to His human agents. Therefore, He chose as His representative, Moses, the most humble of men, a man who was universally acclaimed as His servant (Alshich).

אַהֲרֹן אֲשֶׁר בָּחַר בּוֹ — Aaron whom He had chosen.

Since Moses suffered from a speech impediment, God chose Aaron to be his spokesman (Radak). Indeed, Moses himself refused the honor and glory of representing God and chose Aaron to speak for him. This was another demonstration of Moses' extreme humility (Alshich).

27. שָׂמוּ בָם דִּבְרֵי אֹתוֹתָיו — They placed among them the words of His signs.

Midrash Shocher Tov interprets that the name of every sign (i.e., plague) was etched [אתות can also mean letters] into the flesh of the Egyptian victims, for Exodus 10:2 says: וְאֶת אֹתֹתַי אֲשֶׁר שַׂמְתִּי בָם And the signs [or, letters] which I placed upon them.

וּמֹפְתִים בְּאֶרֶץ חָם — And wonders in the land of Ham.

105

23-28

and make his elders wise.

²³ Thus Israel came to Egypt
and Jacob sojourned in the land of Ham.
²⁴ And He made His nation exceedingly fruitful,
and made them mightier than their oppressors.
²⁵ He turned their heart to hate His nation,
to plot against His servants.
²⁶ He sent Moses, His servant,
Aaron whom He had chosen —
²⁷ They placed among them the words of His signs.
and wonders in the land of Ham.
²⁸ He sent darkness and made it dark,
and they did not defy His word.

[Ham was Noah's lustful son; he was preoccupied with physical gratification. The *Talmud (Sanhedrin* 108b) relates that Ham cohabited with his wife while he was in Noah's ark despite the prohibition against indulging in this pleasure during the tragic period of the great flood. God therefore revealed His wonders in Ham's country (i.e., in the land of his son, Mitzrayim), to introduce an element of spirituality in that depraved land.]

28. שָׁלַח חשֶׁךְ וַיַּחְשִׁךְ — *He sent darkness and made it dark.*

Now the Psalmist begins a description of the signs and plagues which God brought upon Egypt (see *Exodus* chs. 7-12).

The *darkness* which struck Egypt was unprecedented. Rather than an absence of light, the *darkness* of the plague was a tangible substance that immobilized people.

R' Hirsch points out that *darkness,* the next to the last of the ten plagues, is mentioned first in our psalm because it was the most far-reaching in scope of all the plagues. The preceding eight plagues affected only a limited segment of the Egyptian people but the confining darkness enveloped every inch and every person in the vast

Egyptian empire. Every living creature was held captive by the thick cloak of darkness. No one could exercise any control over his own person or his possessions. Thus *darkness* was the most potent demonstration of God's complete mastery over the forces of nature and over the fate of man.

Alshich notes that in this psalm two of the ten plagues are deleted: דֶּבֶר, *pestilence* [afflicting the livestock], and שְׁחִין, *boils* [striking humans]. *Alshich* explains that the purpose of this composition is to *make God's acts known among the nations (verse* 1). The gentiles would not be impressed by these two plagues, for they would deem them commonplace occurrences [not recognizing that the plagues of pestilence and boils struck with unprecedented force and were miraculous in scope].

Ibn Ezra (commentary to *verse* 32) notes that these two plagues even failed to impress the Egyptians, for Pharoah begged Moses to remove every plague with exception of these two.

וְלֹא מָרוּ אֶת דְּבָרוֹ — *And they did not defy His word.*

God said to the ministering angels, "The Egyptians deserve to be punished with darkness!" Immediately, all the

---

קה °דִּבְרוֹ קֹ כט אֶת־°דְּבָרָיו: הָפַךְ אֶת־מֵימֵיהֶם לְדָם וַיָּמֶת

כט-לה אֶת־דְּגָתָם: שָׁרַץ אַרְצָם צְפַרְדְּעִים בְּחַדְרֵי ל

מַלְכֵיהֶם: אָמַר וַיָּבֹא עָרֹב כִּנִּים בְּכָל־גְּבוּלָם: לא

נָתַן גִּשְׁמֵיהֶם בָּרָד אֵשׁ לֶהָבוֹת בְּאַרְצָם: וַיַּךְ לב-לג

גַּפְנָם וּתְאֵנָתָם וַיְשַׁבֵּר עֵץ גְּבוּלָם: אָמַר לד

וַיָּבֹא אַרְבֶּה וְיֶלֶק וְאֵין מִסְפָּר: וַיֹּאכַל כָּל־ לה

---

angels agreed and did not rebel (*Shemos Rabbah* 14:1).

R' Hirsch maintains that this also refers to the eight plagues which preceded *darkness.* God summoned a vast array of creatures and a wide variety of natural forces to execute His judgments and punishments against Egypt. In all instances these creatures complied with God's commands even though God ordered them to do things that were contrary to their nature.

The locusts left their habitat in the distant east and swarmed over Egypt. The beasts of the wild abandoned their remote habitat to attack Pharaoh's land. [Indeed, the frogs obediently entered roasting ovens where their lives were endangered (see *Pesachim* 53b).][1]

29. הָפַךְ אֶת־מֵימֵיהֶם לְדָם — *He turned their waters into blood.*

This sign proved that God was the Master of the world's bodies of water

and all of their inhabitants (*Sforno*).

וַיָּמֶת אֶת דְּגָתָם — *And he killed their fish.*

Some unbelievers scoffed at Moses and denied that he had actually transformed the water into blood. They claimed that he had merely produced an illusion that made the water appear red. However, the death of the fish confirmed the miraculous transformation (*Sforno*).

30. שָׁרַץ אַרְצָם צְפַרְדְּעִים — *Their land swarmed with frogs.*

Frogs sprang out of every body of water, even the smallest pool (*Rashi*).

בְּחַדְרֵי מַלְכֵיהֶם — *In the chambers of their kings.*

No barrier stood in the path of this relentless onslaught of reptiles. Even the strongest palace, built of the hardest marble, was vulnerable. Rabbi Shimon said that this is one of only nine instances in which God gave something

---

1. On a subsequent occasion, we find that the ministering angels *did* challenge God's command. At the sea, God commanded the angels to save Israel by drowning the pursuing Egyptians. The angels protested, saying, "The Egyptians are idolators, but the Jews are idolators as well! Why show preference to the Jews?" God explained that the Egyptians followed the idols voluntarily whereas the Jews were victims of circumstance. [See *Midrash Tanchuma, Parashas Beshalach* 15:5.]

Beis HaLevi (Parashas Bo) explains that the purpose of the plagues was *not* to force Pharaoh to release the Jews. God, the Omnipotent, did not require ten plagues to bring this about. Rather, the plagues were a series of punishments designed measure for measure to recompense Pharaoh and Egypt for their hideous crimes against the Jews. [See *Chiddushei HaGriz HaLevi on the Torah* pp. 24, 88.] Therefore, whenever God gave the command to initiate a plague, there was no protest from the ministering angels (i.e., the forces of nature which carry out God's will), because the plagues were in complete accord with the laws of justice by which God governs the world.

However, the events at the sea were not planned primarily as a punishment for Egypt. At the sea, God's primary objective was to rescue the fleeing Israelites. This rescue appeared to contradict the laws of justice which govern the world, for the Israelites appeared to be unworthy. Thus, the angels (i.e., the forces of nature) would not conform to the Divine imperative until God explained that Israel's rescue was completely justified.

²⁹ *He turned their waters into blood,*
  and he killed their fish.
³⁰ *Their land swarmed with frogs,*
  in the chambers of their kings.
³¹ *He spoke and hordes of beasts arrived,*
  and lice throughout their borders.
³² *He made their rains into hail,*
  flaming fires in their land.
³³ *He struck their vine and fig tree,*
  and he broke the trees of their border.
³⁴ *He spoke and the locust came,*
  and the numberless yellek.

---

soft power over something hard. The frog stood before the marble slab and declared, "Make way! I am a messenger of God!" and the marble crumbled before it (*Midrash Shocher Tov*).

31. אָמַר וַיָּבֹא עָרֹב — *He spoke and hordes of beasts arrived.*

A single word from God prompted hordes of dangerous, mighty beasts to stampede over the land of Egypt (*Radak*).

The plague of *beasts* actually occurred after the plague of *lice*, but the Psalmist mentions the *beasts* first because they were a more severe punishment (*Ibn Ezra*).

כִּנִּים בְּכָל גְּבוּלָם — *And lice throughout their borders.*

The miraculous advent of lice over every inch of Egyptian soil proved that God rules not only over water but over land as well (*Sforno*).

32. נָתַן גִּשְׁמֵיהֶם בָּרָד — *He made their rains into hail.*

[God changed the blessing of gentle rain into a curse of violent hail.]

אֵשׁ לֶהָבוֹת בְּאַרְצָם — *Flaming fires in their land.*

[This constituted a miracle within a miracle, for ordinarily, water douses

fire, yet *Exodus* 9:24 states that *fire flared up amidst the hail.*]

33. וַיַּךְ גַּפְנָם וּתְאֵנָתָם — *He struck their vine and fig tree.*

The Psalmist singles out these two trees because they grow abundantly in Egypt (*Radak*; see 78:47).

Midrash Shocher Tov explains that the damage which the hailstones wrought was most evident in these fragile plants. The hail was like a sledgehammer which smashed them to bits.

וַיְשַׁבֵּר עֵץ גְּבוּלָם — *And he broke the trees of their border.*

[The hail fell with amazing accuracy and precision: not a single stone landed outside Egypt.]

34. אָמַר וַיָּבֹא אַרְבֶּה — *He spoke and the locust came.*

The plague of locusts proved that God's rule is not limited to the sea and the earth but that it also extends to the sky, for the wind swept the locusts into Egypt (*Sforno*).

וְיֶלֶק וְאֵין מִסְפָּר — *And the numberless yellek.*

Ibn Ezra observes that the Psalmist singles out the *yellek*, because it is the worst species of locusts [see commentary and footnote to 78:46].

לו עֵשֶׂב בְּאַרְצָם וַיֹּאכַל פְּרִי אַדְמָתָם: וַיַּךְ כָּל־

לז בְּכוֹר בְּאַרְצָם רֵאשִׁית לְכָל־אוֹנָם: וַיּוֹצִיאֵם

בְּכֶסֶף וְזָהָב וְאֵין בִּשְׁבָטָיו כּוֹשֵׁל: שָׂמַח לח

מִצְרַיִם בְּצֵאתָם כִּי־נָפַל פַּחְדָּם עֲלֵיהֶם:

לט-מ פָּרַשׂ עָנָן לְמָסָךְ וְאֵשׁ לְהָאִיר לָיְלָה: שָׁאַל

מא וַיָּבֵא שְׂלָו וְלֶחֶם שָׁמַיִם יַשְׂבִּיעֵם: פָּתַח צוּר

מב וַיָּזוּבוּ מָיִם הָלְכוּ בַּצִּיּוֹת נָהָר: כִּי־זָכַר אֶת־

מג דְּבַר קָדְשׁוֹ אֶת־אַבְרָהָם עַבְדּוֹ: וַיּוֹצִא עַמּוֹ

מד בְשָׂשׂוֹן בְּרִנָּה אֶת־בְּחִירָיו: וַיִּתֵּן לָהֶם

מה אַרְצוֹת גּוֹיִם וַעֲמַל לְאֻמִּים יִירָשׁוּ: בַּעֲבוּר |

יִשְׁמְרוּ חֻקָּיו וְתוֹרֹתָיו יִנְצֹרוּ הַלְלוּיָהּ:

35. וַיֹּאכַל כָּל עֵשֶׂב בְּאַרְצָם וַיֹּאכַל פְּרִי אַדְמָתָם — *It consumed all grass in their land, and consumed their soil's fruit.*

Any growing thing which was not devastated by hailstones was devoured by the locusts (Ibn Ezra; Radak).

36. וַיַּךְ כָּל בְּכוֹר בְּאַרְצָם — *Then He smote each first-born in their land.*

This final plague was also a punishment measure for measure. For God warned Pharaoh (Exodus 4:22, 23), "Israel is My son, My first-born. And I say to you, let My son go that he may serve Me; and if you refuse to let him go, behold, I will slay your son, your first-born" (Sforno).

רֵאשִׁית לְכָל אוֹנָם — *The prime of all their strength.*

[See commentary to 78:51.]

Midrash Shocher Tov observes that God smote the first-born of men, the first-born of women, the first-born of cattle, and the first-born of every living thing. In a house where there was no first-born, God smote the steward or chief.

37. וַיּוֹצִיאֵם בְּכֶסֶף וְזָהָב — *And He took them out with silver and gold.*

Rabbi Eliezer the Great taught: The lowliest among the Children of Israel brought ninety asses laden with silver and gold when he left Egypt (Midrash Shocher Tov; see Berachos 5b).

וְאֵין בִּשְׁבָטָיו כּוֹשֵׁל — *And among His tribes was none who stumbled.*

The כּוֹשֵׁל is a man who became impoverished and *stumbled* from his original financial level. No Jew who left Egypt could be described as a כּוֹשֵׁל because all were enriched by the booty of their oppressors (Ibn Ezra; Radak).

Ibn Yachya and Sforno describe the כּוֹשֵׁל as a man whose health has deteriorated to the point that he stumbles unless he uses a cane. When the Jews left Egypt, a miracle occurred — not a single person amongst them was sick or debilitated.

38. שָׂמַח מִצְרַיִם בְּצֵאתָם — *Egypt was glad at their departure.*

As the plagues descended upon Egypt, the plagues waited, wondering when the Israelites would leave; and the Israelites waited, wondering when the Holy One, Blessed be He, would redeem them. When Israel departed, both nations were glad. But we did not know which nation was happier until David composed this verse. Then we understood that the Egyptians were even

³⁵ *It consumed all grass in their land,*
    and consumed their soil's fruit.

³⁶ *Then He smote each first-born in their land,*
    the prime of all their strength.

³⁷ *And He took them out with silver and gold,*
    and among His tribes was none who stumbled.

³⁸ *Egypt was glad at their departure,*
    for their fear had fallen upon them.

³⁹ *He spread out a cloud for shelter,*
    and a fire to illuminate the night.

⁴⁰ *They asked and He brought quail,*
    and bread from heaven sated them.

⁴¹ *He opened a rock and waters gushed,*
    and ran like a river through dry places.

⁴² *For He remembered His holy promise,*
    to Abraham, His servant.

⁴³ *And He led out His nation with mirth,*
    His chosen ones with joyous song.

⁴⁴ *He gave them lands of peoples,*
    and they inherited the toil of nations.

⁴⁵ *So that they might safeguard His statutes*
    and observe His teachings. Praise God!

---

happier than the Israelites [because the plagues had imposed such a terrible burden upon the Egyptians] (*Midrash Shocher Tov*).

כִּי נָפַל פַּחְדָּם עֲלֵיהֶם — *For their fear had fallen upon them.*

The plagues made the Egyptians fear for their lives, as they said, (*Exodus* 12:33) "We shall all die [from these plagues]" (*Radak*).

39. פָּרַשׂ עָנָן לְמָסָךְ — *He spread out a cloud for shelter.*

While the Israelites traveled, the pillar of cloud preceded them like a billowing screen of smoke which was *spread out* like a curtain. When they stopped and camped, the cloud *spread out* above them like a protective umbrella (*Radak*).

וְאֵשׁ לְהָאִיר לָיְלָה — *And a fire to illuminate the night.*

This fire radiated light but not heat, for heat would have added to their discomfort in the hot desert (*Alshich*, commentary to 78:14).

40. שָׁאַל וַיָּבֵא שְׂלָו — *They* [lit., *it*, i.e., the nation] *asked and He brought quail.*

Their bodies craved physical pleasure so God supplied them with fat *quail* to still their hunger (*Alshich*).

וְלֶחֶם שָׁמַיִם יַשְׂבִּיעֵם — *And bread from heaven sated them.*

... but God did not wish them to become sensual, lustful creatures, so He treated them like angels and fed them manna, spiritual nutrition *from heaven* (*Alshich*).

41. פָּתַח צוּר וַיָּזוּבוּ מָיִם — *He opened a rock and waters gushed.*

Early in their wilderness sojourn, the Israelites arrived at Rephidim and there was no water. They mutinied, and God instructed Moses to smite the rock; then water gushed forth (*Exodus* 17:1-7; *Radak*).

At first, the rock oozed blood, and the scoffers of that generation complained. But then a mass of water suddenly burst from the rock, drowning many of the scoffers (*Midrash Shocher Tov*).

הָלְכוּ בַּצִּיּוֹת נָהָר — *And ran like a river through dry places.*

[The צִיָה is a parched, arid land which sees no rainfall. Suddenly God flooded this dry ground with rivers of water to supply the needs of a nation.]

Radak cites the *Midrash* which relates צִיָה to צִי, *navy* (see *Isaiah* 33:21). When they camped in the wilderness, each tribal encampment was surrounded by rivers so wide that boats could travel upon them. The Jews actually built a flotilla, a navy with which they would travel from tribe to tribe.

42. כִּי זָכַר אֶת דְּבַר קָדְשׁוֹ אֶת אַבְרָהָם עַבְדּוֹ — *For He remembered His holy promise, to Abraham, His servant.*

God did not redeem the Jews from Egypt [laden with treasure] because of their own merit, but because of the *promise* He made to their worthy forefather, Abraham. In the wilderness, too, the mutinous Jews were sustained miraculously, for God *remembered* the faithfulness of their progenitors, His devoted servants (*Rashi; Radak*).

43. וַיּוֹצִא עַמּוֹ בְשָׂשׂוֹן בְּרִנָּה אֶת בְּחִירָיו — *And He led out His nation with mirth, His chosen ones with joyous song.*

[God did not merely load their saddlebags with material wealth; He filled their hearts with spiritual wealth. The redeemed ones reaped a rich harvest of faith, the outgrowth of the wonders they beheld. This filled their hearts *with mirth* and their mouths *with song.*]

44. וַיִּתֵּן לָהֶם אַרְצוֹת גּוֹיִם — *He gave them lands of peoples.*

[God did not redeem the Jews and give them the Torah in order to leave them stranded in the wilderness. He provided them with a country perfectly suited to their needs, where they could practice the precepts of the Torah in comfort and joy (see *Radak*).]

וַעֲמַל לְאֻמִּים יִירָשׁוּ — *And they inherited the toil of nations.*

When the Jews are faithful they deserve to have the world toil on their behalf. But, if Heaven forbid, they betray God, then their own hard work will come to naught and the marauding gentiles will plunder the fruit of their labor (*Tanchuma, Parashas Kedoshim*).

45. בַּעֲבוּר יִשְׁמְרוּ חֻקָּיו וְתוֹרֹתָיו יִנְצֹרוּ הַלְלוּיָהּ — *So that they might safeguard His statutes and observe His teachings. Praise God!*

God dealt kindly with the Patriarchs' descendants so that they might grow up to follow the example of their forefathers, who zealously safeguarded God's statutes and *teachings.* God gave them the land of Israel so that the Jews would have the proper environment and atmosphere in which to perfect their faith and practice their precepts. God always stands ready to provide a person's material needs so that the effort required for their fulfillment does not interfere with the pursuit of spiritual excellence (*Sforno; Radak*)

[These words provide an appropriate conclusion for this psalm. It was composed when the Holy Ark of the Law was ceremoniously carried into the capital of the Holy Land, Jerusalem, to be installed in the Temple and the Holy of Holies, the center of the Land. The honor accorded to the Holy Ark and to the Torah demonstrated that the purpose of Jewish settlement in Israel is, *So that they might safeguard His statutes and observe His teachings,* so that they might be filled with sacred, joy and sing, *Praise God!*]

See commentary to 111:1 for the implications of the term הַלְלוּיָהּ, *Praise God!*

The preceding composition described the extensive wonders with which God mercifully redeemed our forefathers from Egypt. This psalm resumes the narrative and relates how God miraculously sustained the Jews as they wandered in the wilderness for forty years. Then Hashem led the Israelites into the land of Canaan and empowered them to conquer their adversaries despite overwhelming odds. Throughout these great historic periods, Hashem repeatedly performed so many wonders that the Psalmist exclaims (verse 2), Who can express the mighty acts of HASHEM? Who can declare all of His praise? (Radak).

However, even while God was displaying unprecedented kindness to Israel, the Israelites were negligent in their duties toward God, and they failed to appreciate His wonders. Indeed, they defied God's representative, Moses, and rebelled against his commands. This defiance initiated the spiritual and moral decline which eventually led to the Jew's exile from the Holy Land (Sforno).

The Psalmist completes his description of Israel's infidelity and exile with a prayer for redemption (verse 47), Save us HASHEM, our God, and gather us from among the peoples, to thank Your Holy Name and to glory in Your praise!

This psalm concludes the fourth Book of Tehillim with the declaration, Blessed is HASHEM, the God of Israel, from This World to the World to Come, and let the entire nation say, "Amen!" Praise God!

א הַלְלוּיָהּ | הוֹדוּ לַיהוה כִּי־טוֹב כִּי לְעוֹלָם

ב חַסְדּוֹ: מִי יְמַלֵּל גְּבוּרוֹת יהוה יַשְׁמִיעַ כָּל־

ג תְּהִלָּתוֹ: אַשְׁרֵי שֹׁמְרֵי מִשְׁפָּט עֹשֵׂה צְדָקָה

ד בְכָל־עֵת: זָכְרֵנִי יהוה בִּרְצוֹן עַמֶּךָ פָּקְדֵנִי

ה בִּישׁוּעָתֶךָ: לִרְאוֹת | בְּטוֹבַת בְּחִירֶיךָ לִשְׂמֹחַ

1. הַלְלוּיָהּ הוֹדוּ לַה' כִּי טוֹב — *Praise God! Give thanks to HASHEM for He is good.*

The word הַלְלוּיָהּ [Hallelujah], *Praise God*, is discussed in the commentary to 111:1.

Ibn Yachya and *Malbim* say that this psalm is a continuation of psalm 105, which was composed by David as he took the Holy Ark to Jerusalem. At that time David gave thanks to Hashem for all the goodness He performed throughout Jewish history.

כִּי לְעוֹלָם חַסְדּוֹ — *For His kindness is eternal.*

[The scope of God's kindness transcends the limits of time; His goodness is not temporary nor short-lived. In one generation He may lay the groundwork for kindness which will not be manifested until many generations later.]

2. מִי יְמַלֵּל גְּבוּרוֹת ה' יַשְׁמִיעַ כָּל תְּהִלָּתוֹ — *Who can express the mighty acts of HASHEM?, [Who can] declare* [lit. *make heard*] *all of His praise?*

This psalm, like the preceding one, is dedicated to recounting the wonders which God performed for our forefathers in Egypt, in the wilderness, and in Canaan. Many cannot grasp the enormity of God's actions on behalf of His chosen nation. Countless details endless incidents, and incessant vigilance went into the nation's redemption.

Even the kindness which Hashem performs for an individual is too vast to recount, as 40:6 attests: *Much have You done — You HASHEM, my God, Your wonders and Your thoughts are for us, none can compare to You. Can I relate or speak of them? They are too mighty to recount.* Indeed, the Rabbis noted,

אֵין בַּעַל הַנֵּס מַכִּיר בְּנִסּוֹ, *the beneficiary of God's miracles is not cognizant of his own miracle* (Niddah 31a). God does not always make such miracles known because He is more concerned with the results of His wonders than with appreciation for them.

David's words in 9:15 seem to contradict this verse. Here David says that it is impossible to express all the mighty acts of Hashem. There he says, *That I may proclaim all of Your praises in the gates of the daughter of Zion.* However, the context of that psalm proves that David was referring to his miraculous salvation from specific dangers.

Although no mortal can comprehend or recount *all* of God's mighty acts, David attempted to proclaim *all* of God's praises for specific incidents (*Radak*).

Zohar (*Parashas Yisro*) notes that the customary term for utterance or speech is יְדַבֵּר. The Psalmist uses the obscure word יְמַלֵּל because it is cognate with מָלַל, *to cut down stalks,* as in *Deuteronomy 23:26:* וְקָטַפְתָּ מְלִילֹת בְּיָדֶךָ, *You shall pluck with your hand the stalks which stand to be cut down.* Thus יְמַלֵּל implies *a full grasp of the subject,* to have it in the palm of the hand. Man can attempt to speak (יְדַבֵּר) of God's wonders although he will never complete the list, but man cannot even begin to grasp (יְמַלֵּל) the intricacy and the enormity of God's involvement with human affairs.

According to the above commentaries, the word מִי, *who,* refers to both the first and the second stich of this verse: i.e., מִי יְמַלֵּל, *Who can express?* מִי יַשְׁמִיעַ, *Who can declare?*

Praise God! Give thanks to HASHEM
for He is good;
for His kindness is eternal.
² Who can express the mighty acts of HASHEM?
Who can declare all of His praise?
³ Praiseworthy are those who maintain justice,
and do charity in every time.
⁴ Remember me, HASHEM,
when You show Your nation favor,
recall me with Your salvation —
⁵ To see the good of Your chosen ones,

However, the *Talmud (Horayos* 13b) perceives the first stich as a rhetorical question answered by the second stich: i.e., *Who has the right to express the mighty acts of HASHEM?* [Only] the one who *can declare all of His praise!* Based on this, the Rabbis ruled that the only scholar who can be appointed רֹאשׁ יְשִׁיבָה, *the head of the Academy,* is one who is well-versed in every tractate of the *Talmud* [the work which discusses the *mighty acts of HASHEM*] and who has mastered every aspect of Torah lore. However, if the scholar is not completely fluent in even one tractate, obscure as it may seem to be, he must be relieved of his position, immediately.[1]

3. אַשְׁרֵי שֹׁמְרֵי מִשְׁפָּט — *Praiseworthy are those who maintain justice.*

[It is impossible to *express the mighty acts of HASHEM* or to *declare all of His praise* (verse 2) but the praiseworthiness of a man is summarized succinctly: *Praiseworthy are those who maintain justice.*]

עֹשֵׂה צְדָקָה בְכָל עֵת — *And do charity in every time.*

The *Talmud (Kesubos* 50a) asks if it is actually possible to give charity

constantly, *in every time,* without interruption? The Rabbis of Yavne (some say: Rabbi Eliezer) say that this verse refers to the man who supports his sons and daughters when they are small. (*Rashi* explains that this responsibility weighs on the father's mind at all *times,* day and night.) Rabbi Shmuel bar Nachmani says that this verse refers to the one who raises an orphan in his home and arranges his marriage when he comes of age (see *Midrash Shocher Tov).*

4. זָכְרֵנִי ה׳ בִּרְצוֹן עַמֶּךָ פָּקְדֵנִי בִּישׁוּעָתֶךָ — *Remember me, HASHEM, when You show Your nation favor, recall me with Your salvation.*

The Jew looks forward to the time when God will *favor* His nation with the *salvation* of the Messiah's advent, the reconstruction of the Holy Temple, and the resurrection of the dead. The Psalmist pleads that he be remembered and included in these events (*Radak*).

5. לִרְאוֹת בְּטוֹבַת בְּחִירֶיךָ — *To see the good of Your chosen ones.*

Since Israel is *Your chosen* nation, the good which You have reserved as their reward will surely be unique, and I pray that I will deserve to see it *(Radak).*

---

1. The *Talmud (Megillah* 18a) gives our verse a practical application. When engaged in formal prayer, no man can attempt to recite all of God's praises; he must confine himself to the שְׁמוֹנֶה עֶשְׂרֵה, *Eighteen Benedictions,* which were formulated by the one hundred and twenty

ו בְּשִׂמְחַת גּוֹיֶךָ לְהִתְהַלֵּל עִם־נַחֲלָתֶךָ: חָטָאנוּ
ז עִם־אֲבוֹתֵינוּ הֶעֱוִינוּ הִרְשָׁעְנוּ: אֲבוֹתֵינוּ
בְּמִצְרַיִם | לֹא־הִשְׂכִּילוּ נִפְלְאוֹתֶיךָ לֹא זָכְרוּ
אֶת־רֹב חֲסָדֶיךָ וַיַּמְרוּ עַל־יָם בְּיַם־סוּף:
ח וַיּוֹשִׁיעֵם לְמַעַן שְׁמוֹ לְהוֹדִיעַ אֶת־גְּבוּרָתוֹ:
ט וַיִּגְעַר בְּיַם־סוּף וַיֶּחֱרָב וַיּוֹלִיכֵם בַּתְּהֹמוֹת
י כַּמִּדְבָּר: וַיּוֹשִׁיעֵם מִיַּד שׂוֹנֵא וַיִּגְאָלֵם מִיַּד

According to *Chazah Zion*, this refers to the reconstruction of the Third and final Temple. When that is rebuilt, it will be akin to the First Temple in its glory, and the First Temple was the *chosen one*.

לִשְׂמֹחַ בְּשִׂמְחַת גּוֹיֶךָ לְהִתְהַלֵּל עִם נַחֲלָתֶךָ — *To rejoice in the gladness of Your people, and to glory with Your inheritance.*

These two phrases refer to the Second and Third Temples, respectively (*Chazah Zion*).

6. חָטָאנוּ עִם אֲבוֹתֵינוּ הֶעֱוִינוּ הִרְשָׁעְנוּ — *We have sinned like* [lit. with] *our fathers, we have committed iniquity and wickedness.*

The exiled Jews will say: "Our fathers sinned and we have perpetuated their sins" (*Radak*). This statement will fulfill the Scriptural prophecy (*Leviticus* 26:40): *And they shall confess their iniquity and the iniquity of their fathers, and their betrayal with which they betrayed against Me* (*Ibn Ezra*).

7. אֲבוֹתֵינוּ בְמִצְרַיִם לֹא הִשְׂכִּילוּ נִפְלְאוֹתֶיךָ — *Our fathers in Egypt comprehended not Your wonders.*

As our fathers were leaving Egypt,

they already forgot the wonders which You performed on their behalf while they were still in bondage in Egypt. This proves that they never truly comprehended these wonders even while in Egypt (*Radak*).

לֹא זָכְרוּ אֶת רֹב חֲסָדֶיךָ — *They remembered not Your abundant kindnesses.*

As they were leaving Egypt, the Egyptians began to pursue them, and the Jews were terrified. They imagined that God had abandoned them to be slaughtered by their enemies. If they had only remembered the abundance of God's kindness towards them, they could never have imagined that God would suddenly forsake them (*Radak*).

וַיַּמְרוּ עַל יָם בְּיַם סוּף — *They rebelled by the sea, at the Sea of Reeds.*

Rav Hunna teaches that the Israelites of that generation had very meager faith. Although they witnessed the splitting of the sea and clearly saw the waters returning to their former position, they still had doubts about God's salvation. They cried out, "Just as we came out of the sea on this side, the

---

members of the כְּנֶסֶת הַגְּדוֹלָה, *Great Assembly*, because, *Who can express the mighty acts of Hashem?* [Only] *He who can declare all of His praises.*

Rabbi Chaim of Volozhin (*Nefesh HaChaim* II:13) explains that these one hundred and twenty men were not typical mortals, but great prophets and sages who were inspired with the Divine Spirit. These seers saw that the entire universe is in a constant state of flux and transition. The daily prayers must be designed to complement the unique nature of each passing day, hour and moment. Their task was awesome and staggering, for no two situations are the same, no two men are alike. These inspired men incorporated into every word of Jewish liturgy a countless variety of nuances and meanings which capture the never-ending praises of God for all times and in all situations.

to rejoice in the gladness of Your people,
and to glory with Your inheritance.

⁶ We have sinned like our fathers,
we have committed iniquity and wickedness.
⁷ Our fathers in Egypt
comprehended not Your wonders;
they remembered not Your abundant kindnesses.
They rebelled by the sea, at the Sea of Reeds.
⁸ But He saved them for His Name's sake,
to make known His might.
⁹ He roared at the Sea of Reeds and it became dry,
and led them through the depths
as through a desert.
¹⁰ He saved them from the hand of the enemy,
and redeemed them from the hand of the foe.

Egyptians came out on the other side [and we are still in potential danger]." Therefore, God commanded the ministering angel appointed over the sea to spew out the corpses of the drowned Egyptians so that Israel would clearly see them dead on the sea shore (Rashi from Pesachim 118b).

8. וַיּוֹשִׁיעֵם לְמַעַן שְׁמוֹ — But He saved them for His Name's sake.

He saved them because He was known as אֱלֹהֵי הָעִבְרִים, the God of the Hebrews (Exodus 3:18, 5:3; Ibn Ezra).

[Therefore, despite the fact that Israel rebelled, God felt obligated to save them.]

לְהוֹדִיעַ אֶת גְּבוּרָתוֹ — To make known His might.

In Egypt, God displayed His mastery over Creation in order to prove to mankind that He was the mighty architect of the six days of Creation (Ibn Yachya).

9. וַיִּגְעַר בְּיַם סוּף וַיֶּחֱרָב — He roared at the Sea of Reeds and it became dry.

The Psalmist describes the wind which blew upon the sea and dried it as a roar. Similarly, the prophet (Nachum

1:4) says: גּוֹעֵר בַּיָּם וַיַּבְּשֵׁהוּ, He roared at the sea and dried it up (Radak; Ibn Ezra).

וַיּוֹלִיכֵם בַּתְּהֹמוֹת כַּמִּדְבָּר — And led them through the depths as through a desert.

Malbim explains that the seabed dried up and was as arid as the desert.

Rav Nehorai taught that the Jewish mothers crossed the sea with their children in their arms. If a child cried, his mother could calm him by stretching out her hand to pluck the child an apple or pomegranate from the sea. Thus, God led them through the depths as [He led them] through a desert, for just as He provided for all their needs in the wilderness [with manna and the well] so did He provide for them in the sea (Shemos Rabbah 21:9).

10. וַיּוֹשִׁיעֵם מִיַּד שׂוֹנֵא — He saved them from the hand of the enemy.

This refers to Pharaoh (Ibn Ezra).

וַיִּגְאָלֵם מִיַּד אוֹיֵב — And redeemed them from the hand of the foe.

Malbim explains that saving indicates merely a temporary rescue, whereas redemption is for all time. Moreover, since the hatred of the אוֹיֵב, foe, is more

יא אוֹיֵב: וַיְכַסּוּ־מַיִם צָרֵיהֶם אֶחָד מֵהֶם לֹא

יב נוֹתָר: וַיַּאֲמִינוּ בִדְבָרָיו יָשִׁירוּ תְּהִלָּתוֹ:

יג מִהֲרוּ שָׁכְחוּ מַעֲשָׂיו לֹא־חִכּוּ לַעֲצָתוֹ:

יד וַיִּתְאַוּוּ תַאֲוָה בַּמִּדְבָּר וַיְנַסּוּ־אֵל בִּישִׁימוֹן:

טו וַיִּתֵּן לָהֶם שֶׁאֱלָתָם וַיְשַׁלַּח רָזוֹן בְּנַפְשָׁם:

טז וַיְקַנְאוּ לְמֹשֶׁה בַּמַּחֲנֶה לְאַהֲרֹן קְדוֹשׁ יְהוָה:

יז תִּפְתַּח־אֶרֶץ וַתִּבְלַע דָּתָן וַתְּכַס עַל־עֲדַת

---

intensive and manifest than that of the שׂוֹנֵא, *enemy*, it can only be checked by a very forceful and permanent redemption (*Malbim*).

11. וַיְכַסּוּ מַיִם צָרֵיהֶם — *And the waters covered their tormentors.*

A *tormentor* is even worse than a *foe*, because he inflicts pain upon his victim (*Malbim*). [Therefore, Israel's tormentors well deserved the painful death of drowning.]

אֶחָד מֵהֶם לֹא נוֹתָר — *None of them was left* [lit. *one of them was not left*].

Exodus 14:28 records that when Pharaoh's army drowned in the Sea of Reeds, לֹא נִשְׁאַר בָּהֶם עַד אֶחָד, *there remained not among them even* [lit. *until*] *one*. Based on the literal meaning of עַד, *until*, some Sages maintain that all were destroyed *until one* remained. That one was Pharaoh whom God allowed to escape so that he could relate God's miracles and spread His Name among the nations of the world. [Our verse, *none of them was left*, seems to contradict this view. Accordingly, we would have to consider that Pharaoh was not *one of them* but was *above*

them and is thus excluded from our verse.] (*Midrash Shocher Tov*)[1]

12. וַיַּאֲמִינוּ בִדְבָרָיו יָשִׁירוּ תְּהִלָּתוֹ — *Then they believed His words, they sang His praise.*

Even the Jews who were initially doubtful of God's ability to redeem them came to believe in Him completely when they witnessed His wonders at the sea. In the merit of this belief, God's spirit descended upon them and *they sang his praise* (*Mechilta Beshalach; Shemos Rabbah* 23:2).

13. מִהֲרוּ שָׁכְחוּ מַעֲשָׂיו — *Swiftly they forgot His deeds.*

A mere three days after they journeyed from the Sea of Reeds, they arrived at Marah, a place where the water was bitter and unfit to drink (*Exodus* 15:22-26). [They failed to remember that as they had gone through the Sea of Reeds, God had transformed the salty sea water into sweet, fresh liquid.] They complained against God and questioned His ability [to provide water for them in the wilderness] (*Radak; Ibn Yachya*).

---

1. The prophet Jonah warned the people of Nineveh to repent lest their city be overturned. In *Jonah* 3:6 we read: *When word reached the king of Nineveh, he arose from his throne and removed his robe from upon himself. He covered himself with sackcloth and sat on ashes.*
According to *Pirkei d'Rabbi Eliezer* (ch. 43), this king was the Pharaoh of the Exodus who had firsthand acquaintance with God's might at the Sea of Reeds. *Yalkut Shimoni* (*Shemos* 17b) notes that Pharaoh was spared so that he would recount God's greatness and this Pharaoh later became king of Nineveh. When word of Jonah's ominous warning reached him the terrified king decreed: "Let neither man nor beast, herd nor flock, taste anything for three days at the risk of being burned alive for disobedience; let them neither feed nor drink water, for know that there is no God beside Him in all the world; all His words are truth, and all His judgments are true and faithful!"

¹¹ *And the waters covered their tormentors,*
none of them was left.

¹² *Then they believed His words,*
they sang His praise.

¹³ *Swiftly they forgot His deeds,*
they did not await His counsel.

¹⁴ *They craved a lust in the wilderness,*
and tested God in the desolation.

¹⁵ *And He gave them their request,*
but dispatched emaciation to their souls.

¹⁶ *They were jealous of Moses in the camp,*
of Aaron, HASHEM's holy one.

¹⁷ *The earth opened and swallowed Dathan,*

לֹא חִכּוּ לַעֲצָתוֹ — *They did not await His counsel.*

The Jews' reaction was irrational [as well as disloyal]. Since God had performed wonders to help them cross the Sea of Reeds, certainly He did not intend to abandon them in the wilderness by allowing them to die of thirst. [Yet, even if this had been the Divine decree,] it would have been far better for them to die of thirst than to question the will of God! They should have waited patiently for His counsel to unfold. In fact, the Divine plan was revealed finally when God miraculously sweetened the waters of Marah (*Radak; Ibn Yachya*).

14. וַיִּתְאַוּוּ תַאֲוָה בַּמִּדְבָּר וַיְנַסּוּ אֵל בִּישִׁימוֹן — *They craved a lust in the wilderness, and tested God in the desolation.*

[See *Numbers* 11:4 and commentary to 78:18.]

15. וַיִּתֵּן לָהֶם שֶׁאֱלָתָם וַיְשַׁלַּח רָזוֹן בְּנַפְשָׁם — *And He gave them their request, but dispatched emaciation to their souls.*

They searched desperately for physical satisfaction, but they achieved the opposite — a terrible *emaciation* and emptiness of the soul (*Radak*).

16. וַיְקַנְאוּ לְמֹשֶׁה בַּמַּחֲנֶה — *They were jealous of Moses in the camp.*

This refers to Korach and his party; *they were jealous* of the authority which Moses and Aaron had assumed. Korach vehemently demanded of Moses (*Numbers* 16:13), "Why do you persist in making yourself a prince over us?" (*Ibn Ezra*).

The Psalmist blames the entire Jewish nation for Korach's revolt even though only two hundred and fifty men actually joined Korach's ranks. Had all the Jews been perfectly loyal to Moses and steadfast in their support of their leader, Korach would not have dared to defy Moses. The failure of the nation to protest and quell Korach's mutiny is considered tantamount to participation in Korach's crime (*Radak*).

לְאַהֲרֹן קְדוֹשׁ ה' — *Of Aaron, HASHEM's holy one.*

Korach's anger was kindled when he saw that Moses appointed Aaron to the post of the consecrated High Priest. Korach thundered (*Numbers* 16:3) "You have taken too much for yourselves! All members of the congregation are holy, and HASHEM is among them, why do you elevate yourselves above the congregation of HASHEM?" (*Radak*).

17. תִּפְתַּח אֶרֶץ וַתִּבְלַע דָּתָן — *The earth opened and swallowed Dathan.*

יח אֲבִירָם: וַתִּבְעַר־אֵשׁ בַּעֲדָתָם לֶהָבָה תְּלַהֵט

יט רְשָׁעִים: יַעֲשׂוּ־עֵגֶל בְּחֹרֵב וַיִּשְׁתַּחֲווּ

כ לְמַסֵּכָה: וַיָּמִירוּ אֶת־כְּבוֹדָם בְּתַבְנִית שׁוֹר

כא אֹכֵל עֵשֶׂב: שָׁכְחוּ אֵל מוֹשִׁיעָם עֹשֶׂה גְדֹלוֹת

כב בְּמִצְרָיִם: נִפְלָאוֹת בְּאֶרֶץ חָם נוֹרָאוֹת עַל־

[Dathan and Abiram were arch-enemies of Moses for many years. They were Korach's main henchmen in his rebellion against Moses (see Numbers 16:1,12-14).]

Rashi observes that the Psalmist refrains from any open reference to Korach's role in the mutiny and the ensuing disaster out of respect for Korach's illustrious sons, who were psalmists themselves.

Radak explains that Korach's henchmen are singled out because the underlings who assist the wicked leaders are as guilty as the leaders themselves, because if the leader could not find followers, he would not dare to perpetuate his evil acts.

וַתְּכַס עַל עֲדַת אֲבִירָם — And covered over the company of Abiram.

Midrash Shocher Tov says that at one point [even before Korach rebelled], the Israelites sought to appoint Dathan in place of Moses, and Abiram instead of Aaron, saying, "Let us appoint a chief and let us return to Egypt" (Numbers 14:4). However, instead of ascending to greatness, Dathan and Abiram descended to the pit of destruction.

Malbim says that Dathan was swallowed alone; Abiram, however, was part of an עֵדָה, company, of ten people which included his sons, daughters, and other family members who were swallowed with him.

18. וַתִּבְעַר אֵשׁ בַּעֲדָתָם — And a fire blazed amid their company.

As Numbers 16:35 states: And a fire came forth from before HASHEM and consumed the two hundred and fifty men [supporters of Korach] who offered the incense (Rashi).

לֶהָבָה תְּלַהֵט רְשָׁעִים — A flame ignited the wicked.

Malbim says that this refers to the aftermath of Korach's revolt, when, On the morrow, all of the congregation of the Children of Israel murmured against Moses and Aaron saying, "You have murdered the nation of HASHEM" (Numbers 17:6).

In response, anger blazed forth from HASHEM and the plague began (Numbers 17:11). This plague is considered a secondary flame which was ignited as a result of the main fire, which burned amidst the assembly [of Korach's followers].

19. יַעֲשׂוּ עֵגֶל בְּחֹרֵב — They made a calf in Horeb.

The Psalmist emphasizes the sheer irony of the event. In Horeb, the entire congregation received the Ten Commandments from the mouth of God and heard Him say, "You shall not make for yourself a carved idol or any image" (Exodus 20:4), yet it was at this very spot that they defied His command and made the golden calf (Radak).

The original name of the mountain was סִינַי, Sinai. After the Jewish people sinned with the calf, however, it became known as חֹרֵב, Horeb, which literally means destruction, for this sin devastated the Jews and lowered their glorious spiritual level, as Exodus 33:6 recounts: and the Children of Israel stripped themselves of their ornaments by Mount Horeb (Rav Chaim Vital).

וַיִּשְׁתַּחֲווּ לְמַסֵּכָה — And prostrated themselves before a molten image.

[Although the molten image was lifeless, they offered their very lives in complete submission to it.]

and covered over the company of Abiram.

¹⁸ And a fire blazed amid their company,
   a flame ignited the wicked.
¹⁹ They made a calf in Horeb,
   and prostrated themselves
   before a molten image.
²⁰ They exchanged their glory
   for the likeness of a grass-eating ox.
²¹ They forgot God, their Savior,
   Who had done great things in Egypt,
²² Wondrous works in the land of Ham,

20. וַיָּמִירוּ אֶת כְּבוֹדָם בְּתַבְנִית שׁוֹר אֹכֵל עֵשֶׂב — *They exchanged their glory for the likeness of a grass-eating ox.*

The ox is most despicable when it eats grass because it regurgitates, chews its cud, and defecates (*Rashi*). [How foolish were the Children of Israel to choose such a repulsive symbol for worship — especially since this choice made them forfeit their former glorious status as servants of the Almighty.]

21. שָׁכְחוּ אֵל מוֹשִׁיעָם — *They forgot God, their Savior.*

They attributed their salvation to the calf saying, "This is your god, O Israel, who brought you up out of the land of Egypt" (*Exodus* 32:4).

[The *Talmud* (*Sanhedrin* 63b) explains that initially the Jewish people did not really believe in lifeless idols. They worshiped these images only in an attempt to release themselves from the strict demands of Torah law which prohibited satisfaction of many bodily lusts. The Jews only served the idols in order to be able to be publicly lewd with the women prohibited by Torah law. However, the *Talmud* concludes that after the Jews became involved with the idols they began to believe in them and ultimately became fanatically devoted to their new gods.]

עָשָׂה גְדֹלוֹת בְּמִצְרָיִם — *Who had done great things in Egypt.*

Twelve zodiac signs circle the heavens. The sign that is in ascent in a particular month determines man's fortunes. In the month of Nissan, when Israel was redeemed from Egypt, the sign of the טְלֶה, *Lamb* [referred to in English as the Ram] was in ascent. Nissan should have been a specially fortunate month for the Egyptians because the Lamb was their special national idol. Nevertheless, *great things* happened and Egypt fell. The Jews attributed this to the fact that the zodiac sign of the שׁוֹר, *Bull*, follows that of the Ram and the Bull deposed the Ram. Therefore, they made an image of a young bull, a calf, and venerated it. They forgot Hashem who was really responsible for the great events which had occurred (*Abarbanel* and *Akeidah* to *Exodus* 32; see *Me'am Loaz* there).

22. נִפְלָאוֹת בְּאֶרֶץ חָם — *Wondrous works in the land of Ham.*

Ham was the father of Mitzrayim, the progenitor of Egypt. Just as he was accursed and despised, so was the land of his descendants despised and unholy. Nevertheless, God performed wonders there, but Israel forgot God and attributed the miracles to the calf (*Radak*).

כג יַם־סוּף: וַיֹּאמֶר לְהַשְׁמִידָם לוּלֵי מֹשֶׁה
בְחִירוֹ עָמַד בַּפֶּרֶץ לְפָנָיו לְהָשִׁיב חֲמָתוֹ
כד מֵהַשְׁחִית: וַיִּמְאֲסוּ בְּאֶרֶץ חֶמְדָּה לֹא־
כה הֶאֱמִינוּ לִדְבָרוֹ: וַיֵּרָגְנוּ בְאָהֳלֵיהֶם לֹא שָׁמְעוּ
כו בְּקוֹל יְהוָה: וַיִּשָּׂא יָדוֹ לָהֶם לְהַפִּיל אוֹתָם
כז בַּמִּדְבָּר: וּלְהַפִּיל זַרְעָם | בַּגּוֹיִם וּלְזָרוֹתָם
כח בָּאֲרָצוֹת: וַיִּצָּמְדוּ לְבַעַל פְּעוֹר וַיֹּאכְלוּ זִבְחֵי

נוֹרָאוֹת עַל יַם סוּף — *Awesome things by the Sea of Reeds.*

[They attributed these miracles, as well, to the calf.]

23. וַיֹּאמֶר לְהַשְׁמִידָם לוּלֵי מֹשֶׁה בְחִירוֹ עָמַד בַּפֶּרֶץ לְפָנָיו — *He said He would destroy them — had not Moses, His chosen one, stood before Him in the breach.*

This may be compared to the king's son who was accused and put on trial. When the prosecutor condemned the prince, his faithful teacher ejected the prosecutor from the courtroom and stood in the breach to defend the damaged reputation of his beloved disciple. Similarly, Moses, the teacher of Israel, defended the actions of his beloved disciples (*Shemos Rabbah* 43:1).

The *Talmud* (*Pesachim* 119a) notes that the ways of God differ from the ways of mortals, for when a man is bested in an argument he becomes depressed, but when God is 'bested' in an argument, He rejoices. God intended to destroy the Jews, but Moses argued on their behalf and prevailed upon God to change His decision. That God rejoiced over Moses' success is evident from the fact that Moses was only called בְחִירוֹ, *His chosen one,* when he had *stood before Him in the breach.*

לְהָשִׁיב חֲמָתוֹ מֵהַשְׁחִית — *To turn away His wrath from destruction.*

Moses committed a most courageous act in order to save Israel from destruction: he took the tablets of the Law from God's hand and smashed

them. This may be likened to the king who sent his royal agent to his bride with the marriage contract which would complete the bond of matrimony. Meanwhile, the bride betrayed the king and sinned with another man. Seeing this, the compassionate agent tore the contract into shreds, saying, "It is far better for her to be judged as an unwed woman than as the king's wife."

Similarly, when Moses saw Israel betray God with the calf, he smashed the tablets which were their contract with God, saying, "It is better that they be judged as uncommitted bystanders than as partners; better that they be considered innocent and uninformed of the Law than as guilty intentional transgressors" (*Shemos Rabbah* 43:1).

24. וַיִּמְאֲסוּ בְּאֶרֶץ חֶמְדָּה — *And they despised the desirable land.*

[The Jews abandoned their journey to the promised Land when they accepted the evil reports of the spies, who depicted the Holy Land as a dangerous country which devours its inhabitants.]

לֹא הֶאֱמִינוּ לִדְבָרוֹ — *They had no faith in His word.*

[They preferred to believe the evil reports of the spies than to trust God's word that He would bring them to a wonderful land.]

25. וַיֵּרָגְנוּ בְאָהֳלֵיהֶם לֹא שָׁמְעוּ בְּקוֹל ה' — *They murmured in their tents, they heeded not the voice of HASHEM.*

[See *Deuteronomy* 1:27.]

awesome things by the Sea of Reeds.

²³ He said He would destroy them —
    had not Moses, His chosen one,
stood before Him in the breach
    to turn away His wrath from destruction.
²⁴ And they despised the desirable land,
    they had no faith in His word.
²⁵ They murmured in their tents,
    they heeded not the voice of HASHEM.
²⁶ Then He lifted up His hand against them,
    to throw them down in the wilderness.
²⁷ And to throw down their descendants
    among the peoples,
    and to scatter them among the lands.
²⁸ Then they clung to Baal Peor
    and ate the sacrifices of the dead.

---

26. וַיִּשָּׂא יָדוֹ לָהֶם — *Then He lifted up His hand against them.*

God took an oath to punish them (Rashi; Radak).

לְהַפִּיל אוֹתָם בַּמִּדְבָּר — *To throw them down in the wilderness.*

[God instructed Moses to tell the Children of Israel, "Your carcasses shall fall in this wilderness and all of you who ... have murmured against Me shall not come into the land" (Numbers 14:29,30).]

27. וּלְהַפִּיל זַרְעָם בַּגּוֹיִם — *And to throw down their descendants among the peoples.*

When Israel sinned because of the spies, God already decreed their bitter fate and determined that the First Temple would be destroyed. They foolishly cried for naught on the eve of the Ninth of Av and God declared, "You cried for no reason on this night, therefore in the future, I shall provide you with ample reason to cry on this

night, for I will destroy the Temple on the Ninth of Av." After the destruction the Jews were cast out *among the peoples* (Rashi).

וּלְזָרוֹתָם בָּאֲרָצוֹת — *And to scatter them among the lands.*

As Ezekiel 20:28 prophesied: *I lifted up my hand to them also in the wilderness, declaring that I would scatter them among the nations and disperse them among the lands* (Radak).

28. וַיִּצָּמְדוּ לְבַעַל פְּעוֹר — *Then they clung to Baal Peor.*

At Shittim, the daughters of Midian seduced the young men of Israel into serving the idol Baal Peor and clinging to its faith (see Numbers 25:1-9).

וַיֹּאכְלוּ זִבְחֵי מֵתִים — *And ate the sacrifices of the dead.*

From this the Talmud (Avodah Zarah 48b) learns that the meat of an animal which was sacrificed to idols is as טָמֵא, *contaminated*, as is the flesh of a corpse.

כט מֵתִים: וַיַּכְעִיסוּ בְּמַעַלְלֵיהֶם וַתִּפְרָץ־בָּם

ל מַגֵּפָה: וַיַּעֲמֹד פִּינְחָס וַיְפַלֵּל וַתֵּעָצַר

לא הַמַּגֵּפָה: וַתֵּחָשֶׁב לוֹ לִצְדָקָה לְדֹר וָדֹר עַד־

לב עוֹלָם: וַיַּקְצִיפוּ עַל־מֵי מְרִיבָה וַיֵּרַע לְמֹשֶׁה

לג בַּעֲבוּרָם: כִּי־הִמְרוּ אֶת־רוּחוֹ וַיְבַטֵּא

29. וַיַּכְעִיסוּ בְּמַעַלְלֵיהֶם וַתִּפְרָץ־בָּם מַגֵּפָה — *They angered Him with their behavior and a plague broke out among them.*

Numbers 25:9 records that twenty-four thousand died in this plague.

30. וַיַּעֲמֹד פִּינְחָס וַיְפַלֵּל וַתֵּעָצַר הַמַּגֵּפָה — *Phineas arose and executed judgment, and the plague was halted.*

The translation follows *Ibn Ezra* and *Radak*, who perceive וַיְפַלֵּל as cognate with פְּלִלִים, *judges* (*Exodus* 21:22). [When Phineas saw Zimri son of Salu (the prince of the tribe of Simeon) sinning with Kozbi daughter of Tzur (the Midianite princess), he did not hesitate to condemn them to death; he himself *executed judgment* and slew them.]

Targum, however, translates וַיְפַלֵּל as צְלִי, *he prayed*. According to this view, Phineas invoked Divine assistance before he performed his bold deed.[1]

31. וַתֵּחָשֶׁב לוֹ לִצְדָקָה לְדֹר וָדֹר עַד עוֹלָם — *It was accounted to him as a righteous deed, for all generations* [lit. *to generation and generation*], *forever.*

God instructed Moses to tell Phineas, "I shall give to him My covenant of peace, and he and his seed after him shall have it, a covenant of everlasting priesthood, because he was zealous for his God and made atonement for the Children of Israel" (*Numbers* 25:12-13).

32. וַיַּקְצִיפוּ עַל מֵי מְרִיבָה — *They provoked anger at the waters of strife.*

After Miriam died, the children of Israel were no longer supplied with water from her wondrous well. *The people quarreled with Moses and spoke, saying, "If only we had died when our brethren died in the presence of HASHEM! Why have you brought the congregation of HASHEM into this wilderness, that we and our cattle should die there?"* (*Numbers* 20:3-4).

God responded to these demands and issued instructions to Moses: *Take the rod and gather the assembly together, you and Aaron your brother, and speak to the rock before their eyes and it shall give forth its water ... And Moses took the rod ... and gathered the congregation before the rock and said to them* שִׁמְעוּ נָא הַמֹּרִים, "*Hear now, you rebels! Shall we bring you water from this rock?" And Moses lifted his hand and smote the rock twice and abundant water came out ...* (*ibid.,* vs. 7-11).

וַיֵּרַע לְמֹשֶׁה בַּעֲבוּרָם — *And Moses suffered* [lit. *it went ill with Moses*] *because of them.*

As a result of this incident, Moses was punished very severely: *And HASHEM spoke to Moses and Aaron: "Because you did not believe in Me to sanctify Me in the eyes of the Children of Israel therefore you shall not bring*

---

1. The *Talmud* (*Chullin* 134b) states that the כֹּהֲנִים, *priests*, receive three parts from every animal which a Jew slaughters — the foreleg, the cheeks, and the stomach. They deserve these portions by virtue of the heroic act of Phineas, who safeguarded the sanctity of Israel and, as a reward, was initiated into the society of the priesthood.

The priests were granted the foreleg because Phineas threw the javelin at the sinners with his forearm. They were granted the stomach, because Phineas thrust his weapon into their abdomens. They received the cheeks because *he arose,* וַיְפַלֵּל, *and prayed,* for success in his attempt to sanctify God's Name, and a person's jaws and cheeks move when he prays.

²⁹ *They angered Him with their behavior*
    and a plague broke out among them.
³⁰ *Phineas arose and executed judgment,*
    and the plague was halted.
³¹ *It was accounted to him as a righteous deed,*
    for all generations, forever.
³² *They provoked anger at the waters of strife,*
    and Moses suffered because of them.
³³ *Because they defied His spirit,*

---

the congregation into the land which I have given them" (Numbers 20:12).

God's condemnation of Moses and Aaron, *you did not believe in Me*, did not clarify the specific nature of their sin. Indeed, the major commentators offer many interpretations of the sins, although it is clear that only people of Moses and Aaron's greatness would have been held accountable for such an act. It is clear that their error was one of miscalculation, not of a refusal to obey God's command. Among the prominent interpretations of the sin are the following:

— Instead of speaking to the rock as God had commanded him, Moses struck it with his staff (*Rashi*).

— He displayed his own anger with the people thus leading them to assume that God was angry with them. This, however, was not the case for we find no indication in Scripture that God was angered by a legitimate request for water (*Rambam*).

— In his speech to the people, Moses' words *shall we bring you water* could have led the people to infer that the power to provide water lay with him and Aaron, not with God (*R' Chananel; Ramban*).

33. כִּי הִמְרוּ אֶת רוּחוֹ — *Because they defied His spirit.*

According to this translation הִמְרוּ is cognate with מְרִי, *rebellion* (see *Targum*).

Rashi and *Ibn Ezra* here say that this refers to Moses who defied God[1] when he insulted His Chosen people by telling them *(Numbers 20:10)* שִׁמְעוּ נָא הַמֹּרִים, *Hear now, you rebels.* [*Rashi* (there) defines הַמֹּרִים as סַרְבָנִים, *stubborn ones*, and שׁוֹטִים, *fools*, i.e., followers who presume to lead their own leaders.]

Radak perceives הִמְרוּ as related to מָרָה, *bitterness*. The Psalmist here condemns the Children of Israel who provoked Moses to such a state of despair that he bitterly exclaimed, *"Shall we bring you water out of this rock?"* [I.e., these words implied that

---

1. *Rambam* explains the nature of Moses' sin in the fourth chapter of שְׁמוֹנָה פְּרָקִים, *The Eight Chapters*, his introduction to tractate *Avos*:

When Moses became infuriated and shouted, *"Hear now, You rebels!"*, God faulted Moses, because this public display of anger desecrated the Name of God. The Jewish people scrutinized Moses' every word and motion in order to emulate his worthy conduct; thus they might achieve success in This World and in the World to Come. When he displayed unjustified anger, Moses did not provide the people with a good example to follow.

Based on this, *Gur Aryeh* explains the language of God's condemnation of Moses and Aaron: *Because you did not believe in Me to sanctify Me in the eyes of the Children of Israel.* The man of faith feels very close to God, protected by His warm embrace. He graciously and gratefully accepts every act of God and firmly believes that all is for the best. Thus he will never become angry even under the must extreme pressure. Moses' anger, therefore, displayed a lack of faith in God's goodness in all circumstances.

לד בִּשְׂפָתָיו: לֹא־הִשְׁמִידוּ אֶת־הָעַמִּים אֲשֶׁר
לה אָמַר יהוה לָהֶם: וַיִּתְעָרְבוּ בַגּוֹיִם וַיִּלְמְדוּ
לו מַעֲשֵׂיהֶם: וַיַּעַבְדוּ אֶת־עֲצַבֵּיהֶם וַיִּהְיוּ לָהֶם
לז לְמוֹקֵשׁ: וַיִּזְבְּחוּ אֶת־בְּנֵיהֶם וְאֶת־בְּנוֹתֵיהֶם
לח לַשֵּׁדִים: וַיִּשְׁפְּכוּ דָם נָקִי דַּם־בְּנֵיהֶם
וּבְנוֹתֵיהֶם אֲשֶׁר זִבְּחוּ לַעֲצַבֵּי כְנַעַן וַתֶּחֱנַף
לט הָאָרֶץ בַּדָּמִים: וַיִּטְמְאוּ בְמַעֲשֵׂיהֶם וַיִּזְנוּ

Moses questioned God's ability to perform such a miracle. See comm. of *Rabbeinu Chananel* cited by *Ramban* to *Numbers* 20:10.]

וַיְבַטֵּא בִּשְׂפָתָיו — *He pronounced with His lips.*

When Moses and Aaron defied God, He took an oath against them and pronounced it with His lips, saying (*Numbers* 20:12), "*Because you did not believe in Me, to sanctify Me in the eyes of the Children of Israel, therefore you shall not bring the congregation into the land which I have given them*" (*Rashi; Ibn Ezra*).

Alternatively, *Ibn Yachya* and *Ibn Ezra* explain this as a reference to Moses. The people angered him so much that *he pronounced* [something improper] *with his lips*, saying: "*Hear now you rebels!*"

34. לֹא־הִשְׁמִידוּ אֶת הָעַמִּים אֲשֶׁר אָמַר ה׳ לָהֶם — *They did not destroy the nations as HASHEM had told them.*

Hashem commanded that no Canaanite should be allowed to dwell in their midst; indeed, He said, **לֹא תְחַיֶּה כָּל נְשָׁמָה**, *You shall not allow a soul to remain alive* (*Deuteronomy* 20:16).

However, when the Jews conquered the land of Canaan under the leadership of Joshua, they ignored God's command and allowed some Canaanites to remain in their midst so that they could pay tribute in the form of physical servitude (*Rashi*; see also *Metzudos* to *Joshua* 16:10).

35. וַיִּתְעָרְבוּ בַגּוֹיִם וַיִּלְמְדוּ מַעֲשֵׂיהֶם — *But they mingled with the nations and learned their deeds.*

[They assimilated socially and culturally with the gentiles. It was precisely to avoid assimilation that God had wanted the gentiles to leave the land: *So that they should not teach you to imitate their abominable ways which they have practiced towards their gods, and thus cause you to sin towards HASHEM, your God* (*Deuteronomy* 20:18).]

36. וַיַּעַבְדוּ אֶת עֲצַבֵּיהֶם — *And served their idols.*

[Literally, עֶצֶב means *sorrow*. It is used to describe idols for although the Israelites sought happiness and success from the idols of the gentiles, they found only agony and sorrow. (See also footnote to 96:5.)]

וַיִּהְיוּ לָהֶם לְמוֹקֵשׁ — *Which became a snare for them.*

According to *Midrash Shocher Tov*, מוֹקֵשׁ is cognate with הֶקֵּשׁ, *comparison*, and with הַקִּישׁ, *to knock* or *ring a bell*. At first, the gentiles respected the Jews for their firm faith in one God, a creed which set Israel apart from all the nations. But when they saw that Israel, too, served their idols, they said, "The Jews aren't special; they are comparable to us!" Then they began to mock the Jews and to ring bells at them as a sign of derision (*Rav Vidal HaTzorfati*).

37. וַיִּזְבְּחוּ אֶת בְּנֵיהֶם וְאֶת בְּנוֹתֵיהֶם לַשֵּׁדִים — *They sacrificed their sons and*

He pronounced with His lips.

³⁴ They did not destroy the nations
   as HASHEM had told them.
³⁵ But they mingled with the nations
   and learned their deeds.
³⁶ And served their idols,
   which became a snare for them.
³⁷ They sacrificed their sons and daughters
   to the demons.
³⁸ They spilled innocent blood,
   the blood of their sons and daughters
whom they sacrificed to the Canaanite idols;
   and the land was polluted by the bloods.
³⁹ Thus were they defiled by their deeds,
   and went astray through their actions.

---

daughters to the demons.

Even among idolators, demon-worship is deemed the most ignominious form of paganism. Yet Israel was foolish enough to offer *the demons the most precious of sacrifices, their own children* (Yaavetz HaDoresh).[1]

וַיִּשְׁפְּכוּ דָם נָקִי דַם בְּנֵיהֶם וּבְנוֹתֵיהֶם **38.** אֲשֶׁר זִבְּחוּ לַעֲצַבֵּי כְנָעַן — *They spilled innocent blood, the blood of their sons and daughters whom they sacrificed to the Canaanite idols.*

In addition to the sin of idolatry, the Jews were guilty of murdering their own children (Radak).

וַתֶּחֱנַף הָאָרֶץ בַּדָּמִים — *And the land was polluted by the bloods.*

[Wanton bloodshed is an abomination which causes God's holy spirit to depart from the land of Israel, thus leaving the land desecrated and polluted, as Numbers 35:33 states: *And you shall not pollute the land which you are in, for the blood is that which pollutes the land, and the land will have no atonement for the blood which is shed in it, except by vengeance against the blood of he who spilled it.*]

וַיִּטְמְאוּ בְמַעֲשֵׂיהֶם וַיִּזְנוּ בְּמַעַלְלֵיהֶם — **39.** *Thus were they defiled by their deeds, and went astray through their actions.*

They repeatedly *defiled* themselves *through their actions* until their very personalities became utterly corrupt (Malbim).

---

1. In the Ten Commandments we read: *You shall not make yourself a carved image nor any likeness of that which is in the heavens above, or on the earth below, or in the water beneath the earth* (Exodus 20:4). *Ramban* comments that this final category refers to the שֵׁדִים, *demons*, who usually conceal themselves in the water beneath the earth. *Ramban* explains that in early times people began venerating these evil spiritual forces. Some such harmful forces could be harnessed by the magicians and soothsayers of Scriptural times. The magicians of Pharaoh, for example, were able to duplicate the first two plagues because they possessed the now lost art of utilizing these evil powers. Scripture ridicules Jews who believe in demonolatry, saying (Deuteronomy 32:17): *They sacrificed to demons, non-gods, gods that they knew not, new gods that came up of late, which your fathers feared not.*

מ בְּמַעַלְלֵיהֶם: וַיִּחַר־אַף יהוה בְּעַמּוֹ וַיְתָעֵב
מא אֶת־נַחֲלָתוֹ: וַיִּתְּנֵם בְּיַד־גּוֹיִם וַיִּמְשְׁלוּ בָהֶם
מב שֹׂנְאֵיהֶם: וַיִּלְחָצוּם אוֹיְבֵיהֶם וַיִּכָּנְעוּ תַּחַת
מג יָדָם: פְּעָמִים רַבּוֹת יַצִּילֵם וְהֵמָּה יַמְרוּ
מד בַעֲצָתָם וַיָּמֹכּוּ בַּעֲוֹנָם: וַיַּרְא בַּצַּר לָהֶם
מה בְּשָׁמְעוֹ אֶת־רִנָּתָם: וַיִּזְכֹּר לָהֶם בְּרִיתוֹ
מו וַיִּנָּחֵם כְּרֹב חֲסָדָו: וַיִּתֵּן אוֹתָם לְרַחֲמִים
מז לִפְנֵי כָּל־שׁוֹבֵיהֶם: הוֹשִׁיעֵנוּ | יהוה אֱלֹהֵינוּ
וְקַבְּצֵנוּ מִן־הַגּוֹיִם לְהֹדוֹת לְשֵׁם קָדְשֶׁךָ
מח לְהִשְׁתַּבֵּחַ בִּתְהִלָּתֶךָ: בָּרוּךְ יהוה | אֱלֹהֵי
יִשְׂרָאֵל מִן־הָעוֹלָם | וְעַד הָעוֹלָם וְאָמַר כָּל־
הָעָם אָמֵן הַלְלוּיָהּ:

40. וַיִּחַר אַף ה' בְּעַמּוֹ וַיְתָעֵב אֶת נַחֲלָתוֹ —
And HASHEM's wrath was kindled against His nation, and He abhorred His inheritance.

At first, Israel was bound to God by virtue of their purity. Later, however, He despised and rejected them, as a result of their abominable conduct (*Malbim*).

41. וַיִּתְּנֵם בְּיַד גּוֹיִם וַיִּמְשְׁלוּ בָהֶם שֹׂנְאֵיהֶם —
So He delivered them to the hands of the peoples, and their enemies ruled over them.

This refers to the era of the שׁוֹפְטִים, *judges*. When Israel obeyed the word of God, they remained an autonomous, powerful nation, ruled by their own leaders. But whenever they sinned and betrayed Hashem, they were given over to the rule of their enemies such as Eglon, Kushan Rishasayim, Sisera, the Philistines, and the Midianites (*Rashi*).

42. וַיִּלְחָצוּם אוֹיְבֵיהֶם וַיִּכָּנְעוּ תַּחַת יָדָם —
Their foes oppressed them, and they were humbled under their power [lit. *hand*].

[Only when they accepted God's rule were they free from alien oppression.]

43. פְּעָמִים רַבּוֹת יַצִּילֵם וְהֵמָּה יַמְרוּ בַעֲצָתָם —
Many times did He rescue them, yet they were defiant in their counsel.

Tanchuma (Parashas Behar) points out that Hashem is very reluctant to inflict physical harm upon people and only does so as a last resort. The first time a man sins, God inflicts damage upon his property; then the sinner, somewhat impoverished, is forced to sell his fields. If he repents, all is well; but if he refuses to repent, his poverty grows worse and he is forced to sell his home. If he repents, all is well, but if he refuses to mend his ways, he then sinks to such poverty that he must sell himself as a slave. This is the meaning of this verse; God is patient and kind. He repeatedly seeks to deliver people from sin and suffering. However, when the sinners remain stubbornly *defiant in their counsel,* God is forced to make them suffer more and more, until they are crushed by the burden of their own iniquity.

וַיָּמֹכּוּ בַּעֲוֹנָם — *And were impoverished by their iniquity.*

As a result of their sins, they were

⁴⁰ *And HASHEM's wrath was kindled*
   against His nation,
      and He abhorred His inheritance.
⁴¹ *So He delivered them to the hands of the peoples,*
      and their enemies ruled them.
⁴² *Their foes oppressed them,*
      and they were humbled under their power.
⁴³ *Many times did He rescue them,*
      yet they were defiant in their counsel
      and were impoverished by their iniquity.
⁴⁴ *But He took note when they were in distress,*
      when He heard their outcry.
⁴⁵ *He remembered His covenant for them*
      and relented
      in accordance with His abundant kindness.
⁴⁶ *He caused them to be pitied*
      by all their captors.
⁴⁷ *Save us HASHEM, our God,*
      and gather us from among the peoples,
   to thank Your Holy Name
      and to glory in Your praise!
⁴⁸ *Blessed is HASHEM, the God of Israel,*
      from This World to the World to Come,
   and let the entire nation say, "Amen!"
      Praise God!

battered, impoverished, and finally, forced into exile (*Radak*).

The word מָךְ describes abject *poverty.* As the prophet describes Israel in the era of the Judges, וַיִּדַּל יִשְׂרָאֵל מְאֹד, *Israel was greatly impoverished* (*Judges* 6:6). Some Rabbis interpret this to mean that they were spiritually impoverished and had no *mitzvos* to their credit. Other Rabbis interpret this literally to mean that they were in dire financial straits. They were so poor that they could not afford a handful of flour for a מִנְחָה, *meal offering* (*Tanchuma, Parashas Behar*).

44. וַיַּרְא בַּצַּר לָהֶם בְּשָׁמְעוֹ אֶת רִנָּתָם — *But He took note* [lit. *and He saw*] *when they were in distress, when He heard their outcry.*

Despite the sinfulness that caused the exile, God heeds Israel's prayers when it is in distress (*Radak*).

Midrash Shocher Tov (alluded to by *Rashi*) lists five factors which precipitate Israel's redemption; they are enumerated in verses 44, 45, and 47.

First, Israel is saved on account of its distress, as this verse states: *He took note when they were in distress.* Second, they are delivered on account of their prayer, for the verse continues, when He heard their outcry [of prayer].

45. וַיִּזְכֹּר לָהֶם בְּרִיתוֹ — *He remembered His covenant for them.*

Third, Israel is redeemed by virtue of the *covenant* which God struck with their forefathers, Abraham, Isaac, and Jacob (*Midrash Shocher Tov*).

וַיִּנָּחֵם כְּרֹב חֲסָדָיו — *And relented in accordance with His abundant kindness.*

Fourth, Israel is redeemed on account of Hashem's *abundant kindness* (*Midrash Shocher Tov*).

46. וַיִּתֵּן אוֹתָם לְרַחֲמִים לִפְנֵי כָּל שׁוֹבֵיהֶם — *He caused them to be pitied by all their captors.*

[Even in Egypt, after the populace had suffered through plague after plague because of Israel, HASHEM *gave the* (Jewish) *people grace in the eyes of Egypt* (*Exodus* 11:3), and the Egyptians lent the Jews gold and silver vessels when they released them.]

47. הוֹשִׁיעֵנוּ ה' אֱלֹהֵינוּ וְקַבְּצֵנוּ מִן הַגּוֹיִם לְהֹדוֹת לְשֵׁם קָדְשֶׁךָ — *Save us HASHEM, our God, and gather us from among the peoples, to thank Your Holy Name.*

The fifth and conclusive cause of redemption is the arrival of the קֵץ, *final time* of ingathering (*Midrash Shocher Tov*). [The Messiah can come earlier by virtue of our special merits, but even if we lack merits, God has decreed that he must arrive by a certain time and no later.]

Maharam Arma'ah observes that this serves as an appropriate conclusion for the fourth *Book of Tehillim* because the bulk of this book is devoted to prayer and supplication for redemption from exile.

לְהִשְׁתַּבֵּחַ בִּתְהִלָּתֶךָ — *And to glory in Your praise.*

The glory of Israel is to praise God, and no nation can equal the praise we offer to Him (*Radak*).

Similarly, *Deuteronomy* 10:21 states: הוּא תְהִלָּתְךָ וְהוּא אֱלֹהֶיךָ, *He is your praise and He is your God* (*Maharam Arma'ah*).

48. בָּרוּךְ ה' אֱלֹהֵי יִשְׂרָאֵל מִן הָעוֹלָם וְעַד הָעוֹלָם — *Blessed is HASHEM, the God of Israel, from This World to the World to Come.*

Throughout the millennia of the world's existence, throughout every split second of time from the beginning of creation to the end, God is *blessed* and worthy of praise (*Radak*; *Sforno*).

According to *Ibn Ezra*, these are the words of those who *glory in Your* [God's] *praise* (verse 47).

These are the intelligent scholars who have studied every event of history from the dawn of creation. They truly understand why God deserves to be *blessed* for every historical development (*Radak*).

וְאָמַר כָּל הָעָם אָמֵן — *And let the entire nation say, "Amen!"*

The *entire nation* [i.e., the common people] cannot fathom the intricacy and the profound intelligence of the Divine design of history, but they can listen to the praise which the scholars offer to God and respond, "Amen!" (*Radak*).

הַלְלוּיָהּ — *Praise God!*

In the final analysis, there will be no differences among the men who will unite in perfect harmony to sing and proclaim: "Praise God!" (*Radak*).

[See commentary to 111:1.]

This hymn of thanksgiving opens the fifth and final Book of Psalms. Primarily, this composition expresses the thanks of those who were in places of danger but were rescued and arrived home safely. As such, these verses relate to a number of historical settings. Alshich says that the Psalmist is amplifying the thanks which Israel offered to God when they were redeemed from the dangers of Egyptian bondage, where they were threatened by the hazards of both the scorched wilderness and the deep sea.

Ibn Yachya relates this work to David's life. The Philistines captured the Holy Ark, and it was endangered in countless ways. When David returned the Ark to a haven of safety and sanctity, he composed this hymn of thanks.

Sforno says that the Psalmist echoes those who will be redeemed from the present exile. Throughout the centuries they have endured all kinds of danger, only to be ultimately confronted with the greatest danger of all — the war of Gog and Magog, which will threaten to tear the entire world asunder.

The Talmud (Berachos 54b) derives a practical rule of Jewish conduct from this psalm: Four people must offer thanks to God — he who traveled over the sea; he who journeyed through the desert; he who was sick and then healed; and he who was jailed and then released. All four of these perilous situations are vividly described in this psalm.

א־ב הֹדוּ לַיהוה כִּי־טוֹב כִּי לְעוֹלָם חַסְדּוֹ: יֹאמְרוּ
ג גְּאוּלֵי יהוה אֲשֶׁר גְּאָלָם מִיַּד־צָר: וּמֵאֲרָצוֹת
ד קִבְּצָם מִמִּזְרָח וּמִמַּעֲרָב מִצָּפוֹן וּמִיָּם: תָּעוּ
בַמִּדְבָּר בִּישִׁימוֹן דָּרֶךְ עִיר מוֹשָׁב לֹא מָצָאוּ:
ה רְעֵבִים גַּם־צְמֵאִים נַפְשָׁם בָּהֶם תִּתְעַטָּף:
ו וַיִּצְעֲקוּ אֶל־יהוה בַּצַּר לָהֶם מִמְּצוּקוֹתֵיהֶם

1. הֹדוּ לַה' כִּי טוֹב — *Give thanks to HASHEM, for He is good.*

Let all men recognize that when something good happens to them it does not happen by chance; rather, it is ordained by God, the Source of all good (*Radak*).

כִּי לְעוֹלָם חַסְדּוֹ — *His kindness endures forever.*

God's kindness is not confined to one generation. His compassion for the righteous forefathers pours over to their descendants forever (*Alshich*).

2. יֹאמְרוּ גְּאוּלֵי ה' אֲשֶׁר גְּאָלָם מִיַּד צָר — *Let those redeemed by HASHEM say it, those He redeemed from the tormentor's hand.*

Those who recognize that their salvation comes from Hashem and from none other should recite the declaration of thanks expressed in the preceding verse (*Rashi*).

Chazah Zion comments that this applies specifically to the Exodus from Egypt, when Israel recognized that it was God Himself who led them, not an angel or a messenger (see *Exodus* 12:12).

3. וּמֵאֲרָצוֹת קִבְּצָם — *He gathered them from the lands.*

The Sages taught: The Holy One, Blessed be He, said to Israel, "When you were in Egypt you were scattered, but within a short time, I gathered all of you together in Rameses. Now you are scattered in all of the lands, but just as I gathered you together in the past, so shall I gather you together in the future" (*Midrash Shocher Tov*).

מִמִּזְרָח וּמִמַּעֲרָב מִצָּפוֹן וּמִיָּם — *From east and from west, from north and from the sea.*

The Psalmist denotes three directions but deletes the south because the vast majority of the Jews in exile are in the northern hemisphere. Even travelers and merchants who ordinarily put themselves in danger, shun the scorched, forbidding deserts of the south. Instead of the south, the Psalmist speaks of the *sea*, because the exiles are constantly traversing these great bodies of water searching for a haven and a livelihood. Additionally, it alludes to one of the four who is required to offer thanks, namely, the seafarer (*Ibn Ezra; Radak*).

Metzudos understands וּמִיָּם as a reference to the far-flung islands of the sea.

Targum renders: *from the southern sea.*

4. תָּעוּ בַמִּדְבָּר בִּישִׁימוֹן דָּרֶךְ — *They wandered in the wilderness on a path of desolation.*

The caravan trail through the desert is described as a *path of desolation*, because even when some kind of roadway is demarcated by countless travelers, the shifting sands quickly blow over the path and obliterate all signs and directions (*Radak*).

[God guided the Israelites very carefully throughout their forty year sojourn in the wilderness. By day, they followed a pillar of cloud, and by night, a pillar of fire (*Exodus* 13:4). Nevertheless, the Psalmist describes them as

107

Give thanks to HASHEM, for He is good;
His kindness endures forever!

² Let those redeemed by HASHEM say it,
those He redeemed from the tormentor's hand.

³ He gathered them from the lands —
from east and from west,
from north and from the sea.

⁴ They wandered in the wilderness
on a path of desolation;
an inhabited city they did not find.

⁵ Hungry and also thirsty,
their soul fainted within them.

⁶ Then they cried out to HASHEM in their distress;
from their woes He rescued them.

---

pitiful wanderers because they had no idea of where their journeys would take them or how long they would stop at each camp.]

This verse introduces us to the first of the four people in danger who must give thanks to Hashem (*Berachos* 54b), i.e. the man who traveled through the desert and survived (*Rashi*).

עִיר מוֹשָׁב לֹא מָצָאוּ — *An inhabited city they did not find.*

When the shifting sands obliterate all directions, the desert travelers cannot find their way to their destination which is the inhabited city (*Radak*); and while they are in the wilderness they search for an oasis for refreshment or direction, but they can find none (*Sforno*).

5. רְעֵבִים גַּם צְמֵאִים — *Hungry and also thirsty.*

The traveler determined the length of his desert journey before he set out, and he prepared supplies for a certain amount of time. But when he loses his way and wanders aimlessly, his supplies give out and he grows hungry and thirsty (*Radak*).

נַפְשָׁם בָּהֶם תִּתְעַטָּף — *Their soul fainted within them.*

Their strength slowly begins to ebb for lack of food and water (*Radak*).

6. וַיִּצְעֲקוּ אֶל ה׳ בַּצַּר לָהֶם — *Then they cried out to HASHEM in their distress.*

The Rabbis state: A person should always be sure to pray before the moment of trouble arrives. Nevertheless the Psalmist observes that even though these desperate travelers cried out *after* their troubles began, Hashem still listened and saved them (*Alshich*).

The *Talmud* (*Rosh Hashanah* 16b) states: When heaven issues a severe judgment against a person, four things can destroy the edict: charity, prayer, a change of name, and a change of deeds. We learn of the efficacy of prayer from this verse: *They cried out to HASHEM in their distress; from their woes He rescued them.*

מִמְּצוּקוֹתֵיהֶם יַצִּילֵם — *From their woes He rescued them.*

The travelers were beset by *two* forms of distress, i.e., *hunger and thirst,* and God saved them from both (*Chazah Zion*).

ז יַצִּילֵם: וַיַּדְרִיכֵם בְּדֶרֶךְ יְשָׁרָה לָלֶכֶת אֶל־
ח עִיר מוֹשָׁב: יוֹדוּ לַיהוה חַסְדּוֹ וְנִפְלְאוֹתָיו
ט לִבְנֵי אָדָם: כִּי־הִשְׂבִּיעַ נֶפֶשׁ שֹׁקֵקָה וְנֶפֶשׁ
י רְעֵבָה מִלֵּא־טוֹב: יֹשְׁבֵי חֹשֶׁךְ וְצַלְמָוֶת
יא אֲסִירֵי עֳנִי וּבַרְזֶל: כִּי־הִמְרוּ אִמְרֵי־אֵל
יב וַעֲצַת עֶלְיוֹן נָאָצוּ: וַיַּכְנַע בֶּעָמָל לִבָּם כָּשְׁלוּ

7. וַיַּדְרִיכֵם בְּדֶרֶךְ יְשָׁרָה לָלֶכֶת אֶל עִיר מוֹשָׁב
— He led them upon a straight path, to
go to an inhabited city.

Finally, God heard the cries of the lost
traveler. He revealed the trail and
guided him to his destination, where the
traveler offers God thanks (Radak).

Sforno notes that the Psalmist does
not say that the traveler reached מָחוֹז
חֶפְצוֹ, the haven of his desire [as in verse
30]; rather, he reached an inhabited city,
i.e., a settlement or oasis on the way;
and this in itself is ample reason for
gladness and thanks [see comm. verse
30].

8. יוֹדוּ לַה׳ חַסְדּוֹ — Let them thank
HASHEM for His kindness.

When they arrive safely in the
inhabited city (Radak).

וְנִפְלְאוֹתָיו לִבְנֵי אָדָם — And for His
wonders to mankind [lit. children of
man].

When a king favors for his
subjects it is not genuine kindness,
because every leader tries to ingratiate
himself with his followers to inspire
their loyalty. Not so is the kindness of
Hashem, Who has no need for the aid of
any person. Thus, His wonderful works
are truly for the benefit of the children
of man — not for Himself (Alshich).

9. כִּי־הִשְׂבִּיעַ נֶפֶשׁ שֹׁקֵקָה — For He sated
the yearning soul.

When the Jews left Egypt and entered
the parched wilderness they yearned for
fresh sweet water, and God satisfied

their yearning by sweetening the waters
of Marah (Exodus 15:25; Sforno).

Similarly, when the traveler reaches
an oasis or an inhabited city, he satisfies
his parched throat with drink and fills
his hungry stomach with food (Radak).

וְנֶפֶשׁ רְעֵבָה מִלֵּא טוֹב — And filled the
hungry soul with good.

When the Israelites hungered in the
wilderness, God filled them with fat
quail and with manna from heaven
(Sforno).

10. יֹשְׁבֵי חֹשֶׁךְ וְצַלְמָוֶת — Those who sat
in darkness and the shadow of death.

Now the Psalmist turns his attention
to the second category of people in
distress — those who languish in prison.

Rav Avraham Azulai explains that
incarceration in prison is worse than
wandering in the wilderness, because
the man in the wilderness, although in
grave danger, at least retains his
freedom, whereas the prisoner is at the
mercy of his captors, who have the
power to kill or torture him at will.

Furthermore, the Psalmist describes
two types of prison. The first is a dark
dungeon which has no windows. Since
rays of life-giving sun never penetrate
these massive prison walls, the darkness
is called the shadow of death. [This
terrible darkness resembles the depths
of hell, for the Talmud (Eruvin 19b)
states that one of the seven Scriptural
names for hell is צַלְמָוֶת, the shadow of
death.][11]

---

1. Between Rosh HaShanah and Yom Kippur it is customary to perform the penitential ritual
of Kapparos which means atonement [see Rama, Shulchan Aruch, Orach Chaim 605].
One takes a fowl for slaughter and says, "This life in place of my life," or he takes money

⁷ *He led them upon a straight path,*
to go to an inhabited city.
⁸ *Let them thank HASHEM for His kindness*
and for His wonders to mankind.
⁹ *For He sated the yearning soul,*
and filled the hungry soul with good.
¹⁰ *Those who sat in darkness*
and the shadow of death,
shackled in affliction and iron.
¹¹ *Because they defied the words of God,*
and the counsel of the Supreme One
they scorned.
¹² *So He humbled their heart with hard labor.*

Targum says that this verse specifically refers to Tzidkiyahu, the King of Judah, and his noble retinue, who were chained and dragged into Babylonian exile by Nebuchadnezzar. [Babylon is called a place of *darkness* and *death* (see *Sanhedrin* 24a). In addition, Tzidkiyahu was blinded and the man whose eyes are darkened is considered to be dead (see *Nedarim* 64a).]

אֲסִירֵי עֳנִי וּבַרְזֶל — *Shackled in affliction and iron.*

Rav Avraham Azulai continues: The prisoners locked in the dark dungeon (*the shadow of death*) need not be shackled and chained because they have no hope of escape. However, other prisoners are held in rooms that have windows, which can provide a means of escape. These captives must be bound in irons (which inflict bruises and pain) to restrict their movement.

11. כִּי הִמְרוּ אִמְרֵי אֵל — *Because they defied the words of God.*

In connection with the prisoners and

those afflicted by sickness (*verse 17*), the Psalmist refers to their transgressions since these situations of suffering are basically punishments for sin. No one is imprisoned or falls sick voluntarily. God thrusts these situations upon a person as a form of retribution.

However, in reference to those who traverse the wilderness or the sea, no sin is mentioned. Such trips are normal occurrences which the traveler embarks upon voluntarily. Only after the outset of the journey, when the traveler finds himself in a precarious position, does the emergency arise. At that point, God may decide to use this opportunity to frighten the traveler with a threat to his life so that he will genuinely repent of his shortcomings (*Radak*).

וַעֲצַת עֶלְיוֹן נָאָצוּ — *And the counsel of the Supreme One they scorned.*

Radak explains that this prisoner is not being punished for transgressing the commands which were given exclusively to the Jews; rather he is held captive because he defied the universal

and says, "This money to charity to atone for my life." This ritual signifies that the sincere penitent is overwhelmed by the weight of his sins. As Yom Kippur approaches the sinner trembles in awe before the final judgment of the heavenly tribunal and the specter of possible punishment by death looms vividly before his eyes.

The custom is to preface the *Kapparos* ritual with recital of this verse which sets the mood of awe. *Those who sat in darkness and the shadow of death* ... This is followed by verses 14,17-21. The recital concludes with two final verses from *Job* 33:23,24.

יג וְאֵין עֹזֵר: וַיִּזְעֲקוּ אֶל־יהוה בַּצַּר לָהֶם

יד מִמְּצֻקוֹתֵיהֶם יוֹשִׁיעֵם: יוֹצִיאֵם מֵחֹשֶׁךְ

טו וְצַלְמָוֶת וּמוֹסְרוֹתֵיהֶם יְנַתֵּק: יוֹדוּ לַיהוה

טז חַסְדּוֹ וְנִפְלְאוֹתָיו לִבְנֵי אָדָם: כִּי־שִׁבַּר

יז דַּלְתוֹת נְחֹשֶׁת וּבְרִיחֵי בַרְזֶל גִּדֵּעַ: אֱוִלִים

יח מִדֶּרֶךְ פִּשְׁעָם וּמֵעֲוֹנֹתֵיהֶם יִתְעַנּוּ: כָּל־אֹכֶל

rules which bind the gentiles as well. The Psalmist refes to these Noachide laws as אִמְרֵי אֵל, *the words of God*, and עֲצַת עֶלְיוֹן, *the counsel of the Supreme One*, i.e., the supreme code of human conduct which is the basis of society. Those who defy this supreme code are stricken with sickness or thrown into captivity.

Rav Vidal HaTzorfati suggests that *the words of God* are the positive commandments, whereas the *counsel of the Supreme One* describes the negative commands, which are good counsel for staying away from evil.

12. וַיַּכְנַע בֶּעָמָל לִבָּם — *So He humbled their heart with hard labor.*

Conceit and arrogance caused these prisoners to rebel against God and so, measure for measure, their proud hearts are humbled by the forced labor of the prison camp (*Rav Avraham Azulai*).

כָּשְׁלוּ וְאֵין עֹזֵר — *They stumbled — and there was none to help.*

The proud sinners defied God's counsel and direction and chose to follow their own path; therefore, they stumble on that very path and there is no one to come to their aid (*Rav Avraham Azulai*).

13. וַיִּזְעֲקוּ אֶל ה' בַּצַּר לָהֶם — *Then they cried out to HASHEM in their distress.*

In reference to those in danger in the desert or on the seas the Psalmist describes their cry as וַיִּצְעֲקוּ with the letter צ (verses 6, 28), whereas the captive and the sick man (here and verse 19) are described as וַיִּזְעֲקוּ with the letter ז. *Zohar (Parashas Shemos)* says that

there is no difference between these two terms and *Radak* concurs. *Malbim*, however, maintains that צְעָקָה is a stronger term than זְעָקָה. *Chazah Zion* explains that the letter צ is taller and wider than the letter ז. Thus, צְעָקָה is the proper description of the cry of those in distress in the open desert or sea, where there are no walls to hinder their shouts from spreading out far and wide. However, the cries of those confined to the prison cell or the sickroom are contained by restrictive walls, and so their shouts are best described with the word זְעָקָה.

מִמְּצֻקוֹתֵיהֶם יוֹשִׁיעֵם — *From their woes He saved them.*

Radak notes that in reference to the travelers of the wilderness the Psalmist (verse 6) uses the word יַצִּילֵם, *He rescued them.* In reference to one who makes a sea journey, the Psalmist (verse 28) uses the word יוֹצִיאֵם, *He removed them.* However, in the case of both the prisoner and the sick man the choice of words is יוֹשִׁיעֵם, *He saved them.*

Malbim defines *saving* as an action more powerful than *rescuing* (or *removing*). [This can be readily understood in light of *Radak's* commentary to *verse 11*, which explains that imprisonment and sickness are direct punishments for sin. Thus, the danger which they present is most acute and only a major יְשׁוּעָה, *salvation*, can save a man from captivity or sickness.]

14. יוֹצִיאֵם מֵחֹשֶׁךְ וְצַלְמָוֶת וּמוֹסְרוֹתֵיהֶם יְנַתֵּק — *He brought them out of darkness and the shadow of death, and broke open their shackles.*

> *They stumbled — and there was none to help.*
> 13 *Then they cried out to HASHEM in their distress;*
>   *from their woes He saved them.*
> 14 *He brought them out of darkness*
>   *and the shadow of death,*
>   *and broke open their shackles.*
> 15 *Let them thank HASHEM for His kindness*
>   *and for His wonders to mankind.*
> 16 *For He smashed copper gates,*
>   *and cut asunder iron bolts.*
> 17 *The fools — because of their sinful path*
>   *and of their iniquities they were afflicted.*

God is the liberator of captives. He helps the innocent prisoners to escape from their dark dungeons and their heavy chains; God may even implant a spark of compassion in the hearts of the captors, who will be moved to free their prisoners (*Radak*).

15. יוֹדוּ לַה׳ חַסְדּוֹ וְנִפְלְאוֹתָיו לִבְנֵי אָדָם — *Let them thank HASHEM for His kindness and for His wonders to mankind.*

The liberated captive can repay God for His kindness by publicly attributing his freedom to Divine intervention (*Rav Avraham Azulai*) and by teaching mankind that God is Master at all times (*Ibn Ezra*).

16. כִּי שִׁבַּר דַּלְתוֹת נְחֹשֶׁת — *For He smashed copper gates.*

When God decides to liberate the captive nothing stands in His way, not even the heaviest metal gate guarding the dungeon (*Radak*).

וּבְרִיחֵי בַרְזֶל גִּדֵּעַ — *And cut asunder iron bolts.*

Even if the metal gate is reinforced with heavy iron bolts, God will tear them asunder if necessary (*Radak*).

אֱוִלִים מִדֶּרֶךְ פִּשְׁעָם וּמֵעֲוֺנֹתֵיהֶם יִתְעַנּוּ — **17.** *The fools — because of their sinful path and of their iniquities they were afflicted.*

The Psalmist commences his description of the third group of endangered people — the sick. They are described as אֱוִלִים, *fools*, because the Rabbis teach (*Sotah 5a*) that a man only sins when he is overcome by a spirit of foolishness [and sickness is the punishment for sin] (*Ibn Ezra; Ibn Yachya*).

Radak examines the basic difference between captivity and sickness. The captive is seized and imprisoned in one fell swoop, whereas sickness overcomes a person slowly. Indeed, sickness may be compared to a messenger from God warning a man to repent. At the very first sign of illness a man should immediately repent if he has the wisdom to understand the Divine signal, but if he is foolish and ignores the first sign, then the illness is progressively intensified until it cannot be ignored. Therefore, one who ignores the early warning signs of sickness is labeled a fool.[1]

Targum and *Alshich* observe that the Psalmist is specifically referring to King

1. The *Talmud* (*Shabbos 32a*) emphasizes that a person should never underestimate any situation where he is exposed to danger: Even if a person merely goes to the public marketplace he should beware of danger [because even an innocent bystander may be harmed

יט   תִּתְעֵב נַפְשָׁם וַיַּגִּיעוּ עַד־שַׁעֲרֵי מָוֶת: וַיִּזְעֲקוּ
אֶל־יהוה בַּצַּר לָהֶם מִמְּצֻקוֹתֵיהֶם יוֹשִׁיעֵם:

כ   יִשְׁלַח דְּבָרוֹ וְיִרְפָּאֵם וִימַלֵּט מִשְּׁחִיתוֹתָם:

כא   יוֹדוּ לַיהוה חַסְדּוֹ וְנִפְלְאוֹתָיו לִבְנֵי אָדָם:

כב   וְיִזְבְּחוּ זִבְחֵי תוֹדָה וִיסַפְּרוּ מַעֲשָׂיו בְּרִנָּה:

כג   יוֹרְדֵי הַיָּם בָּאֳנִיּוֹת עֹשֵׂי מְלָאכָה   ז

Hezekiah (Chizkiyahu) of Judah whose health progressively deteriorated. No one knew why, until Isaiah the prophet came and clearly informed him of the error for which he was being punished (see *Berachos* 10a).

כָּל אֹכֶל תְּתַעֵב נַפְשָׁם וַיַּגִּיעוּ עַד־שַׁעֲרֵי — **18.** מָוֶת — *Their soul abhorred all food, and they reached until the portals of death.*

[There are many other symptoms of acute illness, such as fever, vomiting, and pain, yet the Psalmist chose the illustration of abhorrence of food because it shows that the sick man has lost his desire to enjoy or even to sustain his life. This proves that he has reached the *portals of death* and has no hope of survival.]

וַיִּזְעֲקוּ אֶל־יהוה בַּצַּר לָהֶם — **19.** — *Then they cried out to HASHEM in their distress.*

The foolish, sick man finally comes to his senses and realizes that there is no hope in potions or pills, in doctors or drugs. There is no one to turn to but the Great Healer of all flesh (*Ibn Ezra; Radak*).

מִמְּצֻקוֹתֵיהֶם יוֹשִׁיעֵם — *From their woes He saved them.*

Salvation can come to the sick man only after he realizes that his distresses are his own sins which plague him, and that he can be saved only by sincere prayer and repentance (*Alshich*).

20. יִשְׁלַח דְּבָרוֹ וְיִרְפָּאֵם — *He dispatched His word and cured them.*

No cure is effective on its own. God Himself must speak and decree, "This herb will cure that disease! This doctor will heal that malady!" (*Ibn Ezra; Alshich*).

וִימַלֵּט מִשְּׁחִיתוֹתָם — *And let them escape their destruction.*

The term שַׁחַת, *destruction*, is one of the names of hell. The sick man was on the brink of death and damnation (*Radak*).

Panim Yafos translates: *And rescued them 'by means' of their destruction.* This refers to King Hezekiah, who was stricken with a severe case of שְׁחִין, *infectious boils*, which threatened his life. God decreed that he be cured after the king repented and prayed for forgiveness. *And Isaiah said, "Let them take hold of a cluster of pressed figs and smear it on the boils," and behold it was cured!* (*Isaiah* 38:21)

Rashi (ibid.) explains that this was a miracle within a miracle. Ordinarily, fig paste is harmful even to healthy skin, yet here God bade that the harmful fig be placed on the harmed skin and behold! — it was miraculously cured! Thus, *God rescued them, 'by means' of the catastrophe*, i.e., the harmful agent.

[*Radak's* original translation of שְׁחִיתוֹתָם as the *destruction* of hell

---

in the market. It is a place of quarrels and strife between vendors and customers, between gentiles and Jews (*Rashi*). If a person feels even a slight headache coming on, he should feel as if he has been placed in shackles. If a person is confined to his bed by sickness, he should feel as if he is accused of a capital crime and stands in the dock waiting to be condemned. Any person accused of capital crime needs a powerful defender to win an acquittal. What is a person's most powerful defense? The merit of his Torah study and his good deeds!

18 *Their soul abhorred all food,*
   and they reached until the portals of death.
19 *Then they cried out to HASHEM in their distress;*
   from their woes He saved them.
20 *He dispatched His word and cured them,*
   and let them escape their destruction.
21 *Let them thank HASHEM for His kindness*
   and for His wonders to mankind.
22 *And let them sacrifice thanksgiving offerings,*
   and relate His works with joyful song.
23 *Those who go down to the sea in ships,*

---

applies to Hezekiah as well. When Hezekiah's prayer for salvation was answered, he exclaimed, וְאַתָּה חָשַׁקְתָּ נַפְשִׁי מִשַּׁחַת, *You yearned to save my soul from destruction* (Isaiah 38:17).]

21. יוֹדוּ לַה' חַסְדּוֹ וְנִפְלְאוֹתָיו לִבְנֵי אָדָם — *Let them thank HASHEM for His kindness and for His wonders to mankind.*

[Restored to life, Hezekiah exclaimed (Isaiah 38:19): "חַי חַי הוּא יוֹדֶךָ כָּמוֹנִי הַיּוֹם, *The Living! The Living! They all thank You as I do today!*" King Hezekiah further pledged himself to relate God's wonderful works to his children, saying (ibid. v. 20): "*The father transmits to his son a tradition of true faith in You, HASHEM, my salvation! And we shall play all of my melodies all the days of our lives in the House of HASHEM."*]

22. וְיִזְבְּחוּ זִבְחֵי תוֹדָה — *And let them sacrifice thanksgiving offerings.*

The Psalmist mentions sacrifices of thanksgiving only in reference to the sick man because his salvation and cure do not occur suddenly, as in the cases

of the prisoner who is released in a moment, the seafarer who is saved when the storm dies down suddenly, and the lost desert traveler who inadvertently finds the path. The sick man is nursed back to health slowly and, as he gets stronger, seeks to assure the continuity of his recovery by making a vow to offer sacrifices of thanksgiving (*Radak*).

וִיסַפְּרוּ מַעֲשָׂיו בְּרִנָּה — *And relate His works with joyful song.*

When the sick man regains his health he does not keep his intense gratitude to God a secret. He publicly tells of God's curative works and recounts them with relish and joy (*Radak*).

23. יוֹרְדֵי הַיָּם בָּאֳנִיּוֹת — *Those who go down to the sea in ships.*

The seafarers are described as *those who go down to the sea* because the seashore at the edge of the water is usually slightly elevated above the sea. Also a seaworthy ship usually rides deep in the water and her bottom holds are below the water line. Thus, whoever boards the ship is described as going down (*Radak*).[1]

---

1. The *Talmud* (Rosh Hashanah 17) notes the strange punctuation sign which precedes this verse and appears seven times in this psalm. It is called a נו"ן הַפוּכָה, *a reversed* נ, or a נו"ן מְנוּזֶרֶת, *a backward* נ, and it is a sign of exclusion or dimunition, i.e., not all who cry out when in peril will be answered; some will be excluded. Once the heavenly decree is issued and sealed it will not be changed. Only the man who cries out before it is sealed will be delivered [see *Minchas Shai*].

כד בְּמַיִם רַבִּים: ן הֵמָּה רָאוּ מַעֲשֵׂי יְהוָה
כה וְנִפְלְאוֹתָיו בִּמְצוּלָה: ן וַיֹּאמֶר וַיַּעֲמֵד
כו רוּחַ סְעָרָה וַתְּרוֹמֵם גַּלָּיו: ן יַעֲלוּ
שָׁמַיִם יֵרְדוּ תְהוֹמוֹת נַפְשָׁם בְּרָעָה תִתְמוֹגָג:
כז יָחוֹגּוּ וְיָנוּעוּ כַּשִּׁכּוֹר וְכָל־חָכְמָתָם ן
כח תִּתְבַּלָּע: ן וַיִּצְעֲקוּ אֶל־יְהוָה בַּצַּר
כט לָהֶם וּמִמְּצוּקֹתֵיהֶם יוֹצִיאֵם: ן יָקֵם סְעָרָה
ל לִדְמָמָה וַיֶּחֱשׁוּ גַּלֵּיהֶם: ן וַיִּשְׂמְחוּ כִי־יִשְׁתֹּקוּ
לא וַיַּנְחֵם אֶל־מְחוֹז חֶפְצָם: יוֹדוּ לַיהוָה חַסְדּוֹ

עָשׂוּ מְלָאכָה בְּמַיִם רַבִּים — *Who do their work in mighty waters.*

The good sailor must perform many arduous and difficult tasks in order to keep his ship afloat. He works with many riggings and ropes, with masts and sails, and with other navigational instruments to steer his way through the *great waters* (Radak).

24. הֵמָּה רָאוּ מַעֲשֵׂי יהוה — *They have seen the deeds of HASHEM.*

Shevet Mussar cites a *Midrash* which says that although David traveled extensively when he fled from Saul and when he campaigned against his enemies, nevertheless, David never once traveled over the sea. David certainly experienced the other three travails described in this psalm — the desert, prison and sickness — but he never felt what it was like to be at the mercy of God on the open, high seas. Therefore, David emphasizes הֵמָּה, *they,* i.e., other people have seen God on the sea, not I!

וְנִפְלְאוֹתָיו בִּמְצוּלָה — *And His wonders in the watery deep.*

The sailor stands on deck and is overwhelmed by the realization that he is surrounded on all sides by roaring waves and dangerous fish. Nothing stands between him and a watery grave except a few planks of wood. Then the sailor appreciates the greatest wonder of God, that He inspired the human

intellect to master the craft of ship-building [including the theories of buoyancy, flotation, water displacement, and navigation]. These are the normal thoughts of the sailor. But when his ship is caught in a howling gale which tosses about his craft like a matchstick and yet he survives, then he is doubly impressed with God's wonders (Radak).

וַיֹּאמֶר וַיַּעֲמֵד רוּחַ סְעָרָה וַתְּרוֹמֵם גַּלָּיו **25.** — *He spoke and the stormy wind stood up and lifted up its waves.*

[No one feels as lost and helpless as the seafarer who is caught in the raging tempest at sea. He knows that it is the word of God (that *He spoke*) which stirred up the storm, and only the word of God can calm it. He is at God's mercy.]

26. יַעֲלוּ שָׁמַיִם יֵרְדוּ תְהוֹמוֹת — *They rise heavenward, they descend to the depths.*

The rolling, storm-tossed waves raise and lower the ship relentlessly (Radak).

נַפְשָׁם בְּרָעָה תִתְמוֹגָג — *Their soul melts with trouble.*

They are filled with terror and fear of imminent death (Radak).

The *Midrash* (*Kiddushin* 82a) teaches: הַסַּפָּנִין רֻבָּן חֲסִידִים, *Most sailors are devout.* Rashi (ibid.) explains: Because they sail to distant places full of

who do their work in many waters —
²⁴ They have seen the deeds of HASHEM,
   and His wonders in the watery deep.
²⁵ He spoke and the stormy wind stood up
   and lifted up its waves.
²⁶ They rise heavenward, they descend to the depths,
   their soul melts with trouble.
²⁷ They reel, they stagger like a drunkard,
   and all their wisdom is swallowed up.
²⁸ Then they cried out to HASHEM in their distress,
   from their woes He removed them.
²⁹ He transforms the storm to calmness,
   and their waves are stilled.
³⁰ They rejoiced because they were quiet,
   and He guided them to their desired boundary.
³¹ Let them thank HASHEM for His kindness

---

danger, they are constantly humbled with trepidation. They realize better than most that only God's protection enables them to survive.

27. יָחוֹגוּ וְיָנוּעוּ כַּשִּׁכּוֹר — *They reel, they stagger like a drunkard.*

The violent rolling and lurching of the ship makes the sailors lose their balance and they cannot walk straight (Radak).

וְכָל חָכְמָתָם תִּתְבַּלָּע — *And all their wisdom is swallowed up.*

All of the seafarers are numbed with fright, which turns their minds blank. The sailors forget their sailing skills and the navigators lose their ability to control and steer the lurching boat (Ibn Ezra; Radak).

28. וַיִּצְעֲקוּ אֶל ה' בַּצַּר לָהֶם וּמִמְּצוּקֹתֵיהֶם יוֹצִיאֵם — *Then they cried out to HASHEM in their distress, from their woes He removed them.*

[This is the only one of the four groups in danger whose rescue is described with the word יוֹצִיאֵם, *He removed them.* The seafarers are

actually enveloped by the water in which they are sinking and drowning and they must be *removed* from these waters. (See commentary to verse 13.)]

29. יָקֵם סְעָרָה לִדְמָמָה — *He transforms* [lit. *stands up*] *the storm to calmness.*

[God brings the storm to its climax and then lets it die down so that the wild sea becomes calm.]

וַיֶּחֱשׁוּ גַּלֵּיהֶם — *And their waves are stilled.*

[The towering waves subside and the surface of the sea becomes smooth.]

30. וַיִּשְׂמְחוּ כִי יִשְׁתֹּקוּ — *They rejoiced because they were quiet.*

When the raging sea quieted down, the terrified passengers rejoiced (Ibn Ezra).

וַיַּנְחֵם אֶל מְחוֹז חֶפְצָם — *And He guided them to their desired boundary.*

When the ship arrived at its destination, its home territory, the passengers rejoiced (Rashi; Ibn Ezra).

[This alludes to the *halachah* (Orach Chaim 219:1) that the blessing of

לב וְנִפְלְאוֹתָיו לִבְנֵי אָדָם: וִירוֹמְמוּהוּ בִּקְהַל־

לג עָם וּבְמוֹשַׁב זְקֵנִים יְהַלְלוּהוּ: יָשֵׂם נְהָרוֹת

לד לְמִדְבָּר וּמֹצָאֵי מַיִם לְצִמָּאוֹן: אֶרֶץ פְּרִי

לה לִמְלֵחָה מֵרָעַת יוֹשְׁבֵי בָהּ: יָשֵׂם מִדְבָּר

לו לַאֲגַם־מַיִם וְאֶרֶץ צִיָּה לְמֹצָאֵי מָיִם: וַיּוֹשֶׁב

לז שָׁם רְעֵבִים וַיְכוֹנְנוּ עִיר מוֹשָׁב: וַיִּזְרְעוּ

שָׂדוֹת וַיִּטְּעוּ כְרָמִים וַיַּעֲשׂוּ פְּרִי תְבוּאָה:

thanksgiving is not recited by the seafarer while he is still out at sea, even though the dangerous storm has completely subsided. Even when the ship stops at a port of call where it docks for a few days and the passengers temporarily disembark, the blessing is not recited. The passenger must give thanks only when he arrives at his final destination and leaves the ship entirely. The same *halachah* applies to those who traverse the desert. They do not recite the special blessing at a safe stopover oasis (although they do express *some* form of praise there, see *verse 7*) but only when they reach their city of destination (See *Mishnah Berurah* ibid.).]

31. יוֹדוּ לַה׳ חַסְדּוֹ וְנִפְלְאוֹתָיו לִבְנֵי אָדָם — *Let them thank HASHEM for His kindness and for His wonders to mankind.*

[The four groups of people who are delivered from danger are obligated to recite a special blessing (*Orach Chaim* 219:2): Blessed are You, HASHEM our God, King of the Universe, Who performs acts of kindness even for the guilty; Who has granted me all the best! (The term *the guilty* may also be rendered: those who are already indebted to You for past kindnesses.) When the assembled congregation hears this blessing they respond: *May He Who has granted you all the best continue to grant you all the best forever!*]

32. וִירוֹמְמוּהוּ בִּקְהַל עָם — *Let them exalt Him in the assembly of people.*

The blessing of thanksgiving must be recited in the presence of a quorum of ten men who constitute a קָהָל, assembly [the one who blesses is included in the quorum] (*Berachos* 54b).

וּבְמוֹשַׁב זְקֵנִים יְהַלְלוּהוּ — *And at the session of the elders praise Him.*

From this the Talmud learns that two of the ten men in the *assembly* should be *elders*, i.e., Torah scholars.

33. יָשֵׂם נְהָרוֹת לְמִדְבָּר — *He turns rivers to a desert.*

The Psalmist embarks upon the second theme of this composition. In the first section the author demonstrated God's ability to transform a situation of danger and suffering into one of security and joy. Now the Psalmist describes how God can change all natural phenomena — the flora, the fauna and the landscape — at will (*Ibn Ezra*).

וּמֹצָאֵי מַיִם לְצִמָּאוֹן — *And springs of water to aridity.*

If God sees fit to punish a sinning nation He can change their fortunes dramatically; He can transform a lush paradise into a parched wasteland (*Radak*).

Targum observes that this refers to the generation of the prophet Joel. When Israel rebelled against God in his days, a drought struck the land and turned the great rivers into dry wadis.

and for His wonders to mankind.

³² Let them exalt Him in the assembly of people,
and at the session of the elders praise Him.

³³ He turns rivers to a desert,
and springs of water to aridity.

³⁴ A fruitful land to a salty waste
because of the evil of its inhabitants.

³⁵ He turns a desert to a pool of water,
and arid land into springs of water.

³⁶ There He settled the hungry,
and they established an inhabited city.

³⁷ They sowed fields and planted vineyards
which yielded a fruitful harvest.

[See chapters 1 and 2 of *Joel* for a complete description of the devastation wrought by locusts and drought.]

34. אֶרֶץ פְּרִי לִמְלֵחָה מֵרָעַת יוֹשְׁבֵי בָהּ — *A fruitful land to a salty waste because of the evil of its inhabitants.*

Targum explains this as a reference to the cataclysmic destruction of Sodom. [This thriving and prosperous city was the center of the green and fertile Jordan Valley. It was utterly destroyed because of the extreme wickedness of its inhabitants.]

35. וְשָׂם מִדְבָּר לַאֲגַם מָיִם — *He turns a desert to a pool of water.*

[The *Midrash* (cited by *Radak* to 105:41) says that in the desert God miraculously surrounded the Israelite camp with pools of water on which the Jews could sail small boats and travel from one tribe's campsite to another's.]

וְאֶרֶץ צִיָּה לְמֹצָאֵי מָיִם — *And arid land into springs of water.*

[Furthermore, *Midrash Shocher Tov* (Psalm 23) relates that the Jews were supplied by בְּאֵרָהּ שֶׁל מִרְיָם, *the well of Miriam*, a fresh water spring that followed the Jews on their journeys through the wilderness.

This well caused verdant meadows and vast flourishing forests to spring up miraculously from the arid desert wherever Israel encamped. Concerning this David said (23:2), *In lush meadows He lays me down, beside tranquil waters He leads me:* and again (78:15, 16), *He sundered rocks in the wilderness, and provided drinks like the abundant depths. He brought forth flowing waters from the rock and caused waters to descend like rivers.*]

36. וַיּוֹשֶׁב שָׁם רְעֵבִים וַיְכוֹנְנוּ עִיר מוֹשָׁב — *There He settled the hungry, and they established an inhabited city.*

[In the wilderness God fed the hungry masses with the manna which fell from heaven until the Israelites came to the land of Canaan. In this Promised Land they established a new and glorious civilization which centered around great *cities for habitation* such as Jerusalem.]

37. וַיִּזְרְעוּ שָׂדוֹת וַיִּטְּעוּ כְרָמִים וַיַּעֲשׂוּ פְּרִי תְבוּאָה — *They sowed fields and planted vineyards which yielded a fruitful harvest.*

[Their every endeavor met with abundant success, and everything which they undertook was productive.]

לח וַיְבָרֲכֵם וַיִּרְבּוּ מְאֹד וּבְהֶמְתָּם לֹא יַמְעִיט:

לט וַיִּמְעֲטוּ וַיָּשֹׁחוּ מֵעֹצֶר רָעָה וְיָגוֹן: ז

מ שֹׁפֵךְ בּוּז עַל־נְדִיבִים וַיַּתְעֵם בְּתֹהוּ לֹא־דָרֶךְ:

מא וַיְשַׂגֵּב אֶבְיוֹן מֵעוֹנִי וַיָּשֶׂם כַּצֹּאן מִשְׁפָּחוֹת:

מב יִרְאוּ יְשָׁרִים וְיִשְׂמָחוּ וְכָל־עַוְלָה קָפְצָה פִּיהָ:

מג מִי־חָכָם וְיִשְׁמָר־אֵלֶּה וְיִתְבּוֹנְנוּ חַסְדֵי יהוה:

---

38. וַיְבָרֲכֵם וַיִּרְבּוּ מְאֹד וּבְהֶמְתָּם לֹא יַמְעִיט — *He blessed them and they multiplied greatly, and He did not decrease their livestock.*

God *blessed them* with wealth, caused them to increase and *multiply* with many children, and protected their *livestock* so that they did not miscarry. Needless to say, their wives also had only successful pregnancies and never lost their children (*Radak*).

39. וַיִּמְעֲטוּ וַיָּשֹׁחוּ מֵעֹצֶר רָעָה וְיָגוֹן — *Though they had been diminished and stooped from lingering trouble and agony.*

[God's bountiful blessing is all the more amazing and well appreciated considering the dire poverty in which the Jews originally found themselves in Egypt (see *Rashi*).]

40. שֹׁפֵךְ בּוּז עַל נְדִיבִים — *He pours contempt upon nobles.*

The Psalmist continues to provide examples of God's ability to effect dramatic transformations in the fortunes of men. If God so wishes, He can turn the honor and glory of princes into degradation and contempt (*Radak*).

וַיַּתְעֵם בְּתֹהוּ לֹא דָרֶךְ — *And makes them wander in a pathless wasteland.*

Even if these nobles attempt to flee the danger and disgrace which now face them, they get lost and cannot find the path which leads to safety (*Radak*).

41. וַיְשַׂגֵּב אֶבְיוֹן מֵעוֹנִי — *He strengthened the destitute from poverty.*

While the fortunes of the rich nobles decline drastically, God raises the needy to prosperity (*Radak*). [As the *Talmud* (*Shabbos* 151b) says: This world is like an eternally rotating wheel; while one man rises, another man falls.]

וַיָּשֶׂם כַּצֹּאן מִשְׁפָּחוֹת — *And makes families like a flock.*

Not only will God make the needy man prosper financially; He will also cause his family to increase (*Radak*).

42. יִרְאוּ יְשָׁרִים וְיִשְׂמָחוּ — *The upright shall see and be glad.*

³⁸ He blessed them and they multiplied greatly,
    and He did not decrease their livestock.
³⁹ Though they had been diminished and stooped
    from lingering trouble and agony.
⁴⁰ He pours contempt upon nobles,
    and makes them wander in a pathless wasteland.
⁴¹ He strengthened the destitute from poverty,
    and makes families like a flock.
⁴² The upright shall see and be glad,
    and all iniquity shuts its mouth.
⁴³ Whoever is wise let him note these things,
    and they will comprehend
        the kindnesses of HASHEM.

The *upright* are the only class of people who can observe the drastic changes described above without being terrified. They do not fear the fate of the deposed and dispossessed nobles, because the noble are corrupt and these men are upright. Furthermore, they can aspire to the new-found prosperity of those who were formerly needy because these *upright* men shared in their poverty (Ibn Ezra).

וְכָל עֵוְלָה קָפְצָה פִּיהָ — *And all iniquity shuts its mouth.*

When criminals and men of iniquity observe the downfall of the unscrupulous men of wealth, they realize that riches are no guarantee of permanent success. The mouth of the criminals are shut and they boast no longer (Ibn Ezra).

43. מִי חָכָם וְיִשְׁמָר אֵלֶּה — *Whoever is wise let him note these things.*

The man who is wise will take pains to carefully study the lessons of this psalm, which vividly illustrates that God is in complete control of every aspect of this world. It is God alone who determines whether man will experience suffering or salvation, captivity or freedom, want or wealth. The wise man will direct all of his prayers to God and confidence in Hashem, the Master of human fortunes (Radak).

וְיִתְבּוֹנְנוּ חַסְדֵי ה׳ — *And they will comprehend the kindnesses of HASHEM.*

Sometimes a person is bewildered by what he sees in this world. It appears as if the wicked prosper and the righteous suffer. But if a person will really examine and contemplate the workings of society, he will surely conclude that for the most part justice *does* prevail. The good people do succeed and the bad ones fail. If there are exceptions to this rule, man must have confidence in God and be assured that certainly the ways of God are perfectly just and for the best (Radak).

מזמור קח 108

This composition is unique in that it is almost an exact replica of sections of previous psalms. Verses 2-6 of this psalm are closely patterned after verses 8-12 of psalm 57, and verses 7-14 of this psalm correspond almost totally to verses 7-14 of psalm 60.

Radak explains that the earlier psalms relate to David's desperate flight from Saul and his ultimate salvation. Psalm 60 tells of David's conquest of Aram. Here these verses take on new meaning, for they refer to the fortunes of Israel as a whole. In the future, the Messiah, scion of David, will deliver Israel from exile and will lead the Jews in triumphant conquest of their enemies.

At that time the refrain of Israel's song will be, Grant us help against the oppressor; futile is the aid of man. Through God we shall form an army, and He will trample our oppressors (verses 13-14).

שִׁיר מִזְמוֹר לְדָוִד: נָכוֹן לִבִּי אֱלֹהִים אָשִׁירָה

וַאֲזַמְּרָה אַף־כְּבוֹדִי: עוּרָה הַנֵּבֶל וְכִנּוֹר

אָעִירָה שָּׁחַר: אוֹדְךָ בָעַמִּים | יהוה וַאֲזַמֶּרְךָ

בַּלְאֻמִּים: כִּי־גָדֹל מֵעַל־שָׁמַיִם חַסְדֶּךָ וְעַד־

שְׁחָקִים אֲמִתֶּךָ: רוּמָה עַל־שָׁמַיִם אֱלֹהִים

1. שִׁיר מִזְמוֹר לְדָוִד — *A song with musical accompaniment, by David.*

See commentary to 30:1 citing the *Siddur Baal HaTanya*, who explains that שִׁיר, *song*, refers to the lyrics of the composition and מִזְמוֹר alludes to the accompaniment of כְּלֵי זֶמֶר, *musical instruments.* [Radak adverts to this in his commentary to the second verse.]

Chazah Zion explains that the initial letters of שִׁיר מִזְמוֹר לְדָוִד form שָׁלֵם *perfect,* which suggests that this psalm echoes the ultimate perfection and excellence which the royal line of David will achieve.

2. נָכוֹן לִבִּי אֱלֹהִים — *My heart is steadfast, O God.*

Although this dismal exile appears to be interminable, I firmly cling to my belief that God will send the redeemer (*Radak*).

One of the most glaring problems of the exile is the absence of strong leadership. This vacuum has allowed the Jews to lapse into moral degeneration which has distorted their hearts and minds. When the Messiah restores strong leadership to Israel he will strengthen the moral fiber of the people and make their straying hearts *steadfast* once again (*Sforno*).

אָשִׁירָה וַאֲזַמְּרָה אַף־כְּבוֹדִי — *I will sing and I will make music even with my soul* [lit. *glory* or *honor*].

[The *soul* is the כָּבוֹד, *glory,* of man, as explained in the commentary to 8:6 and 30:13.]

Malbim [see commentary to 57:9] explains that King Saul's jealousy towards David and his relentless pursuit of him had a great impact on David and left a deep, dark blot on his soul. As an innocent man condemned and vilified, as a helpless fugitive hunted and threatened, David suffered greatly and became withdrawn. The full radiance of David's brilliant personality went into eclipse.

When the threat posed by Saul was finally removed, David's melancholy was dissolved and the full force of his unique personality burst forth. David's *soul* now composed *music* to God, for it surged with renewed hope and vitality. [This same description applies to the metamorphosis which Israel will undergo in the Messianic era, after being redeemed from exile.]

3. עוּרָה הַנֵּבֶל וְכִנּוֹר אָעִירָה שָּׁחַר — *Awake, O* neivel *and harp, I shall awaken the dawn.*

David exclaimed: ''Other kings slumber soundly through the entire night and are awakened by the dawn and its rays of light. I, however, *awaken the dawn!* A harp stands over my bed. At midnight, a north wind blows through my chambers and causes the harp to play by itself. These sounds awaken me and I spend the rest of the night singing psalms and hymns of praise to God'' (*Rashi*).[1]

[Similarly, before the dawn of the Messianic redemption, there will be a universal revival of the Jewish spirit.

1. The commentaries to the *Talmud* (*Berachos* 3b) attempt to explain the phenomenon of the harp and the wind. *Rav Hai Gaon* says that David's harp functioned somewhat like a wind gauge or anemometer. At midnight, the wind would come from the north and reach a certain velocity. David's harp was positioned in such a way as to catch this northerly wind and record

108
1-6

A song with musical accompaniment, by David.

² My heart is steadfast, O God,
I will sing and I will make music
even with my soul.

³ Awake, O neivel and harp,
I shall awaken the dawn.

⁴ I will thank You among the peoples, HASHEM,
and I will sing to You among the nations.

⁵ For great above the very heavens is Your kindness,
and until the upper heights is Your truth.

⁶ Be exalted above heaven, O God,

Then Jews will perceive the presence of God despite the engulfing gloom of exile.]

4. אוֹדְךָ בָעַמִּים ה' — *I will thank You among the peoples, HASHEM.*

In the future, we will thank You for everything which transpired in the course of the exile — both the good and the bad (*Rav Avraham Azulai*).

וַאֲזַמֶּרְךָ בַּלְאֻמִּים — *And I will sing to You among the nations.*

All the nations are destined to converge upon Jerusalem in the future, and they will join Israel in praising God (*Radak*).

5. כִּי גָדֹל מֵעַל שָׁמַיִם חַסְדֶּךָ — *For great above the very heavens is Your kindness.*

57:11 is almost identical, but reads כִּי גָדֹל עַד שָׁמַיִם חַסְדֶּךָ, *For great until the very heavens is Your kindness. Radak* explains that since the earlier psalm speaks of David personally, it states *until the very heavens*, for the kindness which God displays to an individual is limited. However, this psalm describes the future of Israel, when all the nations will be instruments by which God

showers kindness on His chosen people. The gentiles will eagerly transport the Jews back to Israel in splendid carriages and shining chariots. They will dote on Israel and fulfill their every whim, as *Isaiah* 49:23 prophesies: *Kings will serve as your governesses and princes will be your nursemaids.*

The *kindness* which God displays at that time will far surpass any previous kindness and exceed all expectations. Therefore it can be described as *great even above the very heavens* (*Radak*).

[See commentary to 57:11 for the explanation provided by the *Talmud, Pesachim* 50b.]

וְעַד שְׁחָקִים אֲמִתֶּךָ — *And until the upper heights is Your truth.*

This is an exact repetition of the second half of 57:11. *Radak* explains that even though the measure of God's kindness will increase in the future, His *truth* will remain the same. For *truth* is an eternal, unchanging reality, whereas *kindness*, which consists of gratuitous merciful acts, can be exercised in varying degrees.

6. רוּמָה עַל שָׁמַיִם אֱלֹהִים — *Be exalted above heaven, O God.*

---

its speed through the vibrations of the harpstrings. When the wind reached a certain, pre-determined velocity David knew immediately that midnight had arrived.

Rashba describes this harp as a complex apparatus which resembled a water clock. Drops of water were released into a receptacle according to a precise schedule. The drops were released through the night, until at midnight the container was full. The full weight of the receptacle activated a mechanism which automatically strummed the harp strings and awakened David.

וְעַל כָּל־הָאָרֶץ כְּבוֹדֶךָ: לְמַעַן יֵחָלְצוּן יְדִידֶיךָ ז

הוֹשִׁיעָה יְמִינְךָ °וַעֲנֵנוּ: אֱלֹהִים | דִּבֶּר ח

בְּקָדְשׁוֹ אֶעְלֹזָה אֲחַלְּקָה שְׁכֶם וְעֵמֶק סֻכּוֹת

אֲמַדֵּד: לִי גִלְעָד | לִי מְנַשֶּׁה וְאֶפְרַיִם מָעוֹז ט

רֹאשִׁי יְהוּדָה מְחֹקְקִי: מוֹאָב | סִיר רַחְצִי עַל־ י

אֱדוֹם אַשְׁלִיךְ נַעֲלִי עֲלֵי־פְלֶשֶׁת אֶתְרוֹעָע:

מִי יֹבִלֵנִי עִיר מִבְצָר מִי נָחַנִי עַד־אֱדוֹם: יא

הֲלֹא־אֱלֹהִים זְנַחְתָּנוּ וְלֹא־תֵצֵא אֱלֹהִים יב

°וַעֲנֵנִי ק׳

When Israel is downtrodden in exile, God does not appear exalted; but when He redeems Israel, His dominion over all the nations will be manifest. Then God will truly be exalted (Radak).

וְעַל כָּל־הָאָרֶץ כְּבוֹדֶךָ — And above all the earth, Your glory.

In the Messianic Era, the righteous Sages will have the freedom to teach Torah to the ignorant masses of Israel and to draw them to the service of God. Then God's glory, hitherto comprehended only by a handful of individuals, will be spread throughout the earth (Sforno).

7. לְמַעַן יֵחָלְצוּן יְדִידֶיךָ — So that Your beloved ones may be given rest.

This refers to the Jews' release from captivity and oppression at the hands of the nations (Sforno).

הוֹשִׁיעָה יְמִינְךָ וַעֲנֵנִי — Let Your right hand save and respond to me.

Save יְדִידֶיךָ, Your beloved ones, the pious Torah scholars, from exile, and respond to my plea so that they may begin at once to teach Torah to the masses (Sforno).

8. אֱלֹהִים דִּבֶּר בְּקָדְשׁוֹ אֶעְלֹזָה — God said in His sanctity that I would exult.

[God promised Israel world-wide dominion, causing them to rejoice and exult.]

אֲחַלְּקָה שְׁכֶם — That I would divide a portion.

In the future, the Jews will inherit the land of their enemies, and they will divide the territory evenly among themselves (Rashi).

וְעֵמֶק סֻכּוֹת אֲמַדֵּד — And the Valley of Succos I would measure out.

This world is plagued by border disputes between neighboring countries, provinces, and cities. The Messiah will measure all of the lands and settle these disputes (Sforno).

9. לִי גִלְעָד — Mine is Gilead.

In this world, Gilead is a wicked city of violent crime and iniquity, as *Hoshea 6:8* states: *Gilead is a city of evildoers, filled with blood.* But in the future, says the Messiah, "It will be my city." Under his benign influence, it will be transformed into a tranquil metropolis (Sforno).

לִי מְנַשֶּׁה וְאֶפְרַיִם מָעוֹז רֹאשִׁי יְהוּדָה מְחֹקְקִי — Mine is Menashe; Ephraim is the stronghold of my head; Judah is my scholar.

These three tribes were royal families — proud, strong and fiercely individualistic. In this world, they were most reluctant to accept authority; in the future, each will eagerly submit to the rule of the Messiah (Sforno).

The translation of מְחֹקְקִי as *my scholar* follows *Rashi* to Genesis 49:10, according to which the word is derived from חֹק, *law*. Ibn Ezra there renders *scribe. Radak* renders *lawgiver.*

and above all the earth, Your glory.

⁷ *So that Your beloved ones may be given rest,*
let Your right hand save and respond to me.

⁸ *God said in His sanctity that I would exult,*
that I would divide a portion;
and the Valley of Succos
I would measure out.

⁹ *Mine is Gilead, mine is Menashe;*
Ephraim is the stronghold of my head;
Judah is my scholar

¹⁰ *Moab is my washbasin;*
upon Edom I will cast my lock;
I will shout at Philistia.

¹¹ *Who will bring me to the fortified city?*
Who will lead me until Edom?

¹² *Did not You, O God, forsake us,*
and not go forth, O God, with our legions?

---

10. מוֹאָב סִיר רַחְצִי — *Moab is my washbasin.*

The Messiah will conquer all of Israel's traditional enemies. He will treat Moab with contempt, like filthy water which is cast away in disgust (*Rashi*).

עַל אֱדוֹם אַשְׁלִיךְ נַעֲלִי — *Upon Edom I will cast my lock.*

[See commentary to 60:10.] The translation of נַעֲלִי follows *Rashi*, and implies: I will lock Edom into my tight grip. *Metzudos* renders: I will cast iron chains on their feet, in order to fetter them.

Radak, however, translates נַעֲלִי as *my shoe*, in which case the verse means that the Messiah's armies will trample the enemy.

עֲלֵי פְלֶשֶׁת אֶתְרוֹעָע — *I will shout at Philistia.*

I will let out a blood-curdling scream at Philistia in order to terrify their legions (*Rashi*).

11. מִי יֹבִלֵנִי עִיר מִבְצָר — *Who will bring*

me to the fortified city?

Who will give the Messiah the courage and the strength to attack his well fortified enemies? (*Rashi*).

מִי נָחַנִי עַד אֱדוֹם — *Who will lead me until Edom?*

According to *Rashi*, these words are not part of the question but rather form an answer: God, Who led me [i.e., Israel] against Edom [in David's time] and conquered their impregnable bastions, will also bring me to victory over these fortified cities in Messianic times.

12. הֲלֹא אֱלֹהִים זְנַחְתָּנוּ וְלֹא תֵצֵא אֱלֹהִים בְּצִבְאֹתֵינוּ — *Did not You, O God, forsake us, and not go forth, O God, with our legions?*

According to *Radak*, this is the Psalmist's reply to the question posed in the preceding verse: Who brought us victory over the fortified city? It was none other than You, O God! You had originally forsaken us and refused to go out with our legions, but when You

יג בְּצִבְאוֹתֵינוּ: הָבָה־לָּנוּ עֶזְרָת מִצָּר וְשָׁוְא
יד תְּשׁוּעַת אָדָם: בֵּאלֹהִים נַעֲשֶׂה־חָיִל וְהוּא
יָבוּס צָרֵינוּ:

decided to favor us, You granted us an amazing triumph over enemy forces which greatly outnumbered us!

13. הָבָה־לָּנוּ עֶזְרָת מִצָּר — *Grant us help against the oppressor.*

Grant us victory directly from Your hands, rather than through a human intermediary *(Tehillos Hashem).*

וְשָׁוְא תְּשׁוּעַת אָדָם — *Futile is the aid of man.*

[David's general, Joab, realized that success does not depend on armies or on brilliant strategies, for all is in God's hands. Therefore, he addressed the

troops and said, *"Be of good courage and let us prove strong for our people ... and HASHEM will do that which seems proper to Him"* (II Samuel 10:11).]

14. בֵּאלֹהִים נַעֲשֶׂה חָיִל — *Through God we shall form an army.*

With the help of God, the Sages of the Messianic era will band together to form an academic force which will launch an assault upon ignorance and apathy. An army of eager students will gather around these scholars and dedicate themselves to the service of God *(Sforno).*[1]

---

1. The prophet *Isaiah* (12:3) describes the future Messianic era vividly: וּשְׁאַבְתֶּם מַיִם בְּשָׂשׂוֹן מִמַּעַיְנֵי הַיְשׁוּעָה, *With joy you shall draw up water out of the wellsprings of salvation.*

Targum Yonasan ben Uziel interprets this: In the future you will receive fresh intellectual insight and teachings, with joy, from the choicest of the righteous men.

Rambam (Moreh Nevuchim 1:30) and commentary of *Rabbeinu Shem Tov* (ibid.) explain

¹³ *Grant us help against the oppressor;*
futile is the aid of man.
¹⁴ *Through God we shall form an army,*
and He will trample our oppressors.

וְהוּא יָבוּס צָרֵינוּ — *And He will trample our oppressors.*

The military forces of the Messiah will be victorious in the merit of their Torah study, for as the *Talmud* (*Sanhedrin* 45a) states: Had David not stayed behind to study Torah with his disciples, his general Joab would not

have been victorious in battle (*Sforno*).

[The struggle of Messiah is one of light over darkness, of intellect over ignorance. It may well be said that the light of wisdom makes might, and that Torah endows its students with the power to overcome all obstacles and adversaries.]

that Messiah will open men's eyes and make them aware of new intellectual horizons. He will plumb the depths of man's mental capacity and uncover talents and abilities which were hitherto dormant and untapped.

Rabbeinu Shem Tov observes that even in pre-Messianic times a devoted disciple can achieve enlightenment from the teachings of his master, and thus experience a degree of intellectual redemption. In the future, this sort of liberation will be universally shared as the prophet says (*Isaiah* 11:9): *And the earth will be filled with the knowledge of HASHEM as waters cover the sea.*

109 מזמור קט

David composed this psalm as he fled from the wrath of King Saul. Some people had slandered David to Saul and besmirched his name. David was saying: "O God of my praise, be not silent" (verse 1), i.e., recognize, dear God, how I differ from my foes. They praise themselves for their deftness at slander, but I praise myself only for my closeness to You, my Lord!

Midrash Shocher Tov says that these words describe Israel's unique relationship to God. God is Israel's only praise as Deuteronomy 10:21 states: He is your praise, He is your God; and Israel is God's only source of praise, as Isaiah 43:21 states: This nation I fashioned for Myself, so that they might recite My praise.

Therefore, David said to HASHEM, "You are my only praise [and the praise of all Israel]. Do not be silent when we suffer and are oppressed." O God, do not hold Yourself silent; be not deaf and be not still, O God (83:2).

David concludes this work with complete confidence that God will respond, For He stands at the right of the destitute, to save him from condemners of his soul (verse 31).

א לַמְנַצֵּחַ לְדָוִד מִזְמוֹר אֱלֹהֵי תְהִלָּתִי אַל־
ב תֶּחֱרַשׁ: כִּי פִי רָשָׁע וּפִי־מִרְמָה עָלַי פָּתָחוּ
ג דִּבְּרוּ אִתִּי לְשׁוֹן שָׁקֶר: וְדִבְרֵי שִׂנְאָה סְבָבוּנִי
ד וַיִּלָּחֲמוּנִי חִנָּם: תַּחַת־אַהֲבָתִי יִשְׂטְנוּנִי וַאֲנִי
ה תְפִלָּה: וַיָּשִׂימוּ עָלַי רָעָה תַּחַת טוֹבָה
ו וְשִׂנְאָה תַּחַת אַהֲבָתִי: הַפְקֵד עָלָיו רָשָׁע

1. לַמְנַצֵּחַ לְדָוִד מִזְמוֹר — *For the Conductor, by David, a song.*

The Sages of the *Talmud* (*Pesachim* 117a) teach that whenever the name of David (לְדָוִד) appears before the word מִזְמוֹר, *a song*, this indicates that Divine inspiration came first, and culminated in David's song (see *commentary* to 3:1). [One would imagine that when David was a fugitive from Saul (see *Prefatory Remarks*) he would hardly be in a state of mind conducive to Divine inspiration and song. But such was David's nature that adversity served only to evoke his faith and the Divine melody in his heart.]

אֱלֹהֵי תְהִלָּתִי אַל תֶּחֱרַשׁ — *O God of my praise, be not silent.*

Do not be indifferent to those who seek to harm me and to disgrace me (*Radak*).

I am always vigilant to assure that You will be properly praised. Therefore, act on my behalf to destroy those who strip me of praise and cover me with abuse (*Sforno*).

2. כִּי פִי רָשָׁע — *For the mouth of the wicked.*

David's treacherous enemies disguised themselves as friends, while their tongues spoke deceitfully (*Radak*).

David wrote this composition not only in reference to his own personal life, but also as a description of Israel's suffering in exile.

The mouth of the wicked refers to the Romans, the cruel descendants of bloody Esau (*Ibn Yachya*).

These barbaric marauders forced their way into the Holy of Holies and

mocked us with drunken defiance, saying, "Where is your God? Let Him come and do battle with us!" (*Midrash Shocher Tov*).

— וּפִי מִרְמָה עָלַי פָּתָחוּ דִּבְּרוּ אִתִּי לְשׁוֹן שָׁקֶר *And the mouth of the deceitful have opened against me, they have spoken to me the language of falsehood.*

The mouth of the deceitful refers to the Arabs, the crafty and thieving offspring of Ishmael. With their false love they attempted to lure me away from my true God, to follow their false and worthless religion (*Ibn Yachya*).

3. וְדִבְרֵי שִׂנְאָה סְבָבוּנִי — *With words of hatred they encircled me.*

These wicked men incensed Saul with their slanderous reports about me, and Saul pursued and surrounded me in fierce hatred (*Radak*).

The gentiles speak the words of hatred which their forefather taught them, for *Genesis* 27:41 states, *And Esau hated Jacob.* He hated Jacob so much that he took vengeance himself and also instilled his hatred in the hearts of his descendants (*Midrash Shocher Tov*).

וַיִּלָּחֲמוּנִי חִנָּם — *And attacked me without cause.*

They fight against us without provocation. When we sent messengers to Esau, we conducted ourselves with good will, as *Numbers* 20:14 states, *And Moses sent messengers ... unto the king of Edom: "Thus says your brother Israel ..."* On the other hand, *Edom said unto him ... "Lest I come out with the sword against you"* (*Numbers* 20:18).

For the Conductor, by David, a song,
      O God of my praise, be not silent.
   ² *For the mouth of the wicked*
         and the mouth of the deceitful
            have opened against me,
   they have spoken to me
         the language of falsehood.
   ³ *With words of hatred they encircled me,*
         and attacked me without cause.
   ⁴ *In return for my love they accuse me,*
         but I am prayer.
   ⁵ *But they imposed upon me evil in return for good,*
         and hatred in return for my love.

The people of Israel also said, *"I am all peace; but when I speak, they are for war"* (120:7). Therefore, the Holy One, Blessed is He, said to Israel, *"They have not let you live in peace."* Hence, *Amos* 1:11 states: *Thus says Hashem, "For three transgressions of Edom* [Esau], *indeed, for four, I will not reverse it: because he did pursue his brother* [Jacob] *with the sword"* (Midrash Shocher Tov).

4. תַּחַת אַהֲבָתִי יִשְׂטְנוּנִי — *In return for my love they accuse me.*

Because I love You, my God, they hate me and accuse me. But I remain undaunted, for I am *prayer* (see below) and devotion to You (Rashi).

According to *Ibn Ezra, Radak* and *Sforno,* David says: Despite their animosity, I loved my adversaries, but they repaid my love with hate.

Ibn Yachya adds: I loved the Romans because the Torah commands *You shall not despise the Edomite, for he is your brother* (Deuteronomy 23:8). I loved the sons of Ishmael because Ishmael took an Egyptian wife and the Torah says, *You shall not despise the Egyptian, for you were a stranger in his land* (Deuteronomy 23:8). Nevertheless, these nations repaid my tolerance with bigotry and hatred.

וַאֲנִי תְפִלָּה — *But I am prayer.*

Because I always pray to You, I am like a living prayer (Rashi).

Despite their provocations against me, *I do* not respond in kind. Instead I pray even for my enemies (Ibn Ezra).

5. וַיָּשִׂימוּ עָלַי רָעָה תַּחַת טוֹבָה — *But they imposed upon me evil in return for good.*

[As 35:12 states, *They repay me evil for good, death for my soul.*]

Israel said: I sacrifice seventy bullocks every year on the Festival of Tabernacles on behalf of the seventy nations, and I beseech God to send them life-giving rain. But they ignore my intercession on their behalf, and they harm me (Rashi).

וְשִׂנְאָה תַּחַת אַהֲבָתִי — *And hatred in return for my love.*

[David continues: When my enemies were sick I treated them with compassion: *As if for a companion, as if for my own brother, I went about; As if in mourning for a mother, I bleakly bent over. But when I limped, they rejoiced and gathered, against me gathered the lame — I know not why* (35:14,15).]

6-19. According to *Malbim* and *R' Hirsch,* verses 6-19 contain the curses that David's enemies hurled at *him,* not

ז וְשָׂטָן יַעֲמֹד עַל-יְמִינוֹ: בְּהִשָּׁפְטוֹ יֵצֵא רָשָׁע

ח וּתְפִלָּתוֹ תִּהְיֶה לַחֲטָאָה: יִהְיוּ-יָמָיו מְעַטִּים

ט פְּקֻדָּתוֹ יִקַּח אַחֵר: יִהְיוּ-בָנָיו יְתוֹמִים וְאִשְׁתּוֹ

י אַלְמָנָה: וְנוֹעַ יָנוּעוּ בָנָיו וְשִׁאֵלוּ וְדָרְשׁוּ

יא מֵחָרְבוֹתֵיהֶם: יְנַקֵּשׁ נוֹשֶׁה לְכָל-אֲשֶׁר-לוֹ

יב וְיָבֹזּוּ זָרִים יְגִיעוֹ: אַל-יְהִי-לוֹ מֹשֵׁךְ חָסֶד

his response to them. According to most earlier commentaries, such as *Radak* and *Ibn Ezra*, it is the fugitive David who is now cursing his malicious foes, the most notable of whom was Doeg the Edomite who was incessantly inciting King Saul and the nation against David.

Rashi, as is evident from his commentary to verses 14-18, understands this passage as an allusion to Esau's sins and punishment.

[Ordinarily David reacted to his bitterest adversaries with indifferent silence as we read (39:2): *I said: "I will guard my ways from sinning with my tongue, I will guard my mouth with a muzzle while the wicked one still stands before me"* (see also 38:13-15). However, Doeg was in the category of a מוֹסֵר, *an informer*, of such a serious degree that he loses his portion in the World to Come and even forfeits his right to exist in This World. The halachic details concerning an informer are complex, but this term provides a general description of those whom David curses here. He was physically unable to prevent them from pursuing their wicked crimes so he invoked Divine assistance to deter and punish them.]

6. הַפְקֵד עָלָיו רָשָׁע — *Appoint a wicked man over him.*

Let a wicked man have power over my enemies [so that they experience how bitter it is to be dominated by a cruel overlord, as they wished to dominate me]. The Psalmist addresses all of his enemies in the singular form, as one man, because he is referring

primarily to the arch-enemy who led all those who incited against him: Doeg the Edomite [see psalm 52]. It was he who first aroused Saul's blind jealousy against David *(Radak).*

וְשָׂטָן יַעֲמֹד עַל יְמִינוֹ — *And let an adversary stand at his right.*

Radak comments: Let an angel of violence and destruction hound the evil man and bring curses and failure to his every endeavor.

7. בְּהִשָּׁפְטוֹ יֵצֵא רָשָׁע — *When he is judged may he go forth condemned.*

When You judge the wicked in Your heavenly tribunal, condemn them *(Rashi).*

Also, if they come to trial in civil court against any adversary, may they lose their case and be found guilty. Trip their tongues and confuse their minds, so that their arguments and their defenses will be foiled *(Radak).*

וּתְפִלָּתוֹ תִּהְיֶה לַחֲטָאָה — *And let his prayer be turned to sin.*

When the wicked pray, do not view this as a merit, but as a selfish, sinful act. Alternatively, the word חֲטָאָה, *to sin,* also means *to miss the mark (Judges* 20:16). Thus, let their prayers miss their mark and do not let them be accepted *(Radak).*

8. יִהְיוּ יָמָיו מְעַטִּים — *May his days be few.*

[Similarly, David prayed, "Men of bloodshed and deceit shall not live out half their days" (55:24).]

פְּקֻדָּתוֹ יִקַּח אַחֵר — *May another take his position.*

⁶ *Appoint a wicked man over him,*
   and let an adversary stand at his right.
⁷ *When he is judged may he go forth condemned,*
   and let his prayer be turned to sin.
⁸ *May his days be few;*
   may another take his position.
⁹ *May his children be orphans*
   and his wife a widow.
¹⁰ *May his children constantly wander and beg,*
   and may they forage among their ruins.
¹¹ *May the creditor seize all that he has,*
   and may aliens despoil his labor.
¹² *May he have none who extend kindness,*

Many translations are advanced for פְקֻדָּה.

Rashi contends that it means an exalted *position*. According to *Radak*, it is cognate with פִּקָּדוֹן, *an article given for safekeeping*, referring to a person's wife or fortune, which he guards with special care. *Ibn Ezra* observes that the Psalmist prays that the wicked man should lose the precious soul [i.e., his life] which God gave to him for safekeeping.

9. יִהְיוּ בָנָיו יְתוֹמִים וְאִשְׁתּוֹ אַלְמָנָה — *May his children be orphans and his wife a widow.*

[See *Exodus* 22:23 and *Rashi's* commentary.]

When this wicked man dies young, his wife will be a youthful widow, and his infant children will be helpless orphans (*Radak*).

10. וְנוֹעַ יָנוּעוּ בָנָיו וְשִׁאֵלוּ — *May his children constantly wander* [lit. *and wander may his children wander*] *and beg* [lit. *ask*].

The translation of שִׁאֵלוּ as *beg* follows *Radak, Ibn Ezra,* and *Rashi. Rashi* prefers another interpretation, *they are asked after,* for when people see the ruin which befalls the wicked,

they will be amazed and ask what caused this calamity.

וְדָרְשׁוּ מֵחָרְבוֹתֵיהֶם — *And may they forage among their ruins.*

They will scrounge around the rubble and *ruins* of their homes in search of some leftover food. As they stand in the *ruins,* they will stretch out their hands to beg for alms from passersby (*Radak*).

11. יְנַקֵּשׁ נוֹשֶׁה לְכָל אֲשֶׁר לוֹ — *May the creditor seize all that he has.*

Literally, יְנַקֵּשׁ means *may he trap* [related to מוֹקֵשׁ, *snare*]; thus, the creditor will trap the debtor's assets and not let them out of his grip (*Radak*).

Rashi observes that this refers to the wicked Esau, who was forever indebted to Jacob. Esau was in Jacob's service, as *Genesis* 25:23 states: וְרַב יַעֲבֹד צָעִיר, *the elder* [Esau] *shall serve the younger* [Jacob].

וְיָבֹזּוּ זָרִים יְגִיעוֹ — *And may aliens despoil his labor.*

May he be burglarized by night so that the fruits of his day's labor go to waste (*Ibn Yachya*).

12. אַל יְהִי לוֹ מֹשֵׁךְ חָסֶד — *May he have none who extend kindness.*

When the wicked man's children

יג וְאַל־יְהִי חוֹנֵן לִיתוֹמָיו: יְהִי־אַחֲרִיתוֹ
יד לְהַכְרִית בְּדוֹר אַחֵר יִמַּח שְׁמָם: יִזָּכֵר | עֲוֺן
אֲבֹתָיו אֶל־יהוה וְחַטַּאת אִמּוֹ אַל־תִּמָּח:
טו יִהְיוּ נֶגֶד־יהוה תָּמִיד וְיַכְרֵת מֵאֶרֶץ זִכְרָם:
טז יַעַן אֲשֶׁר | לֹא זָכַר עֲשׂוֹת חָסֶד וַיִּרְדֹּף אִישׁ־
יז עָנִי וְאֶבְיוֹן וְנִכְאֵה לֵבָב לְמוֹתֵת: וַיֶּאֱהַב
קְלָלָה וַתְּבוֹאֵהוּ וְלֹא־חָפֵץ בִּבְרָכָה וַתִּרְחַק

---

wander from place to place begging for
food (verse 10), may they be refused
assistance and turned away empty-
handed (Radak).

וְאַל יְהִי חוֹנֵן לִיתוֹמָיו — And may none be
merciful to his orphans.

[May the wicked man die and leave
his orphaned children (verse 9) pen-
niless, helpless, and friendless; for
society will turn its back on the progeny
of the criminal who harmed humanity
so violently (see Radak).]

13. יְהִי אַחֲרִיתוֹ לְהַכְרִית — May his
posterity be cut off.

Literally, אַחֲרִית means that which
one leaves behind, after himself, i.e., his
children. Thus, let the children of the
wicked perish (Ibn Ezra; Radak).

בְּדוֹר אַחֵר יִמַּח שְׁמָם — In a later
generation let their name be erased.

The first two generations, i.e., the
father and his son, will ultimately be
physically cut off, but their memory
will endure as long as they still live. But
in the third generation, the generation
of the grandchildren, the father and son
who were cut off will be completely
forgotten and their memory will be
obliterated (Radak).

14. יִזָּכֵר עֲוֺן אֲבֹתָיו אֶל ה' — May his
fathers' iniquity be remembered by
HASHEM.

This refers to the wicked Esau. The
Rabbis note, however, that Esau's
fathers — i.e., his father Isaac and his
grandfather Abraham — were perfectly
righteous. Thus the Psalmist must

mean: May the iniquity which Esau
perpetrated against his fathers be
remembered.

Esau was responsible for the shorten-
ing of Abraham's life. The Talmud
(Bava Basra 16b) notes that on the day
Abraham died, Esau began his sinful
career. Abraham was originally destined
to live five years more, to the age of one
hundred and eighty, but God wanted to
spare him the pain of witnessing the
corruption of his grandchild.

For this very reason God also caused
Isaac to lose his eyesight. The incense
that Esau allowed his wives to burn in
honor of his idols also contributed to
Isaac's blindness (see Genesis 27:1).

Thus, Esau's iniquities adversely
affected both Abraham and Isaac
(Rashi).

וְחַטַּאת אִמּוֹ אַל תִּמָּח — And may his
mother's sin not be erased.

At the time of Esau's birth, he
damaged his mother's womb so as to
prevent her from bearing any more
children [who would share in the estate
he hoped to inherit from his parents].

Additionally, the Torah says nothing
about the death of the righteous
Rebecca, mother of Esau. Her passing
was purposely concealed so the people
would not condemn her, saying,
"Cursed be the woman, who brought
the evil Esau into the world." Thus Esau
deprived his righteous mother of the last
honors she deserved (Rashi).

15. יִהְיוּ נֶגֶד ה' תָּמִיד וְיַכְרֵת מֵאֶרֶץ זִכְרָם —
May they be before HASHEM at all

and may none be merciful to his orphans.

¹³ May his posterity be cut off,
    in a later generation let their name be erased.
¹⁴ May his fathers' iniquity be remembered
        by HASHEM,
    and may his mother's sin not be erased.
¹⁵ May they be before HASHEM at all times,
    and may He cut off their memory
        from the earth.
¹⁶ Because he remembered not to do kindness,
    and he pursued the poor, the destitute,
    and the brokenhearted unto death.
¹⁷ He loved the curse
    and now it has come upon him;
he desired not blessing
    and it stayed far from him.

---

times, and may He cut off their memory from the earth.

May God remember Esau's crimes forever and cause his memory and the memory of his children to be blotted out forever (*Rashi*).

16. יַעַן אֲשֶׁר לֹא זָכַר עֲשׂוֹת חָסֶד — *Because he remembered not to do kindness.*

Esau dedicated his entire life to self-satisfaction. He never once *remembered to do kindness* to anyone (*Radak*).

On the day of Abraham's death, Isaac was deep in mourning. Jacob performed a kindness for his bereaved father and cooked him a pot of lentils, the traditional meal of consolation [see *Genesis* 25:29], but Esau unfeelingly left to hunt in the field. He did not even take this opportunity to act kindly toward his own father (*Rashi*).

וַיִּרְדֹּף אִישׁ עָנִי וְאֶבְיוֹן — *And he pursued the poor, the destitute.*

[When Jacob left the home of his parents to go to live with Laban, he was laden with riches and gifts. However,

Esau sent his son Eliphaz to pursue Jacob and to kill him. Jacob persuaded Eliphaz to spare his life and to take all of his possessions instead. Consequently, Jacob arrived at Laban's home a poor and needy man (see comm. of *Rashi* to *Genesis* 29:10).]

וְנִכְאֵה לֵבָב לְמוֹתֵת — *And the broken-hearted unto death.*

Radak comments that this verse also refers to David. He considered himself *poor, needy,* and *broken-hearted* because his enemies pursued him until *death.*

17. וַיֶּאֱהַב קְלָלָה וַתְּבוֹאֵהוּ — *He loved the curse and now it has come upon him.*

Esau blasphemed and denied God [see *Bava Basra* 16b], which is tantamount to cursing the Almighty (*Rashi*). In this manner, he invited the curses of God to descend upon him (*Radak*).

וְלֹא חָפֵץ בִּבְרָכָה וַתִּרְחַק מִמֶּנּוּ — *He desired not blessing and it stayed far from him.*

When Esau sold his privileges to Jacob, he said: וְלָמָּה זֶּה לִי בְּכֹרָה, *So of*

יח מִמֶּנּוּ: וַיִּלְבַּשׁ קְלָלָה כְּמַדּוֹ וַתָּבֹא כַמַּיִם

בְּקִרְבּוֹ וְכַשֶּׁמֶן בְּעַצְמוֹתָיו: תְּהִי־לוֹ כְּבֶגֶד יט

יַעְטֶה וּלְמֵזַח תָּמִיד יַחְגְּרֶהָ: זֹאת | פְּעֻלַּת כ

שֹׂטְנַי מֵאֵת יְהֹוָה וְהַדֹּבְרִים רָע עַל־נַפְשִׁי:

וְאַתָּה | יֱהֹוִה אֲדֹנָי עֲשֵׂה־אִתִּי לְמַעַן שְׁמֶךָ כא

כִּי־טוֹב חַסְדְּךָ הַצִּילֵנִי: כִּי־עָנִי וְאֶבְיוֹן אָנֹכִי כב

וְלִבִּי חָלַל בְּקִרְבִּי: כְּצֵל כִּנְטוֹתוֹ נֶהֱלָכְתִּי כג

---

what use to me is a birthright? (Genesis 25:32). When he uttered these words, God exclaimed: וְלָמָּה זֶּה לְךָ בְּרָכָה, *Then of what use to you is a blessing?* [a play on the words בְּכֹרָה, *birthright*, and בְּרָכָה, *blessing*] (Midrash HaGadol).

18. וַיִּלְבַּשׁ קְלָלָה כְּמַדּוֹ — *He donned curse as his garment.*

[Had Esau kept the birthright, he would have been endowed with the sanctity of a priest, who is privileged to bless the people and to offer sacrifices on their behalf. Since he rejected this and embraced idols, he willingly enveloped himself in all the curses which the Torah hurls at these pagan deities (see *Rashi*).]

וַתָּבֹא כַמַּיִם בְּקִרְבּוֹ וְכַשֶּׁמֶן בְּעַצְמוֹתָיו — *And it came like water into his innards, and like oil into his bones.*

[These curses were not merely external; rather, they penetrated the essence of the wicked man's existence, until he became completely identified with curses and tragedy.]

19. תְּהִי־לוֹ כְּבֶגֶד יַעְטֶה — *May it be to him like a garment in which he wraps himself.*

Malbim explains that originally (verse 18) the Psalmist said, וַיִּלְבַּשׁ קְלָלָה כְּמַדּוֹ, *he donned curse as his garment.* The word מַדּוֹ is derived from מִדָּה, *measure*, and refers to a custom-made garment which adheres to the precise dimensions of the individual. Here, the Psalmist goes further and asks that additional curses plague the wicked,

enveloping him like a huge, loose-fitting robe [which obliterates a person's shape].

וּלְמֵזַח תָּמִיד יַחְגְּרֶהָ — *And a belt with which he constantly girds himself.*

The curses which surround the wicked will resemble large garments. A person wearing large, flowing robes must gird himself with a tight belt in order to draw in his skirts. Similarly, the curses will cling tightly and relentlessly to the body of the wicked man (*Malbim*).

20. זֹאת פְּעֻלַּת שֹׂטְנַי מֵאֵת ה׳ — *This is from HASHEM for the deed of my adversaries.*

The aforementioned curses are the just reward which my adversaries will receive for their evil accomplishments (*Radak*).

וְהַדֹּבְרִים רָע עַל נַפְשִׁי — *And those who speak evil against my soul.*

[They especially deserve curses because they spoke evil of me and cursed my soul.]

21. וְאַתָּה ה׳ אֲדֹנָי עֲשֵׂה אִתִּי לְמַעַן שְׁמֶךָ — *But You, HASHEM/ELOHIM, my Lord, deal with me for Your Name's sake.*

Here the Divine Name is spelled יְ־הֹ־וִ־ה, the Holy Name that represents God as *the Dispenser of Mercy*, but it is vowelized with the vowels of אֱלֹהִים, the Holy Name that represents God as *the Dispenser of Strict Justice*. This alludes to David's request that God temper His strict justice with gentle kindness (*Chazah Zion*).

¹⁸ He donned curse as his garment,
and it came like water into his innards,
and like oil into his bones.
¹⁹ May it be to him like a garment
in which he wraps himself,
and a belt
with which he constantly girds himself.
²⁰ This is from HASHEM
for the deed of my adversaries,
and those who speak evil against my soul.
²¹ But You, HASHEM/ELOHIM, my Lord,
deal with me for Your Name's sake;
Because Your kindness is good — rescue me!
²² For poor and destitute am I,
and my heart is dead within me.
²³ Like a vanishing shadow, I am banished,

After David concludes his curses against the wicked, he prays that God bestow blessing and strength upon himself because he feels powerless in the presence of his foes (Ibn Ezra).

כִּי טוֹב חַסְדְּךָ הַצִּילֵנִי — Because Your kindness is good — rescue me!

Save me so that I may have the opportunity to study Your Torah and to perform mitzvos [and acts of charity and kindness] (Sforno).

22. כִּי עָנִי וְאֶבְיוֹן אָנֹכִי — For poor and destitute am I.

[Poor and destitute am I. In my situation, as a fugitive I can only take from others; I have nothing to give. What can I contribute to society if I am barred from the company of my fellow countrymen? Indeed, the poor man is considered to be dead (Nedarim 64b), and I must continue to endure this gruesome, living death.]

וְלִבִּי חָלַל בְּקִרְבִּי — And my heart is dead within me.

[In truth, there was a Divine purpose for David's poverty and suffering, because his pain and sorrow subdued the intensity of his evil inclination. Furthermore, David's ordeal filled him with humility. Gone were his rash pride and strong self-confidence (Chidah; AriZal). Now he fully realized that he depended on God for every breath of life and each precious heartbeat.]

The Talmud (Bava Basra 17a) states that three righteous men were so strong that their evil inclination had no influence over them: Abraham, Isaac, and Jacob. Some Rabbis add David to this list, because David said, My heart [i.e., my evil inclination] is dead within me. However, others disagree, contending that in this verse David literally meant that his heart was deadened with pain because of his sorrows and travails.[1]

23. כְּצֵל כִּנְטוֹתוֹ נֶהֱלָכְתִּי — Like a vanishing shadow, I am banished.

When the sun is high in the sky, its

1. The Talmud (Avodah Zarah 4b) apparently follows the opinion that David did subdue his evil inclination. It states that David's sin with Bath Sheba was completely incompatible with

כד נִגְעַרְתִּי כָאַרְבֶּה: בִּרְכַּי כָּשְׁלוּ מִצּוֹם וּבְשָׂרִי

כה כָּחַשׁ מִשָּׁמֶן: וַאֲנִי | הָיִיתִי חֶרְפָּה לָהֶם

כו יִרְאוּנִי יְנִיעוּן רֹאשָׁם: עָזְרֵנִי יְהוָה אֱלֹהָי

כז הוֹשִׁיעֵנִי כְחַסְדֶּךָ: וְיֵדְעוּ כִּי־יָדְךָ זֹּאת אַתָּה

כח יְהוָה עֲשִׂיתָהּ: יְקַלְלוּ־הֵמָּה וְאַתָּה תְבָרֵךְ

כט קָמוּ | וַיֵּבֹשׁוּ וְעַבְדְּךָ יִשְׂמָח: יִלְבְּשׁוּ שׂוֹטְנַי

ל כְּלִמָּה וְיַעֲטוּ כַמְעִיל בָּשְׁתָּם: אוֹדֶה יְהוָה

לא מְאֹד בְּפִי וּבְתוֹךְ רַבִּים אֲהַלְלֶנּוּ: כִּי־יַעֲמֹד

לִימִין אֶבְיוֹן לְהוֹשִׁיעַ מִשֹּׁפְטֵי נַפְשׁוֹ:

---

rays cast shadows; but as it descends and sets, the shadows begin to lengthen and to vanish until they are completely swallowed by the darkness (*Rashi; Radak*).

The days of my life are swiftly passing and vanishing into nothingness (*Ibn Ezra*).

נִגְעַרְתִּי כָאַרְבֶּה — *I am stirred up like a locust.*

For as long as Saul pursues me, I must run from one hideout to another, and I have no security or rest! Thus, I resemble the scavenging locust which has no permanent nest (*Rashi; Ibn Ezra; Radak*).

24. בִּרְכַּי כָּשְׁלוּ מִצּוֹם — *My knees totter from fasting.*

When David fled from Saul, he abstained from food so that God would notice his suffering and take pity on him. Lack of nutrition drained David of his strength and he could not walk (*Radak*).

וּבְשָׂרִי כָּחַשׁ מִשָּׁמֶן — *And my flesh is lean without fat.*

Fasting and incessant travel as a fugitive robbed my flesh of its fat, and I am now merely skin and bones (*Radak*).

25. וַאֲנִי הָיִיתִי חֶרְפָּה לָהֶם יִרְאוּנִי יְנִיעוּן רֹאשָׁם — *And I have become a disgrace to them, they see me and shake their heads.*

When my enemies saw how thin and emaciated I became, they mocked me and shook their heads as a sign of scorn and derision (*Ibn Ezra; Radak*).

26. עָזְרֵנִי ה' אֱלֹהַי הוֹשִׁיעֵנִי כְחַסְדֶּךָ — *Help me, HASHEM, my God, save me according to Your kindness!*

You have displayed kindness to many others and even to me, on many occasions. Please save me now in accordance with Your long, tradition of kindness (*Radak*).

27. וְיֵדְעוּ כִּי יָדְךָ זֹּאת אַתָּה ה' עֲשִׂיתָהּ — *Let them know that this is Your hand, that You, HASHEM, have acted.*

---

his exalted stature, because he himself testified, "*And my heart is dead within me*" [i.e., I rule over my evil inclination and I am in control of my passions (*Rashi*)].

However, even the most self-disciplined person cannot subdue his evil inclination without Divine assistance, because this inclination is such a potent, relentless spiritual force [see *Kiddushin* 30b]. God did not help David to overcome his passion in the incident of Bath Sheba (*Maharsha, Avodah Zarah* 4b). Ordinarily, David deserved Divine assistance, but in this instance God allowed David to sin so that his subsequent repentance would serve as an inspiration to other sinners. If they become discouraged and despair of atonement, we remind them that when David repented fully, his sin was completely forgiven and erased. He returned to God's good graces like an innocent babe!

> *I am stirred up like a locust.*
>

²⁴ *My knees totter from fasting,*
> *and my flesh is lean without fat.*

²⁵ *And I have become a disgrace to them,*
> *they see me and shake their heads.*

²⁶ *Help me, HASHEM, my God,*
> *save me according to Your kindness!*

²⁷ *Let them know that this is Your hand,*
> *that You, HASHEM, have acted.*

²⁸ *Let them curse, but You will bless.*
> *They rose up, but they will be shamed —*
> *and Your servant will rejoice!*

²⁹ *May my adversaries be clothed in humiliation,*
> *and may they wrap themselves in their shame*
> *as in a cloak.*

³⁰ *I will thank HASHEM exceedingly with my mouth,*
> *and amid the multitude I will praise Him.*

³¹ *For He stands at the right of the destitute,*
> *to save him from condemners of his soul.*

Let everyone know clearly, beyond any doubt, that my success is entirely because of You. Let no one attribute my victory to my own power or brilliance, for You alone *have acted* (*Radak*).

28. וִיקַלְלוּ הֵמָּה וְאַתָּה תְבָרֵךְ — *Let them curse, but You will bless.*

Although my enemies curse me I have no fear, because I am confident that Your blessings will protect me (*Radak*).

קָמוּ וַיֵּבֹשׁוּ וְעַבְדְּךָ יִשְׂמָח — *They rose up, but they will be shamed — and Your servant will rejoice!*

They plotted against me but their schemes will be foiled when they *arise to* execute them. At that time, I, *your servant, shall rejoice* (*Radak*).

29. וְלָבְּשׁוּ שׂוֹטְנַי כְּלִמָּה — *May my adversaries be clothed in humiliation.*

... when they see that their plot has been foiled (*Radak*).

וְיַעֲטוּ כַמְעִיל בָּשְׁתָּם — *And may they wrap themselves in their shame as in a cloak.*

Just as *a cloak* covers every inch of the body, may they be completely covered with *shame*, so that nothing honorable or respectable remains of them (*Radak*).

30. אוֹדֶה ה' מְאֹד בְּפִי — *I will thank HASHEM exceedingly with my mouth.*

[When God saves me, I shall not hide the great event.]

וּבְתוֹךְ רַבִּים אֲהַלְלֶנּוּ — *And amid the multitude I will praise Him.*

I will take pains to publicize the fact that it is You, O God, who deserves all the credit for my victories, not I (*Radak*).

31. כִּי יַעֲמֹד לִימִין אֶבְיוֹן — *For He stands at the right of the destitute.*

The poor and defenseless man who places all of his trust in Hashem has nothing to fear, for Hashem will stand at his side to fight for him (Radak).

להושיע משפטי נפשו — To save him from condemners [lit. judges] of his soul.

The wicked condemn the righteous man to death, but God saves him from his assailants (Radak).

In these words, Alshich perceives an answer to that persistent question of why the righteous languish in exile. Why is an innocent man like David pursued and driven from his homeland?

The answer is that every sin which man commits creates an avenging, accusing angel which is destined to condemn him before the Heavenly Tribunal. The suffering of exile inspires the fugitive to repent and to call upon God to be at his right hand. This merit will save the persecuted exile from the angels which condemn him.

Midrash Shocher Tov *interprets this psalm as a hymn of gratitude which God recited to Abraham. God speaks to Abraham and calls him, "My master!" The* Midrash *explains: Rabbi Reuven said: The nations were in a slumber that prevented them from coming under the wing of God's Presence. Who aroused them to come? Abraham! ... the concept of kindness was also asleep, and Abraham aroused it, for he opened an inn and invited passersby to share his table.*

God Himself was indebted to Abraham because until Abraham proclaimed God as Master, the purpose of Creation had been frustrated. God created the universe so that man could perceive Him and appreciate His works. Until Abraham's time, however, the world failed to achieve its purpose, because men were oblivious of God. By teaching the world to recognize God, Abraham gave meaning to existence. In a sense, therefore, Abraham became the master of the world, for it owed its continued existence to him.

God also called Abraham My master, because Abraham had presented God with a gift that He, despite His infinite power, could not have fashioned for Himself. Because man is a creature of free will, even God cannot guarantee that man will choose good over evil and truth over falsehood. By dint of his indomitable faith, Abraham presented God with the heart and minds of mankind, to whom he had revealed the essence of the Divine. Abraham's mission was continued by David, and it will be completed by the Messiah. This psalm is dedicated to these three pillars of Jewish tradition. [See Overview to Artscroll Bereishis, *vol. II, p. 375.]*

א לְדָוִד מִזְמוֹר נְאֻם יהוה | לַאדֹנִי שֵׁב לִימִינִי
ב עַד־אָשִׁית אֹיְבֶיךָ הֲדֹם לְרַגְלֶיךָ: מַטֵּה עֻזְּךָ
ג יִשְׁלַח יהוה מִצִּיּוֹן רְדֵה בְּקֶרֶב אֹיְבֶיךָ: עַמְּךָ
נְדָבֹת בְּיוֹם חֵילֶךָ בְּהַדְרֵי־קֹדֶשׁ מֵרֶחֶם
מִשְׁחָר לְךָ טַל יַלְדֻתֶיךָ

1. לְדָוִד מִזְמוֹר נְאֻם ה׳ לַאדֹנִי — *Of David — a song. The words of HASHEM: To My master.*

Rashi cites the opinion of the Rabbis that Hashem addressed these words to the Patriarch Abraham. Abraham was universally recognized as *master of the world,* because he taught everyone that God alone is the true Master [see *Berachos 7b*: Rabbi Shimon bar Yochai taught: From the day of Creation there was no person who called the Holy One, Blessed is He, אָדוֹן, *Master,* until our forefather Abraham came and called God אָדוֹן (see Prefatory Remarks)].

The height of Abraham's mastery came when he defeated the four powerful kings who threatened to obliterate him and the truth which he taught to the world [see *Genesis 14*] (*Radak*).

The *Talmud* (*Sanhedrin 108b*) relates that Shem, son of Noah, once met Eliezer, the servant of Abraham, and asked him, "When all the kings of the east and of the west attacked you, how did you defend yourselves?"

Eliezer replied, "The Holy One, Blessed is He, snatched Abraham and placed him at His right side. We threw dust at the enemy and it turned into swords; we threw stones at the enemy and they became arrows" (see *Yad Ramah* and *Rif's* commentary on *Ein Yaakov, Sanhedrin 108b*).

Ibn Ezra attributes this psalm to David's devoted soldiers. As he became older and weaker, they feared for his safety in battle, and demanded that he wait in his palace while they went forth to subdue his enemies.

They felt that if David were to stay behind, immersed in Torah study and fervent prayer, then certainly Hashem

would be the right hand, i.e., the champion of the armies of Israel (see *Malbim*).

שֵׁב לִימִינִי — *Wait* [literally, *sit*] *at My right.*

Hashem said to Abraham: "Your efforts and prowess are unnecessary in this campaign. Sit back and wait for me to vanquish the enemy" (*Rashi*).

According to *Malbim,* God proclaims that it is He, not David, who truly sits on the royal throne of Israel and controls the nation's destiny. Thus God commanded David to sit at His side and to recognize that he, the mortal king, is merely God's assistant.

Midrash Shocher Tov and *Targum* interpret יְמִינִי as a reference to King Saul of the Tribe of בִּנְיָמִין, *Benjamin.* Saul was called יְמִינִי (see commentary to 7:1 and *Moed Kattan 16b*).

God sent Samuel the Prophet to anoint David while Saul still reigned, and the reign of a new king cannot encroach upon the reign of the previous king. Therefore, Hashem said to David, "Wait for Saul, the יְמִינִי, *Benjaminite,* to complete his reign. You, David, will inherit his throne because you are immersed in the study of Torah which was given to Israel by יְמִינִי, *My right hand* [see *Deuteronomy 33:2*]."

Radak quotes *Ibn Ezra's* assertion that immediately after David assumed his throne, he was attacked by the Philistines. [See comm. to 2:1.] He maintains that God renewed David's confidence and resolve with the reassurance expressed in this psalm.

עַד אָשִׁית אֹיְבֶיךָ הֲדֹם לְרַגְלֶיךָ — *Until I make your enemies a stool for your feet.*

Sforno says that this psalm is dedicated to the future King Messiah.

110
1-3
Of David — a song.

The words of HASHEM:
To My master, wait at My right;
    until I make your enemies a stool for your feet.
² The staff of your strength
    will HASHEM dispatch from Zion.
    Rule amid your enemies!
³ Your nation volunteered
    on the day of your campaign,
because of your majestic sanctity

He is on God's right hand and the ministering angels are on the left. The armies of Gog and Magog will attack, but Hashem will subdue them until they come crawling to the feet of the Messiah.

2. מַטֵּה עֻזְּךָ יִשְׁלַח ה' מִצִּיּוֹן — *The staff of your strength will HASHEM dispatch from Zion.*[1]

The מַטֶּה refers to bread, the *staff* of life (see 105:16). After Abraham and his men defeated the four kings, they were hungry and exhausted. Then, Malchizedek, king of [Jeru]salem [Zion], *brought out bread and wine (Genesis 14:19).*

This verse also refers to David, who captured Jerusalem in the beginning of his reign. This well fortified city became the staff of David's strength and sovereignty over the entire realm *(Radak).*

Zion was also the source of David's spiritual strength, for the Holy Ark rested there *(Ibn Ezra).* [The Psalmist alluded to this in 20:3: *May He dispatch your help from the Sanctuary, and support you from Zion.*]

רְדֵה בְּקֶרֶב אֹיְבֶיךָ — *Rule amid your enemies.*

[Jerusalem was originally the capital city of David's foes, an impregnable stronghold *in the midst of his enemies,* but God made it the center of David's kingdom.]

Radak comments that, at first, David ruled only the insignificant Philistine cities which were on his border. Later he penetrated into the *midst of the enemy* and captured the heartland of the Philistine nation.

3. עַמְּךָ נְדָבֹת בְּיוֹם חֵילֶךָ — *Your nation volunteered on the day of your campaign.*

When Abraham went out to battle the kings, *he armed his disciples who had been born in his house (Genesis 14:14).* Abraham did not need to coerce them to join his ranks, because his teachings had already imbued them with the Spirit of God; thus they were infused with the courage to confront even a large army *(Malbim, Genesis 14:14).*

Although Abraham had not sought the assistance of his allies Aner, Eshkol and Mamre, they loyally volunteered to

1. *Midrash Yelamdeinu* perceives this as a reference to the wooden staff which participated in many wondrous events throughout the course of Jewish history. This rod was first used by Jacob when he split the Jordan River *(Genesis 32:11).* Moses and Aaron used the same staff to perform wonders in Egypt before the eyes of Pharaoh *(Exodus 4:3; 7:10).* David held this staff in his hand when he went forth to battle Goliath *(I Samuel 17:40).* It served as a sceptre in the hands of each king of David's dynasty until the Temple was destroyed; then, the staff was hidden. In the future it will be revealed to the Messiah, who will use it to conquer all the nations of the world.

ד מִשְׁחָר לְךָ טַל יַלְדֻתֶךָ: נִשְׁבַּע יהוה | וְלֹא
יִנָּחֵם אַתָּה־כֹהֵן לְעוֹלָם עַל־דִּבְרָתִי מַלְכִּי־
ה צֶדֶק: אֲדֹנָי עַל־יְמֵינְךָ מָחַץ בְּיוֹם־אַפּוֹ

join his ranks (Rashi).

[Similarly, David's men were always willing to rally to his call. Not only were they glad to accept David's leadership, but as he grew older, they also volunteered to go out to battle, while he stayed behind in safety. The Messiah, too, will inspire the masses to enlist in his cause.]

מֵרֶחֶם מִשְׁחָר קֹדֶשׁ בְּהַדְרֵי — *Because of your majestic sanctity from the womb, from emergence.*

Abraham possessed a charismatic holiness that attracted the masses to monotheism. His charm was fresh and innocent because he recognized God when he was only three years old, virtually from the time of his *emergence from the womb.* The purity of Abraham's soul endowed him with an aura of *majestic sanctity* (Rashi).

Radak and *Ibn Ezra* render מִשְׁחָר, *from the dawn,* which is also a euphemism for birth. *Metzudos* renders *investigation,* referring to the fact that Abraham began to investigate God's will and way from his early childhood.

יַלְדֻתֶךָ טַל לְךָ — *You possess youthful innocence like fresh dew* [lit. *to you, dew of your youth*].

From his earliest youth, Abraham was innocent, kind, and gentle; he always desired to aid and sustain his fellow man. Thus, Abraham's kindness is compared to the soft *dew* which enables vegetation to flourish (Rashi).[1]

According to *Radak,* this phrase refers to David, whose monarchy had been destined from the very moment of his birth, from the time of his *youthful innocence.*

4. לְעוֹלָם כֹהֵן אַתָּה יִנָּחֵם וְלֹא ה' נִשְׁבַּע — *HASHEM has sworn and will not relent: "You shall be a priest forever ..."*

After Abraham was forced to slay the troops of the four kings, he was afraid that God would punish him for shedding blood. Therefore, Hashem reassured him, saying, *"Fear not, Abraham, I am your shield; your reward is very great"* (Genesis 15:1).

[Although a priest who has shed blood is normally disqualified from the priesthood (Berachos 32b; see Sotah 39a, Tosafos, s.v. מֵהֲדַר וּכִי) God promised Abraham that he himself would be a גָּדוֹל כֹּהֵן, *High Priest,* (Bereishis Rabbah 46:4) and that priests and kings would emanate from his seed (Rashi).

Radak perceives this as a reference to

---

1. The Midrash (Bereishis Rabbah 39:9) reads this verse as if the word עַמְּךָ, *your nation,* were vowelized עִמְּךָ, *with you,* i.e., I was with you when you volunteered. According to this interpretation, God was with Abraham when he chose to sanctify God's name by exposing the falseness of idol worship. This took place חֵילְךָ בְּיוֹם, *on the day of your masses,* i.e., the day on which all the legions and masses gathered to witness the execution of Abraham, the young heretic who had smashed his father's idols. The name of God was קֹדֶשׁ בְּהַדְרֵי, *sanctified with majesty,* when Abraham was willing to die for Him. But מֵרֶחֶם, *from the womb* of the earth [i.e., from the fiery furnace, which was in a deep pit], מִשְׁחָר, God *liberated* [שִׁחְרוּר] Abraham.

Although Abraham's miraculous rescue reflected the love which God bore him, Abraham was greatly troubled by the fact that he had served idols all the years prior to his discovery of God. But God consoled him, saying, יַלְדֻתֶךָ טַל לְךָ, *You possess youthful innocence like fresh dew,* for just as *dew* evaporates quickly, so had Abraham's sins evaporated without leaving the slightest trace on his soul.

4-5

from the womb, from emergence;
you possess youthful innocence
like fresh dew.

⁴ *HASHEM has sworn and will not relent:*
"You shall be a priest forever,
in accord with Malchizedek's word."

⁵ *My Lord is at your right,*
He crushes kings on the day of His fury.

David, for *II Samuel* 8:18 describes David's family in similar terms: וּבְנֵי דָוִד כֹּהֲנִים הָיוּ, *and the sons of David were priests* [i.e., ministers of state]. God promised David that his dynasty would endure forever, unlike Saul's [which was terminated].

עַל דִּבְרָתִי מַלְכִּי צֶדֶק — *"... in accord with Malchizedek's word."*

When Malchizedek went out to greet Abraham upon his return from battle, *Genesis* 14:18-20 states: *He* [Malchizedek] *was a priest of God, the Most High. He blessed him saying: "Blessed is Abram of God the Most High, Maker of heaven and earth; and blessed be God the Most High Who has delivered your foes into your hand."*

Rav Zechariah said on behalf of Rav Yishmael that the Holy One, Blessed is He, had intended that the priesthood should stem from Shem the son of Noah [who later assumed the title of Malchizedek]. But after Malchizedek uttered this blessing, God decided that the priesthood should stem from Abraham. For when Malchizedek blessed Abraham before God, Abraham had rebuked Malchizedek: "Should a servant's blessing be given precedence over his Master's?"

Therefore, God gave the priesthood to Abraham. *The words of HASHEM ... You shall be a priest forever because of the* דִּבְרַת, *words, of Malchizedek, who accorded Abraham precedence over Hashem.*

Therefore the verse reads (*Genesis* 14:18): *And 'he' was a priest of God the Most High, to indicate that he* [*Malchizedek*] *was a priest, but not his descendants* (*Nedarim* 32b).

Rabbi Moshe (quoted by *Ibn Ezra*) perceives this as a reference to David, who was מַלְכִּי צֶדֶק, literally *a king of righteousness,* for Scripture describes David as performing מִשְׁפָּט וּצְדָקָה, *justice and righteousness to all his people* (*II Samuel* 8:15).

5. אֲדֹנָי עַל יְמִינְךָ — *My Lord is at your right.*

Previously (*verse* 1), Abraham is described as sitting at God's right hand, with God, therefore, at Abraham's left. Now the Psalmist places God at Abraham's right hand. This alludes to the statement of *Yalkut Shimoni,* that, in the future, God will place the Messiah at His right hand and Abraham at His left. Abraham will protest, "Why is the Messiah, my descendant, privileged to sit, at Your right hand, while I sit at Your left?"

Then God will appease Abraham, saying, "Your descendant sits at My right hand, but I sit at *your* right hand."

מָחַץ בְּיוֹם אַפּוֹ מְלָכִים — *He crushes kings on the day of His fury.*

God destroyed the four kings who allied themselves against Abraham. This served as an example of what would happen to all monarchs who attacked Abraham's descendants (*Rashi*).

ו יָדִין בַּגּוֹיִם מָלֵא גְוִיּוֹת מָחַץ רֹאשׁ מְלָכִים:
ז עַל־אֶרֶץ רַבָּה: מִנַּחַל בַּדֶּרֶךְ יִשְׁתֶּה עַל־כֵּן
יָרִים רֹאשׁ:

6. יָדִין בַּגּוֹיִם מָלֵא גְוִיּוֹת — *He shall judge the corpse-filled nations.*

God will deal a stunning blow when He judges the nations which have attacked Israel, and the battlefield will be littered with their corpses (*Radak*).

This occurred already when the entire Egyptian army was drowned at the sea, for their corpses were washed upon the shore, where they lay ignominiously, for all to see (*Rashi*).

Midrash Yelamdeinu interprets this homiletically: the Rabbis taught that God remembers each Jewish soul murdered by Esau and by the gentiles. God dips His regal mantle into the blood of the innocent victims until the entire garment is dyed blood red. When the Final Day of Judgment arrives, God will cloak Himself in this mantle, which will reflect the face of each of these righteous victims.

At that time, the blood of the gentile murderers will be shed and will flow in huge rivers. The scavenging fowl will come to drink from the flowing river

(verse 7), but the turbulent river will make bloody waves, and the bird will raise his head and fly to safety.

מָחַץ רֹאשׁ עַל אֶרֶץ רַבָּה — *He shall crush the leader of the mighty land.*

This translation follows *Rashi*, who renders רֹאשׁ as *head* of state. Thus it alludes to the king and specifically to Pharaoh; אֶרֶץ רַבָּה, literally *great land*, refers to Egypt, which was then the most powerful empire.

Radak interprets רֹאשׁ literally as *head* or *skull*, and he sees רַבָּה, *many*, as modifying *head*. Thus, God will crush many heads to the ground.

Radak also mentions the opinion that רַבָּה, *Rabbah*, alludes to Rabat, the capital of Ammon, the site of a major campaign. According to this view, David composed this psalm at the time of that military action [see *Malbim*].

7. מִנַּחַל בַּדֶּרֶךְ יִשְׁתֶּה — *From a river along the way he shall drink.*

So many corpses lay bleeding on the battlefield that a river of blood began to

⁶ *He shall judge the corpse-filled nations,*
   He shall crush the leader of the mighty land.
⁷ *From a river along the way he shall drink,*
   therefore he may proudly lift his head.

flow from the site. The phrase *he drinks* is a metaphor for victory (*Radak*).

Ibn Ezra comments that these words indicate that the army of the righteous will be extraordinarily large, for ordinarily an invading army can rely on cisterns and wells for its water supply, but this army will be so vast that it will be forced to march near a flowing river to assure its men ample water.

According to *Rashi*, this is a description of the Egyptian empire, which derived its fabulous wealth from the great Nile River. Egypt lifted up her head in pride on account of the Nile, but God crushed her to the ground.

[This punishment is measure for measure. The river was the source of the prosperity which fostered Egypt's arrogance. Therefore, the river will be the site of Egypt's downfall.]

עַל כֵּן יָרִים רֹאשׁ — *Therefore he may proudly lift his head.*

According to *Targum*, this verse

describes the ultimate victory for which all men of faith yearn, because Abraham, David, and the Messiah do not seek blood, but truth. It is destined that a prophet will arise from whom wisdom will gush as water gushes from a flowing river. His teaching will inspire men to lift their heads with a sense of spiritual triumph as they enter God's presence.

[The prophet (*Isaiah* 12:2-6) foretells the triumphant song of the future: *Behold! God is my salvation! I will trust and not be afraid, for God is my strength and my song, He is also my salvation ... And on that day you shall say, "Give thanks to HASHEM, call upon His Name, declare His deeds among the nations, pronounce that His Name is exalted. Sing to HASHEM, for He has done splendid things, this is known throughout the earth. Cry out and shout joyously, You dweller of Zion, for great is the Holy One of Israel in Your midst.*]

Sforno explains that this psalm is a sermon exhorting the common Jew to devote time to Torah study. Usually, simple and uneducated people offer two excuses for their neglect of Torah: they claim that the subject matter is too difficult for them and that their preoccupation with the pursuit of a livelihood leaves them no time for study.

In answer to these claims, the Psalmist responds that Israel is deeply indebted to God for all His kindness. The man who is sincerely grateful to the Almighty yearns to thank HASHEM wholeheartedly (v. 1). The only way to demonstrate this thanks is to study His word in order to fathom His will. If a person dedicates all his heart to comprehend God's will, then no obstacle can deter him! Every person can find some time for Torah and learn to appreciate its lessons.

This truth is the סוֹד, counsel, of the יְשָׁרִים, upright, who have dedicated themselves to Torah, which the Psalmist now communicates to the עֵדָה, congregation (verse 1).

In conclusion, the Psalmist offers the masses the following advice on how to embark on the pursuit of wisdom: The beginning of wisdom is the fear of HASHEM, good understanding to all their [the mitzvos] practitioners (verse 10). If man is determined to fear Hashem and to practice His mitzvos, then the highest heavens are within his reach!

א הַלְלוּיָהּ | אוֹדֶה יהוה בְּכָל־לֵבָב בְּסוֹד
ב יְשָׁרִים וְעֵדָה: גְּדֹלִים מַעֲשֵׂי יהוה דְּרוּשִׁים
ג לְכָל־חֶפְצֵיהֶם: הוֹד־וְהָדָר פָּעֳלוֹ וְצִדְקָתוֹ

1. הַלְלוּיָהּ — *Praise God!*

Literally this means הַלְלוּ, *praise*, יָהּ, *YAH*. There is a great debate as to whether this is considered as one long word or as two separate words. The matter is not merely academic, for if it is one word, then Jewish Law requires that both syllables be written together on the same line [there is no hyphenation in Scrolls of Scripture]; in addition, the entire word takes on special sanctity, because it contains God's Holy Name. If it is two separate words, however, it may be written on two separate lines if necessary, and only the Name itself is sacred (see *Pesachim* 117a and *Minchas Shai*).

The *Talmud* (*Pesachim* 117a) notes that throughout the *Book of Psalms*, the Psalmist uses ten different terms to express praise for God. These include such words as נָגוּן, מִזְמוֹר, שִׁיר, תְּהִלָּה, נִצּוּחַ. However, the most potent and meaningful expression of praise is הַלְלוּיָהּ, because it is composed of two elements: שֵׁם, a combination of a Divine Name and וְשֶׁבַח בְּבַת אַחַת, a term of praise.

Midrash Shocher Tov notes that only the abbreviated form of the Holy name, יָהּ, *YAH*, appears in הַלְלוּיָהּ. This suggests that Hashem's Name is incomplete in עוֹלָם הַזֶּה, *This World*, because mankind is not able to recognize Hashem's complete glory. Similarly, the entire *Book of Psalms* concludes with the words, כֹּל הַנְּשָׁמָה תְּהַלֵּל יָהּ הַלְלוּיָהּ, *The entire soul will praise, YAH!, Praise God!* (150:6). Only in the future world will God's Name be complete; then He will be fully praised.

Rashi and *Radak* point out that the initial letters of the stiches of this psalm [after the first word הַלְלוּיָהּ] follow the sequence of the *Aleph-Beis*, the Hebrew

alphabet. This order indicates that this composition serves as a progressive guide to attaining the truth. Step by step, the novice is initiated into ever higher levels of wisdom (see *Prefatory Remarks*).

אוֹדֶה ה׳ בְּכָל לֵבָב — *I shall thank HASHEM wholeheartedly.*

Wholeheartedly means with all the concentration and feeling which I can muster (*Radak*).

The Psalmist uses the word לֵבָב for *heart* [with a double ב] rather than לֵב, [with a single ב] in order to indicate that two forces, the evil inclination and the good inclination, struggle for mastery of the heart. The person who sincerely strives to give thanks to Hashem will find the way to harness both inner forces to serve his Creator (*Alshich; Ibn Yachya*).

בְּסוֹד יְשָׁרִים וְעֵדָה — *In the counsel* [lit. *the secret] of the upright and the congregation.*

The upright are the select scholars who have attained the highest levels of wisdom and have perfected their character in accordance with the lofty teachings of Torah. They have been initiated into the סוֹד, *counsel*, of Divinity. *The congregation* refers to the novices who come to centers of Torah study to embark upon a program of instruction (*Sforno*).

[The Psalmist encourages those who teach Torah to appreciate the potential of every student, no matter how ignorant he appears to be, because Israel in its entirety is described as a nation of יְשָׁרִים, *upright* scholars (*Numbers* 23:10; see *Radak*). The secret belongs to everyone. If a conscientious teacher bears this in mind even when teaching beginners, he will motivate his classes in

*P*raise God! I shall thank HASHEM wholeheartedly,
in the counsel of the upright
and the congregation.
² *Great are the accomplishments of HASHEM,*
accessible to all who want them.
³ *Majestic and splendid is His work,*

---

the direction of achieving excellence at some point in their academic careers.][1]

2. 'גְדֹלִים מַעֲשֵׂי ה — *Great are the accomplishments of HASHEM.*

[The serious student of creation may view the work of the Creator from one of two possible vantage points:

The world can be analyzed and evaluated in a scientific manner which only pays attention to the physical data which is visible to the viewer. The detached observer of cold, hard facts is oblivious to the broad Divine design which is imprinted on all natural phenomena.

Or, nature can be researched and appreciated by men of religion who discern the intangible but very real spiritual dimension of every creature and appreciate the universal pattern and harmony which unites the vast panorama of Creation. Only the Torah student who has learnt how to identify the signature of Hashem which is inscribed upon every molecule and atom of the universe can exclaim, "Great are the accomplishments of HASHEM!"]

דְּרוּשִׁים לְכָל חֶפְצֵיהֶם — *Accessible to all who want them.*

It is paradoxical that although the *accomplishments* of God are great, even

the simplest person can attain an awareness of God's Omnipotence. All that is necessary is a genuine *desire* to find God (*Radak*).

After a person studies the world from a Torah perspective, he finds such study to be the most sublime of all pleasures. As King Solomon said (*Proverbs* 8:11), *For wisdom is better than pearls and all that can be desired cannot be compared to it* (*Rashi*).

3. הוֹד וְהָדָר פָּעֳלוֹ — *Majestic and splendid is His work.*

Malbim differentiates between Hashem's מַעֲשֶׂה, *accomplishment* (v. 2), and His פְּעֻלָּה, *work.* The former term refers to a completed project, whereas the latter term describes an ongoing activity. God's creation can be considered an *accomplishment* because He completed everything during the first six days, in the sense that nothing new has been created since that time. However, if God had then abandoned His creation, it would have collapsed instantaneously. Thus, sustaining the creation can be viewed as God's *work.*

Malbim concludes that הוֹד, *majesty,* refers to the inner beauty of the world, while הָדָר, *splendor,* describes its external brilliance. Both aspects are to be found in God's works.

---

1. The Rosh Yeshiva of Telshe, *Rav Yoseif Leib Bloch,* זצ״ל, was a renowned orator who would often address the general public on very lofty themes. Once when a devoted disciple complained that Rabbi Bloch's speech was over the heads of his audience, he replied, "I am not speaking to their bodies, I am addressing myself to their souls! Since the souls of all Jews were present at Sinai when God revealed His secret to His chosen people, these Jewish souls are capable of understanding far more than I can teach them. Why should I aim my address at their present intellectual level when I can try to stimulate them to realize their full potential, by speaking to their noble, lofty souls?"

ד עֹמֶדֶת לָעַד: זֵכֶר עָשָׂה לְנִפְלְאֹתָיו חַנּוּן
ה וְרַחוּם יְהֹוָה: טֶרֶף נָתַן לִירֵאָיו יִזְכֹּר לְעוֹלָם
ו בְּרִיתוֹ: כֹּחַ מַעֲשָׂיו הִגִּיד לְעַמּוֹ לָתֵת לָהֶם

וְצִדְקָתוֹ עֹמֶדֶת לָעַד — *And His righteousness endures forever.*

Because the Creator is righteous, He steadfastly adheres to His commitment to maintain the basic laws of nature which will endure forever (*Malbim*).

4. זֵכֶר עָשָׂה לְנִפְלְאֹתָיו — *He made a memorial for His wonders.*

The Jewish calendar is studded with dates which commemorate the works of God. God sanctified the Sabbath as a testimony to His creation in seven days and He consecrated the festivals to celebrate the wonders which He wrought for the Jews. Moreover, each commandment stands for an aspect of God's *work* in the world (*Rashi*).

In particular, many festivals and *mitzvos* serve as a means by which to remember the wondrous works which God performed in Egypt (*Radak*).

חַנּוּן וְרַחוּם ה׳ — *Compassionate and merciful is HASHEM.*

[After the Jews sinned with the Golden Calf, God taught the *Thirteen Attributes of Divine Mercy* to Moses (*Exodus* 34:6-7). In that instance the attribute רַחוּם, *Merciful,* preceded חַנּוּן, *Compassionate.* Tosafos (*Rosh Hashanah* 17b, *gloss*) explains this order. The term רַחוּם refers to *mercy* of a relatively mild intensity, whereas חַנּוּן is much stronger *compassion.*] The reversed order of these attributes as given in this verse can be understood in light of *Malbim's* commentary:

Both God's *compassion* and His *mercy* led Him to perform wondrous works for the enslaved Jews in Egypt. The root of חַנּוּן is חֵן, *charm* or *favor.* This attribute stems from the *favor* which the Patriarchs found in God's eyes, for He promised that He would later release the Jews from bondage for the Patriarchs' sake. When the actual oppression and torture began, however,

God also had רַחֲמָנוּת, *mercy,* on the downtrodden Jews. [Thus, in this case, God's compassion preceded His mercy.]

5. טֶרֶף נָתַן לִירֵאָיו — *He provided food for those who fear Him.*

The word טֶרֶף means *food* or *supplies* as in *Proverbs* 30:8. When the Jews left Egypt, God supplied them with the Egyptians' wealth and the nation was emptied of her riches. They received these riches because God *eternally remembers His covenant* with the Patriarch Abraham. In the בְּרִית בֵּין הַבְּתָרִים, *Covenant Between the Parts* (*Genesis* 15:14), God had promised the Patriarch that at the conclusion of the Egyptian bondage *they* (Israel) *shall leave with great possessions* (*Radak*).

[The Psalmist here employs the uncommon term טֶרֶף rather than the usual word מָזוֹן, *food.* טֶרֶף refers to the predatory beast's manner of feeding itself by snatching and ripping apart its prey (see *Exodus* 22:32). נָתַן, literally *he gave,* implies that they did not snatch but passively accepted what was offered to them. The juxtaposition of טֶרֶף נָתַן, *that which was snatched he gave,* seems paradoxical. The combination alludes to the violent, forceful plagues that God brought upon the Egyptians to shatter their spirits until they gladly gave gold and silver vessels to the departing Jews. Thus, טֶרֶף denotes the plagues whereas נָתַן refers to that which the Egyptians gave peacefully to the Jews (see *R' Hirsch*).]

יִזְכֹּר לְעוֹלָם בְּרִיתוֹ — *He eternally remembers His covenant.*

The *Zohar (Parashas Emor)* points out that God forged another eternal *covenant* with the dedicated Torah scholars who study the Divine word day and night. Since diligence and devotion in Torah study signify that the student sincerely *fears* God, he is therefore

and His righteousness endures forever.

⁴ *He made a memorial for His wonders,*
compassionate and merciful is HASHEM.

⁵ *He provided food for those who fear Him,*
He eternally remembers His covenant.

⁶ *The strength of His deeds*
He declared to His nation,
to give them the heritage of the peoples.

---

guaranteed that God will provide *food* for him.

Indeed, *Megalleh Amukos* notes that the entire world is supplied with food only in the merit of the God-fearing Torah scholar. The *Talmud* (*Taanis* 10a) states: The entire world is sustained with food by virtue of God's son, [the scholar] Rabbi Chanina ben Dosa, and [yet] Rabbi Chanina himself eats no more than a small measure of carob fruit all week!

6. בֹּחַ מֵעֲשָׂיו הִגִּיד לְעַמּוֹ — *The strength of His deeds He declared to His nation.*

[The wondrous events which accompanied the Exodus from Egypt were truly impressive, yet they were not God's most powerful accomplishment. At creation, God designated every area of the globe for a specific nation, and as each nation developed, it flourished on its native soil and became firmly rooted in the land. The nation of Egypt developed where it was supposed to, in the land of Egypt; the nation of Israel did not belong there. Thus, Israel's presence on foreign Egyptian soil was most unnatural. The Exodus, then, represented a restoration of the normal state, for the Egyptian people remained where they belonged and the Israelites were removed from a land where they did not belong.

However, the Jewish occupation of the Land of Canaan triggered a tremendous upheaval. Seven great nations had developed in Canaan, yet God suddenly cast them from their native soil and replaced them with

Israel, an alien nation. The Jewish conquerors of Canaan were comparatively few in number and possessed neither military training nor equipment. Their miraculous conquest of Canaan truly demonstrated *the strength of his deeds*.]

Moreover, *Radak* observes that long before the conquest, God *declared* that He would drive the Canaanites out of the land [because their abominable behavior was totally incongruous with the sacred nature of the Holy Land]. God purposely made this public declaration so that the entire world would recognize that His strength was solely responsible for the Jews' victory; their success could not be ascribed to blind fate.

The *Midrash* (*Bamidbar Rabbah* 23:11) relates that the Holy One, Blessed is He, said to the Children of Israel, ''I could easily have created a new homeland for you, a glorious uninhabited land which you could have occupied without contention or combat. Yet, I specifically assigned you the Land of Canaan, where your settlement would be vigorously challenged. I did this so that I could perform miracles for you and show the world *the strength of* [My] *deeds* on your behalf!''

לָתֵת לָהֶם נַחֲלַת גּוֹיִם — *To give them the heritage of the peoples.*

[This verse serves as the theme of *Rashi's* introduction to his commentary on the Torah.]

Rav Yitzchak noted that since the Torah is a book of law, one might think

ז נַחֲלַת גּוֹיִם: מַעֲשֵׂי יָדָיו אֱמֶת וּמִשְׁפָּט
ח נֶאֱמָנִים כָּל-פִּקּוּדָיו: סְמוּכִים לָעַד לְעוֹלָם
ט עֲשׂוּיִם בֶּאֱמֶת וְיָשָׁר | פְּדוּת | שָׁלַח לְעַמּוֹ
    צִוָּה-לְעוֹלָם בְּרִיתוֹ קָדוֹשׁ וְנוֹרָא שְׁמוֹ:
י   רֵאשִׁית חָכְמָה | יִרְאַת יְהֹוָה שֵׂכֶל טוֹב לְכָל-
    עֹשֵׂיהֶם תְּהִלָּתוֹ עֹמֶדֶת לָעַד:

that it should have begun with, *This month shall be to you the first of the months* (Exodus 12:2), for that verse contained the first commandment given to all Israel. Why, then, did the Torah begin with the narrative of Creation, which is a statement of history rather than of law?

Rav Yitzchak explains: The reason is to establish the highest of all laws, the sovereignty of God over the earth. *The strength of His deeds He declared to His nation, to give them the heritage of the peoples.* If the nations accuse Israel of banditry, of having illegitimately seized the lands of the seven nations of Canaan, Israel will tell them: "The entire universe belongs to God. He created it and He granted its territory to whomever He deemed fit. It was His desire to give it to them, and it was later His desire to take it from them and grant it to us" (see *Tanchuma Parashas Bereishis*).

Rav Eliyahu Meir Bloch, צ״ל, of Telshe explains that *Rav Yitzchak* does not mean to say that this argument will convince the gentiles of the legitimacy of the Jewish claim to *Eretz Yisrael,* for just as they deny the authenticity of the entire Torah, they will deny this truth. Rather, this argument was meant to reinforce the resolve and the faith of the Jews themselves. If the Jews waver and question their own right to dispossess the gentiles who have lived on the holy soil for centuries and millennia, they need merely study the very first verse of the Torah to find the Divine manifesto which declares God's authority to

bequeath the Holy Land to His chosen people!

7. מַעֲשֵׂי יָדָיו אֱמֶת וּמִשְׁפָּט — *His handiwork is truth and justice.*

Let no man say that when God dispossessed the seven nations from the Land of Canaan, He acted with ruthless, lawless hate. For God's accomplishments in Canaan were true and just. He was true to His word to Abraham, for God had promised the Patriarch that his children would inherit Canaan (*Genesis* 17:8). God also meted out justice to the depraved inhabitants of Canaan. They could not possibly have been permitted to remain in the Holy Land, for they were engaged in vile abominations which caused the sanctified soil to repel them (*Radak*).

נֶאֱמָנִים כָּל פִּקּוּדָיו — *Faithful are all His orders.*

Just as there is no question as to the *truth and justice* of God's actions in Canaan, so is there no doubt that God is always faithful in His words and deeds (*Radak*).

8. סְמוּכִים לָעַד לְעוֹלָם — *They are steadfast forever, for eternity* [or, *for the world*].

God provided סְמִיכָה, *firm support,* for the dictates of the Torah with many warnings and with punishment for *those* who transgress (*Rashi*).

The Torah is the *raison d'etre* of the world and the firm support for its continued existence. Thus, סְמוּכִים לָעַד, they [Torah words] *are steadfast forever,* לְעוֹלָם, *for the world* (*Malbim*).

⁷ His handiwork is truth and justice,
  faithful are all His orders.
⁸ They are steadfast forever, for eternity,
  accomplished in truth and fairness.
⁹ He sent redemption to His nation,
  He commanded His covenant for eternity;
  holy and awesome is His Name.
¹⁰ The beginning of wisdom is the fear of HASHEM —
  good understanding to all their practitioners.
  His praise endures forever.

עָשׂוּים בֶּאֱמֶת וְיָשָׁר — *Accomplished in truth and fairness.*

One can totally rely on the dictates of the Torah and base his entire life on them, because, when done in uprightness and truth, the dictates of the Torah are impervious to the vicissitudes of time (*Ibn Ezra*).

9. פְּדוּת שָׁלַח לְעַמּוֹ צִוָּה לְעוֹלָם בְּרִיתוֹ — *He sent redemption to His nation, He commanded His covenant for eternity.*

God redeemed His nation from the bondage of Egypt in order to give them the Torah and strike a covenant with them, as *Exodus* 34:27 states: *Based on these words* [of Torah], *I have made a covenant with you* (*Sforno*).

קָדוֹשׁ וְנוֹרָא שְׁמוֹ — *Holy and awesome is His Name.*

God formed an eternal covenant to elevate Israel above other nations because God Himself is holy and far removed from profanity, as *Leviticus* 11:44-45 teaches: *You shall sanctify yourselves and you shall be holy for I am HASHEM who brought you out of the land of Egypt to*

be your God. You shall therefore be holy, for I am holy (*Radak*).

10. רֵאשִׁית חָכְמָה יִרְאַת ה' — *The beginning of wisdom is the fear of HASHEM.*

[All Torah study is oriented towards one goal: gaining a genuine and sincere fear of Hashem. This fact is repeated often throughout Scripture. King Solomon emphasized it in *Proverbs* 1:7: יִרְאַת ה' רֵאשִׁית דָּעַת, *The fear of HASHEM is the beginning of knowledge*, and he repeated it in *Proverbs* 9:10: תְּחִלַּת חָכְמָה יִרְאַת ה', *The beginning of wisdom is the fear of HASHEM*. (See *Malbim's* commentary on *Genesis* 1:1 for an explanation of the difference between רֵאשִׁית and תְּחִלָּה).]

The Sages say (*Avos* 3:9): When a scholar gives precedence to fear of God over the pursuit of wisdom, his wisdom will endure, but when his pursuit of wisdom takes precedence over his fear of God, his wisdom will not endure.[1]

Radak describes the procedure by which a person acquires the fear of God. The seeker of God must divorce himself from the desires and values of this

---

1. The *Talmud* (*Shabbos* 31a-31b) explains the significance of the fear of God by means of parables:
   Isaiah 33:6 states, יִרְאַת ה' הִיא אוֹצָרוֹ, *the fear of HASHEM is its* [i.e., wisdom's] *storage-house*. This may be compared to the case in which a farmer told his worker to store a measure of grain in his warehouse. Later, the farmer asked, "Did you remember to mix some preservatives into the grain, to guard it from rot?" When the worker admitted that he had not, the farmer told him, "It would have been better if you had not stored the grain in the first

mundane world and concentrate on Divine, spiritual values. Only then will he truly be convinced that nothing matters or exists except God.

שֵׂכֶל טוֹב לְכָל עֹשֵׂיהֶם — *Good understanding to all their practitioners.*

I.e., those who pursue both fear of God and wisdom, as mentioned above, are rewarded with a proper understanding (*Radak*).

[Only those who recognize God's control over the world have a *good understanding* of reality, for those who are oblivious to God's providence are deluded and misguided. Those who practice God's *mitzvos* demonstrate that He is the sole Lawmaker and Controller

of the world.]

Radak observes that שֵׂכֶל can also be translated as *success* (see *I Samuel* 18:14, 30); thus, those who fear God and practice His commandments will merit great success in This World and the World to Come.

תְּהִלָּתוֹ עֹמֶדֶת לָעַד — *His praise endures forever.*

The sincere servant of Hashem is engaged in a pursuit which is timeless. Therefore his achievement will not be obliterated by the passage of time. Even many generations after his death, he will be remembered. Furthermore, his soul will be praised and rewarded forever in the World to Come (*Radak*).

place!" [Similarly, if Torah wisdom is not preserved with sincere fear of Hashem, it can deteriorate into a distortion of the Divine will.]

The *Talmud* (*Shabbos* 31a) continues that a scholar who acquires Torah without fear of Hashem resembles the treasurer who was given the keys to an inner vault but not the keys to the outer treasure chamber leading to the vault. Obviously, he could not reach the vault. [Torah knowledge is the inner secret of God's essence and of His will. Fear of God is the prerequisite (the outer chamber) for the true perception of God. If one is barred from the outer chamber the inner vault remains forever inaccessible.]

Rabbi Yehudah said: 'God created this world for the sole purpose of having men fear Him! Similarly, King Solomon stated (*Ecclesiastes* 3:14): וְהָאֱלֹהִים עָשָׂה שֶׁיִּרְאוּ מִלְּפָנָיו, *And God has made it* [the world] *so that men should fear Him.*

Two rabbis were seated when a great sage passed by. One said, "Let us stand [out of respect] because the one who passes by is God-fearing!"

The other said, "Let us stand because he is a brilliant Torah scholar!"

Said the first rabbi, "When I tell you that this man is worthy because he is God-fearing [which is the greatest of virtues], why do you bother to tell me that he is a scholar [for wisdom is insignificant compared to fear of God]! ... Indeed, Hashem cares for nothing in the world except for fear of God, as Scripture states (*Deut.* 10:12): *And now Israel, what does HASHEM, your God, ask of you, but to fear HASHEM, your God.* Job 28:28 states: *He said to man, 'Behold, fear of my Lord, that is wisdom!'* "

T he preceding psalm concluded with the words The beginning of wisdom is the fear of HASHEM (verse 10). This composition takes up that theme with the declaration, Praiseworthy is the man who fears HASHEM, and proceeds to describe that good fortune (Malbim).

The Midrash (Koheles Rabbah) observes that fear of God is so important that King Solomon, the wisest of all men, concluded two of his books with this very theme: Grace is false and beauty is vain, a God-fearing women — she should be praised (Proverbs 31:21), and The sum of matter, when all has been considered: fear God and keep His commandments, for that is man's whole duty (Ecclesiastes 12:13).

The initial letters of the stiches of this psalm follow the sequence of the Aleph-Beis, the Hebrew alphabet. This indicates that the hero of this psalm, the God-fearing man, painstakingly fulfills every dictate of the Torah from א, the first letter, to ת, the last letter of the Law (Midrash Shocher Tov).

א הַלְלוּיָהּ | אַשְׁרֵי־אִישׁ יָרֵא אֶת־יְהוָה
ב בְּמִצְוֹתָיו חָפֵץ מְאֹד: גִּבּוֹר בָּאָרֶץ יִהְיֶה זַרְעוֹ
ג דּוֹר יְשָׁרִים יְבֹרָךְ: הוֹן־וָעֹשֶׁר בְּבֵיתוֹ
ד וְצִדְקָתוֹ עֹמֶדֶת לָעַד: זָרַח בַּחֹשֶׁךְ אוֹר
ה לַיְשָׁרִים חַנּוּן וְרַחוּם וְצַדִּיק: טוֹב־אִישׁ חוֹנֵן

1. ' הַלְלוּיָהּ אַשְׁרֵי אִישׁ יָרֵא אֶת ה — *Praise God! Praiseworthy is the man who fears HASHEM.*

The righteous man fears Hashem in private just as much as he appears to fear Him in public, because his fear of God is genuine and sincere. He fears God exclusively and has no fear of mortal men (*Radak*).

Rabbi Eliezer Rokeach of Worms notes that this man is not called יָרֵא אֱלֹהִים, *one who fears ELOHIM*, the Dispenser of Strict Justice; rather, he is called a ה' יָרֵא, *one who fears HASHEM*, the Dispenser of Kindness. This teaches that the righteous man's fear of God is not derived from the knowledge that God can punish him, but from the realization that God loves him. In return, he loves God and *greatly desires His commandments.* This man has but one fear: that he may sin and destroy the intimate relationship which he enjoys with God.

בְּמִצְוֹתָיו חָפֵץ מְאֹד — *Who greatly desires His commandments.*

The *Talmud* (*Avodah Zarah* 19a) comments: His great desire is to fulfill God's commandments rather than to receive the reward of His commandments. *Pirkei Avos* 1:3 states: Be not like servants who serve their master for the sake of reward; rather, be like servants who serve their master not for the sake of reward.

Sefer Chassidim explains that he who *greatly desires* God's commands has an extraordinary love for the precepts of the Torah. First, he prays fervently that God provide him with the opportunity to perform commandments. Then he spends large sums of money to enhance the beauty of each *mitzvah*. Finally, he encourages and helps other people to perform God's *mitzvos*.

2. גִּבּוֹר בָּאָרֶץ יִהְיֶה זַרְעוֹ — *Mighty in the land will his offspring be.*

The man who sincerely fears God will be feared and respected by his fellow men in the same way that they fear a mighty warrior. Moreover, the father will pass on his power and prestige to his children; for, as the *Mishnah* (*Eduyos* 2:9) teaches, a father bequeaths five things to his son: beauty, strength, wealth, wisdom, and longevity (*Radak*).

דּוֹר יְשָׁרִים יְבֹרָךְ — *A generation of the upright who shall be blessed.*

Although most mighty men use their power for personal gain, the man who fears Hashem uses his power to persuade his contemporaries to follow the path of righteousness, so that they may merit God's blessing (*Alshich*).

3. הוֹן וָעֹשֶׁר בְּבֵיתוֹ — *Wealth and riches are in his house.*

Because this man was *forever righteous*, the wealth in his house never diminished (*Malbim*).

וְצִדְקָתוֹ עֹמֶדֶת לָעַד — *And his charity* [or *righteousness*] *endures forever.*

In this world, the God-fearing man will enjoy abundant material wealth; and in the next world, he will *forever* enjoy the reward of צִדְקָתוֹ, *his charity*, which he performed with his wealth (*Radak*).

The *Talmud* (*Kesubos* 50a) describes two cases which epitomize the lesson of this verse. The first example is the man who studies Torah himself and teaches it to others; he retains the wealth of his

112
1-5

Praise God! Praiseworthy is the man
    who fears HASHEM,
    who greatly desires His commandments.
2 Mighty in the land will his offspring be,
    a generation of the upright
    who shall be blessed.
3 Wealth and riches are in his house,
    and his charity endures forever.
4 Even in darkness a light shines
    for the upright;
    He is compassionate, merciful, and righteous.
5 Good is the man who is compassionate and lends,

Torah knowledge in his own house, while his charity to others endures forever. The second is the man who writes scrolls of the Scriptures and lends these to others. The scrolls remain his personal property, and he performs an act of charity which endures forever.

4. זָרַח בַּחשֶׁךְ אוֹר לַיְשָׁרִים — *Even in darkness a light shines for the upright.*

Troubles are described as *darkness;* Hashem's salvation is *a light,* as *Michah 7:8* states: *When I sit in darkness, HASHEM shall be a light to me (Ibn Ezra; Radak).*

חַנּוּן וְרַחוּם וְצַדִּיק — *He is compassionate, merciful, and righteous.*

God is *compassionate* to those who pray and beg for compassion; He is *merciful* to those poor and ignorant souls who cannot pray; and He is *righteous* in that He gives each man the portion he deserves (*Sforno*).

5. טוֹב אִישׁ חוֹנֵן וּמַלְוֶה — *Good is the man who is compassionate and lends.*

[The true philanthropist is highly sensitive to the feelings of his beneficiaries. Realizing that some needy people are too proud to accept charity, he compassionately offers the poor man an opportunity for financial rehabilitation by lending him funds (see *Radak*).

Rambam (Hilchos Matnos Aniyim

10:7) describes eight levels of virtue in the art of giving charity properly. He rules that the highest level of philanthropy is to lend a poor person money so that he can establish himself in a dignified manner and thereby avoid becoming a public charge.

Lesser philanthropists prefer to give outright gifts to the poor. They allocate a certain portion of their income for charity, and they are eager to dispense these funds and discharge their obligation. Although their actions are charitable and praiseworthy, they have not yet reached the highest pinnacle of generosity. They are reluctant to grant requests for loans, for issuing a loan would require that they draw from their working capital and keep a record of the loan for an extended period of time. Whenever they think of the money which they lent out, interest-free, they calculate the profit they could have gained by investing that amount.

Nevertheless, despite these numerous considerations, the genuinely *good man is compassionate* and lends his money willingly (see *Rashi*).]

The *Midrash (Shemos Rabbah 31:16)* emphasizes that lending and borrowing are an integral part of the world order. No creature is self-sufficient; each must derive some help from another creature

וּמַלְוֶה יְכַלְכֵּל דְּבָרָיו בְּמִשְׁפָּט: כִּי־לְעוֹלָם ו

לֹא־יִמּוֹט לְזֵכֶר עוֹלָם יִהְיֶה צַדִּיק: מִשְּׁמוּעָה ז

רָעָה לֹא יִירָא נָכוֹן לִבּוֹ בָּטֻחַ בַּיהוָה: סָמוּךְ ח

לִבּוֹ לֹא יִירָא עַד אֲשֶׁר־יִרְאֶה בְצָרָיו: פִּזַּר | ט

in order to survive and function properly.

Another *Midrash (Shemos Rabbah* 31:1) says that this verse describes the Holy One, Blessed is He, to whom every creature is deeply indebted for God granted it the gifts of life and sustenance. But instead of paying their debt to God, many people anger God with disobedience and sin. Nevertheless, He remains *compassionate;* He forgives their sins and lends them additional years of life and sustenance.

יְכַלְכֵּל דְּבָרָיו בְּמִשְׁפָּט — *He conducts his affairs with justice.*

The generous man may appear to be reckless with his money because he lends it out readily, but this is not the case, for he is extremely careful and scrupulous in his personal financial dealings *(Rashi).* [This prudence stems from the realization that the money is not his own, for he is merely a trustee for the disbursement of God's funds. Thus once the God-fearing man understands that he must be *compassionate* and *lend* he also realizes that he must *conduct his private affairs with justice.*][1]

6. כִּי לְעוֹלָם לֹא יִמּוֹט — *Surely he will never falter.*

The charitable man will always remain physically healthy and financially secure. He will suffer no loss *(Radak).*

[See psalm 15, which describes the

man who is scrupulous in his dealings with his fellow man. That psalm concludes *(verses 5, 6): Who lends not his money at interest ... Whoever does these shall forever not falter.* The *Talmud (Bava Metzia* 71a) says that this implies that whoever *does* lend his money at interest will falter financially and ultimately will lose all of his money *forever,* i.e., he will never recoup his losses.]

לְזֵכֶר עוֹלָם יִהְיֶה צַדִּיק — *An everlasting remembrance will the righteous man remain.*

Even after death, the memory of the righteous man will live on *(Radak).*

[And every time people mention his name they will bless the righteous man as Solomon said *(Proverbs 10:7):* זֵכֶר צַדִּיק לִבְרָכָה, *the memory of the righteous is a blessing* (Yoma 38b).]

7. מִשְּׁמוּעָה רָעָה לֹא יִירָא — *Of evil tidings he will have no fear.*

No adversary nor catastrophe can frighten him *(Sforno).*

The God-fearing man thus stands in contrast to the wicked man, of whom Scripture states קוֹל פְּחָדִים בְּאָזְנָיו, *the sound of terror echoes in his ears* (Job 15:21).

There are many reasons to fear bad news. Some people have children or relatives abroad, and they are always apprehensive about their well-being. Others are afraid of attack by enemies

---

1. Based on this verse, the *Talmud (Chullin* 84b) advises that man should always spend less than his means on food and drink and clothe himself in accordance with his means. However, he should provide for his wife and children in a dignified manner, even if this exceeds his means. For they are dependent on their husband and father, but he himself is dependent solely on God, He who spoke and the world came into being [see *Rambam, Hilchos Deos* 5:10].

Maharsha explains that a man should be willing to subsist on bare essentials and *conduct his affairs with justice.* However, he should be prepared to be *compassionate* to his family and even to borrow, if necessary, to clothe and maintain his kin with dignity.

he conducts his affairs with justice.

⁶ *Surely he will never falter,*
an everlasting remembrance
will the righteous man remain.
⁷ *Of evil tidings he will have no fear,*
his heart is firm — confident in HASHEM.
⁸ *His heart is steadfast, he shall not fear,*
before he sees judgment upon his tormentors.
⁹ *He gave a distribution to the destitute,*

or robbers. Everyone has ample cause for tension and anxiety, except for the man who finds security in Hashem. He places no confidence in his money, relatives, or friends, but only in his Father in Heaven (*Radak*).

נָכוֹן לִבּוֹ בָּטֻחַ בַּה׳ — *His heart is firm — confident in HASHEM.*

The *Talmud* (*Berachos* 60a) relates: When Hillel the Elder was on the road approaching his hometown he once heard a loud scream. He said, "I am certain that this scream did not come from my home." It is the perfect faith displayed by men such as Hillel to which the Psalmist refers here: *Of evil tidings he will have no fear, his heart is firm — confident in HASHEM.*

However, the commentaries take issue with Hillel's declaration, for it appears to reflect an unwarranted, overconfident attitude. After all, evil tidings come even to the most righteous of men, for no one is immune to tragedy and suffering. How, then, could Hillel be so sure that no evil would befall his family? Some commentators contend that the truly righteous man, such as Hillel, always has a premonition of evil and danger. Since tragedy occurs as a signal of Divine displeasure, the truly devout man is so close to God that he would undoubtedly sense Divine displeasure before the wrath of God actually erupted.

Shaloh Hakadosh and *Maharam Almosnino* explain that although Hillel

was no stranger to tragedy and misfortune, he knew that no scream would emanate from his home. For Hillel's *heart* was *firm* in its faith in God, and he knew that everything which the Almighty ordains is for the best. He accepted calamity with calm, and he taught his family to react similarly in times of trouble.

8. סָמוּךְ לִבּוֹ לֹא יִירָא עַד אֲשֶׁר יִרְאֶה בְצָרָיו — *His heart is steadfast, he shall not fear, before he sees [judgment] upon his tormentors.*

[We have inserted the word *judgment* to help convey the sense of the phrase.]

The intensity of his faith does not waver; he constantly places his complete confidence in God and has no doubt that he will ultimately witness the ruin of his tormentors. His faith remains strong even before he witnesses the downfall of the wicked (*Radak*).

9. פִּזַּר נָתַן לָאֶבְיוֹנִים — *He gave a distribution to the destitute.*

The juxtaposition of these words presents an apparent contradiction, for פִּזַּר literally means *to scatter* [wildly], whereas נָתַן means *to give* [carefully].

In explanation, *Radak* cites the *Talmudic* dictum (*Kesubos* 50a) which cautions the philanthropist to be judicious and prudent in his distribution of alms to the poor. Even when a person wishes to be magnanimous, he should not give away more than a fifth of his capital, lest he seriously jeopardize his

נָתַן לָאֶבְיוֹנִים צִדְקָתוֹ עֹמֶדֶת לָעַד קַרְנוֹ
תָּרוּם בְּכָבוֹד: רָשָׁע יִרְאֶה| וְכָעָס שִׁנָּיו יַחֲרֹק
וְנָמָס תַּאֲוַת רְשָׁעִים תֹּאבֵד:

---

own financial security. The significant element in the practice of philanthropy is not the amount of the gifts but the frequency of giving. Thus, rather than giving away large sums to a few charities, the philanthropist should scrupulously respond to every request made of him. Thus, the psalmist says, נָתַן לָאֶבְיוֹנִים, *he distributed freely*, פִּזֵּר, by giving [something] *to every needy person*.[1]

צִדְקָתוֹ עֹמֶדֶת לָעַד — *His charity [or righteousness] endures forever.*

Zohar (Parashas Beha'aloscha) explains that whenever a man gives charity and assures a poor man a living, this act strengthens the עֵץ הַחַיִּים, *Tree of Life;* as a result the *Tree of Life* then protects the philanthropist and adds vitality and joy to his life.

קַרְנוֹ תָּרוּם בְּכָבוֹד — *His pride is exalted with glory.*

The philanthropist enhances his portion in the World to Come, which *endures forever.* In addition, all the days of his sojourn on earth are *exalted with*

---

1. [See *Avos* 3:15, וְהַכֹּל לְפִי רוֹב הַמַּעֲשֶׂה, *all depends upon the frequency of the action.* *Rambam* comments that a small action, repeated often, forms a strong habit, whereas a major act, performed but once, leaves no lasting trace on one's personality. If a man gives a pauper a single present of one thousand gold pieces, this act will not make the donor a generous person. But if a man gives one gold coin apiece to one thousand paupers, he repeatedly stirs his heart to compassion and generosity; then the quality of generosity will become well-rooted in his character.]

Maseches Kallah relates that Rabbi Tarfon was a very wealthy man, but he did not give charity in proportion to his means. Once Rabbi Akiva asked him, "Would you like me to buy you a city or two?" Rabbi Tarfon eagerly accepted the offer and gave Rabbi Akiva forty thousand gold coins, which Rabbi Akiva immediately divided among the poor.

After a while, Rabbi Tarfon met Rabbi Akiva again and asked, "Where are the cities which you purchased with my gold coins?"

Rabbi Akiva then took Rabbi Tarfon to the study hall, where they found a young boy learning from the *Book of Psalms.* They all recited together from the text until they arrived at the verse, *He gave a distribution to the destitute, his charity endures forever.* Rabbi Akiva exclaimed, "This *mitzvah* is the [enduring, permanent] city which I purchased for you!"

Rabbi Tarfon rose and kissed Rabbi Akiva, exclaiming, "My rabbi! My guide! My rabbi in wisdom — My guide in proper conduct!"

Rabbi Tarfon then gave Rabbi Akiva an additional sum of money to distribute among the poor.

his charity endures forever,

his pride is exalted with glory.

¹⁰ The wicked man shall see and be angered,

he will gnash his teeth and melt away,

the ambition of the wicked shall perish.

the *glory* of a fine reputation and of Divine favor (*Sforno*).

10. רָשָׁע יִרְאֶה וְכָעָס — *The wicked man shall see and be angered.*

The wicked man dedicated his life to the pursuit of avarice. He sought to amass wealth, in order to gain the power to dominate and exploit people.

When the wicked man observes the success of the God-fearing man he is infuriated, because the pious man's way of life repudiates everything the wicked man prizes. The pious man distributed freely and gave to the needy, yet *his pride is exalted with glory.* This fact demonstrates that giving — rather than taking — strengthened the God-fearing man (*Sforno*).

שִׁנָּיו יַחֲרֹק וְנָמָס — *He will gnash his teeth and melt away.*

If the wicked man could destroy the pious one, he would do so without hesitation (*Radak*), but he will never realize this desire. His heart will grow faint and *melt away* because his desire to harm the righteous remains unfulfilled (*Sforno*). [1]

תַּאֲוַת רְשָׁעִים תֹּאבֵד — *The ambition of the wicked shall perish.*

The wicked are obsessed with one overriding ambition: they yearn to see the downfall of the righteous. This ambition will come to naught because the wicked themselves will perish and the righteous will prosper (*Radak*).

1. The *Talmud* (*Pesachim* 49b) describes the ignorant people of older times who refused to accept the teachings of the rabbis, yet were jealous of their Torah knowledge. These coarse people were bitter and frustrated, and invariably rejected the rabbis' offers to teach them.

Rabbi Akiva testified, "Before I studied Torah, I was an ignoramus who used to say: 'Who will put a Torah scholar into my clutches so that I can bite him as a donkey bites!' "

Rabbi Akiva's disciples asked him, "Why did you compare your proposed bite to that of a donkey and not to that of a [more common] dog?"

Rabbi Akiva replied, "The dog bites only into the flesh but breaks no bones. The donkey bite is far more powerful; it crushes the bones as it tears the flesh."

113 מזמור קיג

Psalms 113-118 are collectively known as הַלֵּל, Hallel [praise]. Although they are so designated throughout Rabbinic literature, these psalms are sometimes called הַלֵּל הַמִּצְרִי, the Egyptian Hallel, to distinguish them from psalm 136 which is referred to as הַלֵּל הַגָּדוֹל, the great Hallel.

The Talmud (Pesachim 118a) explains that the הַלֵּל הַמִּצְרִי surpasses the הַלֵּל הַגָּדוֹל because its themes are essential articles of the Jewish faith. They include the exodus from Egypt, the splitting of the sea, the revelation at Mount Sinai, the resurrection of the dead, and the cataclysmic advent of the Messiah (see footnote to 115:1).

Hallel is included in the liturgy. It is recited in its entirety on all the days of Sukkos, Shemini Atzeres, Chanukah, the first day of Pesach, both at the seder and again in the morning service, and on Shavuos (Arachin 10a). [In the Diaspora, the entire Hallel is also recited on the second day of Pesach.] On Rosh Chodesh (the festival of the New Month) and on the remaining days of Pesach, Half Hallel is recited, i.e., 115:1-11 and 116:1-11 are omitted.

א הַלְלוּיָהּ | הַלְלוּ עַבְדֵי יהוה הַלְלוּ אֶת־שֵׁם
ב יהוה: יְהִי שֵׁם יהוה מְבֹרָךְ מֵעַתָּה וְעַד־
ג עוֹלָם: מִמִּזְרַח־שֶׁמֶשׁ עַד־מְבוֹאוֹ מְהֻלָּל שֵׁם

1. הַלְלוּיָהּ — *Praise God!*

[See commentary to 111:1.]

The *Midrash* notes that the numerical value of הַלְלוּיָהּ is 71, which alludes to the Egyptian exile. Jacob and his family descended to Egypt as a group of seventy people. Since they were accompanied by the Divine Presence, however, their total number was 71. When God redeemed them, His Divine Presence was in their midst. Therefore, יָהּ, *YAH,* should be praised with the word הַלְלוּ.[1]

הַלְלוּ עַבְדֵי ה׳ — *Give praise, you servants of HASHEM!*

At first, the Jews were the servants of Pharaoh. Only after their liberation could they be considered the *servants of HASHEM.* For as *Leviticus* 25:55 states, כִּי לִי בְנֵי יִשְׂרָאֵל עֲבָדִים, *For unto Me* [alone] *the Children of Israel are slaves.*

Midrash Shocher Tov adds: twenty-six generations elapsed from the moment of Creation until the time when the Jews left Egypt; throughout all this time, no man ever said *Hallel* to Hashem. But when God redeemed the Jews from Egypt, they sang *Hallel.*

Specifically, they sang *Hallel* after the last plague, in which God smote the בְּכוֹרוֹת, *the first-born.* In the middle of the night, Pharaoh was aroused by cries of anguish which burst from every house, for no home was spared this plague of death. He ran through the streets and knocked on every door in search of Moses and Aaron [for he wanted the Jews to leave Egypt immediately]. When Moses and Aaron sent word to Pharaoh that they would not leave until the next morning, Pharaoh pleaded, ''I beg you to leave now, if something is not done immediately all of Egypt will be destroyed!''

Moses and Aaron replied, ''If you want the plague to cease, you must issue an official proclamation of emancipation for the Jews.''

At this Pharaoh shouted, ''In the past you were my slaves, but now you are free men! You are on your own, so you must give praise, you servants of HASHEM!''

הַלְלוּ אֶת שֵׁם ה׳ — *Praise the Name of HASHEM.*

When God wrought His miracles in Egypt, the entire world was aware of it,

---

1. The *Talmud* (*Pesachim* 117a) cites numerous opinions concerning the authorship of *Hallel.*

Rabbi Yosi said that Moses and all of Israel said *Hallel* when they emerged safely from the sea.

Rabbi Eliezer said that Moses and all of Israel said *Hallel* when they stood before the sea.

Rabbi Yehoshua said that Joshua and all of Israel said *Hallel* when all the kings of Canaan gathered against them.

Rabbi Eliezer HaModei said that Devorah and Barak said *Hallel* when Sisera threatened them.

Rabbi Elazar ben Azariah said that King Chizkiyahu and his court said *Hallel* when the wicked Sennacherib threatened them.

Rabbi Yosi HaGalli said that Mordechai and Esther said *Hallel* when Haman threatened them.

The Sages said that the prophets of Israel composed *Hallel* so that the people could recite it upon every great event and in every period of danger; they will also recite *Hallel* upon the final redemption.

The *Talmud* also mentions the view that David composed *Hallel.*

There is truth to all these opinions. The basic framework for *Hallel* was established by the

Praise God! Give praise, you servants of HASHEM!
    Praise the Name of HASHEM!
  ² Blessed be the Name of HASHEM
    from this time forth and forever.
  ³ From the rising of the sun to its setting,
    HASHEM's Name is praised.

and sang His praises (Sforno).

However, the most intense recognition of God took place among the pagans of Egypt who initially ignored Hashem and denied His power, for God proclaimed, "And the Egyptians will know that I am HASHEM" (Exodus 7:5).

The comprehension of the true meaning of the Name 'ה, HASHEM, was a tremendous accomplishment, and it first occurred in Egypt. God told Moses that even the patriarchs Abraham, Isaac, and Jacob had not known this Name (Exodus 6:3): וּשְׁמִי ה' לֹא נוֹדַעְתִּי לָהֶם, And with my Name, HASHEM I was not known to them (Rabbi Yaakov of Lissa).

The Midrash points out that the word הַלְלוּ appears here for the third time in this verse. This alludes to the idea that Hallel should preferably be recited by a group of three people. One man arises and exhorts the other two [who serve as witnesses, bearing testimony to God's praise], הַלְלוּ, Give praise! [See Orach Chaim 422:2 and gloss of Ramah and Mishnah Berurah.]

2. יְהִי שֵׁם ה' מְבֹרָךְ מֵעַתָּה וְעַד עוֹלָם — Blessed be the Name of HASHEM from this time forth and forever.

In this world, the Name יְהֹוָה, HASHEM, appears in abbreviated form as יָהּ, YAH, because God's presence is partially concealed. However, from this time forth and forever [i.e., from the time of miraculous revelation], more and more blessings will be added to God's Name, as He reveals more and

more of His power and kindness to humanity. Finally, when the measure of blessing is full, the complete name, יְהֹוָה, HASHEM, will appear (Rav Nosson Shapiro, Megalleh Amukos).

Midrash Shocher Tov observes that, in this world, Israel's behavior is erratic: sometimes the Jews please God and praise Him, but at other times they anger Him. As time progresses, however, the acts of obedience and praise will exceed the acts of defiance and God will increase His providence and protection accordingly, as 125:2 states: HASHEM surrounds His nation from this time forth and forever.

3. מִמִּזְרַח שֶׁמֶשׁ עַד מְבוֹאוֹ מְהֻלָּל שֵׁם ה' — From the rising of the sun to its setting [see 50:1], HASHEM's Name is praised.

Similarly, God says of Himself (Malachi 1:11): כִּי מִמִּזְרַח שֶׁמֶשׁ וְעַד מְבוֹאוֹ גָּדוֹל שְׁמִי בַּגּוֹיִם, Because from the rising of the sun to its setting, my Name is great among the peoples (Radak).

[When the Jews left Egypt, the wonders which God wrought for their sake amazed the entire world. At that time, praise for God was heard even from idolators in the furthest corners of the earth. Similarly, the wonders of the future redemption from exile will evoke praise from all the people of the earth.]

Alshich comments that the sun's daily journey across the sky is a source of wonder which prompts man to praise God.

Sunrise symbolizes good times and

early prophets, but this was elaborated upon in successive generations as a result of historic occasions which stimulated an outpouring of praise for Hashem. Later the master Psalmist, David, put these chapters of Hallel into their final form in the Book of Psalms (Teshuvah Me'Ahavah Vol.II, responsa 264).

ד יְהֹוָה: רָם עַל־כָּל־גּוֹיִם | יְהֹוָה עַל הַשָּׁמַיִם
ה כְּבוֹדוֹ: מִי כַּיהֹוָה אֱלֹהֵינוּ הַמַּגְבִּיהִי לָשָׁבֶת:
ו־ז הַמַּשְׁפִּילִי לִרְאוֹת בַּשָּׁמַיִם וּבָאָרֶץ: מְקִימִי
ח מֵעָפָר דָּל מֵאַשְׁפֹּת יָרִים אֶבְיוֹן: לְהוֹשִׁיבִי
ט עִם־נְדִיבִים עִם נְדִיבֵי עַמּוֹ: מוֹשִׁיבִי | עֲקֶרֶת
הַבַּיִת אֵם־הַבָּנִים שְׂמֵחָה הַלְלוּיָהּ:

rising expectations, while sunset symbolizes decline. Both the Jewish nation and each individual member have experienced these two aspects of life. Nevertheless, whatever we undergo, whether Hashem seems to smile at us or to frown, מְהֻלָּל שֵׁם ה׳, *HASHEM's Name is praised by us.* Always recognizing that God's ways are just, we bless Him in every situation [see *Haggadah Treasury*].

4. רָם עַל כָּל גּוֹיִם ה׳ — *High above all nations is HASHEM.*

Minchas Shai draws our attention to the פָּסִיק, *separation line,* which separates the word גּוֹיִם, *nations,* from the Name ה׳. This separation serves to emphasize the alienation of the gentile peoples from our God.

In 99:2, we read ה׳ בְּצִיּוֹן גָּדוֹל וְרָם, *HASHEM is great in Zion, and He is high above all the nations.* Something גָּדוֹל, *great,* resembles a tower, which rises to the sky but is based on earth. Thus does the Jewish people (Zion) view God: He is great and lofty, yet He is also involved with this world. The word רָם, *high above,* refers to an elevated object which is completely divorced from the earth, such as a soaring bird. Thus do the gentile nations conceive of God. He is deemed רָם, *aloof* and *remote.* (See commentary to Psalm 47:3.)

עַל הַשָּׁמַיִם כְּבוֹדוֹ — *Above the heavens is His glory.*

Although all the peoples will attempt to praise and exalt Hashem, no one can truly grasp His *glory,* for it is *above* and beyond the comprehension of the

heavens and the celestial legions. They too attempt to sing of God's wonders but fail to exhaust His infinite praises *(Radak).*

The scholars of Kabbalah *(Maseches Heicholos,* 3) note that the words of the Psalmist seem to contradict the prophet's statement, כְּבוֹדוֹ מְלֹא כָל הָאָרֶץ, *His glory pervades the entire earth* (Isaiah 6:3), which implies that God is Omnipresent rather than aloof or distant *above the heavens.*

The Rabbis explain that although the true essence of the שְׁכִינָה, *Holy Presence,* is concentrated *above the heavens,* the influence and power of this Divine glory radiates throughout the universe and *pervades the entire earth.* Any manifestation of glory which we behold on earth, particularly the majestic glory of emperors and kings, is merely a reflection of God's glory which is *above the heavens.*

5. מִי כַּה׳ אֱלֹהֵינוּ הַמַּגְבִּיהִי לָשָׁבֶת — *Who is like HASHEM, our God, Who is enthroned on high —*

As long as wickedness fills the earth and the sacred message of the Torah has not yet permeated the world, Hashem's Presence remains aloof, enthroned on high. Because God's presence on earth is incomplete, His Name remains incomplete as יָהּ, *YAH.* The Psalmist alludes to this by using the poetic form הַמַּגְבִּיהִי, the first and last letters of which form the Name יָהּ, to suggest that since Hashem is מַגְבִּיהַּ, *raised on high,* His name on earth is incomplete *(Alshich).*

6. הַמַּשְׁפִּילִי לִרְאוֹת בַּשָּׁמַיִם וּבָאָרֶץ — *Yet deigns to look* [lit. *bends down low to*

⁴ *High above all nations is HASHEM,*
   above the heavens is His glory.
⁵ *Who is like HASHEM, our God,*
   Who is enthroned on high —
⁶ *Yet deigns to look*
   upon the heaven and the earth?
⁷ *He raises the needy from the dust,*
   from the trash heaps He lifts the destitute.
⁸ *To seat them with nobles,*
   with the nobles of His people.
⁹ *He transforms the barren wife*
   into a glad mother of children. Praise God!

---

see] *upon the heaven and the earth?*

[This is the challenging and exciting aspect of God's relationship to man: as we act towards God, so does He react to us. If we ignore His presence, He withdraws high *above the heavens*, but if we welcome His proximity, He lovingly involves Himself in every phase of our lives.]

According to *Maharam Alvilada*, this explains why five key words in this psalm הַמַּגְבִּיהִי, הַמַּשְׁפִּילִי, מְקִימִי, לְהוֹשִׁיבִי (מוֹשִׁיבִי) bear the seemingly superfluous suffix י. The appended י usually means *me*, here implying that all the actions of God, whether He ascends on high or descends below, all these actions are controlled *by me*, [i.e., undertaken in response to my individual behavior] and are done *for me* [i.e., to benefit me].

7. מְקִימִי מֵעָפָר דָּל — *He raises the needy from the dust.*

In exile, Israel is considered as low and worthless as the dust (*Sforno*), but this very humiliation leads to their salvation. For when the Jews humbly submit to God, He will raise them from their degradation (*Alshich*).

מֵאַשְׁפֹּת יָרִים אֶבְיוֹן — *From the trash heaps He lifts the destitute.*

[The poverty of the אֶבְיוֹן is even greater than that of the דָּל, because the אֶבְיוֹן is תָּאֵב לְכָל, *in need of everything*. Therefore, he scours the אַשְׁפָּה, *dungheap*, in order to take anything that he can salvage. God will lift this wretched soul, too, if he will only put his life into God's hands.][1]

8. לְהוֹשִׁיבִי עִם נְדִיבִים — *To seat them with nobles.*

God does not merely lift the poor and needy out of degradation, but He also actually elevates them to the highest

---

1. *Rav Eliezer Nachman Puah* in *Midrash B'Chiddush* illustrates this verse with the following tale. When Sultan Suleiman ruled over Palestine in the sixteenth century, he sought the remnants of the Holy Temple, which had long since vanished. The excavator charged with this task looked all over the Holy City without success, until one day he noticed an old lady carrying a basketful of dung and putrid refuse, which she deliberately dumped in a certain spot. Upon his inquiry, she told the excavator that she had come all the way from Bethlehem.

Incredulous, the excavator asked, "Are there no garbage dumps in Bethlehem, that you must haul your refuse all the way to Jerusalem?"

The old woman replied, "Our priest claims that this spot is where the Temple of the Jews once stood and that whoever [shows contempt for it and] covers it with additional waste earns tremendous merit."

The excavator relayed this information to Sultan Suleiman, who then scattered thousands of coins throughout the area. Afterwards, the Sultan invited the populace of the city to dig there

ranks of nobility (Radak).

עם נְדִיבֵי עַמּוֹ — With the nobles of His people.

... The needy and poor who are elevated are not placed among the ranks of the gentile nobles. Rather they enter the aristocracy of God's chosen nation, Israel (Radak).

[Specifically, this refers to the princely Patriarchs, led by Abraham; for, as 47:10 relates, נְדִיבֵי עַמִּים נֶאֱסָפוּ עַם אֱלֹהֵי אַבְרָהָם, the nobles of the nations gathered, the nation of the God of Abraham. (See comm. to 47:10.)

The lives of the poor and the needy are distinguished by the self-sacrifice with which they uphold the tradition they received from their fathers. Therefore, their ultimate reward will be to sit among their forefathers who exemplified the virtue of self-sacrifice.]

9. מוֹשִׁיבִי עֲקֶרֶת הַבַּיִת — He transforms the barren wife [lit. barren woman of the house].

The Creator exercises complete control over nature. This control is vividly demonstrated when God suddenly transforms the barren woman into a mother (Radak).

The Midrash (Bereishis Rabbah 53:6) perceives here an allusion to the many righteous but barren women who were initially spurned and humiliated but were later transformed into the matriarchs and heroines of Jewish history.

The Matriarch Sarah was barren for many years before God miraculously rejuvenated her. Not only did she give birth to Isaac, but she was also sufficiently robust to nourish many additional infants.

[Other barren women who were transformed include Rebecca, Leah, Rachel, Samson's mother (Tzlalphonis; see Bava Basra 91a) and Hannah, mother of the prophet Samuel.]

Rashi suggests that we interpret this verse as a reference to Israel in exile, for Isaiah 54:1 says, רָנִּי עֲקָרָה לֹא יָלָדָה, Sing joyously, O barren one who did not bear children, meaning that because of the destruction, Jerusalem is empty and barren of her populace.

אֵם הַבָּנִים שְׂמֵחָה הַלְלוּיָהּ — [Into] a glad mother of children. Praise God!

In the future, Zion and Jerusalem will be teeming with inhabitants and the celebration in the city will resemble a joyful homecoming, as Isaiah 66:8 foretells: For Zion has gone through travail and she has given birth to her sons [who will return from the four corners of the earth] (Rashi).

and search for these precious coins. While sifting through the waste to find the coins, the people cleared away tons of refuse, until the Western Wall and other remnants of the Holy Temple were revealed. Then the Sultan had the area thoroughly cleared, and he sprinkled fragrant rose water over the area to destroy the foul stench of refuse.

This is the symbolism of this verse: because our holiest place became a dunghill it was in desperate need of salvation; therefore God caused it to be discovered and cleansed of its filth and shame.

T*his second chapter of Hallel continues the theme of the first chapter, which praises God: He raises the needy from the dust, from the trash heaps He lifts the destitute. To seat them with nobles, with the nobles of His people (113:7-8).*

Israel achieved this level of nobility when the Jews left Egypt and displayed tremendous self-sacrifice at the sea. For they willingly risked their lives by entering the sea at God's command (Exodus 14:22). Then, as the second and third verses of this psalm state: Judah became His sanctuary, Israel His dominion. The sea saw and fled, the Jordan turned backward (Rav Vidal HaTzorfati).

The ultimate self-discipline was achieved when Israel accepted the burden of the Torah at Sinai and agreed to conform completely to the will of God. At that moment, the entire creation was born anew.

Throbbing with new energy, bounding with fresh hope, the post-Sinaitic world is eloquently described by the Psalmist in the fourth verse: The mountains skipped like rams, the hills like young lambs.

The brief revelation and transformation at Sinai provided the world with a glimpse of the metamorphosis which will occur in the redemption of the future. Indeed, it is not nature which is destined to change; rather it is man whose eyes and ears will suddenly be opened, for the earth shall be filled with knowledge of HASHEM, as water covers the sea (Isaiah 11:9). Thus, says the Psalmist, God will turn the rock into a pond of water [i.e., a reservoir of knowledge], the flint into a flowing fountain (verse 8).

א בְּצֵאת יִשְׂרָאֵל מִמִּצְרָיִם בֵּית יַעֲקֹב מֵעַם
ב לֹעֵז: הָיְתָה יְהוּדָה לְקָדְשׁוֹ יִשְׂרָאֵל
ג מַמְשְׁלוֹתָיו: הַיָּם רָאָה וַיָּנֹס הַיַּרְדֵּן יִסֹּב

1. בְּצֵאת יִשְׂרָאֵל מִמִּצְרָיִם — *When Israel went out of Egypt.*

According to *Midrash Shocher Tov*, the Children of Israel merited redemption from Egypt because:

לֹא שִׁנּוּ אֶת שְׁמָם, *They did not change their names;* לֹא שִׁנּוּ אֶת לְשׁוֹנָם, *They did not change their tongue* (i.e., the Hebrew language); and שֶׁהָיוּ גְּדוּרִים בָּעֲרָיוֹת, *They were restrained against immorality.*

The first two verses of this psalm allude to these three merits. *When 'Israel' went out* indicates that the Jewish nation remained *Israel*, retaining their Jewish names; *from a people of alien tongue* indicates that the language of Egypt was still *alien* to the Jewish people. *Judah became His sanctuary* implies that Israel was not defiled by the immorality of Egypt, for, as our Sages have taught (*Vayikra Rabbah* 24:6), restraint against sexual immorality is a precondition of holiness (*Chasam Sofer*).

בֵּית יַעֲקֹב מֵעַם לֹעֵז — *Jacob's household from a people of alien tongue.*

This statement poses a puzzling question: since Israel sojourned in Egypt for two hundred and ten years, how did the Egyptian language remain *alien* to them? *Radak* explains that although many Jews left their quarters to work among the Egyptians (and thus *did* learn the language of their oppressors), there was a group that remained in the Jewish territory of

Goshen. It was these Jews who spoke only the Holy Tongue. *Alshich* identifies this group as the tribe of Levi, who did not serve the Egyptians. *Ibn Yachya*, however, says that this verse refers to the Jewish women, who stayed home and did not mingle with the aliens. Therefore, the Psalmist uses the expression בֵּית יַעֲקֹב, *the household of Jacob*, which is the name reserved specifically for Jewish women (see *Exodus* 19:3 and *Rashi's* commentary there).

Radak concludes that even the Jews who were forced to communicate with the Egyptians only did so under duress. Among themselves, however, the Jews spoke only the Holy Tongue and regarded Egyptian as a foreign language.[1]

2. הָיְתָה יְהוּדָה לְקָדְשׁוֹ — *Judah became His sanctuary.*

God singled out the tribe of Judah to be the family of royalty, and He sanctified them for this role when they displayed outstanding leadership at the Sea of Reeds. Led by their prince, Nachshon ben Aminadav, this tribe was the first to jump into the threatening waters. God's name was sanctified by Judah's willingness to face martyrdom (*Rashi*).

In 68:28, the Psalmist described how, when the tribe of Benjamin attempted to usurp Judah's leadership by jumping into the sea first, שָׂרֵי יְהוּדָה רִגְמָתָם, *the princes of Judah stoned them.* Since

---

1. At first, Moses refused to be God's representative to Pharaoh, with the excuse that he was tongue-tied. *Rashbam* explains that Moses was *not* suffering from a physiological speech impediment, but that he found his speech impaired when he spoke the Egyptian language.

The *Rogatchover Gaon* points out that Moses should have been quite comfortable and fluent in the Egyptian language, because he had spoken it ever since his infancy in the king's palace. Nevertheless, this language silenced Moses, for it reflected the depravity of the Egyptian people. Since Moses was a holy man of the spirit, he simply could not communicate in a language devoted to lust and gratification of the flesh. His tongue could only speak freely in the Holy Tongue, the language of the soul.

$\mathbf{W}$hen Israel went out of Egypt,
Jacob's household from a people of
alien tongue.
² *Judah became His sanctuary,*
Israel His dominion.
³ *The sea saw and fled,*

---

leadership meant so much to Judah that he was even prepared to stone [רֶגֶם] his adversaries, his descendants [specifically Daniel] were rewarded by being cloaked in אַרְגְּוָן, *royal purple* [cognate to the root רֶגֶם] (see *Daniel* 5:16 and *Midrash Shocher Tov*).[1]

The commentaries note the unusual feminine usage here: the verse states הָיְתָה יְהוּדָה, whereas the masculine form is הָיָה.

Maharal explains that because of Judah's devotion to Him, God entered into an intimate relationship with Israel. This relationship resembled matrimony, with God as the bridegroom and Israel as the bride. [The word קָדְשׁוֹ, *His sanctuary*, may homiletically be rendered *His marriage partner*, for the word קִדּוּשִׁין, literally *sanctification*, also means *betrothal*.] Since Judah is styled as the bride, the feminine form, הָיְתָה, is used here.

יִשְׂרָאֵל מַמְשְׁלוֹתָיו — *Israel His dominion.*

At the sea, Israel finally left the dominion of Egypt. Thenceforth they were under the total sovereignty of God, Who had proclaimed (*Exodus* 19:6): *And you shall be for Me a kingdom of priests and a holy nation*, i.e., a nation completely divorced from the immorality of Egypt (*Radak*).

This may also be interpreted as a specific reference to the tribe of Judah, for when Judah became sanctified, he i.e., King David of the tribe of Judah, was anointed to rule the entire nation, and *Israel became his dominion* (Ibn Yachya).

3. הַיָּם רָאָה וַיָּנֹס — *The sea saw and fled.*
[The verse alludes to the Sea of Reeds which miraculously split [fled] to allow the Jews to escape their Egyptian pursuers.] What did the sea see that caused it to flee? *Midrash Hallel* says that it saw the upraised staff of Moses, which had God's great name engraved upon it.

---

1. *Yalkut Me'am Loez* (Parashas Beshalach 14:21) explains the deeper meaning of the quarrel which raged between Judah and Benjamin at the sea. Indeed, it is difficult to understand why they had to quarrel over who should jump first because there was ample room at the seashore for both tribes to plunge in at the same time.

In truth, this apparently suicidal plunge into the sea was a tremendous demonstration of faith in Hashem, a public act of Sanctification of God's Name. God's Name is sanctified to an even greater extent when an act of faith is spearheaded by the most distinguished Jews, because they set an example for the masses to follow, saying: "If the tribe of kings shows submission and subservience before God, certainly the rest of us must faithfully surrender to His will!"

Therefore, the royal tribe of Judah felt that if any other tribe attempted to usurp their prerogative it was an open defiance of God's will and the sea would not split for them. They cried out to Benjamin, "You are committing suicide by jumping into these waters. You deserve to be stoned for this crime."

In response, Benjamin argued: "God commanded בְּנֵי יִשְׂרָאֵל, *the Children of Israel*, to descend into the sea. The forerunners of the other tribes were born while our father was still called יַעֲקֹב, *Jacob*. Only Benjamin was born after Jacob was awarded the title of victory, *Israel* (see *Genesis* 32:29). Thus, only we Benjaminites are the true Children of Israel and only we are fit to lead the Jewish people triumphantly across the sea."

ד לָאָחוֹר: הֶהָרִים רָקְדוּ כְאֵילִים גְּבָעוֹת כִּבְנֵי־

ה צֹאן: מַה־לְּךָ הַיָּם כִּי תָנוּס הַיַּרְדֵּן תִּסֹּב

ו לְאָחוֹר: הֶהָרִים תִּרְקְדוּ כְאֵילִים גְּבָעוֹת

ז כִּבְנֵי־צֹאן: מִלִּפְנֵי אָדוֹן חוּלִי אָרֶץ מִלִּפְנֵי

ח אֱלוֹהַּ יַעֲקֹב: הַהֹפְכִי הַצּוּר אֲגַם־מָיִם

חַלָּמִישׁ לְמַעְיְנוֹ־מָיִם:

According to a more familiar version of the *Midrash* (*Bereishis Rabbah* 87:10), the sea saw the אֲרוֹן שֶׁל יוֹסֵף, *the casket of Joseph.*

This means that the waters were reluctant to halt their natural flow; they maintained that they were obliged to obey the natural law under which God had placed them. But Joseph's coffin reminded them of how that righteous man had transcended his nature to resist being seduced by Potiphar's wife (*Genesis* 39:13). The sea concluded that if a frail human being could control his nature and flee from sin, then it, too, could restrain its natural flow and flee for the sake of Israel [see *Haggadah Treasury*].

Yet another *Midrash* (*Tanchumah, Parashas Nasso*) emphasizes the idea that the sea is described as seeing Joseph's coffin because Joseph excelled at sanctifying his own vision. Since Joseph refused to become degraded by gazing at another man's wife, he was rewarded when the sea fled upon seeing his coffin.

הַיַּרְדֵּן יִסֹּב לְאָחוֹר — *The Jordan turned backward.*

According to *Rashi* this, too, refers to the miracle of the splitting of the sea, for all the bodies of water in the world — including the Jordan — miraculously parted at that time.

Malbim, however, says that this describes the miracle which occurred in Joshua's time (see *Joshua* 3:16), rather than the miracle at the Sea of Reeds. The Jordan River parted when Joshua led the Jews into Canaan, but the

splitting of this river differed from the splitting of the sea. The sea was a flat, relatively placid body of water, and God sent a wind to push back the water from the two sides; thus the sea seemed to flee in all directions before these gusts.

The Jordan, in contrast, was a flowing river. When God held back the current, the water piled up into a wall, but only on one side. Therefore, the Psalmist here uses the term יִסֹּב, *turned backward*, to indicate that the current was diverted from its usual path.

4. הֶהָרִים רָקְדוּ כְאֵילִים — *The mountains skipped like rams.*

[At the sea, Israel achieved complete autonomy from the physical bonds of Egypt. Yet the Jews did not totally release themselves from the spiritual and cultural influences of Egypt until they purged their souls at Sinai, when they received the Torah. At that time, all the mountains gathered around Sinai (see 68:16) and trembled in awe before the Presence of God. They skipped and pranced, because the world was reborn at Sinai and filled with fresh energy.]

Since *mountains* are very steep and sharp, they are described as *rams* which are large [and have pointed horns] (*Malbim*).

גְּבָעוֹת כִּבְנֵי צֹאן — *The hill like young lambs.*

Since *the hills* are low and shaped in soft curves and ridges, they are compared to *young lambs*, which are small and tender (*Malbim*).

5. מַה־לְּךָ הַיָּם כִּי תָנוּס הַיַּרְדֵּן תִּסֹּב לְאָחוֹר — *What ails you, O sea, that you flee? O*

the Jordan turned backward.

⁴ *The mountains skipped like rams,*
the hills like young lambs.

⁵ *What ails you, O sea, that you flee?*
O Jordan, that you turn back?

⁶ *O mountains, that you skip like rams?*
O hills, like young lambs?

⁷ *Before the Lord's Presence did I, the earth, tremble,*
before the Presence of the God of Jacob.

⁸ *Who turns the rock into a pond of water,*
the flint into a flowing fountain.

Jordan, that you turn back?

[The aforementioned cataclysmic events had a tremendous impact on every phase of creation. Every human being was startled by the tremors which convulsed the world when all the waters split because of the events at the Sea of Reeds and again at the moment of Divine revelation at Sinai. The Psalmist captures the sense of awe and bewilderment which then seized mankind.]

הֶהָרִים תִּרְקְדוּ כְאֵילִים גְּבָעוֹת כִּבְנֵי צֹאן — *O mountains, that you skip like rams? O hills, like young lambs?*

[What metamorphosis has caused you to prance with such renewed vigor?]

7. מִלִּפְנֵי אָדוֹן חוּלִי אָרֶץ — *Before the Lord's Presence did I, the earth, tremble.*

The *earth*, which includes both the mountains and the seas, answers the question posed in the preceding verses: the mountains shook and the seas split because that was the will of God who is *the Lord* and Master over all (*Radak*).

When Moses saw that the sea had split, he laughed and danced for joy. He asked, "O sea, why do you flee?"

The sea replied, "Before you ask me, ask the Jordan why it turned back!"

Moses then posed this question to the Jordan, which replied, "Before you ask me, why don't you ask the mountains why they skip?"

Moses then put this query to the mountains, who responded, "Before you inquire of us, why don't you ask the entire earth why it shook and jumped out of place?"

Moses then questioned the earth, which replied, "Rest assured that it was not because of Moses the son of Amram that we convulsed! It was *before the Lord* alone that the earth trembled" (*Midrash Hallel*).

מִלִּפְנֵי אֱלוֹהַּ יַעֲקֹב — *Before [the Presence of] the God of Jacob.*

Mahari Sagis says that this phrase refers back to the Jordan River which, as explained, did not flee but merely turned backward (*verse* 3). This implies that the Jordan felt less awe before the Presence of God than did the sea. The Jordan did not *flee* in awe upon being split by God because it had previously parted in deference to the Patriarch Jacob (*Genesis* 32:11), when he wished to cross it. Therefore, in Joshua's time, the Jordan merely *turned backward before the Presence of the God of Jacob.*

8. הַהֹפְכִי הַצּוּר אֲגַם מָיִם — *Who turns the rock [into] a pond of water.*

According to *Radak*, this refers to the incident described in *Exodus* 17:6. When the Jews thirsted for water in the wilderness, God instructed Moses, *"You shall smite the rock and water shall come out of it, so that the people may drink."*

חַלָּמִישׁ לְמַעְיְנוֹ מָיִם — *The flint into a flowing fountain.*

[As explained in the *Prefatory Remarks,* this also alludes to the future, when, *the earth shall be filled with knowledge of HASHEM as water covers the sea* (Isaiah 11:9). Even cold rock and hard flint, which seem utterly lifeless, show evidence of the Creator's complete mastery over all of nature.]

The interpolation of the word *into* in the first stich of this verse is based on its parallelism with the second stich. Thus, the prefix ל, *into,* of the word לְמַעְיְנוֹ, *into a fountain,* is tacit in the word אֲגַם, *pond.* Absence of this prefix, however, allows for an alternative interpretation.

Dorash Moshe translates: *Who turns, into rock, a pond of water.* This is a description of Israel crossing the sea. At that time, God performed a double miracle. First, He transformed the pool of water into solid rock and dry land so that Israel could walk through the sea. When the Jews became thirsty during the crossing, God instructed them to strike the frozen walls of water, which resembled stone dikes. Miraculously, the walls, which had been like *flint,* turned into deliciously sweet springs of water which refreshed the Jews and their cattle (*Yalkut Me'am Loez, Parashas Beshalach*).

T he preceding psalm vividly depicts the profound and immediate
awe which HASHEM's miracles inspired in all of mankind. This psalm,
however, describes the long-term effect of these wonders. God's
appearance left an indelible mark of faith upon the Jewish heart from
all generations, but the gentiles were quick to forget the miraculous
display of Divine might. The moment God concealed His presence,
the gentiles taunted the Jews saying, ''Where now is their God?''
(verse 2).

Therefore, we beseech God to intervene again, in order to teach the
scoffers a lesson, Not for our sake, HASHEM, not for our sake, but for
Your Name's sake give glory, for the sake of Your kindness and Your
truth! (verse 1). Give us an opportunity to silence the heretics who
mock You, and thus, we will praise HASHEM, henceforth and forever!
Praise God! (verse 18).

א לֹא לָנוּ יהוה לֹא לָנוּ כִּי־לְשִׁמְךָ תֵּן כָּבוֹד
ב עַל־חַסְדְּךָ עַל־אֲמִתֶּךָ: לָמָּה יֹאמְרוּ הַגּוֹיִם
ג אַיֵּה־נָא אֱלֹהֵיהֶם: וֵאלֹהֵינוּ בַשָּׁמָיִם כֹּל
ד אֲשֶׁר־חָפֵץ עָשָׂה: עֲצַבֵּיהֶם כֶּסֶף וְזָהָב
ה מַעֲשֵׂה יְדֵי אָדָם: פֶּה־לָהֶם וְלֹא יְדַבֵּרוּ עֵינַיִם

1. לֹא לָנוּ ה' לֹא לָנוּ כִּי לְשִׁמְךָ תֵּן כָּבוֹד —
*Not for our sake, HASHEM, not for our
sake, but for Your Name's sake give
glory.*

We beg You to redeem us, Hashem,
but not because we are personally
worthy, nor because of the merit of our
forefathers (*Iyun Tefillah*). Rather we
urgently strive to protect Your glorious
Name, so that the gentiles have no
opportunity to deny Your mastery and
dominion (*Radak*).

Some commentaries note that the
numerical value of לָנוּ is eighty-six,
which is equivalent to the numerical
value of אֱלֹהִים, *ELOHIM, the Dispenser
of Divine Justice.* Thus we plead לֹא לָנוּ,
do *not* punish us with the strict justice
inherent in the Name *ELOHIM,* ה', but
rather with the kind mercy exemplified
by the Name *HASHEM.* לֹא לָנוּ, but it is
not for our sake that we make this
request for leniency, but because this
harsh punishment would cause a
desecration of Your Name in the eyes of
the gentiles (*Rav Vidal HaTzorfati;
Nachal Eshkol*).

עַל חַסְדְּךָ עַל אֲמִתֶּךָ — *For the sake of
Your kindness and Your truth!*

Our personal merit is insufficient to
warrant Your assistance; however, You
are the God of *Kindness* Who helps
even those who are unworthy. You also
made a covenant with the Patriarchs and
promised not to abandon their children,
and You must abide by this *truth*
(*Malbim; Iyun Tefilla*).

2. לָמָּה יֹאמְרוּ הַגּוֹיִם אַיֵּה נָא אֱלֹהֵיהֶם —
*Why should the nations say, "Where
now* [or, *please*] *is their God?"*

The translation of נָא, *now,* follows
Targum and *Metzudos* (see comm. to
116:14).

The nations admit that God performed miracles for Israel in the past,
but they claim that *now* He has
withdrawn into His heavenly abode and
abandoned them (*Maharam Arma'ah*).

In 79:10, the very same question is
asked, but without the word נָא, *please*
(which is a form of entreaty). *Chasam
Sofer* explains that the question
concerning God's whereabouts is all too
often a rhetorical one, meant to mock
us. However, as the nations become
disillusioned with their idols, they will
earnestly ask us to *please* tell them
about God. [Here the Psalmist laments
that it will be a pity if we cannot explain
to them why God had hidden His face.]

3. וֵאלֹהֵינוּ בַשָּׁמַיִם כֹּל אֲשֶׁר חָפֵץ עָשָׂה —
*Our God is in the heavens, whatever He
pleases, He does!*

Those fools who mock us do not
recognize the vast difference between
their false idols and our true God. [Their
idols are helpless even though they
reside in their midst, yet] although our
God is in the highest heavens, He rules
all that is upon the earth and in the
heavens above (*Radak*)[1].

4. עֲצַבֵּיהֶם כֶּסֶף וְזָהָב מַעֲשֵׂה יְדֵי אָדָם —
Their idols are silver and gold, the

1. The *Brisker Rav* (*Chiddushei HaGriz HaLevi* on the Torah) provides a deeper insight into
this verse. The *Talmud* (*Yoma* 69a) says that when the gentile hordes desecrated the Holy
Temple, all asked, "Where is Israel's awesome God?" When the cruel nations oppressed God's
chosen children, all wondered, "Where is God's strength?"

In reply, the Sages explained that these events provide a most dramatic display of God's

Not for our sake, HASHEM, not for our sake,
    but for Your Name's sake give glory,
      for the sake of Your kindness and Your truth!
² Why should the nations say,
    "Where now is their God?"
³ Our God is in the heavens,
    whatever He pleases, He does!
⁴ Their idols are silver and gold,
    the handiwork of man.
⁵ They have a mouth, but cannot speak;

---

handiwork of man.

The word עֲצַבֵּיהֶם is cognate with עֶצֶב, *sorrow,* because the helpless idols only disappoint their worshipers, causing them heartbreak and sorrow. How can the idols help a man, since they are the work of his own hands? Certainly they have no more power than their maker (*Ibn Ezra; Radak*).

Homiletically, the *Rabbi of Kotzk* would teach concerning this verse that man suffers from sorrow (i.e., עֲצַבֵּיהֶם) because he mistakenly thinks that כֶּסֶף וְזָהָב מַעֲשֵׂה יְדֵי אָדָם, *silver and gold* [i.e., material riches] *are the handiwork of man.* Consequently, he abuses himself to make money and is sorrowful at its loss, not realizing that a man's income is determined by the will of God.

5. פֶּה לָהֶם וְלֹא יְדַבֵּרוּ — *They have a mouth, but cannot speak.*

These illustrations emphasize the complete impotence of man-made idols, which even lack the five senses which any ordinary man possesses.

Indeed, although the pagans themselves are aware of the inadequacies of these lifeless objects, this does not concern them, because they consider the idols to be no more than symbols representing potent spiritual forces which control the world (*Abarbanel*).

[Here the Psalmist mocks the entire concept of paganism, which is nothing more than a selfish deception. Judaism teaches that man was molded in God's image and that he must serve God by constantly refining and improving himself, in order to bear increasingly greater resemblance to God's lofty attributes of mercy and sanctity (see *Shabbos* 132a).

The pagan, however, selfishly believes that the entire world must serve him. He molds the representative of the spiritual forces in the shape of man so that all of these forces will be channeled towards man. The pagan does not even want his idol to talk, for then it might dictate to him. His true desire is that the power which the idol represents should be transferred to himself.]

awesome power, because the brutality which the conquerors displayed towards Israel infuriates God, yet, He holds back His intense anger and is patient with them.

It is God's desire to allow men to exercise their free will [although, of course, they must be prepared to suffer the consequences of their choices]. God does not allow emotions such as anger and revenge to interfere with His design for the world.

Therefore, when the nations ask, "*Where now is their God?*" i.e., why does He allow Israel's enemies to do all that they desire?, the answer is that it is God's desire to let them exercise free will. Thus, *whatever he,* i.e., the nations, *pleases, he does,* and God does not prevent him from doing so.

ו לָהֶם וְלֹא יִרְאוּ: אָזְנַיִם לָהֶם וְלֹא יִשְׁמְעוּ אַף

ז לָהֶם וְלֹא יְרִיחוּן: יְדֵיהֶם | וְלֹא יְמִישׁוּן
רַגְלֵיהֶם וְלֹא יְהַלֵּכוּ לֹא־יֶהְגּוּ בִּגְרוֹנָם:

ח כְּמוֹהֶם יִהְיוּ עֹשֵׂיהֶם כֹּל אֲשֶׁר־בֹּטֵחַ בָּהֶם:

ט־י יִשְׂרָאֵל בְּטַח בַּיהוָה עֶזְרָם וּמָגִנָּם הוּא: בֵּית

יא אַהֲרֹן בִּטְחוּ בַיהוָה עֶזְרָם וּמָגִנָּם הוּא: יִרְאֵי

עֵינַיִם לָהֶם וְלֹא יִרְאוּ — *They have eyes,
but cannot* [or, *do not*] *see.*

[The repetition of לָהֶם, *for them*,
throughout this sequence would be
unnecessary if the word is a reference to
the idols. Rather לָהֶם refers to the men
who made the idols. They put eyes into
these lifeless dolls solely for their own
selfish purposes. Therefore they are not
concerned with the fact that the idols
לֹא יִרְאוּ, *cannot see* (see *Ohr Hameir*).]

6. אָזְנַיִם לָהֶם וְלֹא יִשְׁמְעוּ — *They have
ears, but cannot hear.*

[The idol-worshipers are deaf to the
truth and to admonitions to change their
ways.]

אַף לָהֶם וְלֹא יְרִיחוּן — *They have a nose,
but cannot smell.*

[The Creator fashioned Adam, the
father of all mankind, in His own image
and blew the breath of life into Adam's
nostrils. With every breath of fresh air
he inhales, man reminds himself that
God is his Creator and that his life is in
God's hands. The idolator has a nose
which is physically identical to the nose
of the believer. Yet, the idolator fails to
sense the presence and the kindness of
the Creator with every breath he takes.]

7. יְדֵיהֶם וְלֹא יְמִישׁוּן רַגְלֵיהֶם וְלֹא יְהַלֵּכוּ —
*Their hands — they cannot feel; their
feet — they cannot walk.*

The expressions *their hands* and *their
feet* are noteworthy, because the
previous two verses had established a
different pattern. Why didn't the
Psalmist state, *they have hands and
cannot feel; they have feet and cannot
walk?* This choice of words is based on

the *Mishnah* (*Avodah Zarah* 41a). If
pieces break off an idol, most of them
may be used, because they are no longer
considered part of the idol. The idol's
hands and feet however, are deemed
essential. [For, as *Rav Hirsch* points out,
these limbs signify the power and free
will which the heathens impute to their
gods.] Therefore, even once the hands
and feet are broken from the idol, they
remain forbidden. Thus פֶּה לָהֶם, *they*
[the idols] *have a mouth* indicates that
the mouth is not considered an integral
part of the idol. But יְדֵיהֶם, *their hands*,
implies that the hands are always
considered part of the idol (*Chanukas
HaTorah*; see *Haggadah Treasury*,
comm. to *Hallel*).

לֹא יֶהְגּוּ בִּגְרוֹנָם — *They cannot utter a
sound from their throat.*

Radak describes הֶגֶה as a grunting
sound which comes from the throat.
Not even so minimal a sound emanates
from the lifeless idols.

8. כְּמוֹהֶם יִהְיוּ עֹשֵׂיהֶם — *Those who
make them should become like them.*

Rav Zeira (*Yerushalmi Avodah Zarah*
4:7) notes that the verse does not say
*those that worship them should be like
them*, for how could those who worship
the sun, moon, and stars become like
them? Therefore, this curse applies only
to man-made images, for it is possible
for the craftsmen *who make them* to
become as lifeless as their creations.

Rav Mannah, however, maintains
that indeed, the Psalmist *could have
said*, *those who worship them should be
like them*, implying that the worshipers

they have eyes, but cannot see;

⁶ *They have ears, but cannot hear;*
they have a nose, but cannot smell.

⁷ *Their hands — they cannot feel;*
their feet — they cannot walk;
they cannot utter a sound from their throat.

⁸ *Those who make them should become like them,*
whoever trusts in them!

⁹ *O Israel! Trust in HASHEM —*
He is their help and their shield!

¹⁰ *House of Aaron! Trust in HASHEM —*
He is their help and their shield!

---

of the celestial bodies and their gods will all be disgraced, for *Isaiah 24:23* prophesies: *Then the moon will be humiliated and the sun ashamed, when HASHEM of Legions will reign in Mount Zion and Jerusalem.*

כּל אֲשֶׁר בֹּטֵחַ בָּהֶם — *Whoever trusts in them!*

[Anyone who places his trust in these inanimate objects will lose his own resemblance to God and will become as lifeless as the idols.]

9. יִשְׂרָאֵל בְּטַח בַּה׳ — *O Israel! Trust in HASHEM.*

The Psalmist contrasts the Children of Israel, who trust in Hashem alone, with those described in the previous verse, who trust in the lifeless and helpless idols (Ibn Ezra).

Maharal comments that there are three groups of Jews, and each has a different motive for serving God. Some Jews cling to God simply because they feel that He is their Father, and they are His devoted sons. These are called יִשְׂרָאֵל, *Israel*, God's chosen, beloved nation.

עֶזְרָם וּמָגִנָּם הוּא — *He is their help and their shield!*

Israel trusts in God because the Jews have a tradition of faith and know that throughout all generations, God *is their help and their shield* (Radak).

When those who merited the title Israel undertake any action, they put their trust in God and *He is their help.* When they need protection from any negative, harmful force, *He is their shield* (Rav Vidal HaTzorfati).

10. בֵּית אַהֲרֹן בִּטְחוּ בַה׳ עֶזְרָם וּמָגִנָּם הוּא — *House of Aaron! Trust in HASHEM — He is their help and their shield!*

According to *Maharal*, this verse refers to the second group of Jews, composed of those who serve God out of love. [They do not approach God sporadically, when seized by a fleeting impulse; rather, they constantly concentrate their hearts on His service and cling to God in all situations. Thus they resemble the *House of Aaron*, i.e., the *Kohanim*-priests, who never betrayed God and were therefore designated to stand in His presence, in the Temple, for all time.][1]

---

1. *Maharsha* (comm. to *Pesachim* 117a) asks: Since *Hallel* was first composed when the Jews crossed the Sea of Reeds — before Aaron had been chosen for the priesthood — how could the Jews single out his family for special blessing?

Harav Moshe Feinstein, שליט״א *(Iggros Moshe, Orach Chaim,* vol. IV, responsa 40, part 12) answers: At that time the Jews merely said: "He will bless the House of Priests" without

יב יְהוָה בָּטְחוּ בַיהוָה עֶזְרָם וּמָגִנָּם הוּא: יְהוָה
זְכָרָנוּ יְבָרֵךְ יְבָרֵךְ אֶת־בֵּית יִשְׂרָאֵל יְבָרֵךְ
יג אֶת־בֵּית אַהֲרֹן: יְבָרֵךְ יִרְאֵי יְהוָה הַקְּטַנִּים
יד עִם־הַגְּדֹלִים: יֹסֵף יְהוָה עֲלֵיכֶם עֲלֵיכֶם וְעַל־
טו בְּנֵיכֶם: בְּרוּכִים אַתֶּם לַיהוָה עֹשֵׂה שָׁמַיִם
טז וָאָרֶץ: הַשָּׁמַיִם שָׁמַיִם לַיהוָה וְהָאָרֶץ נָתַן

The Psalmist assures these devotees that they can *trust* wholeheartedly that God will be their unfailing *shield* (Radak).

11. יִרְאֵי ה׳ בִּטְחוּ בַה׳ עֶזְרָם וּמָגִנָּם הוּא — *You who fear HASHEM! Trust in HASHEM — He is their help and their shield!*

This refers to a third group of Jews, who serve God out of fear and awe (Maharal). Radak identifies them as scholars who are totally immersed in their studies in the seclusion of the House of God. Their intensive research has led them to the conclusion that there is no force in the world which should be feared or trusted, other than God.

Radak also suggests that this may refer to those righteous gentiles who fear God. Indeed, Rashi maintains that these are the gentiles who ultimately converted to Judaism.

Malbim takes note of the refrain עֶזְרָם וּמָגִנָּם הוּא, *He is their help and their shield,* which is thrice repeated. Since each successive group possesses a higher level of faith, it deserves a totally different degree of divine protection. Thus God's reaction to each group is mentioned separately.

12. ה׳ זְכָרָנוּ יְבָרֵךְ — *HASHEM Who has remembered us will bless.*

[Hashem *has remembered* the com-

plex makeup of the Jewish nation and recognizes the diverse levels of faith. He will bless each group and each individual in accordance with his special characteristics. The word יְבָרֵךְ, *will bless*, is included in this stich, even though it is immediately repeated in the following one, in order to emphasize the fact that the root of all blessing is God's mindfulness of us. Indeed, God's concern is, in itself, a blessing worthy of mention.]

יְבָרֵךְ אֶת בֵּית יִשְׂרָאֵל יְבָרֵךְ אֶת בֵּית אַהֲרֹן — *He will bless the House of Israel; He will bless the House of Aaron.*

[The term יְבָרֵךְ, *He will bless*, is repeated three times in this verse because an event which recurs three times creates a חֲזָקָה, *a firmly established reality* (see Yevamos 64b), as King Solomon said: *A three-ply cord is not easily severed* (Koheles 4:12).]

13. יְבָרֵךְ יִרְאֵי ה׳ הַקְּטַנִּים עִם הַגְּדֹלִים — *He will bless those who fear HASHEM, the small as well as the great.*

[When the Psalmist exhorted all elements of the Jewish nation to *trust in HASHEM* (verses 9-11), he made no special reference to the small children because minors lack the experience and maturity which are pre-requisites for complete trust in Hashem. However, now that the Psalmist calls upon God to

knowing who the priests would be. When David later included this phrase in *Hallel*, he substituted the word Aaron.

[According to comm. of *Maharal* to verse 10, the 'House of Aaron' is a general term for all Jews who follow the example of Aaron and serve God out of love. Even before he was appointed to the priesthood Aaron was an example of devoted service to God and was thus worthy of a special blessing as the Jews crossed the sea.]

¹¹ *You who fear HASHEM! Trust in HASHEM —*
   He is their help and their shield!
¹² *HASHEM Who has remembered us will bless —*
   He will bless the House of Israel;
   He will bless the House of Aaron.
¹³ *He will bless those who fear HASHEM,*
   the small as well as the great.
¹⁴ *May HASHEM add upon you,*
   upon you and upon your children!
¹⁵ *You are blessed of HASHEM,*
   Maker of heaven and earth.
¹⁶ *As for the heavens — the heavens are HASHEM's,*
   but the earth He has given to mankind.

bless *those who fear HASHEM* the children are included because they observe the piety of their elders and learn from their example.

Radak suggests that this verse may be interpreted: *He will bless* the small ones in the merit of the older and greater ones (*Radak*).

יֹסֵף ה' עֲלֵיכֶם וְעַל בְּנֵיכֶם .14. *May HASHEM add upon you, upon you and upon your children.*

These words provide a most accurate description of the true nature of בְּרָכָה, blessing. Blessing means increase and abundance, whereas the closest definition of קְלָלָה, curse, is decrease and loss (*Ibn Ezra*).

Abarbanel explains that the Psalmist foresaw through the Holy Spirit that Israel would suffer from attrition in exile. Israel will be concerned lest they never be redeemed because they will be so close to extinction. Therefore, the Psalmist encourages Israel with the assurance that, at the advent of Messiah, their numbers will increase dramatically.

בְּרוּכִים אַתֶּם לַה' עֹשֵׂה שָׁמַיִם וָאָרֶץ .15. *You are blessed of HASHEM, Maker of heaven and earth.*

Because Hashem is the Maker of heaven and earth, all is His, and He is truly the Master, who controls all blessing (*Radak*).

At Creation, God blessed *heaven and earth;* however, as human history unfolded, man's corruption brought curses upon *heaven and earth.* In the future, however, *heaven and earth* will be restored to their pristine state of blessed purity (see Isaiah 66:21). This will be a blessing to all (*Sforno*).

הַשָּׁמַיִם שָׁמַיִם לַה' וְהָאָרֶץ נָתַן לִבְנֵי אָדָם .16. *— As for the heavens — the heavens are HASHEM's* [lit. *to HASHEM*], *but the earth He has given to mankind.*

Although God made both heaven and earth (*verse 15*), it is only the heavens which remain under God's exclusive control, for God gave man control over the earth, as Psalm 8:7 states: *You gave him dominion over the works of Your hand, You placed everything under his feet.*

Since the heavens remain under God's firm control, all celestial bodies are forced to act in accordance with the will of God, without freedom of choice. On earth, however, man was granted the freedom to determine his own actions and beliefs (*Maharit*).

יז לִבְנֵי־אָדָם: לֹא הַמֵּתִים יְהַלְלוּ־יָהּ וְלֹא כָּל־
יח יֹרְדֵי דוּמָה: וַאֲנַחְנוּ | נְבָרֵךְ יָהּ מֵעַתָּה וְעַד־
עוֹלָם הַלְלוּיָהּ:

Many commentaries explain this verse homiletically. Heaven is already *to God*, i.e., dedicated to the holiness of God, thus man need not perfect heaven. But the earth is man's province. We are bidden to perfect it and transform its material nature into something spiritual. Indeed, we are charged to make the earth heavenly (see *Haggadah Treasury*).

[בְּנֵי אָדָם, *mankind* (literally, *Sons of Adam*), alludes to the most distinguished members of the human race. It is they who recognize God's omnipresence and bless Him. Thus they resemble Adam, who comprehended all the secrets of creation.]

The *Talmud* (*Berachos* 35a) notices an apparent contradiction. 24:1 states לַה' הָאָרֶץ וּמְלֹאָהּ, *HASHEM's is the earth and its fullness*, yet here it states: *the earth He has given to mankind*. The *Talmud* explains that if man fails to recognize that the entirety of creation belongs to Hashem, and if he offers no

blessings for the food which he eats, then *the earth and its fullness* remains the property of Hashem. But when man blesses God for the food he eats and pays homage to the Creator, God gives the earth and its bounty to the children of man.

The *Talmud* (*Yevamos* 63a) derives from this verse that it is important to own a piece of real estate, for property gives a person a measure of financial security in addition to a degree of dignity and stature. The *Talmud* states that any man who does not own a piece of land is not considered a man, for the Psalmist says that Hashem gave the earth to the sons of man [i.e., a person only merits the title *son of man* after he possesses a tract of earth].

17. לֹא הַמֵּתִים יְהַלְלוּ יָהּ — *Neither the dead can praise YAH.*

The people who fail to recognize God's omnipresence and influence over the world resemble *the dead*, who are insensitive to all external stimuli and

17 *Neither the dead can praise YAH,*
        nor any who descend into silence.
18 *But we will praise HASHEM,*
        henceforth and forever. Praise God!

who are oblivious to reality (*Rabbi Azariah Figo*). However, the righteous, who are stirred by God's presence, continue to praise God even after their souls depart from their bodies (*Ibn Ezra*).

The Sages (*Yalkut Shimoni* 873) cite this verse in their ruling that a *lulav* (palm branch) which is dried out, bleached, or brittle is invalid for use during the Festival of Succos, because the *lulav* symbolizes the human spine, which enables man to lead an active life. Thus the *lulav* must be fresh and supple, for *the dead cannot praise HASHEM!*

וְלֹא כָּל יֹרְדֵי דוּמָה — *Nor any who descend into silence.*

[The angel who guards the dead is called דוּמָה, *Silence* (see *Chagigah* 5a, *Rashi, s.v.* וְדָרְעִינָא). Those who kept silent in this world and refused to praise God will remain silent in the grave.]

18. וַאֲנַחְנוּ נְבָרֵךְ יָהּ מֵעַתָּה וְעַד עוֹלָם
הַלְלוּיָהּ — *But we will praise HASHEM, henceforth and forever. Praise God!*

Those who praised Hashem in this world will do so *forever*, even in the world of souls [beyond the grave] (*Radak*).

Beis Avraham comments that a person's prayers are often disturbed by the memories of the many sins he has committed, causing him to wonder how he can pray to Hashem. Thus does the Evil Inclination seek to depress man's spirits, for as long as someone is depressed, he cannot raise himself to higher spiritual levels. Therefore, someone who is beset by thoughts of his deficiencies should resolve to begin anew and to forget his earlier failures. This is the Psalmist's call, *We will praise HASHEM, henceforth and forever;* even though we have failed previously, we are determined to make a fresh start.

When David was fleeing from Saul, he felt forlorn and abandoned. Forsaken by family and friends, David proclaimed, I love Him, for HASHEM hears my voice, my supplications (verse 1). Despite the constant harrassment he suffered at Saul's hands, David was sincerely disturbed by the news of Saul's death. When the bearer of these tidings proudly boasted of having slain David's 'enemy,' Saul, David ordered the man executed for having dared to send his hand to destroy the anointed of HASHEM (II Samuel 1:14). Yet, since Saul's death brought a measure of relief to David, he composed this hymn of praise to God (Rashi).

The Psalmist foresaw that Israel would also feel completely alone in exile. The nations taunt them, "Your prayers and pleas are worthless, because God has turned a deaf ear to you." Therefore, this psalm was composed to encourage the downcast exiles with the assurance that indeed, HASHEM hears my voice, my supplications.

The Talmud (Rosh HaShanah 16b-17a) explains that this psalm describes the day of Final Judgment at the time of תְּחִיַּת הַמֵּתִים, the Resurrection of the Dead. The בֵּינוֹנִים, the average people, who are neither completely righteous nor completely wicked, will be saved from hell because God will hear their cries, and He will forgive them. In gratitude, they will sing, "I love Him, for HASHEM hears my voice, my supplications."

‫א אָהַבְתִּי כִּי־יִשְׁמַע | יְהוָה אֶת־קוֹלִי תַּחֲנוּנָי:‬
‫ב-ג כִּי־הִטָּה אָזְנוֹ לִי וּבְיָמַי אֶקְרָא: אֲפָפוּנִי |‬
‫חֶבְלֵי־מָוֶת וּמְצָרֵי שְׁאוֹל מְצָאוּנִי צָרָה וְיָגוֹן‬

1. אָהַבְתִּי כִּי יִשְׁמַע ה' אֶת קוֹלִי תַּחֲנוּנָי — *I love [Him], for HASHEM hears my voice, my supplications.*

The translation follows *Radak*. However, other interpretations of this verse have been offered. According to the *Talmud (Pesachim* 118b), the Jewish people declare: *I am beloved by HASHEM when He hears my voice,* for God's attention proves His love and concern.

Midrash Shocher Tov maintains that the Jewish people here plead with God: We are sick and our hearts ache — not from physical pain, but from love and yearning for You, O God. Oh, how we wish that You would hear our prayers and our pleas and draw us near (see *Rashi* and *Ibn Ezra*).

As explained in the *Prefatory Remarks,* the *Talmud (Rosh Hashanah* 17a) interprets this entire psalm as a reference to the day of Final Judgment, when the dead are resurrected. The בֵּינוֹנִים, *average people,* who are neither completely righteous nor completely wicked, will descend to the fires of hell until God heeds their screams of pain and takes pity on them.

Of this, the School of Hillel taught: וְרַב חֶסֶד מַטֶּה כְּלַפֵּי חֶסֶד, [If the scales of justice are exactly balanced and a man's merits and sins are equal, God] *the abundantly kind One will tilt the scales toward the side of merit.* Thus the unfortunate one who is on the verge of being condemned to hell will be lifted from danger (*Rashi, Rosh HaShanah*).

2. כִּי הִטָּה אָזְנוֹ לִי — *For He has inclined His ear to me.*

Alshich explains that the word שְׁמִיעָה, *hearing,* implies a distance,

whereas אֹזֶן, הִטָּה, *to incline the ear,* connotes proximity and very close attention. At first, God merely *hears* the prayers of Israel, but as our relationship grows more intimate, He inclines His ear to pay heed to our every wish.

וּבְיָמַי אֶקְרָא — *In my days I will invoke [His Name].*

In the days of my exile I called upon Him, and in the days of my triumphant redemption, I give praise to His Name (*Rashi*).

I have learned from experience that I can confidently invoke God under all circumstances, even when I am not entirely worthy of His assistance (*Sforno*).

Midrash Shocher Tov contends that בְּיָמַי, *in my days,* refers to the very best days of life, i.e., the holidays, when Israel reads the special portions of the Torah which relate to the sanctity of these days. [God then responds by imbuing Israel with an additional dimension of holiness which enhances their festival.]

Arugas Habosem (vol. II, p. 234) cites this verse as the reason why *Hallel* is not recited on the Sabbath, despite its immense sanctity. The Sabbath was consecrated by God Himself during the first week of Creation, whereas the festivals have been sanctified by the Jews throughout history. Moreover, it is the Jewish court on earth, rather than the Heavenly Tribunal, which determines the calendar and designates the dates of the festivals. Therefore, when the Psalmist declares וּבְיָמַי [lit., *in my days*] he is alluding to the festival days whose sanctity he and his fellow Jews have created. Only then, אֶקְרָא, *I will call* upon God with *Hallel.*[1]

1. The recital of *Hallel* is restricted to special days. the *Talmud (Shabbos* 118b) rules that one who recites *Hallel* every day is blaspheming and insulting God because the prophets

I love Him, for HASHEM hears
    my voice, my supplications.
² For He has inclined His ear to me,
    in my days I will invoke His Name.
³ The pains of death encircled me;
    the confines of the grave have found me,
    trouble and sorrow I would find.

3. אֲפָפוּנִי — Encircled me.

[This phrase also appears in 18:5; see comm. there. The word אֲפָפוּנִי appears to be cognate with אוֹפַן, wheel or circle.]

Midrash Shocher Tov (Psalm 18:5) suggests several homiletic interpretations: David may be saying, ''My misfortunes are so many that they reach my אַף, nose'' [i.e., they threaten to suffocate me]; or, ''Miseries constantly roll over me, like a never ending אוֹפַן, wheel''; or, ''My misfortunes come in pairs, like the אֲפָפוּן, doubled thread of the loom.'' This word can also be interpreted as if it were spelled עֲפָפוּנִי, cognate with עוּף, bird, suggesting: Sorrows soar over my head like עוֹפוֹת, flying birds.

חֶבְלֵי מָוֶת — The pains of death.

The translation follows Radak and Metzudos, who translate חֶבְלֵי as pains or travails, i.e., I was in the throes of death. Rashi and Targum render groups and interpret: I was surrounded by hostile bands of murderers who sought to kill me. [See commentary to 18:5,6.]

Abarbanel remarks that this is an apt description of the exile, for Israel is encircled by violent enemies who seek to kill them.

According to Tosafos (Rosh Hashanah 17a) this refers to the man who is imprisoned by the deadly bands which inflict eternal punishment in hell. He cries out to God for release.

וּמְצָרֵי שְׁאוֹל מְצָאוּנִי — The confines of the grave have found me.

Rashi views מְצָרֵי as cognate with מֵיצָר, boundary. Radak identifies it with צָר, adversary [i.e., deadly antagonist].

Radak also notes that the strange usage מְצָאוּנִי, lit. they found me, indicates that a person cannot evade the fate which heaven has ordained for him. A man never knows his own destiny. Sometimes he journeys a great distance anticipating that he will meet with success, yet he actually meets his death and the confines of the grave.[1]

צָרָה וְיָגוֹן אֶמְצָא — Trouble and sorrow I would find.

designated Hallel as the hallowed hymn to commemorate the most auspicious occasions in Jewish life. If one recites it daily, he lowers Hallel to the status of a common song and detracts from God's praise (Rashi, Shabbos 118b).

Meiri explains that constant recital of God's miracles diminishes a person's awe for them. Lacking reverence, the person will ultimately deny the veracity of these miracles and blaspheme God.

Meshech Chochmah (Parashas B'Chukosai) observes that God's control over the world is not confined to the performance of extraordinary miracles. God completely controls and directs every aspect of nature. If a man recites Hallel every day it is as if he only praises God for the extraordinary marvels and denies the daily ongoing wonder of God's mastery over nature. This attitude truly insults God.

[See Talmidei Rabbeinu Yonah, Berachos chapter 5, and Magen Avraham to Orach Chaim 684:1.]

1. Radak cites an incident from the Talmud (Sukkah 53a) to illustrate this point. Rabbi Yochanan said: The feet of a man are his bond, for they take him to the place where his

ד אֶמְצָא: וּבְשֵׁם־יהוה אֶקְרָא אָנָּה יהוה
ה מַלְּטָה נַפְשִׁי: חַנּוּן יהוה וְצַדִּיק וֵאלֹהֵינוּ
ו מְרַחֵם: שֹׁמֵר פְּתָאיִם יהוה דַּלּוֹתִי וְלִי
ז יְהוֹשִׁיעַ: שׁוּבִי נַפְשִׁי לִמְנוּחָיְכִי כִּי־יהוה
ח גָּמַל עָלָיְכִי: כִּי חִלַּצְתָּ נַפְשִׁי מִמָּוֶת אֶת־עֵינִי
ט מִן־דִּמְעָה אֶת־רַגְלִי מִדֶּחִי: אֶתְהַלֵּךְ לִפְנֵי

Alshich defines צָרָה, *trouble*, as physical pain, and יָגוֹן, *sorrow*, as mental anguish. [Both of these agonies beset David and the nation of Israel in exile.]

4. וּבְשֵׁם ה' אֶקְרָא — *Then I would invoke the Name of HASHEM.*

[When endangered, I called upon ה', HASHEM, the Dispenser of Kindness.]

אָנָּה ה' מַלְּטָה נַפְשִׁי — *"Please HASHEM, save my soul!"*

The word אָנָּה denotes fervent pleading. It may be spelled either אָנָּה as here and in verse 16 or אָנָּא as in 118:25 (*Radak*).

5. חַנּוּן ה' וְצַדִּיק וֵאלֹהֵינוּ מְרַחֵם — *Gracious is HASHEM and righteous, our God is merciful.*

The Psalmist explains that before He invoked Hashem's Name, these thoughts passed through his mind (*Ibn Ezra*).

[He recognized that ה', the Dispenser of Divine Kindness, is not wanton in His goodness, He is *righteous*, just as אֱלֹהִים, the Dispenser of Divine Justice, is *merciful* and understanding.]

6. שֹׁמֵר פְּתָאיִם ה' — *HASHEM protects the simple.*

HASHEM protects those whose faith

is *simple* and innocent, who do not weave elaborate schemes and plots to protect themselves. God protects the intelligent man who does not use his mind to assure his personal security but trusts in Hashem. God also watches over the feeble-minded, *simpletons* who lack the mental ability to protect themselves (*Radak*).

דַּלּוֹתִי וְלִי יְהוֹשִׁיעַ — *I was brought low, but He saved me.*

Sforno perceives this verse as a reference to the dark days of Israel's exile: Wandering and suffering robbed me of my knowledge, and I became a *simpleton* who could not even protect himself with prayer. I was defenseless because my intellect was *brought low*, yet God *saved me.*

According to the *Talmud* (*Rosh Hashanah* 17a), this alludes to a man who was on the verge of sinking into the depths of hell, but was saved by God's abundant kindness.

Tosafos suggests that דַּלּוֹתִי is related to דַּל, *poor*, implying: Since I was impoverished by a lack of *mitzvos* and merits, I was about to sink. *Tosafos* also suggests that דַּלּוֹתִי is related to דָּלָה, *to raise up*, indicating, "When I was *low*, God raised me up and saved me."

presence is required. Two Ethiopians were once in the service of King Solomon and acted as his scribes. One day, the Angel of Death confided to Solomon that he needed to take the lives of the two men. To preserve their lives, Solomon sent his scribes to the city of Luz, for the Angel of Death cannot enter Luz, because all its inhabitants are careful to speak only the truth.

Yet, when the two Ethiopians reached the gates of Luz, they died. Afterwards, the Angel of Death told Solomon, "You sent those two to the very place where I was commanded to take their lives!"

Then Solomon observed, "The feet of a man are his bond for they bring him to the place where his presence is required."

⁴ *Then I would invoke the Name of HASHEM:*
"Please HASHEM, save my soul!"
⁵ *Gracious is HASHEM and righteous,*
our God is merciful.
⁶ *HASHEM protects the simple;*
I was brought low, but He saved me.
⁷ *Return to your rest, my soul;*
for HASHEM has been kind to you.
⁸ *For You delivered my soul from death,*
my eyes from tears,
my feet from stumbling.

---

7. שׁוּבִי נַפְשִׁי לִמְנוּחָיְכִי — *Return to your rest, my soul.*

When misery and persecution upset me, I told my soul that it would find peace and comfort only if it would *return* to Hashem (*Radak*). For the prophet (*Hosea* 14:2) exhorts, *Return* [i.e. *repent*] *O Israel, unto HASHEM your God* (*Abarbanel*).

Similarly, when it is time for the ingathering of the exiles, they will be encouraged to return to Hashem through Torah study and *mitzvah* observance (*Sforno*).

Tosafos (ibid.) teaches that these words reflect the relief and joy of the soul which was *saved* from the fires of hell and returned to its *rest* in paradise by God's kindness and mercy.

כִּי ה׳ גָּמַל עָלָיְכִי — *For HASHEM has been kind to you.*

Past history clearly indicates that Israel's return to God has always achieved favorable results (*Radak*).

8. כִּי חִלַּצְתָּ נַפְשִׁי מִמָּוֶת — *For You delivered my soul from death.*

In exile, I was in mortal danger on countless occasions, and You rescued me (*Sforno*).

אֶת עֵינִי מִן דִּמְעָה — *My eyes from tears.*

I broke down and cried bitterly when the cruel tyrants ruthlessly forbade the practice of Your precepts. However, You wiped my tears away by nullifying their decree (*Sforno*).

אֶת רַגְלִי מִדֶּחִי — *My feet from stumbling.*

When I wished to pursue the path of righteousness, the gentiles placed obstacles in my way. You removed these difficulties and kept *my feet from stumbling* (*Sforno*).[1]

---

1. The *Brisker Rav* (*Chiddushei HaGriz HaLevi on Torah, Tehillim*) explains how this entire verse relates to the day of Final Judgment, for there are three terrible judgments which can be rendered at that time, and the Psalmist thanks God for salvation from all of them.

The worst punishment is כָּרֵת, *cutting off*, of the soul. For, as *Rambam* teaches (*Hilchos Teshuvah* 8:5): The greatest revenge which the Almighty can take is to cut the soul off from eternal life. Thus, the Psalmist states, *For You delivered my soul from* [eternal] *death*.

The next level of punishment is for the בֵּינוֹנִים, *average people*, who retain a portion in the eternal afterlife, but must first suffer the pains of *Gehinnom* (hell), to purge them of their sins (see *Hilchos Teshuvah* 3:5).

The Psalmist (84:7) calls *Gehinnom*, עֵמֶק הַבָּכָא, *the Valley of Weeping*, because all who burn there shed constant tears (see *Rashi* on 84:7 and *Eruvin* 19a). When saved from *Gehinnom* the Psalmist says, *You delivered ... my eyes from tears*.

The *Talmud* (*Rosh Hashanah* 17a) describes a third punishment of Judgment Day; after twelve months in *Gehinnom*, the body of the wicked man is completely destroyed and his soul

י יהוה בְּאַרְצוֹת הַחַיִּים: הֶאֱמַנְתִּי כִּי אֲדַבֵּר
יא אֲנִי עָנִיתִי מְאֹד: אֲנִי אָמַרְתִּי בְחָפְזִי כָּל־
יב הָאָדָם כֹּזֵב: מָה־אָשִׁיב לַיהוה כָּל־
יג תַּגְמוּלוֹהִי עָלָי: כּוֹס־יְשׁוּעוֹת אֶשָּׂא וּבְשֵׁם

9. אֶתְהַלֵּךְ לִפְנֵי ה׳ בְּאַרְצוֹת הַחַיִּים — *I shall walk before HASHEM in the land of the living.*

Saul chased me out of the land of Israel, the home of the living God, to dwell in foreign lands where idolators worship lifeless gods (*Rashi*).

How I yearn to return to Israel, where the very air makes men healthy and robust and the holy atmosphere grants the mind renewed vitality and alertness (*Radak*).[1]

Indeed, continues *Radak*, Israel deserves to be called the *land of the living*, for the exiled Jew lives in constant fear of death, but in Israel he dwells in safety.

The *Talmud* (Yoma 71a) cites the opinion of Rav Yehudah, who identifies the *land of the living* as מְקוֹם שְׁוָקִים, *the market place.* When David fled from his pursuers and when Israel wandered in exile, they lacked the income to provide the necessities of life. Therefore a market place became of vital importance for them (*Rashi* and *Tosafos Yeshanim, Yoma 71a*).

Harav Mordechai Gifter, א שליט״, observes that David's piety was not confined to the synagogue or the House of Study. He recognized that he was before Hashem even while engaged in financial matters of the market place and his rigid honesty and morality were as steadfast in the market place as they were in the synagogue.

Rambam (Hilchos Teshuvah 3:5, 8:7) identifies אַרְצוֹת הַחַיִּים, *the land of the living,* as the World to Come, for the man who is delivered from hell praises God for bringing him to his eternal reward (see *Tosafos, Rosh Hashanah 17a*).

10. הֶאֱמַנְתִּי כִּי אֲדַבֵּר אֲנִי עָנִיתִי מְאֹד — *I kept faith although I would say, "I suffer exceedingly."*

Ibn Ezra renders: I trust that which I said — *Return my soul, unto your rest* — for I believe that God can redeem me from my deep suffering and restore my tranquility.

According to *Rashi*, this verse expresses David's frustration in exile. When David's son Absalom rebelled against him, many of David's former friends and allies also turned against him. David was particularly shocked when Tziva, the servant of Mefiboshes (the son of King Saul), falsely claimed that his master had treacherously joined the revolt against David and sought the throne for himself. Tziva ingratiated himself to David by supplying David with sorely needed provisions and transportation. In sincere gratitude, David declared that Mefiboshes would be stripped of all his possessions and that those would then be given to the faithful Tziva (*II Samuel 16:1-4*).

Later Tziva's accusations proved to be false [see *Shabbos 56a*]. David

is burned. The wind then scatters his ashes beneath the feet of the righteous.

Thus the Psalmist thanks God: *You delivered ... my feet from stumbling*, i.e., from becoming dirt under the feet of the righteous.

1. Numerous sources identify *Eretz Yisrael* as the *land of the living* beause the dead are destined to be resurrected there. For this reason, the Patriarchs and righteous Sages in all generations yearned to be buried in the holy soil. Those who are interred in foreign soil will roll to Israel through subterranean passages prior to their resurrection (*Pesikta Rabbasi 1; Yerushalmi Kesubos 12:3*).

⁹ *I shall walk before HASHEM*
     in the land of the living.
¹⁰ *I kept faith although I would say,*
     "I suffer exceedingly."
¹¹ *I said in my haste,*
     "All mankind is deceitful."
¹² *How can I repay HASHEM*
     for all His kindness to me?
¹³ *I will raise the cup of salvations*

---

bitterly lamented the fact that he had been duped and said, הֶאֱמַנְתִּי, *I trusted*, Tziva like a gullible fool; my confidence in Tziva was so great כִּי אֲדַבֵּר, *that I spoke out*, and condemned Mefiboshes. For this rash act, *I suffer exceedingly*, because (verse 11), *in my haste, I said, 'All mankind* [even the faithful Mefiboshes] *is deceitful' "* (Chida, Simchas HaRegel).

[The incident with Tziva proved to David that one of the deepest pains of exile is the uncertainty it breeds, for one never knows who his true friends are.]

11. אֲנִי אָמַרְתִּי בְחָפְזִי כָּל הָאָדָם כֹּזֵב — *I said in my haste, "All mankind is deceitful."*

Rashi (based on *Midrash Shocher Tov* to Psalm 18) comments that this refers to the incident at סֶלַע הַמַּחְלְקוֹת, *the Rock of Division* (See *I Samuel* 23:19-29), in which the treacherous people of Zif revealed David's mountain hideaway to Saul. Saul's army then encircled the mountain, leaving no avenue of escape. In his despair David demanded of Hashem, "What happened to the promise You made to me when the prophet Samuel anointed me king? If I am slain now, I will never ascend to the throne!"

Suddenly God sent an angel who called Saul away from the pursuit, saying, "Hurry away, for the Philistines have spread out to attack the land." Thus David was saved.

Others contend that Hashem miraculously split the mountain in two

with David and his warriors on one side and Saul's army on the other. Therefore, the mountain was called סֶלַע הַמַּחְלְקוֹת, *the Rock of Division*.

At that time, David admitted that he had been hasty in condemning Samuel as deceitful [see footnotes to 18:3 and 24].

Abarbanel perceives this verse as a reference to the bleak, dismal exile [for the exile discourages the Jews and leads them to the hasty, premature conclusion that all the prophets' promises concerning redemption were *deceitful*].

12. מָה אָשִׁיב לַה׳ — *How can I repay HASHEM?*

When God gathers in the scattered survivors of the long exile, they will remember that God delivered them from many extremely dangerous situations, and they will feel incapable of expressing their apprecation (*Sforno*).

What gift can I give to the King who owns everything? (*Ibn Ezra*). How can I possibly repay His acts of kindness for they are too numerous to recount? (*Radak*).

How can I even approach Him? He is eternal and I am finite; He is the highest, and I am the lowest! (*Ibn Yachya*).

תַּגְמוּלוֹהִי — *His kindness.*

Radak draws our attention to the uncommon spelling תַּגְמוּלוֹהִי. (This word is usually spelled תַּגְמוּלוֹ.) He explains that the הִי ending is in the Aramaic literary and grammatical style.

יד יהוה אֶקְרָא: נְדָרַי לַיהוה אֲשַׁלֵּם נֶגְדָה־נָּא
טו לְכָל־עַמּוֹ: יָקָר בְּעֵינֵי יהוה הַמָּוְתָה

[When the Psalmist refers to the kindness which Hashem displayed in the exile, he writes kindness in foreign style.]

Etz Yosef cites the Talmud (Menachos 29a) which teaches that the World to Come was created with the letter י, and This World was created with the letter ה. By adding these letters to תְּגְמוּלוֹ, the Psalmist thanks God for the kindness which He bestows upon us in both worlds.

13. כּוֹס יְשׁוּעוֹת אֶשָּׂא — I will raise the cup of salvations.

Rashi translates כּוֹס literally as a cup of wine, a reference to the thanksgiving offerings which the fugitive exile will bring when he returns safely to his homeland, for the animal sacrifices

[קָרְבַּן תּוֹדָה] are accompanied by wine libations upon the altar. At that time, the Levites sing hymns of praise for God's salvation.[1]

16:5 reads ה׳ מְנָת חֶלְקִי וְכוֹסִי, HASHEM is my allotted portion and my share.

Ibn Ezra comments that here, too, כּוֹס, cup, (which contains an exact measurement) refers to man's share in this world. Thus, whatever a man's lot, he must lift it up (i.e., dedicate it) to the service of God and give thanks for his destiny.

וּבְשֵׁם ה׳ אֶקְרָא — And I will invoke the Name of HASHEM.

Here David thanks God for His acts of salvation. Earlier (verses 3-4) David used the same words to praise God even in times of suffering. Verse three

1. The Talmud (Pesachim 119b) teaches that God will host a special banquet as a reward for the righteous. It will be called the Banquet of Loving-Kindness. After the meal, the cup of benediction will be handed to the Patriarch Abraham, in order that he may lead the grace. Abraham will demur, "I cannot lead the grace because I begot Ishmael."

Isaac will refuse to lead the grace, saying, "... I begot Esau."

Jacob will refuse, saying, "... I married two sisters at once, something which the Torah was destined to prohibit."

Moses will turn down the offer to lead the grace, saying, "... I never had the privilege of entering the Land of Israel, not in my lifetime and not even [in burial] after my death."

Joshua will refuse, saying, "... I was not granted the privilege of sons."

Finally, David will be asked to lead the grace and he will respond enthusiastically, "Indeed, it is most fitting that I should bless [God]. I will raise the cup of salvations and I will invoke the Name of HASHEM."

[David's wholehearted acceptance is puzzling, because the defects which disqualified the other candidates also applied to David: David bore sons who shamed him — Absalom and Adoniyahu; he married Bath Sheba under questionable circumstances; and he was responsible for the death of Uriah the Hittite.

To understand the refusal of the Patriarchs and other Jewish leaders, we must realize that at this future Banquet of Loving-Kindness, mankind will offer its gratitude for all the kindness which God showed throughout history. Mankind will finally recognize that even when God visited suffering and tragedy upon them, it was for the best.

However, the person who leads the final grace must be one who fully appreciated God's kindness in each and every event of his lifetime.

Thus, Abraham will disqualify himself with the confession, "There was one event in my life which I did not fully appreciate: I did not accept the birth of a wicked son like Ishmael, with a full heart." Our other luminaries will make similar confessions.

Only David can claim with full confidence, "Although many tragedies befell me, I accepted every Divine decree with a full heart and appreciated the kindness concealed in every blow! I always lifted the cup of salvation and called upon the Name of HASHEM," i.e., I recognized Him as Dispenser of loving-kindness.]

and I will invoke the Name of HASHEM,
14 My vows to HASHEM I will pay,
in the presence of His entire people.
15 Precious in the sight of HASHEM
is the death of His devout ones.

concludes, צָרָה וְיָגוֹן אֶמְצָא, *trouble and sorrow I would find;* and verse four begins, וּבְשֵׁם ה' אֶקְרָא, *then I would invoke the Name of HASHEM.*

The only difference between the two references is that at the time of salvation and triumph, David can immediately lift up his cup to God. In times of trouble and sorrow, however, David must pause briefly to absorb the shock and to meditate upon each manifestation of God's Will. After a moment of reflection, David even appreciates the value of personal tragedy. Then he begins a new sentence, and invokes the Name of Hashem (*Chazah Zion*).

14. נְדָרַי לַה' אֲשַׁלֵּם — *My vows to HASHEM I will pay.*

As I was fleeing and wandering in exile, I made many vows to Hashem. I promised that if He would return me safely to Israel, I would render thanksgiving offerings to His Name (*Radak*).

Sforno views this as a pledge by the Jewish people to rededicate themselves to the very first vow which they made at Sinai, נַעֲשֶׂה וְנִשְׁמָע, *We shall do and we shall listen* (Exodus 24:7).

נֶגְדָה נָא לְכָל עַמּוֹ — *In the presence of His entire people.*

I will fulfill my vow in the presence of all Jews especially the sinners who have neglected their own obligations and vows, either intentionally or unintentionally. My service will set an example for them (*Sforno*).

According to *Metzudos* and *Targum* (see *Targuma D'HaTargum* and comm. to 115:2) נָא means *now* and refers to the time when David promises to pay his vows, which is immediately.

Radak is of the opinion that נָא means

please and he also says that it refers back to אֲשַׁלֵּם [implying that this is not a declaration but a humble request: May I please be given the opportunity to pay my vows].

15. יָקָר בְּעֵינֵי ה' הַמָּוְתָה לַחֲסִידָיו — *Precious in the sight of HASHEM is the death of His devout ones.*

Rashi and *Ibn Ezra* comment that יָקָר actually means *a great undertaking* or *a difficult thing.* It is difficult for God to remove a devout man from this world, for his fulfillment of God's precepts and his Torah study are extremely precious. [The Psalmist predicts that when he pays his vows to Hashem and serves Him devoutly, the righteous man will enter the ranks of those whose service is *precious in the sight of HASHEM.*]

Rav Yosef Caro explains that God must entice the soul of a righteous man away from his body by showing him the יָקָר, *precious,* spiritual reward which awaits in the afterlife. When God draws the pious soul to Himself in this fashion, it is known as מִיתַת נְשִׁיקָה, *Death by Divine kiss* (*Maggid Meishorim*).

The *Midrash* (*Shemos Rabbah* 52:3) relates that Rabbi Abahu was depressed on his deathbed because he thought that he had wasted his life. But God displayed before him thirteen rivers flowing with perfume, symbolic of the Torah and *mitzvos* of Rabbi Abahu's life. Then Rabbi Abuhu died confident that his piety had been precious to God and that his eternal reward would be equally precious.

Midrash Shocher Tov observes that it is so difficult for God to remove the righteous from this world that He cannot do it, so to speak, unless He

טז לַחֲסִידָיו: אָנָּה יהוה כִּי־אֲנִי עַבְדֶּךָ אֲנִי־
יז עַבְדְּךָ בֶּן־אֲמָתֶךָ פִּתַּחְתָּ לְמוֹסֵרָי: לְךָ־אֶזְבַּח
יח זֶבַח תּוֹדָה וּבְשֵׁם יהוה אֶקְרָא: נְדָרַי לַיהוה
יט אֲשַׁלֵּם נֶגְדָה־נָּא לְכָל־עַמּוֹ: בְּחַצְרוֹת | בֵּית
יהוה בְּתוֹכֵכִי יְרוּשָׁלָ͏ִם הַלְלוּ־יָהּ:

receives their permission. God convinces the devout that they must make way for the next generation who are waiting to make their own precious contributions to the advancement of God's glory.

When the pious are about to leave the world, the common masses begin to realize how precious their presence had been, for it is the virtue and merit of the pious which protects their contemporaries from many punishments and catastrophes.

As the precious soul of the pious ascends heavenward, three legions of ministering angels greet with the traditional welcome, יָבֹא בְשָׁלוֹם, come in peace.

16. אָנָּה ה' כִּי אֲנִי עַבְדֶּךָ — Please, HASHEM — for I am Your servant.

Targum translates אָנָּה as בְּבָן, please. Sforno interprets: Please, God, let me live to see the days of the Messiah. I realize that precious reward awaits the pious in the afterlife [yet since I am Your servant, I wish to live to see the time when all men will serve You].

Ibn Ezra renders אָנָּה as I thank You, i.e., I give thanks to Hashem for allowing me the privilege of being His servant.

Sifri (Parashas Va'eschanan) stresses the unique distinction of being awarded the title עַבְדּ, servant, of God: Some men called themselves God's servant, yet God did not regard them as such. Other men were called עַבְדּ, servant, by God, but they did not call themselves servant. David, however, referred to himself as God's servant and recognized that this conferred special obligations upon him. Moreover, God endorsed this title by

calling him עַבְדּ as I Kings 11:32 states: לְמַעַן עַבְדִּי דָוִד, for the sake of David, My servant.

Meshech Chochmah explains that God only awards the title עַבְדִּי, My servant, to men who never accepted the mastery of another person and never called any other man אֲדֹנִי, my master. [See ArtScroll comm. to Joshua 1:1 and Overview to Joshua.]

אֲנִי עַבְדְּךָ בֶּן אֲמָתֶךָ — I am Your servant, son of Your handmaid.

[See Radak on 86:16.]

The slave who is born to a mother who is also a slave [i.e., handmaid] is far more submissive than a slave who was born free (Rashi). The former serves his master naturally and instinctively, whereas the latter serves him only in response to external threats (Sforno).

Panim Yafos explains that this repetition of the expression עַבְדְּךָ, Your servant, alludes to the dual aspect of David's identity. David received the seventy years of his life as a gift from Adam [see Overview, vol. I] who was God's servant, but not the son of His handmaid [for Adam had no mother]. Later Adam's soul came into David who was not only God's servant, but also the son of Your handmaid [for David's devout mother exerted a great influence over her son. Here David pays homage to her contribution to his success].

David also recognized that his greatness was inherited from his grandmother Ruth, who was a humble servant of God and of all those who represented God (see Bava Basra 75b; Tanchuma Vayishlach 1).

When Ruth spoke to Boaz, the Torah leader of Israel, she referred to herself as

16 *Please, HASHEM — for I am Your servant,*
   I am Your servant, son of Your handmaid —
      You have released my bonds.
17 *To You I will sacrifice thanksgiving offerings,*
      and I will invoke the Name of HASHEM.
18 *My vows to HASHEM I will pay,*
      in the presence of His entire people.
19 *In the courtyards of the House of HASHEM,*
      in your midst, O Jerusalem. Praise God!

---

a mere שִׁפְחָה, *woman-servant* (*Ruth* 2:13). But Boaz responded: Heaven forbid! Do not deprecate yourself! You will not go down in history as one of the lowly אֲמָהוֹת, *handmaidens*, but as one of the holy אִמָּהוֹת, *matriarchs*, of the Jewish nation (*Pesikta D'Rav Kahana*).

פִּתַּחְתָּ לְמוֹסֵרָי — *You have released my bonds.*

The slave who is purchased in the market resents the bondage which is forced upon him and constantly seeks avenues of escape; therefore he must be tightly bound and shackled. However, the born slave has an ingrained allegiance to his master and gladly remains under his jurisdiction. His bonds may be loosened for he will not attempt to escape (*Alshich*).

Thus, David declares: I have inherited a legacy of love for You, O God! My grandmother Ruth made immense sacrifices in order to join the Jewish people and to accept the yoke of Torah. From her I inherited an instinctive devotion to do your will, so I need no external bonds to harness me to Your service (*Bach*).

The *Talmud* (*Yevamos* 77a) relates that God planned David's birth many years before he was born. The Torah prohibits Ammonites and Moabites from entering the Congregation of God, but the restriction applies only to male converts. This is because God foresaw that David was destined to descend from Ruth the Moabite and that

Rechavam, king of Judah, grandson of David and progenitor of the Davidean dynasty, was to be born from Solomon's wife, Na'amah the Ammonite.

David sang: *You have released my bonds.* Sovereign of the Universe, two binding prohibitions restricted me until You excluded females from the injunction against the Ammonites and the Moabites. [See commentary to *Psalm* 40:6.]

17. לְךָ אֶזְבַּח זֶבַח תּוֹדָה — *To You I will sacrifice thanksgiving offerings.*

David promises to offer these sacrifices in appreciation of the wonders which God performed for his sake (*Rashi*).

The Sages teach (*Tanchuma Emor* 14) that all sacrifices will be discontinued in the Messianic era except for the thanksgiving offering. Here David expresses his yearning to witness the advent of that long-awaited era (*Sforno*).

וּבְשֵׁם ה' אֶקְרָא — *And I will invoke the Name of HASHEM.*

I will bring my thanksgiving offerings publicly, so that I can proclaim my gratitude to You, before the Jewish masses (*Radak*), and in the presence of the gentile nations (*Sforno*).

18. נְדָרַי לַה' אֲשַׁלֵּם נֶגְדָה נָּא לְכָל עַמּוֹ — *My vows to HASHEM I will pay, in the presence of His entire people.*

Ibn Ezra explains that verse 14 is repeated here to indicate the exact place where the Psalmist intends to fulfill his vows: *In the courtyards of the House of HASHEM* (verse 19).

19. בְּחַצְרוֹת בֵּית ה' — *In the courtyards of the House of HASHEM.*

The vows will be paid in the location of the Holy Ark, where Hashem's Presence resides (*Radak*).

בְּתוֹכֵכִי יְרוּשָׁלָיִם — *In your midst, O Jerusalem.*

This refers to the ultimate sanctity. The Tabernacle in the wilderness was sacred but its sanctity was limited, for it was not intended to be the perpetual home of the Holy Ark. However,

Jerusalem was ordained as the permanent resting place of the Holy Ark. Therefore, it is most appropriate that God be praised *in the midst* of this holy city (*Abarbanel*).

הַלְלוּיָהּ — *Praise God!*

This constitutes the public declaration which David promised to make (verse 17), הַלְלוּיָהּ, *praise God!* (*Ibn Ezra*)

[This declaration is more meaningful than any animal sacrifice for it indicates a submission of the entire soul to God. See commentary to 111:1 for its significance.]

117 מזמור קיז

This psalm, composed of only two verses, is the shortest chapter in all of Scripture. Radak explains that its brevity symbolizes the simplicity of the world order which will prevail after the advent of the Messiah.

Today the world is composed of countless groups which are divided by differences in religion, politics, economics, race and nationality. In the future, however, there will be but two groups: the Children of Israel who will scrupulously follow all six hundred and thirteen precepts of the Torah and the remainder of mankind who will faithfully fulfill the Torah's seven Noachide laws. The first verse of psalm 117 speaks of the gentiles, who will eventually recognize God; the second verse describes Israel, who has always recognized Him.

א הַלְלוּ אֶת־יהוה כָּל־גּוֹיִם שַׁבְּחוּהוּ כָּל־
ב הָאֻמִּים: כִּי גָבַר עָלֵינוּ | חַסְדּוֹ וֶאֱמֶת־יהוה
לְעוֹלָם הַלְלוּיָהּ:

1. הַלְלוּ אֶת ה' כָּל גוֹיִם — *Praise HASHEM, all you peoples.*

Ibn Ezra attributes this exhortation to David, who [at one time] ruled over *all the peoples* of the world (see *I Kings* 18:10 and *Megillah* 11a).

שַׁבְּחוּהוּ כָּל הָאֻמִּים — *Laud Him, all you nations!*

Midrash Shocher Tov defines גּוֹיִם, *peoples,* as those groups who oppressed Israel and אֻמִּים, *nations,* as those who did *not* oppress Israel.

In the future, the benevolent and friendly *nations* will ensure that the formerly hostile *peoples* will recognize the truth and praise Hashem. The *nations* will say: If the hostile and cruel *peoples* can repent and sing, God's praises we certainly should do so! [Thus all gentile groups will rally around God's banner.]

Chazah Zion identifies גּוֹיִם as the *ministering angels* in heaven whom God has appointed as His agents to control the אֻמִּים, *nations,* down on earth.

Iyyun Tefillah notes that הָאֻמִּים is spelled with the ה' הַיְדִיעָה, *definite article,* whereas גוֹיִם is spelled without it. This teaches that the אֻמִּים are the powerful, well-known *nations,* whereas the גוֹיִם are the *peoples* of the small, backward countries which lack international prominence.

2. כִּי גָבַר עָלֵינוּ חַסְדּוֹ — *For His kindness to us was overwhelming.*

Why should *gentile peoples* and *nations* praise HASHEM for overwhelming Israel with Divine kindness?[1]

Radak explains that the gentiles constantly mock God and deny His ability to extricate Israel from exile. However, when they witness Israel's miraculous redemption, at which time God will overwhelm us with kindness, they will be forced to admit God's supremacy and praise His Name.

Yaavetz Hadoresh observes that Israel will merit overwhelming kindness because of the extraordinary service which the Jews rendered to God. Therefore all the gentiles are destined to become Israel's servants and they will

---

1. One might expect that the martyrs of Israel would seek Divine revenge against their gentile persecutors and executioners. Yet, when the holy souls of the martyrs ascend to heaven, God showers them with such spiritual bliss that they immediately forget the physical suffering which they endured at the hands of the gentiles. Therefore: *Praise HASHEM, all you peoples; laud Him, all you nations,* because God's *kindness to us was* so *overwhelming* that our anger is forgotten and we do not demand revenge for the torture and suffering which you inflicted upon us.

117
1-2

Praise HASHEM, all you peoples;
laud Him, all you nations!
²*For His kindness to us was overwhelming,*
and the truth of HASHEM is eternal. Praise God!

praise God for this opportunity to make amends for their original cruelty to Israel.

Once, a Russian prince asked *Rav Yitzchak (Reb Itzaleh)* of Volozhin to explain why *non*-Jews, instead of Jews, are expected to praise God for his kindness to Israel. *Rav Yitzchak* replied without hesitation, ''You princes plan countless anti-Semitic schemes with which to destroy us, but our Merciful God always manages to foil your plots. Your secret councils are so well guarded that we Jews don't even realize all the

ways in which you intended to harm us, nor how God saved us. Only you gentiles see clearly how God's *kindness to us was overwhelming;* therefore only you can praise Him adequately!'' *(Chiddushei HaGriz HaLevi on the Torah, Yisro 18:10; Iyun Tefillah.)*[1]

וֶאֱמֶת ה' לְעוֹלָם הַלְלוּיָהּ — *And the truth of HASHEM is eternal. Praise God!*

God's promise to redeem us from exile is *the truth which endures forever,* i.e., for the duration of the exile. Therefore, Praise God *(Radak).*

1. In the times of the Vilna Gaon, Valentin Potocki, a young noble and heir to Count Potocki, converted to Judaism and assumed the name of Abraham ben Abraham. The Catholic church was infuriated by his conversion and condemned him to be burned at the stake. As he was lead to his death, his executioner realized that he was about to kill a holy man and begged Abraham ben Abraham not to seek revenge against him in the afterlife.

The kindly convert calmed the executioner, saying, ''When I was a little boy I wandered from the palace and got lost in the woods. A farmer took me into his home and treated me like his own son. Once I made some soldiers out of clay but the farmer's son was jealous and smashed my precious soldiers. I was both sad and angry.

''Eventually I was found and returned to my palace. A few days later the farmer and his son, trembling with fear, came to see me. The farmer begged me not to punish his son for breaking my soldiers.

''I calmed him, saying, 'When I was with you I had nothing but those mud soldiers and so their destruction grieved me. But in my palace I have more splendid toys and playthings than I can ever use. Now, the loss of coarse mud figurings means nothing to me.'''

Passionately, the devout convert turned to his executioner, ''While I lived, my body, my flesh and blood, were precious to me and certainly I would be bitter towards anyone who hurt me. But now I am entering a new world, a spiritual palace of eternal bliss and glory. In that world, my body will seem like crude clay and mud and its pain and destruction will be meaningless to me.''

מזמור קיח 118

Radak detects two levels of meaning in the text of this psalm. On a personal level, these verses express David's relief at the death of King Saul, who had pursued him relentlessly. As he ascended the throne, David envisioned the many wonderful improvements which he planned to make for the enhancement of his kingdom and for the welfare of his subjects.

On a national level, this composition reflects the joy which Israel will experience at the final redemption, when Israel will return to its former glory and will revive its noble traditions and institutions. Every segment of Jewish society will be affected by God's concern, and all will enthusiastically proclaim: His kindness endures forever!

Verses 5-9 of this psalm are included in the main portion of the Tashlich service.

א הוֹדוּ לַיהוה כִּי־טוֹב כִּי לְעוֹלָם חַסְדּוֹ:
ב־ג יֹאמַר־נָא יִשְׂרָאֵל כִּי לְעוֹלָם חַסְדּוֹ: יֹאמְרוּ־
ד נָא בֵית־אַהֲרֹן כִּי לְעוֹלָם חַסְדּוֹ: יֹאמְרוּ־נָא
ה יִרְאֵי יהוה כִּי לְעוֹלָם חַסְדּוֹ: מִן־הַמֵּצַר
ו קָרָאתִי יָּהּ עָנָנִי בַמֶּרְחָב יָהּ: יהוה לִי לֹא

1. הוֹדוּ לַה׳ כִּי טוֹב — *Give thanks to HASHEM, for He is good.*

Abarbanel explains that this is a general expression of thanks to God. No matter what occurs, God is always good and everything He does is for the best, even though this may not be immediately apparent to man.

כִּי לְעוֹלָם חַסְדּוֹ — *His kindness endures forever!*

Abarbanel explains that this phrase refers to clearly revealed acts of kindness. Often, this visible *kindness* is followed by periods of הֶסְתֵּר פָּנִים, *concealment of the Divine Presence.* The Psalmist reassures Israel that God's *kindness endures forever* and that it will definitely manifest itself again after each period of concealment.

In the next three verses, the Psalmist exhorts various groups to repeat the second part of the verse (but not the first part) because although these groups will praise God for specific acts of Divine *kindness* which they have witnessed, they do not always appreciate God's constant, unfailing goodness (which is lauded in the first section of this verse).

2. יֹאמַר נָא יִשְׂרָאֵל כִּי לְעוֹלָם חַסְדּוֹ — *Let Israel say: "His kindness endures forever!"*

Let Israel constantly recount the kindness which God bestowed upon them when He took them out of Egypt and sustained them in the desert for forty years (*Midrash Shocher Tov*).

According to *Radak*, David is speaking: Now that I have become king, Israel surely has reason to praise God's kindness. Even during the reign of King Saul, I was Israel's protection, but how

much more can I be Israel's defender now that I am invested with royal power! They have nothing more to fear from their enemies.

3. יֹאמְרוּ נָא בֵית אַהֲרֹן כִּי לְעוֹלָם חַסְדּוֹ — *Let the House of Aaron say: "His kindness endures forever!"*

David noted that the priests, in particular, suffered at the hand of King Saul, for he ordered the massacre of the priestly city of Nob, which took eighty-five lives. These sons of Aaron certainly must praise God for the kindness He showed in ending Saul's reign of terror and beginning David's benign rule.

Radak explains that, in the future, the sons of Aaron will also have special reason to rejoice, because they were particularly hurt by the Temple's destruction and by the exile, which deprived them of the opportunity to perform their priestly duties. When they witness the ingathering of the exiles and the reconstruction of the Temple, they will see that God's *kindness endures forever* (*Radak*)

4. יֹאמְרוּ נָא יִרְאֵי ה׳ כִּי לְעוֹלָם חַסְדּוֹ — *Let those who fear HASHEM say: "His kindness endures forever!"*

Those who fear God have special cause to rejoice at my assumption of royal power, because I will assure the peace and security of the land. This atmosphere of tranquility is essential for establishing a nation-wide awareness of God's presence.

Similarly, at the advent of the Messianic era, Israel will thank God for releasing them from the need to fear other men, thereby enabling them to concentrate on the fear of God (*Radak*).

Midrash Shocher Tov comments that

Give thanks to HASHEM, for He is good;
"His kindness endures forever!"

² Let Israel say:
"His kindness endures forever!"

³ Let the House of Aaron say:
"His kindness endures forever!"

⁴ Let those who fear HASHEM say:
His kindness endures forever!

⁵ From the straits I called upon YAH,
YAH answered me with expansiveness.

---

a number of individuals especially deserved the title יְרֵא ה', *one who fears HASHEM*; these included Phineas [who killed Zimri, the prince of the tribe of Shimon], Chananyah, Mishael, and Azariah [who did not fear Nebuchadnezzar when he threw them into the furnace], and the gentiles who convert to Judaism in every generation [and do not fear those who condemn their conversion act].

5. מִן הַמֵּצַר קָרָאתִי יָּהּ עָנָנִי בַמֶּרְחָב יָהּ — *From the straits I called upon YAH, YAH answered me with expansiveness.*

Literally, מֵצַר means *confines* or *limits* and מֶרְחָב means *wide open space.* David said: When Saul pursued me, I was confined to narrow caves. Now that I am king, however, I openly display my royal majesty (*Radak*).

[The stress which results from suffering and from being in danger constricts a person's spirit, but God's deliverance creates joy and relief, which cause the spirit to expand.]

[In this verse, the Psalmist addresses God with the abbreviated Name יָהּ, *YAH*, which signifies the concealment of the Divine Presence when the Jews are in exile. Since God's involvment in Israel's affairs becomes limited (צַר), His Name is reduced from the four letters of יהו״ה to the two letters of יָהּ, *YAH*.

The Psalmist notes that although the Jew is in exile, when God's name is limited (מֵצַר) to YAH, nevertheless, YAH

answered with (מֶרְחָב) *expansiveness*, i.e., unlimited relief.]

Abarbanel adds that the Jews here recall the difficult days in the מֵצַר of מִצְרַיִם, *Egypt* [מִצְרַיִם may be read as מֵצָרִים, *limits, straits*]. Just as God responded at that time when we called out to Him, so does He respond whenever we plead before Him in distress.

[In 4:2 we read: בַּצָּר הִרְחַבְתָּ לִי, *You have relieved me of my distress.* צָר, *distress*, literally means a *tight, constricted place*, and הִרְחַבְתָּ, *relieved*, literally means *widened, enlarged.*

David said to the Holy One, Blessed is He, "Master of the Universe, whenever I was constricted by difficult circumstances, You provided an avenue of relief and set me free. When I was caught in the dilemma of Bath Sheba, You presented me with a wonderful son, Solomon. When I was embroiled in the distress of all Israel, You eased my burden and gave me permission to prepare for the construction of the Holy Temple" (*Yerushalmi, Taanis* 2:9).

This declaration is an eloquent expression of one of David's most cherished credos: Never be discouraged by the terrible burdens and pressures of life, for every frustrating, enfeebling situation is actually a Divinely ordained opportunity to overcome adversity by fully utilizing one's talents and abilities. Thus, every distress which threatens to limit or diminish an individual, can

---

ז אִירָא מַה־יַּעֲשֶׂה לִי אָדָם: יהוה לִי בְּעֹזְרָי
ח וַאֲנִי אֶרְאֶה בְשֹׂנְאָי: טוֹב לַחֲסוֹת בַּיהוה
ט מִבְּטֹחַ בָּאָדָם: טוֹב לַחֲסוֹת בַּיהוה מִבְּטֹחַ

serve to broaden his scope and to enlarge his soul. (See comm. to 4:2.)]

6. ה' לִי לֹא אִירָא — *HASHEM is with me, I have no fear.*

[In the despair of exile, God's full presence is not revealed on earth and His limited involvement in human affairs is signified by the abbreviated Name יָהּ, YAH. Yet the Psalmist teaches that, in the uppermost heavens, יהוה, HASHEM the full Divine Name, indicating God's total involvement with man), sympathizes completely with those in exile.

God Himself is an infinite power. He is the source of all power, from whom every man draws his strength. The Psalmist asks, "What threat can any man pose, since I am fortified by the omnipotent God?"]

מַה־יַּעֲשֶׂה לִי אָדָם — *How can man affect me?*

No individual can harm me (Radak). Even an entire nation cannot overwhelm me or tear me from my faith (Sforno).

[Man derives all his strength from God. If God has not ordained my death, how can my adversary destroy me?]

Abraham asked, "What can my enemy Abimelech do to me?"

Jacob asked, "What can my malicious brother Esau do to me?"

David asked, "What can my gigantic rival Goliath do to me?"

This may be compared to the King's favored attendant who was envied by the other courtiers. When they grew jealous and threatened his life, the favorite merely said, "The king loves me and protects me. What, then, can the others do to me?" (Midrash Shocher Tov).

7. ה' לִי בְּעֹזְרָי — *HASHEM is with me, through my helpers.*

I have many helpers, but I place confidence in them only because

HASHEM is with them. If my helpers were not granted strength by God, their assistance would be futile and worthless.

I recognize that Hashem, who is the source of all power, has stripped my enemies of their power and has invested power in my helpers and friends. Now I can have full confidence in my helpers, because I am sure that they are vehicles for the fulfillment of God's will (Ibn Ezra; Radak).

Indeed, once Hashem is with a person, everyone will become the man's helper, as Solomon said (Proverbs 16:7), בִּרְצוֹת ה' דַּרְכֵי אִישׁ גַּם אוֹיְבָיו יַשְׁלִם אִתּוֹ *When HASHEM is pleased with a man's ways, He causes even his enemies to make peace with him* (Abarbanel).

Iggeres Hatiyul comments that David was prompted to write this verse because he had reason to believe that his ranks had been infiltrated by traitors and spies, who posed as his helpers and friends. He pleaded: ה' לִי בְּעֹזְרָי, *HASHEM be with me among my helpers,* to expose those who masquerade as my friends; וַאֲנִי אֶרְאֶה בְשֹׂנְאָי, *and I myself will vanquish those enemies who challenge me openly.* [See also Rav Vidal HaTzorfati and Chasam Sofer.]

וַאֲנִי אֶרְאֶה בְשֹׂנְאָי — *Therefore I can face my foes.*

When Hashem comes to my aid, I shall witness the downfall of my enemies in any way that I desire (Radak).

Radak also notes that the Psalmist says something similar in 54:9: *From every distress has He rescued me, and upon my foes has my eye looked.*

The Sages teach that a person who *deserves* salvation is granted the privilege of witnessing the downfall of his enemies, as when Israel saw the death of the Egyptians at the Sea.

⁶ HASHEM is with me, I have no fear;
   how can man affect me?
⁷ HASHEM is with me through my helpers,
   therefore I can face my foes.
⁸ It is better to take refuge in HASHEM
   than to rely on man.
⁹ It is better to take refuge in HASHEM
   than to rely on nobles.

However, he who is saved by the merits of others does not deserve this privilege. Therefore, Lot, who was saved by virtue of Abraham's merit, was forbidden to look back upon the destruction of Sodom. Here the Psalmist expresses confidence that he will be righteous enough to witness his enemies' defeat (Navah Tehillah).

Rabbi Yoseif Leib Bloch of Telshe interpreted the verse homiletically, noting that a man is known by his enemies. If one's enemies are righteous people, then he surely must be at fault; but if he is hated by the wicked, then he must be highly commendable. David is confident that Hashem is for him through his helpers, because he sees [the character of] his enemies: they are people who have cast off the yoke of Torah and mitzvos. Since David is hated by such people, then he can feel confident that he is serving God and will merit His help (Haggadah Treasury).

8. טוֹב לַחֲסוֹת בַּה׳ מִבְּטֹחַ בָּאָדָם — It is better to take refuge in HASHEM than to rely on man.

Rabbeinu Bachya and Vilna Gaon explain the difference between the two closely related words חָסִיוֹן, taking refuge, and בְּטָחוֹן, reliance. The former denotes absolute confidence even though no guarantees have been given. Thus, one may seek מַחֲסֶה, refuge, behind a boulder or under a sturdy roof, for although neither the boulder nor the roof has pledged shelter, one has confidence in their indestructibility. The word בְּטָחוֹן, reliance, however, presup-

poses a promise of protection. Thus, one may receive a הַבְטָחָה, pledge, of protection from a military power. The Psalmist says that it is far better to put one's trust in Hashem's protection, even without a pledge from Him, than to rely on the most profuse assurances of human beings (Haggadah Treasury).

Radak cites the words of the prophet (Jeremiah 17:5): Cursed be the person who relies on man and makes mortal flesh his supporting arm. Even if circumstances do force a person to rely on his fellow man, he should place his main confidence in God, for it is He Who implants the desire to help in the heart of the human benefactor.

9. טוֹב לַחֲסוֹת בַּה׳ מִבְּטֹחַ בִּנְדִיבִים — It is better to take refuge in HASHEM than to rely on nobles.

Not only is God's protection better than that of a common man (verse 8), but it even surpasses the protection afforded by all the powerful nobles of the world (Ibn Ezra).

Ibn Yachya determines that the נְדִיבִים are the seventy ministering angels, who are God's agents for governing the seventy peoples of the earth.

These seventy angels compose the Heavenly Tribunal which surrounds God's celestial throne. Those who are positioned on God's left are harsh and unrelenting in their demands for strict justice, whereas those who stand at God's right are נְדִיבִים [lit. generous] in their desire to treat mankind with compassion.

Nevertheless, it is far better to take refuge in the mercy of Hashem than to

 י   בְּנֶדֶיבִֹים: כָּל־גוֹיִם סְבָבֻוּנִי בְּשֵׁם יהוה כִּי

יא   אֲמִילַם: סַבּוּנִי גַם־סְבָבֻוּנִי בְּשֵׁם יהוה כִּי

יב   אֲמִילַם: סַבּוּנִי כִדְבֹרִים דֹּעֲכוּ כְּאֵשׁ קוֹצִים

יג   בְּשֵׁם יהוה כִּי אֲמִילַם: דָּחֹה דְחִיתַנִי לִנְפֹּל

יד   וַיהוה עֲזָרָנִי: עָזִּי וְזִמְרָת יָהּ וַיְהִי־לִי

rely on [the kindness of these] noble angels (Mahari Gikatalla).

10. כָּל גוֹיִם סְבָבֻוּנִי בְּשֵׁם ה' כִּי אֲמִילַם — *All the peoples surround me; in the Name of Hashem I cut them down!*

Radak maintains that this refers to two incidents in David's life: the first took place when David sought refuge at the court of King Achish and he was immediately surrounded by hostile enemies. He escaped, feigning insanity, until the frustrated Achish had him driven away, a clever ruse which Hashem had implanted in his mind.

The second incident occurred when the Amalekites surrounded the city of Ziklag, burned it to the ground, and carried off David's wives and family. [Then David asked for help in *the Name of HASHEM.* David sought out Eviasar, the High Priest, and requested that he seek guidance from the sacred breastplate, the *Urim V'Tumim,* which would light up and relay messages to him in the name of Hashem. Through the *Urim V'Tumim,* Hashem assured David that he would pursue the enemy and *cut him down* (see *I Samuel* 30).]

11. סַבּוּנִי גַם־סְבָבֻוּנִי בְּשֵׁם ה' כִּי אֲמִילַם — *They encircle me, they also surround me; in the Name of HASHEM I cut them down!*

Midrash Shocher Tov and *Rashi* view this verse and the preceding one as alluding to the future war of Gog and Magog. The Psalmist repeats that the enemy surrounds him three times, an allusion that Gog and Magog will attack Israel three times and ascend three times against Jerusalem, even as Sennacherib ascended three times against the land of Israel and as Nebuchadnezzar ascended

three times against Jerusalem.

Vilna Gaon (commentary to *Isaiah* 5:26) differentiates between the root סָב which means *to encircle from close by* and סָבַב, which means *to surround from a distance.* Thus the Psalmist reasons: The first to attack me were the neighboring peoples who סְבָבֻוּנִי, *encircled me* (verse 10) — from a distance. Then they closed in and tightly encircled me [סַבּוּנִי]. Meanwhile, the distant nations arrived to join the hostilities. First they, too, surrounded me from a distance and then *they encircled me like bees,* as all the attackers pressed against me, in a mad frenzy (*Etz Yosef, Otzar HaTefillos*).

12. סַבּוּנִי כִדְבֹרִים — *They encircle me like bees.*

Midrash Shocher Tov comments that just as a bee gathers honey for her masters, so the Holy One, Blessed is He, will gather all the nations of the world and bring them to ascend against Jerusalem. [This symbolism is most appropriate, for when the bee gathers honey, it thinks that it is collecting the sweet nectar for its own use, not realizing that the beehive is under the control and supervision of a beekeeper. Similarly, the nations will gather around Jerusalem under the impression that they are fighting for their own gain. In truth they are mere pawns manipulated by God to fulfill His design for the world.]

Maharam Arma'ah observes that a bee stings only once in its lifetime, and for that one sting it pays with its life, because it leaves its stinger inside its victim and remains mortally wounded. Similarly, David's enemies were so consumed with hatred that they fought

¹⁰ *All the peoples surround me;*
in the Name of HASHEM I cut them down!
¹¹ *They encircle me, they also surround me;*
in the Name of HASHEM I cut them down!
¹² *They encircle me like bees,*
but they are extinguished as a fire does thorns;
in the Name of HASHEM I cut them down!
¹³ *You pushed me hard that I might fall,*
but HASHEM assisted me.
¹⁴ *My strength and my song is YAH,*

---

him even though they knew that they would surely forfeit their lives in the conflict.

דַּעֲכוּ כְּאֵשׁ קוֹצִים — [But] they are extinguished as a fire does thorns.

When dried-out thorns are ignited, the flame blazes immediately, but subsides quickly and then dies out (Ibn Ezra, Sforno). The thorn fire does not spread to other trees. Similarly, David's enemies flared up against him, knowing that they themselves would be consumed in the conflict, but hoping that they could destroy David with them. To their vast dismay, however, although they were consumed in the flame of their own hatred, the blaze failed to spread and David remained unscathed (Maharam Arma'ah).

13. דָּחֹה דְחִיתַנִי לִנְפֹּל וַה׳ עֲזָרָנִי — You pushed me hard [lit. pushing you pushed me] that I might fall, but HASHEM assisted me.

In the preceding verses, the Psalmist speaks of his enemy indirectly; now, however, he addresses the foe directly. Zohar (Parashas Vayishlach) identifies this foe as man's greatest adversary, the Evil Inclination, which always tempts him. This foe must be dealt with directly and decisively.

Chazah Zion says that the Psalmist is referring to the physical personification

of evil, the serpent which struck at Eve again and again and pushed her against the tree, saying, ''Just as you have touched the tree and remained unharmed, so can you also safely eat of its fruit.'' The serpent intended to make Adam and Eve fall, but HASHEM helped them.

Maharam Arma'ah says that David made this statement to King Saul after Saul inadvertently entered David's cave hideway. David could have slain Saul, but he allowed the King to leave unscathed. David cried out after Saul, ''You attempted to strike me down again and again, but Hashem is with me and you have failed. Let Hashem judge between us and may Hashem avenge me from you'' (see I Samuel, 24:12).

According to Ibn Yachya, this verse refers to the future war of Gog and Magog. At first the enemy will be successful and מָשִׁיחַ בֶּן יוֹסֵף, the Messiah, son of Joseph, will be slain. The enemy will strike again and again, chasing the defeated Jews to the mountains and the wilderness. Ultimately, Hashem will help me (i.e., Israel) with the advent of the eternal Messiah, the son of David.[1]

14. עָזִי וְזִמְרָת יָהּ וַיְהִי לִי לִישׁוּעָה — My strength and my song is YAH, and He has been my slavation.

[This verse is an exact replica of

---

1. The Talmud (Succah 52b) introduces the tradition of two Messiahs. We have at least two detailed descriptions of how events leading from one Messiah to the next are destined to

טו לִישׁוּעָה: קוֹל | רִנָּה וִישׁוּעָה בְּאָהֳלֵי צַדִּיקִים
טז יְמִין יְהוָה עֹשָׂה חָיִל: יְמִין יְהוָה רוֹמֵמָה
יז יְמִין יְהוָה עֹשָׂה חָיִל: לֹא־אָמוּת כִּי־אֶחְיֶה
יח וַאֲסַפֵּר מַעֲשֵׂי יָהּ: יַסֹּר יִסְּרַנִּי יָּהּ וְלַמָּוֶת לֹא
יט נְתָנָנִי: פִּתְחוּ־לִי שַׁעֲרֵי־צֶדֶק אָבֹא־בָם אוֹדֶה

Exodus 15:2, where these words serve
as the introduction to the Song at the
Sea [.אָז יָשִׁיר].

[I received *My strength* from God
alone, and when I used it to overcome all
of my foes, Hashem's goodness was the
theme of *my song.* Even in exile, when
God limits the *strength* of His
involvement in Israel's affairs and His
full Name is abbreviated to יָהּ, *YAH,* He
is still *my (only) salvation.*]

15. קוֹל רִנָּה וִישׁוּעָה בְּאָהֳלֵי צַדִּיקִים — *The
sound of rejoicing and salvation is in the
tents of the righteous.*

When *HASHEM's right hand does
valiantly* for the sake of His chosen
people then *the righteous* will respond
by filling their *tents* with *with sounds of
rejoicing* over this *salvation* (Radak).

יְמִין ה' עֹשָׂה חָיִל — *"HASHEM's right
hand does valiantly …"*

Radak explains that חָיִל [literally
power] refers to energy and wealth:
when God bestows these upon man,
there is ample reason to rejoice.

Rashi holds that these words and
those of the following verse are the
joyous proclamations made by the
righteous.

16. יְמִין ה' רוֹמֵמָה — *HASHEM's right
hand is raised triumphantly.*

Rashi quotes *Midrash Aggadah,*
which says that since God created the
upper celestial world with His right

hand, Death can exercise no power
there. As *Isaiah* 48:13 states: *My hand*
[i.e., the left hand] *has laid the
foundation of the earth, and My right
hand has spanned the heavens.*
Similarly, the Psalmist says here, the
right hand of Hashem created the
exalted heavens. This very same right
hand shall do valiantly for the righteous
in the future. The right hand will
resurrect them and they will live
forever, as the Psalmist proclaims, *I
shall not die! I shall live!* (verse 17).

יְמִין ה' עֹשָׂה חָיִל — *"… HASHEM's right
hand does valiantly."*

This is a repetiton of the end of the
preceding verse. Why is *HASHEM's
right hand* mentioned twice, while no
mention is made of the left? *Tanchuma
(Parashas Beshalach)* explains that when
the Jews abide by the will of God, they
have the power to transform His left
hand (which is relatively inferior) into a
right hand. But if Israel defies God's
wishes, His *right hand* becomes a left
hand as we read הֵשִׁיב אָחוֹר יְמִינוֹ, *He has
withdrawn His right hand* (*Lamentations* 2:3).

17. לֹא אָמוּת כִּי אֶחְיֶה וַאֲסַפֵּר מַעֲשֵׂי יָהּ — *I
shall not die! I shall live and relate the
deeds of YAH.*

No! I will survive the murder
attempts of my enemies and live to
*recount the deeds of God, Who saved
me from my foes* (Radak).

untold: that of *Rav Saadiah Gaon* in his *Emunos Vedeos* (8,2,5) and *Ramban* in commentary
to *Shir HaShirim* (8:13).

The common thread which runs through both commentaries is that initially there will be a
Messiah descended from Joseph who will bring about a degree of independence in a rebuilt
Jerusalem where many of the former exiles will have gathered. However, this Messiah is
destined to be killed in battle and only after that will the events be set in motion which will
culminate in the rule of the Davidic Messiah [see ArtScroll *Ezekiel,* comm. to 37:8].

and He has been my salvation.

¹⁵ *The sound of rejoicing and salvation*
is in the tents of the righteous:
"HASHEM's right hand does valiantly.

¹⁶ *HASHEM's right hand is raised triumphantly;*
HASHEM's right hand does valiantly!"

¹⁷ *I shall not die! I shall live*
and relate the deeds of YAH.

¹⁸ *YAH has chastened me exceedingly,*
but He did not let me die.

¹⁹ *Open for me the gates of righteousness,*
I will enter them and thank YAH.

Michlal Yofi translates these words: *I shall not die while I live*, for as the *Talmud (Berachos* 18b) says, the wicked are considered dead even while they are alive, because their souls are cut off from God, the source of all life. David says, "I shall be counted among the righteous who are considered alive even after death. Certainly, I will not be considered dead even while I live!"

Yaavetz HaDoresh paraphrases: *I shall not die when I relive*, i.e., after I am resurrected. This alludes to the statement of the *Talmud (Sanhedrin* 92b) that the righteous who will be resurrected will never again return to dust. Their restored bodies will be endowed with a spiritual dimension which will make them perfectly attuned to the performance of God's will (see *Ramban, Shaar HaGemul*).

18. יִסֹּר יִסְּרַנִּי יָּהּ וְלַמָּוֶת לֹא נְתָנָנִי — *YAH has chastened me exceedingly* [lit. *chasten has He chastened me*], *but He did not let me die.*

Throughout the duration of the exile, *YAH has chastened me exceedingly*, However, I survived because God never intended to kill me. He decreed that I should suffer only because suffering would atone for my sins (*Rashi*).

Indeed, יִסּוּרִים, *suffering*, is the most positive assurance of life, as Solomon

taught (*Proverbs* 6:23): וְדֶרֶךְ חַיִּים תּוֹכְחוֹת מוּסָר, *and instructive chastisement is the path of life* (*Bereishis Rabbah* 9:10) [see Overview to Vol. I part III, *The Kindness of Affliction*].

19. פִּתְחוּ לִי שַׁעֲרֵי צֶדֶק אָבֹא בָם אוֹדֶה יָהּ — *Open for me the gates of righteousness, I will enter them and thank YAH.*

In *Sefer HaMaggid*, Rav Yoseif Karo ponders this request: If the righteous man is truly deserving, then the gates of heaven will be opened for him by Divine command, and a request is unnecessary; if the righteous man is undeserving, however, how can pleading help?

Kedushas Levi explains that this plea reflects the yearning of the righteous man to ascend to new heights of sanctity and devotion. When he reaches a plateau of piety, the righteous man remains unsatisfied and immediately seeks to climb even closer to Hashem. It is precisely this intense yearning which infuses the righteous man with the strength to overcome all obstacles in his path. Thus, although certain doors may in fact be closed even to righteous men, the yearning expressed in this verse is itself the key to opening them.

Zohar (Parashas Emor), explains that this plea is the righteous man's response to Hashem's call to all who love Him,

כ יָהּ: זֶה־הַשַּׁעַר לַיהוה צַדִּיקִים יָבֹאוּ בוֹ:

כא־כב אוֹדְךָ כִּי עֲנִיתָנִי וַתְּהִי־לִי לִישׁוּעָה: אֶבֶן

כג מָאֲסוּ הַבּוֹנִים הָיְתָה לְרֹאשׁ פִּנָּה: מֵאֵת

כד יהוה הָיְתָה זֹּאת הִיא נִפְלָאת בְּעֵינֵינוּ: זֶה־

for from heaven there rings out a cry: "Open your hearts to Me, even with an opening as tiny as a pinpoint, and I will open for you the massive gates of heaven!"

Midrash Shocher Tov explains the significance of the plural usage שַׁעֲרֵי צֶדֶק, *the gates of righteousness.* In the future, they [i.e., the angels] will ask a man, "On which *mitzvah* did you concentrate?"

If he answers, "I fed the hungry," they will tell him, "This is the gate for those who fed the hungry; you may enter!"

If a man answers, "I gave drink to the thirsty," they will tell him, "This is the gate of those who gave drink to the thirsty; you may enter!"

The same will happen to those who clothed the naked, provided homes for orphans, practiced loving-kindness or concentrated on any of the *mitzvos.* Thus David says, "I concentrated on *all* the *mitzvos*; therefore, let all *the gates of righteousness open for me!*"

20. זֶה הַשַּׁעַר לַה' צַדִּיקִים יָבֹאוּ בוֹ — *This is the gate of HASHEM; the righteous shall enter through it.*

[One special gate is reserved only for the truly righteous: the gate of song. All who enter there fill their mouths with words of appreciation for Hashem's kindness.]

Targum and *Rashi* identify this gate as the gate of the Temple, which leads to

the House of Hashem. When the exile is over, the righteous will enter through this gate, and they will thank God for answering their plea for redemption.

Yaavetz HaDoresh explains that the שַׁעֲרֵי צֶדֶק, *gates of righteousness*, are the gates of Jerusalem, which is destined to be called עִיר הַצֶּדֶק, *the city of righteousness* (Isaiah 1:26). When the armies of Gog and Magog besiege Jerusalem, the gates will be locked tight. Refugees and exiles from all over the world will come to these gates, begging for asylum: *Open for me the gates of righteousness* (verse 19). However, only one gate will be opened, and only the deserving will be granted entry: *This is the gate of HASHEM,* [only] *the righteous shall enter it!*[1]

21. אוֹדְךָ כִּי עֲנִיתָנִי וַתְּהִי־לִי לִישׁוּעָה — *I thank You for You have answered me and become my salvation.*

The translation עֲנִיתָנִי, *You have answered me,* follows *Targum, Radak,* and *Sforno.* Other commentaries view עֲנִיתָנִי as cognate with עִנָּה, *suffering,* in which case the verse would mean: *I thank You for causing me to suffer* — because the suffering purged me and made me worthy of being answered and saved.

According to *Midrash Shocher Tov,* the suffering itself is the salvation. This may be likened to the case of a man who had made elaborate preparations for a long caravan journey and was bitten by

1. The *Talmud* (*Tamid* 32b) relates the story of Alexander the Great who explored the world. One day he sat by a fresh stream of water and ate salted fish which had a very powerful fish odor. Alexander washed the salty fish in the stream and was amazed to find that the fishy smell was replaced by an extraordinarily fresh, and delicate fragrance. Alexander thought that this stream's source must be in the Garden of Eden. He carefully followed the stream to its source and found himself standing at the gates of paradise. As the most powerful conqueror and emperor of the world, Alexander demanded entry, but a voice rang out and denied his request saying: *"This is the gate of HASHEM,* [only] *the righteous shall enter through it!"*

118

20-23

²⁰ *This is the gate of HASHEM;*
the righteous shall enter through it.
²¹ *I thank You for You have answered me*
and become my salvation.
²² *The stone which the builders despised*
has become the cornerstone!
²³ *This has emanated from HASHEM;*
it is wondrous in our eyes.

a snake as soon as the caravan left the settled area. Since he was delirious with fever, his fellow travelers left him behind. In agony and despair, the abandoned man poured out his heart to God and asked, "What terrible sin did I commit that I deserve such a miserable fate?"

His fever passed, and he was able to return home. A few days later, however, the man received word that the caravan had been destroyed in the wilderness. Immediately he rose and praised God: "I thank You that You caused me to suffer and thus brought me salvation."

22. אֶבֶן מָאֲסוּ הַבּוֹנִים הָיְתָה לְרֹאשׁ פִּנָּה — *The stone which the builders despised has become the cornerstone!*

This verse refers to David, who was despised and rejected by his own father and brothers (*Targum*). They sent him out to watch the sheep in the hope that the unprotected youngster would perish in the wilds, mauled by a lion or a bear. When the prophet Samuel visited, searching for the son of Jesse who was fit to be anointed king, no one even thought of summoning David, who was out with the sheep. Ultimately, of course, David was chosen as king and as the founder of Israel's royal dynasty, thus becoming the *cornerstone* of the nation (*Rav Shmuel Laniado*). [See *Overview ArtScroll Ruth*, and *Book of Our Heritage, Sivan*, by Rabbi Eliyahu Kitov, for a complete explanation of why David's family despised him.]

Similarly, Bath Sheba was initially rejected because people thought that David had committed adultery with her.

In the end, she gave birth to Solomon, David's successor (*Peh Echad; Chida*).

Israel is also called אֶבֶן, *stone* (*Genesis* 49:24), for Israel is the cornerstone of God's design for the world. The world endures only by virtue of Israel's observance of God's laws, a fact which has influenced all nations to appreciate and accept certain aspects of Hashem's commands. If not for the order and meaning which Israel has brought to the entire world, the world would long ago have sunk into chaos.

Ironically, the nations of the world never appreciated Israel's essential role in their survival. The *builders*, i.e., the rulers of the nations, despised the Jews; they demanded that the Jews be expelled or annihilated, claiming that they were parasites who made no contribution to the common good.

But when the dawn of redemption arrives, all nations will realize that Israel is the *cornerstone* of the world (*Radak*).

23. מֵאֵת ה׳ הָיְתָה זֹּאת הִיא נִפְלָאת בְּעֵינֵינוּ — *This has emanated from HASHEM; it is wondrous in our eyes.*

[When the despised David was anointed by Samuel, a heavenly voice proclaimed, "This one shall be king!" Then all realized that David's anointment was Hashem's doing, and they marveled at David's sudden transformation from lowly shepherd to saintly monarch (see *Targum*).]

Midrash Shocher Tov observes that David himself was amazed when he was suddenly catapulted to greatness. As a common shepherd, he had been engaged in the most menial of tasks. He

כה הַיּוֹם עָשָׂה יְהוָה נָגִילָה וְנִשְׂמְחָה בוֹ: אָנָּא
יהוה הוֹשִׁיעָה נָּא אָנָּא יהוה הַצְלִיחָה נָּא:

כו בָּרוּךְ הַבָּא בְּשֵׁם יְהוָה בֵּרַכְנוּכֶם מִבֵּית

כז יְהוָה: אֵל | יהוה וַיָּאֶר לָנוּ אִסְרוּ־חַג

כח בַּעֲבֹתִים עַד־קַרְנוֹת הַמִּזְבֵּחַ: אֵלִי אַתָּה

כט וְאוֹדֶךָּ אֱלֹהַי אֲרוֹמְמֶךָּ: הוֹדוּ לַיהוה כִּי־טוֹב
כִּי לְעוֹלָם חַסְדּוֹ:

painstakingly plucked tender grass for the young lambs and found tall, hard blades of grass for the older rams. Hashem proclaimed, "This man is worthy of being shepherd for all of My children of Israel."

When David was crowned, all were amazed by the metamorphosis, but David said, "This is even more surprising and *wondrous* to me than it is to anyone else!"

Similarly, Israel will be catapulted to glory and tranquility in the future. The nations who persecuted the Jews will ask in surprise, "Aren't these the very Jews who were once despised and afflicted?"

The Jews will respond, "We are even more amazed than you are, for only we know the depths of degradation we suffered!"

Then a heavenly voice will proclaim *"This has emanated from HASHEM!"*

24. זֶה הַיּוֹם עָשָׂה ה' נָגִילָה וְנִשְׂמְחָה בוֹ — *This is the day HASHEM has made; we will rejoice and be glad in Him!*

In the future it will be obvious that the marvelous events which are transpiring for the benefit of Israel are supernatural. Then everyone will admit: *This is the day HASHEM has made* (*Radak*).

25. אָנָּא ה' הוֹשִׁיעָה נָּא אָנָּא ה' הַצְלִיחָה נָּא — *O HASHEM, please save us! O HASHEM, please make us prosper!*

[First we request that *HASHEM save us* from negative influences and from danger; only then do we ask that He

make us prosper.]

Sforno perceives this as a plea for the future: *Save us* from the travails of the war of Gog and Magog and *make us prosper* under the influence of the righteous and holy scholars who will lead the nation in the Messianic era.

Alshich points out that the advent of the Messiah may occur in either of two ways. At the very outset of the exile, God pre-determined a date by which the Messiah must arrive, even if Israel doesn't merit redemption. If however, Israel repents before this time, as a result of their hardships in exile, then God will hasten to send the Messiah even before the appointed date.

In reference to the set date, the Psalmist declares: *This is the day HASHEM has made, we will rejoice and be glad in Him.* Nevertheless, we cannot be satisfied to wait for that unknown date; rather, we must plead with God to accept our prayers and penitence. In this vein, we beseech: *O HASHEM, please save us ... make us prosper*, by sending the Messiah immediately.

26. בָּרוּךְ הַבָּא בְּשֵׁם ה' — *Blessed be he who comes in the Name of Hashem!*

[In the course of the exile, many Jews unfortunately became estranged from their own tradition and no longer felt at home with their own heritage. In the future, however, righteous and congenial teachers will welcome back all those who strayed from the fold and will bless them *in the Name of HASHEM* (see *Sforno*).]

²⁴ *This is the day HASHEM has made;*
We will rejoice and be glad in Him!
²⁵ *O HASHEM, please save us!*
O HASHEM, please make us prosper!
²⁶ *Blessed be he who comes in the Name of HASHEM!*
We bless you from the House of HASHEM.
²⁷ *HASHEM is God; He illuminated for us;*
bind the festival offering with cords
to the corners of the altar.
²⁸ *You are my God, and I will thank You,*
my God, I will exalt You!
²⁹ *Give thanks to HASHEM, for He is good;*
His kindness endures forever!

Yaavetz HaDoresh translates *Blessed be he who comes with the Name of HASHEM.* This alludes to the Talmudic statement (*Bava Basra* 10b): Praiseworthy is he who arrives in heaven with the entirety of his Torah studies in hand, for such a person has a secure position in the most blessed and sublime part of Paradise.

בָּרַכְנוּכֶם מִבֵּית ה׳ — *We bless you from the House of HASHEM.*

In the future, blessing and abundance will pour forth from the rebuilt Temple. Israel will effortlessly enjoy unprecedented prosperity and contentment, enabling them to study God's Torah undisturbed (*Sforno; Rambam, Hilchos Melachim* 12:4).

In earlier days and better times, the Temple was always a center of hospitality and blessing for all who approached it. The priests would go out to welcome and bless the pilgrims who arrived for the festivals and those who brought their בִּיכּוּרִים, *first fruits,* to the Temple (*Rashi; Radak*).

27. אֵל ה׳ וַיָּאֶר לָנוּ — *HASHEM is God; He illuminated for us.*

Exile is equated with darkness, as in 43:2, *Why must I walk in gloom*

because of the foe's oppression? The advent of the King Messiah is likened to light, as in 43:3, *Dispatch Your light and Your truth — they will guide me.* 132:17 states, *I prepared a candle for my Messiah.* Hashem will restore the light of prophecy to Israel. Thus the Jew prays daily: אוֹר חָדָשׁ עַל צִיוֹן תָּאִיר וְנִזְכֶּה כוּלָּנוּ מְהֵרָה לְאוֹרוֹ, *Shine a new light upon Zion and may we all speedily merit to see its light* (see *Radak* and commentary to 43:3).

אִסְרוּ חַג בַּעֲבֹתִים עַד קַרְנוֹת הַמִּזְבֵּחַ — *Bind the festival offering with cords to the corners of the altar.*

Radak renders: Tie the animal with ropes and then bring it to the altar.

[The four corners of the altar symbolize the four corners of the earth; indeed, the expanse of the earth is no more than a huge altar, dedicated to God. The word קָרְבָּן, *sacrifice,* literally means *a vehicle for coming* קָרוֹב, *close,* to God, and this closeness is the purpose of the entire creation. In the future, life will be a constant חַג, *festival,* of rejoicing in God's service. As long as man is far from the altar (i.e., far from God), the festive spirit is still dormant within him — bound up, pent up *with cords,* as it were. But in the environs of the altar, man escapes these bonds and attains a lofty, free spirit of total festive celebration.]

28. אֵלִי אַתָּה וְאוֹדֶךָּ — *You are my God, and I will thank You.*

When the light of redemption shines upon Israel and the Jews arrive at the Temple, they will praise God as אֵל [literally *the strong One*, see footnote to 22:2], because He used His strength to extract Israel from the iron grip of the nations (*Radak*).

The Psalmist emphasizes that Israel will *give thanks* unto God because, in the future, all sacrifices will be discontinued, except for the תּוֹדָה *thanksgiving offering* (*Tanchuma, Emor* 19; *Yaavetz HaDoresh*. See commentary to 50:14).

אֱלֹהַי אֲרוֹמְמֶךָּ — *My God, I will exalt You!*

Israel will exalt God because He appeared as אֱלֹהִים, *the Divine Dispenser of Strict Justice* and punished the gentile nations who persecuted them

(*Radak*). Thus, all will recognize that our God, the only true one, is *exalted above all false gods* (*Sforno*)[1].

29. הוֹדוּ לַה' כִּי טוֹב כִּי לְעוֹלָם חַסְדּוֹ — *Give thanks to HASHEM, for He is good; His kindness endures forever!*

As explained in the commentary to verse twenty-six, the priests will first welcome all the exiles to the newly rebuilt Temple. The exiles will proclaim, "You are my God, and I will thank You" (*verse* 28). Finally, both the priests and the Levites will respond, "*Give thanks to HASHEM, for He is good*" (*Ibn Ezra*).

[These words are a repetition of the very first verse of this psalm. The theme of this composition is that every action which God takes is inspired by *His kindness*. At the very outset of the exile, Israel knew this to be true, although the fact was not readily apparent. At the end of the exile, however, Israel will *see* this to be true, for God's *kindness* will be clearly visible to all mankind.]

---

1. The *Talmud* (*Pesachim* 119a) teaches that verses 21-28 were said in conjunction with David's anointment. David said: *I thank You for You have answered me.*

His father Jesse said: *The stone which the builders despised has become the cornerstone.*

David's brothers said: *This emanated from HASHEM, it is wondrous in our eyes.*

Samuel the prophet said: *This is the day HASHEM has made, we will rejoice and be glad in Him.*

David's brothers said: *O HASHEM, please save us.*

David said: *O HASHEM, please make us prosper!*

Jesse said: *Blessed be He who comes in the Name of HASHEM.*

Samuel said: *We bless you from the House of HASHEM.*

Everyone together said: *HASHEM is God, He illuminated for us.*

Samuel said: *Bind the festival offering with cords.*

David said: *You are my God, and I will thank You.*

Everyone in unison concluded: *My God, I will exalt You!* (See *Rashbam* and *Maharsha* to *Pesachim* 119a.)

When this psalm is incorporated into the liturgy as part of *Hallel*, each of these verses are recited twice to emphasize that each verse stands independently and was spoken by a different person (*Abudraham*; see *Otzar HaTefillos*).